P9-AOD-284

THE ARTS
AND THE ART OF
CRITICISM

LONDON: GEOFFREY CUMBERLEGE
OXFORD UNIVERSITY PRESS

ALINARI

The Deposition, Michelangelo

THE ARTS
AND THE ART OF CRITICISM

BY

THEODORE MEYER GREENE

PRINCETON
PRINCETON UNIVERSITY PRESS
1947

SECOND PRINTING, 1947

PRINTED AT PRINCETON UNIVERSITY PRESS
PRINCETON, NEW JERSEY, U. S. A.

To

my innumerable collaborators

PREFACE

THE *Arts and the Art of Criticism* epitomizes the scope and orientation of the present volume. It is a study of the work of art as an object of delight, a vehicle of communication, and, at least potentially, a record of significant insight. But it is also concerned with those aspects of the art of criticism which lend themselves to philosophical analysis. In dealing with the arts I have attempted to discover their essential nature; in analyzing man's critical response to art I have tried to formulate as precisely as possible the basic principles and norms to which the artistically sensitive layman and critic both appeal, however unconsciously, in all artistic appraisal. The volume thus deals with certain broad issues which have been discussed for centuries by critics and philosophers. But it considers them with greater philosophical rigor than is usual in critical essays, and with far greater attention to primary artistic data than is common in philosophical treatises. For it has been written by a philosopher in close collaboration with experts in the several arts under review, and is, in sum, the record of our cooperative explorations over a period of years. These distinguishing features of the book invite a word of explanation.

The empirical material has been deliberately limited to the "pure" major arts, in order to simplify the problem and to facilitate the formulation of certain basic categories of artistic analysis. Music and the dance, architecture, sculpture, painting, and the art of literature were found to be sufficiently rich and various to permit illuminating comparison and to provide a basis for sound inductive generalization. Had all the arts been examined *seriatim*, the minor as well as the major, and the "mixed" arts along with those which rely primarily upon a single medium, our investigation would either have had to be indefinitely extended or else condemned to superficiality. And had attention not been focused upon certain arts in all their specificity, my desire to eschew mere abstract theorizing would have been frustrated from the outset. I have tried to steer a middle course between the Scylla of theory divorced from fact and the Charybdis of isolated fact unilluminated by interpretative generalization.

My procedure has been to explore, with copious illustration, each of the six arts in turn, with special reference to their respective media, their several types of formal organization, and their expressive potentialities and limitations. This analysis has set in sharp relief the distinctive characteristics of each art, but it has also revealed analogical relationships between them, and has made possible the formulation of certain basic categories which are applicable to all art as such. It has also prepared the way for a systematic analysis of critical principles and a formulation of artistic norms at once more general and more empirically oriented than would have otherwise been possible.

The region thus explored has proved to be a no-man's land which most philosophers have shunned as too empirical for philosophical inquiry, and which most critics have avoided as too abstract for their aesthetic tastes and aptitudes. The further my collaborators and I pushed our investigations, the more acutely did we come to realize that critics and philosophers of art need one another's help. The critic cannot avoid appealing to general concepts and universal criteria, but he is frequently unable, particularly in this age of specialization, to forge the conceptual tools requisite to precise critical analysis and evaluation. The philosophical aesthetician as frequently exhibits the opposite deficiency. Lacking sufficient orientation in the several arts, he is too often content with tenuous generalizations concerning Beauty, Art, and Genius. Both critics and philosophers have tended to forget their mutual dependence, and both alike have suffered from unhealthy isolation.

A modern Aristotle or Hegel might perhaps be able to master the several arts in all their historical complexity, develop the capacity for competent philosophical analysis and interpretation, and thus achieve the desired historico-philosophical synthesis single-handed. But failing the advent of such a genius, the only practical solution would seem to be a resolute attempt at cooperation among specialists. This book, at all events, is to a very unusual degree the product of such association. I willingly assume full responsibility for the entire volume, since it was I who have expressed our findings in their present form. But my indebtedness to my friends and colleagues in Princeton University is so extensive that, for better or worse, they must be regarded as collaborators in the truest sense.

Thus, the classification of the artistic categories was initiated by conversations with A. E. Hinds, of the Department of English, and the specific application of many of these categories to literature was made under his expert guidance. A. M. Friend, Jr., of the Department of Art and Archaeology, contributed much of the critical analysis of the plastic arts, suggested nearly all of the illustrations here reproduced, and gave me his invaluable assistance in preparing the plates for publication R. D. Welch, of the Department of Music, corrected and enriched the sections dealing with music, provided a large part of the empirical documentation, and, in addition, wrote the supplementary essay on the expressed content of music, which so markedly enhances the value of the book. D. F. Bowers, of the Department of Philosophy, read and re-read the manuscript and contributed greatly to the articulation of the more philosophical sections. Had these colleagues of mine not promised me their assistance, this project would never have been undertaken, and had they not fulfilled their promise with unparalleled generosity of time and effort, it could never have been developed to its present state.

W. J. Oates, in Classics, and D. A. Stauffer, in English, have also read the entire manuscript and made many helpful suggestions. C. W. Kennedy, in English, and D. D. Egbert, in Art and Archaeology, have contributed richly with their counsel. F. R. B. Godolphin, in Classics, G. H. Forsyth, Jr., in Art and Archaeology, and Erwin Panofsky, of the Princeton Institute for Advanced Study, have helped me greatly in the analysis of various problems. Mrs. Eyler Simpson (Keith Coppage) has given me the benefit of her experience as a dancer, and M. L. Beck, of the School of Architecture, has checked some of the passages on architecture. H. P. Robertson, in the Departments of Mathematics and Physics, has discussed with me some of the sections on science. W. B. C. Watkins and S. A. Larrabee, of the Department of English, have helped me illustrate my analysis of literary content. F. F. A. Comstock, of the School of Architecture, designed the cover and jacket and assisted me in other ways. Miss Helen Woodruff, Director of the Index of Christian Art, read part of an early draft and made many useful suggestions, and, more recently, J. F. A. Taylor, in Philosophy, has been tireless in his detailed scrutiny of the thought and style of the manuscript. And to this long catalogue of collaborators must be added the many students and colleagues, too numerous to be mentioned here by name, whose critical and constructive interest has so effectively demonstrated the feasibility of cooperative effort in this field.

The volume which has finally emerged from these conjoint labors makes no pretense at finality or completeness, for it is the log of a first voyage of discovery over relatively uncharted seas. Far more remains to be done than has yet been accomplished, and some indication should be given of what lies ahead in critical investigation and philosophical interpretation.

Philosophers will discover that such traditional problems as the generic character of the aesthetic experience, the subjectivity or objectivity of aesthetic quality in its various manifestations, and the significance of art and beauty viewed in larger philosophical perspective, have been dealt with very cursorily. My effort has been rather to establish a factual basis for philosophical theory—to examine the arts and their appraisal with empirical honesty and without philosophical prejudice. An inquiry of this type must of course rest on certain philosophical presuppositions, and its findings must entail certain metaphysical and epistemological implications. Some of these have been explicitly recognized. But no synoptic epistemology or metaphysic has been developed or endorsed in these pages. If the analysis has any objective validity, its conclusions must be taken into account by every philosopher of art, whatever his philosophical persuasion; but it is left to him to interpret them in any manner that seems most reasonable and adequate. The volume should therefore be regarded as a propaedeutic to more formal philosophical speculation, for it investigates what most philosophers ignore and stops where most philosophers begin their philosophical inquiries.

Students and critics of the several arts will find that the volume is concerned entirely with the formulation and documentation of basic artistic categories and critical principles. It makes no attempt to trace the history of the arts or to reproduce representative works of famous artists. The pictures have been chosen solely to illustrate phases of a systematic analysis. Nor does this analysis pretend to be exhaustive. Every section in the book invites extensive empirical elaboration. I have pushed the analysis as far as seemed appropriate in a volume of this type; but innumerable specific problems in the six arts here considered and in the other arts remain to be explored. This task must be undertaken by students of the several arts who possess the requisite historical and technical orientation, and, in addition, the taste and aptitude for systematic analysis and generalization. For example, only one reference has been made to the art of the Far East; I have concerned myself exclusively with the art of Europe and the Near East. This is a serious limitation. For not only could many of the conclusions here reached have been illustrated more aptly in terms of Far Eastern, and particularly Chinese, art; a comparable study of the art of Asia might well dictate important revisions in my list of basic categories, and it would certainly lead to a notable extension of the factual basis for inductive generalization. Or again, no attempt has been made to analyze the complex and vital art of the motion picture. If my approach to the other arts is soundly conceived it should be applicable, with suitable modification, to this art which today provides one of the richest fields for systematic investigation. These and other limitations have been self-imposed in the belief that if less were attempted, more would be accomplished in an initial survey. But my colleagues and I sincerely hope that others may now be impelled to join with us in further studies along the general lines here laid down.

I also hope that the volume will interest the sensitive and reflective layman who finds in art a source of perennial enjoyment, enlightenment, and inspiration. The response of Princeton undergraduates to this type of analysis, and the interest expressed by various laymen who have been in touch with the investigation, would seem to justify the hope that thoughtful art-lovers may find that a study of these pages will increase their understanding of the basic principles of the art of criticism and thus enrich their appreciation of the world's artistic treasures.

I would even make so bold as to invite the attention of the creative artist who, by temperament and profession, is properly an individualist preoccupied with his own creative labors. I realize that he normally turns to the works of other artists primarily for inspiration and technical suggestion, and that his standards of criticism are largely the product of solitary reflection upon his own creative projects and achievements. I also realize that rigorous systematic analysis is likely to dampen his spirits and to repel him as too remote from his own immediate and vital concerns. Yet the creative arts today are in a state of unprecedented confusion. Tradition is discounted, conventions are repudiated, time-honored objectives are renounced, and artists are put to it to find appropriate and satisfying substitutes. As a result, many have been impelled to devise new theories of art, and for this task they are not always ideally equipped. My collaborators and I believe that our analysis may suggest to the contemporary artist solutions to some of his most immediate problems by providing him with the underlying artistic principles of which he is in search.

This volume is accordingly addressed to all critics and philosophers of art, all sensitive laymen and creative artists, who feel the need for an analysis of the arts and the art of criticism which is at once empirical and theoretical; which studies the arts from the artistic point of view, yet with appropriate philosophic rigor; and which formulates concepts and principles universal in applicability, yet rooted in artistic fact.

I wish gratefully to acknowledge the generous financial aid of the American Council of Learned Societies. The travelling fellowship which was awarded me in 1932 made possible a cherished year of study in Europe, and more recent grants have enabled me to include the unusually large number of illustrations in collotype. I also wish to thank the Princeton University Council of the Humanities for its financial assistance towards publication. The Princeton University Press, and, in particular, Mr. Joseph Brandt, have outdone themselves in helpful suggestion and willing cooperation. Mr. Harold H. Hugo, of The Meriden Gravure Company, has been most efficient and understanding in supervising the preparation of the plates. Professor and Mrs. E. Von der Muhll were very helpful the last days before publication, and Mr. J. F. A. Taylor, Dr. W. H. Cerf, and Dr. and Mrs. F. B. Agard have been of great assistance in the reading of proof. I am also grateful to Mr. Taylor for preparing the Index of Proper Names and Titles. My wife's assistance in the preparation of the entire volume has been so extensive that words of appreciation fail me; only she can know how impossible would have been my task without her aid and counsel.

THEODORE M. GREENE

Princeton, Nov. 1, 1939

PREFACE TO THE SECOND EDITION

I HAVE often been tempted, during the last six years, to rewrite various portions of this book, not because I have changed any of my basic ideas regarding the nature of art and criticism, but because further study and reflection have made me want to express some of these ideas somewhat differently. But the book, as first published, has, it seems to me, sufficient internal unity to demand complete revision if any part of it were to be rewritten or amplified, and for such revision I have neither the time nor the inclination. I shall therefore restrict myself, in this Preface, to a few observations which may be helpful to the reader.

The only analysis in the book which I have come somewhat to question relates to the role of interpretation in pure or absolute music. My question is this: Would it be more correct to say that the composer merely evokes, explores and exhibits his subject-matter, that is, man's emotive-conative states, with unparalleled subtlety and precision, or was I right in saying that he also interprets these emotions, impulses and moods? I have had many interesting conversations on this subject since 1940 and must confess that I am still genuinely puzzled. The reader will find it profitable to explore this alternative interpretation of musical content.

The only part of the book which I could perhaps amplify is the account of artistic greatness, in Chapter XXIV. Greatness might, it seems to me now, be described helpfully in terms of the concept of inexhaustibility. One of the characteristics of truly great art in any medium is the fact that the most sensitive and informed critic can return to it again and again and always find in it formal relationships not previously observed, insights, perspectives and evaluations not previously noted or comprehended. A great work of art is thus, as it were, a perpetual challenge to fresh discovery, a continuing stimulus to growth, an inexhaustible source of refreshment and delight. This in no way contradicts my analysis of artistic greatness in terms of "breadth" and "depth." On the contrary, it seems to me to unite these two conditions of greatness under a single, inclusive and illuminating concept.

The chief limitation of the book as a whole has been pointed out by at least one reviewer and deserves explicit mention in this Preface. My systematic analytical approach has entailed a necessary sacrifice. The book does not give the reader a sense of the excitement of artistic creation and enjoyment, of the surging exploring quality of artistic invention and discovery or of critical rediscovery and appraisal. I do not feel obliged to apologize for this lack because I made no attempt to deal in these terms with these aspects of the total artistic transaction. But the reader should be warned at the outset that he must look elsewhere, e.g. to Augusto Centeno's Introduction to "The Intent of the Artist" (Princeton University Press, 1941) and Donald Stauffer's Introduction to "The Intent of the Critic" (Princeton University Press, 1941), for accounts of artistic creation and enjoyment which complement my prosaic analyses.

Finally, the teacher of aesthetics or the philosophy of art who may be inclined to use my book as a text should be warned of the positive harm which it can do a certain type of student, namely, the plodding student without much artistic sensitivity and imagination. The danger is that he will memorize my categories and definitions and try to apply them to this or that work of art mechanically and slavishly. This can only result in blinding him to the unity, the originality and the artistic vitality of the work of art in question, in short, in making it harder for him to understand and enjoy it for itself. If, on the other hand, my categories are really understood and intelligently used they can help a student, even of average ability, better to explore, understand and appreciate works of art in the several media.

THEODORE M. GREENE

Princeton, 1946

ACKNOWLEDGMENTS

PERMISSION to quote from other volumes has been kindly granted by the various publishers. The Clarendon Press, Oxford, has permitted me to quote from W. D. Ross' translation of Aristotle's *Ethica Nicomachea*, H. S. Macran's *The Harmonics of Aristoxenus*, and E. A. Milne's *Relativity, Gravitation, and World-Structure*; the Oxford Press, New York, from Shelley's *A Defense of Poetry* and Erwin Panofsky's *Studies in Iconology* (The Mary Flexner Lectures for 1937); Macmillan and Co., Ltd., London, from Walter Pater's *Appreciations* and *Grove's Dictionary of Music and Musicians*; the Macmillan Company, New York, from Davies and Vaughan's translation of Plato's *Republic*; George Bell and Sons, from M. D. Hottinger's translation of H. Wölfflin's *Principles of Art History*; Longmans Green and Co., from William James' *Pragmatism*; Harcourt Brace, from T. S. Eliot's *Essays Ancient and Modern*; E. P. Dutton and Co., from J. Cuthbert Hadden's *Haydn*; The Harvard University Press, from G. D. Birkhoff's *Aesthetic Measure*; Charles Scribner's Sons, from J. Loewenberg's *Hegel, Selections*; the American Library of Musicology, from Josef Yasser's *A Theory of Evolving Tonality*; and A. C. Barnes and Co., from John Martin's *The Modern Dance*. I am particularly indebted to Mr. John Martin and The Dodge Publishing Company for their kind permission to quote so extensively from *America Dancing*.

Due acknowledgments for the use of photographs, and their sources, will be found in the List of Illustrations and under the reproductions at the end of the volume.

TABLE OF CONTENTS

CONTENTS

ILLUSTRATIONS

THE following works of art have been selected for reproduction in this volume to illustrate various phases of the argument. No attempt has been made to include representative masterpieces or to document any historical movement. But, for the most part, well known and more significant works of art have been chosen rather than less known ones which might better have illustrated a single phase of the discussion.

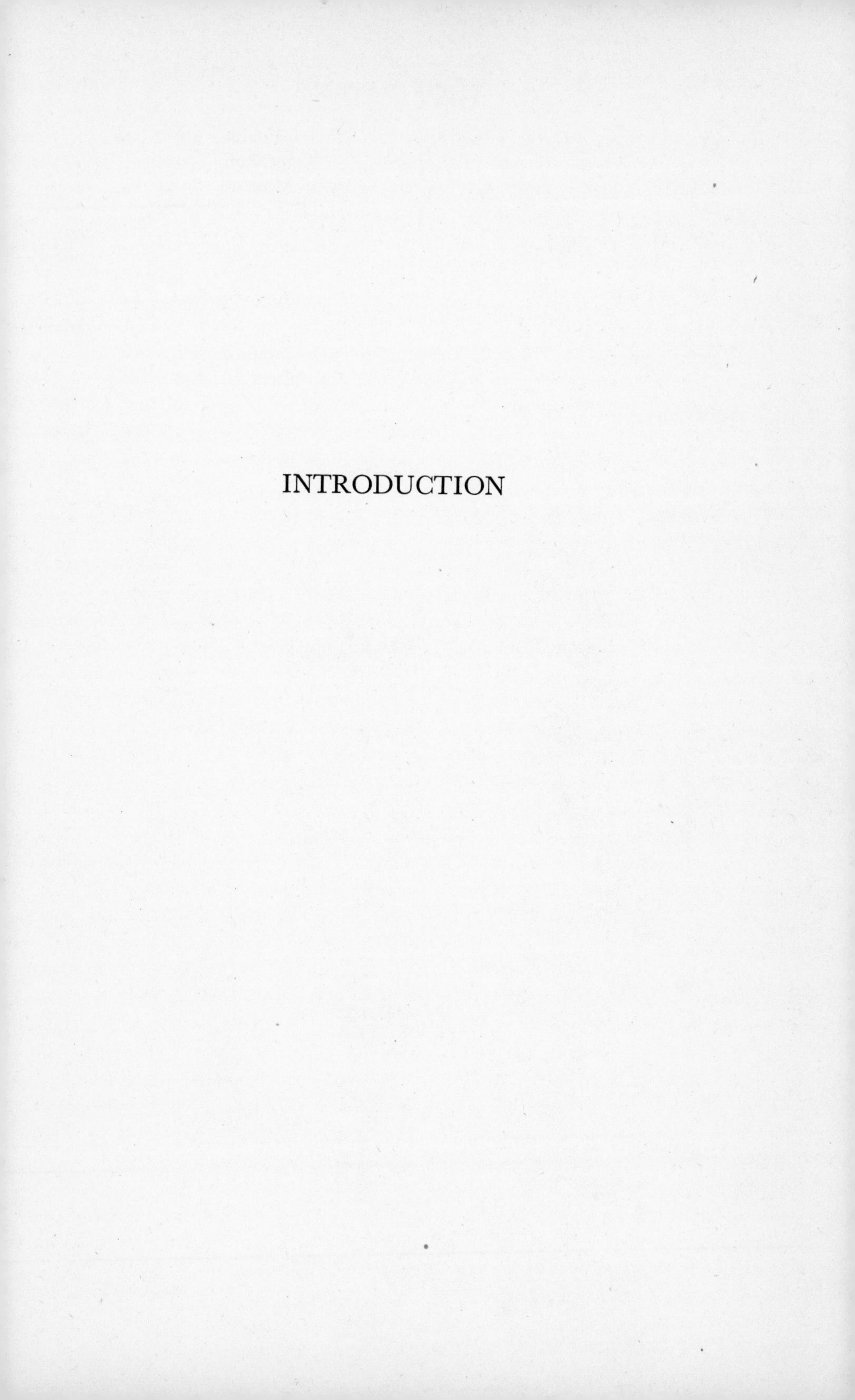

INTRODUCTION

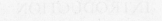

INTRODUCTION

THE nature and scope of the present inquiry can best be indicated by relating it to the more inclusive enterprise of philosophical[1] aesthetics, which may be defined as the synoptic analysis and interpretation of the aesthetic experience and its object. By "aesthetic experience" is here meant both aesthetic creation and re-creation—processes which resemble one another but which are clearly distinguishable. The "object" of the aesthetic experience includes both man-made objects and natural phenomena. "Aesthetic analysis" is "synoptic" if it takes into account every type of investigation which can throw light on the empirical nature of the aesthetic experience and its object. The "interpretation" of this empirical evidence is "synoptic" in proportion as it does justice, both systematically and historically, to all the relevant facts.

Philosophical analysis and interpretation are primarily systematic, since the philosopher is chiefly concerned with the timeless characteristics of his subject-matter. But the subject-matter of the aesthetician includes works of art which cannot be understood adequately save in historical and biographical perspective; and the philosopher's own theories, like those of his predecessors and contemporaries, are themselves historically and biographically conditioned. It is therefore essential that his interpretations and evaluations be historically oriented. Philosophical aesthetics is therefore the systematic, though historically oriented, analysis and interpretation of the processes of aesthetic creation and response and of their characteristic objects, both natural and man-made.

I shall be concerned in the following pages with only certain aspects of this ambitious undertaking, namely, the analysis of the medium, form, and content of art in the six major media, and with man's critical apprehension and evaluation. But it is important, particularly in a restricted undertaking of this type, to formulate in advance the basic presuppositions which constitute the writer's frame of reference. These relate to (1) the objectivity of aesthetic quality, (2) the relation of a work of art to other objects capable of

[1] The qualifying adjective is necessary to differentiate aesthetics as a philosophical discipline from the more restricted and scientifically oriented discipline of psychological aesthetics.

evoking aesthetic response, (3) the nature and limitations of aesthetic inquiry, and, (4) the relation of philosophical inquiry in this field to scientific investigations, on the one hand, critical analysis and appraisal, on the other.

1. The objectivity of aesthetic quality

It is possible to interpret aesthetic response in a purely subjectivistic manner by denying that aesthetic quality actually characterizes the object of awareness. The subjectivist admits that aesthetic response has psychological characteristics which distinguish it from other types of response. But he denies that some objects of awareness actually possess in greater or less degree an objective aesthetic character of their own. He explains the *apparent* objectivity of aesthetic quality by saying that we unconsciously project our aesthetic feelings into the object of our awareness, and thus ascribe to it a quality which the object itself completely lacks. The subjectivist may admit that some objects occasion this projection more readily than other objects, and that some aesthetic preferences are idiosyncratic, some more general, and some very widespread. But this fact is explained solely in terms of temperamental variations, social habits, and cultural traditions, and not at all in terms of the presence or absence of an aesthetic quality in different objects of awareness. Aesthetic quality is thus asserted to be merely a function of aesthetic evaluation, and evaluation, in turn, is not conceived to be the discovery of an objective quality in things.

This interpretation, if correct, would not invalidate my factual analysis (in Parts I, II, and III) of the work of art in the several artistic media. But it would profoundly affect my interpretation of the results of this analysis, and of man's critical response to art. I cannot here review the arguments which have been urged in support of the subjectivistic position, but must content myself with a brief indication of the alternative position which I have adopted.

Aesthetic quality is, I believe, *as* objective as the secondary qualities of color and sound, and may (following G. E. Moore) be entitled a tertiary quality. It is "objective" in the sense of actually characterizing certain objects of awareness and not others, and therefore as awaiting discovery by the aesthetically sensitive observer. It is correctly described as "objective" because it satisfies the generic criterion of objectivity, namely, coercive order. Aesthetic quality is apprehended by the aesthetically-minded observer as a quality which presents itself to him with compelling power; which characterizes different objects in different degrees and in conformity to certain basic principles; which he can rediscover on different occasions and explore as he explores other objective qualities; and which other aesthetically sensitive observers can also discover and investigate.

I have adopted this position because it seems to me to do full justice to the sensitive layman's and the thoughtful critic's normal interpretation of the aesthetic experience, whereas the subjectivistic interpretation does unnecessary violence to this experience. I admit that subjectivism has the merit of offering an easy solution to certain difficulties—notably, variations in aesthetic taste and critical appraisal. But these difficulties permit of an alternative solution, as I shall try to indicate in due course. I would also admit that the philosopher must always reinterpret the conventional beliefs of the layman and the conclusions of the specialist, and that he is sometimes compelled to do violence to these conclusions and beliefs. But I would suggest that such violence is justifiable only as a last resort, and that the burden of proof must rest with the iconoclastic philosopher. And no defense of subjectivism yet formulated seems to me to be compelling or even plausible. I shall therefore presume the objectivity of aesthetic quality in the following analysis.

2. The work of art as a distinctive type of aesthetic object

My second presupposition concerns the definition of a "work of art" and the relation of works of art, so defined, to other types of objects capable of evoking man's aesthetic response. A work of art is here conceived of as a distinctive type of man-made object endowed with formal beauty; beauty, as a function of aesthetically satisfying form; and aesthetic quality, as the generic *differentia* of all aesthetic objects as such.

Anything may be said to possess "aesthetic quality" which evokes an aesthetically re-creative response in a sensitive person. But aesthetic quality may be either "formless" or "formal." Certain sensory qualities possess aesthetic quality quite apart from all formal organization. The aesthetic quality of most aesthetic objects of awareness, on the other hand, is a function of their formal organization. The term "beauty" will be restricted to apply only to formal aesthetic quality. Beauty, in turn, may be either "natural" or "man-made." We find beauty in nature, and we can interpret this beauty in a variety of ways. But formal beauty is most perfectly exemplified in man-made "objects." Finally, aesthetically satisfying objects of human construction may be either artistically inexpressive or artistically expressive. Many utilitarian objects possess beauty but lack all artistic expressiveness. A "work of art," in contrast, is here conceived of as necessarily expressive. Artistically expressive beauty is thus a species of man-made beauty, which, in turn, is a species of generic beauty or formal aesthetic quality, which, finally, is a species of aesthetic quality as such. These relationships, which I must now attempt briefly to explain and justify, may be summarized as follows:

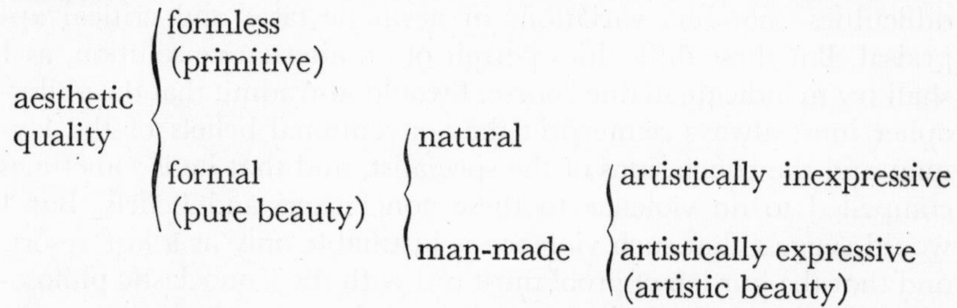

(a) The term "aesthetic" is here used to signify the distinctive common quality of *any* object of awareness which is capable of evoking a *re*-creative response in an aesthetically sensitive spectator, whatever more specialized aesthetic character the object in question may have. Hence the category of the "aesthetic" is my most inclusive and philosophically basic category. Aesthetic quality is the lowest common denominator of all aesthetic objects, for by an "aesthetic object" is meant an object which actually possesses the unique generic quality designated as "aesthetic." This quality, like other ultimates, is unique and therefore indefinable. It can be apprehended only by "direct acquaintance."

(b) Aesthetic quality manifests itself most simply and primitively in "formless" sensory qualities. Certain colors and sounds possess a positive (or negative) aesthetic character quite independently of all formal organization. They are in themselves immediately attractive or repugnant to primitive aesthetic sensitivity. For example, the hue, clarity, depth, intensity, or "value" of a color may be intrinsically satisfying irrespective of the shape or immediate environment of the colored area; the timbre, pitch, or volume of a single sound may have aesthetic value irrespective of the sound's tonal relationships to other sounds. Other colors and sounds are in themselves aesthetically disagreeable, while still others are aesthetically neutral, i.e., devoid of aesthetic quality. We shall discover that this primitive aesthetic quality can profoundly affect the formal beauty of a more complex object of awareness, both positively and negatively. But we shall also find that a sensuous quality which is aesthetically pleasing in itself may become aesthetically displeasing in a formal context, or a displeasing quality, pleasing, or an aesthetically neutral quality either pleasing or displeasing. The primitive aesthetic character of sensuous qualities cannot be ignored in aesthetic analysis; but the analyst must expect surprising alterations in the aesthetic character of sensuous qualities when they are organized into more or less complex patterns.

I have chosen to limit the term "beautiful" to "formal" aesthetic quality, that is, to the positive (or negative) aesthetic character of formal organization, whatever the medium thus organized and whatever the nature of this organization. So delimited, "beauty" is a distinctive type of aesthetic quality and, as such, sharply to be distinguished from its primitive or formless manifestations. This conception of beauty as a function of formal organization is in line with traditional philosophical usage and permits the ascription of beauty to the greatest variety of formal patterns in the most diverse media. For example, it justifies the recognition of formal beauty in mathematics (where it is usually entitled "elegance"), in purely geometrical configurations (whether diagrammatic or physical), in utilitarian objects (such as machines), in the most varied types of individual and social processes and organizations (political, industrial, athletic, moral, religious, etc.), in every kind of natural phenomenon, including the human body, and, finally, in works of art in the various artistic media. *Any* formal organization or pattern which is intrinsically satisfying may be said to possess beauty. Any formal organization, in contrast, which is aesthetically repugnant may be entitled "ugly." If a formal pattern evokes neither aesthetic pleasure nor displeasure it is aesthetically neutral, i.e., devoid of formal aesthetic quality.

The term "formal" must not be misconstrued. Form must not be abstracted, as Kant tended to abstract it, from the medium in question. The distinction between what is organized and its formal organization is valid and useful for purposes of analysis. But in any concrete case the form which is designated as beautiful is not autonomous or independent of the medium; it is merely the manner in which the medial elements are related to one another. In a pictorial "abstraction," for instance, the form which occasions our aesthetic delight must not be identified with the lines, outlines, or shapes of the composition irrespective of color and "value" relationships between the discernible parts of the composition.

Beauty, as a species of generic aesthetic quality, is the proper object of "taste," itself a species of aesthetic sensitivity. Beauty and taste are both species of wider genera. Just as generic aesthetic sensitivity enables the observer to distinguish between primitive aesthetic value, neutrality, and disvalue, so the man of taste is able to distinguish between formal beauty, formal aesthetic neutrality, and formal ugliness. This three-fold distinction is empirically verifiable. Just as specific secondary qualities present themselves to the aesthetically sensitive observer as aesthetically neutral, i.e., without occasioning either aesthetic pleasure or pain, while others are apprehended with varying degrees of aesthetic satisfaction or dissatisfaction, so do certain patterns or arrangements in any given medium present themselves to a man whose taste is cultivated in this medium as either beautiful or ugly, while others seem to him to lack all formal aesthetic quality. Ugliness is not mere absence of beauty. It is not a mere void, but an aching void. It is the violation of an aesthetic requirement and the source of positive aesthetic pain which is different in kind from aesthetic indifference and aesthetic delight. Ugliness is the aesthetic analogue of vice in the moral sphere, as beauty is the analogue of virtue and as formal aesthetic neutrality is the analogue of the unmoral or the morally neutral.

(c) Man finds in nature not only formless but formal aesthetic quality—in the human body, in the structure and movements of animals, in vegetation, and even in inorganic configurations. He may also see in natural beauty the expression of a cosmic purpose. The Psalmist is not alone in believing that the heavens declare the glory of God and that the firmament showeth His handiwork. But it is possible to challenge this teleological interpretation of natural beauty, and it is very necessary to distinguish between such formal beauty as nature actually possesses, on the one hand, and, on the other, the beauty which originates in the creative imagination of the artistically sensitive spectator and which he unconsciously projects into nature. Let us consider these two problems in the reverse order.

To isolate natural beauty for purposes of analysis we must distinguish between the subjective processes of artistic creation and aesthetic re-creation. The process of artistic creation is the process of bringing into being a new form endowed with aesthetic quality, and it involves the activities of selection, interpretation, and arrangement. The process of aesthetic re-creation, in contrast, is essentially docile and assimilative. Though never wholly passive, it is a process motivated by a desire not to create something new, not to impose upon some medium a beautiful and meaningful form, but rather to discover and enjoy what has already been aesthetically ordered. It therefore presupposes the objective reality of what is thus discovered with aesthetic delight.

When, therefore, we ascribe beauty to nature we refer to instances of formal organization in nature which are capable of evoking man's aesthetically re-creative response and are not merely a stimulus to his artistically creative impulses. That nature actually manifests such beauty cannot be doubted. It is a question, however, as to how complete, perfect, or flawless such beauty ever is. A work of art may seem to us to be aesthetically so perfect that the slightest change would, in our opinion, be a change for the worse. Can any natural object be said to be as perfectly beautiful?

This question must be answered in the negative if for no other reason than that nature itself never provides us with any indication as to how much to include and exclude in our aesthetic response to natural phenomena. No natural object or scene is ever bounded by a "frame," i.e., any set limits indicative of where the aesthetic object in question begins and ends. For example, how much should be included in a "sunset," or a "forest glade," or a "mountain peak," if these are to be viewed as aesthetic objects? What are the boundaries of nature's "works of art"? These questions nature herself always leaves unanswered. But if we supply the answer and assume the responsibility of bounding an object of natural beauty, we contribute, by that very act, to whatever beauty may appear within these boundaries. To this extent our response has been creative rather than strictly re-creative. And even if we impose a frame on nature and arbitrarily decide to include in our aesthetic apprehension this much and no more of what lies before us, is it ever possible to find a natural scene or object whose formal organization is as aesthetically satisfying as a work of art? Is nature ever perfectly beautiful in the sense that every element of a given whole is organically related to every other element and to the whole in an aesthetically satisfying manner?

However this question be answered, it is undeniable that man's aesthetic response to nature is predominantly creative rather than re-creative. What he normally does, however unconsciously and incompletely, is to indulge in that preliminary artistic selection, organization, and interpretation which constitute the initial stages of the artist's creative activity. His aesthetic reaction to nature resembles that of the painter and the poet rather than that of the critic. It is predominantly an act of artistic creation, not of re-creative discovery. The subjectivistic interpretation of the aesthetic experience *does* therefore apply in large measure to man's aesthetic response to nature. He does project himself into nature and he does tend to ascribe to it the expressive forms in terms of which he aesthetically apprehends it. It is not strange that some philosophers have been led to adopt a subjectivistic interpretation of *all* aesthetic response by an illegitimate generalization from man's characteristic aesthetic response to nature.

The full-fledged artist goes to nature for inspiration just because natural beauties are themselves so incomplete and fragmentary. Were nature itself perfectly beautiful, either in part or in whole, the artist could do no more than copy as faithfully as possible what lies before him, that is, translate the natural object or scene without emendation into some artistic medium. Artistic beauty would also necessarily be inferior to the beauty of nature, and Plato's remarks on art in Book X of the *Republic* would have to be accepted as sound. But, as we shall see, good art is never imitative in this sense. On the other hand, were nature wholly devoid of fragmentary beauty, it could hardly stimulate the creative impulse of the artist and the sensitive observer as it does. Nature spurs man on to artistic endeavor because it is so rich in partial and incomplete beauty of form, so subtle and diverse in its hints as to what might be artistically accomplished by the creative artist himself.

The expressiveness of natural beauty must be interpreted in an analogous way. If we take the whole of nature as a unified cosmic process we can, no doubt, believe it to manifest whatever we conceive ultimate reality to be—a divine providence, or a cosmic principle indifferent to spiritual and moral values, or a satanic impulse to destruction and decay. But can we reasonably assert that nature as a whole, and, more specifically, such formal beauty as nature itself manifests, does unequivocally exhibit any such inner cosmic character? Could the Psalmist have conceived of the heavens as a declaration of the glory of God had he not *already* been possessed of an assured religious faith? Did he not merely find in nature confirmation of an already well-established belief in Divine Providence?

We must here distinguish between mere natural manifestation and artistic expression. The *differentiae* of artistic expression will be examined in considerable detail in later chapters of this volume. Here it must suffice to define a work of art as an intrinsically satisfying and, at the same time, a *meaningful* organization of some appropriate medium. A work of art always expresses in a unique manner an interpretation of some subject-matter. It is the expression, *via* artistic form, of an intelligible artistic content. This expression, in turn, differs in kind from the mere manifestation of universal traits and underlying processes. Now every natural phenomenon does, of course, manifest many properties and underlying processes. But can the objective beauty of a natural phenomenon ever be said to express an underlying meaning in a manner analogous to that in which an artist expresses his interpretations of his subject-matter *via* artistic form? Is nature in the raw ever expressive as art is expressive? It seems indubitable that whatever meaning man may be able to discover in nature is not expressed by nature itself as the artist's meaning finds expression in his art.

This must suffice to indicate the fragmentariness of natural beauty and to suggest that such beauty as nature does possess differs in kind from the expressive beauty of a work of art. No close analogy to artistic expressiveness is to be found either in specific objects and scenes in nature or in nature as a whole.

(d) The distinction between artistically expressive and artistically inexpressive products of human creation can best be indicated by comparing machines and works of art. If a machine is well adapted to its utilitarian function it will manifest this function to the discerning eye. But this does not make the machine artistically expressive. Some industrial products are, in addition, aesthetically satisfying; that is, they may possess an aesthetically pleasing surface, and they may even be beautiful in formal structure. But normally this beauty is quite inexpressive of the object's utilitarian function. Finally, some industrial products, such as polished ball-bearings and aesthetically stream-lined automobiles, may express their utilitarian purpose aesthetically.[2] The polished surface of a ball-bearing or a billiard ball (Fig. 93) emphasizes its smooth rotundity and enhances our appreciation of its mechanical function. The stream-lining of a motor car gives aesthetic expression to the use for which the car was created. But the most that a machine can express is its immediate utilitarian function, whereas a work of art expresses the artist's *interpretation* of a given subject-matter. This difference between a work of art and a machine is of profound importance for a true understanding of art. It will become increasingly evident as we proceed with our investigation of artistic form and artistic content.

The terms "aesthetic," "beautiful," and "artistic" have all been defined, and are still defined, in a variety of ways, and no finality is claimed for the definitions here suggested But if the following analysis is to be intelligible, crucial terms such as these must be accorded some clear definition and must be used consistently. I shall attempt to use them in the manner indicated.

3. The nature and value of aesthetic inquiry

There are two methodological questions which the philosopher of art must ask himself at the beginning of his inquiry. The first relates to the initial delimitation of his subject-matter, the second, to the potentialities and limitations of conceptual analysis in the field of art.

Assuming that his inquiry must be empirically oriented if it is to be illuminating, how can he know where to begin his empirical investigations? He must decide at the start what objects to investigate. But how, prior to such investigation, can he recognize a work of art when he sees it? Is he not caught in a vicious circle by having to presuppose at the outset the very knowledge which his inquiry is designed to produce?

The critic of art and literature is faced with the same predicament. It is his task to re-create, interpret, and evaluate specific works of art in their historical contexts. To perform this task he must know what man-made objects to investigate. But how, prior to critical analysis and evaluation, can he know what it is that makes an object a work of art? However paradoxical it may appear, it is

[2] Cf. Philip Johnson, *Machine Art* (New York: W. W. Norton & Co., 1934), for excellent illustrations of the purely formal beauty versus the functionally expressive beauty of various mechanical products.

the critic and the thoughtful art-lover who "make" certain objects "works of art" by deciding that they possess the requisite quality to merit inclusion in this class. Such recognition of artistic quality presupposes critical competence, and the critic can acquire this competence only through actual critical investigation. How can he possess this competence prior to such investigation? And how can he start his investigation without any critical knowledge of what it is that he is to investigate?

The same difficulty arises in other fields of inquiry. The student of ethics seeks to describe and formulate the nature of moral goodness, and if his investigation is not to be entirely *a priori* it must be based upon an empirical study of concrete instances of moral character and conduct, motives and ideals. But how, prior to all ethical inquiry, can he delimit his subject-matter or know what type of empirical phenomenon to analyze and interpret? The student of religion is confronted with the same predicament. Nor is this difficulty restricted to the normative disciplines. The scientist must base his interpretations of nature upon relevant sensory observations; his theories must "do justice" to the empirical "facts." But the relevance of an observation and the factuality of a "fact" can be determined only within the framework of a scientific theory. Thus, scientific observation presupposes scientific theory; yet a theory, to be scientific, must be based on observation. Even the scientist would therefore seem to require, at the outset of his scientific investigations, the very knowledge to which these investigations are intended to lead.

The solution of this difficulty is not far to seek. Students in every field of inquiry, including the aesthetic, find themselves at the outset in a state neither of complete ignorance nor of adequate knowledge, but in a state of opinion. For they have inherited some portion of the funded knowledge of the race. The experiences and reflections of past generations have crystallized at both the conventional and the critical levels of discourse into a body of beliefs which provides the investigator with preliminary hypotheses and working criteria adequate to his immediate needs.

In the realm of art, critics and artistically cultured laymen are in substantial agreement that certain musical compositions, buildings, paintings, and literary works unquestionably possess artistic merit. The would-be critic can therefore start with these works as his initial subject-matter. He can train himself to a more and more adequate appreciation of their distinctive characteristics and thus acquire a finer sensitivity for artistic quality in general. He can then broaden his investigation, venture into new fields, reformulate his definitions and criteria in the interest of greater catholicity and precision, revise earlier critical estimates, and, finally, discover artistic quality in unsuspected places. The philosopher of art can follow the same procedure. He can start with accepted critical estimates, consider their implications, formulate generic artistic categories, and then revise these in the light of new empirical evidence and more synoptic philosophical theory. Here, as in other fields of investigation, earlier conclusions are the basis of subsequent inquiry, while theory and observation go hand in hand, each conditioning the other. What at first appears to be a vicious circle is thus found to be a spiral of continued advance in breadth of outlook, refinement of theory, and fresh empirical discovery.

Aesthetic inquiry, then, need not be blocked at the very outset by a methodological dilemma. But it is important to realize that aesthetic quality in its various forms can never be logically demonstrated but must be accepted as a primary datum which must be immediately apprehended to be known. Like life, consciousness, rationality, and moral goodness, aesthetic quality and its variants are ultimate and unique. As such, they cannot even be defined, since definition always involves the description of the defined objects in terms of something else. All that can be defined are the *conditions* under which they make their appearance; their qualitative essence can be apprehended only through immediate first-hand aesthetic experience.

There may be some unfortunate individuals who lack not only a developed aesthetic sensitivity but even a latent aesthetic capacity which might be cultivated by suitable training. Like the congenitally color-blind who can never really know what color is, such individuals, if they exist, would be deprived irremediably of all artistic insight and debarred from all aesthetic enjoyment. But it would be difficult to prove that any such individuals actually do exist; it is more likely that everyone possesses some capacity for aesthetic response. Men certainly differ enormously in native aesthetic sensitivity and in the kind of aesthetic training which they have received. Nor can it be denied that man's most sensitive aesthetic responses and his deepest artistic insights are the product of unusual aesthetic aptitude subjected to unusually fortunate cultivation. But this need not preclude the possibility that all men have *some* capacity, however latent, for aesthetic insight and enjoyment.

The similarity between aesthetic and other ultimate qualities, and between the conditions of their respective apprehension, is too obvious to require lengthy exposition. Moral goodness remains, despite all attempts at atomistic reduction, irreducible and unique in the judgment of those who possess moral sensitivity and who have responded to moral instruction. The quality of holiness which pervades and characterizes objects of religious veneration is also unique; were this not so, the generic term "religious" could have no assignable meaning. And, like aesthetic response, religious insight presupposes both native endowment and its appropriate cultivation. The same is true of rational reflection, which involves the ability to recognize that ultimate logical relationship which we entitle logical consistency, and to distinguish it from its opposite, logical inconsistency. These ultimates are simply *given* in relevant first-hand experience; their phenomenological factuality must be accepted as final and irreducible, incapable of rational demonstration. Whoever, through ignorance or perversity, denies them altogether automatically excludes himself from the universes of discourse which presuppose their empirical reality, for only if this reality is admitted can their nature and import even be discussed.

The philosopher's examination of art is therefore conditioned by a disciplined sensitivity to artistic quality. In his investigation of works of art in the several artistic media, he must be guided at the outset by the consensus of critical and philosophical opinion, just as the critic must, at the start, tentatively accept the verdict of his predecessors. But both the critic and the philosopher must rely ultimately upon their own artistic sensitivity, for it is this capacity alone which can enable them actually to recognize objective artistic quality when they see it.

The question now arises as to the potentialities and limitations of systematic inquiry in this field. What light can conceptual analysis be expected to throw upon the distinguishing characteristics of works of art in the several artistic media?

"Artistic quality" is the generic character common to all "works of art." Each work of art in turn, exists in a distinctive medium which determines its artistic quality in essential ways. It follows that no adequate translation of a work of art into another medium is ever possible. Such translation may be approximated when the two media involved are similar, as in the case of the pianoforte and the clavichord, bronze and silver, or French and English. But in proportion as a work of art possesses real artistic quality, translation, even into a similar medium, tends to be specious rather than genuine. How, then, can the theorist hope to analyze and express, in the very different medium of conceptual prose, that unique, irreducible, and untranslatable quality which pervades works of art in the media of music, the dance, architecture, sculpture, painting, or literature? I shall presently argue that the creative artist is well advised not only to exploit the expressive potentialities of his medium but to refrain from ignoring or denying its limitations. As theorists in the realm of art, we should similarly make clear to ourselves what such an analysis as we are about to undertake can and cannot be expected to accomplish.

Since artistic quality reveals itself only to immediate intuition, aesthetic theory, far from rivalling such intuition, must presuppose it from first to last. And since artistic quality is essentially untranslatable, it defies adequate description in conceptual prose. Once and for all, theoretical analysis is no substitute for immediate aesthetic response or sensitive critical re-creation.

But analysis can isolate the generic characteristics and conditions of the artistic experience and its object. It can disclose the generic characteristics of the several artistic media, of artistic form, and of art's expressed content; it can distinguish between artistic creation and re-creation; and it can formulate the criteria of critical appraisal. Such analysis need not distort its subject-matter; the conclusions to which it leads may be accurate and illuminating, provided they are not misconstrued. Aesthetic theory is merely limited in the *kind* of insight which it yields. Meanwhile, rigorous analysis is the *only* method at our disposal for apprehending the generic structure of art and the factors which condition artistic quality. It is of the utmost importance that its cognitive limitations never be forgotten; but it is equally important to recognize the contributions which it alone can make.

Aesthetic theory can also prepare the way for fresh artistic experience. All who have benefited from the systematic study of music, literature, painting, or any of the other arts, will testify to this.

Though no intelligent student of music would dream of substituting the study of harmony and counterpoint for first-hand musical appreciation, he would insist that such study sharpens the ear, trains the memory, and indirectly enriches subsequent musical response by clarifying the structure of music in general and of particular musical compositions.

Our analysis of art, if wisely conducted, will therefore have value both as an end in itself and as a means to deeper artistic insight. It will possess intrinsic interest for those who are intellectually curious in this realm; but it should also contribute indirectly to our immediate artistic understanding and enjoyment of specific works of art in the several artistic media.

4. Complementary approaches to art and the aesthetic experience

The work of art and the processes of artistic creation and re-creation can be investigated from three different points of view, the scientific, the critical, and the philosophical.

(a) The scientific approach is characterized by a predominant interest on the part of the inquirer in the physical, psychological, sociological, or historical *contexts* of art, artistic creation, and critical response. He must rely on artistic sensitivity, whether his own or that of others, for the delimitation of his subject-matter, since his purpose is to study *artistic* phenomena in a scientific manner. But once he has learned what phenomena to investigate, his chief concern is to explore with scientific objectivity and rigor the *non-artistic* aspects and conditions of the artistic experience and its object.[3]

Some scientific investigations are more immediately relevant to art than others. The science of acoustics exemplifies the less relevant type, since it is concerned with the physical conditions and character of sound as such, which is merely the "raw material"[4] of music. Investigations can be pursued in this field without musical training or a musical ear. The sounds which are analyzed are produced by instruments, e.g., tuning forks, constructed with scientific precision to emit pure tones of given frequencies of vibration; they are investigated by means of laboratory experiment; and the results of these experiments are interpreted in terms of physical laws and are expressed whenever possible in mathematical formulae. Primary

[3] Cf., e.g., George D. Birkhoff, *Aesthetic Measure* (Cambridge: Harvard University Press, 1933); Sir James Jeans, *Science and Music* (New York: Macmillan, 1937).

[4] Cf., below, pp. 39*ff*.

interest is thus focused upon sound as a physical, not as an artistic, phenomenon. The resultant discoveries relate to music indirectly, since music has a physical basis; they constitute a scientific explanation of the sounds and sound relationships which the musician uses, and they facilitate the construction of musical instruments. Experiments can even be conducted and acoustical theories formulated with specific reference to musical theory and practice. When this is done, it is of course necessary to apprehend the ultimate objective in musical terms, with due reliance upon a musical ear and the requisite musical training. But even when these investigations are musically motivated, the conclusions arrived at are only indirectly related to music as such, for they can never disclose the strictly *musical* conditions of musical excellence.

Musical theory exemplifies a second type of investigation, for it is concerned not with the "raw material" of art but rather with its "artistic medium"[5] and its effective exploitation. Investigations of this type are *directly* relevant to an adequate understanding of art and its creation and re-creation. The musical theorist must depend continually upon a musically trained ear and a cultivated musical intelligence, for it is his task to explore the *musical* operations, conventions, and forms of his art with systematic rigor. The Greek musical theorist, Aristoxenus, was the first in our western tradition to differentiate this "science" of music from the mathematico-physical science of acoustics.

It will be recalled that Plato distinguished in the *Republic*[6] between the purely empirical approach to music of "those good men who tease and torture the chords and rack them upon the pegs" and who are preoccupied with "the blows given by the plectrum, and the peevishness, reserve and frowardness of the strings," and the more scientific approach of the Pythagoreans who "investigate the numerical relation subsisting between these *audible* concords." He criticized the former for "postponing their reason to their ears," and for thus making themselves "quite ridiculous"; but he was also critical of the Pythagoreans who are "content to measure the notes and concords distinguished by the *ear*, one against another, and therefore toil without result." They should rather, he believed, "apply themselves to problems, with the object of examining what

[5] Cf., below, pp. 39*ff*.

[6] VII, 531. The quotations are from the translation of Davies and Vaughan (New York: Macmillan, 1921). The italics are mine.

numbers are, and what numbers are not, consonant, and what is the reason of the difference." In short, Plato conceived of the true science of harmony in purely mathematical terms.

Aristoxenus, in contrast, regarded a musical ear and a musical intelligence as the absolutely necessary prerequisites to genuine musical theory. He too was critical of the musical empiricists as well as of the Pythagoreans, but for reasons very different from those advanced by Plato.[7] Macran has admirably described these two contemporary approaches to music and Aristoxenus' own conception of musical theory.

"Until Aristoxenus appeared upon the scene the limits of Musical Science had been wholly misconceived. There existed, indeed, a flourishing school of Musical Art; there was conscious preference of this style of composition to that; of this method of performance to that; of this construction of instruments to that; and the habits formed by these preferences were transmitted by instruction. To facilitate this instruction, and as an aid to memory, recourse was had to diagrams and superficial generalization; but with principles for their own sake the artist, empiricist as he was, did not concern himself. . . . Over against these empiricists there stood a school of mathematicians and physicists, professing to be students of music, and claiming Pythagoras as their master, who were busied in reducing sounds to air vibrations, and ascertaining the numerical relations which replace for the mathematical intellect the sense-distinctions of high and low pitch. Here we have a genuine school of science, the soundness of whose hypotheses and the accuracy of whose computations have been established by the light of modern

[7] "Some of [our predecessors] introduced extraneous reasoning, and rejecting the senses as inaccurate fabricated rational principles, asserting that height and depth of pitch consist in certain numerical ratios and relative rates of vibration—a theory utterly extraneous to the subject and quite at variance with the phenomena; while others, dispensing with reason and demonstration, confined themselves to isolated dogmatic statements, not being successful either in their enumeration of the mere phenomena. . . . Our method rests in the last resort on an appeal to the two faculties of hearing and intellect. By the former we judge the magnitudes of the intervals, by the latter we contemplate the functions of the notes. We must therefore accustom ourselves to an accurate discrimination of particulars. . . . For the student of musical science accuracy of sense-perception is a fundamental requirement. . . . Musical cognition implies the simultaneous cognition of a permanent and of a changeable element and . . . this applies without limitation or qualification to every branch of music." *The Harmonics of Aristoxenus*, ed. and tr. H. S. Macran (Oxford: The Clarendon Press, 1902), pp. 188-90.

discovery. Nevertheless, musical science was still to seek. For if the artists were musicians without science, the physicists and mathematicians were men of science without music.[8] Under the microscope of their analysis all musical preferences are levelled, all musical worth is sacrificed; noble and beautiful sounds and melodies dissolve, equally with the ugly and base, into arithmetical relations and relations of relations, any one of which is precisely as valuable and as valueless as any other. . . . So busy were the Pythagoreans in establishing the mere physical and mathematical antecedents of sounds in general, that they never saw that the essence of musical sounds lies in their dynamical [i.e., musically functional] relation to one another. Thus they missed the true formal notion of music, which is ever present to Aristoxenus, that of a system or organic whole of sounds, each member of which *is* essentially what it *does* [i.e., musically], and in which a sound cannot become a member because merely there is room for it, but only if there is a function which it can discharge."[9]

Aristoxenus was quite correct in believing that purely physical and mathematical investigations of sound are, strictly speaking, irrelevant to an understanding of music as such, however interesting they may be to the natural scientist or to the mathematician, and however helpful they may be indirectly to musical theory and practice. They are not strictly relevant to music because it is never possible to determine musical excellence or the musical conditions of such excellence on a purely physical or mathematical basis. Only a trained musical ear and a disciplined musical intelligence can recognize musical quality or explore the musical devices whereby it is achieved. Once it has been recognized and its *musical* conditions determined, *their* physical basis can, in turn, be explored and interpreted in terms of pure physics and mathematics; but no invocation of a physical law or a mathematical formula can either justify or condemn the conclusions of a musical theorist or the critical judgments of a competent music critic. And what applies to music applies equally to the other arts; artistic quality and its artistic conditions, in whatever medium, are discoverable only by those whose innate aesthetic sensitivity has been suitably cultivated and whose

[8] Cf. Berlioz' distinction between "les musiciens: *Ils ne savent pas*" and "les musiciens: *Ils ne sentent pas*." H. Berlioz, *A Travers Chants* (Paris: Calmann-Lévy, 1927), p. 4.

[9] H. S. Macran, *op. cit.*, pp. 87-9.

artistic intelligence has been trained to a mastery of the relevant artistic conventions.

The scientific approach to art may also take the form of anthropological, sociological, and archaeological investigations. These studies contribute more directly to an understanding of art and its creation and reception than do those of the natural scientists. They are animated by the scientific ideal of impersonal objectivity, verification, and conceptual precision; but since they treat art as a *human* product and seek to relate it to its *social* context, the facts which they discover are more immediately relevant to critical understanding and philosophical appraisal. Thus the anthropologist and the sociologist study various manifestations of man's artistic consciousness as significant aspects of a culture pattern, and these throw light on the relation of artistic to religious, moral, and utilitarian attitudes and practices. The archaeologist makes an essential contribution to the study of art by rediscovering works of art and by setting them in their historical context. Without the aid of these disciplines, the critic and the philosopher of art would be hopelessly handicapped, for they would lack the empirical knowledge which is essential to the true understanding of their subject-matter. None the less, these disciplines are all primarily concerned not with the inner essence of art but with its social and historical context.

Psychological investigations of man's aesthetic experiences are too varied in character to permit of a summary description or appraisal.[10] Some are no more directly relevant to the artistic enterprise than is the science of acoustics to music. Others, e.g., the studies of Lipps and Bullough issuing in the doctrines of "empathy" and "psychical distance," are directly relevant and very illuminating. There can be no question that psychology can make a unique contribution in this field. The aesthetic, as opposed to the purely scientific, value of psychological studies depends upon the adequacy with which aesthetic phenomena are themselves apprehended and upon the way in which these phenomena are interpreted. The psychologist who states his problem with genuine artistic insight and who succeeds in exploring the psychological aspects of the artistic experience without doing violence to this insight can make an invaluable contribution to our knowledge of artistic creation and response. Most psychological studies thus far have been conducted

[10] Cf., e.g., Robert Morris Ogden, *The Psychology of Art* (New York: Scribners, 1938).

at a sub-artistic level; that is, the psychologist has usually, and quite naturally, been concerned with the simpler and more primitive types of aesthetic response rather than with the very complex activities of man's artistic creation of, and critical response to, genuine works of art.

Each of these variants of the scientific approach may therefore be said to make some contribution to an understanding of art and the aesthetic experience. But however relevant to art this type of investigation may be, it differs in kind from the investigations of the critic of art and literature.

(b) The term "critic" is here used in its most generic sense to include not only the professional critic but the sensitive art-lover. Criticism, whether lay or professional, has three essential aspects, the re-creative, the historical, and the judicial. The critic seeks to re-create the individual work of art with true artistic sensitivity, and to do so he must set it in its historical context. He also seeks to evaluate it in terms of appropriate artistic standards. I shall examine these complementary activities of the critic, and the hierarchy of critical norms to which he appeals, in Part IV of this volume. Here I am merely concerned to indicate the generic difference between the critical and the scientific approaches to art.

The critic's chief concern is to apprehend the work of art as an "agent" rather than as an "observer." Professor Fite[11] has formulated this valuable distinction in his discussion of morality, but it applies equally well to art. By an agent he means anyone who participates in an experience at first hand and who comprehends its object with sympathetic understanding based upon immediate intuition. An observer, in contrast, is one who approaches his object as an alien, externally, in the spirit of cold, dispassionate inquiry. Thus, in the moral sphere, a man adopts the rôle of agent when he enters imaginatively into the life of another human being with genuine sympathetic insight; he functions as an observer when he regards a human being with scientific detachment. Similarly, man approaches art as an agent whenever it is his prime concern to comprehend it with true artistic insight, whereas his approach is that of an observer when his dominant interest is focused upon the non-aesthetic context of art rather than upon its unique artistic essence.

[11] Warner Fite, *The Living Mind* (New York: The Dial Press, 1930), Chap. II.

So far as the scientifically-minded inquirer relies upon aesthetic sensitivity for the delimitation of his subject-matter, his approach to art is that of an agent rather than that of an observer. The critic, in turn, frequently investigates art as an observer, particularly in his historical studies. The scientist in the field of art is therefore not a mere observer, and the critic is not exclusively an aesthetic agent; each, to be effective, must be able to assume either rôle as occasion demands. But the critic's predominant interest is that of an agent intent on establishing artistic *rapport* with the work of art, whereas the scientist's chief concern is to explore art's non-artistic contexts. Thus the activity of the archaeologist or philologist is, from the scientific point of view, an end in itself, and artistic intuition is for them but a means to an end. The critic reverses this emphasis and values relevant scientific studies as essential means to the end of more adequate re-creation and appraisal.

(c) The essential task of the philosopher of art is analytical and evaluative. To perform this task competently he must assimilate the relevant discoveries of the scientist as well as the specific insights and evaluations of the critic. All that relates to art, whether directly or indirectly, is grist to his mill; and the value of his distinctively philosophical contribution will in large measure depend upon the precision and adequacy of his empirical orientation. This orientation need not, of course, take the form of first-hand scientific investigation or critical inquiry and appraisal. It is not his duty to participate in archaeological exploration or sociological surveys, any more than it is the duty of the philosopher of science to make actual laboratory experiments or to devise new scientific hypotheses. All that is required is a thorough understanding of the scientific approach and a familiarity with the results of scientific inquiry. Nor need the philosopher of art be a professional critic in his own right, though the more competent he is as a critic, the better will he be able to understand the methods and conclusions of critical analysis and appraisal. The philosopher's perennial temptation is to underestimate the importance of empirical orientation and to hurry into premature speculation. But there is also the theoretical danger of focusing his attention too closely upon this or that body of scientific or critical material and of failing, as a result, to perform his own distinctive task.

This task is to analyze the work of art *as such* in the several artistic media; to formulate the presuppositions of critical analysis and the norms of critical appraisal; and, finally, to attempt a philosophical evaluation of art in general and of the aesthetic experience as a whole. The critic must, in the nature of the case, limit himself to one field of critical endeavor, and even were he equally competent in every realm of art, his lack of philosophical training would perforce disqualify him for a philosophically rigorous analysis of the work of art as such. The critic is also seldom equipped to formulate with conceptual precision the presuppositions of his own critical methodology or the implicit norms of his own critical appraisals. Finally, the comparison of the artistic enterprise as a whole with other human enterprises, and the evaluation of the contribution of art and the aesthetic experience to human life is essentially a philosophical undertaking. The scientist *qua* scientist takes the order of nature for granted and assumes the possibility and value of scientific inquiry. The critic *qua* critic accepts without doubt or demonstration the objective reality and intrinsic value of art, and never questions the significance of his own critical endeavors. No specialist, as such, is equipped for the philosophical task of *comparative* analysis and appraisal, since it involves the raising of every major philosophical issue, metaphysical, epistemological, and axiological, presupposes familiarity with the essential methods and discoveries of the more specialized disciplines, and requires, in addition, the maintenance of an historical perspective. Only the philosopher of art who possesses the requisite philosophical training and who is scientifically, critically, and historically oriented can venture on this ambitious undertaking with any hope of reasonable success.

This must suffice to indicate the larger framework of the present inquiry. It will, as I have said, be limited to the systematic investigation of the work of art in the six major artistic media and to a discussion of certain principles of artistic and literary criticism. The more technical determination of the ontological and epistemological status of aesthetic quality and its variants, and the systematic evaluation of the aesthetic experience as a whole in its relation to other major types of human experience, must be postponed to another occasion, since it would involve the development and reasoned defense of an entire theory of knowledge, reality, and value. My empirical analysis would have been enriched by the introduction of anthropological, sociological, and psychological material, and my interpretation would have been clarified and strengthened by references to the writings of philosophers of art, past and present. I have had to forego the advantages of such orientation in this volume for lack of space. I have attempted to compensate for this lack by a special concern for the critical approach, and by the introduction of as much philosophical precision as possible. But I must ask any critics who may read this book to remember that all my references to specific works of art are introduced merely by way of illustration. If they object to my selection or use of any particular work of art in a specific context, they are invited to substitute a work which seems to them to illustrate the point at issue more effectively. And I must ask philosophers to recall the dictum of Aristotle: "Our discussion will be adequate if it has as much clearness as the subject-matter admits of. . . . It is the mark of an educated man to look for precision in each class of things just so far as the nature of the subject admits; it is evidently equally foolish to accept probable reasoning from a mathematician and to demand from a rhetorician scientific proofs."[12]

[12] *Ethica Nicomachea*, tr. W. D. Ross (Oxford: The Clarendon Press, 1925), 1094b.

PART I

THE ARTISTIC CATEGORIES AND THE MATTER OF ART

CHAPTER I

THE CATEGORIES OF ART

1. *The investigation of a work of art*

WHATEVER its medium, a work of art has an organic character. It is not internally undifferentiated and homogeneous, but is complex in quality and structure. Yet if it is to be considered a work of art at all, it must possess some measure of inner unity and coherence. Its parts must be artistically related to one another so as to contribute to the artistic vitality of the composition. The task of artistic analysis is to differentiate these parts and aspects in the work of art and to study them in abstracted isolation. The task of artistic synthesis is to comprehend the whole work of art as a fusion of aspects and an organization of parts. Both analysis and synthesis are essential to the apprehension of a work of art as an organic whole.

The term "organic" is of course taken from biology and applied to art metaphorically. A biological organism is a living entity composed of parts which, while contributing to the life of the whole, also depend upon one another and upon the whole organism for their own being. Thus a tree is a living organism because its life depends upon the healthy activity of its branches, leaves, and roots, and because these, in turn, depend upon the tree as a whole, and thus upon one another, for their own vitality and growth. A work of art is obviously not a living organism in the strict biological sense; at the pre-artistic level it is, save in the dance, an inanimate thing. But, as a work of art, it has an artistic vitality of its own. Its parts derive their artistic significance from the larger whole of which they are the constituent members, and its artistic unity, in turn, depends upon the contributions of its several parts and aspects.

We can press the biological metaphor a step further to apply to the process whereby a work of art is artistically apprehended. Analysis and synthesis "organically" condition one another, for analysis presupposes some prior awareness of the whole to be analyzed, and recognition of the whole as an artistically unified entity involves some realization that it is composed of related parts. Analysis and synthesis are thus complementary aspects of a single organic process of investigation.

In our normal artistic response to art, analysis and synthesis take place simultaneously and cooperate so smoothly that we are unaware of their respective contributions to artistic insight and enjoyment. Yet there can be no doubt that both are operative even here. To listen to music with any degree of musical intelligence involves distinguishing the notes, intervals, phrases, melodies, and movements, and it also involves observing their relation to one another in the composition. To appreciate a picture of artistic worth we must distinguish its colored areas, its two-dimensional shapes, and its representational subject-matter, and we must also note the contribution of these elements to the picture as a unified composition.

The philosophical analysis and synthesis of art is much more self-conscious and articulate. The philosopher is interested in the generic character of art in the several artistic media. It is, therefore, his task explicitly to differentiate these media from one another and to describe the structure of typical works of art in each medium, and of the individual work of art as such, with maximum precision. This is possible only if analysis is sharpened by the evocation of powertul abstract categories, rigorously defined. But the generic factors distinguished in such analysis must also be studied synthetically in their organic relation to one another and to the artistic unity which they condition.

In such investigation analysis tends to precede synthesis; we are inclined to attempt to complete the task of dismemberment before we undertake to reunite the parts into a whole. This procedure tempts the investigator to conceive of the object which he is studying as a mere aggregate of parts, and to forget that an organic whole is more than the sum of its parts. The biologist, who must dissect in order to learn, may forget that what he is dissecting is no longer alive but dead. The philosopher of art must be on his guard against a similar error. He must make every effort to remember that the expressive vitality of art, which is its most essential characteristic, reveals itself only to synthetic apprehension.

When a subject of investigation does not permit of actual dissection, analysis takes the form of ideational abstraction; factors which actually exist only in organic relation to other factors are isolated *in thought* and then studied *seriatim*. The analysis of art is predominantly of this type. The analyst must distinguish aspects and ingredients which in the work of art have their artistic being only in concrete artistic relation to one another. Genuine knowledge can be gained by such discriminations. But, once again, the analyst must be careful not to suppose that what is thus distinguishable is itself distinct, or that what has been abstracted in thought has any reality apart from the individual work of art itself.

2. *The categories of artistic analysis*

An artistic category may be defined as a concept which is essential to artistic inquiry and in terms of which alone art can be systematically explored.

Some artistic categories are, in a sense, more basic than others because they refer to characteristics which *every* work of art must, by definition, possess. "Matter," "form," and "content" are categories of this type. Other categories are useful to artistic analysis because they suggest questions which are relevant to any work of art in any medium, even though some works of art lack the character which the category specifies. Negative answers are as illuminating as affirmative answers, for it is as important to discover what generic characteristics works of art in this or that medium lack as it is to know what characteristics they possess.

The use of the term "category" to designate a concept which in one way or another is essential to artistic inquiry need not imply that such concepts are necessarily *a priori*. The whole philosophical dispute regarding the *apriority* of certain concepts is irrelevant to the present investigation. But it would be possible to argue that the more basic categories, for example, the categories of matter, form, and content, are *a priori* in the sense of being necessarily and affirmatively applicable, by definition, to every work of art in any medium. I make no claim, meanwhile, that my list of categories is either exhaustive or final, although a sincere effort has been made to define each category with precision and not to neglect any category of major importance.[1]

Every work of art exists in some medium, possesses some form, and, if it has any artistic merit whatever, has some expressed content. These three essential aspects of the work of art are clearly distinguishable; but since they are so mutually dependent it will be well to define them in such a way as to show their relation to one

[1] A diagrammatic chart of the categories applicable to works of art in the six major artistic media will be found at the end of the book. This chart is too condensed to be self-explanatory, but a preliminary scrutiny of it, and occasional reference to it during the reading of the text, is recommended.

another. The "matter"[2] of a work of art is that in it which has been expressively organized. The "form" of a work of art is the expressive organization of its matter. The "content" of a work of art is that which finds artistic expression through such formal organization of its matter.

The category of matter as here defined includes all the material, of whatever kind, which is available to the creative artist for artistic manipulation. Prior to its formal organization it has no artistic value whatever, though it may have an aesthetic character of its own. But it has certain artistic potentialities which are normally hidden from the layman but of which the creative artist must be aware, since only such awareness can dictate his choice of materials suited to artistic organization. The matter of any particular work of art is, of course, only a fragment of the large mass of material from which the artist makes his selection. We must therefore distinguish the category of the generic matter of art as such from the concept of the specific matter of any particular work of art.

The category of artistic form is the inclusive concept under which must be subsumed all of the innumerable ways in which the artist can organize his material. The actual form which an artist impresses upon a specific work of art is of course unique, and, as such, an aspect of the work's individuality. But comparison of various works of art with one another reveals certain generic forms which specific works exemplify. These generic forms do not exhaust the possibilities of formal organization, for these are infinite in number. Hence, just as the specific matter of any particular work of art is but a minute portion of the sum of available matter, so the specific form of any specific work is but one of an infinite number of ways in which the artist might have organized his material.

Artistic form is the peculiar locus of artistic quality, and the *sine qua non* of all artistic excellence.[3] Without artistic form an object is not a work of art at all. Non-artistic objects also possess form and individuality; but their form and their uniqueness are non-artistic in character. Aestheticians who have insisted on the preeminence of artistic form are quite justified in urging its importance. But artistic form is never merely an end in itself. It is a means of expression. Expression, in turn, must be the expression of something, however

[2] I shall distinguish presently between "matter" and "medium"; for the moment they may be considered synonymous.

[3] Cf., below, Chap. XXII, §1.

true or false, trivial or profound. To say that the form of a composition is artistically inexpressive is to deny it all artistic quality, while to claim that its form *is* expressive and therefore artistic is to assert that the artist has been at least in some degree successful in expressing, *via* artistic form, something which a sensitive and well-trained observer should be able to discover in the work of art itself.

Whatever is thus actually expressed in a work of art constitutes its artistic content. This content is never adequately translatable into another medium of communication, such as conceptual prose, nor can it even be perfectly re-expressed in another work of art in the same medium.[4] Artistic content has, it is true, a generic character which reappears in different artistic compositions in different media, and which can be analyzed and described. But the *specific* artistic content of every work of art is unique. This unique content is a function of the work's specific matter as well as of its specific form.

Further explanation of the artistic categories of matter, form, and content can best be given by means of a somewhat detailed analysis of the six major arts in their purer forms. This will be attempted in subsequent chapters.

3. The "major" and "minor" arts and the "pure" and "mixed" arts

The distinction between a "major" and a "minor" art is partly conventional. In some cultures no such distinction was recognized, and when it has been recognized, different cultures and periods have classified the arts in different ways. Today the distinction is usually taken for granted, but it is not easy to formulate its basis.

Perhaps the most essential characteristic of a major art is its potential expressiveness. The medium of a major art permits of a degree of artistic expressiveness which that of a minor art cannot rival. This is evidenced by the fact that the most expressive products of a minor art have a far thinner and less significant artistic content than that of equally distinguished products of a major art. Compare, for example, the finest lace, or china, or silver, with the finest architectural, pictorial, or literary productions.

A second basis for distinction is the artist's primary intent and objective. In the case of the minor arts, this intent is utility and decoration, not the artistic expression of a significant interpretation of human experience. The silversmith or the cabinet-maker is

[4] Cf., below, pp. 437*ff*.

primarily a craftsman with a well-developed decorative sense. His concern is to produce an article which is at once useful and aesthetically satisfying, rather than to create a work of art whose sole or primary function is to express genuine artistic insight. But this criterion, taken by itself, leaves the status of architecture somewhat ambiguous.

A third possible criterion is artistic self-sufficiency. The products of a major art may be said to be normally self-contained objects of artistic contemplation, whereas those of a minor art are normally objects which are not self-contained works of art in this sense. Compare, for example, a painting and a fine piece of embroidery, or a free-standing statue and a finely wrought balustrade. This distinction is again not absolute; how, for example, shall we classify a Gobelin tapestry? It has the merit, however, of indicating that the same art can be used both as a major and as a minor art. Thus a sculptor can create a self-contained figure or sculptural group, but he can also subordinate himself to an architect and provide him with statues and sculptural decorations which are specifically intended to articulate, enrich, and intensify an exterior or interior architectural effect.

No one of these criteria can justify an absolute distinction between the major and minor arts. The so-called major arts differ from the minor arts only in degree of expressiveness and self-sufficiency, not in kind. The one group shades imperceptibly into the other. But there can be no doubt that music and the dance, sculpture and painting, architecture and literature, are major arts, and the fact that each of these has its own distinctive primary medium justifies the differentiation of each from the other five. No further defense is needed for their selection for special study in this volume.

The distinction between the "pure" and the "mixed" arts is also a pragmatic rather than an absolute distinction, and it too must be based upon the nature of the primary medium employed. An art, whether major or minor, may be said to be "pure" if it relies on *one* generic primary medium, "mixed," when *two or more* generic primary media are employed. Instrumental music is a pure art according to this definition, while the opera is obviously a mixed art since it makes use not only of music but of words, acting, stage-setting, and the dance. I shall restrict myself for the most part to the pure major arts, since their analysis should precede that of the mixed arts, but I shall discuss the problem of how the arts may profitably be combined in my analysis of vocal music and various mixed forms of the dance.

The following analysis of art will therefore be by no means exhaustive. But if it is sound and basic within the prescribed limits, the method of analysis employed, as well as the more essential conclusions arrived at, should be applicable, *mutatis mutandis*, to the minor arts and to the more complicated mixed arts as well.[5]

4. Preliminary description of the media of the six pure major arts

Before attempting a more detailed analysis of the media of the major arts, let us quickly survey the field by means of a brief, non-technical description of the primary and secondary[6] media of the arts here considered.

The primary medium of pure or absolute music consists of musically related tones and rests which permit of formal organization into abstract musical patterns. These patterns are not visible, as are architectural compositions, but auditory; they are not "imitative" or representational, and therefore differ from those of pantomime and of representational sculpture and painting; and they are not, in whole or in part, symbolic of ideational meaning as are words, taken both singly and in combination. The secondary medium or subject-matter of pure music is human emotion and conation. In vocal and program music both media are more complicated.

The primary medium of the non-mimetic dance is the human body in motion and at rest. Its secondary medium, like that of music, is human emotion and conation. The dance has, since earliest times, been accompanied by music, or at least by an audible rhythmic beat. So accompanied, it is not, strictly speaking, a pure art. Even with an auditory accompaniment, the dance need not be mimetic; its three-dimensional patterns, like musical patterns, can be directly expressive of inner emotional states and attitudes. But the dance is

[5] It is with genuine regret that I have had to ignore the art of the motion picture. This is undoubtedly a major art according to any significant criterion, and it is, in addition, one of the most living arts today. But it is too new and too complicated to permit of adequate analysis in this volume. I am confident, however, that my analysis of the other arts can provide a useful basis for its systematic exploration.

[6] This distinction will be discussed in the next section. It is, in a word, the distinction between the partly or wholly sensuous medium (here called "primary") which is *directly* manipulated by the artist, and the subject-matter (here called the "secondary" medium) whose interpretation achieves artistic expression only *indirectly* through the organization of the primary medium.

often more or less mimetic. Pantomime is the "imitation" or mimicry, by means of bodily movement and facial expression, of the appearance and behavior of human and other individuals and types. It is also possible by means of pantomime to tell a simple story. Hence the secondary medium of pantomime includes whatever lends itself to silent mimicry. The art of acting also involves bodily movement. But acting is a mixed art because it makes use not only of bodily movement but of the spoken word. The dance is therefore the purest exemplification of the generic art of bodily movement.

The primary medium of architecture is three-dimensional solids and voids. Like music and the non-mimetic dance, architecture is essentially an "abstract" art which achieves artistic expressiveness directly through non-representational forms. It thus differs basically from the representational arts of sculpture and painting. It differs also from literature because its primary medium and its forms are not essentially symbolic, as are words and phrases, though architectural forms may acquire symbolic meaning, as may musical figures and the movements of the dance.

Architecture differs from the other major arts in one important respect. I am not referring, as might be supposed, to its dependence upon engineering principles—a dependence which has received much attention from contemporary architectural "functionalists." Architecture is no more enslaved by the non-artistic laws of its primary medium than are the other arts by the analogous laws of their respective media. I have in mind the social function of architecture. The use to which a building is put is its distinctive secondary medium. The architect must know, from the beginning, not only the site and available building materials but also the manner in which the building is to be employed. This is an artistic, not merely a utilitarian, necessity, for the artist is under artistic obligation to express in architectural form the spirit of the building's social function. All art, of course, has a general social function, and particular works of art in other media may be created for particular social uses and occasions. But it is only in architecture, among the major arts, that a more specific "program" constitutes an essential part of the secondary medium. Like certain minor arts, architecture is in this sense peculiarly utilitarian in character; the artistic expression of its practical use is integral to architectural excellence.

Sculpture and painting can be considered together. Their primary or physical media are of course different; the sensuous medium of sculpture is a three-dimensional solid, that of painting, a two-dimensional surface. But these arts resemble each other in inviting representational treatment, though their primary media can be organized non-representationally. In sculptural and pictorial abstractions the respective primary media are organized, as are musical tones, into non-representational patterns which give direct artistic expression to inner emotive and conative states. But unlike the primary media of music and architecture, the physical media of painting and sculpture lend themselves so effectively to the representation of visible objects that the potentialities of these arts cannot be said to have been adequately exploited in pure "abstractions." These arts, like the pantomimic dance, have, therefore, as their secondary medium all objects which might be regarded as potential representational subject-matter.

Sculpture and painting may also be treated symbolically. Symbolic meaning can be attached both to abstract and to representational forms, whether pictorial or sculptural. But such symbolism is no more essential to these arts than it is to music, architecture, and the dance. It is only literature whose primary medium is essentially symbolic.

The primary medium of literature is words in meaningful relation. This medium is more complex than that of any of the other arts, for words themselves have a complex character. They have, on the one hand, a sensuous aspect, for they are audible sounds to which are assigned visible symbols in all civilized languages. But these sounds (and visible signs) also have ideational meanings. These meanings, in turn, are in essence conceptual, but they may also, in addition, be imagistic, emotive, and conative. The relation of sensory symbol and ideational meaning is arbitrary (save in the case of onomatopoeia), since meanings become attached to signs by fiat or convention. The meaning of a verbal symbol must therefore be learned, and only through translation does such a symbol become intelligible.[7]

The sound-patterns of words used in various combinations may be directly expressive of emotional attitudes in a way somewhat analogous to the way in which musical patterns can be directly expressive. But complete reliance in literature on the immediate non-symbolic expressiveness of the spoken word is even more of a *tour*

[7] This is less true of ideographic writing.

de force than is complete reliance on wholly abstract form in sculpture and painting, and constitutes an even greater failure to exploit the potentialities of the primary medium. The meanings of words used singly and in combination constitute an essential part of the primary medium of literature.

The referential meanings of words refer us to "objects" of one type or another which, in aggregate, constitute the potential subject-matter or secondary medium of literature. This medium is much more extensive and varied than that of any of the other arts. Music and the dance are, for the most part, restricted to the interpretation of man's emotive and conative states. The chief subject-matter of architecture is man's social activities which require to be housed. Sculpture lends itself best to the representation of the human body, and even painting can directly represent only the visible world of nature. Literature, in contrast, can treat of every type of object and every kind of human experience. It cannot, it is true, make its physical subject-matter visible to the eye, as can sculpture and painting, nor can it express man's emotive and conative states in the way in which music expresses them. It too has its expressive limitations. But what it cannot "represent" to sense it can conjure up for the imagination, and what it cannot directly evoke by sound alone it can evoke by its own methods of indirection. Because of its complex primary medium literature has a far richer secondary medium than any of the other major arts.

These six arts can be classified in several different ways with reference to their respective primary media. Music, the dance, and literature, for example, are "temporal" arts in the sense of unfolding themselves to the percipient in a determined temporal order and at a tempo more or less dictated by the composition itself; in them time plays a rôle which it does not play in architecture, sculpture, or painting. Again, music and literature are "auditory" arts, whereas the other major arts are "visual." This means that the latter are spatial in the sense of actually existing, in one way or another, in space. Yet spatial associations attach themselves to musical tones and patterns, and literature is rich in spatial imagery. Both of these classifications are likely to be misleading unless the precise relation of each art to space and time is formulated with great precision.

The classification most useful for my purpose is that which distinguishes between the "abstract" arts of music, the pure dance, and architecture, the "representational" arts of sculpture and painting, and the "symbolic" art of literature. These descriptive terms will be explained and justified in due course.

5. "Raw material" and "artistic medium," "primary" and "secondary"

The matter of art can be analyzed with precision only in terms of two basic distinctions which cut across one another in such a way that neither distinction can be defined save by reference to the other. The first is that between the "raw material" and the "artistic medium." The raw material of art includes whatever might be of use to the artist as material for *ultimate* artistic manipulation and interpretation, considered *prior* to all preliminary selection and organization. The artistic medium is this same material *after* it has been selected and organized in such a way as to be *immediately* available for artistic use. The distinction between "primary" and "secondary" applies both to the raw material and to the artistic medium. The primary raw material of any art is the sensuous (in the case of literature, the partly sensuous) material which, once it has been organized into a language or vehicle of artistic expression and communication, constitutes its primary artistic medium. The secondary raw material of any art is its potential subject-matter prior to all pre-artistic selection and appraisal; its secondary artistic medium is this same subject-matter after it has been scrutinized with an eye to its immediate availability for the art in question. The relation of these two distinctions to one another can be indicated diagrammatically as follows:

	Primary	*Secondary*
Raw material	Primary raw material	Secondary raw material
Artistic medium	Primary artistic medium	Secondary artistic medium

The precise nature and import of these distinctions will be evident only after we have explored the primary and secondary raw materials and artistic media of the six major arts in turn. But a preliminary and non-technical explanation of them is desirable.

The distinction between the primary raw material and the primary artistic medium can be illustrated most simply in music. The primary raw material of pure instrumental music is sound and silence as such. But the composer does not start with sound and silence "in the raw." His primary medium consists of readily producible sounds organized into a system of musically related tones expressible in a scale. A scale may be defined as a series of tones ordered with relation to their pitch and accepted by convention as the basis for musical composition. Many different kinds of scales have been and still are used as the basis for musical composition, but all music is necessarily based upon some scale or other. It is the scale, then, or rather the system of tonal relations whose distinctive character finds expression in the scale, which constitutes the basic structure of the "language" of music. This language includes in addition not only the many timbres and degrees of volume and intensity which musical instruments can produce, as well as variations in duration and tempo, but also musically pregnant silences or rests. For a musical rest is clearly not mere silence or absence of sound; it is a silence endowed with musical significance by the tones which precede and follow it. As part of a specific musical composition a rest is, of course, created by the musical forms. But as an aspect of the medium of music the rest, considered generically, is silence apprehended in terms of its musical potentialities.

In the case of music, the primary raw material must be subjected to a good deal of selection and organization before it is transformed into a primary medium suited to the requirements of artistic composition. In most of the other arts such preliminary ordering of the primary raw material is not carried so far and the distinction between it and the primary artistic medium is not so apparent. But there too the distinction exists, and is, as we shall see, of importance.

Sculpture and painting, regarded as representative arts, provide the simplest illustration of the distinction between the secondary raw material and the secondary artistic medium or subject-matter. Their secondary raw material includes all that might conceivably be interpreted in any of the primary sculptural or pictorial media. In the case of sculpture it includes all three-dimensional physical objects which a sculptor might conceivably represent in a sculptural medium, and, in addition, whatever physical events and activities, emotive-conative states, and ideas permit of sculptural interpretation either directly or indirectly, i.e., *via* representation or symbolism. All these "objects" of human awareness constitute in aggregate the potential subject-matter of sculpture as such. But when a sculptor applies himself to the problem of what subject-matter is best adapted to sculptural interpretation in general, and when he considers the more specific problem of what types of subject-matter are most amenable to interpretation in this or that specific primary sculptural medium, he discovers that some subjects lend themselves to sculptural treatment far better than others, and that each of the several primary sculptural media has its own expressive potentialities and limitations.

Thus, if the expressive potentialities of the primary sculptural medium, regarded generically, are contrasted with those of the primary pictorial medium in its generic character, it is evident that there are many aspects of the visible world of nature which can be represented with ease in painting and only with difficulty, if at all, in sculpture. For example, clouds can be magnificently represented on canvas, whereas the medium of stone is strained to the limit in the representation of clouds in all their billowy, soft insubstantiality (Figs. 111, 113, 114, 125). The sculptor can, in his own way, represent water (Fig. 112) and rays of light (Fig. 113); but he cannot portray a stormy sea or an atmosphere bathed in light, whereas the painter can treat these subjects with the greatest ease (Figs. 114, 169). The ideal physical subject-matter of sculpture is the human body, either nude or clothed in drapery substantial enough to allow of sculptural handling and yet pliable enough not wholly to obscure the contours of the body underneath it (Figs. 109, 110, 115, 116).

Each of the primary sculptural media (e.g., various types of stone, metal, and wood, ivory, porcelain, stucco, etc.) also lends itself better to the treatment of some types of representational subject-matter than to other types. Thus stone is ideally suited to the sculptural rendering of heavy, massive bodies, and of whatever aspects of man's experience are characteristically associated with such bodies (Figs. 128, 152); bronze is the ideal sculptural medium for the expression of sinuous and tensile grace (Figs. 117, 119); terracotta and colored porcelain are perfectly adapted to soft and delicate rococo subjects (Figs. 122, 124).

That each of the primary media in each of the major arts has its own expressive potentialities and limitations is recognized by every competent artist. Were an artist equally at home in all the primary artistic media he would, given a certain subject-matter, prefer to treat it in one medium rather than another; or conversely, an artist who was restricted to a given primary medium and who was sensitive to its expressive potentialities and limitations, would realize that some subjects lend themselves to effective treatment in that medium far better than others. This is not to deny the artist's right to interpret in a given primary medium a subject not ideally suited to that medium. If his attempt is successful, when judged by artistic standards, this success testifies to his unusual skill. If his work merely exemplifies his precocity, we entitle it a *tour de force* (Figs. 103, 109); if he fails completely to achieve his objective, his failure may be attributed either to his technical incompetence or to his unwise choice of subject-matter. All things are allowable in art provided the artist succeeds in achieving genuine artistic expressiveness in his chosen primary medium. What I am here concerned to urge is merely the necessity, which the artist cannot escape, of delimiting the potential subject-matter of his generic primary medium and of recognizing the specific potentialities and limitations of his specific primary medium. For it is precisely this preliminary selection and appraisal of art's secondary raw material which transforms it into a secondary artistic medium or subject-matter immediately available for artistic use in specific works of art in this or that primary medium.

This principle of selection differs radically from the principle, frequently invoked in the nineteenth century, i.e., that only those subjects which are themselves beautiful are appropriate subjects for artistic interpretation, and that whatever is ugly or aesthetically neutral in its own right is automatically unfit for artistic treatment. The choice of subject-matter here referred to is dictated entirely by the expressive potentialities of the primary medium and by considerations of artistic technique, and not at all by the objective beauty, ugliness, or aesthetic neutrality of the subjects available for artistic treatment.

On the other hand, the fact that the secondary raw material of art frequently does have an aesthetic character, and sometimes possesses formal beauty as well, cannot be a matter of indifference to the creative artist. The musical composer cannot afford to ignore the aesthetic appeal of certain sounds and timbres, nor can the sensitive sculptor or painter ignore the beauty of the human body and of natural forms and scenes. In his own way, and with due regard to the work of art itself which he is in process of creating, the artist will often attempt to incorporate this aesthetic quality and this formal beauty into his art. But it is essential that both he and the critic clearly discriminate between mere aesthetic quality as such and mere formal beauty, on the one hand, and genuinely artistic form, on the other, for it is only the latter which, by definition, is expressive of an artistic content.

It is also very important to distinguish subject-matter from artistic content. The tendency of the artistically untutored layman to confuse subject-matter and content in art is notorious. No less notorious has been the tendency of certain artists, and particularly sculptors and painters in certain periods, to attempt to reproduce a given subject-matter as literally as the medium allows (Figs. 103-105), and of certain philosophers, notably Plato,[8] to condone this practice. Were subject-matter and artistic content the same thing, works of this type would exemplify art at its very best.

The fallacy involved in such identification of subject-matter and expressed content will be at once apparent to all who have genuine critical discernment. I have used the term "artistic content" to signify that which the artist expresses *via* artistic form in an artistic medium. A work of art is expressive in proportion as the artist succeeds in "telling us something," in *revealing* something about human experience and the reality of which we are a part. There is all the difference in the world between "just talking" and "saying something" worth while, between mere statement of atomistic fact and illuminating interpretation. Sheer prosaic statement of fact in its unrelieved particularity is, in every universe of discourse, wholly unilluminating and uninteresting. What we crave as intelligent beings is a commentary on our human experience and on the world around us. We want to escape the boredom of sheer particularity by discovering the inner nature of things, their relation to one another, and their larger meaning and significance. At their best, science, philosophy, and history all contribute such illumination, each in its own way, and so does art at its best. Art too is expressive or revelatory of significant aspects of man's inner and outer experience. In the abstract arts this expression is for the most part achieved directly, *via* abstract form. The primary media of the representational arts can also be organized into more or less immediately expressive "surface" patterns. But sculpture and painting achieve expressiveness primarily through suitable choice and treatment of a representa-

[8] Cf., *Republic*, Book X.

tional subject-matter, yet not through mere literal reproduction of the appearance of things but by means of selection, arrangement, distortion, and other interpretative devices. The rôle of interpretation in literature is equally essential. In all the arts, subject-matter as such is no more artistically expressive than is the primary medium as such. *Both* await artistic manipulation, and success or failure in artistic expressiveness depends entirely upon how *both* media are handled by the creative artist. Merely to introduce a subject-matter into a work of art is to indulge in a meaningless statement of particular fact. *What* is artistically expressed (i.e., the artistic content) depends upon *how* the primary medium is organized to express in the manner of art the artist's interpretation of his subject-matter.

The chief types of subject-matter available to the artist for artistic selection and interpretation are (i) physical objects and events, and their perceptual attributes; (ii) man's social or communal needs and activities, religious, civic, domestic, and the like; (iii) man's emotive-conative states; and (iv) the ideas, whether conceptual or imagistic, and whether religiously, socially, or introspectively oriented, in terms of which man interprets his experiences and the objects of his awareness. This is not offered as a philosophically rigorous classification, but merely as a convenient and useful basis for a more detailed empirical analysis of the secondary media of the major arts. When I come, in Chapter XVI, to the analysis of artistic content, I shall discriminate between different generic types of content with somewhat greater precision.

When the distinctive subject-matter of each of the six major arts is analyzed in terms of this classification, it is found that whereas each art can, in one way or another, treat of each of the generic types of subject-matter, different types are basic to different arts. Thus music can interpret abstract ideas and the perceptual world only very inadequately and indirectly, *via* musical symbolism and "programmatic" suggestion. Its basic subject-matter is man's emotive-conative states. The same applies to the non-mimetic and the mimetic dance. Architecture does not lend itself at all to the representation of perceptual objects, but it can express, *via* architectural form, certain perceptual attributes and, *via* symbolism, certain general ideas. Its basic subject-matter consists of various types of social activity, with which are associated various emotive states and conative attitudes. The basic subject-matter of sculpture is the human body in motion and at rest, but the sculptor can also express, directly *via* artistic form, indirectly *via* symbolism, but primarily by his representational handling of the human body, certain emotive-conative states and ideas. He can also, within limits, interpret certain types of events and activities. The subject-matter of painting resembles that of sculpture except that it can represent the whole visible world as effectively as sculpture can the human body. Finally, the unrivalled scope of literature is indicated by the fact that it can deal with equal ease with all four types of subject-matter, and that no one type can be considered basic in this medium.[9] In my analysis of the secondary media of the six major arts I shall follow this classification of the generic types of artistic subject-matter.

[9] Cf. the chart at the end of the volume.

CHAPTER II

THE MATTER OF MUSIC

1. The raw material of music

(a) *The primary and secondary raw material of pure music.* The primary raw material of pure music is auditory sound with variations of pitch, timbre, intensity, and duration, plus silence, regarded as the mere absence of such sound. Tempo, conceived in purely physical terms as rate of speed, should also be included, since it provides the physica basis for tempo in a musical sense, and, in combination with duration, intensity, and other factors, for musical rhythm. By physical tempo is meant the rapidity with which successive sounds follow one another in time.

This primary raw material of music is, as such, entirely pre-artistic in character and constitutes the subject-matter of the physical science of acoustics. That is, the physicist can study sound as a purely physical phenomenon with the aid of laboratory experiment and physico-mathematical theory and can analyze its structure in terms of scientific concepts and mathematical formulae. He can, for example, determine with accuracy the vibration rates of "pure" sounds of this or that pitch and express the relations of pitch between one sound and another in terms of mathematical ratios. But "no physical conclusion is of musical value which the ear does not endorse."[1]

The secondary raw material of pure music comprises all the emotions and conative[2] attitudes which might conceivably find expression in pure music, for example, such emotional states as joy and sorrow, and such conative attitudes as hope and despair, endeavor and resignation. The emotive and conative aspects of man's inner experience are distinguishable in theory but are so intimately related in actuality that we are justified, in the present context, in considering them together, as "emotive-conative" states. A composer usually strives, consciously or unconsciously, to express certain

[1] A. H. Fox-Strangways, in the article entitled "Interval" in *Grove's Dictionary of Music and Musicians*, 3rd edition, ed. H. C. Colles (London: Macmillan, 1927-1928).

[2] Conation includes all dynamic tendencies and processes, such as wishing, willing, and striving, at various stages of conscious reflection.

emotive-conative states and moods through pure musical pattern. Such terms as *scherzo* (a joke, jest, or pleasantry), *rhapsody*, *allegro* (originally meaning cheerful, gay, merry, though often used merely to designate tempo), *dolce* (sweet and gentle), *con brio* (with vivacity and spirit), and *con fuoco* (with fire and passion), are not only instructions to the performer but also indications of the mental states or moods which the music is written to express.

As expressed in music, these emotive-conative states constitute its content, and I shall have occasion to deal with them as such in due course. But prior to all selection and musical interpretation they constitute the secondary raw material of music. Were man incapable of experiencing such states, it would be impossible for the musician or any other artist to express them *via* artistic form in an artistic medium.

(b) *The secondary raw material of program music and of occasional music.* Music, I have said, does not lend itself readily to the representation of perceptual objects, scenes, or events. The attempt is often made to introduce such representational subject-matter by means of "imitation"[3] or programmatic suggestion. The brief passage in Beethoven's *Pastoral Symphony* (the Sixth), in which the songs of the cuckoo, the nightingale, and the quail are reproduced with considerable fidelity, may be cited in illustration, as may also the braying of the ass in Mendelssohn's *Overture* to *A Midsummer Night's Dream*, the vivid suggestion of thunder and lightning in Wagner's Introduction to the first act of *Die Walküre* and in the fourth movement of Beethoven's *Pastoral Symphony*, the bleating of lambs in Richard Strauss' *Don Quixote*, and the sound of musketry and cannon in Beethoven's *Battle Symphony*. Programmatic intent varies greatly, ranging all the way from a more or less faithful reproduction of sounds such as the humming of bees, the gentle lapping of water, the shriek and turmoil of the wind, and the steady crashing of machinery, to the suggestion of moods associated with typical periods and seasons, scenes or events, such as the night, the spring, a well or a forest glade, a farewell or a victorious return.[4] In many cases a

[3] The term "imitation" is here used in the more general sense of "reproduction of recognizable sounds," not in the technical musical sense, i.e., as referring to that type of music in which the contour of one statement is reproduced or suggested by another.

[4] Such effects may be found in Rimsky Korsakov's *The Flight of the Bumblebee*, Debussy's *La Mer*, Mendelssohn's *Fingal's Cave*, Rachmaninoff's *Toteninsel*, Wagner's *Overture* to *The Flying Dutchman*, Honegger's *Pacific 231*, Haydn's *Creation*, Spohr's

poem, drama, or picture is consciously used as the basis of musical invention or organization, as in Liszt's *Les Préludes*, Debussy's *L'Après-Midi d'un Faune*, or Moussorgsky's *Pictures at an Exhibition*. In order to clarify his descriptive intention the composer himself sometimes supplies his hearers with program notes, as did Berlioz in the case of his *Fantastic Symphony*, though it is oftener the critic who writes such notes to indicate what the music "is about." It is, on the other hand, not unusual for a composer to suggest the mood or general subject of his composition in the title; *vide* Schumann's *Carnaval* and his *Scenes from Childhood.*

This is not the place to assess the artistic merits of such attempts at musical representation.[5] That program music exists and that some of it possesses genuine musical value must be admitted. If we could be certain that the representational factors in good program music are wholly irrelevant to its musical excellence, and that such music is good music in spite of, and never even partly because of, these factors, we could ignore them altogether in an account of music's raw material and artistic medium. In order not to prejudge the issue, however, let us assume that these representational ingredients may at least occasionally make some contribution to the final artistic effect of such compositions. On this assumption, all aspects of nature which might conceivably allow of representational treatment in music must be included under the heading of its secondary raw material.

I have mentioned the fact that architecture seems to differ from the other major arts in having as an essential part of its secondary medium a more or less specific social function. Music and the other arts may, though they need not, be adapted to characteristic social uses and even to specific social occasions. Examples of socially functional music written for characteristic types of human activity are marches (including funeral and wedding marches) and dance music of all sorts. Examples of music not only written for special occasions, but in a manner specifically suited for such occasions, include much of the music written for the liturgy of the Roman

Ninth Symphony, *The Seasons*, Mendelssohn's Nocturne for *A Midsummer Night's Dream*, Ravel's *Jeux d'Eau*, and Bach's *Caprice on the Departure of a Well-beloved Brother*.

[5] For discussions of this problem see Ernest Newman, *Musical Studies* (New York: John Lane, 1905), Chap. III: "Programme Music"; Percy C. Buck's article, "Programme-Music," in *Grove's Dictionary of Music and Musicians*; and Frederick Niecks, *Programme Music in the Last Four Centuries* (London: Novello, 1906).

Catholic Church, in which not only the *Proprium* is treated with special reference to the place and the occasion under which it is to be heard, but the *Ordinarium* is given characteristic treatment as well. Bach's *Wedding Cantata*, Beethoven's Overture, *Die Weihe des Hauses*, and Mozart's Masonic music are also clear instances of compositions conditioned by the time and occasion for which they were written. To the extent to which such activities and occasions can influence musical composition artistically and contribute to the artistic whole of the composition, these too, taken generically, must be included in the secondary raw material of music.

(c) *The primary and secondary raw material of music with words.* We cannot neglect vocal music in our discussion of the matter of music, since vocal music has bulked so very large in our own European tradition as well as in that of other cultures.[6] The problem of whether the music or the text is, or should be, artistically dominant in vocal music is irrelevant here.[7] Except where the words are wholly subordinated to the music and where their meaning is so completely ignored that they are merely a device for facilitating the production of musical tones by the human voice, the words and the ideas which they express are at least of some artistic importance. In such compositions as Bach's *B Minor Mass* and Brahms' *Vier ernste Gesänge* the importance of the words is very great. Both the primary and secondary raw material of literature become in this case part of the raw material, primary and secondary, of music, although clearly there are many potentialities of language as such, and a great many types of subject-matter with which language can deal, which can have no place in vocal music.

2. *The artistic medium of music*

The broad distinction between the raw material and the artistic medium of any art consists, I have said, in the fact that the raw material is the medium prior to all preliminary selection, organization, and interpretation from the point of view of artistic potentiality; the medium, both primary and secondary, is the raw material already subjected to these processes. The raw material may

[6] A survey of the history of music not only in Europe but in other cultures shows that instrumental music unaccompanied either by words or the dance or both together is the exception rather than the rule. Even in our western tradition pure music really came into its own only after 1600.

[7] Cf., below, pp. 61-2.

be aesthetically pleasing, displeasing, or neutral. The artistic medium may be called aesthetic but "pre-artistic" since it has passed through a preliminary process of artistic selection but still lacks the artistic quality or character which even an uncompleted work of art possesses.

(a) *The primary artistic medium of pure music.* Three essential factors must here be taken into account: first, the tonal relationships of pitch expressed in a scale; second, the qualitative characteristics of the timbre of different instruments and different human voices; and third, the quantitative variations of intensity, duration, and tempo. The first of these factors is basic to all formal structure in music, the second is the chief source of musical "color," i.e., of its sensuously qualitative character, and the third is the basis of musical rhythm. These three factors are closely interrelated and are all essential parts of the primary medium. The composer cannot afford to neglect any of them in his creative work, though prior emphasis can be given now to one factor, now to another.

(i) The basis of musical structure consists of a system of related tones expressible in a scale. A musical "tone" is a sound of a given pitch which stands in definite relation to other sounds, each of a different pitch. In this sense no sound, taken by itself, can be called a musical tone, although some individual sounds are more pleasing to the musical ear than others, partly because of their purity and partly because of their pitch, timbre, overtones or absence of overtones, etc. A sound takes on musical significance only when it stands in a definite relation of pitch to other sounds. These relations or musical "intervals" may or may not differ within a given musical system, and musical systems differ by virtue of the characteristic intervals between tones as expressed in a basic scale.

In a "tonal" system or scale, each tone stands in definite relation to one tone which is the tonal center or "tonic." The tonic is the original starting point and the continual point of reference. Certain intervals in any tonal system are more immediately satisfying to the musical ear of anyone at home in this system than are other intervals. Examples of such intervals are the Octave and the perfect Fourth and Fifth, which are elementary relations in most musical systems, and the major Third, which is so important in modern European music but which had no place as an elementary relation in the tonal system of ancient Greece. Relations of this type are called concords. Other relations demand "resolution" into these elementary concords, because they first announce themselves to the ear as discords and leave the hearer dissatisfied until they have been transformed into relations which he is able to accept as concords.

Tonal scales allow of various modifications which, taken together, define the distinctive character of the musical system as a whole. The basis of modern diatonic music, for example, is the heptatonic scale which, with its interpolated (chromatic) degrees, has twelve major and twelve minor related keys. A "key" is a specific set of relations among scale tones with reference to a tonic, and the terms "major" and "minor" signify the two pervasive "modes" within one or the other of which every key in the diatonic scale must fall. These keys and modes are of essential musical importance since the character of a composition depends notably upon the key or keys and the mode or modes in which it is written. For though in the system of tuning accepted by us at present all keys in the same mode are identical save for pitch, pitch is none the less felt by sensitive ears to be so significant emotionally that composers discriminate carefully in the use of one or another of the possible pitches. Beethoven, for example, felt C minor a tragic key (*vide* his *Fifth Symphony* or *Opus 111*), though identical relationships would exist in C sharp minor or any other key.

I have summarized a few of these well-known facts[8] to give some indication of the complex ways in which mere sound, the raw material of music, is selectively organized into an artistic medium. Many different musical systems have been devised which differ with

[8] Cf. Joseph Yasser, "The Future of Tonality," *Modern Music*, Special Supplement to Vol. VIII, No. 1 (Nov.-Dec. 1930), p. 2; reprinted as *Addendum II*, in Yasser, *A Theory of Evolving Tonality* (New York: American Library of Musicology, W. W. Norton and Co., Inc., 1932), p. 331: "Tonality is a principle which organically and tonocentrically unites the melodic and harmonic functions of a certain number of systematically arranged sounds as most simply represented in a musical scale.

To expand this definition and describe the two functional aspects in reference to our present (diatonic) system which is governed by the above principle, we may add that the tonal center represents a single note (Tonic) from the melodic point of view, and a chord of three notes arranged by Thirds (tonic Triad) from the harmonic point of view. Again, that in the melodic aspect this system manifests a characteristic distribution of its seven regular (diatonic) degrees within an Octave, forming various chains of whole steps and half steps (Modes) which, by the aid of the additional set of five auxiliary (chromatic) degrees interpolated between the former, can be freely transposed into twelve different keys. Finally, that from the harmonic viewpoint this system divides all its possible tonal combinations into two distinctly opposed groups of consonances and dissonances, the latter inevitably 'requiring' resolution into the former."

respect to their basic tonal intervals and their resultant musical quality but which are alike in all being tonal in some sense.[9] Even the so-called "atonal" music of Schönberg and his followers does not entirely divorce itself from the fundamental principle of tonality. It makes a resolute and partly successful effort to disorganize our classical tonal system as a system and to introduce a certain degree of musical anarchy. Yet even it is based on an arbitrarily constructed scale of twelve tones no one of which may be considered a tonic, and thus recognizes the principle of tonality by the very act of systematically and consistently repudiating it. Even atonal music, therefore, is far from employing mere sound *as such* as its artistic medium; it is based upon a scale of tones precisely related to one another, and its compositions, like all musical compositions, are in large measure determined by the musical potentialities and limitations of its carefully chosen medium.

Musical systems such as our diatonic system are so complex in character that a composer who wishes to make use of them, and a critic who aspires to competence in the understanding and appraisal of compositions based upon them, must study them with "scientific" rigor. This study[10] is the aesthetic but pre-artistic equivalent of the true science of acoustics, whose subject-matter is natural sound as such. It differs from the latter in presupposing a musical ear. It differs also from the wider discipline of musical criticism which is concerned with the analysis and appraisal of specific musical compositions suitably rendered, rather than with musical theory as such.

(ii) Every actually sounded musical tone has a distinctive timbre whose nature is determined by the physical organ from which it issues. Each musical instrument produces sounds of one or more characteristic timbres, and so does the human voice, adult and adolescent, male and female, tenor and bass, etc. The same musical score played on different instruments, such as the piano and the harpsichord, for instance, may sound so different that the com-

[9] Cf., for example, the ancient scales or "modes" of the Greeks and Romans, the pentatonic (five tone) scale common in primitive and folk music, the "whole tone" (six whole steps) scale of Debussy, etc.

[10] The "theory of music" is the systematic study of the primary medium of music and of the accepted forms of musical composition. "Musicology" is the sum of collective disciplines relating to music which employ a rigorous technique, including the study of scales, tonality, systems of notation, etc., and the analysis of compositions, styles, etc.

positions as executed are in effect two different compositions rather than two different renderings of the same composition. Timbre, then, is an essential aspect of music and of its artistic medium. It is, of course, only one of the factors determining musical quality, other factors such as tonality, tempo, dynamics, etc. being at least as important; but it is the chief source of that aspect of musical quality sometimes called musical "color."

To the physicist, timbre is a function of air vibrations. To the musician, it is a musically essential quality of sound. The composer, in the effort to master his medium, must accordingly learn the characteristic timbre of available instruments and is well advised to compose for specific instruments. Adaptation of a composition to another instrument is often possible and may even enhance the musical effect; but this does not alter the fact that such an adaptation, whether or not it be considered an improvement, is in essential respects a new composition.

(iii) A sound of any pitch or timbre can be louder or softer, more or less prolonged, and more or less closely followed by other sounds. An auditory beat may be a function of alternating intensity or "accent" (—́ — —́ — ; — — —́ — — —́), or of alternating quantities (——— — ——— — ; — — ——— — — ———), or of a combination of both (——́— — ——́— — ; — — ——́— — — ——́—). A group of beats, while maintaining their metrical relation, may also vary in tempo by being produced more rapidly or more slowly.

These quantitative variations are of course physical and can be measured by the physicist. When their musical potentialities are appreciated they become part of the primary artistic medium of music and the other temporal arts (e.g., the dance and literature). Musical rhythm, meanwhile, like other forms of artistic rhythm, is a product of compositional organization and, as such, is a basic characteristic of musical form.[11] These quantitative variations enter essentially into the structure of musical rhythm but do not exhaust its nature, for rhythm can also be produced, or at least enriched, in music by a balancing of musical phrases, by a succession of entries, and by other compositional devices which are not wholly reducible to purely quantitative variations. The latter, however, remain the basis, in the artistic medium, of musical rhythm.

[11] Cf., below, Chap. XI, §3.

Such, then, is the "language" of music. The "language" of any art might be defined to include the entire medium, since an artist makes use of both his primary and his secondary media to express what he wishes to express in his compositions. But the primary medium is always more basic in providing the vehicle by which alone the secondary medium can be brought into use. Defining the language of music in this more restricted sense, it can, in summary, be said to consist of a system of musical tones and intervals productive of at least some degree and type of tonality, plus musically related timbres, plus quantitative variations which possess potential musical significance. Every tonal system, in turn, has its own rules of tonal organization which constitute its grammar and syntax. As in the case of verbal languages, obedience to these rules cannot in itself guarantee artistic excellence or even intelligibility, but their neglect must lead inevitably to musical incoherence and chaos. No musical language is absolute, but every musical language has a degree of social objectivity proportional to its conventional acceptance, and is thus capable of becoming, like our diatonic system, a vehicle of communication. The radical innovator in music who wishes to change the accepted system in fundamental ways must not only construct an alternative system which possesses enough musical potentiality to justify a break in the tradition, but must persuade his audience to learn and accept the new language which he has invented. Unless he can accomplish this, his efforts are doomed to insignificance and social neglect.

(b) *The unusual complexity of the primary medium of pure music.* We shall find that none of the other major arts has nearly so highly organized a primary artistic medium. Much of the world's music, it is true, is simple when compared, for example, with a great modern symphony. Yet even the simplest and most primitive music is *based* on a well-organized tonal system. The layman, singing or listening to music which he likes and with which he is familiar, is usually unaware of the intricate musical grammar and syntax which underlies all musical compositions, the simple as well as the complex. But he is equally unconscious of the grammatical and syntactical structure of his own mother tongue. He can speak his own language without a theoretical knowledge of grammar, and he may be able to enjoy music, invent a melody, or even manifest an untutored sense of harmony, without knowing anything about the theory of music. The relative simplicity of some music and the layman's ignorance of musical theory in no way disproves the structural complexity of the musical medium.

To explain why this medium has become so highly organized we must appeal to several different factors taken in conjunction. It is important to note, in the first place, that music, like the other arts, is essentially a mode of expression and communication. It may also, and simultaneously, give sublimated satisfaction to primitive instincts and be a form of play, an exemplification of the conditioned and unconditioned reflex, and many other things besides. But these additional characteristics and uses must not be allowed to obscure its all-important expressive and communicatory function. And it can perform this function effectively *only* if its basic structure is adequate to the task. The more subtle and complex the emotive-conative states to be expressed and communicated, the more sensitive and adaptable must be its forms and therefore their underlying medium.

Secondly, music differs from the other arts in not finding at its disposal a medium already developed for non-artistic uses. It has had to create and develop a primary medium of its own adequate to its own particular needs.[12] Literature has not had to create a language; it has found language ready made and in universal use. The writer has merely had to adapt the language of common speech to his own expressive requirements. (Not that this is as easy a task as the word "merely" might seem to suggest; the very fact that his medium is put to such varied non-artistic uses actually complicates the writer's problem.) The sculptor and the painter can both lean heavily on the familiar "language" of visual representation and the still older language of ideographic script. The actor, dancer, and mimic need merely develop the universal language of voice inflection, expressive bodily movement, and pantomime to satisfy the material requirements of their arts. And even the architect starts with a whole body of engineering principles already systematized for the utilitarian construction of buildings. These dictate innumerable three-dimensional forms and patterns which the architect is free to adapt to his own expressive purposes. The pri-

[12] Cf. *The Harmonics of Aristoxenus*, "Introduction," p. 3. Aristoxenus, according to Macran, remarked that music does not find its material ready-made "in nature, but provides for itself, by creating out of the chaos of infinite sounds a world of sound-relations, a system in which each member has its relation to every other determined. . . ."

mary medium of music, in contrast, has been developed solely for the sake of music itself and even now, in its highly developed state, can be employed for no other ends. Completed musical compositions can, of course, be put to many non-artistic uses; but the primary medium cannot be non-artistically employed.

Moreover, the fact that absolute music is in essence neither a representational nor a symbolic art but an abstract art means that it must rely entirely upon abstract tonal patterns for the conveyance or expression of meaning. And these patterns can be created and interrelated with the subtlety and precision requisite to musical intelligibility only if the primary medium, i.e., the system of interrelated tones and intervals, is itself subtly and precisely organized. Literature makes extensive use, for purposes of artistic expression, of the symbolic meanings of the words and phrases it employs, and therefore need not rely exclusively upon formal, abstract, non-symbolic patterns. Sculpture and painting can lean upon the effective manipulation of representational subject-matter; the dance and the art of acting can exploit familiar and immediately intelligible bodily movements; and even architecture can count on familiar associations of typical structures with typical utilitarian uses. But a musical composition must rely for its intelligibility upon abstract tonal patterns based upon a system of auditory units and relations employed by and significant for music alone. Hence the need for a highly developed artificial language as a vehicle for sensitive musical utterance.

Finally, the development of music as a temporal art is essentially dependent upon musical notation which, in turn, presupposes musical theory. Buildings, paintings, and statues are created once and for all, and endure until they are destroyed. A musical composition, in contrast, can achieve and maintain its artistic reality only by being so recorded and comprehended that it can be executed again and again by different individuals. It is true that simple folk music, both instrumental and vocal, can live in the memory of the musically gifted and be passed on from person to person and generation to generation without the aid of explicit theory or a musical score. But more complicated musical compositions can neither be created, preserved, nor performed without the aid of a well-defined musical theory and a method of precise musical notation. Music as we know it today became possible only with the invention of modern notation, and it owes its development as well as its widespread enjoyment very largely to the modern score and underlying musical theory.

The development of the ballet is hardly to be compared with that of modern music, but such development as it has had has been made possible in large measure by an analogous definition of steps and other bodily motions which constitute its primary artistic medium. Extreme sculptural and pictorial abstractions, on the other hand, tend to be unintelligible not only to the layman but to many artists and critics partly because the abstractionists, while imitating the musician in their attempt to achieve direct artistic expression through abstract form, have scarcely begun to organize their primary media as the musical theorists have through the centuries organized theirs. It is, indeed, a question as to whether the primary media of the representational arts allow of such organization; but unless they do, and until abstract units and relations comparable to musical tones and intervals are defined with a precision approaching that of musical theory, the abstractionists in sculpture and painting must expect their art to remain esoteric to the point of solipsism. They must devise and teach an abstract language as intelligible as that of music if they wish their compositions to be received and understood as widely as is music today.

These various considerations, taken in conjunction, suggest at least some of the reasons for the high degree of pre-artistic organization to which the primary medium of music has been subjected. I am not claiming that musical *compositions* are necessarily more complex than are compositions in other media, or that the primary raw material of music is in itself more subtle or varied than that of the other arts. I have merely been considering the indisputable fact that musical theorists have organized the primary medium of music with incomparably greater precision and detail than have the theorists in the other arts,[13] and I have sought to explain this fact by calling attention (i) to the unusual *artificiality* of the primary medium of music, i.e., its having been specifically invented (partly through the creation of musical instruments productive of sounds which do not exist in nature) for musically expressive purposes; (ii) to its *abstractness*, i.e., its non-representational and non-symbolic character; and

[13] The nearest approaches in the other arts are the definition of modular systems in architecture, the formulation of sculptural canons like those of Polycleitos, analyses of color and form such as those of Pope and Birkhoff, and the enunciation of principles of versification in literature.

(iii) to the fact that music is a *temporal* art whose more complicated musical compositions can be composed, preserved, and performed only with the aid of a highly organized and widely accepted system of notation and a well developed musical theory.

It was partly man's *need* for an adequate vehicle for musical expression and communication that in diverse ways led to the amazing organization of the musical medium. Once created, this vehicle has invited the expression and communication of inner states which, in its absence, would have had to remain unexpressed. Thus the need led to the perfecting of the medium, while the medium, once perfected, awakened new needs. It was the need for a more adequate vehicle that led Bach to perfect the well-tempered scale and the well-tempered clavichord. This invention, in turn, has made possible a host of compositions which, without it, would never have been created.

(c) *The secondary artistic medium of pure music.* The secondary raw material of pure music without words consists, I have said, of all those emotive-conative states which might conceivably be given interpretative musical expression. This raw material is transformed into a secondary artistic medium through the creative artist's selective apprehension of these states in their more universal aspects.

Every actual emotive-conative state is both particular and universal, that is, both unique and similar, in various ways, to other actual and possible states of this generic type. Were a given emotion or conation entirely unique, it would be unintelligible and incommunicable. Man's emotive-conative experiences lend themselves to artistic (as well as scientific) interpretation only because the emotions and conations of different individuals, and of the same individual at different times, have common or universal characteristics. The composer, in turn, must be aware of these common characteristics if he is to express in his music an intelligible interpretation of this aspect of human experience.

Like other men, the composer can achieve direct acquaintance with human emotion and conation only through immediate first-hand experience. He is accordingly concerned at the outset with his own emotions and impulses in all their particularity, uniqueness, immediacy, and warmth. So strong is this interest that he is constantly tempted, as are other creative artists, to rest content with mere "self-expression," that is, the expression of his own inner states from moment to moment in all their distinctive particularity, and the critics who are partial to the Romantic emphasis tend to insist that this is just what the creative artist should do, i.e., that it is his primary task to express as clearly and as vividly as possible his own *individual* emotions and desires in all their uniqueness. Unlike the conceptual thinker, his chief interest, they believe, is and should be centered upon the particular instance rather than the universal which it manifests—the individual emotion rather than the type.

There is truth in this conception of the artist's task. But it is only half the truth. For every artist must, if he is to speak for the man in men, be interested also in the more or less *common* characteristics of men and their environment. Only through recognition and expression of such universal traits, whether in nature or in man, can he hope to endow his art with a meaning intelligible and valuable to others than himself. Indeed, he himself can find only that significant (whether within himself or in the world around him) which stands in meaningful relation to other aspects and moments of his own wider experience. The artist cannot therefore neglect universals with impunity. This is a fact which critics in the Neo-classic tradition have been particularly concerned to emphasize. Hence, though the composer must himself experience with poignant vividness the emotions and conative attitudes which he proposes to express in his musical compositions, he must also manage to express what is universal in man's emotive-conative experience.

How in music is this to be accomplished? Only through transformation by the creative artist of his own and other men's specific emotive-conative states (the secondary raw material of music) into their more universal types (music's secondary artistic medium). Thus transformed, these emotions and attitudes can then be taken up into the work of art and given individual expression in and through specific musical patterns. This account, in terms of distinct stages through which a given emotion must pass before it finally achieves artistic expression in the completed work of art, must not be interpreted to mean that the composer need be consciously and explicitly aware of these successive stages, or that he himself must pass, during the act of creation, from one stage to the next in orderly temporal sequence. Rather, endowed with a temperamental capacity for intense emotive-conative experience, the composer, in proportion to the profundity of his character and insight, is able to experience more vividly and deeply than the normal individual what all men experience in some measure and perhaps only on rare occasions, and to realize, during these experiences of his, their universal human character and import. His own emotive-conative states, taken as typical not of man's usual experience but of what all men, suitably endowed, might experience at their best, thus become the artistic "subject-matter" or secondary medium of his art. As such, they are translated into expressive musical patterns and these patterns, in turn, if adequately performed in the presence of men with sensitive hearing, cultivated musical intelligence, and the power imaginatively to understand profound human emotion, are found by them to express emotional states which were not merely private to the composer but generic to the human race.

If this analysis is correct, it appears that the transformation of the secondary raw material of music into its secondary artistic medium differs from the analogous transformation of primary material into primary medium in several important respects. In both cases some transformation must take place. But whereas the organization of the primary medium has been achieved through the cooperative efforts of musicians and musical theorists over a long period of time, the organization of the secondary medium must be undertaken by each individual composer whenever he attempts musical composition. And whereas the pre-artistic organization of tones into a musical system is the result of explicit conceptual codification, the artist's pre-artistic apprehension of the universality of specific emotive-conative states is a half-conscious process that takes place during the mysterious act of artistic creation. Hence, whereas a precise analysis of the composer's primary medium is possible at the pre-artistic level, no such analysis of his secondary medium can be given. But some such transformation as I have tried to describe in necessarily general terms must take place if significantly expressive music is to come into being.

This account of the secondary artistic medium of pure music applies *mutatis mutandis* to the secondary media of all the other arts. For however much they may differ from music in other respects, and whatever additional material may be available to them as part of their secondary media, all the arts express, each in its own way, the emotive and conative aspects of man's inner life. Accordingly, every creative artist must, during the process of creation, apprehend and express his own emotional states in their more universal generic character. In my discussion of the secondary media of the other arts

I shall therefore merely refer to the foregoing analysis and not attempt to reproduce it for each medium.

(d) *The secondary medium of program music, occasional music, and music with words.* A very cursory account of the additional secondary media employed in these types of music will suffice. As regards program music, what is required of the artist is a realization of what representational subject-matter can and cannot be dealt with effectively in and through his primary medium. Such realization involves, on the one hand, an adequate understanding of the representational potentialities and limitations of tonal patterns, and, on the other, judicious selection of possible representational subject-matter according to criteria dictated by the primary medium itself. It is a safe generalization that program music which is artistically dependent upon program notes or other non-musical aids must be condemned on strictly artistic grounds. When, on the other hand, program music is able to suggest scenes and events in the outer world without fortuitous assistance, or at most with the aid of a title, such music can be regarded as successful.[14]

In the case of occasional music, what is required again is a keen sense of what the primary medium will permit, and, in addition, genuine understanding of the social function or specific occasion to be celebrated. Music which is *merely* occasional, i.e., so narrowly adapted to special circumstances as to be unintelligible in all other contexts, can hardly be conceived of and would in any case lack all larger musical significance. Occasional music, like portraiture in sculpture, painting, and literature, must try to do justice to the individual occasion and at the same time express what it and other occasions have or might have in common.[15]

Music has been combined in many ways both with the dance and with words, and in every specific instance the question must arise as to whether a perfect balance between the two media should be attempted or whether one medium should be more or less subordinated to the aesthetic requirements of the other. In such combinations priority is given now to the words and what they express, now to the music. Sometimes the composer's interest in the words is relatively incidental; he is preoccupied with the melody for its own

[14] Cf. Ernest Newman, *op. cit.*, p. 186: "The only aesthetic fact we can be sure of is this, that no piece of representation [in music] will be tolerated unless it is at the same time *music*."

[15] Cf., below, Chap. XVIII, on portraiture.

sake and chooses his text primarily on the basis of whether or not the words can easily be sung, and secondarily with reference to the appropriateness to the music of the ideas which the words suggest. Mozart's "*La ci darem la mano*" in *Don Giovanni*, for example, is an exquisite melody that may be, and often is, heard with artistic satisfaction apart from the text and that certainly does not conform musically to the more precise meaning of the words. Sometimes, on the other hand, the composer starts with a significant literary text and seeks to discover how best to express in music the meaning and spirit of the words. Bach's religious music (*vide* his *B Minor Mass*) and Brahms' *Vier ernste Gesänge* exemplify this procedure.[16] Here the meaning of the words, and often the very rhythm of the language, is preserved, intensified, and interpreted by the music. So heavy may be the reliance on the words, as in the "Epic Declamation" of Wagner and the lyrically suffused song-speech of Debussy's *Pelléas*, that the composition is next to meaningless musically apart from its text. Many of the great songs, finally, mediate between these extremes. The composer, having chosen an appropriate text, gives musical expression to the general spirit and mood of the text as a whole and brings out the more subtle emotional overtones of certain words and phrases. Meanwhile, the more poetic the text, that is, the more successful the writer has been in expressing himself in the purely verbal medium, the less adapted is the literary composition to serve as a text for music, for what is gained through *musical* interpretation is balanced by loss of *literary* expressiveness.

The task of combining words and music is a difficult one involving all the artistic principles basic to the mixed arts. Here I can merely point out that when words are set to music, whatever the particular nature of the combination, their sounds at once constitute part of the composer's primary medium and their meaning becomes part of his secondary medium. The composer must therefore always select and use his literary text with the greatest care if it is to enhance rather than mar the unity and expressiveness of his composition.

[16] Cf. Albert Schweitzer, *J. S. Bach*, 2 vols., tr. Ernest Newman (London: A. & C. Black, 1923).

CHAPTER III

THE MATTER OF THE DANCE

1. The chief types of dance and their relation to the other arts of bodily movement

DANCING may be (i) unaccompanied by music, or even (at least theoretically) by an auditory rhythmic beat, or it may be accompanied, as it usually is, by rhythmic sound or music; (ii) it may be pantomimic to a greater or less extent, or it may rely wholly on non-mimetic bodily movement; (iii) it may possess a formal conventional structure in part or in whole, or it may be free from, and independent of, rigidly prescribed conventions and rules; and (iv) it may rely more or less upon costume and setting (including the whole art of the theater), or it may dispense with all setting as a *mise en scène* and even with all forms of costume and drapery. In analyzing the raw material and the artistic medium of the dance we must keep in mind these basic variations.[1]

I have selected the dance as the richest, purest, and most diverse art of bodily movement. But it is not the only art which makes use of this primary medium; there are also the arts of pantomime, public speech, and acting. Pure pantomime or "dumb show," as such, is a minor art and need not be examined here in detail. But we must note its chief characteristics, since the dance as well as the arts of public speech and acting frequently resort to pantomime as an aid to direct bodily expression.

Bodily movement itself need be neither expressive nor pantomimic, though it will always be in some sense symptomatic to the discerning eye. Most of our movements are primarily reflex and habitual; they constitute our unconscious efforts to adapt ourselves to our physical environment. But we also indulge, some of us more frequently and more eloquently than others, in spontaneously expressive motions such as facial contortions, gestures, and bodily postures. Many of these expressive motions and overt attitudes seem to be natural to man and constitute a "language" which cuts across the frontiers of nationality, race, and culture. Typical bodily manifestations of

[1] Cf., below, Chap. IX, §2 and Chap. X, §2, for a fuller account of the generic forms of the dance.

rage, joy, sorrow, fear, curiosity and other basic emotive-conative attitudes are as native to the child as to the adult, to the savage as to civilized man, and are therefore everywhere intelligible. Such behavior is not in essence imitative or pantomimic. It is the immediate expression, in the most primitive and natural of all languages, of man's inner feelings and impulsive strivings.

Pantomime introduces a new factor, that of imitation. But what is it that is imitated in pantomime? The mimic cannot accurately be said to "imitate" his own inner states or those of others; he can imitate, by means of bodily movement, only what has *already* been manifested in bodily movement. Pantomime must be defined as the physical imitation of the characteristic *physical appearance*, both static and dynamic, of human and non-human individuals and types.

The chief primary medium of the mimic is his own body; costume may be used as an aid but is not essential. He imitates the visual appearance of his subject, whether in motion or at rest. Animals and even plants or inorganic objects can be imitated (e.g., cats and dogs, the flight of birds, trees swaying in the wind, and machinery), but the chief subject of pantomime is of course man. Usually it is a type (e.g., the importunate suitor, the lovely heroine, the angry father, or the stupid policeman) or a form of typical behavior (e.g., dancing with joy, cowering with terror, busy bustling, cautious investigation) that is imitated; but it is also possible to mimic characters (e.g., Napoleon, Mussolini, or Punch).

As a self-contained art pantomime aims higher than this; in its more ambitious forms the attempt is made to act out in dumb show a more or less complicated plot which may be original and in which the characters are not familiar types but newly created and clearly individualized personalities. Here pantomime is less imitative of bodily action than illustrative of a story, and much use is made of immediately expressive bodily movements. The limitations of pantomime as a self-sufficient art are obvious and justify its classification as a minor art, since the body is hardly adapted to serve as the *sole* vehicle for extended dramatic action or the portrayal of a complex personality. Our chief concern, meanwhile, is with pantomimic *quality*, that is, with pantomime as a device occasionally resorted to by the arts as a supplementary aid.

Public speech and acting must be distinguished from the dance and from pure pantomime. Both use the medium of the spoken word as well as the medium of bodily movement. Acting may also rely extensively on stage-setting. The term "acting" is here used to signify the drama as performed upon the stage, and may be defined as the visible and audible interpretative rendition of the written drama. So defined, it is a "mixed" art which includes (i) the "lines" which the dramatist has composed and (ii) the actor's and producer's interpretation of them. Here the medium of bodily movement is important but not as important as the medium of language. If acting be defined more narrowly, to exclude the literary contribution of the dramatist and the supplementary arts of the theater, and to include only the actor's own interpretative presentation of the character in the play, expressive bodily movement assumes a relatively more important rôle. But even according to this restricted definition the actor must not only make expressive use of his body but must also use his voice effectively. Both body and voice, meanwhile, must remain the servants of the actor's reconstructive and constructive imagination, by means of which alone he can interpret the writer's words, identify himself with a dramatic character, and thus translate the dramatist's literary creation into visible and audible actuality on the stage. However acting be defined, then, bodily movement is *not* as basic to it as it is to the dance, though the importance of such movement must not on that account be underestimated.

Both public speech and acting may also assume, to a greater or less extent depending upon the context, the quality of pantomime. But the most effective public speaking and acting rely much less on pantomime than on immediately expressive bodily movement and voice control.

The chief similarities and differences of the arts of the dancer and the actor may accordingly be summarized as follows. (i) Bodily movement is the *basic* primary medium of the dance (and also of pantomime, regarded as a self-contained art); it is an important but *not* the basic medium of acting. (ii) The dance is usually accompanied by music, but even in the accompanied dance the body in motion and at rest, not the music, is the chief expressive vehicle. This is true of all serious accompanied dancing, even when the music possesses the highest artistic merit, and even though the dancer be consciously attempting to interpret in his own medium the spirit of the music. In acting, on the other hand, bodily movement is always (except in pure pantomime) accompanied by speech, but here the order of artistic priority is reversed, the words and what they signify constituting the basic medium, and bodily movement remaining, however invaluable, merely an aid to the expressive interpretation of the words. (iii) *Both* dancing and acting can take on pantomimic quality and tend to do so on appropriate occasions. In their purest forms, however, both rely only incidentally and sparingly on pantomimic effect, and achieve their artistic ends primarily through immediately expressive bodily movements and postures. Undue reliance on mimicry tends to transform both arts into the very different and essentially minor art of pure pantomime.

These distinctions justify the conclusion that the dance is the best exemplification of the generic art of bodily movement. Let us turn now to a more systematic analysis of the raw material and the artistic medium of the dance in its chief forms, beginning with the pure dance and then considering what is added with the introduction of music, pantomime, and stage setting.[2]

2. *The raw material and the artistic medium of the pure dance*

By the "pure" dance is meant the forms of the dance which are wholly self-contained and which rely neither on music, pantomime, nor stage setting. Actual dances of this type are rare and, for the most part, esoteric; but they exemplify the dance in its simplest form. The pure dance can be studied, of course, in the more complex forms of the dance by ignoring all additional factors which appear in these forms and by attending only to bodily movement and to what such movement can express.

(a) *The primary raw material* of the pure dance is bodily motion and rest. This includes all overt movements of any part of the body or of the whole body, as well as the absence of such movement. Both movement and rest must of course be in space and time. Hence tempo, duration, and acceleration and retardation of bodily movement, as well as the three basic spatial planes (the horizontal, vertical, and third-dimensional, together with all their possible variants) must be included. This raw material is non-artistically exploited in such activities as calisthenics, eurythmics, gymnastics, acrobatics, etc.

[2] I shall have to anticipate in part the problem of form in the dance as a completed work of art. Such anticipation is necessary not only in the dance but in all the arts, since no empirical account can be given of an artistic medium save by reference to characteristic forms of actual works of art in that medium.

(b) *The secondary raw material* of the pure dance includes all the emotions and conative attitudes which might conceivably be expressed directly through bodily movement. Here pure music and the pure dance closely resemble one another. But the pure dance can also express with great eloquence the primary sensations of weight and lightness, thrust, rising and falling, floating, soaring and sinking, opening and closing, and the like. Thus a whole range of subject-matter foreign to music is made available to the dance by the fact that its primary raw material is not disembodied sound but visible three-dimensional bodily movement, and, more particularly, because it is the human body which is here the vehicle of artistic expression.

The pure dance can also, like music, be more or less symbolic. That is, symbolic meaning can be given to various movements and gestures and to more complicated dance patterns. This symbolic meaning may have its orientation in religious belief or social convention (*vide* primitive religious dances, which are highly symbolic but in which a line can seldom be drawn between religious and secular symbolism[3]) and may therefore be widely understood as part of the cultural tradition; or it may be devised by individual dancers and comprehensible only to a limited esoteric group. Whatever its form, such symbolism introduces into the secondary raw material of the dance new factors which must be taken into account.

(c) *The primary artistic medium* of the pure dance is the primary raw material subjected to preliminary selection and organization. Here a sharp distinction must be noted between the "free" and the "conventional" dance.[4] In the former no specific steps or detailed rules of dance technique are prescribed; the term "free" signifies this absence of methodological prescription. In the conventional dance, in contrast, many steps, arm movements, and more inclusive bodily movements have been reduced to rigorous systematization, and an elaborate and highly exacting technique has been evolved. The pre-artistic organization of the primary medium thus approximates, particularly in the ballet, to the pre-artistic organization of

[3] A certain step (stamping to the side, in front, and again to the side) in a Mexican folk dance was recently described by an Indian girl in Mexico City first as "the sign of the cross" and then as "a step that the wild turkey makes."

[4] Cf. Elizabeth Selden, *Elements of the Free Dance* (New York: A. S. Barnes, 1930), for an illuminating discussion of certain essential differences between the "rhythmic" (or "free") dance and the ballet, taken as representing the conventional dance.

the primary medium in music. The same is true, though in a more informal and less professional way, of most forms of folk and social dancing. These dances allow of precise description in terms not only of floor-patterns but of steps to be executed in certain specific ways.[5] But even in the free dance certain basic principles can be formulated concerning the handling of various parts of the body (e.g., the "center" of movement, the "pulse" of movement, muscular control, change of weight), and more specific types of "action modes" (folding-unfolding, rise-fall, press-pull, bending-reaching, rotating-twisting, swaying, vibrating, etc.) which include the body as a whole. Hence, though no formal instruction can be given in the free dance comparable to ballet instruction in the execution of the *saute*, *entrechat*, *rond de jambe*, or *pirouette*, the student can be taught its underlying principles and instructed in the general methods in which direct bodily expression can be achieved (e.g., through explanation of the "arc of motion," favored by some dancers, involving a beginning, ascent, crest, descent, and end).

The primary artistic medium of the pure dance includes, then, all those bodily movements and rests which possess artistic or expressive potentialities, which permit of more or less detailed preliminary organization, and which invite technical mastery.[6] It should be noted that just as a musical rest is not mere silence but silence impregnated with artistic significance by a surrounding pattern of musical tones, so, in the dance, what is sheer absence of movement at the level of the raw material can become, in conjunction with bodily movement, profoundly expressive. Witness, for example, the eloquent moment of "rest" which precedes a soaring spring, or the thrilling instant of floating suspension in mid-air at the crest of a mobile arc, or a landing, expressive of achievement and completion. The competent dancer, in surveying his raw material, is as well aware of the positive artistic potentialities of such moments of rest as he is of what can be achieved by a sequence of bodily movements.

[5] Cf. Cecil J. Sharp and A. P. Oppé, *The Dance, An Historical Survey of Dancing in Europe* (New York: Minton Balch, 1924), for descriptions of such dances.

[6] The fact that I have used for this analysis forms which are almost invariably accompanied by music, and which often also introduce pantomime and rely on costumes and stage settings, does not invalidate my description, since *all* forms of the dance should exemplify the basic principles of the pure dance and should differ from it not by omission but only by the addition of new factors.

As in the case of music, rhythm in the dance is an aspect of its form, not of its matter as such, though it is of course based on the regular or irregular physical beat which is an ingredient both of its raw material and of its artistic medium.

(d) *The secondary artistic medium* of the pure dance is the secondary raw material subjected to preliminary interpretative selection. Here the situation is strictly analogous to the situation in music. Before beginning to create a dance or to execute an already created dance the dancer must know, whether explicitly or implicitly, what emotions, conations, and other primary experiences allow of immediate or symbolic expression by means of bodily movement. This involves, as in music, a thorough understanding of the primary medium and the ability to recognize in his own inner states what is wholly idiosyncratic and therefore not communicable and what, in contrast, is more universal and therefore of wider human significance. The transformation of secondary raw material into secondary artistic medium necessitates not only rich first-hand experience and keen observation but also a capacity to generalize and to interpret. Once again, however, the artistic medium, whether primary or secondary, is not itself a work of art, and mere technical mastery of the medium falls far short of significant artistic creation.[7]

3. *The enrichment of the raw material and of the artistic medium of the dance through the addition of music, pantomime, costume, and stage setting*

All additions to the pure dance should, at least ideally, enrich the art of the dance, although the more ambitious the combinations attempted and the greater the resultant complexity, the harder it is to achieve artistic unity. But whatever ultimately appears in the

[7] My references to dances as works of art and my description of some of the artistic requirements for successful communication might seem to rule out, as lacking in artistic quality, all spontaneous self-expression which is in no way designed for public exhibition. Such self-expression is certainly possible in all the arts, including the dance. We can sing for the sheer joy of it, or dance because we cannot help ourselves, or paint or write merely for our own satisfaction. May not the products of such activity be truly artistic? The answer is of course affirmative. The only relevant criterion is the presence or absence of artistic quality; does the end product satisfy or does it not satisfy the basic requirements of art? Strictly speaking, the intention to communicate is irrelevant to the definition of art, as is also the artistic response of the onlooker, although in actual practice most artistic creation is motivated, at least in part, by the desire to communicate and to please, and is conditioned in many important ways by anticipated public and critical reception.

dance in any of its forms must be present in an artistically unorganized state in the raw material and, partly organized, in the artistic medium. We must therefore briefly consider the nature of these complicating factors.

(a) *Auditory accompaniment.* As has already been indicated, some auditory accompaniment to the dance is almost, though not absolutely, indispensable. Even in a free dance which is unaccompanied by musical or percussion instruments, the dancer is very likely to resort to stamping, hand-clapping, or slapping the body to emphasize in sound the visible rhythm of bodily movement. In primitive dances drums, cymbals, and bells are often used to proclaim and strengthen the rhythm. All such sounds are, as primary raw material, mere sounds with intervening silences, the sounds varying in timbre, intensity, duration, and tempo. The equivalent secondary raw material includes all that can be expressed by sound. This raw material is transformed into a part of the artistic medium of the dance through appropriate selection in terms of artistic potentiality. It obviously does not permit of extensive pre-artistic organization.

When melody and musical harmony are added, the dance's raw material and artistic medium, both primary and secondary, are correspondingly enriched. My entire analysis of the medium of music now becomes applicable with one important exception. Not all music allows of combination with the dance. Hence only the raw material and the artistic medium of that music which might conceivably accompany the dance should here be included. The dance and music, in short, are distinct major arts. Much can be expressed in music which cannot be interpreted by bodily movement, and the body can express what music can only vaguely suggest.[8]

(b) *Pantomime.* The pantomimic dance is not a fusion of two arts but a natural extension of expressive bodily motion into the realm of imitation or mimicry. The basic requirement from the point of view of the dance is that all pantomimic action should be rigorously disciplined by the rhythm and motifs of the dance itself. Pantomime cannot simply be added; the movements of the dance must take on pantomimic quality without loss of the dynamic rhythm of the dance itself. Through suitably controlled addition of pantomimic quality the dance becomes distinctly representational, and when this hap-

[8] The majority of modern dancers first compose their dances, noting down their measures, tempo, etc., and then have music composed to fit the dance which they have created.

pens its raw material and its artistic medium become correspondingly enriched by the inclusion of subject-matter permitting of pantomimic representation. This subject-matter comprises human and other individuals and types, their respective static and dynamic appearances, and whatever inner states they may possess which allow of pantomimic rendering. The primary raw material of the pantomimic factor is thus bodily action, and its primary artistic medium is bodily action regarded as potentially imitative or illustrative. Its secondary raw material includes whatever can thus be represented, prior to its pre-artistic selection; its secondary medium is this material subsequent to such selection.

(c) *Costumes and stage setting*. When the dance makes use of costume and of the several arts and crafts (other than acting) which pertain to the synthetic art of the theater, it does not combine with a major art (as in the case of the accompanied dance), nor does it merely extend the scope of its own proper medium (as in the case of the pantomimic dance). It now calls to its aid various *minor* arts whose rôle must remain subsidiary. Whenever these arts acquire ascendancy the result is not a dance in the true sense but rather a "spectacle" with dances introduced as diversions or interludes.[9] Wisely used, however, i.e., as an enhancement of the effect primarily achieved by the dance itself, costumes and stage settings can contribute greatly to the expressiveness of the dance. Flowing drapery which emphasizes the contours and movements of the body, stylized costumes, and stage settings can all, if kept in their proper place, help greatly to convey the spirit of the dance itself and portray dramatic action. I can leave it to the reader to apply to these minor yet not unimportant additions to the dance the formulae for distinguishing between primary and secondary raw material and artistic medium.

[9] "Spectacles" which not only profess but achieve artistic selt-sufficiency are even more of a *tour de force* than pure pantomime. Usually they are mere exhibitions of facile ingenuity and vulgar financial expenditure, and remain, artistically considered, mere incoherent aggregations of parts which even in themselves possess little artistic quality.

CHAPTER IV

THE MATTER OF ARCHITECTURE

1. Factors relevant and irrelevant to architecture as an art

ARCHITECTURE is the third of the great abstract arts. Ruskin called attention to its eloquent abstractness in the phrase "frozen music";[1] architecture defies representational use even more successfully than music. The rare attempts at realistic representation in architecture are uniformly grotesque. Consider, for instance, the façade of *St. John Nepomuk* in Munich (Fig. 66), into which large unhewn rocks have been built on either side of the doorway (to suggest, presumably, that the church stands on a rocky eminence instead of on a flat city street); or the interior of the *Laiterie* of *Château Rambouillet* (Fig. 16), where the whole end of the interior is a huge rocky grotto; or Hubert Robert's *Grotte d'Apollon* in the gardens of Versailles (Fig. 15), where the line between nature and architecture is almost completely lost; or finally, as a glorious *reductio ad absurdum*, some of the designs submitted for the *Tribune Building* in Chicago (Figs. 17-19).[2] Much has been made by some writers of the forest motif in Gothic architecture; they would have

[1] Sculpture might analogously be described as the art of the "frozen dance," since the pose of the sculptured figure is, at least ideally, expressive of either bodily motion or significant repose. But all such comparative characterizations are valuable only as metaphorical suggestions.

[2] The designs here reproduced are from the volume entitled *The International Competition for a New Administration Building for the Chicago Tribune MCMXXII.* They are not, of course, to be considered as typical of the 259 designs included in the book, but as the individual reactions of certain architects to the problem. The entire collection forms an unusually interesting and valuable document. Many of the designs submitted anticipate important developments in modern architecture.

These pictures illustrate three distinguishable types of architectural imitation, (i) of nature (Figs. 66, 15, 16), (ii) of sculpture (Fig. 19), and (iii) of other buildings or parts of buildings (Figs. 17, 18). A much commoner form of architectural imitation is exaggerated adaptation or the unimaginative copying of a particular style or building. Cf. *Fonthill Abbey* (Figs. 20, 21), built for domestic use, and *Mereworth Castle* (Fig. 23), built in slavish imitation of Palladio's *Rotonda* (Fig. 22) in total disregard of climatic necessities. The absurdity of this particular imitation is evidenced by the fact that the ribs of the dome have been transformed into flues which carry the smoke up to the peak of the dome where it issues forth in grotesque fashion.

the soaring columns represent tree trunks, and the vaulted ribs, the interlacing boughs. This too is sheer fantasy not only misapplied but fundamentally misleading, since it suggests a representational motivation essentially alien to the medium, spirit, and development of architecture.

On the other hand, architecture does lend itself to symbolism, though even here we must exercise caution. Various types of architectural form, as for example the Greek Orders, the pointed Gothic arch, or the secular Baroque façade, have acquired various symbolic associations. But these associations are hardly comparable in precision and uniformity to the meanings of words as conventionally accepted symbols. Architecture in itself (apart from the details of architectural ornament) is no more symbolic in essence than is music. Both arts can *acquire* symbolic meaning, but neither art exemplifies primary symbolism as does the art of literature.

There are two factors present in all architecture which deserve brief consideration for somewhat different reasons—the economic factor, because it so clearly illustrates the presence in art of determining influences which lack artistic significance, and the engineering factor, because its indisputable artistic significance is so often misinterpreted in contemporary aesthetic theory.

Every architect has learned from bitter experience how restrictive may be the lack of available funds. He suffers in this respect more than other artists, because it costs more to build a building than to create a work of art in most of the other media. Money is therefore a factor which may powerfully influence architectural creation for good or ill. But money is no more of an *artistic* factor in architecture than it is in the other arts. The cost of materials and workmanship is wholly irrelevant to the artistic nature and expressive quality of the completed building. We can therefore dismiss the economic factor in our consideration of this and all other arts.

The engineering factor, in contrast, is of great importance to architecture, yet not as it is interpreted by most modern "functionalists." Their contention, stated somewhat crudely, is that good engineering guarantees good architecture; architecture is good, they say, in proportion as it exemplifies engineering strength and economy of means. There is an element of truth in this contention, but stated in this bald and extreme form it is as fallacious as is the saying of Henry Ford that what is economically right is also morally right.[3] Mr. Ford has here confused two entirely different realms of value, extrinsic economic value and intrinsic moral value. His dictum, if pressed, would result in the reduction of right to might, that is, in the denial or destruction of all morality. Yet economic values must be assigned a place in the larger scheme of the moral life. The architectural functionalists, like Mr. Ford, confuse two quite different things—structural efficiency, which is the product of the applied science of engineering, and architectural quality, which is the product of the artistic imagination and cannot be reduced to non-artistic engineering factors. Yet engineering does make its own distinctive contribution to the art of architecture. We must presently attempt to define this contribution more precisely.

So much for factors which are not, in themselves, actual components of architectural excellence. There are other aspects of architecture which do immediately and essentially contribute to its artistic being. A building is fundamentally a hollow shell, and the primary effect of architecture depends on how this shell *appears* to be constructed. Every building has also a physical site; its outer surface invites ornamental treatment; and its interior demands suitable decoration and furnishing. These last three factors are all essential to the building as an architectural unit and will engage the serious attention of a conscientious and imaginative architect.

(a) The architect usually has no voice in the selection of the *site* but must accept it as a brute fact to be dealt with in the best way possible. There is in every site much that defies artificial change. But this fact need not spell artistic frustration. For every site has, at least ideally, certain distinctive characteristics which the skillful architect can exploit by adapting his building to them and by making it express in its own way what they suggest. Examples of such successful adaptation may be found among the stone houses of the Cotswolds (Figs. 13, 14) or the flat-roofed Spanish haciendas with their patios, or the castles of Northern Europe, each of which, at its best, is perfectly adapted to and expressive of its physical environment. *Mont St. Michel* (Fig. 10) and *Kloster Melk* on the Danube are famous instances of effective exploitation of the site. The failure to recognize the architectural importance of a site finds illustration in F. Gilly's project for a memorial to Frederick the

[3] Quoted by James Truslow Adams, *The Epic of America* (Boston: Little Brown, 1931), p. 400.

Great (Fig. 11), in which he proposed to build a copy of the *Parthenon* (Fig. 51) on a rectangular elevation in flat Berlin. (Compare also Fig. 18.)

On the other hand, it is often possible to adapt the site to the building without destroying the site's distinctive features. The art of landscape gardening is a highly developed minor art which has, on notable occasions, achieved relative artistic self-sufficiency (compare the *Kew Gardens* or the gardens of *Villa d'Este*, *Versailles*, or *Caserta*). But its chief architectural function is to adapt the site to the building and the building to the site. This can be done in many ways, the two outstanding solutions being the formal garden (Fig. 12), where a maximum of regularity is imposed upon nature, and the informal or "English" garden (Fig. 13), where nature is skillfully tamed without being subjugated to completely formal symmetry. These two very different conceptions of a garden can be combined according to the principle of maximum regularity in the vicinity of the formal architectural structure, and an increasing concession to the informality of nature as the boundaries of the estate are approached—the whole garden thus providing a transition, gradual yet unconfused, from architecture to nature in the raw.

(b) The minor art of architectural *ornament* is so rich and varied that it would require volumes to do it justice. It ranges all the way from abstract design (Fig. 1), usually geometrical in its simplest forms, to sculptural representation (Fig. 2), and from architectural modelling, through more or less elaborate mosaic and fresco, to sculpture in relief (Fig. 112) and in the round (Figs. 7, 42-46). The basic principle of all architectural ornament, whatever its nature, is that it remain subordinate to the artistic requirements of the architectural whole and justify its existence artistically by expressing and emphasizing in its own way what is already expressed in the larger architectural forms. (Compare Figs. 4 and 5 for successful and unsuccessful architectural ornament.)

(c) This principle holds for *interior decoration*. A building remains artistically incomplete until it has been furnished in a manner appropriate to the style of the building and to its intended use. The architect is more often aware of this requirement than is the patron, and is frequently compelled to see a building which he has designed ruined artistically by inappropriate furnishings. Yet many examples can be found in every type and style of architecture which illustrate the ways in which furniture, drapery, and ornament can not only be made to harmonize with, but notably to enhance, the artistic effect of an architectural interior (Fig. 6).

Thus the site, the exterior and interior decorations, and the furnishings all have an important place in the art of architecture. They constitute, especially in private dwellings, a perfect bridge from nature to man and a perfect example of graduated artistic adaptation of nature to man and man to nature. Man gathers around him in his own private dwelling intimate personal belongings which reflect his own habits and tastes. His furniture and movable wall and floor decorations are somewhat more impersonal and formal, although, at least ideally, they too should typify his character in their own way. The more permanent interior and exterior decorations of his house are still more formal, and frequently more impersonal outdoors than indoors. Thus far nature has been adapted to his ends; the raw materials which it provides have been manipulated and combined in a markedly artificial manner. Even in the most formal gardens, in contrast, nature remains relatively untamed, and the more informal the garden becomes, the more completely are natural shapes and colors allowed to remain what they were. Man thus may be said to have constructed for himself an intimate and artificial immediate environment which passes, by a series of gradual but well-defined steps, into less and less intimate and artificial stages of adaptation until all organization ceases and nature reappears in its pristine state. This happens, it is true, only in ideal circumstances. The principle of gradual transition does not permit of rigorous formulation or application. It merely indicates the relation in which site, ornament, and furnishings stand to architecture as such.

2. *The primary and secondary raw material of architecture*

The primary raw material of architecture includes all the physical substances (e.g., wood, brick, stone, steel, concrete, etc.) which can be used in building construction; plus their visible color and texture; plus the physical laws (e.g., gravity, elasticity, durability, etc.) to which they are obedient, and the three-dimensional structural shapes which, in conformity to these laws, they can be made to assume; plus the three-dimensional space in which they exist and portions of which they can be made to enclose; plus physical light.

This raw material, prior to all aesthetic pre-artistic selection and interpretation, is *par excellence* the subject-matter of engineering. The physicist, chemist, and geologist, i.e., the natural scientist, studies these physical materials and phenomena from various approaches, and some of their investigations are indirectly relevant to the applied science of engineering. The engineer, in turn, is interested only in those physical principles and mathematical processes which he can use in his profession of building physical structures. He need not know, for example, the geological explanation of glacial deposits, but it is essential that he know the tensile strength and durability of various kinds of rock. Equipped with the requisite information regarding his materials, and with a knowledge of mathematics sufficient for purposes of computation, he applies himself to the task of discovering how various types of structure can be built effectively —"effectiveness" being definable ultimately in terms of economy of means to envisaged ends. These calculations are based on the nature of the raw materials of engineering already transformed into building materials adapted to immediate use. The engineer starts not with the living rock but with rock quarried and hewn into suitable sizes and shapes; with clay not in the pit but already fashioned and baked into bricks; with trees already converted into beams and planks, iron ore into steel girders, etc. Even the engineer, therefore, has a medium which is distinguishable from his raw material. But aesthetic considerations are as completely irrelevant to the applied *science* of engineering as such as are moral considerations to the applied *science* of medicine as such, though engineers may *also* be aesthetically sensitive and may make concessions to aesthetic principles, just as doctors are, and should be, guided in their practice by moral as well as by purely scientific principles.

The secondary raw material of architecture consists primarily of all those aspects of human existence which necessitate or invite building construction. Man requires shelter from the elements, storage for his possessions, and buildings in which to work and meet his fellow men for various social activities. Without these primary social activities and needs architecture would never have come into existence.

It is possible to study these aspects of human life in their own right, for they constitute part of the subject-matter of the disciplines of social psychology and sociology, anthropology, history, and economics. These investigations need not, it is true, wholly ignore the artistic factor. But they are usually conducted without specific reference to art in general or to architecture in particular. Like the primary raw material of architecture, these social activities and needs are, as such, non-artistic. They need not, though they frequently do, find satisfaction in structures which express them through architectural form.

This does not exhaust the secondary raw material of architecture. For abstract architectural forms can, like the abstract patterns of music or the dance, directly express emotive and conative states. But in architecture the emotive-conative states which are thus expressed are usually the psychological manifestations of the basic social activities just described. Man's need for protection and privacy, or for corporate religious worship, for example, is naturally accompanied by a variety of emotions and attitudes, and it is primarily these which successful architecture expresses *via* architectural form. If the secondary raw material of architecture is equated with man's "social activities and needs," this phrase must therefore be defined to include all the emotive-conative states which reflect these needs.

Architecture, then, is more essentially a social art than are any of the other major arts. A building can, of course, be contemplated in solitude, just as, conversely, music and the dance, painting, sculpture, and literature can be enjoyed in a social setting and have a social function. We must not insist on too sharp a distinction between architecture and the other arts. But the fact remains that buildings are almost invariably built for social rather than individual use. This applies not only to palaces and churches, office buildings and factories, theaters and libraries, but also to private dwellings, which are normally designed to house not solitary individuals but a family. The secondary raw material of architecture is therefore to an unusual extent social in character; the human needs to be satisfied are social, and so are the emotive-conative states awaiting architectural expression.

3. The primary and secondary artistic media of architecture

These two media are, respectively, the primary and secondary raw materials of architecture subjected to aesthetic pre-artistic selection and organization.

In the case of the primary medium this selection and organization can be carried a long way. The architect has ample opportunity to exercise artistic discrimination in his choice of building materials with an eye to their color and surface texture—factors which enter powerfully into the final artistic effect of the completed building (Fig. 32). He can also become aware of the artistic potentialities of basic engineering structure, noting that some types of structure *visibly* express better than others the physical phenomena of weight and mass, thrust and counter-thrust, height, breadth and volume, flexibility and inflexibility, etc. He can realize how both space and light can be controlled by suitable construction so as to produce new architectural effects whereby a façade or a hall, for example, can be made to appear larger or smaller than other façades and halls of identical physical measurements. None of these considerations is relevant to the science of engineering as such; all are motivated by artistic interest and determined according to artistic criteria.

But the "science" of architecture can go further than this in its preliminary organization of its primary material. It can define architectural units of various types, such as columns, pedestals, and capitals, trabeated and arcuated openings, flat ceilings and vaults, roofs of innumerable shapes, etc., not to mention the many species of architectural ornament; and it can then proceed with Vitruvius to define, in historical perspective, architectural "Orders" such as the Doric, Ionic, and Corinthian (Figs. 51-53), whose essence consists in a proportionality of architectural solids and voids to one another. The latter type of organization may develop into a "modular" system, a module being definable as a variable unit of measure determined primarily by a basic architectural form (e.g., the diameter of a column at its base) and translatable into mathematical units of measure. Here the parallel to music is striking. Just as a tonal musical system is organized with reference to a "tonic" or basic tone of specific pitch, so the Greek Orders tend to be organized (we can speak here only of tendencies, not of absolute prescriptions) with reference to a characteristic column of specific proportions, this column, or architectural "tonic," determining the spaces between the columns of the colonnade, the relation of the colonnade to the main shell, the shape and size of the pediment, etc. It is clear that definitions and principles of this type are not those of a natural science but are essentially artistic in character; it is the artistically sensitive eye, not the foot-rule, which creates and approves them. They cannot in themselves guarantee architectural excellence, any more than can the rules of musical harmony and counterpoint guarantee musical expressiveness. Mastery of them is a condition of successful artistic creation within the architectural framework prescribed by a Greek Order; but only creative architectural genius can so apply these rules and principles as to produce truly expressive architecture.

But the analogy to music must not be pressed too far. All successful architecture does indeed depend upon *some* principle of architectural proportion which, in turn, involves the existence of artistically measurable units and relations, solids and spatial intervals, of some sort. But not all architecture is created with the aid of a strictly modular system of the Classic type. The Gothic tradition predicates, for example, a radically different architectural approach.

The secondary medium of architecture is characterized by a noticeably greater specificity of pre-artistic definition than in the other arts. I have already referred to the fact that architecture requires for its very creation a far more precise determination of the social function which it is to satisfy than is the case elsewhere in the artistic realm. Ideally, the architect should know not only the general but the more specific nature of these social requirements and fully appreciate their import. The builders of a Greek temple or a Gothic cathedral, for instance, had to enter into the spirit of their respective religions, know the beliefs and ritualistic observances of Greek polytheism or Christian worship, and possess this knowledge with imaginative precision and intensity, in order to be able to create architectural structures expressive of these religious faiths. Similarly, the architect of a private dwelling must appreciate not only the architectural requirements of domestic life in general, but must be prepared to satisfy the particular needs of his patron, for only thus can he hope to express in the language of architecture both the universal traits of private life and the specific character and temper of the prospective owner. In a word, a completed building can have "character" or expressed content only if, prior to its creation, the architect can clearly envisage his "program," i.e., the social function which constitutes the secondary medium of his art.

As in the case of the primary medium, however, a clear appreciation of a specified program cannot of itself guarantee success in its architectural expression. The prospective owner may know very well what building needs he wishes to have satisfied, but he has to hire an architect with the ability to translate his wish into architectural reality, and architects differ, of course, in the skill with which they are able to perform the required task. Hence, preliminary realization of specific and general social function and of the relation of this function to architectural construction cannot assure appropriately expressive architectural form. We are still at the level of the medium and not yet in the presence of the finished work of art.

The fact that buildings constructed for one social function can often be used with considerable artistic appropriateness for some other more or less similar function in no way alters the principle here enunciated. For, on the one hand, the new use to which the building is put cannot differ too radically from its original use without disastrous artistic consequences. Imagine a Gothic cathedral used as a railway terminal, or a house suited to an Oscar Wilde acquired by an Immanuel Kant. But where two social functions are in essence similar we need not be surprised by the possibility of new uses without too great artistic loss. Mohammedanism and Christianity, for example, are both religions, and religions which have much in common; hence the possibility of transforming *Hagia Sophia* (Fig. 63) from a Christian church into a Moslem mosque with relatively little architectural alteration. As another example, the Roman institution of the public bath had a good deal in common with the activities which are housed in a modern railway terminal. Both are large-scale secular enterprises requiring a central concourse leading to numerous larger and smaller areas. Hence the measure of success with which the general architectural plan of the *Baths of Caracalla* (Fig. 27) has been utilized in the *Pennsylvania Station* in New York City (Fig. 26). But the finest architecture of every culture is more indigenous than this and closer to the cultural and social soil. The buildings which most profoundly satisfy our artistic sense are those which have been built with the keenest realization of the specific primary and secondary media, interpreted in the light of a deeply rooted and authentic cultural tradition.

Much that has been said regarding the secondary medium of architecture applies *mutatis mutandis* to the other arts. This is clearly evident in national and folk music and dancing, and it is equally evident in the arts which we still have to analyze. But the peculiar rôle of a specific social function in the creation and artistic being of architecture remains one of the distinguishing characteristics of this art.

CHAPTER V

THE MATTER OF SCULPTURE AND PAINTING

SCULPTURE and painting are alike in both being essentially representational arts. They differ in primary medium and in scope of subject-matter or secondary medium. Their similarities and differences can best be explored by considering them together.

1. The primary raw material and artistic medium of sculpture

The primary raw material of sculpture consists of three-dimensional solids of various types of material capable of assuming various shapes, plus the space in which these solids exist, plus the light which illumines them.

All sculpture, whether free-standing or in relief, is essentially three-dimensional. A purely linear relief which consists merely of lines cut into a flat surface (Fig. 145) belongs, for purposes of classification, in the twilight zone between the generic arts of "sculpture" and "painting."

The sculptor makes use of many types of material—of all sorts of stone and wood, of many kinds of metal, of baked clay with a variety of surfaces, etc. (Figs. 99, 120-125, 128, etc.). Each of these materials has its own natural weight and tensile strength as well as its own color, texture, and often its characteristic grain or stratification. The surface color and texture of sculpture can be more or less radically altered by the use of wax polish, pigmentation, enamel, and other types of surface treatment. All the materials so used must be included in sculpture's primary raw material.

The rôles of space and light are different in sculpture from what they are in architecture. A building not only exists in space; it can, as we have seen, enclose space in such a way as to transform it artistically by endowing it with a new aesthetic dimension—a dimension which, furthermore, can be apprehended by the actual presence in it of the beholder himself. The architect can also control the light which is allowed to flood such enclosed space and to transform it into a factor of great architectural significance (Figs. 41, 60, 62, 63, 74, 75). Sculpture can control neither space nor light in this way. It must of course exist in space, and, in addition, it can achieve an artistically powerful interplay of space and solid, as for example in Baroque sculpture (Fig. 135). But it cannot enclose space as architecture can, or alter its aesthetic nature in the same manner; space remains primarily the environment which surrounds the sculptural figure and which the latter can control only by thrusting itself into it with greater or less dynamic emphasis.[1] Similarly in the case of light. Sculpture must indeed be illuminated to be seen, and sculptural forms can often be seen effectively only if the illumination is such as to produce high lights, deep shadows, and many intervening degrees of "value" and illumination. Light is thus an important factor in sculptural effect, both as primary illumination and as controlled *chiaroscuro*, although in proportion as *chiaroscuro* is made a *primary artistic* factor, as for example in Rodin's *Porte de l'Enfer* (Fig. 153), sculpture again moves in the direction of painting. But sculpture cannot itself control light and change its aesthetic quality as can architecture by an effective use of clerestory illumination and colored glass.

As regards shape, every physical object has, in any of its natural states, some three-dimensional shape. These shapes are normally irregular, though they may approximate to geometrical regularity even in nature. The basic physical materials of sculpture, such as wood and stone, can also be fashioned by man in a purely mechanical way into a great variety of regular and irregular shapes. The sum of these shapes, actual and possible, constitutes an additional part of sculpture's raw material, since every sculptural shape is but an instance of one or more of these pre-aesthetic shapes capable of being selected by the artist and put to artistic use.

This primary raw material of sculpture invites strictly scientific study (e.g., in the geological and chemical analysis of rocks and metals and in mathematical investigations of three-dimensional geometric forms). It also invites mechanical manipulation by a variety of techniques (e.g., casting of metal, modelling of clay, wood carving and stone cutting) considered as crafts innocent of artistic motivation or control. When a craftsman in these media submits in any way to artistic guidance, the product of his labors

[1] Because of its inability to control space by enclosing it, sculpture does not lend itself to the representation of a large group of figures without architectural assistance. Rodin's *Burghers of Calais* exploits this limited sculptural potentiality about as effectively as is possible.

ceases to be mere sculptural raw material and falls under the category of sculpture's primary artistic medium.

The primary artistic medium of sculpture is its raw material apprehended in terms of its artistic potentialities and submitted to preliminary aesthetic pre-artistic organization. The immediate attractiveness of various colors, textures, and surfaces, and of various three-dimensional geometrical patterns; the empathic effect of various types of form such as the triangular, pyramidal, circular, spherical, and spiral; the emotive power of *chiaroscuro*—these and other pre-artistic considerations enter into the transformation of the primary raw material of sculpture into its primary artistic medium. Scientifically-minded investigators such as Lipps and Birkhoff,[2] who are also endowed with aesthetic sensitivity and have attempted to adapt their methods of investigation to the nature of their subject-matter, have studied various aesthetic pre-artistic types of organization with great ingenuity and precision, and have shown how various arts tend to favor certain elementary patterns whose "aesthetic measure" is mathematically determinable. These studies cannot be classified as artistic or literary criticism, though they contribute to these disciplines. They are not concerned with the historical emergence of styles and do not aim at an evaluation of works of art as historical phenomena. They seek only to discover what types of arrangement and proportion are *immediately* satisfying in themselves and how they can enter into works of art as elementary aesthetic factors.

The creative artist, meanwhile, is more apt to trust to his artistic intuition for the preliminary selection and appraisal of his primary raw material. He need not be explicitly aware of any of these aesthetic relationships; it suffices that he be directly sensitive to them and thus be able to exploit man's more or less uniform and spontaneous aesthetic preferences and aversions. A conceptual apprehension of these relations, and a prosaic obedience to mathematically formulated principles based upon a disciplined study of them, would, in any case, never suffice to bring into being vital and expressive works of art. This is true, as we have seen, in music, the dance, and architecture; it is equally true in sculpture and painting.

[2] George D. Birkhoff, *Aesthetic Measure* (Cambridge, Mass.: Harvard University Press, 1933). This interesting book considers polygonal forms of various types as exemplified in ornaments, tiles, and vases. It also deals with aspects of diatonic harmony, melody, and the music of poetry.

In sculpture, as in the other arts, the creative artist decides to work in one physical medium rather than another, selects a particular block of stone or wood to work on, and consciously or unconsciously favors certain elementary color, texture, and geometrical relationships, all with reference to the specific work of art about to be fashioned. There seems to be no parallel in sculpture to the elaborate and precise pre-artistic organization of sound which distinguishes the primary artistic medium of music from its raw material. Whatever pre-artistic selection and ordering there is in sculpture is part of the actual, ever newly initiated, process of creation. But it represents an early stage in this process and is one which might easily be completed with reasonable success without being followed by successful fulfilment of the later and preeminently creative stage of actual composition. Hence the primary artistic medium of sculpture is not, on the one hand, to be identified with its raw material nor, on the other hand, with sculpture in its finished, artistically expressive state.

2. *The primary raw material and artistic medium of painting*

"Painting" is a generic term which subsumes works of art executed on a two-dimensional surface. The species of this genus are, of course, numerous and varied. Many types of surfaces are used, ranging all the way from baked clay and plaster to canvas, vellum, and many kinds of paper. The rendering may be in black and white with all the intermediate shades or "values," or in color. The technical processes employed include the use not only of the brush and palette-knife, but of the various tools employed in etching and engraving, drypoint and silverpoint, lithograph and aquatint. It is not my task to describe or even to enumerate all these contrasting modes of painting, but we must bear in mind their variety if we are to do justice to the raw materials and artistic media of this art.

The primary raw material of painting includes all the two-dimensional surfaces which allow of treatment in any species of painting, plus all the materials which can in one way or another be applied to these surfaces. Both the materials applied and the underlying surfaces vary in texture, color, saturation, and "value."

The three-dimensional space in which a painting, as a physical object, must exist, and the light which must illumine it if it is to be seen effectively, also constitute part of the primary raw material of painting in certain cases—for example, in Mantegna's *Camera degli*

Sposi (Fig. 197), in Velasquez' *Las Meninas*, and in certain Baroque paintings, where the picture plane is deliberately destroyed to establish a continuity between the space and even the light of the picture and of the room. But save in these cases they merely comprise essential but non-aesthetic conditions of its physical existence and visibility. Painting as a major art is therefore, as regards space and light, peculiarly self-contained. The use of the picture-frame makes this apparent, its primary function being to indicate the frontiers of the picture and to emphasize its artistic self-sufficiency. Even a statue normally rests on a pedestal which, like the picture-frame and proscenium arch over a stage, gives visual indication of the fact that a work of art is, as such, a world apart and requires, for proper artistic apprehension, the right amount of "psychical distance."[3] I have observed that statues may relate themselves to the surrounding three-dimensional space in an artistic manner through calculated interpenetration with it. In painting, on the other hand, the actual three-dimensional space in which the picture exists has (except in the cases indicated) no essential artistic import; space normally takes on artistic significance in this art only indirectly through representation—it has to be visually created on the two-dimensional surface within the work's own proper boundaries. Natural light is also normally of aesthetic significance in painting only as creatively introduced into the picture itself *via* representation. That paintings can be hung and lighted effectively or ineffectively is true. But this fact merely means that certain physical and psychological conditions must be satisfied if works of art in this medium, as in any other, are to be effectively apprehended.

When painting is used specifically as a minor art, that is, as making a contribution to a larger artistic whole which exists primarily in some other medium, the picture's *milieu* assumes genuine artistic importance. Murals, for example, should conform to the artistic requirements of their architectural setting. Some interiors, for example, architecturally demand a flat handling (Fig. 130) of the representational subject-matter, for otherwise a "hole" is created in the wall with serious architectural loss; other interiors permit and may even invite a realistic representation of solid objects and figures in three-dimensional space (Figs. 131, 132). But these requirements are not strictly relevant to painting as a major or self-

[3] Cf., below, pp. 240-1.

contained art, and merely exemplify the fact that wherever one art is made to serve another, concessions and adaptations become necessary. The proper hanging of pictures in a furnished room raises similar problems which need not be considered here.

The raw materials of painting allow of scientific analysis and of pre-aesthetic manipulation, as in the chemical analysis of paint and in the craft of the house painter. Such investigations and techniques, though indirectly useful to the painter[4] and worthy of consideration by the critic, are strictly pre-aesthetic in character. Like other artists, the painter must be enough of a scientist and craftsman in knowledge and technical manipulation of his primary raw material to ensure technical efficiency at the artistic level. But the pre-aesthetic and pre-artistic approaches need not, for that reason, be identified.

The primary artistic medium of painting is its raw material considered with respect to its potential artistic use and, so far as possible, subjected to aesthetic, pre-artistic organization. The general evaluation of this raw material as potentially useful in the art of painting is similar to all such selection and appraisal, and requires no further comment. But two special types of pre-artistic organization possible in this art should be mentioned.

The first of these relates to color. Colors differ in saturation or intensity, in "value" (light and dark) and "warmth" (hot and cold), and in "visual distance" (hot colors, such as red, appearing to come forward towards the spectator and cold colors, such as blue, to recede into the background). They are also related to one another by mixing, harmonizing, complementing, and clashing in various ways which can be accurately determined and recorded. These relationships are strictly analogous to the tonal interrelationships of sounds. Colors, like sounds, can be translated into wave lengths and vibration rates and analyzed at this pre-sensuous scientific level. They can also be studied from the point of view of aesthetic, pre-artistic vision, just as musical tones can be investigated with the aid of the musically sensitive ear. The pure colors can, for example, be organized into a "color scale" which constitutes the basis of different color palettes, and these, in turn, are differentiated with reference to the use of different color triads, such as yellow-red-blue; orange-green-violet; orange-yellow, violet-red, green-

[4] Whistler's blackened oils bear witness to the tragic penalty of using impermanent pigments.

blue; and orange-red, yellow-green, blue-violet. Useful scales of "values" and intensities can also be devised, and these scales can then be combined in systematic fashion, for example, in terms of Professor Pope's "tone solid." This type of investigation leads to accurate and diagrammatic descriptions of the basic principles of color harmony, sequence, and balance, to such concepts as those of high or low "key," and to the enumeration of possible and of actually used "scaled palettes." Such systematization of the fundamental aesthetic principles of color cannot achieve the order and complexity which characterize the aesthetic "science" of music, and it must usually fall short of complete mathematical precision. Such scales, says Professor Pope, "are of course not mathematically accurate, but must be thought of as adjusted or tempered for the convenience of the painter."[5] But the primary medium of painting has certainly been organized much more elaborately than that of sculpture. No comparable analysis of the primary medium of sculpture has, to my knowledge, been attempted, and there is reason to doubt its possibility.

Professors Ross, Pope, Birkhoff, and others have also shown how much can be done to analyze with systematic precision the basic elements of form in painting. Leaving out of account the all-important factor of representation, all pictures can be reduced by analysis to regular and irregular patterns of color, area, and line. Every area, in turn, has some specific two-dimensional shape. These shapes, and even individual lines, are found, when considered by themselves in ideal abstraction, to vary in immediate aesthetic attractiveness, some evoking marked satisfaction, others appearing aesthetically neutral, and still others arousing more or less pronounced feelings of dislike or repugnance. Some scientifically-minded aestheticians have attempted to invent a scale for measuring "normal"[6] reactions to such simple lines and shapes. Professor Birkhoff, for example, defining his "aesthetic measure" in terms of

[5] Arthur Pope, *An Introduction to the Language of Drawing and Painting*, 2 vols. (Cambridge, Mass.: Harvard University Press, 1929), Vol. I, p. 11. See the entire work for an excellent example of the pre-artistic analysis in this medium. Cf., also, Denman W. Ross, *A Theory of Pure Design* (New York: P. Smith, 1933).

[6] The invariable and perhaps unavoidable appeal to the "normal" is open to serious question, first, because it is impossible to define normality with any degree of precision or to determine normal reactions by means of practicable scientific tests; and second, because in the aesthetic as in other normative realms normal reactions, even if they

a ratio between order and complexity ($M = \frac{O}{C}$), and defining these factors, in turn, in terms of such "formal associations" as repetition, similarity, contrast, equality, symmetry, balance, and sequence, has devised a method whereby the inherent aesthetic value of an indefinite number of polygonal forms (he lists ninety such forms) can be computed with accuracy up to two decimal places. Investigations of this type are inevitably subject to the dangers of erroneous interpretation. They easily lead to the fallacy of atomicity, that is, to the belief that a work of art is merely the sum of its parts, and that aesthetic response to the work as a whole is merely the sum of individual responses to individual ingredients which can be isolated by analysis. They also tempt the investigator to conclude, often contrary to his own better judgment, that sheer obedience to the rules suggested by his own analytical investigations may suffice to produce real art.[7] But these temptations can be withstood and do not justify the abandonment of such investigations. On the contrary, they are not only interesting from the experimental scientific angle

could be determined with reasonable precision, would throw but little light on the nature of the values under consideration.

As regards the first point, is normality to be defined in terms of the entire human race, including men and women, children and adults, of every race and color, stage of culture, and degree of intelligence, from every type of environment, in every stage of health, and with however much or little native aesthetic sensibility? If so, the practical difficulties of determining normal reactions are wellnigh insuperable; if not, on what basis is a selection to be made, and how is this basis to be *scientifically* justified?

But even if we waive these difficulties and assume that suitable tests can be devised and applied to a fair sample of all mankind, or even of a large, specially selected group, what would the results prove regarding artistic creation of works of art and artistic response *at their best*, since it is only at their best that their true nature stands revealed? Professorial generalizations regarding "normal" reactions, based on results obtained from experiments in a college class of highly selected students already conditioned in innumerable ways, demand the most critical, if sympathetic, scrutiny.

[7] Cf. Birkhoff's admirable repudiation of any such possibility in his "Preface," *op. cit.*, p. ix: "Of course it would be absurd to think of the basic mathematical formula as a *deus ex machina*. . . . The true function of the concept of aesthetic measure is to provide systematic means of analysis in simple formal aesthetic domains. There is a vast difference between the discovery of a diamond and its appraisal; still more, between the creation of a work of art and an analysis of the formal factors which enter into it." He ventures, none the less, to use his formula "in a more or less mechanical fashion for purposes of construction," hopefully leaving it to the reader "to judge for himself to what extent the vase forms, simple melodies, and short poems so obtained are successful." Here Professor Birkhoff is clearly on dangerous ground.

but, wisely interpreted, facilitate analysis of concrete works of art by calling attention to recurrent forms in pictorial and other artistic patterns. They might even on occasion be of value to the creative artist who is faced with a technical problem which he cannot solve by his own unaided efforts.

Once again, however, I must emphasize the pre-artistic character of color harmonies and of the immediate attractiveness or unattractiveness of lines and shapes. Our responses to them are indeed aesthetic responses, and they themselves are essential aspects of the painter's artistic medium. Yet everything depends on *how they are used in actual creative composition.* No artistic medium and no part of an artistic medium is, as such, a work of art, but remains unequivocally pre-artistic. Only in actual works of art (which cannot be turned out according to rule but require the creative imagination for their conception and birth) can true artistic quality be found, and in such works these elementary color relationships and these simple forms acquire a very different aesthetic character and import.

3. Representation and abstraction in sculpture and painting

Sculpture and painting have been described as "representational" arts. I have assumed throughout this chapter that each of the component factors entering into a completed work of art may be found in a more or less unformed state at both the pre-aesthetic and the pre-artistic levels, and I have attempted to offer some justification for this assumption in my analyses of music, the dance, and architecture. The representational factor in sculpture and painting is no exception to this rule. It appears, by definition, in all representational sculptures and paintings; it appears at the aesthetic pre-artistic level as the chief constituent of the secondary artistic medium; and it also exists, in its pristine state, as part of the secondary raw material of these arts. My account of the factor of representation at the levels of raw material and artistic medium will be simplified by some preliminary definitions.

"Representation" in general may be defined as the reproduction, imitation, or re-presentation, in a suitable medium, of the visible appearance of objects, scenes, or events in the physical world. I shall presently have to emphasize the prime importance of selective and interpretative alteration of the natural appearance of things in all truly artistic or expressive representation. The ideal limit of non-artistic, mechanical representation is "literal reproduction." This may be defined as the most exact possible duplication, in a given medium, of the visual appearance of physical objects, scenes, and events. The best example of such literal reproduction on a two-dimensional surface would be a technically perfect color photograph, unretouched, and taken of *any* object at random in perfect focus and under suitable lighting conditions. In the three-dimensional medium the perfect illustration of literal reproduction would be an ideally faithful replica of any man or woman in wax, accurately painted and correctly clothed.[8]

Questions as to the artistic value or lack of value of such literal reproduction must be postponed.[9] We are here concerned only with the fact that, of all the pure major arts, none can compete with sculpture and painting in literal reproduction.[10] But even in these two arts the term "literal reproduction" must not be interpreted in the strictest sense, for the most faithful reproduction is "literal" only in a relative and qualified sense. *Strictly* literal reproduction would mean actual reduplication in every detail, both inner and outer, and the impossibility of such perfect reduplication, either in art or in nature, is evident.[11] In sculpture and painting, moreover, it is clearly only the visible outer appearance of objects that can be reproduced, and even this appearance must be *translated* into an artistic medium.

This translation, in turn, necessitates extensive alteration. In the most faithful sculptured copy of the human body, for instance, living flesh and blood must be rendered in an inanimate substance. If the medium is unpainted wood, metal, or stone, the color and texture of skin and hair must be translated into the very different color and texture of, e.g., oak, bronze, or marble. Movement cannot be literally reproduced at all but can only be suggested by catching the moving model in a posture which is indicative of motion just com-

[8] The term "realism" is used by critics in many different ways. It would be possible to define it as ideally close approximation to "literal reproduction." According to this definition, the photograph and the wax figure just described would be ideally "realistic." But, to avoid possible ambiguity, I shall usually refer to this type of imitation as "literal reproduction" rather than as "realism."

[9] Cf., below, Chap. XIX, §1.

[10] The art of the theater can, for obvious reasons, achieve even greater literalism, but since it is a mixed, not a pure, art we need not consider it here.

[11] Cf. Leibniz' principle of "the identity of indiscernibles."

pleted or about to take place. In painting even more extensive translation is required. The third spatial dimension in nature must be visually *created* on a two-dimensional surface by means of technical devices such as perspective, the use of hot and cold colors, modelling, *chiaroscuro*, skillful handling of line, and the like. Some selection of subject-matter, moreover, is unavoidable. The painter, even as a mere technician or craftsman, must choose to depict this object rather than that, in one position rather than another, and as seen from some particular angle and at some specific distance. The fact of light must also be recognized in one way or another by the painter, i.e., either by exclusion or by selective inclusion, for objects can be made pictorially visible without being illuminated (Fig. 162, cf. 163), or illuminated by a "spotlight" (Fig. 166), or by light from an indeterminate source (Fig. 167), or by natural light (Fig. 168). And, finally, a literalistic rendering of certain visual aspects of an object is often incompatible with an equally literalistic rendering of other aspects of the same object. Attention to microscopic detail, for example, must preclude a "realistic" treatment of motion or of the blurred and simplified appearance of objects seen at a distance through an atmospheric haze (Fig. 35). Selection of certain aspects of nature for literal reproduction at the expense of other aspects is therefore unavoidable.

Even ideally painstaking literal reproduction in these arts, then, is inescapably artificial. The most faithful of copies are still notably selective and cannot help being interpretative, just because the very technique of translation into a sculptural or pictorial medium requires selection and modification. Even the camera in the hands of a wholly unartistically-minded photographer must be selective and interpretative in this sense. The term "literal reproduction" has, none the less, pragmatic value in aesthetic analysis. For it indicates a potentiality of sculpture and painting of the utmost importance. Were these arts as unsuited to representation as are music and architecture, a wholly different account would have to be given of them as artistically expressive vehicles. The term also marks the limit beyond which they cannot be pushed in a naturalistically faithful rendering of the visual appearance of things. The opposite limit may be designated by the term "abstraction."

"Abstraction" in painting and sculpture can be defined as the wholly non-representational organization of the primary medium.

A pure abstraction (Figs. 94, 96-98) in sculpture and painting resembles no concrete physical object, scene, or event in the physical world. Its colors and shapes will of course resemble certain colors and shapes exemplified in nature, but only when the latter are considered by themselves, that is, abstracted from natural objects in all their complex individuality. Thus the term "abstraction" is also a relative term; its meaning can best be understood by reference to the process whereby a part or aspect of nature is, as it were, lifted out of its context, apprehended in isolation, and introduced into a new context in a wholly artificial and non-naturalistic manner. For example, many natural objects are red. This redness can be perceptually apprehended, and actual red pigment can be manufactured. This pigment can then be applied to canvas in ways not to be paralleled in nature. Similarly, natural shapes tend to approximate to regular geometrical shapes. These natural shapes can be abstracted from the objects which they characterize and be purified and multiplied by geometrical construction. These geometrical shapes can then be introduced in non-naturalistic fashion into pictorial and sculptural compositions. No abstraction is therefore wholly unlike nature in all respects; abstraction from nature can never be absolute. But the characteristic appearance of concrete physical objects can be systematically ignored. Artificially created patterns in stone or on canvas need not suggest any specific type of natural object and may justify no referential interpretation.

Abstraction in painting and sculpture is artistically more significant than literal reproduction, its opposing counterpart. For although a pure abstraction must fail to exploit the full expressive potentialities of the media of these arts, it can be directly expressive in the way (though certainly not in the same degree) in which abstract, non-representational patterns in music, architecture, and the dance can be expressive, whereas literal reproduction of nature in sculpture and painting must, as we shall see, be judged to lack all, or almost all, expressive value. The great masterpieces and most of the lesser works of art in these two media will be found to mediate between these limits or poles of literal reproduction and abstraction, and it is partly in terms of this mean that the conditions of artistic quality in these arts will ultimately have to be defined.[12]

[12] Cf., below, Chap. XXII.

4. The secondary raw materials and artistic media of sculpture and painting

Let us now examine more closely the potential subject-matter of these two representational arts, following the classification[13] of the chief generic types of artistic subject-matter.

(a) The *representational subject-matter* of sculpture and painting includes everything in the perceptual world which can be directly represented in either art. As secondary raw material, these natural objects and events simply exist in their own right; as secondary artistic medium, their adaptability to representational treatment in the primary pictorial and sculptural media is taken into account. The criterion of such adaptability is not intrinsic beauty but the technical possibility of effective rendition in the primary medium. The potential representational subject-matter of painting is clearly much greater in variety and range than that of sculpture; there are innumerable aspects of nature which can be represented only in pictures, and many other aspects which can be reproduced in sculpture only inadequately and with difficulty.[14] Sculpture, on the other hand, can represent three-dimensional objects such as the human body with a degree of immediacy and actuality unrivalled in painting (compare Figs. 133 and 134) because a sculptured figure actually exists in three dimensions while a pictorial representation of a similar figure exists physically only as a flat area. This fact complicates rather than simplifies the sculptor's problem, however, since too great "literalism," as defined above, is harmful to artistic expressiveness, and it correspondingly facilitates the task of the painter, since what has already been translated from three into two dimensions lends itself more easily to effective artistic manipulation.

The subject-matter allowing of representation in these arts may be historical, general, or fictitious. Historical persons are represented in portraiture more or less as they actually appeared (Figs. 239, 242-245, 249, 263) and they can be treated in "historical" sculptures and paintings either as they appeared or as they might have appeared (Figs. 256, 259, 262, 264-269). Or the individuals represented may bear no historical reference and may be chosen or created primarily for the more or less universal characteristics which they embody (Figs. 126, 127, 254, 255, 257). Or, finally, the artist can give free rein to his imagination and invent a subject-matter

[13] Cf., above, p. 44.

[14] Cf., above, pp. 40*ff*.

which resembles actual objects only in certain respects, e.g., fabulous monsters, fantastic scenery, etc. Compare the paintings of Bosch and Dali, which resemble one another in this respect despite a profoundly different motivation and expressive intent. The painter is more free in this respect than the sculptor because of the greater representational potentiality of his primary medium. In such fantastic creations the secondary raw material consists of those parts or aspects of nature which can be combined into new and wonderful representational forms, while the secondary artistic medium consists of these forms themselves.

(b) *Emotive-conative states* constitute most of the secondary material and medium of sculptural and pictorial abstractions, in the same way (though not in the same degree) in which they constitute the secondary material and medium of music and the non-pantomimic dance. But such states can be far more effectively expressed in sculpture and painting indirectly by means of representation. That is, human beings can be depicted in such a way as to convey, through facial expression, gesture, posture, action, and setting, the greatest variety of emotions and conative attitudes (Figs. 113, 121, 237, etc.). The motivation of these states can also be indicated by means of representational treatment as it cannot in pure abstractions. Not only can grief and exaltation, for example, be depicted in the faces and postures of attendant figures in a pietà or transfiguration; the cause of this grief and the reason for this exaltation can also be indicated by an appropriate handling of the central figure and of the representational setting (Figs. 184, 209-211). Sculpture and painting can express a greater variety of determinate aspects of man's inner life than can the abstract arts. All those inner states, cognitive, emotive, and conative, which permit either of abstract or representational treatment must be included in the secondary material and medium of these arts.

(c) The possibility of *symbolism* is greater in sculpture and painting than in the abstract arts. For in the latter only "abstract" (i.e., non-representational) forms can be used as symbols, whereas in representational works of art it is possible for representational forms (e.g., the cross, the halo, or the symbols of the martyrs, etc.) and events (e.g., the Annunciation, Adoration, Crowning with Thorns, and Crucifixion) to act as eloquent vehicles of symbolic meaning. The secondary raw material and artistic medium of sculpture and painting must therefore include whatever permits of symbolic representational treatment (Figs. 3, 211).

(d) Reference has been made to "occasional" music and dances in which some of the special characteristics of the occasion in question found explicit artistic recognition, and the rôle of *specific and more general social function* in architecture has been emphasized. It is relatively easy to introduce into painting or sculpture, *via* representation, a reference to a specific occasion (Figs. 264-270) or to a general social function (Figs. 223-229). But we must avoid confusion here between paintings and sculptures which are socially functional in this sense, and pictures and sculptures which are specifically designed to have a more particular social function. Rubens' *Medici* series, for example, was not only explicitly painted to celebrate the marriage and reign of Marie and Henry IV; a knowledge of where these pictures were intended to hang and the social function they were meant to perform is a definite aid to our understanding and appraisal of them. Similarly, altar-pieces successfully adapted to a specific religious function can most adequately be appreciated in the light of this function. This is not to deny that even here the work of art is, in a real sense, self-contained. I am merely urging that pictures and statues can, somewhat analogously to buildings, be created for more or less specific social uses and can, furthermore, be adapted to these uses so effectively that they cannot be *completely* understood unless the latter are taken into account. Wherever this is the case, this social function, whatever its nature, must also be included as part of the secondary raw material and artistic medium of these arts.

I need not labor the distinction between raw material and artistic medium in each of these four types of secondary matter available for sculptural and pictorial treatment. Nor need I discuss here the distinction between secondary medium and artistic content. But this distinction must never be forgotten. It is one thing for a painter or sculptor to decide to represent a joyful man; it is another to succeed in portraying him in such a way as to express, by representing certain of its visible manifestations, the emotion of joy. Or again, it is often easy to perceive, without much artistic sensitivity, the representational, symbolic, or functional subject-matter of a sculpture or painting. But only trained artistic perception can discover the artist's expressive interpretation of this subject-matter, as revealed in the language of his art. Artistic content is only latent and potential in the secondary medium. The subject-matter must receive artistic treatment before it can become artistically expressive.

CHAPTER VI

THE MATTER OF LITERATURE

1. Verbal languages

THE task of analyzing the primary medium of literature is complicated, first, by the inherent complexity of words, and secondly, by the radically different uses to which they are put, only one of which is expressive in the strictly "literary" or artistic sense. Before considering the essentially symbolic character of words, let us briefly note some of the generic ways in which words are used as a medium of exploration and communication. These can be distinguished most simply in terms (i) of contrasting interests and objectives, and (ii) of the several aspects of words which are exploited in satisfying these interests and attaining these objectives.

I shall have occasion in later chapters[1] to analyze more adequately the scientist's distinctive subject-matter, his characteristic attitude towards this subject-matter, and his highly specialized use of verbal and other symbols to record and interpret the results of his investigations. The typical subject-matter of scientific inquiry is the spatio-temporal world of natural process, including man as a psycho-physical organism. The scientist as such is concerned primarily with the skeletal structure or recurrent pattern of these events, and seeks to describe and interpret as precisely as possible what observation and experiment reveal in terms of universal laws and principles. His attitude is dispassionate and impersonal; his goal is the attainment of valid insights whose criteria are defined in a strictly scientific manner.

The scientist's use of words is dictated by this interest and goal. It is itself conceptually precise and impersonal. The "music" of the spoken word is entirely ignored. Emotive and conative overtones are deliberately avoided or suppressed. The only images which are countenanced are illustrations and diagrams which indicate what can usually be expressed more accurately in scientific prose or mathematical formulae. Every effort is made to invoke *only* the conceptual meaning of words, and merely to *assert* what is believed to

[1] Cf., below, Chaps. XIII-XV, XXIII.

be the abiding character of natural phenomena. The scientific use of words is thus essentially "prosaic" and differs profoundly, as we shall see, from their "poetic" or "literary" use in artistic expression.

The disciplines of history and philosophy are more catholic in interest and orientation. The subject-matter of history is, at least ideally, the whole sweep of past events regarded as an intelligible interconnected sequence of temporal occurrences; that of philosophy, the whole of reality reviewed *sub specie aeternitatis*. The findings of the more specialized disciplines, as well as man's everyday experiences, are as relevant to historical inquiry as they are to philosophical interpretation. These disciplines differ primarily in their major emphases, history stressing the temporal, philosophy, the abiding or eternal, aspect of things. But this difference of emphasis is, of course, of great importance.

The historian is more concerned than the philosopher with the unique events and characters in human history, and one of his chief tasks is so to describe these events and characters that they will "come to life" for the contemporary reader. He must, accordingly, attempt an imaginative reconstruction, from available documents, of concrete situations and occurrences in all their specificity. The philosopher, in contrast, is primarily interested (like the scientist) in recurrent patterns and (like the common man in his moral, aesthetic, and religious preoccupations) in the validity of norms or standards of evaluation. He is therefore given to abstract analysis and to a type of systematic appraisal foreign to the strictly historical enterprise.

Yet even this difference of emphasis, important as it is, is overshadowed by what these two disciplines have in common. For if history is defined more narrowly, as it usually is, as the study and interpretation of social and cultural phenomena of the past, and if philosophy is defined more broadly than it is by some contemporary philosophers so as to include normative evaluations, both history and philosophy differ from the natural sciences in dealing not only with fact but with value. Even historical fact-finding of the "scientific" type has significance for the historian only in proportion as the facts thus established can be made to contribute to his understanding of history as a process of profound human import; and the most abstract philosophical inquiries in logic and epistemology, which aim at scientific and mathematical precision, take on philosophical meaning only in proportion as they contribute to the philosopher's synoptic description and appraisal of reality in its relation to human life. Neither the philosopher nor the historian can ultimately ignore social standards and individual values, whether aesthetic, moral, or religious. Both history and philosophy are essentially humanistic disciplines.[2]

The "languages" of philosophy and history are, at their best, ideally adapted to these distinct though related enterprises. Philosophical discourse of the more analytical type resembles that of science in being abstract, conceptually precise, and logically demonstrative, whereas much historical writing is more akin to that of the art of literature in its greater use of concrete description and imagery. But the philosopher cannot ignore the illustrative value of imagery, and historians must make use of innumerable concepts with analytical rigor. Moreover, the most distinguished historians and philosophers of the past have not hesitated to exploit the emotional overtones of words in their depiction and appraisal of the normative aspects of their subject-matter. Historians have given us a vivid sense of what it must have felt like to live in other periods and to participate in major and minor historical events of the past. Like the poets, they have vitalized their subject-matter and brought home to us its perennial human interest. Similarly, the philosophers of the great tradition have not hesitated to use words and phrases heavily weighted with emotional overtones in their attempt to express in language their own evaluations of those aspects of reality whose structure they have laid bare by means of conceptual analysis. Witness the contrasting normative appraisals, and the corresponding variations in the use of emotive language, of such philosophers as Plato and Aristotle, Aquinas and Descartes, Spinoza and Hume, Kant and Schopenhauer, or, among the moderns, of Russell and Santayana, Bergson, James, and Dewey. Each exhibits an expressive style not to be duplicated in scientific exposition.[3] Finally, neither the philosopher nor the historian can afford to ignore the expressive sound and rhythm of effective prose, since these factors so

[2] Cf. the author's "Introduction" in *The Meaning of the Humanities* (Princeton: Princeton University Press, 1938), pp. xiii-xxxix.

[3] Logical positivists recognize this characteristic of metaphysical writing, deplore it, and make every effort to model philosophical discourse as closely as possible on that of science. The possibility, and indeed the desirability, of such repudiation of a tradition more than two thousand years old is, to say the least, open to serious question.

notably enhance the clarity and vividness of verbal exposition in these fields.

The common man (including the specialist on all matters not connected with his speciality) uses language with greater informality and less consistency than do the natural scientists, historians, and philosophers. He employs both the spoken and the written word for prosaic assertion of fact and for naïve speculation, for command, persuasion, and suggestion, for evaluations of every type, and for more or less untutored artistic expression. Even he is usually a specialist in his own trade or profession and adept in the use of its technical vocabulary and distinctive idiom. But in other fields he remains a layman—a scientist, philosopher, historian, and poet only in embryo.

As we proceed with our analysis of the medium, form, and content of the art of literature, the similarities and dissimilarities between the use of words for artistic expression and their various non-artistic uses will become increasingly apparent. It is, of course, quite impossible to draw an absolute line of demarkation between strictly literary prose and eloquent historical or philosophical prose—literary biography and the reflective essay are authentic mediating genres—or, at their farther boundaries, between historical prose of the more factual type and scientific description, or between rigorous philosophical analysis and scientific analysis. Yet, despite this imperceptible shading off of one generic use of words into another, these uses do, in their most characteristic form, differ in significant ways. For in each case the specialist transforms the language of the common man into a more or less specialized "language" which is better adapted to his own particular needs. Let us examine the essential nature of words, i.e., the primary raw material of both the non-literary writer and the literary artist, and see how writers transform this raw material into primary media for scientific, historical, philosophical, and artistic expression.

2. *The primary raw material of literature*

(a) *Signs, symbols, and words.* A word is a sound, or visible mark, with an ideational meaning, and is therefore *essentially* symbolic in character. But it is a distinctive type of symbol, for not all symbols are verbal. Symbols, in turn, are signs of a special type, for there are signs which cannot accurately be described as symbols.

Anything may function as a "sign" if it is so related to something else that the acute observer is enabled to pass in thought from it to that to which it stands in the specified relation. Natural phenomena, for example, function as signs in being related to one another as cause and effect, condition and conditioned, for this relation, once it is perceived, makes possible the prophetic anticipation of future events and the discovery of causes and conditions previously unknown. Thus, even to the layman, black clouds signify the likelihood of rain, and a poor harvest is the sign of spring drought or some other cause. The scientist is more expert than the layman in reading the sign-language of nature. With the aid of scientific instruments, experiment, and mathematical calculation, he can interpret familiar natural events with greater precision and discover causes and conditions hidden from the layman's view. But however expertly or inexpertly nature is observed and interpreted, natural phenomena only *become* signs as the result of human interpretation. In and of themselves, they are merely particular entities or occurrences standing in various spatio-temporal and dynamic relations to one another. They *acquire* significance as signs only for a *mind* which has discovered their natural order.

"Symbols," in turn, are signs which are *entirely* the product of human contrivance. In pure symbolism the relation of symbol and meaning symbolized is wholly arbitrary. It has no basis in nature or in logic; the meaning of a pure symbol is arbitrarily attached to it by individual *fiat* or social convention. Most words are pure symbols in this sense. Save in the case of onomatopoeia, the ideational meaning of verbal sounds has no natural basis, and it cannot be ascertained by logical inference save within a wider linguistic context. The meaning of verbal symbols and linguistic conventions must therefore simply be accepted as arbitrary facts.

There are, of course, many types of non-verbal symbols. Flags may symbolize nationality; a bent arrow along a highway symbolizes a curve in the road; the Cross and Crescent symbolize the Christian and Mohammedan faiths. Words are only one type of symbol, as symbols are only one type of sign.

Symbols, both verbal and non-verbal, differ in complexity and purity. A flag is a relatively simple symbol; the Lord's Supper is a highly complex symbol, commemorative in the Protestant tradition, sacramental in the Catholic. Arabic numerals are pure symbols since they are neither imitative nor directly expressive, whereas words like "buzz," "thump," and "cuckoo" are imitative in resembling the sounds of the objects or processes symbolized,[4] and ejaculations are immediately expressive symbols whose meaning is often intelligible to foreigners. Symbols differ also in origin. Some are established by *fiat*. Flags and mathematical symbols are usually of this type, and scientific terms are often deliberately coined. Most words, in contrast, have an obscure social origin. But whatever their origin, all symbols are man-made, and, as such, arbitrary. They cannot, therefore, function as symbols unless their meaning is established with sufficient precision to allow of translation or passage from sign to meaning signified. Symbols can serve as intelligible records for the solitary individual only if he remembers the meanings which he has assigned to the symbols he has used; and they can be vehicles for inter-personal communication only if communicator and communicant can agree, by special arrangement or by participation in a common heritage, on the meanings of the symbols to be employed.

A verbal language, accordingly, is a system of auditory symbols (often with a visual equivalent) which have arbitrary individual meanings and which can be made to generate new meanings by being combined syntactically. As a sensuous phenomenon, a word is an audible sound and a visible mark on paper or on some other physical surface. As such, it has its own auditory and visual qualities and its own linguistic history. But as symbols, these sounds and marks possess a meaning by virtue of which they point beyond themselves to some aspect of man's inner or outer experience. This meaning, even in the case of a single word, is itself complex. The real unit of language is of course not the single word but the phrase or sentence. But we will do well to start by distinguishing the chief generic meanings of the individual word.

(b) *Three types of verbal meaning*. The three types of meaning here in question may be entitled "conceptual," "imagistic," and "emotive-conative."[5]

[4] Chinese and Egyptian ideograms have a representational basis, picturing in simplified form some aspect of the object or activity symbolized.

[5] The term "meaning" is here used broadly and in a somewhat unorthodox manner to signify whatever a word (or combination of words) arouses in the mind, irrespective of the nature of what is thus aroused. Thus a word, by virtue of its "conceptual meaning," *refers* us to one or more *universals* that are *public* to human experience. By virtue of its "imagistic meaning," it *conjures up* one or more *images* which, as mental objects, are necessarily *private* to each individual, but which may none the less closely resemble one

All words except proper names and their equivalents have, in the first place, one or more conceptual meanings which the dictionary attempts to define. Proper names and demonstratives must be excepted, since they refer us to particular individuals. But all other words have a more or less well established universal meaning, that is, they signify a class of individuals or a qualifying attribute which is or might be exemplified in two or more particular instances.[6] Thus, "Fido" and "Henry James" are proper names signifying particular individuals,[7] whereas "dog" and "man," "brown" and "angry," are terms signifying *types* of individuals or qualifying *attributes* which do or might characterize many different individuals. I shall follow a convenient philosophical usage and entitle these more or less common characteristics "universals."[8] Since universals can be apprehended in abstraction by means of conceptual analysis and definition, and since all common names must necessarily have an essential meaning of this type, I have entitled it the word's core of conceptual meaning.

Secondly, many common names tend to arouse or suggest sensuous images. These may be relatively clear-cut and specific, or they may be hazy and confused. They may also be visual, auditory, olfactory, tactile, thermal, or kinaesthetic, or a combination of these. Words themselves differ greatly in imagistic association. The meaning of some is so predominantly abstract (e.g., "contradiction" and "whole") as to be hostile to associated images; others (e.g., "dog" and "table") strongly tend to conjure up images in the mind; still others, such as the names of specific colors, sounds, and other sensuous qualities, refer so directly to specific sensations or perceptions that it is almost impossible to distinguish their imagistic from their conceptual meanings.

another in two or more minds. By virtue of its "emotive-conative meaning," it *evokes* characteristic *emotions and attitudes* which, again, are *private* but potentially similar. Universals, images, and emotive-conative states differ from one another radically, and they differ also as regards the relation in which they stand to the word. I have found it convenient to designate all three types of verbal effect as "verbal meaning."

[6] Articles ("a," "an," and "the") and such words as "any," "all," and "some" have a meaning which requires the special consideration given them in logic but which need not concern us here.

[7] That the same proper name is applied to different individuals is again irrelevant to the present argument.

[8] The use of this term need not imply any particular philosophical interpretation of the ontological status of universals. Cf., below, pp. 243*ff*.

Thirdly, many words come to acquire more or less powerful emotive and conative overtones, and tend to arouse in us more or less specific emotions, feelings, and desires. Political terms, such as "democracy," "fascism," and "communism," are today heavily weighted with such dynamic overtones, and words like "justice," "father," and "love" are always prone to arouse in men a variety of emotions and attitudes whose nature depends on the context in which they are used.

Of these three types of meaning, the core of conceptual meaning changes least from generation to generation and enjoys the greatest degree of social objectivity. Imagistic associations vary not only from individual to individual but even for one and the same conscious agent, since new experiences are always storing the mind with new images or forcing the revision or abandonment of older images. The emotions and conative attitudes aroused by words (and all words can acquire this power if rightly used) are also subject to change, the same word provoking anger or resignation, joy or sorrow, depending on the circumstances of its use. But even the conceptual meaning of a word may change with social usage; it may be affected by the specific context in which it is used; and it may be interpreted differently even by men with a similar cultural background. Hence the difficulty which we all experience in trying to communicate our ideas to one another verbally.

Words could not be used at all as communicatory symbols if they did not possess their core of conceptual meaning. They owe their amazing adaptability to the fact that every common name signifies not a concrete individual object but a universal trait or quality. One way of describing the world of our inner and outer experience is to say that it consists of individual objects and events which manifest universals shared (actually or potentially) with other individuals. A language can be used effectively in the description and analysis of these individual objects and events, each of which is unique, only in proportion as the words which constitute its vocabulary signify these universal traits and the recurrent relations in which they stand to one another. A word whose only meaning was a specific concrete image would be almost useless as a vehicle of communication. To attempt to rely exclusively on words of this type would be like trying to conduct a conversation by using nothing but proper names. Were the word "dog," for instance, to signify merely a specific image or a particular dog, all discussion of dogs in general would be impossible. But since the words "dog," "brown," "my," and "is" all possess a core of conceptual meaning by virtue of which they refer to universal traits and relations, we can so combine these words as to describe with reasonable accuracy a particular fact such as that "my dog is brown." Thus, *universal* reference is, in language, the basic condition of the applicability of words to specific instances. If words lacked these universal meanings all conceptual abstractions and all reasoning would also be impossible. The conceptual core of meaning which common names possess is the linguistic basis of science, philosophy, history, and related disciplines.

But this need not affect the importance of imagistic associations. For images are the echoes or reflections, now simple and now the product of combination and fusion, now clear and now obscure, of our first-hand perceptual contacts with the outer world. Conceptual analysis breaks up this world of spatio-temporal objects into its universal ingredients and leads to their apprehension in isolation. The reproductive imagination, in contrast, revives in memory our immediate, coercive sense-perceptions of the concrete objects themselves in all their concrete individuality. Hence words which arouse sensuous images in our minds bring us back to physical reality itself with unrivalled directness and immediacy.

Finally, our emotions and feelings, desires and volitions are the *subjective* condition of all normative apprehension and appraisal. Certain professional and lay philosophers defend the subjectivity of values on the ground that the values which most men regard as objective are actually the hypostatized projections of their own desires, feelings, and emotions. I should be prepared to argue that this subjectivistic interpretation of values is neither coercive nor reasonable, though its falsity cannot be absolutely demonstrated. Yet, even if we grant that beauty, goodness, and holiness have at least some kind of objective status, it is clear that, were we incapable of emotional and conative response, *we* could never discover or appraise them. Just as our innate capacity for reasoning and our instinctive curiosity subjectively condition our apprehension of truth, so too do our instinctive tendency to like and dislike and our innate ability to experience emotion subjectively condition all our evaluations. And it is because many words suggest preferences and emotional states that they are such essential instruments for the preservation and communication of normative judgments.

(c) *New emergent meanings*. So far I have considered only the referential meanings of words taken in isolation. The primary raw material of every verbal language includes, in addition, the meanings which may emerge from their grammatical and syntactical combination. Every verbal language has a grammar and syntax in obedience to which words may be combined into larger linguistic units. These relationships are the linguistic equivalent of the basic relationships of pitch in music, mechanical relationships in architecture, etc. Obedience to them is a necessary (though not a sufficient) condition of linguistic intelligibility. Words may be combined in conformity to these linguistic conditions so as to express meanings which cannot be expressed by individual words alone. This fact is of the utmost importance for the understanding of literary meaning.

I have said that the conceptual, imagistic, and emotive-conative meanings of a single word are always more or less indeterminate. But as soon as a word is meaningfully combined with other words the meanings which it and they are meant to carry are more clearly specified. These individual meanings, now become precise, may also be combined to express new and complex meanings with notable exactness. No better instance could be adduced of an organic relationship, in which the whole is more than the sum of its parts and is yet conditioned by them, while they, in turn, are significantly determined by participation in the whole. This applies to each of the three types of meaning which I have described. The conceptual core, the associated images, and the emotive-conative overtones of individual words can all acquire greater precision in a meaningful context, and words can, by skillful combination, be made to convey new concepts, fresh images, and novel emotive-conative states devoid of ambiguity.[9]

(d) *Verbal tonality*. One additional characteristic of words as the raw material of literature must be mentioned. This is their tonal character. Words as uttered, whether vocally or sub-vocally, and whether singly or in combination, are sensuous patterns of sound whose timbre, pitch, intensity, and duration constitute, in conjunction with intervening pauses, the basis of metrical and non-metrical rhythm and make possible that "musical quality" of the spoken word which is so essential to all genuine literary excellence. It is to be noted that, even in common speech, this factor contributes in two

[9] Cf. W. Empson, *Seven Types of Ambiguity* (London: Chatto, 1930), for an excellent discussion of this point.

ways to inter-subjective communication: first, as *directly* expressive of emotive and conative meaning (as in ejaculations of joy, anger, or pain); and secondly, by clarifying the *symbolic* meaning of the words. Words spoken in a monotone without inflection or cadence are much harder to understand than words spoken rhythmically, with suitable variations of pitch, etc.

(e) *"Primary" and "secondary" symbolism.* The primary raw material of literature, then, as of the non-literary verbal disciplines, is *essentially* symbolic, since a word is an auditory sound or visual mark signifying an arbitrarily assigned meaning. This symbolism is so basic to the very nature of language that it merits the designation "primary symbolism." The art of literature may therefore be said to be "symbolic" in the same sense in which music, the pure dance, and architecture have been referred to as "abstract," and the arts of sculpture and painting as "representational." This "primary" symbolism may be distinguished from "secondary" symbolism by defining the latter as an *additional* symbolic meaning which may be attached to the objects or ideas referentially specified through the primary symbolism of words. Words which are not onomatopoetic are pure primary symbols. But when they are so combined as to generate referential meanings to which *further* symbolic meaning is attached, this *new* meaning is symbolic in the "secondary" sense. Thus, the primary symbolic meaning of the word "cross" is, roughly, its dictionary meaning. But the cross has itself come to be accepted as the symbol of Christianity. This symbolic meaning is "secondary." Similarly, the symbolism in the poems of Yeats is a "secondary" symbolism. The primary raw material in each of the other arts, in sharp contrast to that of literature, is essentially *non*-symbolic, i.e., devoid of primary symbolism. But compositions in these arts can acquire, both in part and in whole, a secondary symbolic meaning strictly comparable to that which characterizes certain literary compositions. In short, primary symbolism (as here defined) is basic, but only in the art of literature; secondary symbolism is ancillary, but permits of use in any of the arts.

3. The non-literary and literary primary linguistic media

Verbal languages may be classified in two ways, only one of which marks the distinction between the primary raw material and the primary medium. They can be classified, on the one hand, according to race, nationality, period, and the like (e.g., into Greek and Latin; Anglo-Saxon, Elizabethan English, and modern English; English dialects in various localities, etc.). Each of these languages is a more or less flexible and precise vehicle for inter-subjective communication, and each permits, at least in theory, of more specialized use; but none is in itself a specialized verbal medium in the stricter sense in which the "languages" of science and philosophy, history, and the art of literature are specialized. These specialized "languages" use one of the "cultural" languages as their primary raw material and, by judicious selection, addition, and distinctive employment, transform it into a vehicle uniquely adapted to a highly specialized use.

I have already indicated the general ways in which the natural scientist, the philosopher, and the historian exploit the language of the common man. Each makes a distinctive use of those aspects of his native tongue which serve his special expressive purposes.[10] The creative writer's use of language is equally distinctive. He too transforms his mother tongue, as his primary raw material, into a flexible primary artistic medium by recognizing and exploiting its expressive potentialities.

This transformation takes place *during* the actual process of literary composition. No rules can be laid down to determine what words, phrases, or syntactical constructions have potential literary value; it must be left to the writer to sense what is appropriate and expressive in a specific literary context, and what is not. One mark of the literary artist is a complete mastery of language, i.e., the ability to transform the verbal raw material at his disposal into a powerful primary medium for literary expression. This "sense of language" is partly an innate gift, partly the product of study and cultivation. Three devices constantly employed by the literary artist to achieve his expressive ends make clear some of the literary potentialities of words and the ways in which these potentialities can be exploited.

(a) *The metaphorical dimension.* The first and most important of these devices is the literary use of metaphor.[11] The creative writer must, for reasons already indicated, make use of the conceptual meaning of words and the possibility of expressing more complex concepts by combining words in an appropriate manner. He must also exploit their imagistic associations and, with their aid, create

[10] Cf., below, pp. 259*ff*., on the scientific use of language.

[11] I am particularly indebted to Professor A. E. Hinds for the following interpretation of the "metaphorical dimension."

new images, the synthetic products of his own imagination. But literature as a fine art is primarily concerned neither with abstract concepts (whether simple or complex) nor with concrete images (whether original or reproductive) merely for their own sake. Its outstanding characteristic is its use of concepts and images in metaphorical relation.

A metaphor may be defined narrowly as the "application of [a] name or descriptive term to an object to which it is not literally applicable,"[12] as, for example, in "a glaring error" or "a marble brow." Errors do not literally glare, and human foreheads are not actually of marble. But as here used, these adjectives perform the important function of emphasizing certain distinguishing characteristics of the object named by analogical reference to other objects in which these qualities are unmistakably and vividly present. An obvious error obtrudes itself upon us like a blinding or glaring light. A brow, like marble, may be cool and white. These metaphors bring home to us, with imaginative power and great economy of means, what is prosaically asserted when an error is merely said to be very obvious and a forehead to be white, cool, or smooth.

In every metaphor two ideas are related in such a way as to illumine and vitalize one another. The metaphorical relation is essentially one of revealing analogical comparison. Analogy is of prime importance in every universe of discourse, in mathematics and science, philosophy and history, as well as in literature.[13] But in literature it takes a special form, for it almost invariably involves a juxtaposition of ideas one of which is more general, the other, more particular. In the phrase, "a glaring error," for example, "error" is more general and abstract, "glaring," more imagistic and concrete; in "a marble brow," "marble" (here meaning marble-like) is more abstract and general than "brow."

A metaphor in this narrower sense is the simplest and clearest example of the literary relation of the more general to the more particular. But the same relation obtains within still narrower limits on the one hand, and on a much larger scale on the other.

Most words in such languages as English, French, or German have themselves undergone a change not only in form but in meaning. This change in meaning is frequently in the direction of a greater generality (and often looseness). "Limbo," for example,

[12] *Concise Oxford Dictionary* (Oxford: The Clarendon Press, 1934).

[13] Cf. Scott Buchanan, *Poetry and Mathematics* (New York: John Day, 1929).

meant in the Middle Ages a region on the border of hell where pre-Christian men of virtue and unbaptized infants were confined, while today it signifies a condition of neglect or oblivion.[14] But the change of meaning may also be from the more general to the more particular. Thus, "curry" originally meant (O.F. *conreer*) to prepare, and has come to signify (in one of its modern uses) the process of rubbing down or dressing a horse. When words are so used as to bring out one of these etymological meanings, a metaphorical relation is established between the older and the contemporary meaning, with the result that the word itself, as well as the words with which it is combined in the context, takes on new life and significance. Note, for example, the use of the words "oblivion" and "gross" in Hamlet's soliloquy (IV, iv):

> Now, whe'r it be
> Bestial oblivion, or some craven scruple
> Of thinking too precisely on the event,

and

> . . . Examples gross as earth exhort me.

"Oblivion" is here used not in the more common sense of "being forgotten" but in the older sense of "being oblivious to," i.e., of *not* thinking, like a beast. This older meaning is clearly indicated by the context; "oblivion" is contrasted with "thinking too precisely." Similarly, "gross" is used primarily in its older sense of "large" or "big" (F. *gros*, *grosse*), not in the later sense of "coarse."

A metaphor may, on the other hand, be expanded into a simile (e.g., "as punctual as a star"), where the comparison is usually marked by the words "as" or "like." And similes, in turn, can be developed into parables or fables, and, finally, into allegories in which abstract ideas of great complexity are set in analogical relation to images of comparable complexity, as for example in *Pilgrim's Progress*, *The Divine Comedy*, *The Faery Queen*, and *The Hind and the Panther*.

In literature, analogical comparison is most often made between concrete images and abstract concepts. "A glaring error" is a metaphor of this type, and so is the simile: "Life [an abstract concept], like [marking the comparison] a dome of many-coloured glass

[14] Cf. "depend"—*hang from*; "egregious"—*selected from the herd*; "precocious"—*too early ripe*; "thrill"—*to bore or drill*; "front"—*forehead*. Cf. J. B. Greenough and G. L. Kittredge, *Words and their Ways in English Speech* (New York: The Macmillan Company, 1922), Chap. II.

[a concrete image], stains the white radiance of eternity [metaphorical development of the comparison]." Here the literary image is explicit and somewhat developed; in a simple metaphor it is undeveloped and merely suggested. But it is also possible to bring together with metaphorical effect two images, as in "the wine-dark sea," "blind mouths," or in Wordsworth's comparison of the dancing daffodils with the "stars that shine and twinkle on the Milky Way." Or, alternatively, two concepts may be metaphorically related, as in "cold sin" (in George Herbert's *Decay*), a "crowd of cares" (in his *Misery*), or, with the aid of imagery, in:

> O loose this frame, this knot of man untie,
> That my free *soul* may use her wing,
> Which now is *pinioned with mortality*,
> As an entangled, hampered thing.[15]

In short, the means by which the metaphorical relationship can be established are very varied. But what is important in each case is that, in one way or another, one of the terms compared be *more* abstract and general, the other *more* concrete, restricted, and particular. Whenever this relationship is set up in the medium of words it may, for convenience, be entitled a "metaphorical relation."

It does not follow, of course, that all metaphorical comparisons possess literary quality or value. They do so, as we shall see,[16] only in proportion as they succeed in heightening our sense of reality by endowing abstract concepts (or their equivalent) with life through concrete application, and by giving concrete images (or their equivalent) significance through conceptual interpretation. From the strictly literary point of view, pure concepts are cold and dead in their abstract aloofness from the concrete world of man's experience; and from any point of view, sheer particularity, whether perceptual or imagistic, is blind and meaningless. It is only through meaningful application of the abstract to the concrete, and through interpretation of the concrete in terms of the more abstract, that interest can be aroused and the imagination stimulated into fruitful activity. To accomplish this it is not enough merely to bring more and less general ideas into juxtaposition. They must be so selected and combined as to fructify one another, each preserving its essential character while taking on new significance through lit-

[15] George Herbert, *Home*. My italics.

[16] Cf., below, Chap. XXII, §4,d.

erary fusion. Only thus can that dynamic tension be created which constitutes the very essence of literary quality.[17]

This quality is, of course, the product of literary form; it does not exist in the primary literary medium as such. Yet it is the character of words, taken individually and in combination, which conditions the very possibility of the literary metaphor in its various forms. The author who achieves literary vitality by invoking the metaphorical dimension is, in effect, exploiting the literary potentialities of words and using them not as mere raw material but as a primary linguistic medium for literary expression.

(b) *Emotive-conative overtones*. The competent literary artist also exploits the emotional and conative overtones of words, and, in so doing, again transforms his verbal raw material into an artistic medium. Here the problem arises as to how he can succeed in controlling these overtones and express the precise emotions and attitudes which he wishes to express, since the word tends, as we have seen, to evoke different emotions and attitudes in different men and in the same individual on different occasions. He can do so in several ways, and he is likely to use them all simultaneously. He has at his command, in the first place, such words as "gay," "pensive," and "sad" which refer the reader directly to specific emotional states and moods. With these he can explicitly describe or suggest the emotions, moods, and feelings which he wishes to express. Note Milton's use of words of this type in his description of the nun in *Il Penseroso*:

> Come, pensive Nun, devout and pure,
> Sober, steadfast, and demure. . . .

[17] For an example of a series of superb literary metaphors, see Gaunt's speech on England, in *Richard II* (II, i):

> This royal throne of kings, this sceptred isle,
> This earth of majesty, this seat of Mars,
> This other Eden, demi-paradise,
> This fortress built by Nature for herself
> Against infection and the hand of war,
> This happy breed of men, this little world,
> This precious stone set in the silver sea,
> Which serves it in the office of a wall
> Or as a moat defensive to a house,
> Against the envy of less happier lands,—
> This blessed plot, this earth, this realm, this England. . . .

Secondly, he can create images which tend to arouse the emotion or mood in question, as does Coleridge in *Kubla Khan*:

> A savage place! as holy and enchanted
> As e'er beneath a waning moon was haunted
> By woman wailing for her demon-lover!
>
> A sunny pleasure-dome with caves of ice!

or William Cowper in *The Castaway*:

> But I beneath a rougher sea,
> And whelm'd in deeper gulphs than he.

Thirdly, he can make use of words and phrases which normally carry several different overtones only some of which are relevant to the theme. Here the context must determine which associations are intended; hence, single lines, taken out of context, cannot be instanced by way of illustration. When these and other devices are skillfully used in conjunction, the artist's emotive intent becomes quite unambiguous.

In *The Daffodils*, to cite a very familiar and simple illustration, Wordsworth wishes to express the joy and gaiety which may follow upon loneliness, and the feeling of pleasure which may accompany a pensive mood. The initial sense of loneliness is suggested by "wander'd," specifically referred to in "lonely," and metaphorically intensified by the image of "a cloud that floats on high o'er vales and hills." The contrasting feeling of pleasure is suggestively anticipated in the phrase "all at once," indicating a transition and a contrast. Then comes the image:

> . . . a crowd,
> A host, of golden daffodils;
> Beside the lake, beneath the trees,
> Fluttering and dancing in the breeze.

This image will suffice of itself to arouse in all who are sensitive to nature a feeling of pleasurable delight. But some of the words used in painting the picture further specify a happy mood, e.g., "dancing." Others, e.g., "host," "golden," "fluttering," and "breeze," might, in another context, express different emotions, but here the context leaves no doubt as to the emotive and affective states which they are meant to evoke. After the effect of this image has been intensified by further metaphorical allusions to the "twinkling stars" and the "sparkling waves," the dominant mood is expressly stated in:

> A poet could not but be gay,
> In such a jocund company. . . .

The poem concludes with a reflective comment, predominantly conceptual in character, on the value of memory, as illustrated by the poet's recollection of this joyful scene in an idle or pensive moment. Wordsworth thus succeeds in making perfectly clear to us the emotional attitudes which he intended to express. Indeed, he expresses these attitudes far more precisely and vividly than is possible in mere unimaginative prose.

The artistic expressiveness of a poem is of course not a function of the individual words and phrases in isolation but of the poem as a whole; and its artistic quality is a direct function not of the primary medium as such, but of artistic form. Yet no poem could be expressive of emotive-conative states if the individual words and phrases employed lacked all emotive and conative associations. What the poet does is to exploit these associations by combining the right words in the right way.

(c) *The sound of the spoken word.* Finally, language is transformed into the primary artistic medium of literature through recognition and suitable exploitation of the sound of the spoken word. From the literary point of view, the sounds of words are much more important than their visible marks. Good poetry and literary prose can be fully appreciated only if heard, at least by the inward ear.[18]

The rhythm of language may be defined as the measured flow of words in verse and prose. The "measure" is, at the sensuous level, a function primarily of the tonic and secondary accents or pitch of words (in the Germanic languages) or of the quantity or duration of syllables (in the Latin languages), though, ultimately, accent and quantity really imply one another. In metrical verse the time intervals are more regular than in prose and are felt to be basically equal. But the regular or irregular measured flow of sound in literature is not artistically autonomous, as it is in music. It is largely conditioned by the accepted pronunciation of words and by the meaning of the words and phrases used. Verse is characterized by

[18] A fine page of manuscript or print is a delight to the eye and helps to clarify and enrich the literary quality of the words. But this effect is hardly comparable in literary significance to that of auditory rhythm and timbre.

an arbitrarily adopted, more or less regular, auditory pattern. But this pattern must never be allowed seriously to distort the correct pronunciation of words or to destroy their meaning. It is their meaningful pronunciation, rather, which gives the clue to the metrical pattern. Iambic pentameter, for instance, is a metrical form consisting of a line of five feet, each foot (the smallest metrical unit) consisting of an unaccented syllable followed by an accented one, thus: ——́ ——́ ——́ ——́ ——́. When such a line as "Of Man's first disobedience, and the fruit" is read aloud intelligently, the accents fall thus: Of Mán's fírst disobédience, and the frúit. The first and last accents are here determined by the meaning, the third, by normal pronunciation. To read the line in slavish conformity to the metrical form would involve serious distortion of meaning: Of Mán's first dísobédience ańd the frúit. Three of the four normal and meaningful accents, meanwhile, correspond with the accents of the abstract metrical form of iambic pentameter. In the next line four more metrical accents (the second, third, fourth, and fifth) are determined by pronunciation and meaning, and in the third line four more accents (the first, third, fourth, and fifth) receive recognition.

> Of Mán's fírst disobédience, and the frúit
> Of that forbídden trée, whose mórtal táste
> Brought déath into the wórld, and áll our wóe. . . .

Thus the metrical pattern is well established within the first three lines by a meaningful and unforced reading of the words. The meaning dictates certain accents (such as the accent on "first" in the opening line), certain unaccented words and syllables (such as "and" in the first line), and certain pauses (as after "disobedience" in the first line and after "world" in the third), which break into the strictly metrical pattern and save the lines from mechanical, uninspired conformity. (Compare: "My heart aches, and a drowsy numbness pains. . . .")

Most verse forms also make use of consonance, assonance, alliteration and rhyme[19] to intensify the meaning through direct musical expressiveness. Even literary prose can be musically expressive,

[19] Consonance is identity of consonant sounds (e.g., "The mellow ousel fluting in the elm"); assonance, of vowel sounds (e.g., "grieve, bleed"). Alliteration is consonance of first sounds of accented syllables. Rhyme is consonance plus assonance, but without alliteration at the beginning of rhyming words.

though good prose, by definition, avoids the meter and rhyme of verse. In both prose and verse, auditory rhythm, determined by proper pronunciation and meaning, is thus essential to literary style, and the direct musical expressiveness of words as sounded is an important factor in the production of literary quality. Here, as elsewhere, this quality is always the product of literary form, never merely of the primary medium as such. Yet its actuality is conditioned once again by the nature of words as the primary raw material of literature. In proportion as the musically expressive potentialities of this raw material are appreciated, the latter is transformed into the artistic medium of the art of literature.

4. The secondary raw materials and media of the non-literary linguistic disciplines and of the art of literature

It remains to consider the secondary raw material of linguistic composition as such, and the various secondary media of the more specialized forms of writing.

The generic secondary raw material available to the writer includes all subjects which permit of linguistic treatment, i.e., the whole range of man's "inner" and "outer"[20] experience, and all the objects of inner and outer awareness. But, as has already been indicated, the natural scientist, the philosopher and historian, and the creative writer in the narrower sense, each approaches reality and human experience with a more or less specialized interest, and each selects from this enormously diverse and extensive subject-matter those objects and events and those pervasive characteristics which are immediately relevant to this interest. This selection normally takes place *during* the process of inquiry or act of literary composition, and is, accordingly, implicit rather than explicit. The generic secondary raw material is transformed into a specific secondary medium or subject-matter while the task of specialized investigation or creative composition is in progress. But this must not be allowed to obscure the fact that the writer must always approach his generic subject-matter selectively.

The distinctive secondary media of science, philosophy, and history have already been indicated. The scientist concerns himself with the structural characteristics of the physical world and of man as a psycho-physical organism. The philosopher is distinguished for

[20] Cf., below, pp. 247*ff*.

breadth of interest and generality of interpretation. The historian's primary interest is directed to the individuality of things in their temporal sequence. Each of these specialists, accordingly, adopts a distinctive approach to reality and human experience and selects a distinctive subject-matter for observation and interpretation.

The creative writer's approach to reality is no less distinctive. He is primarily concerned to reveal with imaginative power the nature and import of every type of human experience and of the objects to these generic experiences. His secondary medium is, accordingly, much more extensive and varied than that of artists in the other primary media, for it includes the artistically relevant aspects of (i) physical objects and events, and their perceptual attributes, (ii) man's social activities, (iii) his emotive-conative states, and (iv) the entire range of concepts and images in terms of which he reflects upon his own inner experiences and upon his relation to his fellowmen, the world of nature, and Deity. His secondary medium thus includes every subject that permits of strictly literary (as opposed to merely verbal) treatment.

Once again, no subject-matter, in and of itself, can endow a literary composition with artistic merit. Its literary potentialities must not only be recognized but *realized* through artistic organization and expressive interpretation. But such literary actualization would be impossible were there not available to the writer a variety of subjects of genuine human import. All that he can do is to make explicit in his own primary media, *via* literary form, what is implicit in the nature of things. Subject-matter and literary content must never be confused, but subject-matter does, none the less, essentially condition literary content.

This concludes my analysis of the matter of art in general and of the primary and secondary raw materials and artistic media of the six major arts. The following synoptic definitions of the primary and secondary artistic media—definitions equally applicable to all the arts, major and minor, pure and mixed—may be offered in summary of what has been accomplished.

The primary artistic medium of any art may be said to consist of (i) "measurable" or determinable units, elements, or aspects of the primary raw material, (ii) which are selected with an eye to their expressive potentialities and more or less systematically organized prior to, or coincidental with, artistic creation, and (iii) which thus constitute a "language" available to the artist for the artistic expression of his interpretation of his chosen subject-matter. (iv) This language must enjoy some degree of conventional acceptance if it is to serve as a vehicle of communication; (v) it determines in important ways the distinctive character of the works of art created in it; (vi) but, in itself, it neither possesses nor guarantees artistic merit.

The secondary artistic medium of any art consists of (i) those aspects of the generic subject-matter which permit of interpretative treatment in a specified primary medium, and which therefore possess potential artistic significance. (ii) These potentialities are recognized by the artist before or during the act of artistic creation, and (iii) are exploited by him through formal organization of his primary medium. (iv) This secondary artistic medium must permit of public exploration if its interpretation is to be intelligible to others; (v) it conditions the truth and significance of artistic content in essential ways; (vi) but, in itself, it possesses no actual artistic merit and must be sharply distinguished from expressed artistic content.

These definitions, which anticipate certain distinctions pertaining primarily to artistic form and artistic content, will be clarified by the analysis of form and content in the following chapters.

PART II

ARTISTIC FORM

CHAPTER VII

THE NATURE AND ANALYSIS OF ARTISTIC FORM

IN my preliminary account[1] of the chief categories of artistic analysis I defined the artistic form of a work of art as the artistically expressive organization of its matter or, more accurately, of the medium in which it has its being. I pointed out that all phenomenal objects necessarily have some form or other, and that the *artistic* form of a work of art must therefore have certain special characteristics which serve to distinguish it from non-artistic forms. I also called attention to the fact that all form, whether possessing or lacking artistic quality, is in each particular instance unique, but that when various works of art are compared they are found to resemble each other in various significant ways.[2] And, finally, I suggested that although the artistic form of a work of art is the *peculiar* locus of its artistic quality, this form is not merely an end in itself but also, and essentially, a means, in fact the only means, whereby the artist can express himself and communicate his ideas to others. Part II will be devoted to a fuller exploration of these and other aspects of form in art.

The distinctive form of a work of art is indeed an end in itself in the sense of being intrinsically satisfying. This is, no doubt, what the exponents[3] of the doctrine of "significant form" have primarily in mind when they insist that in painting, for example, the pattern of colors, lines, and shapes, considered *in itself* and without any reference to representational subject-matter, possesses an artistic quality whose value is intrinsic. There is truth in their contention, for not only the creative artist himself but the sensitive artistic and literary critic and the enlightened lover of the fine arts and literature delight in sheer aesthetic form or beauty for its own sake. Note with what deep interest and satisfaction we can explore the polyphonic inter-

[1] Cf., above, Chap. I.

[2] I shall refer to the unique form of a work of art as its "specific" form, and to the patterns which works of art may share as "generic" forms.

[3] Cf. Clive Bell and, less narrowly, Roger Fry; also D. W. Prall's discussion of "surface texture" in his *Aesthetic Judgment* (New York: Thomas Y. Crowell, 1929) and *Aesthetic Analysis* (New York: Thomas Y. Crowell, 1936).

play of "voices" in music, the rhythmic figures of a dance, the thrust and counter-thrust of architectural solids (Fig. 29), the harmonious balance of an abstract sculptural shape (Figs. 94, 96, 99), the essential rightness of a line or a color in a pictorial abstraction (Figs. 97, 98, 100), or the inner vitality and contextual appropriateness of a poetic metaphor.

This satisfaction is partly a delight in mere technical skill. The more we know about the technique of any human activity, the better do we understand the problems, perennial yet ever new, which the creative artist has set himself to solve, and the better can we appreciate and appraise his technical achievement. In art, as in all fields of human endeavor, we cannot help admiring the mastery of a medium (where mastery means unforced control and the exploitation rather than the denial of the potentialities of the medium), the apt solution of a problem (where the solution exemplifies both economy of means and complete attainment of the end in view), and that creative originality which strikes a happy mean between sheer arbitrary novelty and sheer mechanical obedience to convention or rule. Every type of human activity, whether mathematical or scientific, political or industrial, artistically expressive or aesthetically formalistic, has its own craft and its own technique, and in each, pride of craftsmanship is a sign of creative integrity and a promise of technical proficiency.

Aesthetic form, however, is not the product of mere technical craftsmanship, for it exhibits a distinctive aesthetic quality. The aesthetic quality of achievement in fields of human endeavor differs also from one activity to another. The conditions of aesthetic "rightness" can therefore never be defined adequately in the abstract, but only with explicit reference to the type of activity concerned, and, ultimately, in terms of a particular task and its specific context. And only the expert can competently detect and evaluate degrees of aesthetic excellence in any particular realm. Only the trained mathematician, for example, can sense the presence or absence of mathematical "elegance."

The ascription of aesthetic quality to mathematical and other types of excellence is quite justifiable, since notable achievements in any medium may exhibit an aesthetic character. But this ascription must not be allowed to obscure the significant differences between artistic and mere aesthetic quality. *Artistic* quality, as exemplified in *bona fide* works of art, has its *own* essential nature which reveals itself only to the *artistically* sensitive eye and ear and can be appraised only with the aid of the *artistically* cultivated imagination. Only the artistically discerning, moreover, can sense the special problem which the artist has set himself in any particular composition (and all compositions are particular), and only they can appraise the degree of his success or failure in this specific composition. Both specific and general artistic forms, then, have their own unique characteristics, and it is our task to devise conceptual tools which will facilitate their exploration.

Artistic form differs from merely formal beauty in being not only a distinctive object of immediate and intrinsic aesthetic satisfaction but, in addition, the artist's vehicle for self-expression and significant communication. One-sided preoccupation with the purely aesthetic character of artistic form is no less myopic than is Plato's moralistic overemphasis on subject-matter in the earlier books of the *Republic*, or Tolstoy's similar emphasis in *What is Art?* The formalist and the moralist in art are both partly correct in what they assert or wish to assert, but both tend to be short-sighted to the point of perversity in what they ignore or repudiate. Genuine art is *both* aesthetically satisfying *and* profoundly revealing. Art exists "for life's sake" as well as "for art's sake." Its form is both a self-sufficient end of aesthetic response and also the means to the end of significant expression.

In his *Aesthetic*,[4] Croce is curiously indifferent to many essential features of the artistic medium and artistic form (though, as a critic, he often does justice to the very aspects of art whose unimportance he so vigorously proclaims in his theoretical writings); but by his eloquent insistence on the preeminent importance of expression in art he has put us all in his debt. A wholly inexpressive "work of art" is really a contradiction in terms. If it merely possesses a surface texture indicative of aesthetically sensitive craftsmanship, it may satisfy our interest in technical proficiency and give us a certain aesthetic delight, but it can "mean" nothing to us. We cannot even classify such work as minor art, because the distinguishing characteristic of the minor arts is not lack of expressed content—at their best they are rich in meaning.[5] All art worthy of the name is in some sense and to some degree expressive of something and possesses not only surface pattern but artistic content as well. Most formalists will

[4] Benedetto Croce, *Aesthetic*, tr. D. Ainslie (London: Macmillan, 1909).
[5] Cf., above, Chap. 1, §3.

probably admit this, since their real *bête noire* is artistically *misused* subject-matter rather than artistic content as such. The very phrase "significant form" suggests that the form which they value is not merely aesthetically satisfying in itself but "signifies" or expresses something beyond itself.

I shall devote Part III to an analysis of artistic content. The expressiveness of artistic form has been insisted upon here only because we must continually remind ourselves that the aspects of art which we are considering *seriatim* have no artistic being in isolation from one another. The ultimate fact in all aesthetic theory is the completed work of art in all its concreteness and organic unity. To analyze it we must tear it apart and so do violence to its living structure, and such procedure is methodologically defensible since no alternative presents itself. But to hypostatize the factors thus isolated, or to consider the work of art as a mere aggregate of ingredients and thus suggest that any ingredient, such as form or content, may be either present or absent without essential artistic gain or loss, is to commit the unpardonable sin in the study of art.

Form in art can be analyzed in two ways. Attention can be directed to the inner formal structure of a work of art, considered generically, and the attempt can be made to discover the chief categories in terms of which this inner structure can most conveniently and accurately be analyzed. Chapter VIII will be devoted to an analysis of these "structural ingredients." But works of art can also profitably be compared with one another in the effort to discover the more important ways in which compositions in the same medium and in different media resemble and differ from one another in formal organization. Chapters IX to XI will be concerned with an analysis of these intra-medial and inter-medial aspects of artistic form.

This does not mean, of course, that it is possible completely to explore the inner structure of a work of art without comparing it with other works in the same or in different media, or, alternatively, to compare different works of art without analyzing the inner structure of each. These two approaches are strictly complementary; comparison reveals individual characteristics which were previously unnoticed, while intensive study of individual structure suggests new comparisons the institution of which may throw light on the formal potentialities and limitations of the several artistic media.

CHAPTER VIII

THE STRUCTURAL INGREDIENTS OF A WORK OF ART

EVERY work of art is a complex organism of artistic parts or units artistically related to one another. These units and relations have a non-aesthetic basis which can be apprehended without aesthetic sensitivity and which can be described in non-aesthetic terms. Thus a musical phrase can be analyzed into successive sounds of differing pitch, and sounds, in turn, can be analyzed scientifically into air vibrations. A color "harmony" or "discord" can be "reduced" to non-aesthetic color contrasts which can then be expressed scientifically in terms of light waves. A poetic image or metaphor can be analyzed into its non-poetic ingredients, and the words which are used to create it can be examined in various non-aesthetic ways. We cannot, however, reverse this process, that is, start with non-artistic distinctions and argue from these to artistic units in artistic relation. Our approach, even in systematic and critical analysis, must be an artistic approach from the outset, for the boundaries of an artistic unit and the precise artistic relation of one unit to another can be made only by the artistically sensitive eye or ear and the artistically trained intellect operating in conjunction.

1. "Ideas" and "elements"

The two main types of artistic units may be entitled artistic "ideas" and artistic "elements." An artistic idea may be defined as a relatively self-contained, more or less complex, artistic unit which, while standing in definite artistic relation to the work of art as a whole, has artistic quality and an artistic individuality of its own. An artistic element, in contrast, may be defined as an artistic unit which, *taken by itself*, has *no* artistic quality or individuality of its own, is in no sense artistically self-contained, and derives its artistic significance *entirely* from the artistic context in which it appears, but which, none the less, directly or indirectly, makes a definite artistic contribution to the work of which it is a part.

The term "idea" is in many respects unfortunate because it lends itself to serious misinterpretation. It is *not* intended to connote an idea in the mind, that is, a moment or state of consciousness private to a single individual (e.g., my present idea of anything). Nor does it signify an idea in the more abstract logical sense of a concept which can be expressed in a conceptual medium and communicated through this medium by one individual to another (e.g., the concept of God, or of tree, or of sorrow).[1] Nor, finally, does it refer to an Idea in the Platonic sense, that is, an hypostatized "universal" which again can be adequately comprehended only conceptually. An artistic "idea" is as concrete and as objective to sense and imagination as is the work of art of which it is a part, and it is apprehensible only through imaginative artistic re-creation. Students of architecture, sculpture, and painting often refer to artistic ideas in their respective arts as "motifs." I have refrained from using this term instead of the term "idea" only because "motif" has so specialized and limited a meaning in music and so general and indeterminate a meaning in some of the other arts. I have chosen "idea" partly for lack of a better term, partly because it is not infrequently used by artistic and literary critics in exactly the way in which I have here defined it.

The term "element" also has certain irrelevant connotations (e.g., chemical and physical). These connotations can be excluded by using the qualifying adjective "artistic" in contexts where the meaning might otherwise be ambiguous.

Artistic ideas differ in inner complexity, in inner artistic coherence, and in the relations in which they stand to other artistic ideas and to the work of art as a whole. They also tend, as artistic units, to conform to one of two clearly distinguishable types which may, for convenience, be entitled "unitary" and "repetitive."

A "unitary" artistic idea may be defined as an idea which has its artistic being in one and only one sensuous pattern. A "repetitive" artistic idea, in contrast, is an idea which exists or has its artistic being in two or more distinguishable sensuous patterns. A repetitive idea may be either "reiterative" or "developmental." It is reiterative if the relevant sensuous pattern is repeated without

[1] In literature an artistic idea may be predominantly conceptual. Hegel was right in his insistence that literature tends to pass over into other realms, e.g., religion and philosophy. This does not, however, make it the "highest" of the arts, or any the less artistic.

variation, developmental if it is repeated with variations designed to express with progressively greater adequacy the full artistic import of the idea in question. The general nature of an artistic idea, and the distinctions between different kinds of ideas can be illustrated in terms of the several major arts.

2. "*Unitary*" *and* "*repetitive*" *ideas in the major arts*

(a) *Music.* The simplest and most fundamental artistic "idea" in music is a musical "figure," i.e., a pattern of tones (whether melodic, polyphonic, harmonic, or a combination of these) which has its artistic being as a *relatively* self-contained tonal organization. A figure has been defined by Sir Hubert Parry[2] as "any short succession of notes, either as melody or a group of chords, which produces a single, complete and distinct impression. . . . It is in fact the shortest complete idea [*sic*] in music, and in subdividing musical works into their constituent portions, as separate movements, sections, periods, phrases, the units are the figures, and any subdivision below them will leave only expressionless single notes, as unmeaning as the separate letters of a word." So defined, a musical figure perfectly exemplifies, in the medium of music, the type of artistic unit which I propose to call an artistic idea.

It is difficult, however, to illustrate in Western[3] music the distinction between "unitary" and "repetitive" ideas because most of its ideas are repetitive rather than unitary. Western music is in very essence repetitive, that is, the primary task of musical composition is to *use* every figure which is introduced by repeating it with suitable variations and transformations in other portions of the work. In a well-constructed fugue, for example, *every* figure, however slight, is woven into the composition in such a way as to appear again and again, in part or in whole, with or without variations. A fugue is therefore by definition wholly devoid of unitary ideas. Not all musical compositions are constructed as tightly as a successful fugue,

[2] *Grove's Dictionary of Music and Musicians* (London: The Macmillan Company, 1935) in the article on "Figure." Sir Hubert uses the term "idea" exactly as I am using it.

[3] The musical processes dealt with here and in subsequent references are those found chiefly in instrumental music of the Western world. Primitive and certain oriental peoples think musically in substantially the same way. But there is music, especially Hindu, Persian, and Gregorian, in which repetitive patterns are the exception rather than the rule. These types, however, for all their free "melismas," do tend to repeat certain tones or to move within certain intervals which have the effect of unifying the diverse ideas.

and in music of certain types, in program music, for example, it is possible to find rare instances of figures which might be described as unitary ideas. The descending octaves representing final judgment on Til Eulenspiegel, in Richard Strauss' tone poem, is a unitary idea, not used a second time. This figure is not part of the thematic material of the work and is not woven into its essential texture, but is introduced rather for contrast and for dramatic or "pictorial" effect. The more faulty a musical composition, meanwhile, the more likely is it to contain figures which the composer has failed to employ effectively. Nothing distinguishes the competent from the incompetent composer more clearly than the ability of the former (as contrasted with the inability of the latter) to use the material contained in his figures in other portions of the composition.

Repetitive ideas, then, abound in music; almost any musical figure exemplifies this type of artistic unit. Musical figures differ greatly in length, complexity, and musical interest or fecundity. To serve successfully as a musical "subject" a figure must be "a phrase of melody, with or without harmony, of sufficient distinction to be regarded as a musical thought. . . . Each form [e.g., sonata, symphony, or suite] has had its own kinds of subjects suitable to its special method of development."[4] A composer like Beethoven, an acknowledged master in the handling of musical subjects, was able to make the richest use of figures of only a few notes. Compare, for example, the opening of the *C Minor* Symphony:

or of the *Ninth:*

or the initial measures of the piano sonatas, *Opus 31, No. 2* and *No. 3.* Bach's figures are normally somewhat longer than these of Bee-

[4] H. C. Colles in the article on "Subject," in *Grove's Dictionary of Music and Musicians.*

thoven. In the first book of the *Well-Tempered Clavichord* one of the most famous figures in all music forms the basis of the first *Prelude*:

It is repeated twice, at different tonal levels, in every measure save the last two, and reappears even in these last measures in an altered form. The genius of these composers shows itself in their ability not only to invent figures which lend themselves to musical treatment but to realize the musical potentialities of a figure and to exploit (i.e., make the fullest use of) these potentialities with imaginative power.

A repetitive idea, I have said, is one which has its artistic being in two or more sensuous patterns. A musical subject is a perfect case in point. *As a subject* it exists only in the sum of its various manifestations or forms. We may, in critical analysis, refer to the first statement of a subject, i.e., to the initial figure, as the subject; but were the figure in question not subjected to treatment in what follows it would not be a musical subject at all. A musical figure *is* musically what it *does*; it *becomes* a subject only when put to use, and it exists as a subject only in its several appearances taken in conjunction with, and in relation to, the composition as a whole.

It is also clear that a "repetitive" figure in music may be either "reiterative," i.e., literally repetitive without variation, or else "developmental," i.e., repetitive with significant variation. A figure may be, and often is, repeated without any variation whatsoever. More frequently, however, it is repeated at different tonal levels and with many kinds of variation. A somewhat longer figure may, for example, be broken up into subordinate figures which are treated severally, or two figures which are introduced as distinct musical units may be combined and developed in conjunction. There is no end to the variety of treatment to which musical figures can be subjected, and the generic term "repetitive" is intended to cover all types of repetition, however literal and however varied.[5]

[5] For further illustration of "repetitive" ideas in music the reader may be referred to the fugues of J. S. Bach's *Well-Tempered Clavichord*, the dances of his *D Major Suite* (*No. 3*), and the *Crucifixus* from the *B Minor Mass*. The literature of music as a whole abounds in illustrations. Only declamations, songs, rhapsodic improvisations and certain forms of chant or Gregorian song are constituted otherwise.

Some of the other arts, and notably the plastic arts, contain, as we shall presently discover, many examples of unitary ideas. The fact that such ideas can occur in well-knit compositions in these arts, but are hardly to be found in music, points emphatically to an important characteristic of music which distinguishes it sharply from the other arts. Music is in essence more repetitive than any of the other arts. The reason for this is not far to seek. Unlike the plastic arts, music is a temporal art. The unity of a musical composition can be apprehended, therefore, only with the aid of memory. In looking at a statue or a picture we have the whole composition before our eyes from first to last, and the exterior or interior of a building can be surveyed more or less at a glance. We can therefore apprehend with comparative ease the organic relation in which ideas stand to one another and to the composition as a whole. In music, on the other hand, we would be lost without repetition. A musical idea must be introduced again and again to make its impress upon our memory and to establish its contribution to the composition as a whole. This is also true of the dance and literature which, like music, are temporal arts. But the necessity for repetition is greater in music than in the dance because it is so "disembodied," whereas the medium of the dance is the human body, itself a visible unit, indulging in expressive movements whose artistic relations to one another are more easily apprehended without the aid of repetition. The purer, i.e., the less pantomimic, the dance becomes, however, the more will it manifest a tendency to repetition with variations analogous to musical repetition. Even literature is given to repetition with variation, but the symbolic character of language, and the resultant use of concepts and images in this art, makes possible a much richer use of unitary ideas than is possible in music.[6]

(b) *The dance*. In the dance any pattern of movement or rest which possesses some measure of inner artistic structure, which has a "beginning, a middle, and an end," and which, though not repeated, is in itself artistically expressive, is a unitary artistic idea. A reitera-

[6] The fact that good music proves to be singularly devoid of unitary ideas illustrates the analytical value of the artistic categories. These categories, I must repeat, are primarily designed to suggest questions which may profitably be asked regarding *any* work of art in *any* medium. The answers to these questions need not be affirmative to be of value; a negative answer is just as revealing as an affirmative one. Thus the fact, elicited by our question regarding unitary ideas, that music does not in general possess such ideas, is just as important for artistic analysis as the fact that architecture, for example, abounds in such ideas.

tive or developmental rhythmic pattern, on the other hand, is a repetitive idea if this repetition emphasizes or enriches the total artistic expressiveness of the idea so that the new whole is artistically more than any one of its unitary constituents. In the non-mimetic dance, for example, "action modes" such as "folding and unfolding," "rising and falling," "swinging and swaying," exemplify (if artistically handled) genuine repetitive ideas or motifs. An effective rendition of Mary Wigman's *The Seven Dances of Life*[7] would provide more complicated examples of repetitive ideas in the dance of the mimetic type.

(c) *Architecture*. The distinction between unitary and repetitive ideas can easily be illustrated in the plastic arts. In architecture a single column, an architecturally expressive doorway or window, or even a complete façade whose architectural pattern is not repeated elsewhere on the building, is a unitary idea if, from the point of view of architectural quality, it is *relatively* self-contained. The main entrance of the *Palazzo del Grillo* in Rome (Fig. 37) is an elaborate, highly ornamented unitary idea, the entrance to the *Palazzo Giraud-Torlonia* in Rome (Fig. 36), a much simpler unitary idea. The dome of *St. Peter's* (Fig. 64) is a unitary idea of unusual complexity and importance. A colonnade, a tier of identical windows, twin spires or towers, or the front and rear pediments of a Greek temple, are reiterative ideas (Figs. 62, 36, 40, 51); contrasting spires (Fig. 38) are a repetitive idea with variation, while an architectural pattern of openings which exemplify a development from the more simple to the more complex, e.g., from plain windows to more ornate windows (Fig. 32), may be entitled a developmental architectural idea or motif.

Architecture also provides clear illustrations of the way in which unitary and repetitive ideas may organically include one another. In the portico of the *Pantheon* in Rome (Fig. 60), for example, each of the eight Corinthian columns is, *taken by itself*, a relatively simple unitary idea. The *whole* colonnade, including the bays between each column, constitutes a repetitive idea. This colonnade, in turn, is part of an unusually self-contained architectural unit—the portico as a whole—which stands in sharp stylistic contrast to the circular building to which it is attached. This portico is, therefore, a complex unitary idea.

[7] Cf. Mary Wigman, *Die Sieben Tänze des Lebens* (Jena: Eugen Diederichs, 1921).

To describe complicated and artistically important architectural units such as the dome of *St. Peter's* or the portico of the *Pantheon* in Rome as unitary ideas suggests that even music might be said to have unitary ideas in this larger sense. A movement of a symphony may be even more self-contained than an architectural dome, for its distinguishing patterns need not be repeated in any other movements. It is therefore more of a unitary idea than a dome or a portico in architecture. The question arises, however, as to whether the artistic function of such a movement is really analogous to the artistic function of the dome or the portico of a building. This is a problem which I cannot pause to discuss. I would merely note that analogical arguments from one art to another, or even from one composition to another in the same medium, are exceedingly dangerous. The absolute artistic requirement for some larger all-embracing unity in the composition as a whole is indubitable. *Every* work of art, as a single "work of art," *must* possess an essential unity of some type, or be open to the charge of grave artistic defect. But this unity can be achieved through the use of many different types of generic interrelation and an infinite variety of specific artistic devices.

(d) *Sculpture*. Whereas architecture is peculiarly rich in repetitive ideas (both reiterative and developmental), sculpture makes greater use of unitary ideas. The head and the torso of a single figure are necessarily unitary ideas. Proof that these are artistic units is the fact that the surviving torso or head of a mutilated statue often possesses unquestionable artistic quality (Figs. 115, 201). Heads and torsos may also, of course, be created as wholly self-contained works of art (Figs. 202, 256). As such, however, they are no longer mere "ideas." The arms and legs of a single figure may, in their modelling but more particularly in their arrangement, suggest a rhythmic, more or less repetitive, pattern (Fig. 117), but more frequently they are directly related to the torso and to the composition as a whole and are not repetitively related to one another (Fig. 135). In sculptural groups, both in the round and in relief, repetitive motifs are naturally more common (Figs. 115, 120, 207, 208).

(e) *Painting*. Poussin's *Et in Arcadia Ego* in the Duke of Devonshire's Collection (Fig. 136) provides a splendid illustration of unitary and repetitive ideas in painting. The three figures of the shepherdess and the two shepherds are, considered severally, unitary ideas. Taken as a group, they constitute a closely knit and powerfully rhythmic repetitive idea of the developmental type. The eye is quickly caught by the vertical figure of the shepherdess on the left and moves irresistibly from her to the shepherd nearest to her and then on to the second shepherd, whose main axis, intensified by gesture and gaze, is strongly inclined towards the sarcophagus on the extreme right. This repetitive idea or motif, whose basic "figure" (to use a musical analogy) might be said to be the second shepherd's crook, is repeated in reverse by the trees, which are quite vertical at the extreme right and incline more and more as the eye moves from right to left. (Their basic "figure" is the first shepherd's staff which is so clearly silhouetted behind his head.) These two repetitive motifs, then, combine almost in contrapuntal fashion to constitute an unusually clearly defined unit of marked developmental complexity.

The seated male figure in the foreground, meanwhile, is a perfect example of a unitary idea. It is itself a rhythmic and somewhat repetitive organization of more or less self-contained units (note the shoulder, arms, and foot). It also epitomizes, with remarkable economy of means, the complicated contrapuntal idea just mentioned. The right edge of the torso recalls the vertical tree trunk above the sarcophagus. The lighted axis of the torso, with the head, carries out the diagonal of the leaning tree trunk and the first shepherd's crook. The draped foreleg is parallel to the diagonal legs of the shepherds. Thus the natural structure of his body provides the resolution for the vertical and diagonal motifs otherwise only contrasted, and the figure as a whole, itself a very complex unitary idea, sums up the whole picture.

As examples of actually isolated artistic ideas in painting, compare such studies as Leonardo da Vinci's or Dürer's sketches (Figs. 246, 247).

(f) *Literature*. Here the problem is not so much to find illustrations of unitary and repetitive ideas, for they are legion, as to indicate in a few words the enormous variations in complexity and type of both kinds of ideas. The simplest examples of unitary ideas are single literary images possessing true literary quality, such as "the rosy-fingered dawn," "the wine-dark sea," the "ring-giver," or the "swan-bath." From these we can pass through an indefinite number of stages of complexity to the *Inferno*, *Purgatorio*, and *Paradiso* of Dante's epic, where each part is a relatively self-contained and more or less unified section of the entire work.[8] The best examples of a simple repetitive idea without variation are "identical refrains," such as Poe's "Quoth the raven Nevermore," or the refrain of Spenser's *Prothalamion.* Since the subject-matter enters so essentially into a literary composition it too provides admirable examples of "repetitive" themes, as in the analogy, emphasized throughout *King Lear,* between Lear and his cruel daughters, Gloucester and his cruel son. Indeed, the still more general theme of cruelty is a repetitive idea which, like a musical motif, runs through the entire play with innumerable "developmental" variations. Jealousy is an analogous idea in Othello, ambition in Macbeth.[9] Sometimes the dominant mood or theme, itself a repetitive idea, is expressed by means of repetitive language, as in Tennyson's *Mariana,* "I am aweary, aweary, I would that I were dead," or in Coleridge's "Water, water, everywhere."

3. Artistic elements

An artistic element has been defined as any portion of a composition which, of itself, does not possess artistic or expressive quality, and which therefore derives its artistic significance entirely from the compositional pattern to which it belongs and from the contribution which it itself makes to the work of art as a whole.

There are two main kinds of artistic elements, just as there are two main kinds of artistic ideas. An "ideational element," as the adjective is meant to indicate, is a component part of an artistic idea; detached from the idea to which it belongs it has no artistic quality. Examples of such elements are individual musical tones or groups of tones not sufficiently expressive to constitute figures; individual gestures or steps which, though perhaps indicative of

[8] Here an analogy between musical and literary organization at once suggests itself.

[9] Cf. Shakespeare's *Antony and Cleopatra,* where the death of Antony's followers, Enobarbus and Eros, is balanced against the death of Cleopatra's ladies, Iras and Charmian; also the Liebestod "motif" throughout, and minor ideas repeated with variations, as in

"Unarm, Eros; the long day's task is done,
And we must sleep." (Antony, after hearing Cleopatra
is dead, IV, xii, 35-6)
"Finish, good lady; the bright day is done,
And we are for the dark." (Iras to Cleopatra, after
Antony's death, V, ii, 192-3)

emotion, lack artistic expressiveness; part of a finger or a single fold of drapery in sculpture; a single line or colored area in painting; or, in literature, a single word or a phrase devoid of metaphorical suggestion. No whole can exist without its parts, and the more organized the whole, the more essential the contribution of each constituent. But just as the ultimate chemical and physical constituents of a living body are themselves mere physical substance devoid of life, so the smallest discernible elements of a work of art are themselves not artistic in any true sense of the term, though without them the artistic ideas to which they belong could not possess the character or artistic value which they do possess.

Not all the elements of every composition, however, are ideational elements. Many compositions contain at least some elements which may be labelled non-ideational because, while making a contribution to the work as a whole, they do so directly and not indirectly through participation in an artistic idea.

It would be possible to argue that the presence of such non-ideational elements in a composition indicates a lack of inner artistic cohesion and thus constitutes a compositional defect. Sir Hubert Parry, for instance, writes: "In music of an ideally high order, everything should be recognisable as having a meaning; or, in other words, every part of the music should be capable of being analysed into figures, so that even the most insignificant instrument in the orchestra should not be merely making sounds to fill up the mass of the harmony, but should be playing something which is worth playing in itself. . . . In proportion as music approaches to this ideal, it is of a high order as a work of art."[10] Most artists, but more particularly those who are usually identified with the Neo-classic tradition, have consciously striven to approximate to this ideal and at times have actually reached it. Poussin's *Et in Arcadia Ego* (Fig. 136) is, like most of his other paintings, an illustration of such an achievement. One hunts in vain among the leaves of the trees, in the clouds, or even in the foreground, for an area, line, or shape, however small, which is not part of an artistic idea. The larger artistic patterns include smaller patterns, and the whole

[10] In the article already mentioned. For illustration of Sir Hubert's contention, compare the texture of a Bach fugue or a Beethoven symphony (or indeed of many another work of the first order) with almost any sentimental or popular song. In the former every tone is functional in some figure or subject; in the latter, tones are thrown in to "fill up" harmonic or instrumental "space."

composition is interwoven in innumerable and complex ways. Neo-classic criticism has been distinguished for its insistence on the ideal of intra-compositional organization.[11]

But there are other criteria of artistic excellence to which artists and critics of a different persuasion have attached greater importance. In general, the more typical works of the Romantic tradition have emphasized originality, emotional expressiveness, contrast, verisimilitude, and other qualities more than organic structure, and many works of this tradition have been designedly looser in inner structural cohesion. Much contemporary art, though Romantic only in an elusive and subtle way, exhibits the same tendency to a marked degree. It is, for example, almost as hard to find artistic ideas in some of Kandinsky's abstractions (Fig. 98) as it is to find non-ideational elements in a Poussin landscape. These compositions are almost entirely devoid of ideational organization. They consist of lines, colors, and shapes which, taken by themselves, have no artistic quality (though they may be aesthetically pleasing), but which are made to contribute directly to the total artistic effect.

4. "Solitary" artistic ideas and elements

It remains to mention a somewhat rare type of artistic ideas and elements which can be used with great artistic effectiveness because of its distinctive character.

I have described artistic ideas as "relatively" self-contained units in a composition and as "more or less" closely related to the remaining portions of the work. Sometimes, in order to achieve a particular kind of artistic effect, an idea is set in unusually sharp contrast to the rest of the composition. One of Callot's pen and ink drawings (Fig. 155) clearly illustrates this procedure. The swaggering soldier in the foreground contrasts as sharply as does the heavily inked-in frame with the delicate handling of the city square. The cello solo of three measures which interrupts the mad frenzy of Ravel's *La Valse*; the rectangular portico of the Roman *Pantheon*, so different in line and shape from the main building (Fig. 60); an "anti-masque," the prologue of *Romeo and Juliet*, the grave-diggers' scene in *Hamlet*, and the porter's scene in *Macbeth*; the figure of the donor in the *Avignon Pietà* (Fig. 211) or the figure of Mary in the *Entombment* at Solesmes (Fig. 209)—these are all instances of artistic

[11] It goes without saying that the more ambitious the composition, the more difficult it is successfully to translate this ideal into actuality.

ideas which more or less successfully endow the composition as a whole with added vitality by creating a uniquely significant differentiation between a part and the larger whole.

These artistic units I propose to call "solitary" artistic ideas. But the term "solitary" must not be construed too literally. Were part of a composition *completely* solitary and artistically unrelated to the larger whole, it would of course destroy the artistic integrity of the work, whether this unit itself possessed artistic quality as an independent minor composition or not. The "solitariness" here in question can be described with precision only in terms of the requirements which a solitary artistic idea must satisfy if it is to perform its artistic function successfully. (i) The distinctive character of the solitary idea must be negatively determined by the rest of the composition, since it must differ from it in some marked way. (ii) This difference must be such as to emphasize the distinctive characteristics of the main body of the work, by "keying it up" and endowing it with increased vitality and individuality. (iii) To accomplish this end, the solitary idea must not seriously rival the main composition in interest or artistic importance. It must act rather as a foil or (to change the simile) as an artistic measure by reference to which the beholder is helped to appreciate more fully the essential features of the larger work. (iv) The solitary idea, to have artistic significance, must therefore be an essential part of the larger composition; like other artistic units, it *is* what it *does*. Its distinctive character consists in the fact that it relates itself to the composition as a whole primarily by way of *significant contrast*. Its pronounced difference from the rest of the composition is an artistically *functional* difference.

A "solitary" artistic element is necessarily non-ideational, and differs from other non-ideational elements in the same way in which solitary artistic ideas differ from other artistic ideas. Chirico's *Delights of the Poet* (Fig. 140) contains several examples of such solitary elements. The prevailing palette of the picture is cool and subdued, with dominant blues, lemon yellows, greens, and blacks. But on two flagpoles on the building facing the spectator there appear two small bright red flags. These spots of color intensify the color scheme of the whole composition to a remarkable extent; with them the composition takes on added life and power—without them, the picture loses noticeably in vitality and interest. The round clock and the solitary figure in white are also solitary elements. Examples of solitary artistic elements in other artistic media are the chords played on the celeste in the *Rosenkavalier*, which are not harmonically related to the theme, or the ascending notes immediately preceding the final chord in the *Sacre du Printemps*;[12] a violent gesture contrasting sharply with an otherwise smoothly flowing dance rhythm; a realistically executed necklace on a nude sculptural figure (Fig. 139); unadorned round windows or clocks on a building otherwise innocent of curves (Fig. 79); and exclamations such as "Fie!", "Alack!", "God, God!", or rhetorical questions such as Hamlet's "Heaven and Earth, must I remember!"

The more strictly a composition conforms to the Neo-classic canons of structural organization, the less likely is it to contain solitary artistic elements. On the other hand, only compositions with a clearly recognizable plan of organization can be said to contain "solitary" elements or ideas, since the latter possess their distinctive character only by virtue of contrast to what is ordered and organized. Hence the more chaotic a composition and the more carelessly its component parts are thrown together, the less artistic significance or distinction can any one of its units, whether elemental or ideational, possess.

5. *Artistic relations*

The artistic unity of a work of art can never be merely the oneness of an aggregate of units. The units must be related in an artistically functional manner. Hence the relations which unite the ideas and elements to one another are artistically quite as important as are the units themselves.

These relations may be classified by reference to the types of units which they relate. They may be "inter-ideational," i.e., between two distinct ideas in the composition, as, for example, between the river god and the group of shepherds in Poussin's *Et in Arcadia Ego* (Fig. 136); or "intra-ideational," i.e., between elements within an idea (*vide* the relation of the individual leaves to one another in the same picture); or both simultaneously, i.e., when two related ideas are organic members of an idea of a higher order (*vide* the relations

[12] The horn call in the Beethoven *Leonora Overture* (*No. 3*) is a solitary idea, highly dramatic in its effect; the cry of the crowd, "Barabbas!", in the *St. Matthew Passion* of Bach is an equally dramatic solitary element. Strauss' *Don Juan* introduces almost at the end a single tone which suggests the fatal sword-thrust; this tone is a solitary artistic element so far as the thematic structure of the work is concerned, although it is the most striking moment in the passage in which it occurs.

between the shepherds (i) as separate ideas, and (ii) as members of an artistically unified group). They may also be purely "inter-elemental," as in some modernistic pictorial abstractions (Fig. 98). And, finally, they may be "unit-compositional" relationships of contrast, namely, when solitary artistic ideas or elements are successfully related by dynamic contrast to the composition as a whole (Figs. 140, 209).

Conscientious analysis of any work of art involves explicit recognition of as many of these relationships as possible. It would be easy to enumerate an indefinite number of artistic relations of one type or another actually present in any specific work of art. But the richer and subtler the composition, the more difficult and, ultimately, the more impossible it becomes to exhaust its relationships. For one of the characteristics of great art is just its inexhaustibleness; we can return to it again and again and always discover new relationships which we had previously not noticed. Moreover, although it is possible to call attention to these artistic relationships when we are in the actual presence of the work of art in any medium, they defy adequate conceptual description. They have to be seen or heard, and apprehended by the artistic imagination, really to be known for what they are.

This chapter has been devoted to the discrimination and definition of certain basic artistic categories which are requisite to the analysis of individual works of art in any artistic medium, and to an indication of their applicability to specific compositions in the several media. They are, I believe, necessarily invoked in all critical analysis and appraisal—often unconsciously and therefore only implicitly, but sometimes consciously and explicitly. Critics in the several arts are continually analyzing specific compositions into what I have here called unitary and repetitive ideas, ideational and non-ideational elements, and the artistic relations between them. All that I have done is to suggest a terminology and a set of definitions which are, I believe, equally applicable to all the arts. Such common terms should facilitate comparisons of one art with another and aid precise analysis of artistic tendencies and traditions as well as of individual works of art.

But these categories, I must repeat, cannot be applied to specific works of art without artistic discernment. The structural characteristics of a work of art to which they direct our attention reveal themselves neither in purely sensory response nor in purely conceptual abstraction. They have a sensuous locus, but transcend the merely perceptual and imagistic by virtue of their artistic character; and though they are, in a sense, conceptually analyzable and permit of prosaic description, their true nature reveals itself only to the artistically sensitive eye and ear and to the artistically disciplined intellect and imagination.

Finally, the artistic interdependence of these units and relations cannot be overemphasized. No work of art is merely the sum of its units and relations, and no unit or relation, when isolated, remains what it was in its specific artistic context. The more artistically unified the composition, the more profound the artistic repercussions throughout its entire extent when any of its parts suffers the slightest alteration. In short, a work of art is an organic whole comprising that unity of the ideas and elements *and* the relationships between them which gives significant meaning to them all.

CHAPTER IX

BASIC "MANNERS OF TREATMENT" IN THE SIX MAJOR ARTS

THUS far we have been considering ways of analyzing the structural ingredients of any individual work of art in any medium. When works of art are compared with one another, new aspects of formal organization reveal themselves. Some of these aspects are "inter-medial," that is, they do not reflect the special characteristics of any one medium but cut across these boundaries and vary from work to work quite irrespective of what medium has been employed. These inter-medial variables will be dealt with in Chapter XI. This and the following chapter will be devoted to "intra-medial" generic forms, that is, to types of formal organization which are in large measure determined by the media and which, despite analogical similarities dictated by similarities of the underlying media, tend to differ from medium to medium.

Intra-medial generic forms are discoverable *only* by comparing works of art in the same medium. It is always possible to discover structural ingredients by examining a single work of art, but however much a given composition may actually resemble or differ from other compositions, these generic similarities and differences cannot be apprehended except by a process of selective and interpretative comparison. This applies to the generic structure of man and animals, plants and rocks, psychological processes, and cultural traits. It applies also to works of art.

There are two basic types of intra-medial formal organization. (i) Every artistic medium can be subjected to a variety of "manners of treatment." A manner of treatment may be defined as a generic way of handling the primary medium, this manipulation, in turn, frequently (though not always) involving a distinctive approach to the generic subject-matter or secondary medium of the art in question. Some of these manners of treatment are mutually exclusive; others permit of combination or fusion, either in different or in identical portions of the same composition.[1] (ii) Every work of art,

[1] The reader is referred to the Chart at the end of the volume for a schematic indication of the basic manners of treatment in the six major arts and their intra-medial relation to one another.

in any artistic medium, must also have a "compositional pattern" which approximates more or less closely to one or more generic types of compositional arrangement. A compositional pattern may be defined as the formal organization of the primary (and frequently, though not always, the secondary) medium which constitutes the formal structure of the work of art and determines the type and degree of formal unity of the work of art as a whole.

These two basic types of formal organization are clearly distinguishable, but they are related to one another in various ways. (i) Every work of art must participate in *both* types of organization. (ii) The same manner (or manners) of treatment may be employed in works of art of very different compositional patterns, and different manners of treatment may be used in the same work of art or in two or more works of art of very similar compositional pattern. (iii) Yet certain manners of treatment seem to be peculiarly appropriate to certain generic types of compositional pattern.

Critics of art and literature often refer both to "manners of treatment" and to "compositional patterns" as "styles." This usage is inaccurate, for style is, as we shall see,[2] a function of the work of art *as a whole*, that is, of its medium, form *and* content, fused into a complex artistic organism. Yet it is easy to see why critics have used the term "style" to refer to intra-medial generic forms. For the style of a work of art reveals itself most clearly in its intra-medial generic forms, and it is therefore just these forms with which the student of style is normally most concerned. The more accurate terminology here suggested involves no repudiation of what these critics have in mind; it should, rather, facilitate their critical comparisons and generalizations.

I am particularly anxious that my analysis of these types should do full justice to the empirical evidence with which the critics in the several arts are so intimately concerned, because the problems here to be considered are frontier problems whose effective solution requires active cooperation between empirically oriented critics and philosophers trained to systematic generalization. Intra-medial generic forms in art cannot be arrived at by *a priori* deductive inference; they can be discovered only by the method of artistic induction. This necessitates a wider acquaintance with actual works of art in the several media and in each of the major cultures and artistic traditions than most philosophers possess, as well as a type of

[2] Cf., below, Chap. XXI.

systematic comparison which the average critic is seldom qualified to undertake. It is with some trepidation, therefore, that I shall attempt to isolate and describe, as systematically as possible, the more basic generic forms in each of the six media. I must leave it to the critics to confirm or modify these categories in the light of their wider empirical orientation.

It should be added that an account of the basic manners of treatment in the six major media can, at least in principle, be made relatively exhaustive, whereas this is impossible in the case of typical compositional patterns in most of the arts. This is because each medium determines a field of possibility in the former case as it usually does not in the latter. A medium, being what it is, can be treated only in certain fundamental ways, whereas the number of possible compositional patterns into which most media may be organized is well-nigh infinite.

1. Music

The chief manners of treatment in music may be classified into three groups which can be schematically indicated as follows:

music without words	melodic	"absolute" or "pure"
	polyphonic	
music with words	harmonic	"programmatic"

(a) "Music without words" is instrumental music which is unaccompanied by a verbal text. "Music with words" requires no definition. Music with words is older than music without words, and though, strictly speaking, it is a mixed art, it occupies a place of such importance in every culture, including our own, that it must be recognized as a basic manner of treatment in this art. I have already pointed out that in music of this type the importance assigned to the text varies greatly. But despite these variations it remains true that, if the composition is to fall under the category of music, the music rather than the words must be the chief expressive vehicle. Even when the words are assigned the maximum importance consistent with artistic unity and expressiveness, they can do no more than suggest musical expression by their sounds and inflection, provide an ideational theme, and dictate the ever changing moods which the music seeks directly to express.

(b) Musical tones are treated "melodically" when they are organized into a single linear pattern; "polyphonically," when two or more melodic lines run along simultaneously in more or less intimate relation; and "harmonically," when the musical relations between tones heard simultaneously, as in a chord, or between successive chords, receive primary emphasis.

Pure melodic music, entirely free from harmonic implication, is exemplified in the Gregorian or Plain song of the Roman Church, in the majority of folk songs, in the surviving remnants of the music of classical (i.e., Greek and Roman) antiquity, and in many kinds of oriental and primitive songs. The *Seaman's Song* at the beginning of Wagner's *Tristan and Isolde*, and the *Shepherd's Melody* at the beginning of the third act of the same music drama, are specific instances of the melodic manner of treatment.

Polyphonic[3] music is exemplified in the motets, madrigals, and masses of most sixteenth and early seventeenth century composers, although harmonic implications had already begun to appear. The famous *Missa Papae Marcelli* of Palestrina is an illustrious example of the best polyphonic "manner" of this period, though it does not ignore the euphony and feeling for terminal (or other) conclusiveness that result from harmonic considerations. Other examples of the polyphonic manner of treatment are Palestrina's *Sicut Cervus*, the *Penitential Psalms* of Orlando Lassus, and Thomas Weelkes' madrigal *As Vesta was from Patmos Hill Descending*.

The most common treatment of hymn tunes is strictly harmonic; here all the tones other than those of the melody function primarily as parts of chords supporting the melody. Compare, for example, the familiar setting by Sir Arthur Sullivan to "Onward Christian Soldiers," Croft's tune *St. Anne* sung to the words "Oh God, our Help in Ages Past," or Le Jeune's *Urbs Beata* for "Jerusalem the Golden." On a larger scale and with more intense concern for artistic expressiveness much—indeed the larger part—of the music of the late eighteenth and most of the nineteenth century employs tones, other than those of the predominant melody, to support this melody by harmonies. The opening of Wagner's *Overture* to *Tannhäuser* is a harmonized melody, as is the beginning of the *Prelude* to the *Meistersinger*. Beethoven harmonizes the familiar melody at the

[3] A distinction is made between the polyphonic and contrapuntal "styles" or manners of treatment. The first signifies mutually independent melodies heard simultaneously; the second, the accompanying of one melody by others, complete or fragmentary, which are subordinate to it and could, in fact, hardly have any great interest independently of it.

opening of the second movement of his *C Minor Symphony* (the *Fifth*). Most of the symphonies, quartets, and operas of this period, indeed, illustrate this manner of treatment; a major factor in these works is the emphasis on harmonic progressions and, in general, on harmonic relationships.

As these illustrations indicate, these manners of treatment are not mutually exclusive. They more often than not appear in combination. For example, the main theme of the last movement of Beethoven's *Ninth Symphony* is heard first as pure unharmonized melody, and this simple statement is followed by a passage in which the bassoon and double basses add counter melodies to the original subject in the polyphonic manner. Brahms uses the same method in his *Variations on a Theme by Haydn.* The harmonic manner of treatment is never employed at length quite independently; it is invariably used in conjunction with the melodic or polyphonic manners. In the purest polyphonic manner, in contrast, no one voice predominates. But in many polyphonic works of a high order one of the two or more melodies or melodic fragments which are heard simultaneously, and which are thus polyphonically related, is more evident and complete than the other or others. Handel's choral manner is characterized in part by such passages, as in the *Hallelujah Chorus* in the *Messiah.* Compare also the opening chorus *Come Ye Daughters* in J. S. Bach's *St. Matthew Passion,* and the development section or the extended coda of the first movement of Beethoven's *Third Symphony* (*Eroica*). Most melodies, in short, have a polyphonic or harmonic accompaniment; in polyphonic music one voice may be melodically predominant and the harmonic relationships between the chords created by the tones of the several voices may possess great musical significance; while music which is predominantly harmonic will invariably be also more or less melodic or polyphonic in character. But any given portion of a musical composition and many compositions as a whole, tend, as I have said, to be predominantly melodic, polyphonic, or harmonic in manner of treatment. This is true of music in many different historical styles, though some styles favor one manner of treatment rather than another (*vide* ancient Greek music, which was chiefly melodic; medieval music, which was primarily polyphonic; or nineteenth century symphonies, so characteristically harmonic despite their rich use of melodic line and counterpoint).

Musical theory is largely concerned with a detailed and systematic investigation of the innumerable ways in which these three basic manners of treatment can be exploited and combined. Fugue and canon, for example, are variants of polyphonic writing; counterpoint is the more inclusive art of polyphonic composition. Music, in short, has not only its own rules of key and modal relationships (analogous to the rules of syntax in a verbal language); it also has rules which serve to define different manners of treatment (analogous to the rules of various types of metrical composition in poetry).[4] Mastery of these rules ensures musical *correctness*, and a knowledge of them is as important for the composer who may wish to modify or break them in order to secure a particular expressive effect as it is for the more orthodox musical composer. This is, of course, equally true of composition in other media. In no medium, on the other hand, does mere knowledge of the rules of generic treatment suffice for the production of works of artistic distinction.

The musical historian, in turn, is concerned to trace the historical rise and development of musical forms as far back in time, and in as many cultures, as possible. The historically-minded critic (and all true critics must be historically oriented) is also interested in the specific ways in which various composers have employed one or other manner of treatment in specific compositions. It is only in the light of such systematic and historical investigations that we can venture to generalize regarding the fundamental manners of treatment in music.

(c) Finally, "absolute" (or "pure") music is instrumental music not directly associated with ideas outside itself, whereas "program" music is instrumental music that is thus associated. I have already cited a number of examples of program music[5] and discussed its musical significance. Most music, whether with or without words, is definitely non-programmatic.

It should be clear from the discussion and illustrations that the manners of treatment in the three groups here distinguished combine in various ways. All music is either with or without words (or partly with and partly without) and *also* either predominantly or purely melodic, polyphonic, or harmonic, and *also* either absolute or

[4] Rules can also be formulated to define more inclusive compositional patterns, such as the chant, rondo, sonata, etc. (compare the structure of the 14-line sonnet), but with these I am not at present concerned: cf., below, Chap. x, §1.

[5] Cf., above, pp. 47-8.

programmatic (or partly the one, partly the other). We shall discover similar interrelationships between the manners of treatment in the other arts.

2. *The Dance*

The chief manners of treatment of the dance are related in a somewhat complicated way.

silent	solo	"free"	non-mimetic
with sound	dual		
(usually music)	choral	conventional	mimetic

These distinctions are again dictated by the nature of the primary medium. The basic primary medium of the dance consists, we have seen, of potentially expressive movements and rests of the human body in three-dimensional space. The dance may be silent or it may be accompanied by sound; one, two, or more people can take part; it may be relatively free from, or obedient to, conventional rules; and it may avoid or make use of pantomime. All more specific dance forms are modifications or combinations of these basic types.

(a) Just as music may or may not be accompanied by words, so the dance may, at least in theory, be either accompanied or unaccompanied by music. Here, however, we must be on our guard. *Some* auditory indication of the rhythm would seem to be quite essential; in the absence of music, dancers almost invariably rely on the rhythmic beat of a percussion instrument or its equivalent. The completely silent dance is even more of a *tour de force* than is wholly non-representational sculpture and painting, and is almost as unnatural as would be the use of words for literary effect without any regard to their meaning.

Certain enthusiasts for the free dance feel that music, in contradistinction to a merely rhythmic beat, is not absolutely essential to the dance.[6] It is extremely unlikely, however, that the musically

[6] Hanya Holm, for example, has not only solo dances which are entirely unaccompanied, but has one group number that depends exclusively on a common dance pulse. Such unaccompanied group dancing is possible only when the group has worked together for a long time and when each member of the group has acquired an almost "primitive" awareness of what is going on around him at every instant.

Unaccompanied dancing would certainly lose its expressive quality and become monotonous if used for a full-length program. Wisely conceived and used, however, it can be extraordinarily effective. It is a safe generalization that music is made to contribute to the dance now as much as ever. Modern dancers are merely coming to a clearer realization of its proper function in the dance.

unaccompanied dance will ever develop into a completely self-contained and expressive art form. One measure of the potential self-sufficiency of any art is the degree to which its primary medium can be subjected to preliminary pre-artistic organization. Before pure music could become artistically self-contained its primary medium had to be developed enormously, and this development was made possible by the coopèrative labors of many individuals who, together, created and participated in a musical tradition which gradually received the sanction of convention. This tradition, in turn, was made possible chiefly by the invention and wide-spread acceptance of an accurate, flexible, and uniform system of notation. Without the device of the modern musical score, pure music, as we know it today, would never have been possible. It is a significant fact that, at least up to the present time, no comparable tradition or accepted system of notation exists in the dance.[7]

The effort to divorce the dance from music is therefore highly questionable. Most students of the dance not only recognize the rôle of music in the past but assume that it will continue to make an essential contribution in the future.[8] Whereas pure sound, duly organized, is capable of expressing man's inner emotive-conative experience without reliance on words, musically unaccompanied bodily movement can probably never be expressively self-sufficient and must continue to rely on musical motivation and accompaniment.

[7] In the ballet, a good many steps and figures have, it is true, been handed down from one generation of dancers to another, yet almost entirely by means of first-hand instruction, and none of the various dance scripts which choreographers have devised and used in their own work has received general acceptance. Some exponents of the free dance, like Rudolf von Laban, have devised dance scripts, and Elizabeth Selden has made a sincere effort to introduce some order into the chaotic terminology of the dance. Irma Otte-Betz has done a great deal to advance the study of dance notation in this country. But to record a dance according to her system, and to be able to read the score, once it is prepared, requires a very special course of study. No one can prophesy what reception such efforts may eventually receive. But it is certain that until the primary medium of the dance has been organized in a manner comparable to the organization of the musical medium, and until a dance script and an accurate terminology have been devised and widely accepted, we cannot expect the musically unaccompanied dance, or indeed the dance in any of its forms, to develop into as artistically expressive a vehicle as pure music.

[8] Cf. Elizabeth Selden, *op. cit.*, pp. 21*ff.*, 33*ff.* Cf., also, Cecil J. Sharp, *op. cit.*, p. 11: ". . . Isolated steps and postures are merely the raw material, the vocabulary of the dance, and have no significance unless, and until, they are combined into rhythmical phrases or sentences *and associated with their musical accompaniment.*" (My italics.)

(b) The "solo," "dual," and "choral" manners of treatment parallel more or less closely the melodic, polyphonic, and harmonic manners of treatment in music. The mobile pattern woven in space by a solo dancer is analogous to the flowing melodic line of music sung by a single voice or played on a single instrument; dual dancing is analogous to polyphonic music—it too is capable of contrapuntal organization, and the two dancers may even, in their movements, suggest fugal and canonic patterns; while the rhythmic movements of a group of dancers suggest musical harmony. Furthermore, just as a musical composition may be entirely melodic, polyphonic, or harmonic, so an entire dance may be performed by one, two, or several dancers. On the other hand, a dance may, like a musical composition, make use of any two or of all three of these manners of treatment. Thus a dance which is primarily dual or choral may have solo interludes; a solo dancer may from time to time be assisted by a partner or a chorus; etc. Here, as in music, the possible permutations are almost infinite.

(c) Whether solo, dual, or choral, and whether silent or musically accompanied, the dance may be either "free"[9] or "conventional." It is free in proportion as it acknowledges obedience to no specific rules regarding steps, figures, etc., as prescribed by convention. It is conventional to the extent to which its distinctive character is definable primarily in terms of such rules. In one sense the free dance can express what conventionally unorganized sound can never express, for it is based upon, and is really a development of, mankind's untutored movements which, in their spontaneity and variety, are so common to the race and so natural that they are universally intelligible. Gestures, facial expressions, running and leaping for joy, the sagging of shoulders in weariness or grief, etc., constitute man's most primitive language. Spontaneous sounds do, of course, tend to accompany such movements, and they too are directly indicative of emotive-conative states. But they do not seem to permit of unconventional artistic exploitation as do man's silent bodily movements. "Free" music (where "freedom" is defined as it is in the "free" dance) would seem to be as much of a *tour de force* as wholly silent dancing. The expressive potentialities of the free dance, in contrast, have in recent years been amply demonstrated by such dancers as

[9] Cf. John Martin, *The Modern Dance* (New York: Barnes, 1936) and *America Dancing* (New York: Dodge, 1936); Martha Hill, *Symposium on Modernism in the Arts: The Dance* (mimeographed, Bennington College, 1933).

Isadora Duncan, Mary Wigman, Hanya Holm, Martha Graham, Doris Humphrey, Ted Shawn, and Charles Weidman.

(d) Finally, the dance may be more or less "mimetic" or "non-mimetic," that is, it may rely to a greater or less extent on pantomime. The only forms of pantomime which the free dance can assimilate without losing its "freedom" are those familiar and immediately intelligible forms which we associate in our every-day experience with various types of emotive-conative attitudes. But the goal of the free dance is freedom not only from prescribed convention but also from pantomime in general; it aims at direct dramatic expressiveness. In the conventional mimetic dances, such as the traditional ballet or the primitive ritualistic dance, on the other hand, the pantomimic factor also tends to be conventionalized in the direction of more and more abstract symbolism, and this conventional symbolism must be learned by the observer before the mimetic meaning of the dance can be fully understood. The rôle of pantomime is more pronounced and artistically significant in the dance than is the factor of auditory verisimilitude in program music. Bodily movement can be made representational and can be used for purposes of narration far more effectively than can pure musical patterns.

Once again it must be left to the critic and the historian of dance forms to give an empirically adequate account, at once systematic and historically oriented, of the more specific ways in which the primary media of the dance can be formally exploited in these generic manners of treatment.

3. Architecture

The chief architectural manners of treatment are:

trabeated	cubistic	illuminated
arcuated	plastic	

Trabeation and arcuation are primarily types of *engineering* structure; they are ways of employing building materials to bridge and enclose space. They are not, in themselves, principles of architectural expression, but they condition all architectural form and permit of architecturally expressive exploitation.

The cubistic and plastic manners of treatment, in contrast, are essentially *architectural* in character and must be defined in terms of artistically distinguishable relations of architectural solids and voids to one another. They have a physical and geometrical basis but are not reducible to mere physical and geometrical relationships.

Architectural illumination is also an essentially architectural manner of treatment, since it is a function of architectural, i.e., expressive, *control* of light and shadow. All buildings are visible in daylight and admit light through various types of openings, but light can be put to architectural *use* with varying degrees of architectural effectiveness.

Each of the first four manners of treatment is, in its purest form, incompatible with the manner of treatment with which it is paired, but permits of various combinations with one or other member of the other pair and with architectural illumination. Before considering these relationships let us define and illustrate each of these manners of treatment in turn.

(a) The epitome of trabeation is a horizontal lintel supported at either end by vertical posts, as in the *Temple of the Sphinx* in Ghizeh (Fig. 47). This basic engineering principle can be employed in the construction of a building in two distinguishable ways.

(i) The vertical uprights can be expanded horizontally into supporting walls, and the lintel into a slab (ceiling and roof) the edges of which rest on these walls. A building constructed of walls of solid masonry supporting a flat roof would be a simple exemplification of this type of construction.[10]

(ii) Or, alternately, a skeletal framework of upright posts and horizontal beams supported at either end by these posts can first be constructed, and the intervals between these uprights and between these beams can then be filled in with any type of suitable building material. In this mode of construction the walls carry little, if any, load. Chinese buildings (Fig. 84) and modern skyscrapers (Figs. 85-87) are the clearest exemplifications of this type of construction, since both are essentially structures of wooden or steel uprights and horizontal beams or girders carrying the load.

In both types of trabeated construction the basic mechanical principles are compression and tension—compression on the supporting walls or uprights and on the upper surface of the horizontal

[10] Historically, man started with supporting walls and a supported roof, and only gradually came to conceive of the post-and-lintel motif as an epitome of trabeation. From this epitome developed the Greek Orders.

members which span empty space; tension, on the lower surface of these members.

Many different kinds of building materials can be employed in this manner. The supporting uprights can be wooden posts, stone monoliths, steel supports, piers of masonry, etc.; the supported horizontal members can be of any material whose strength is sufficient to span the interval between the supporting uprights; and when the walls do not carry the main load but merely enclose the interior space, they can be constructed of any material adapted to this function.

The epitome of arcuation is, as the term indicates, the arch, which is constructed of individual units, such as bricks or wedge-shaped blocks of stone, so arranged that the supported weight is transmitted from unit to unit (e.g., in stone construction, along the voussoirs) and passed on partly to the vertical supports, partly to the buttressing masonry which is frequently required in this mode of construction. Here the basic mechanical principle is compression.

Any building is in the arcuated manner of treatment in proportion as this principle of arcuation is invoked. The simplest exemplification would be the horizontal expansion of a rounded arch into a barrel vault and of the supporting uprights into supporting walls.[11] Cross-vaults, ribbed vaults, and the like are more complicated variants, as is the dome, which makes a distinctive and peculiar use of this principle of arcuation (Figs. 59, 41, 63). Any type of building material which can sustain the compression induced by the supported weights can be employed in the arcuated manner of construction.

These two manners of treatment, in their purest forms, are mutually exclusive;[12] a specific engineering unit must exemplify one or the other, but cannot exemplify both. But both manners of treatment can be employed in the same building. The rectangular Greek temple (Fig. 51) and the typical modern skyscraper (Fig. 85) exemplify pure trabeation; the *Salle de l'Aquilon* in Mont St. Michel (Fig. 59), pure arcuation; trabeation and arcuation are combined in the interior of the *Pantheon* in Rome (Fig. 60) and of *San Paolo fuori le mura* (Fig. 62).

[11] Here again this process may, historically considered, be reversed. My analysis is systematic, not historical, in orientation.

[12] The "flat arch" is, of course, an arch, though it looks like a post and lintel.

The discovery of new building materials and new methods of engineering construction has made possible an enormous extension of both of these manners of treatment. The basic principle of construction is identical in a wooden frame house and a modern skyscraper, a small brick tomb with a barrel vault and a Gothic cathedral. The second edifice is in each case merely a richer exploitation of the same manner of treatment. New achievements have been made possible by the discovery of such primary media as steel and reinforced concrete. The relation of a modern suspension bridge (Fig. 80) to a primitive bridge of vines or ropes illustrates this identity of engineering principle and extension of its application.

The use of the cantilever principle in modern architecture is a good illustration of the extension of trabeation made possible by new building materials. A cantilever is a horizontal (or diagonal) member resting on a single vertical support according to the lever principle, its stability depending upon the position of the fulcrum (i.e., of the supporting post or wall), the manner in which the supported member is anchored, and the strength of the material out of which it is constructed.[13] This principle is illustrated in an unsupported balcony projecting from a wall, or in a flat unsupported projecting roof. Heavy wooden beams may have the requisite strength for such use, but they are harder to manipulate than reinforced concrete. The discovery of this mode of construction, accordingly, makes possible, at least theoretically, an extended application of the cantilever principle: *vide* Gropius' project for the Chicago Tribune Building (Fig. 87) and many of the buildings of Frank Lloyd Wright (Fig. 89).

This modern use of cantilevers illustrates one important way in which engineering is conditioned by available building materials. But these materials control engineering more radically when a structure quite impossible in one medium becomes feasible in another. A modern suspension bridge or skyscraper could never be built entirely of stone or brick; steel and reinforced concrete are absolute prerequisites.

Reinforced concrete has, in addition, introduced a new principle of engineering construction which is so important that it deserves special notice. This is the principle of the "continuous structure."

[13] Thus the lintel in trabeation, which is supported at *both ends* by *two* vertical uprights, becomes a cantilever when it is supported at *one* point by a *single* upright functioning as a fulcrum.

Typical pre-modern trabeated and arcuated buildings, such as a wooden frame house or a brick vault, are composed of units which, however firmly attached to one another, remain separate and distinct members. A structure of reinforced concrete, in contrast, can be "all of a piece." After the poured concrete has set, the structure can become one continuous unit, not an assemblage of separate units. So important is this new method of construction that it may be regarded as, at least potentially, a new basic manner of treatment meriting some such designation as "continuous" or "monolithic." The engineering and architectural potentialities of reinforced concrete have only begun to be explored, but certain modern structures, like the new *Stadium* at Florence (Fig. 81) or the *Hangar* at Orly (Fig. 82) are so revolutionary from the strictly engineering point of view, and so unique in architectural expressiveness, as to suggest architectural possibilities of major importance.[14] If these possibilities are ever actualized there may emerge a distinctive manner of treatment radically different from both trabeation and arcuation. Meanwhile, reinforced concrete still is used primarily as a substitute for older building materials and in the trabeated and arcuated manners, or in a combination of them, though with increasingly notable extension.

Trabeation and arcuation, then, are the engineering principles either or both of which older architects have employed from engineering necessity, and modern architects partly from necessity and partly from convention. They can be used with greater or less engineering skill and with varying degrees of architectural competence. The more skillful the architect *qua* architect, the more successfully will he be able to exploit the potential architectural expressiveness of these engineering forms. The nature of the artistic content thus expressed, and the ways in which it achieves expression *via* architectural form, will be discussed in a later chapter.[15] Arcuation and trabeation, considered with respect to these expressive potentialities, are thus part of the "language" at the disposal of the architect. The engineer as such considers only their utility and invokes them solely with an eye to such factors as strength, durability, economy, and the like. The architect must take all of these factors into account. But

[14] Cf. the somewhat analogous potentialities of glass, which, like concrete, is poured and solidifies into a continuous unit. These too the modern architect has only begun to exploit.

[15] Cf., below, Chap. XIX, §2.

for him they are not paramount. What to the engineer are ends in themselves are, to the architect, merely means to the achievement of his artistic objective, i.e., the expression, *via* architectural form, of a distinctive architectural content.

(b) The cubistic and plastic manners of treatment, in contrast, are essentially architectural rather than engineering principles, and are therefore ultimately describable not in scientific but only in artistic terms, that is, in terms of the type of artistic impression which different kinds of structure make upon the artistically (i.e., architecturally) sensitive observer. Yet both manners of treatment have a physical basis which can, in each case, be defined with reference to strictly physical relationships.

Cubism and plasticity in architecture are both primarily functions of the relation of solids and voids to one another, that is, of architectural forms to enclosed and enclosing space. In the purest cubistic manner of treatment, the solids and the adjacent spaces exist, as it were, in sheer juxtaposition, without mutual interpenetration or interplay. The blank surface of a flat wall best epitomizes this manner of treatment, and the *Temple of the Sphinx* in Ghizeh (Fig. 47), the *Gate of Ishtar* in Babylon (Fig. 54), and the *Larkin Building* in Buffalo (Fig. 55) exemplify its more extended use. Here the flat surface (or surfaces) constitute a continuous and uncompromising boundary between the solid structure and the surrounding space. The corresponding epitome of the plastic manner of treatment is a broken concave[16] surface which, taken as a whole, gives way to the space which presses in upon it and, simultaneously, protrudes its edges into space, while this interplay of solid and void is repeated still more plastically in the indentations and projections of the surface itself. The moulded arches and ribbed vaults of a Baroque or Gothic church (Figs. 65, 41) clearly exemplify this manner of treatment, while the Rococo architecture of Southern Germany provides abundant examples of architecture whose pronounced plasticity of architectural form is further intensified (when it is not submerged) by very plastic sculptural and pictorial decoration (Figs. 30, 66, 67). In architecture of this type, solids and voids are in continual and dynamic interplay,[17] the solids flowing easily, as it were, in and out

[16] A convex surface would, of course, serve as well.

[17] Hence the term "plastic," which originated as a sculptural term primarily applicable to that type of sculpture which was produced by the modelling of clay or some other soft and malleable material. It is unfortunate that the same term should have to

of space, while the enclosing and enclosed spaces are aesthetically related to the enclosed and enclosing structure in innumerable ways.

The transition from the cubistic to the plastic manners of treatment is clearly illustrated in a series of six architectural uprights selected and ordered as follows: (i) A square pier of masonry (or an analogous monolith) with four flat sides and no capital or base, as in the *Temple of the Sphinx* (Fig. 47), illustrates the most uncompromising antithesis of solid and void, verticality and horizontality,[18] i.e., architectural cubism in its purest form. (ii) An eight-sided post with an abacus block, as in the *Tomb of Beni Hassan* (Fig. 49) marks the beginning of a sympathetic relationship of solid and void. Here the multiplication of sides facilitates the flow of space around the vertical solid, while the abacus block relates the supporting vertical member to the horizontal member by affording a diagonal transition. (iii) The flow of space around the vertical support is further facilitated by the rotundity of a cylindrical vertical shaft, and a more complete transition from the horizontal to the vertical is afforded by a rounded capital (Fig. 50).[19] (iv) The channellings of a Doric column effect a further dynamic interplay of solid and void, the solid curving again and again out into space, only to retreat each time to harbor the encroaching space, while the echinus (or rounded portion of the capital) intensifies this relationship. The entasis (or outward bulge of the column) further accentuates this effect (Fig. 51). (v) The Ionic capital with its twin volutes and its rounded base establishes a still more plastic relationship between solid and void, vertical and horizontal (Fig. 52). (vi) Finally, the Corinthian capital, with its frontal concavity and its curling acanthus leaves projecting into space and creating innumerable interstices,

be employed in such different contexts; but it is preferable to use a term now in common use in architecture than to invent a new one, and no confusion need result if its precise architectural meaning is specificd. The term "cubistic" suffers from an analogous limitation because it suggests that all cubistic architecture is necessarily four-square and trabeated, whereas, as we shall see, the cubistic and arcuated manners of treatment are actually compatible. But here again careful definition can obviate confusion. Meanwhile, the more literal meaning of the term "cubistic" (i.e., like a cube) is directly applicable to architecture in that a building constructed like a plain cube or some geometrical variant of a cube always exemplifies the architecturally "cubistic" (i.e., static) manner of treatment.

[18] The specific rôle of the vertical-horizontal relationship in the cubistic and plastic manners of treatment will be discussed presently.

[19] Thus far the motivation was, historically, utilitarian rather than aesthetic. But this is irrelevant to the argument.

carries the interplay of solid and void and the artistic transition from vertical to horizontal to its ultimate culmination in Greek trabeated architecture (Fig. 53).

This transition from the cubistic to the plastic manner of treatment can be illustrated analogically by comparing a series of sculptural figures on the exterior of five Gothic churches—figures whose dates range from about the middle of the twelfth to the end of the fourteenth centuries. The first of these examples (Fig. 42) is a notably cubistic *trumeau* figure; it is still completely conditioned by the rectangular block of stone from which it was hewn, and clearly manifests the cubistic character of this original stone block. The next figures (Fig. 43) in the series are still made to conform rigorously to the architectural requirements. They are greatly elongated, to emphasize the powerful vertical thrust of the architecture; their drapery is stiff in its geometrical regularity; and the figures themselves are rigidly frontal in pose, thus emphasizing their subservience to strictly architectural demands. The figures in the third example (Fig. 44) are handled in a more plastic manner. Now for the first time a definite architectural space is provided for *each* figure by a *separate* canopy. This space enables the figure to turn on its own axis and to advance one foot. The drapery hangs in easy flowing folds. In the fourth example (Fig. 45) the figures are as completely plastic as they can be made without sacrificing their architectural function. A *continuous* canopy above them creates a *common* architectural space in which they can move in relation to one another; hence they are no longer separate figures but members of a sculpturally unified group. Their sculptural movement and vitality is the proof of their plastic quality, and is the eloquent sculptural expression of the representational theme, i.e., the Presentation in the Temple. The culminating example in the series is the sculptural group by Claus Sluter for the portal of the *Chartreuse of Champmol* at Dijon (Fig. 46). Here all the figures form one scene, the patron saints presenting the kneeling donors to the Virgin. The lateral figures have now no longer any relation to the architecture, and the Virgin, although a *trumeau* figure, is one of the most striking examples of plasticity in the history of sculpture. The first four examples in the series thus illustrate in sculpture, here used as a minor art (i.e., as an expressive adjunct to architecture), the transition from cubistic rigidity to plastic movement, from less to greater interplay of solid and void, from the static to the dynamic. In the last example sculpture emancipates itself from architecture to become a plastic art in its own right.

It is evident from the foregoing illustrations that cubism and plasticity are only distinguishable as artistic, i.e., architectural, manners of treatment, and are definable in terms of their effect upon the artistically sensitive observer. Each necessarily has its own distinctive physical characteristics, to which due reference has been made. But in physical actuality space does not "flow"; the protrusions and recesses of a solid are physically as "static" as the flat surface of a cube; and a diagonal or curve is, scientifically considered, no more of a "transition" from the vertical to the horizontal than an angle of ninety degrees. *Architectural* cubism and plasticity are evident only to the artistically sensitive eye of an observer endowed with the capacity for architecturally conditioned empathic response. In this respect, these manners of treatment differ essentially from those of trabeation and arcuation.

Yet they relate themselves to trabeation and arcuation in a manner deserving of precise analysis. In contrasting the six increasingly plastic vertical supports, two factors were emphasized, (i) the relation of solid to void, and (ii) the relation of the vertical to the horizontal; and it was suggested that architectural cubism and plasticity are functions of *both* types of relationship. In the cubistic manner of treatment, solids exist in sheer juxtaposition to voids, and, in addition, verticals are opposed to horizontals without transition; whereas, in the plastic manner of treatment, there is an architecturally dynamic interplay of solids and voids, *and* an architecturally effective transition is achieved between verticals and horizontals. Now trabeation and arcuation are essentially sympathetic to architectural cubism and plasticity, respectively, with respect to this *second* factor, namely, the vertical-horizontal relationship. When a flat lintel rests on two vertical uprights without sculptural moulding of any sort, no transition from the one to the other is afforded, whereas the plainest arch provides a perfect transition from the vertical to the horizontal. In other words, mere trabeation is, architecturally considered, quite static, whereas the simplest arch is, in itself, architecturally dynamic. In this respect, but only in this respect, arcuation is essentially plastic; trabeation, essentially cubistic. But, as is evident in the Greek Orders, trabeated architecture can become pronouncedly plastic, its plasticity being proportional to the success with which, *within* the basic requirements of trabeation, an interplay of solid and void is achieved by various means. And, on the other hand, arcuated architecture can be predominantly cubistic, as is the case in the interior of Germigny-des-Prés (Fig. 56).

Cubism and plasticity can also be combined in a single building, as, for example, in the interior of the chapel in *Aix-la-Chapelle* (Aachen) (Fig. 57), where the lower story is predominantly cubistic in effect, and the upper, with its columns and Corinthian capitals, more plastic in architectural treatment; or in the interior of *San Paolo fuori le mura* (Fig. 62), whose flat clerestory walls rest on a plastic colonnade supporting plastic arches, and whose rectangular and prevailing cubistic nave ends in a pronouncedly plastic apse.

Modern building materials, notably reinforced concrete and glass, should, at least theoretically, greatly extend the plastic potentialities of architecture. But thus far little progress has been made in this direction, for, with certain exceptions, contemporary architects have been primarily intent on exploiting the possibilities of the cubistic rather than the plastic manner of treatment in the new engineering media.

(c) The third type of architectural manner of treatment may be entitled "illuminated." Once again, the term must be defined with care. For by "illumination" we cannot here mean sheer physical illumination, since all buildings are necessarily bathed in light during the daytime and admit light into their interior through all available openings. The illumination here in question is *architecturally controlled* light and shade, and when this manner of treatment is invoked as it should be, the expressive potentialities of architecturally controlled light are appropriately exploited.

In a typical modern office building the use of light is entirely utilitarian; the architect's sole objective is efficient interior illumination. The lighted cupola of the third chapel of *S. Maria in Trastevere* in Rome (Fig. 74) clearly illustrates the architectural control of light and shade. Similarly, in the Roman *Pantheon* (Fig. 61), the light admitted through the oculus intensifies the visible rotundity and affects the apparent size of the interior. In certain Roman basilicas (Fig. 62) the light admitted through clerestory windows emphasizes the complex architectural character of the interior. In *Hagia Sophia* (Fig. 63), the size and lightness of the dome is visibly enhanced by the admission of light through the windows at the base of the dome. And, finally, in a Gothic cathedral (Fig. 41), the eye, travelling upwards, is made to pass from comparative darkness into a region of light and then on into a region of mysterious shadow in the soaring, vaulted roof.

Stained glass provides the architect with an additional and powerful control of light, producing, as it does, a type of illumination which differs qualitatively from natural light. Thus the colored light inside a Gothic cathedral greatly intensifies the sense of supernatural mystery which this type of architecture so notably expresses.

Light and shade can be controlled with architectural effectiveness on the exterior as well as in the interior of a building. Witness, for example, the calculated play of light and shade in the colonnade of a Greek temple (Fig. 51), and particularly in the pteroma, that is, the space between the colonnade and the cella wall. Or note the visible lightness of the *Temple de l'Amour* at Versailles (Fig. 73). Here the colonnade and dome create an architectural space in which the external light of nature is caught and given a new architectural character. Or consider, finally, the use of light and shade in the portico of *S. Maria* in the Via Lata in Rome (Fig. 75), where the brilliant light reflected from the pavement is made to illumine the space of the vault and thus to intensify the plasticity of the vault and the columns.

These illustrations clearly indicate the relation of illumination to the cubistic and plastic manners of treatment. Both cubistic and plastic architectural effects can be intensified by a wise use of light and shadow, on the exterior as well as in the interior, and the artistic effect of both manners of treatment can be seriously diminished by the failure to control exterior and interior illumination.

The position here adopted has been that light and shade are aspects of the architect's primary medium which he, as an architect, has no business to ignore. On this premise only those buildings in which light and shade are architecturally controlled can be said to possess complete artistic, i.e., architectural quality. There is therefore no such thing as a non-illuminated *architectural* manner of treatment; non-illumination is merely a form of architectural deficiency.

This is of considerable importance for the analysis and appraisal of modern architecture. For despite occasional effective control of exterior light and shadow, the contemporary architect has hardly begun to exploit the luminous potentialities of his new building materials. Despite the extensive use of glass in modern buildings, the light thus admitted has more often been used for purely utilitarian purposes than to create new architectural effects by a control of light and shadow (Fig. 91). It is primarily in the use of electricity that contemporary architects have manifested a genuine architectural control over interior illumination (Fig. 92).

Baroque architecture may be cited as the European style which manifests the richest fusion of these five manners of treatment (Fig. 65). It combines arcuation and trabeation with notable success. It expresses the strength and solidity of architectural cubism, in combination with the grace and dynamic vitality of architectural plasticity. And it uses light and shadow with great architectural effectiveness. As a result, it quite perfectly exemplifies a synthesis of horizontals and verticals in which a transition is effected without the loss of what each has to contribute; and through the interplay of architectural solids and voids which it achieves, partly by means of pure architectural form, partly by a control of light and shade, and partly by skillful use of color and sculptural decoration, it possesses, at its best, a degree of expressive architectural unity not often equalled in European architecture. This unity, with its rich control of all the architectural manners of treatment, expresses an ecumenical dignity never before achieved in architecture.

This concludes my account of the basic manners of treatment in the abstract arts of music, the dance, and architecture. As might have been expected, it was the primary medium in each case, rather than the secondary medium, which here determined the several manners of treatment. The secondary medium is equally influential, as we shall discover, in the production of a distinctive style, but this is not the place to discuss this influence. The control exercised by these primary media, meanwhile, is negative rather than positive. It is man's inventive and creative genius which has discovered the potentialities of these media and translated them into actualities; the media themselves condition the forms which we have been considering only in the sense of determining their physical possibility. Some media lend themselves to several manners of treatment. Stone, for example, permits of both cubistic and plastic manipulation. Each medium, however, has its peculiar limitations which can be transcended, if at all, only by a *tour de force*, and which can never be completely negated. A modern steel bridge or skyscraper cannot be built merely out of stone, wood, or brick, and polyphonic and harmonic music cannot be produced on a one stringed instrument or by one voice. The primary medium, then, defines the field of possibility but cannot of itself bring about artistic actuality.

In passing now to the representational arts of sculpture and painting and to the symbolic art of literature, our problem becomes progressively more complex, because the subject-matter or secondary medium comes to assume an ever greater importance in the determination and definition of the basic manners of treatment of these three arts. The determining influence of subject-matter is least evident in sculpture, which resembles architecture in many important ways. In painting, several of the basic manners of treatment are, we shall discover, essentially conditioned by representational subject-matter. In literature, the primary medium is itself symbolic, and the meanings symbolized carry us inevitably beyond the bare sensuous medium into a world of inner and outer reality. This complicating factor does not lessen the importance of the primary media in these arts; they continue to be as influential as they are in the abstract arts. The subject-matter merely enters in as an additional and increasingly important determining agent which, in conjunction with the primary medium, negatively conditions the basic manners of treatment in these arts.

4. Sculpture

We can distinguish in sculpture between three sets of manners of treatment, the second and third of which are analogically related to the second and third sets in architecture.

	linear	
relief		
	{planear / cubistic}	luminous
free-standing		
	plastic	

If the possibility of *completely* non-representational sculpture is admitted, a fourth set of sculptural manners of treatment, which might be entitled "representational" and "non-representational," should be added, paralleling "music without words" and "music with words." That sculpture can *approach* complete abstraction without losing all sculptural quality must be admitted (Figs. 95, 99); and a few wholly non-representational compositions in three dimensions have been created which are usually classified as sculpture and which have been admired for their sculptural expressiveness (Figs. 94, 96). The applicability of the manners of treatment listed above to compositions of this type must be considered in due course. Meanwhile, I shall assume that crucial importance should be assigned to the representational factor in this art as well as in the art of painting,[20] and shall therefore proceed at once to discuss the applicability of these manners of treatment to representational[21] sculpture.

(a) The categories of sculptural "relief" and "free-standing" sculpture, or sculpture "in the round," are, like those of trabeation and arcuation in architecture, essentially pre-artistic, and, as such, accurately definable in physical terms. In sculptural relief the representational figures are carved, cast, or otherwise created in such a way as to be integrally attached to the background, whereas in free-standing sculpture they are not so attached and are visible, at least theoretically, from every side. These two manners of treatment are readily distinguishable in French's *Longfellow Memorial* (Fig. 143), where the bust of Longfellow is free-standing (though in this case it is intended to be viewed from in front and is artistically related to the background), whereas the carved figures in the background are in low relief. The same artist's *Death and the Sculptor* (Fig. 144) exemplifies the transition from low relief (the Sphinx) to high relief (the symbolic figure of death) to free-standing sculpture (the youthful artist), and, incidentally, the various degrees of low and high relief which are possible. Donatello's *Dance of Salome* (Fig. 150) illustrates this differentiation of low and high relief in a series of well-defined sculptural planes.

These sculptures also illustrate the fact that both of these manners of treatment have a distinctive aesthetic character which is intensified when they are juxtaposed in a single composition. Thus the three-dimensionality of the bust of Longfellow is artistically accentuated by the low relief of the background (an effect which is further enhanced by the difference in media, color, etc.), just as the flatness of this relief is made more evident by the bust. *Death and the Sculptor* illustrates the difficulty of achieving compositional unity when these diverse manners of treatment are both resorted to in a single work. The *Dance of Salome*, which is completely in relief, and most of

[20] Cf., below, p. 168; Chap. XXII, §4.

[21] "Representational" being taken in the widest possible sense to include *all* forms of sculpture which are not *mere* abstract three-dimensional designs.

the statues illustrated in this volume, possess far greater artistic unity partly because this difficult fusion is not attempted. The very emergence of the problem as to whether a single sculptural composition can be in both manners of treatment indicates their artistic significance.

(b) The manners of treatment in the second group are, like architectural cubism and plasticity, primarily artistic rather than physical in character, and must be defined with reference to the different types of impression made upon an artistically sensitive observer. Yet, as in architecture, these manners of treatment have a physical basis which permits of accurate description.

Sculpture is "linear" in proportion as visible lines or edges are given artistic emphasis. No sculptural composition is exclusively in the linear manner of treatment; when line is the only expressive device employed, as in the prehistoric *Charging Mammoth* from La Madeleine (Fig. 145), the composition lacks all sculptural quality and should be classified as "painting." In sculpture, lines and edges are always used in conjunction with one or more of the other manners of treatment in this group. Thus a line may be employed to achieve or intensify sculptural plasticity (Figs. 146-148), or a sharp edge, to define the boundaries of a sculptural plane (Fig. 149). The resultant effect is consequently only partly linear. But this does not deprive the sculptural use of line of its artistic importance, for a linear emphasis makes its own distinctive contribution to the total artistic effect of the composition.

Free-standing statues lend themselves less readily to a linear treatment than do reliefs, but even in them a linear effect can be achieved, notably in the handling of drapery (Fig. 115). But it does not follow that low relief is more amenable to linear treatment than high relief. In Agostino di Duccio's relief (Fig. 148), for instance, the linear effect is most pronounced in the handling of the fire, which is in very low relief, whereas in the bas-relief bust of *Scipio* (Fig. 147) the helmet, in higher relief than the armor, is treated in quite as linear a manner as the armor.

The "planear" and "cubistic" ways of handling the sculptural media are really the same manner of treatment applied, in the one case, to sculptural relief and, in the other, to free-standing sculpture.

In planear reliefs representation is achieved by means of superimposed flat two-dimensional areas or planes. Several overlapping planes may be combined, each plane being distinguished from the next by greater or less indentation or protuberance (as in high, middle, and low relief) with respect to the plane of the original surface (Fig. 149). In the most pronounced examples of planear relief these planes are sharply distinguished from one another and are not related by gradual transitions. The more sharply each planear boundary is thus defined, and the flatter the surfaces of the several planes, the more static the resultant effect, since the representational objects in the several planes are rigidly confined within their planear boundaries.

Free-standing sculpture is cubistic in proportion as the three-dimensional figures or shapes represented are characterized by a geometrical rigidity (Figs. 151, 152). In statues which are pronouncedly cubistic, vertical and horizontal shapes are sharply juxtaposed, and the representational figures are, as a result, deprived of all capacity for visible movement in space.

The difference between sculptural cubism and plasticity has already been discussed in terms of Gothic sculpture employed for architectural adornment. But when sculpture is used as an adjunct to architecture it cannot achieve its maximum plasticity, for, were it to do so, it would cease to perform its architectural function by insisting upon its own sculptural self-sufficiency.

Sculptural relief and free-standing sculpture are both plastic in proportion as the figures represented are so modelled as to emphasize their mobile and dynamic character (Figs. 172, 126). This effect is achieved by avoiding flat planes, sharp edges, and harsh transitions of every type. Whether or not the statue was actually first conceived and executed in soft clay which the sculptor could fashion with ease into the desired shape, the final effect of plastic sculpture suggests this mode of creation. But this does not mean that plastic sculpture is soft and amorphous. What it expresses is rather the dynamic vitality of a living form, and this sense of vitality, in turn, is effected by representing the figures or objects in such a way that they seem capable of unimpeded movement in space. This plastic effect can be achieved as easily in relief, and, indeed in very low relief, as it can in free-standing sculpture.

(c) All sculpture, to be seen effectively, must not only be appropriately illuminated; the relation of lighted passages to passages in shadow cannot be ignored with sculptural impunity. In this respect the rôle of light in sculpture is analogous to its rôle in architecture.

In both cases, a failure to recognize and control the factor of light and shade constitutes an artistic deficiency.

But as the architect can control light in a variety of ways to serve his architectural ends, so the sculptor can deal with the problem of illumination variously. He can, for example, create a statue which can be seen with equal effectiveness from whatever direction the light falls (Fig. 202), or, alternatively, he can so model his figure that its sculptural effectiveness depends upon its being illuminated from one particular point. It is essential, for example, that Michelangelo's *Lorenzo de' Medici* (Fig. 253) be illumined primarily from a point in front of, and above, the figure, in order that the shadow cast by the helmet be correctly placed. But sculptures also vary in the degree and type of importance that is attached to light and shadow. In some statues, light and shade are made relatively unimportant (Fig. 178), in others, quite essential (Figs. 201, 202); and in most statues they are used to intensify sculptural cubism or plasticity (Figs. 152, 134), whereas in others they are used to achieve a distinctive sculptural effect which now deserves special mention.

"Impressionistic" sculpture, whether in relief (Fig. 153) or free-standing (Fig. 180), is characterized by its uneven surface which is deliberately calculated to exploit the play of light and shade. Here the dominant effect is neither linear, planear, cubistic, nor plastic—it is distinctively luminous. Sculpture of this type can be seen effectively only when it is illuminated from a specified direction, and it must be seen from a certain distance and from a more or less restricted angle of vision. And whereas non-impressionistic sculpture frequently awakens in us tactile and kinaesthetic associations so strong that we are impelled to run our hands over the smooth surfaces, the roughened surface of impressionistic sculpture tends to arouse in us an equally strong aversion to the very thought of such tactile contact. Its artistic effect upon us, in short, is exclusively visual; our impulse is to view it in exactly the way in which we would view a painting. A preponderant emphasis on the play of light and shade in this medium thus tends, like an exclusive reliance on line, to make sculpture pictorial rather than sculptural in artistic quality.

How, now, are these sculptural manners of treatment applicable to sculpture which is almost or completely non-representational? Sculptural relief which is completely non-representational can be nothing but sheer ornament or decoration, and is normally geometrical in character (Fig.1). *Entirely* non-representational free-standing sculpture is extremely rare but is more or less closely approximated by some contemporary sculptors (Figs. 94-96, 99). It, too, necessarily tends to be geometrical in character. Sculpture of this type can be said to be linear, planear, cubistic, or plastic in a physical and non-sculptural sense in proportion as visible use is made of strings or wires, planes, cubes (and their variants), and curved surfaces; and, at least theoretically, it can exemplify these manners of treatment artistically by patterning itself on architecture and by reproducing, in miniature, the effects which are achieved in that art by the relations of verticals to horizontals, and solids to enclosing (but not enclosed) space. But it is a grave question as to how much artistic expressiveness can actually be achieved in this manner.

In any case, there can be no question that representational sculpture possesses far richer expressive potentialities than non-representational sculpture. For not only can each of the manners of treatment listed above be more effectively exploited in different statues of this type; several can be employed simultaneously to achieve still greater sculptural unity, vitality, and expressive eloquence. Here, as in architecture, the Baroque style provides some of the best illustrations of how this can be accomplished.

In Bernini's *Longinus* in St. Peter's (Fig. 135), for example, the linear, plastic, and luminous manners of treatment are all employed with masterly skill, each being made to contribute to the effectiveness of the other and to the total sculptural effect.

The statue is linear in three distinguishable respects, (i) in its silhouette which, as in all good statues, is of great sculptural importance, (ii) in the handling of the hair and drapery, and (iii) in the contrapuntal relationships of staff, legs, and outstretched arms. The silhouette, which has been studied with the greatest care,[22] is a highly dynamic edge which contributes notably to the total plastic effect. This effect is further intensified by the clearly defined pattern of elongated passages of luminosity and darkness—*vide* the drapery, the left leg, and the right arm. Finally, the outstretched arms, the legs, and the staff may all be said to be linear in a larger sense, since they constitute, in conjunction, a dynamic pattern of major elon-

[22] Bernini, like Poussin, often made two types of sketches for his projected compositions, one linear, in which the silhouette and modelling received special attention, the other, a wash-drawing specifically directed to the problem of luminosity. Cf., below, p. 170.

gated forms in dynamic interplay. They are all diagonal by reference to the vertical and horizontal axes. The straight staff deviates from the vertical axis with a propulsive outward thrust. The visible curvature of the legs contrasts with the straightness of the staff, and each leg repeats the outward thrust of the staff in the reverse direction, the right leg at a more pronounced diagonal than the left. The two arms (which together constitute a diagonal whose relative horizontality contrasts with the relative verticality of the staff), the legs, and the torso, create a broken yet continuous line from the right hand to the left shoulder, down the left upper arm, and along the extended forearm to the left hand with its outstretched fingers. The figure is thus an eloquent pattern of repetitive ideas (compare Fig. 136) which are linear in a variety of ways.

The plasticity of the figure is immediately evident. The dramatic pose, the waving drapery, the rapt expression of the face, all contribute, each in its own way, to its sculptural and highly expressive vitality. It is to be noted, moreover, that the figure is set in a niche which provides it with an architectural space in which to move. This niche makes possible the dynamic interplay of sculptural form and architectural space, the figure thrusting itself into a space which already possesses a pronounced artistic character and thus invites sculptural exploration. The figure's plasticity is therefore not wholly self-contained or self-determined but derives to a considerable extent from its relations to the controlled architectural space in which it stands. This relation of sculptured figure to architectural setting is further intensified by the way in which the statue contrasts in color and design with the architectural decoration of the niche, its white marble being set off by the colored marble and its modelled irregularity by the geometrical pattern on the wall.

Finally, the statue is a typical exemplification of Baroque sculptural luminosity. The light, already architecturally controlled, is made to fall upon the statue from in front and above so as to set in sharp relief the upturned face, the chest, the outstretched arms, the billowing drapery, and the staff, while the subtly graded and sharply contrasted lighted and shaded passages combine greatly to intensify the plasticity and vitality of the statue as a whole.

That Bernini was explicitly aware of this factor of sculptural luminosity is evidenced by the many wash-drawings which have been preserved, in which he studied this particular problem prior to the final execution of various other statues. In his studies for the angels in the *Chapel of the Sacrament* in St. Peter's (Fig. 141), for example, his preoccupation is entirely with the pattern of sculptural light and shade. Such drawings as these help us to appreciate the essential rôle of sculptural light and shade in the finished product (Fig. 142), and they prove beyond all doubt that Bernini was acutely conscious of the importance of this manner of treatment.

As in architecture, then, a rich exploitation of several complementary manners of treatment can result in a type of artistic vitality and expressiveness which can be achieved in no other way.

5. Painting

Painting differs generically from sculpture in being physically two-dimensional rather than three-dimensional.[23] But its basic manners of treatment, like those of sculpture, fall into three groups, as follows:

black-and-white	linear planear	non-luminous
colored	cubistic plastic	luminous

(a) The first two pictorial manners of treatment are, like trabeation and arcuation in architecture and like sculptural relief and free-standing sculpture, essentially pre-artistic in character, though not, on that account, devoid of artistic significance. Each is definable in terms of the primary medium employed, and this medium is, in each case, varied. The black-and-white media include pencil, charcoal, pen and ink, etching, engraving, etc.; the colored media include oil, water-color, fresco, etc. And each of these subsidiary media has, of course, its own distinctive surface, tools, and technique, which must be taken into account in any adequate description of the several pictorial media. Each has, moreover, its own distinctive artistic potentialities, and it is these which the artist must appropriately exploit if the resultant manner of treatment is to have artistic significance.

The first two pictorial manners of treatment are as applicable to abstractions as to representational compositions. A composition of either type must be in one or other of these manners of treatment, or in a combination of the two. But the remaining manners of treat-

[23] Painted sculptural reliefs, like painted free-standing statues, should be classified as "sculpture" rather than as "painting."

ment are, with one exception, applicable only to representational compositions.

(b) The manners of treatment in the second group are, like the analogous ones in architecture and sculpture, primarily artistic in character; they are definable in each case in terms of the total artistic effect of the completed composition. Yet each has its appropriate physical basis. I shall first consider the use of these manners of treatment in representational painting, and then discuss their applicability, or non-applicability, to pure pictorial abstractions.

A representational composition is "linear" in proportion as lines are emphasized as representational and expressive vehicles. In representational paintings lines are always made to serve representational ends by creating, clarifying, or emphasizing the visible structure of the object or scene depicted. Thus, in a black-and-white composition, the objects depicted, e.g., a group of human figures, can be created entirely by a series of lines outlining the structural members of the figures in question (Fig. 156); or lines can be used in a scene which is primarily a study in pictorial light and shade (Figs. 215, 216); or lines can be employed to define a silhouette or to introduce plasticity by means of chiaroscuro (Fig. 163). In colored compositions, the "line" may be a clearly defined edge of a representational area (Fig. 158), or it may be a structurally significant elongated light or shadow, as in drapery (Figs. 137, 247). In short, line can be used in painting either to represent what presents itself to us in nature as non-linear, or, alternatively, to represent the visibly linear characteristics of natural objects. But it can also be used in a strictly non-representational manner to enhance a representational effect. Thus Marin (Fig. 157) frequently intensifies the perspective and sense of distance in his landscapes by drawing horizontal, vertical, or diagonal lines which have no *direct* representational function whatever.

All pictures in the pictorially linear manner of treatment make use of visible lines of one type or another, and the artistic impression which this use of line makes on us is to a greater or less degree qualitatively linear. But the mere fact that lines are actually employed does not suffice to make the composition *pictorially* linear in manner of treatment, for lines can be used *merely* to establish or enhance a dominant planear, cubistic, plastic, or luminous effect. Few representational compositions are exclusively linear in pictorial manner of treatment; most pictures in which line receives artistic emphasis are both linear *and* planear, cubistic, or plastic in synoptic pictorial effect.

The planear, cubistic, and plastic manners of treatment in painting are applicable only with the aid of pictorial representation, whereas it is possible for a line to achieve artistic expressiveness in a completely non-representational abstraction. This is because a line drawn on a two-dimensional, wholly non-representational, surface is visibly a line, whereas a flat area is not, in and of itself, visibly a plane or, *a fortiori*, a cubistic or plastic three-dimensional object. The term "abstractions" is often used loosely to designate pictorial compositions in which the factor of representation is reduced to a minimum, e.g., to the representation of solid geometrical shapes or even two-dimensional planes visibly related to one another in three-dimensional space (Fig. 100). But it is clear that even this effect can be achieved only representationally, for the simple reason that, in painting, three-dimensional space must always be pictorially *created* on a two-dimensional surface. If no such space is representationally created, a flat area, whether colored or uncolored, is merely a flat area whose plane is visibly identical with that of the paper or canvas. It is not, pictorially considered, a plane at all, but merely a colored or uncolored portion of the physical two-dimensional surface. Most modern "abstractions" are therefore not pure abstractions, since the juxtaposed areas do normally occupy different planes to the discerning eye and, in addition, frequently combine to create solid objects quite definitely related to one another in a visually created space.

But, once again, it is possible representationally to create pictorial planes without resorting to the *pictorially* planear manner of treatment. A composition can be said to be in this manner of treatment only when the planes thus created receive artistic emphasis, that is, in proportion as the composition as a whole makes a planear impression upon the artistically sensitive observer. Manet's *Fifer* (Fig. 158) clearly exemplifies this manner of treatment. Representation is achieved by the juxtaposition of flat areas of carefully contrasted colors, values, and intensities; these areas occupy, in the picture, visibly well-defined planes; and these planes, in turn, receive artistic emphasis. Compared with pictorial figures which are notably three-dimensional, this painting is relatively flat and two-dimensional, though not to the point of serious representational distortion or loss of representational reality. In Ingres' *Bather* (Fig. 159), in contrast, the nude figure is pictorially plastic, though largely composed of flat unmodelled areas. Notice the handling of the arms and legs.

The "cubistic" and "plastic" manners of treatment in painting differ in essentially the same way in which the analogous architectural and sculptural manners of treatment differ from one another. Pictorial "cubism," in the more generic meaning of the term, must not be restricted to an artistic emphasis upon representational cubes or other geometrical solids, though compositions of this type are, as a rule, pronouncedly cubistic in manner of treatment. The hall-mark of pictorial cubism is rather a static rigidity. The solids represented appear immovable and stand in no visibly dynamic relationship to one another or to an enveloping space. A composition is plastic, in contrast, in proportion as objects are represented as possessing an inner vitality and as standing in dynamic relation to one another and to the space which envelops them.

Here two factors must be distinguished for purposes of analysis: (i) the handling of the individual objects which are depicted, and (ii) the handling of their spatial environment. For it is possible to treat a single object, e.g., a human body, in a markedly plastic manner without creating an atmospheric space in which this object might conceivably move. If, for example, we ignore the painted background of one of Michelangelo's *Slaves* on the ceiling of the Sistine Chapel (Fig. 133), and regard only the nude figure, this figure must be admitted to be markedly plastic in pictorial manner of treatment.[24] But it is significant that Michelangelo actually created a pictorial space for the figure to occupy and in which to move—witness the pictorial architecture in successive planes. By this device Michelangelo endowed the entire composition (as here reproduced) with dynamic actuality. The slave's relation to his pictorial environment is clearly established, and this relation permits him to move freely in the space pictorially created for him.

The distinction between these two factors conditioning pictorial plasticity is again evident if we compare the *Avignon Pietà* (Fig. 211) with Rubens' *The Peasants' Dance* (Fig. 204). In the former, the donor is treated in a plastic manner, and the space in which he finds himself differs in kind from the non-representational space

[24] Here Michelangelo's sculptural training is evident: compare Fig. 134. The plasticity of the figure, taken by itself, is sculptural in quality, and is achieved by means of chiaroscuro.

(witness the gold background) in which the other figures statically exist; whereas, in the latter, the figures are portrayed in various stages of potential or actual physical movement through a space which is entirely representational. Hence *The Peasants' Dance* is plastically treated throughout, as the term "plastic" is here defined.

(c) In both sculpture and architecture, light is so unavoidable an ingredient of the primary raw material that the failure to control it and put it to effective artistic use is an artistic defect. Architectural non-illumination and sculptural non-luminosity are not positive artistic manners of treatment. But this is not the case in painting, for if light is to be introduced in a pictorially significant manner (i.e., apart from the sheer physical illumination which is requisite if the picture is to be seen), it must be introduced representationally, and need therefore not be introduced at all. Hence both "luminosity" and "non-luminosity" are potentially valid and expressive pictorial manners of treatment. Thus, though the representational objects in Schongauer's *Crucifixion with Four Angels* (Fig. 162) are eloquently delineated, there is in the picture no representational light, whereas in Dürer's *Crucifixion* (Fig. 163) the corresponding objects are bathed in pictorially created and controlled light. Dürer's *Erasmus* (Fig. 164) clearly illustrates the difference between plain white paper (*vide* the square area of the inscription) and shimmering representational light (*vide* the drapery and the open book). A pictorial composition may therefore be said to be in the luminous manner of treatment in proportion as light and shade are (i) representationally introduced and (ii) artistically controlled.

The rôle of light and shade in painting can be indicated with greater precision by means of a further distinction between chiaroscuro and pictorial luminosity. (i) Pictorial representation can be achieved without resort either to modelling (chiaroscuro) or to genuine luminosity (Fig. 156). (ii) Chiaroscuro can be employed to define the representational objects and achieve plasticity without any pictorial representation of light (Fig. 162). That is, a perceptual object can be modelled in light and shade without the creation of pictorial light and darkness, and the scene containing such shaded objects need not itself be luminous, as is evidenced by the fact that the objects need cast no shadow, or, if they do, that these cast shadows can be used not to create pictorial luminosity but merely to establish the pictorial pattern or to achieve some other pictorial end. (iii) Genuine pictorial luminosity can be introduced representationally. Furthermore, (a) this luminosity can either be assigned major representational importance or used primarily to achieve pictorial plasticity; and (β) the light representationally created can be of various different kinds. Both types of variations deserve consideration.

(a) Light can be represented pictorially only with the aid of "solid" objects (including such ephemeral forms as clouds) which are illumined by it. No painting can be *merely* luminous. In Turner's *Norham Castle at Sunrise* (Fig. 169), for example, the use of solid objects is reduced to the bare minimum. The faintly suggested cliff and the barely indicated cow with its cast shadow play a proportionately essential rôle; without them the picture would cease to represent light altogether and would be merely an abstract medley of brightly colored pigment.

But pictorial luminosity can receive major representational emphasis, as in *Norham Castle*, or it can be employed primarily to define the three-dimensionality of the solid objects represented, as is the case in Poussin's *Ordination* (Fig. 165). Here the function of pictorial luminosity and the representation of solid objects is reversed. Light and shadow are now used to make the figures three-dimensional and plastic, whereas, in *Norham Castle*, the objects were introduced to make the whole scene luminous. Hence, though the relationship of luminosity and objects illumined is clearly reciprocal (perceptual objects conditioning luminosity, and light enhancing physical plasticity), either can be accorded prior emphasis.

Rembrandt's portraits (Fig. 260) exemplify a distinctive fusion of both processes—a fusion in which luminosity and perceptual plasticity are equally emphasized. Here the figure and the background are so handled as to create an atmosphere unusually saturated with luminosity and darkness. This atmosphere, in turn, with its luminous areas and its dark shadows so eloquent of spatial depth, helps to establish the three-dimensionality of the human form. Thus the figure, as depicted, is simultaneously a product and a source of pictorial luminosity and darkness, and the composition is, as a whole, an amazing pattern of solid form and atmospheric space, of luminosity and gloom, of perceptual substantiality and insubstantiality.

(β) The type of light represented pictorially may be naturalistic outdoor light, as in Vermeer (Fig. 168); or the subtle luminosity of the Rembrandt portrait just considered; or theatrical spotlight

(Fig. 166); or, finally, a wholly unreal mystical light from an indeterminable source and of mysterious quality (Fig. 167). Meanwhile, the representational character of pictorial luminosity, of whatever type, is evident if we compare the pictures just mentioned with paintings which make use of gilt or any highly burnished surface. The striated glory in Fra Angelico's *Coronation of the Virgin* in the Uffizi (Fig. 160), or the shimmering gold background of *St. John Prochorus* (Fig. 161), for example, are not *pictorial representations* of light at all. The gilt reflects actual physical light far more effectively than colored pigment, and the light thus introduced into the picture is not pictorial luminosity which has been created by representational means, but mere natural light reflected as in a mirror. It is no more than the artistically controlled physical luminosity of the painter's primary medium.

As in the case of the arts already considered, the several manners of treatment in painting can be employed simultaneously with great artistic effectiveness. Cézanne, for example, in his delicate yet powerful water-colors (Fig. 285), combines the use of color, line, plane, plasticity, and luminosity in a truly amazing way. Note how, with the utmost economy of means, he exploits the expressive potentialities of line, differentiates between flat and rounded surfaces, establishes visible solidity and space, relates solids to one another and to the pictorially created voids, and, in the process, transforms white paper into dancing light and blue pigment into vibrant shadow.

These pictorial manners of treatment are obviously determined in part by the nature of both the primary media and the representational subject-matter. The influence of the latter is greater in painting than it is in sculpture. But, once again, this determination is merely negative. A pictorial subject may invite one manner of treatment rather than another, and may discourage or even prohibit one or more manners of treatment (it would certainly be hard, for example, to represent light, and not merely symbolize or reproduce it, in a *purely* linear manner). But the artist's own creative imagination remains the ultimate source and final arbiter of all manners of treatment in this as in the other arts.

6. Literature

The basic manners of treatment in the abstract arts could be distinguished almost entirely in terms of their primary media, while in the representational arts the subject-matter was found to determine the manners of treatment to only a limited extent. In literature the subject dealt with, and the writer's approach to it, condition most of the manners of treatment so profoundly that these categories must be defined primarily in terms of generic subjects and attitudes. Here, more than in any of the other arts, *how* a thing is said is predominantly a function of *what* is being said and for *what purpose*.

The scientist's distinctive use of language is in the manner of sheer assertion without imagery or emotive evocation. This assertion is not, of course, limited to the bald announcement of isolated facts. It includes all statements concerning premises, descriptions of methodological procedure, accounts of observations and experiments, formulations of scientific theories, and indications of the degree of their reliability. But in all his utterances the scientist merely announces, without use of literary metaphor or emotive overtones, the results of his highly impersonal investigations.

The historian and the philosopher must also indulge in assertions of this type. In his logical and epistemological inquiries, for instance, the philosopher, like the scientist, merely asserts what he believes to be the "facts" in question as precisely, impersonally, and prosaically as he can. Similarly, the historian must indulge in prosaic assertion in reporting on documentary evidence, announcing established historical "facts," and formulating and defending his explanatory theories.

But the larger tasks of the philosopher and the historian are reconstructive and normative, and these activities demand a more flexible and less prosaic use of language. Sheer factual assertion will not suffice to make imaginatively real to us a cultural epoch, a social event of historical import, or the biography of an historical character. Literary devices must be invoked to portray the past with imaginative vitality. Similarly, the philosopher can share his normative insights with us and persuade us of the reasonableness of his normative appraisals only by using language with literary or quasi-literary expressiveness.

The outstanding characteristic of the speech of the common man is its lack of uniformity, its rapid oscillation from one linguistic manner of treatment to another. The complexity of our environment and the variety of our needs and interests are reflected in the diverse uses to which we put our mother tongue. We resort to sheer assertion, we indulge in reflective speculation, we command, exhort, rebuke, petition, and expostulate as occasion requires, and we may even indulge in quasi-poetic utterance. Our varied use of language anticipates prophetically, though incompletely and unsystematically, the more specialized manners of treatment of the scientist, historian, philosopher, and creative writer.

Whatever the more specialized manner of treatment in the art of literature, the *differentia* of literary composition is its dynamic vitality and imaginative power. Sheer factual assertion, however clear, precise, or intellectually convincing, is never literary in an artistic or expressive sense. It is of the very essence of literature that, whatever the subject treated and in whatever manner it is dealt with, it be so presented as to quicken our imaginative comprehension and to evoke our emotive and conative response. Only in proportion as language is used to accomplish this end can a composition be described as "literary" in an artistic sense. The several literary manners of treatment do not differ, then, in imaginative vitality. They must be distinguished on other grounds.

The generic manners of treatment in literature fall into three groups, as follows:

prose	lyrical reflective	timeless
verse	dramatic descriptive	temporal

The distinction between prose and verse is primarily a function of rhythm and depends in large measure upon the use of the primary medium. The remaining manners of treatment, in contrast, must be defined entirely in terms of a distinctive approach to a distinctive subject-matter.

(a) It must be made clear at the outset that "literary prose" is *not* "prosaic." I have defined expressive literature as non-assertive in order to obviate this confusion. Good literary prose manifests literary vitality as clearly as does good literary or "poetic" verse, and differs as sharply from mere prosaic utterance. Literary prose and metrical poetry are both expressively rhythmic, and differ only in the *type* of rhythm employed.

Literary rhythm may be defined as any recurrent emphasis which engages the attention more strongly at the points of emphasis and which, though ultimately dictated by the meaning, finds audible expression in the primary medium in a variety of ways, such as the use of pauses, the change of auditory pitch and intensity, quantitative variations and repetitions, etc. All of these devices are employed in both prose and verse.

Verse is distinguished from prose by various types of metrical organization which are restricted to the several forms of versification. Prose is essentially non-metrical while verse is metrical. By "metrical organization" is meant the use of a wide variety of devices such as rhyme, assonance, alliteration,[25] and the like, to emphasize the *felt* regularity of the rhythms. But this distinction between prose and verse, though sharper than that between the other manners of literary treatment, is not absolute. Highly decorative prose may in places briefly exhibit metrical organization (*vide* Sir Thomas Browne's *Urn Burial*), though if this organization is maintained far enough to suggest a metrical line pattern, as in Dickens' description of little Nell's death in *Old Curiosity Shop*—a passage which lapses unmistakably into pentameter blank verse—it is almost universally condemned as bad taste. Free verse, on the other hand, is characterized by a corresponding departure, partial or complete, from metrical line organization (*vide* the poetry of Amy Lowell, which is only partially metrical, or the English translation of the *Psalms*, which is magnificently rhythmic without being metrical). The same literary composition, moreover, may pass from literary prose to poetic verse and back again, as so frequently happens in the plays of Shakespeare. Such variants and combinations of literary prose and verse do not, however, destroy the validity of the distinction between these basic manners of treatment.

(b) The "lyrical," "reflective" (sometimes called "philosophical" or "metaphysical"), "dramatic," and "descriptive" manners of treatment are used in both prose and verse. They can be distinguished partly in terms of the type of subject-matter which invites their employment, partly in terms of the characteristic approach to this subject-matter. The lyrical manner of treatment is particularly appropriate to the literary interpretation of human emotion; the reflective, to man's reflections on his own nature and destiny and his relation to the physical world, his fellow men, and Deity; the dramatic, to man's volitional and impulsive strivings, usually in a social context; and the descriptive, to the perceptual world of individual objects and events. The characteristic approaches to these four types of subject-matter, in turn, are indicated

[25] Cf., above, p. 116, n. 19.

by the names here assigned to these four manners of treatment respectively.[26]

These manners of treatment are not sharply distinguishable save in their most typical manifestations. They are as distinct, and as closely interrelated, as are man's basic psychological capacities for feeling and emotion, for more or less abstract speculation, for conation ranging all the way from blind impulsion to deliberate volition, and for perceptual apprehension. There is of course no such thing in actual experience as pure feeling or emotion wholly unaccompanied by thought or conative impulse, or pure thought untouched by emotion and entirely non-conative. All reflection and all emotive and conative response are conditioned, directly or indirectly, by sense-perception, and perception is always accompanied by some degree of reflection, emotion, and conation. Yet human experience is, at different times, *predominantly* emotional or reflective, perceptual or volitional. Similarly, all literature deals, in one way or another, with the objects of sense-perception and with man's reflective *and* emotive *and* conative responses to his complex environment. Yet the literary artist can emphasize now one and now another generic aspect of man's inner or outer experience. It is these contrasting emphases to which appeal must be made in distinguishing between the lyrical, reflective, dramatic, and descriptive manners of treatment in literature.

A literary passage, whether long or short and whether in prose or verse, is "lyrical" in proportion (i) as it deals primarily with the feelings and emotions of either a single individual or of a group of individuals who are united by common sentiments and ideals, and (ii) as these feelings and emotions are dealt with chiefly for their own sake and expressed with unusual vividness. Such emotional states will normally be more or less explicitly motivated by social, religious, or other considerations. The lyrical emphasis, however, falls less on what has occasioned the emotions than on the emotions themselves. The subject or theme of a lyrical passage tends to be simple and unitary; it is treated with single-minded intensity; and this intensity of feeling tends to achieve verbal expression in a con-

[26] Special attention is called to the fact that we are here concerned *not* with literary "genres," i.e., not with *the* lyric in its various forms, or *the* epic, *the* drama, *the* novel, or *the* essay, but with the lyrical, reflective, dramatic, and descriptive manners of treatment, in whatever type of compositional pattern they may appear. Cf., below, pp. 210*ff*., for the generic compositional patterns in literature.

centrated and rich use of language. Lyrical verse tends to be characterized by strongly marked regularity of meter, stanzaic organization, and the use of repetitive refrain, while lyrical prose is at once strongly and variously rhythmic and particularly rich in vivid metaphor. The lyrics of Herrick and Keats, Heine and Alfred de Musset, and the essays of Thoreau and Charles Lamb may be cited as illustrations of this lyrical manner of treatment in verse and prose.[27]

A longer or shorter passage is "reflective" in proportion (i) as it deals primarily with man's thoughts or reflections about himself and the larger reality of which he is a part, and (ii) as it emphasizes the normative significance of these reflections. Technical philosophical analyses, speculations, and arguments are reflective, but not in a literary manner. Or perhaps it would be more correct to say that they are rational in the narrower sense rather than reflective, since "reflection" seems to imply a sense of perspective and a realization of the significance of intellectual inquiry and its discoveries which are often lacking in wholly analytical and argumentative discourse. Really to reflect is to consider with truly imaginative insight the complexities of human life in a highly diversified environment, and to take stock of what reality signifies for human life. Such reflection, as expressed in literature, tends to be either "philosophical" in the larger cultural sense, i.e., when it deals with its subject in terms of more enduring problems (whether moral, religious, aesthetic, or more abstractly speculative), or else (and perhaps less frequently) "historical," i.e., when it emphasizes the importance to man of time and historical change, and the significance, for men in every generation, of historical persons and events. No sharp line can therefore be drawn between philosophical and historical treatises of the more cultural type and reflective literature in the more limited sense. The more literary the writing, however, the greater the emphasis on adequate expression of the conclusions, whereas the greater the emphasis on evidence and logical argument, the less likely is it that the result will satisfy the requirements of literature as an expressive art. Examples of the reflective manner of treatment in literary verse and prose respectively are *Death* by John Donne, Pope's *The Dying Christian to his Soul*, and the essays of Francis Bacon and Sir Thomas Browne.[28]

[27] Cf., below, pp. 360*ff*.

[28] Cf., below, pp. 360*ff*.

Literary expression is "dramatic" in manner of treatment in proportion (i) as it deals with the human will in inner or outer "action," normally as revealed in moments of crisis, and (ii) as it depicts such voluntary action, and whatever dynamic conflict may ensue, with unusual vividness and power. Here again we can speak only of tendencies and emphases. All literature, in its inevitable preoccupation with human life, is necessarily "moral" in the largest sense; that is, it reflects man's deep-seated impulse to translate ideals into actualities by volitional effort. This effort is always attended by feeling and emotion, and volition differs from purely reflex, instinctive, or habitual behavior in being guided by past and present reflection. Reflective and lyrical passages, accordingly, may give no less eloquent expression to those inner tensions which characterize vital human experience than do the literary passages and compositions usually entitled "dramatic" in manner of treatment. Yet it is possible for a writer[29] to focus our attention upon those situations and occurrences in which man is impelled to speech and action in the effort to adapt himself to his physical and social environment and to mould this environment to his own needs and desires. Whenever this type of conflict receives special literary emphasis the resultant manner of treatment may be said to be predominantly "dramatic" in character. In his most dramatic moments, as in the murder scene in *Othello*, Shakespeare provides the clearest illustrations of this manner of treatment, but it is also exemplified in such poems as Goethe's *Erlkönig* and Browning's *Men and Women*, and in such novels as Hardy's *Tess of the d'Urbervilles* and Victor Hugo's *Les Misérables*.

Literature may also be primarily "descriptive." In a sense, the literary treatment of any subject—of man's inner life and overt actions as well as of natural phenomena, animate and inanimate—might be called descriptive, but the term "descriptive" is usually used to signify longer or shorter passages whose subject-matter is the world of nature, or man as part of nature.[30] Such literary description differs from prosaically utilitarian or scientific description in its preoccupation with nature as seen from the human point of view, and with man's emotive-conative response to natural things and processes. Hence the tendency of the descriptive writer to por-

[29] I am here considering only dramatic *writing*, not the performance of dramas on the stage.

[30] Cf., below, pp. 358-9.

tray nature anthropomorphically, i.e., as alive and quasi-human. He is inclined to the "pathetic fallacy," and emphasizes the feelings and reflections which nature inspires in him. Thus Tennyson records at length his despair in the face of a universe which he describes as mechanistic, dead, and meaningless—"The stars, she whispers, blindly run"; Lucretius finds deep satisfaction in an atomistic universe; Wordsworth feels nature, both animate and inanimate, to be expressive of a higher purpose and therefore akin to his own nature and aspirations. Writing such as this, whether in prose or verse, is "descriptive" as this category is here defined.

These four manners of treatment are not, I must repeat, mutually exclusive. For not only can an author pass from one manner of treatment to another in different portions of a composition (as Shakespeare does, for example, in the *Tempest*); two or more manners of treatment can be employed simultaneously. Thus, the religious poems of George Herbert are both lyrical and reflective, and Herman Melville's account of the final chase of the great white whale in *Moby Dick* is not only descriptive but highly dramatic in manner of treatment.

(c) The last two manners of treatment, which I have entitled "timeless" and "temporal," relate to the "presentational time" of the passage or entire composition, that is, to the author's deliberate neglect or varied use of the temporal character of his subject-matter. What I have here designated as "presentational" time (for lack of a better term)[31] is distinct from, though not independent of, the time factor in the primary medium as such. It must not be identified with the fact that literature, like music and the dance, is a temporal art whose constituents must be apprehended in a given temporal order and at a tempo which can be varied only within certain limits. Presentational time is the temporal character which is deliberately attributed by the author to his *subject-matter*, as this subject-matter is verbally evoked and interpreted.

A writer can, on the one hand, treat his subject in such a way as not to raise the question of time at all. He can do so by emphasizing those "eternal" aspects of his subject-matter which recur in human experience through the centuries without significant change,

[31] The term "presentational" is here used to distinguish what is presented by *literary* means from what is manifest in direct experience. "Representational" might be used as a synonym, had I not already used it in this volume with a different meaning to characterize the "representational" arts of sculpture and painting.

and by avoiding all orientation of the states, processes, or events portrayed either to the author's (and the reader's) temporal frame of reference, or to that of the character or characters depicted. Most sonnets dealing with love, for instance, treat of this passion in one or other of its timeless manifestations and without regard to *when* the feelings and emotions here described were entertained.[32] In poems of this type we find no significant reference to the poet's past, present, or future, or to that historical sequence of events which marks the flow of historical or socially objective time. The "time" of the poem is an eternal "present"—as "present" today as it was when the poem was written, and likely to be as "present" for future generations.

This timelessness is not, of course, the timelessness of pure conceptual abstraction—that eternity which characterizes all the truths of which the philosopher and the natural scientist are in search. The "specious present"[33] in its literary form plays an essential rôle in all literary compositions of this type. Rossetti's famous definition, in the proem to *The House of Life*: "A sonnet is a moment's monument," acknowledges the importance of the "moment" of experience and also proclaims the poet's desire to eternalize this moment. In dealing with *some* "moment" of experience, and necessarily with some moment rendered imaginatively *concrete*, the sonnet differentiates itself from all philosophical and scientific preoccupation with timeless universals abstracted from a temporal context. But it also distinguishes itself from those types of literary composition which I have entitled "temporal" by selecting for literary treatment a moment which might be *any* moment (of this imaginative type) in the experience of the author or his public, without regard to his or their relation to any specified past or future. Again in the words of Rossetti, a sonnet is a

> Memorial from the Soul's eternity
> To one dead deathless hour.

Poetry of this type is the immediate yet timeless ("deathless") concretion of timeless ("eternal") yet ever-recurrent universals.[34]

[32] Cf. the lines quoted below, pp. 358*ff*.

[33] i.e., the "present" of actual experience, the "now" of human consciousness, which varies in scope and richness but which is never reducible to the durationless instant of clock-time.

[34] This literary timelessness is, of course, quite unrelated to the fact that *all* literary compositions, like all other cultural products, inevitably "date," not necessarily in the

In the "temporal" manner of treatment, in contrast, the events and experiences which constitute the subject-matter are so dealt with as to emphasize their temporal orientation either to the socially objective time of history or to a temporal frame of reference established *within* the literary composition as a self-contained universe of discourse. In both cases, the time factor is deliberately introduced as a factor of literary importance. The temporal orientation is woven into the expressive fabric of the composition in such a way as to acquire positive literary significance.

(i) When the temporal orientation is explicitly "historical," the events or experiences which constitute the subject-matter of the composition are described as having taken place either in a "past" which is common to both the author and the reader as members of a society with a common history; or in the historical "present," i.e., at a time immediately prior to the moment of actual narration; or, as a third alternative, as transpiring in the historical "future," this "future" being defined in relation to the historical "present" of the narration. In each case this historical orientation is given genuine significance and made to contribute to the total expressed content of the composition. Thus, Shakespeare's Roman Tragedies are not only faithful in individual characterization to Plutarch's *Lives*; they clearly reflect the writer's haunting sense of the splendor that was Rome's. Similarly, Shakespeare's English historical plays proclaim his love for England and the reality to him of its historical tradition. A somewhat comparable preoccupation with the past is evident in the epics of Homer and Virgil, and an interest in the historical past is particularly apparent in Scott's historical novels.

Where the reference is to the historical future, as in Aldous Huxley's *Brave New World*, the significance of the time factor is intensified by the fact that the situations and events described are explicitly located in what, from the author's point of view (and so from the reader's, so far as he identifies his "present" with that of the author) is the future, though they are usually described by the author as having taken place in a time already past.[35] This dual

sense of possessing only passing interest, but in the more profound sense of reflecting the cultural period in which the author lived and wrote. The most timeless poetry "dates" in this sense, the poetry of the eighteenth century in England, for example, bearing a different stylistic impress from that which distinguishes nineteenth century or contemporary English poetry.

[35] In prophetic and apocalyptic literature future events are sometimes described in an entirely anticipatory manner, i.e., as not yet having been experienced even by the

reference to time gives additional literary emphasis to the factor of historical futurity, because this future is set in sharp relief by being contrasted with a literary or presentational past.

A vivid sense of historical contemporaneity is conveyed when the author, as narrator, describes (often as an eye-witness, or as an actual participant) events which are alleged to be actually transpiring in the historical present; *vide* the *Battle of Brunanburh* and Stephen Spender's *Vienna. The Fall of the City*, written by Archibald MacLeish for the radio and recently broadcast, suggests that the radio may possess unique expressive potentialities in precisely this literary manner of treatment, i.e., that it may be developed into a vehicle for the artistic expression of historical contemporaneity far more powerful than compositions written to be read or even to be acted on the stage. For in a written description of a contemporary event some time must necessarily elapse between the actual occurrence of the event described and its verbal portrayal, and an additional period of time must elapse between the writing of the text and its perusal by the reader. From the reader's point of view, the historical present, as portrayed, has already been pushed back twice over into the historical past, whereas the radio announcer can not only describe what is occurring in his own present, but is able to convey to the listener a vivid sense of actual participation in events which are just as contemporaneous to him.

My reference to the radio may serve as a reminder that mere historical orientation, as such, whether to the historical past, present, or future, cannot be said to possess any *literary* significance whatever in and of itself. To achieve a literary character it must be put to artistically expressive *use.* I have remarked that historical writing shades imperceptibly into strictly literary composition. But the generic difference between these two types of verbal composition must not be lost sight of even in this border-line region between literary history and literature oriented to historical time. The historian attaches greater importance to the precise sequence of his-

author himself in the rôle of one who has projected himself into the future. A writer can simply describe what he believes will happen in the future, saying, in effect: "I prophesy (or I assert) that such and such an event will take place." Or, alternatively, he can project himself, as narrator, into the future and purport to be describing what has already happened in *his* past (as narrator), though these events still lie in his own actual future (i.e., as an author living in the historical present) and therefore in the future of all living men. It is this second approach to which I have referred in the text.

torical events and resorts to literary expression as a means to an end—the end, namely, of vivid imaginative reconstruction of the historical past for its own sake. This past, and the historical present and future which it illumines, have for him an *intrinsic* interest and value. In the art of literature this emphasis is largely reversed. For the creative writer who chooses to make historical time part of his literary subject-matter is interested in it not primarily for its own sake but rather for its potential contribution to the *universal* literary content which he desires to express by literary means. In literature, historical time is made to serve literary ends. The historical present, past, and future are introduced *primarily* as unique occasions which can be made to yield abiding insights into eternal truths.[36]

(ii) But the temporal orientation of a literary composition need not be historical; the time factor can be emphasized without any indication as to whether the events described precede, follow, or coincide with any particular moment in historical time. The distinctiveness of a non-historical literary narrative depends in large measure upon the fact that, although the events are portrayed as having already transpired in the *narrator's* more remote or more immediate past, this past is not synchronized with historical time.

An author who wishes to push the events narrated into a presentational past may resort to various devices to achieve this effect. He can tell the story himself, or have one of his characters tell it, as a series of happenings in which he himself (or the character) participated; or he can have a character recount what he, the character in the story, alleges to have heard from someone else. When the intermediary rôle of the narrator is introduced in a colorless way, without literary emphasis, the effect of non-historical temporality is correspondingly weakened. When, on the other hand, it receives literary emphasis, as it does in Coleridge's *Ancient Mariner*, Emily Brontë's *Wuthering Heights*, or Conrad's *Lord Jim*, it notably enhances the effect of actuality, even in a fantasy. These things, we are made to feel, actually happened to the Ancient Mariner. The narrator had the story from his own lips; surely, therefore, we must give it credence despite its apparent incredibility.

An analogous projection of events into a presentational, non-historically oriented future occurs when the characters in a composition are made to speculate on coming events whose futurity is

[36] Cf., below, Chap. XVIII, §2, on portraiture, for a further discussion of this problem in terms of artistic content.

relative to their own present. Compare Hamlet's famous soliloquy in which he contemplates suicide, or Claudio's speech in *Measure for Measure* (III, i),

> Ay, but to die, and go we know not where;
> To lie in cold obstruction and to rot. . . .

or the speeches of the fallen angels in Book II of *Paradise Lost*. Or, alternatively, the author may himself, at the end of a composition, anticipate the future of his characters with literary omniscience for the benefit of the reader. But such anticipation can hardly be compared in importance with the narration, in whatever form, of events in the presentational past. They bear the same general relation to the narration of such past events as do anticipations of an historical future to the recording of the historical past.

It is also possible for an author to endow the presentational present with literary importance by depicting the experiences, thoughts, and emotional states of his characters as though these were in actual process of occurrence. Compare, for example, the novels of such "naturalists" or "realists" as Zola. This emphasis on the moving "present" of the narrative is unusually evident in portions of *Tristram Shandy*, for instance in Book VII, Chapter 28, where Sterne calls specific attention to a paradoxical overlapping of three distinguishable "present" moments in his narrative.

"—Now this is the most puzzled skein of all—for in this last chapter, as far at least as it has helped me through Auxerre, I have been getting forwards in two different journeys together, and with the same dash of the pen—for I have got entirely out of Auxerre in this journey which I am writing now, and I am got half way out of Auxerre in that which I shall write hereafter—There is but a certain degree of perfection in every thing; and by pushing at something beyond that, I have brought myself into such a situation, as no traveller ever stood before me; for I am *this moment* walking across the market-place of Auxerre with my father and my uncle Toby, in our way back to dinner—and I am *this moment* also entering Lyons with my post-chaise broke into a thousand pieces—and I am moreover *this moment* in a handsome pavillion built by Pringello, upon the banks of the Garonne, which Mons. Sligniac has lent me, and where I *now* sit rhapsodizing all these affairs.

"—Let me collect myself, and pursue my journey." (My italics.)

The "stream of thought" and the "slice of life" (*tranche de vie*) modes of literary treatment occasionally exhibit complicated variants of this use of literary contemporaneity, the former sometimes emphasizing the character's *present* recollection of past events (*vide* Proust), the latter, the repeated occurrence of a social or individual pattern of thought and behavior (*vide* Becque's *La Parisienne* or Maupassant's *En Famille*).

But we must be particularly careful not to confuse this literary manner of treatment with that "presentational immediacy" which is not one of the manners of treatment at all but rather the distinguishing mark of literary vitality as such, in whatever genre or manner of treatment. A literary composition is devoid of artistic value if it fails to arouse in us a vivid sense of immediate participation. Unless we are enabled to identify ourselves with the subject as presented, the composition must remain for us dead, inert, and artistically inexpressive. This "identification" should never, it is true, be complete. It is as essential in literature as in the other arts to maintain a sense of "psychical distance," i.e., not to confuse art and life or to relate ourselves to the artist's subject-matter as we would to actual objects and events. The identification of ourselves with what has been interpretatively recorded must always be an unconscious act of the *literary*, i.e., artistic, imagination controlled by the total artistic frame of reference. Yet, *within* this frame of reference, we must be able to "lose ourselves" in the composition and share as completely as possible in the experiences which the author has recorded in literary form. A writer is under prime obligation to evoke and direct this response, whatever manner of treatment he employs, and we, his audience, are under comparable obligation to respond in this way to authentic literature of whatever literary type.

Thus, a sonnet exemplifying the timeless manner of treatment, or a non-historical narrative exemplifying the exploitation of a presentational past, should give us as vivid a sense of "presentational immediacy" as an historical narrative; and a treatment of the historical past or future should be as immediate in literary effect as a literary account of the historical present. Similarly, a lyrical, reflective, or descriptive passage of literary excellence will arouse in us, if we are sensitive to literary values, as poignant a sense of immediate participation (though always in a way appropriate to the manner of treatment in question) as will a passage in the more explicitly dramatic manner of treatment.

Our sense of presentational immediacy, in short, is a subjective index, in re-creative response, to objective literary vitality, and this vitality, in turn, is essentially the expression, by literary means, of the vitality of human experience itself. To be alive as conscious human beings is to live in what I have referred to, following philosophical usage, as the "specious present." Now this specious present is not a durationless instant, for such an instant can never actually be experienced but can only be arrived at by calculation with the aid of clocks (or their physical equivalents) and an appeal to scientific abstraction. The specious present has been happily described by William James[37] as a "saddle-back" of time. It is not only experienced as an appreciable duration but as a "present" flowing out of a "past" (itself once a "present") and into a "future," that is, a "present" still to be. As James points out, we never hear a clap of thunder, for example, as a wholly isolated or atomic sound; what we are aware of is always "thunder-breaking-upon-silence-and-contrasting-with-it." In hearing this "thunder-breaking-upon-silence," moreover, we also anticipate the silence which will ensue when, as we presume it must, the thunder ceases. Human consciousness, in short, is an awareness of a present emerging from a past and passing into a future. Reminiscence and longer-range anticipation are merely extensions of these temporal dimensions of "specious" awareness. Human experience, which is necessarily always present experience, is thus in very essence both reminiscent and anticipatory, and its vitality is directly proportional to the span of the specious present and the tension in it between a remembered past and an imaginatively projected future. The more vividly we are able to recall the past and to anticipate the future, the more apparent is the determination of the present by the past, and the stronger the pull of the future upon the present—hence, the greater our sense of being alive "here and now."

Of all the arts, literature is best qualified to express by artistic means this sense of the vital present. It can do so because its primary medium permits a more richly articulated interpretation of human experiences of every type than is possible in any of the other arts. For the writer enjoys a unique control over his subject-matter. In comparing sculpture and painting we found that a painter has a greater control over his representational subject-matter than a

[37] William James, *Principles of Psychology* (New York: Holt, 1890), Vol. I, pp. 608-10.

sculptor, just because he has to create the third dimension on a two-dimensional canvas. Literature stands in the same relation to painting in this respect that painting does to sculpture. Its primary medium, which is not representational but symbolic, does not permit the writer to "represent" perceptual objects in the way in which they can be represented by the painter. The author must *evoke* images by his use of words, and he must depend upon the reader to use his reproductive imagination and "see" what the author wishes him to see. This is, in a sense, a handicap. But the writer's reward is correspondingly great. For he can control what he thus evokes, as the painter can control space and light. He can create, combine, and shift his images with lightning speed, and, in addition, imbue them with conceptual meaning more richly and surely than can those artists whose primary media are essentially non-symbolic. In short, literature not only enjoys a more extended and diverse subject-matter than any of the other arts; its expressive control over this subject-matter is, at least potentially, unexcelled in the other artistic media. As a result, it can arouse in us an unusually vivid sense of "presentational immediacy" by interpreting human experience as significantly conditioned by a past and as pregnant with future consequences of human import. And it can do so in the timeless as well as in the temporal manner of treatment—in a sonnet, regarded as "a *moment's* monument," as well as in an epic or a novel, in which events which may never have occurred are infused with a life-like immediacy. This is not to mimimize the unique contributions to human insight of the other arts, or to proclaim, with Hegel, that literature is the "highest" of the arts. Each art has its own peculiar excellence. But each has also its special limitations which demand recognition.

My classification of the chief literary manners of treatment has not been exhaustive, nor have the categories here enumerated been exhaustively analyzed. Literature is far too complex to permit of adequate exploration in brief compass. I am, however, prepared to defend the omission of certain categories usually included in such a list, on the ground that they are not on a par with those which we have just considered.

For example, the "narrative" and "allegorical" manners of treatment have not been included as distinctive manners of treatment because they are not simple generic ways of handling the literary media. "Narratives" are either in prose or verse; they are frequently dramatic, and often contain long descriptive, lyrical, and reflective passages; and though, as "narratives" in the narrower literary sense, they must be said to be in the temporal manner of treatment, yet some compositions, e.g., certain novels, which may be described as "narratives" in a more catholic sense, fall rather into the "timeless" category. In short, the term "narrative," as used in critical literature, is an omnibus term which is neither simple in reference nor self-explanatory, and it is only with the aid of more carefully delineated categories that its generic nature and varied exemplifications can be understood.

The term "allegory" has a more precise critical meaning. But, once again, this meaning can best be defined in terms of the manners of treatment listed above. It too may be either in prose or verse, and its distinctive character can best be described as a unique combination of the reflective and dramatic manners of treatment on the one hand, the timeless and the temporal on the other. An allegory is in essence a more or less dramatically developed story in which the characters and events are given a "secondary" symbolic meaning into which the reader is continually invited to translate them. This meaning is reflectively expounded, usually in the timeless manner of presentation, whereas the events depicted are usually accorded a temporal orientation.

It is clear, then, that the basic manners of treatment permit of combination in the greatest variety of ways. No passage can be simultaneously in prose or verse, or timeless and temporal, though these manners of treatment can be employed in close succession. But a passage can be simultaneously in two or even more of the manners of treatment in the second group (i.e., lyrical, reflective, dramatic, and descriptive), although, when this is the case, one or other of them will normally receive predominant emphasis. On the other hand, any literary passage *must* be *either* in prose or verse, and *either* timeless or temporal, and *necessarily* in one or more of the four manners included in the second group. Thus, John Donne's *Death* is in verse, in the reflective manner of treatment, and timeless; *Lord Randall* and Thomas Campbell's *Lord Ullen's Daughter* are metrical, primarily dramatic though in part both descriptive and lyrical, and temporally oriented. I have isolated these manners of treatment not with the intention of suggesting that they actually appear in isolation in any specific composition, but rather because they appear only in combination and because such combinations allow of precise analysis only if the ingredients combined have been clearly differentiated.

CHAPTER X

GENERIC COMPOSITIONAL PATTERNS IN THE SIX MAJOR ARTS

THE generic compositional patterns in art resemble and differ from the artistic manners of treatment in several important respects.

They resemble them (i) in being essentially intra-medial, since both types of formal organization are conditioned, at least to some extent, by the primary medium and, to a lesser extent and only in certain arts, by the subject-matter, and (ii) in having a generic character which manifests itself uniquely in each specific work of art. Thus, despite analogical similarities between certain basic compositional patterns in different arts, each art has its own distinctive generic patterns of composition. And though, as we shall see, the basic compositional patterns in each of the arts are limited in number, a specific work of art in any medium has its unique formal pattern, which is a specific instance of one or other of the generic types of compositional structure, and which alone determines the work's artistic merit.

A "compositional pattern" differs from a "manner of treatment" in characterizing the work of art *as a whole*. For it is, by definition, the most inclusive type of organization to be found in a work of art. It is that organization of the specific medium which constitutes the basic structure and organic unity of the work of art in its entirety. Thus, different manners of treatment can be employed in different portions of the same work of art and still be harmonized to produce artistic unity, whereas an artist who, in any specific composition, has committed himself to a specific compositional pattern must conform to this pattern throughout.

It follows that these two types of formal organization can vary independently of one another. The same generic compositional pattern can be executed in different manners of treatment, while the same manner of treatment can be employed in works of radically different compositional pattern.

Exhaustive classifications of the generic compositional patterns in the major arts have occasionally been attempted but without notable success. No such attempt will be made here because, save in the case of architecture, no basic principle of classification has been discovered comparable to the general principles which were invoked in the classification of the basic manners of treatment. But it is important that certain familiar compositional patterns in the several major arts be enumerated by way of illustration.

There has also been a tendency, particularly in the Classic and Neo-classic tradition, to attach undue importance to generic compositional patterns—an emphasis which has sometimes had a disastrous effect both upon artistic creation and upon critical appraisal. The academic mind has found it all too easy to discover compositional similarities in the works of the "masters," to formulate these similarities into canons of compositional construction, and then to appraise the artistic merit of specific works of art in terms of rigid obedience or disobedience to these canons. And even the creative artist has sometimes been intimidated by the authority of academic critics into sacrificing vital artistic expressiveness to compositional orthodoxy.

On the other hand, no artist can free himself entirely from convention, and every artist, to be expressive and intelligible, must discipline his originality in this as in other respects and conform in some degree to one or other basic compositional pattern in each specific creation. The true master in every art has always known that, though artistic merit is, in the last analysis, a function of the work's *specific* form, genius will show itself in the ability to pour new wine into old bottles, i.e., to endow with new vitality a compositional pattern which, in and of itself, can guarantee no artistic distinction whatever. This attitude towards rules and canons is perfectly expressed by the composer Haydn who, on the one hand, "admitted that the rigid rules of harmony should rarely be violated, and 'never without the compensation of some inspired effect,' " but "when asked according to what rule he had introduced a certain progression, replied: 'The rules are all my very obedient humble servants.' "[1]

1. Music

The song, chant, motet, madrigal, fugue (considered as a complete composition, and not adjectivally, as a "fugal" manner of treatment), sonata, and symphony may be cited as representative

[1] J. Cuthbert Hadden, *Haydn* (New York: Dutton, 1934), p. 150.

examples of major and minor compositional patterns in music. Some of these are more regular than others and permit of less variation once they have been adopted for use in any particular composition. The fugue and sonata, for example, in their modern connotations, are among the less variable types, both having basic procedures which are followed in practically all works given these classificatory names. The symphony, string quartet, trio, etc., are essentially sonatas, their several movements more often than not lacking a well-defined structural unity when taken as a whole.[2] Other compositional patterns, such as the song, prelude, and nocturne, lack compositional uniformity and can be described only in such general terms as approximate length, variability of structure, and characteristic mood, though musical convention or the habits of a composer have sometimes led to the crystallization of more rigorous formulae.

In proportion as a more precise compositional pattern is consciously adopted, it is essential that its accepted character be understood if the skill with which the composer has made use of it is adequately to be appreciated. I have already remarked that one of the marks of musical genius is the ability, so pronounced in men like Bach and Beethoven, to combine obedience to rule with creative originality. The resultant beauty is all the greater when an artist can capitalize on these requirements and make them a means to more eloquent artistic expression. Comprehension of such achievements presupposes a knowledge of the compositional patterns thus employed as well as familiarity with their historical development and with other compositions in which they have also been used. But however notable the success which has accompanied the faithful employment of such patterns, they must never be forced upon the composer as inviolable precedents. The most time-honored compositional forms were once new and tentative and would themselves never have been created or accepted had perfect orthodoxy triumphed and all innovation been impossible.

[2] The movements of many symphonies are related to one another and to the work as a whole somewhat in the way in which the three parts of a triptych are related. They may have certain factors in common—a distinctive manner of treatment, a pervasive mood, a common formal austerity or tonal coloration, etc.; and they may, in combination, produce a satisfying organic effect, while yet lacking unity of basic structure or compositional pattern. Formal structure is not the only way to achieve artistic unity, though it is certainly one of the most important and effective means to this end.

Great as are the allowable variations in the use of generic compositional patterns in music, such patterns tend to be more uniform and more clearly definable here than in any of the other arts.[3] In general, the abstract arts incline to greater formal regularity than do the representational arts. Just because they are abstract, they are unable to rely on a skillful use of representational or symbolic, i.e., literary, subject-matter for artistic expression, and are forced to lean the more heavily on conventionally accepted types of formal organization. Literary prose, in contrast, is unquestionably the freest and most variable in formal organization, and depends far more than do any of the other arts on manipulation of the secondary medium for expressive purposes. Metrical poetry is perhaps the art which most richly exploits the expressive potentialities of *both* formal organization and subject-matter. Though it is less discursively articulate than prose, and though it is formally less expressive than music, poetry can, by combining in happy synthesis the special virtues of each of these arts, achieve a unique type of expressiveness.

2. *The dance*

It is particularly difficult to describe the generic compositional patterns of the dance because of the complexity and transitoriness of even the simplest dance. An accurate notational transcription of a dance would have to include a record of the "track" or floor pattern traced by the dancer's feet, the "plane" patterns described by the movements of his arms and legs in the horizontal, vertical, and all intermediate planes, and the "spatial" patterns formed by the movements of the body as a whole in three-dimensional space. And these records, to be adequate, would have to be so annotated as to show how these three sets of patterns are themselves related to one another, since each pattern merely records one aspect of a single, continuous, and unified set of movements of the body and its several members. It is easy to appreciate the problems encountered by the inventors of dance scripts and to understand why their efforts have thus far not been accorded more universal approval.

The "free" dance conforms, by definition, to no common or generic compositional patterns. Its cherished freedom from such conventions is, indeed, its most distinctive characteristic. The "conventional" dance, on the other hand, has assumed many different forms which are related by historical influence and by varying

[3] A somewhat comparable regularity characterizes the verse forms of poetry.

degrees of similarity. The oldest form of the conventional dance is the folk dance, itself of many more or less related types. The *Sword* and *Morris* dances, with all their variations, and the many country dances such as *Rounds*, *Square-eights*, and *Longways*, are among the more important of these traditional folk dances. They, in turn, have profoundly influenced the social dance in its complex and nationally diversified evolution through the centuries. The reader must be referred to histories of the dance for a description of the nature and evolution of such social dances as the *Basse*, *Pavane*, and *Gaillard*; the *Courante*, *Gavotte*, *Allemand*, *Bourrée* and *Sarabande*, which were popular in the sixteenth century; the *Minuet*, which came in in the seventeenth century; the eighteenth century *Cotillon* and *Quadrille*; the nineteenth century *Waltz*, *Lancers*, *Polka*, and *Schottisch*; and such more recent dances as the *Turkey-trot* and *One-step*. These dances have had their influence on the ballet, which, in addition, has also developed many original compositional patterns of its own. But the ballet has tended to be more conventional in its individual steps and postures than in its larger compositional structure. The mimetic and dramatic factors have made for greater originality and have tended to limit structural regularity to individual movements and to more or less segregated interludes.

The more formal a dance, whether solo, dual, or choral, and whether folk, social, or ballet in type, the greater the insistence on correctness of execution, though here, as elsewhere, mere correctness is not to be identified with elegance, grace, or expressive vitality. A more detailed examination of the art of the dance would necessitate fuller recognition of the fact that in the conventional dance, more than in any other art, the locus of artistic quality is not the compositional pattern of formal generic structure but rather its creative or interpretative rendition on each particular occasion. A somewhat comparable importance attaches to the rendition of a musical composition. But since music is usually the product of a previous creative effort on the part of the composer, it has its *own* artistic quality as dance figure patterns do not. The latter are really not in themselves works of art at all, but merely skeletal structures which the dancer must, as it were, transform into clothed and living vehicles of artistic expressiveness. In the other arts, the artist creates a work which others must *interpret* by rendering it with re-creative fidelity (as in music or literature) or by re-creative observation of it (as in architecture, sculpture, and painting); whereas in the conventional dance, and *a fortiori* in the "free" dance, it is the individual dancer or dancers who, on successive occasions, are really the original and creative artists. The chief exception to this is the ballet which, in its more developed forms, is in large measure the creation of the choreographer and of the painters, musicians, costumers, etc., associated with him. But even in the most carefully planned and elaborately constructed ballet it is dancers like Pavlova, Karsovina, and Nijinsky who alone are able to infuse it with expressive vitality. Without them it would be little more than an agreeable and ingenious spectacle. The works of a great musical composer are, no doubt, dependent upon the performer and the conductor for translation into living actuality, but the chief task of these artists is to interpret the musical ideas which have originated in the mind of the composer and have been more or less adequately recorded in the score. The contribution to a ballet of such artists as Nijinsky is different in kind. For the choreographer can, after all, do little more than provide the *mise en scène*. He can merely set the stage, and he must leave it to the genius of his leading dancers both to create and execute patterns of movement which are, to the accompaniment provided, what the living soul is to a beautiful body.

3. Architecture

Since architecture is in essence three-dimensional, its basic compositional patterns can be recorded only in ground-plan *and* elevations; and even this dual record is merely a notation which stands in the same relation to the completed building as seen, as a musical score does to a musical composition as heard. Yet a ground plan and an elevation, taken in conjunction, do have the merit of recording diagrammatically what is most essential to architectural composition, namely, the horizontal and vertical axes in their relation to one another.

An architectural axis is a directional or regulating line (horizontal or vertical) which determines the architectural frame of reference, provides the key to architectural proportion, and is a fundamental source of architectural vitality. Its function is exemplified in the proportions of a room. A room which is visually a hollow cube, as long and high as it is wide, has no architectural axis. It accordingly lacks architectural articulation (i.e., definition of proportional relationship of parts to one another, regardless of actual size), and, as a result, has no architectural character and vitality. This has been recognized by architects since time immemorial. One of the inviolable rules of architecture is that no building, or room in a building, should be, or at least appear to be, a perfect cube.[4]

The first distinction to be made, accordingly, is between pre-axial or non-axial composition, on the one hand, and architectural composition, on the other hand, the latter being axial by definition. Very primitive pre-axial construction is either "unitary" or "agglomerative." That is, it may consist of a single unit, such as a round hut of thatch or a square flat-roofed dwelling of mud, with a single room; or, alternatively, several units of this sort may be attached to one another around an irregular courtyard but without reference to any horizontal or vertical axis. Such construction is pre-architectural, since it is innocent of all axial determination and architectural proportion.

An edifice can achieve architectural character only through the establishment by architectural means of a vertical axis, or of one or more horizontal axes, or of a combination of vertical and horizontal axes. The phrase, "by architectural means," is important as a reminder that it is only the *apparent* proportional dimensions, i.e., the axis or axes made architecturally apparent to the sensitive eye, which possess architectural significance. Thus, in the *Pantheon* in Rome (Fig. 61), the height of the dome (141 feet above the pavement) is *actually* the same as the largest diameter of the interior. Yet the height *appears* greater than the diameter, partly because the side walls rise vertically for about seventy-five feet, and partly because these walls are in two levels separated by a full entablature which rests on Corinthian columns and pilasters. These and other architectural and decorative devices, such as the rectangular recesses or coffers which emphasize the upward over-arching lines of the cupola,[5] accentuate the *visible* height of the interior and thus establish "by architectural means" the all-important central vertical axis of the building.

The compositional pattern of buildings with a circular ground plan, like the Roman *Pantheon*, *Il Tempietto* in the courtyard of *San Pietro in Montario*, the *Baptistery* in Pisa, or the *Temple de l'Amour* in

[4] The same analysis is applicable to a perfect sphere. Thus, despite its utilitarian and symbolic function, the *Perisphere* at the 1939 World's Fair in New York has, in and of itself, i.e., apart from the Trylon, no exterior architectural quality whatever.

[5] Cf. D. M. Robb and J. J. Garrison, *Art in the Western World* (New York: Harpers, 1935), pp. 59*ff*.

Versailles (Fig. 73), may be entitled uni-axial because they possess no major horizontal axis but depend exclusively for their architectural proportion upon the single vertical axis. This axis can, as we have just seen, be architecturally established even when the height and the maximum diameter are equal. But normally the height is in fact greater or less than the width, and, in any case, is visibly emphasized, both on the exterior and in the interior, by a dome, one of the most effective architectural devices for accentuating the vertical axis. This axis, moreover, can be established only by reference to a horizontal plane, and, in addition, to the shape and dimensions of this plane and of the walls which enclose it and support the dome. What is lacking, then, in a composition of this type is *merely* one or more horizontal axes such as appear, for example, in buildings with a rectangular or transeptual ground-plan.

The only other type of vertical uni-axial composition would be that of a building which had a square ground-plan and which achieved a vertical axis either by being built around a square open courtyard or by some comparable architectural device. The courtyards of most, if not all, Pompeiian houses and Spanish haciendas are not square but rectangular (*vide* the *House of the Vettii* in Pompeii, Fig. 78) and thus provide an additional horizontal axis—a fact which testifies to the architectural difficulty of square uni-axial composition.[6] But what is here of primary interest is the manner in which the vertical dimension is established in buildings with an open courtyard. When the courtyard is surrounded not by four blank walls but by a covered colonnade, a sharp visual contrast is established between the partly enclosed space under the colonnade and the space which is vertically unconfined. This contrast gives the sensitive observer an architecturally controlled sense of height, for his eye is made to travel from the enclosed colonnade out into the courtyard and then upwards (whether overtly or incipiently) to the open sky. Were the courtyard enclosed by a flat roof no higher than the roof of the colonnade, this effect would be lost, with the resultant loss of the architecturally all-important vertical axis and, as a consequence, of all architecturally satisfying proportion.

The perfect horizontal equivalent of such vertical uni-axial composition would be an architectural composition which merely

[6] Comparable open-air circular structures are equally rare. The Roman *Colosseum* and the *Theater* at Verona, for example, are not circular but oblong, i.e., built on a horizontal axis.

possessed a single major horizontal axis. But so far as I am aware no such buildings exist. All buildings of architectural merit have either a vertical as well as a horizontal axis, or, as we shall see in a moment, *several* horizontal axes. Thus, architecturally proportioned buildings with a rectangular or oblong ground-plan, such as the *Parthenon* (Fig. 51), *San Paolo fuori le mura* (Fig. 62), or the *Residenz Chapel* in Würzburg (Fig. 67), invariably manifest, either on the exterior or the interior or both, an architectural control of height as well as length; they are, in compositional pattern, bi-axial, i.e., with one vertical and one major horizontal axis.

PROJECT FOR A HOUSE, EXTERNAL VIEW
Mies van der Rohe

The nearest approach to architectural neglect of the vertical axis is to be found in modern domestic architecture in which horizontality is emphasized largely at the expense of significant verticality. But this style of architecture has three characteristics which must

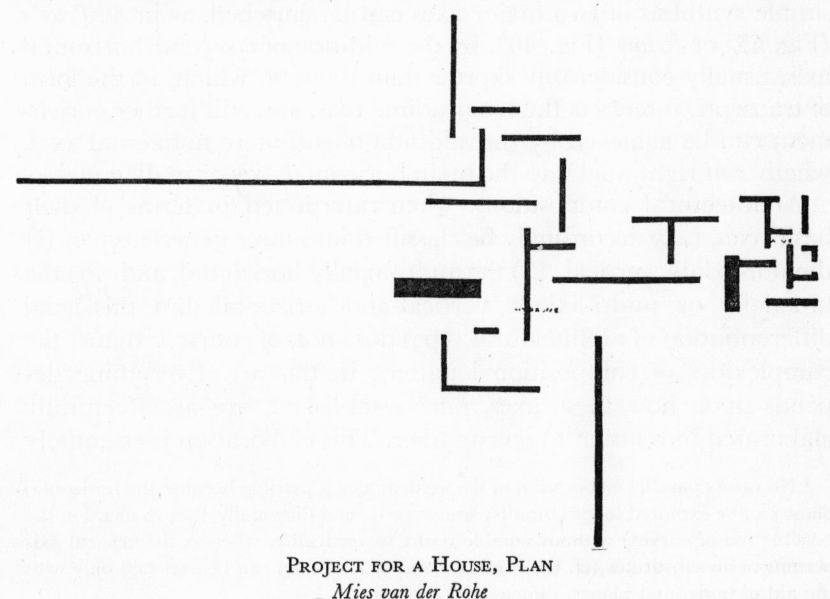

PROJECT FOR A HOUSE, PLAN
Mies van der Rohe

be borne in mind. (i) The competent modern architect never confines himself to a single horizontal axis but articulates the horizontal plane by establishing a number of subtly related longitudinal and transverse axes which are apparent not only in ground-plan but in exterior view. Thus the neglect of architectural verticality is compensated for by richness of horizontal articulation.[7] (ii) Moreover, the vertical dimension does, as it were, receive a negative recognition through explicit architectural denial. For a skillfully conceived building of this type creates in the sensitive observer a sense of flatness or deliberate horizontality as pronounced, though not as richly articulated, as is the sense of height or soaring verticality in a Gothic cathedral. (iii) And, finally, this modern exploitation of the horizontal plane is as appropriate to certain natural sites as is the Gothic exploitation of the rocky cliff in *Mont St. Michel* (Fig. 10). A terrain that is either quite flat or else falls away in a series of relatively flat terraces lends itself ideally to architecture whose compositional pattern is predominantly horizontal.

It cannot be denied, however, that most of the world's great architecture derives its architectural excellence, at least in part, from the establishment of *both* vertical and horizontal axes. This is the case in the bi-axial buildings already mentioned. The relatively simple synthesis of two major axes can be enriched, as in *St. Peter's* (Fig. 65) or *Reims* (Fig. 40), by the addition of a second horizontal axis, usually considerably shorter than the first, which, in the form of transepts, intersects the longitudinal axis, and still further enrichment can be achieved by the addition of still more horizontal axes, whether at right angles to the main horizontal axis or in diagonal.

Architectural compositions, when interpreted in terms of their basic axes, may accordingly be classified into three generic types, (i) the uni-axially vertical, (ii) the multi-axially horizontal, and (iii) the bi-axially or multi-axially vertical-and-horizontal. But this axial differentiation of architectural types does not, of course, exhaust the complexities of compositional pattern in this art. Everything depends upon how these axes, once established, are architecturally elaborated in relation to one another. This elaboration is essentially

[7] No *strictly* parallel elaboration of the vertical axis is possible because the horizontal plane can be explored longitudinally, transversely, and diagonally (not to mention the possible use of curves) without notable resort to verticality, whereas the vertical axis permits of no substitutes (cf. the leaning *Tower of Pisa*) and can be enriched only with the aid of horizontal planes, dimensions, and axes.

a function of the architectural manners of treatment which have already been discussed, i.e., of the use of arches and other devices to relate the horizontal to the vertical, of the plastic or cubistic treatment of solids and voids, and of the architectural control of light. That is, the primary medium can be so used as either to negate or emphasize the basic axes, either to assert them with stark architectural simplicity or to elaborate them with varying degrees of architectural subtlety, and either to set them in violent contrast or to bring them into dynamic, modulated interplay.

Hagia Sophia (Fig. 63) is an unusually eloquent example of rich compositional complexity and pronounced organic unity. The immense dome, visually lightened and raised by the row of windows encircling its base, is supported by four gigantic arches forming a square on the ground plan. The spherical pendentives, which overhang the angles of this square, form a circle on which the dome rests. At the east and west ends are immense apses, as wide as the dome, and each of these, in turn, is subdivided into smaller apses, three in the one case, two in the other. The two larger apses establish the major horizontal axis. This axis is reinforced by the presence of flat walls rather than apses on the north and south walls. But these walls are rendered notably plastic by two colonnades, one above the other, of round columns supporting rounded arches, and by the two high rows of arched windows of graduated size. These colonnades and windows also emphasize the vertical axis by drawing the eye upward towards the encircling dome. The columns and arches, in turn, give scale to the smaller apses, these to the larger apses, and they to the dome. The building is thus a miracle of subtle architectural synthesis of opposing axes and contrasting forms. In ground plan it is a circle, boxed by a square, elongated into an oval with subsidiary

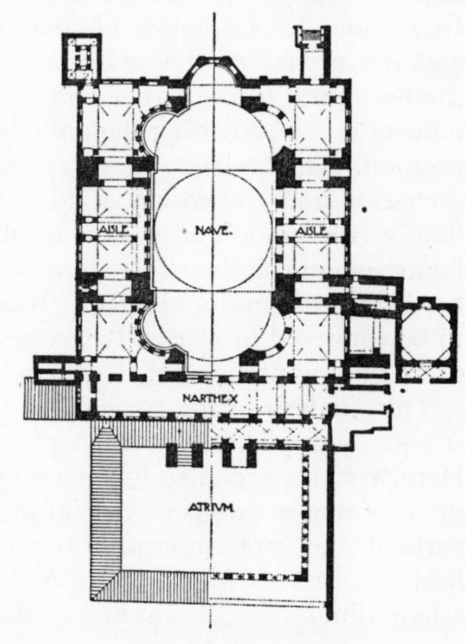

Hagia Sophia, Plan

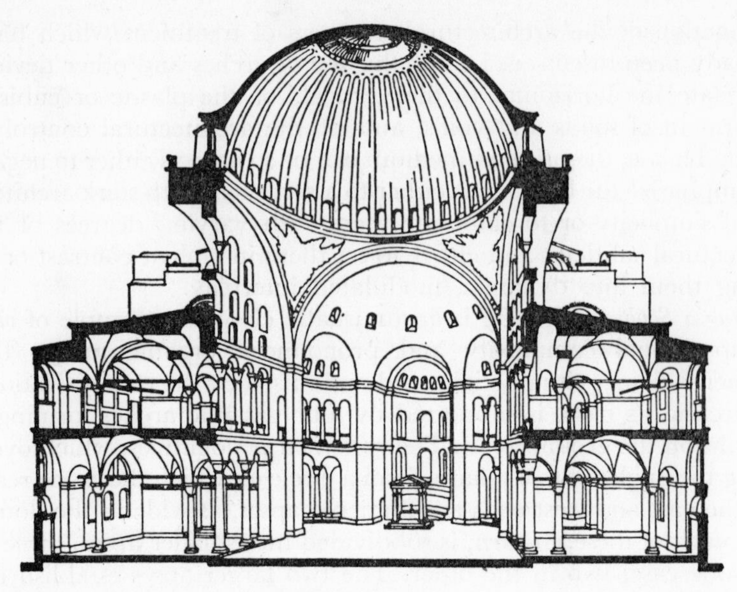

Hagia Sophia, Section

half-circles, and the whole is enclosed in an all-embracing rectangle. In section, it is a series of arcuated forms, graduated from the gigantic arches of the main apses to the smaller arches of the smaller apses, to the larger and smaller arched windows, the magnificent dome providing the architectural climax of the entire composition. The plastic interplay of verticality and horizontality, arcuation and trabeation, solid and void, light and shadow, and, finally, the color and gleam of the mosaics and marbles—each factor enhancing the effect of every other and all contributing to the total three-dimensional effect—is far too subtle and over-powering to be conveyed in words. It is a complex unity which must be seen to be fully apprehended.

This analysis of the basic compositional patterns in architecture is equally applicable to town planning and landscape gardening. Here, as in the organization of a single building, the visual establishment of major axes is of crucial importance. In town planning the vertical axes are important though usually subordinated to the horizontal axes (*vide* the *Place de la Concorde* in Paris, with its major longitudinal axis culminating in the *Louvre* and the *Arc de Triomphe*, its transverse and diagonal axes, and its circles, on the one hand,

and its use of verticality in the controlled height of the buildings, statues, and fountains, on the other). In formal landscape gardening (Fig. 12) the horizontal plane receives still greater emphasis; yet even here the vertical dimension cannot be ignored as is evident from the importance of the height of trees, hedges, statuary, and fountains.

4. Sculpture and painting

The basic compositional patterns in sculpture and painting may profitably be considered together, since representational subject-matter enters as a determining factor into both arts. Additional compositional patterns in painting which are made possible by its primary medium will be considered after the patterns which these arts have in common have been briefly indicated.

(a) *Vertical, horizontal, and diagonal compositions.* Here the composition is built on one or more straight axes. The vertical pattern is exemplified, in varying degrees of complexity, by single standing figures or groups of two or more vertical figures (Figs. 105, 106, 139, 178-182, etc.); the horizontal, by Barye's *Lion* (Fig. 279), Giorgione's *Venus*, or Leonardo da Vinci's *Last Supper*; the diagonal, by Tintoretto's *Bacchus and Ariadne* and *Adam and Eve* (Tintoretto was especially partial to this compositional pattern), or Bernini's *Apollo and Daphne.* In Perugino's *Crucifixion* (Fig. 174) the vertical motif is combined with the horizontal (note the Cross) and is repeated with variations in the standing and kneeling figures. In Poussin's *Shepherds in Arcady* (Fig. 137) diagonals mediate between major verticals and horizontals, as they do in Kolbe's *Heinedenkmal* (Fig. 120).

(b) *Triangular and pyramidal patterns.* Free-standing sculpture is triangular in formal organization, rather than pyramidal, in proportion as a basic triangular pattern is visible only in the frontal plane, or, at the most, only from front and rear; compare the *Laocoön* group (Fig. 171) and Coustou's *Horses of Marly* on the Champs Elysées in Paris. It is pyramidal if it appears triangular from every side; *vide* the *Farnese Bull* in Naples (Fig. 170). A painting is triangular in composition if its two-dimensional surface-pattern is triangular, as in Raphael's *Madonna del Prato* (Fig. 177) and Brouwer's *The Gamesters* (Fig. 227). It becomes pyramidal if the objects or figures represented are not only plastically treated so as to appear emphatically three-dimensional, but are also grouped so as to form a representational pyramid. Leonardo da Vinci's *Madonna and Saint Anne* (Fig. 176) is pyramidal in this sense. Looking at it we feel, as we do not feel before the *Madonna del Prato*, that the group depicted would actually appear triangular if seen from any angle. In short, a statue may appear triangular only from the front or rear, but since it exists in three dimensions it can also actually *be* pyramidal and therefore *appear* triangular from every angle; whereas a painting, which exists physically only in two dimensions, can *appear* but never actually *be* pyramidal. A three-dimensional pyramid can be introduced into a painting only representationally, and the surface-pattern, considered non-representationally, must remain essentially triangular in compositional structure.

(c) *Circular, spherical, and spiral patterns.* Low reliefs are frequently circular in compositional pattern, as are many pictures; compare Michelangelo's medallion of the *Madonna and Child* in the Royal Academy (Fig. 172) and Botticelli's *Madonna of the Magnificat* (Fig. 173).[8] The higher and the more plastic the relief, the more does the circular pattern tend to become three-dimensional and spherical. Free-standing sculpture can be not only representationally but actually spherical in basic compositional pattern, as is the case in Maillol's *Seated Woman* (Fig. 126), while Renoir's *Seated Woman* (Fig. 127) illustrates the possibility of treating the representational subject-matter in painting in such a way as to create a spherical compositional pattern. Sculpture and painting differ in their use of circular and spherical patterns as they do in the use of triangular and pyramidal patterns.

Spiral compositions, which are necessarily three-dimensional (whether actually or only in representation), are so constructed that the eye is drawn upwards along a spiral path, sometimes leisurely and sometimes more violently and rapidly. Giovanni da Bologna's *Mercury* (Fig. 119) is a graceful spiral culminating in the upturned finger of the raised and twisted arm, while his more complicated *Rape of the Sabines* (Fig. 118) achieves the same effect more violently with three skillfully related figures. Titian's *Bacchus and Ariadne* (Fig. 175) is compositionally an interplay of two spirals, the one in reverse motion from the other.

This analysis of the compositional patterns in painting in conjunction with those in sculpture is in line with the Renaissance ap-

[8] A circular frame will obviously not suffice to make the internal structure of either a sculptural relief or a painting circular.

proach to the problem and has the merit of showing what the two arts have compositionally in common. It was only after the Renaissance, with Venice showing the way, that painting gradually came into its own through the discovery of the unique potentialities of its distinctive primary medium. What here primarily distinguishes painting from sculpture is the factor of color and the factor of representationally created and controlled light. So great is the potential importance of these factors that it is possible to make a pictorial composition essentially luminous, i.e., a patterned play of light and shade, or essentially "coloristic," i.e., a pattern of colored areas of different hues and intensities. In both cases the size, shape, and mutual relation of colored areas or luminous and dark passages is, of course, of major importance, but the resultant pattern is frequently not a variant of any one of the classical compositional patterns already described. It is *in essence* coloristic or luminous or a combination of the two.

Thus, many of the paintings of Matisse (Fig. 282) are not predominantly geometrical, as are those just considered, but rather compositions of carefully arranged areas of different sizes and shapes of complementary and contrasting colors and intensities. And some of Cézanne's water-colors (Fig. 285) are, compositionally considered, an ordered and dynamic play of color-impregnated light and shade. Compositions of this type do not permit of further generic classification and must be studied in their specific manifestations; but the possibility of this distinctively pictorial mode of composition must certainly be recognized.

Reference must also be made to non-representational pictorial and sculptural compositions which, though essentially geometrical rather than coloristic (or luminous), cannot be described as variants of the conventional compositional patterns mentioned above. They rely for compositional unity and articulation upon unique formal relationships which do not easily permit of further generic classification.

As in the case of architecture, these generic compositional patterns in sculpture and painting permit of infinitely rich and varied combination. Consider, by way of illustration, the intricate pattern of Watteau's *Embarkation for Cythera* (Fig. 235). The observer starts his investigation with the pronounced, yet infinitely graceful, verticality of the statue, the tree trunk, and the seated figures on the right. He next becomes conscious of the basic pictorial structure of the foreground, which is partly triangular, partly pyramidal, the courtier and his lady standing on the crest of the knoll constituting the apex of the triangle or pyramid. The horizontal axis, already visually established by the horizontality of the canvas, is pictorially intensified by the modulated line of figures stretching across the canvas. A sense of great pictorial depth and, simultaneously, of great pictorial vitality is created by the gradually initiated, leisurely movement of the eye from the right foreground, over the brow of the knoll, to the far distant mountains of Cythera. The statue at the right actually leans slightly to the right and thus expresses a preliminary state of complete rest. The movement is initiated by the main tree-trunk, which leans slightly to the left, and is intensified by the heavy diagonal branch which points us along the path of visual exploration. The two figures at the extreme right of the group are still seated; the next couple is beginning to move, the courtier helping the lady to her feet; while the third couple is already in motion, the lady glancing back, the courtier looking ahead. The remaining figures on the left are either standing still or walking up the gentle rise, but our eye is nevertheless carried irresistibly *down* the hill and out over the water to the distant mountains, and, by another path, along the dynamic spiral of hovering putti off to the faraway land of Cythera through the intervening luminous atmosphere. For the relatively naturalistic light and shade on the right have become by imperceptible degrees the shimmery, misty haze of an imagined luminosity which enhances the compositional diversity amid unity. This effect is further enriched by extraordinarily varied use of the major color triad and its derivatives and complements.

This bald enumeration of a few of the compositional components of this picture, which suffers more than most from such prosaic analysis, must suffice to indicate the literally indescribable subtlety with which the generic compositional patterns in the representational arts can be combined and modified by artistic genius.

5. *Literature*

In literature the generic compositional patterns are reasonably uniform and determinate in verse, variable and amorphous in prose. Both in prose and in verse a compositional form, such as "the lyric" or "the epic," "the essay" or "the novel," must be defined partly in terms of larger structure, partly, of typical subject-matter and manner of treatment.

Thus "the lyric" (e.g., a ballad), considered as a poem of a distinctive compositional type (and not adjectivally, as the lyrical manner of treatment) may be defined as a short literary composition (i) whose typical subject-matter is the emotional life of man both as an individual and as a conscious member of a social group, (ii) whose characteristic manner of treatment is lyrical, though it may also be reflective, and (iii) whose typical verse form tends to strongly marked regularity of meter and stanzaic organization (frequently involving a repetitive refrain). The distinction between compositional form and manner of treatment is exemplified in the difference between the song-lyric and the reflective lyric. In proportion as a lyric is simple, unreflective, and predominantly musical, written to be sung or as if to be sung, it approaches the ideal song-lyric; in proportion as it becomes thoughtful and is handled in the reflective manner, it approaches the reflective lyric.

Or again, in "the epic," (i) the characteristic subject-matter consists of the adventures of a hero of unusual fortitude and virtue who, in his character and actions, typifies the aspirations and exemplifies the culture of a nation, race, or civilization; (ii) its typical manner of treatment is metrical, both dramatic and descriptive, and temporal; and (iii) its typical form is characterized by its considerable length, its metrical and rhythmic dignity, its division into parts or books instead of stanzas, etc. More detailed formal distinctions can be made by comparing the metrical patterns of the great epics and noting the use by Homer and Virgil of a quantitative hexameter, by the author of *Beowulf* of a four-stress, alliterative line, by Milton of the five-stress iambic pentameter, etc.

Other basic compositional patterns, such as "the drama," can be analyzed in the same way in terms of typical subjects, manners of treatment, and more inclusive formal structures. Analysis of the drama, for instance, would lead to descriptive definitions of such familiar dramatic forms as tragedy, comedy, tragi-comedy, romantic comedy, social drama, farce, etc.; to an account of the tendency of the seventeenth century English dramatists to use blank verse and of the contemporary French dramatists to use a twelve-syllable rhymed Alexandrine line; to the recognition in both countries of the conventional five acts, each act containing several scenes, etc. The historical and more detailed systematic study of these and many other aspects of literary compositional patterns is the task of the literary critic and historian. The more regular these forms and the greater their literary significance, the more precise and detailed will be these investigations; the more amorphous and irregular the compositional form, on the other hand, the less profitable are such comparative analyses. Style, rhythm, dynamic movement, and other pervasive aspects of literary quality remain of prime importance, of course, in all forms of literary composition; and in every literary work, whether in verse or prose, the individual compositional pattern is necessarily a basic aspect of its artistic unity, intelligibility, and expressiveness. It is only the generic compositional patterns which become less and less easily discernible as we pass from the more regular and commonly accepted verse forms to the more discursive types of literary prose.

CHAPTER XI

THREE INTER-MEDIAL FACTORS OF FORMAL UNITY

IN the last two chapters we have been considering those types of formal organization which were entitled "intra-medial" because their nature is so largely determined by the primary media. Despite analogical similarities, the manners of treatment and the compositional patterns in the several arts differ more from medium to medium (except possibly in the case of sculpture and painting) than they agree. But the artistic form of a work of art possesses, in addition, certain inter-medial characteristics which vary less from medium to medium than from one composition to another, irrespective of the primary medium. These characteristics determine in essential ways the formal unity and structural vitality of the composition as a whole. I shall not attempt to discuss all of these inter-medial factors but shall consider three by way of illustration, namely, complexity, integration, and rhythm.

Each of these factors is present in every work of art, though more pronouncedly and effectively in some than in others. A composition in any medium must be more or less complex (or simple) in formal organization, more or less integrated (or unintegrated), and more or less rhythmic (or lacking in artistic rhythm). These factors are partly independent of one another, but they tend to vary concomitantly. For example, it is easier to achieve integration in a simple than in a complex composition, though many simple compositions are less integrated than compositions with a more complex formal pattern. Similarly, the rhythmic factor, though often pronounced in both simple and complex and both fractional and well-integrated compositions, is in some measure dependent upon the other two factors and they on it. Thus, a very simple composition does not provide the material for great rhythmic complexity and an unintegrated composition must lack rhythmic coherence; but the rhythm of a composition itself determines to a notable extent its degree of simplicity or complexity, fractionality or integration.

These three inter-medial aspects of artistic form are, in each case, partly pre-artistic, partly the product of artistic manipulation. Each has a non-artistic basis, but each achieves artistic significance only through artistic exploitation and control. Each is, moreover, a conditioning and conditioned factor in the work of art as a whole, for each is integrally related both to the medium and to the expressed content of the composition. Yet the immediate locus of artistic complexity, integration, and rhythm is neither the content nor the primary or secondary medium but rather the artistic form regarded as the artistic organization of the two media for expressive purposes. This will become apparent as we proceed.

1. *Artistic simplicity and complexity*

The complexity of a work of art is to some extent determined by the scope, complexity, and variety of the primary and secondary media actually employed. But it is also, and more significantly from the artistic point of view, a function of the degree and type of formal organization. Considered in purely quantitative terms of length or size and number of component parts, a symphony is necessarily more complex than a prelude, an epic than a sonnet, a cathedral than a private dwelling, a large and ambitious canvas than a study in charcoal. But the *artistic* complexity of these works is primarily a function of the number and variety of the *artistic* relations obtaining between its several *artistic* ingredients, ideational and elemental. Artistic complexity depends upon the extent and subtlety of the artistic organization imposed upon the media. All that is required of the latter is that they be sufficiently complex to receive such formal impress. It is this artistic complexity which the artist finds it so hard to achieve and the art-lover adequately to comprehend. A single torso (Fig. 202) is, no doubt, simpler in subject-matter and primary medium than a monumental sculptural group, but it can be treated with such imaginative power and artistic sensitivity that the finished work manifests an artistic complexity far too subtle to be appreciated by the casual observer or even to be exhausted by the repeated observations of the most sensitive critic. The same is true of many apparently simple songs, buildings, dances, paintings, and poems. Their artistic complexity is frequently greater than that of more pretentious works of inferior artistic quality.

It would be a mistake to assume that artistic complexity can, of itself, guarantee artistic excellence. A relatively simple work of art can be as "perfect"[1] as a more complex work. Indeed, the simpler

[1] Cf., below, Chap. XXII.

the project, the greater the likelihood of its being carried through with artistic success, while the more ambitious the undertaking, the more difficult it is to achieve unity of artistic form or coherence of artistic expression.

A work of art whose medium is relatively restricted and whose form is correspondingly simple can even be "great,"[2] if by greatness is meant profundity of a *restricted* insight eloquently expressed by artistic means. But when artistic greatness is more adequately defined in terms of breadth of insight as well as depth, medial complexity takes on a new significance. For since human experience is itself complex, and since the reality to which it is directed is endlessly rich in interrelations of every type, no insight can be described as truly profound which is not organic rather than atomic, and complex rather than simple. And the more far-reaching and deep-delving the insight to be expressed, the more artistically complex must be the vehicle which is adequate to the expression of this insight. Just as St. Thomas Aquinas could never have recorded his theological interpretations of God, man, and nature in a brief essay, so no small chapel, however exquisite, can make as visible as do the great Gothic cathedrals the Catholic spirit of medieval Christendom; no simple song can express what is expressed in one of Beethoven's great symphonies; no line drawing, what shines forth in a great *Crucifixion* (Figs. 214, 216); no sonnet, what is presented with such literary power in a Shakespearean tragedy or an ancient epic. Viewed in this light, complexity of artistic form *is* a necessary condition of artistic greatness.

Our present enthusiasm for simplicity, particularly in architecture, is understandable as a natural and healthy reaction against Victorian over-elaboration. But it is also a symptom of cultural impoverishment and weakness of spiritual insight. We seek to escape from the perplexities of our civilization by embracing a simplist philosophy of life. In architecture, we tend to idealize engineering and utilitarian functionalism and to worship convenience, cleanliness, and financial and engineering economy for their own sake, whereas the true artistic end of architecture is the significant expression of man's spiritual and cultural achievements. This passion for simplicity (not to be confused with a proper regard for economy of means adequate to the desired end, which is as important in art as it

[2] Cf., below, Chap. xxiv.

is in science, mathematics, politics, and business) reveals itself in our love for primitive musical rhythms, in our enthusiasm for pictorial and sculptural abstractions, and in the popularity of literary compositions which are as naïve in their lack of literary overtones as they are brutal in their power and directness.[3] This passion for simplicity bespeaks relative spiritual poverty and blindness.

Yet it would be foolish to strive for artistic complexity merely for its own sake. A complexity which is merely the product of an ebullient and undisciplined imagination, and which does not derive its artistic justification from the complexity of valid insights demanding artistic expression, is entirely devoid of artistic merit. Contemporary artists, whose work is on the whole far simpler than that of artists of other periods, must be commended for their artistic honesty. Having relatively little to say, they at least exhibit the integrity of the good craftsman in saying what they have to say with simplicity and directness. Only when new insights of greater subtlety and scope are culturally possible will the need, and with it the justification, arise for richer and more complex compositions.

2. Artistic integration

The factor of artistic integration differs from the factor of complexity in being an essential *desideratum* in all art, whatever its medium and whatever its expressive intent. It is self-evident that a work of art must possess some degree of integration and that, other things being equal, the greater the integration, the greater the artistic value of the whole. No product of artistic endeavor which is purely atomistic[4] can be called a "work of art" at all. To merit this designation its parts must be sufficiently related for the work to present itself to us as a whole and not merely as an aggregate of artistically unrelated units. Sheer atomicity is therefore an ideal limit to which a composition may approximate to its demerit but which it can never reach without excluding itself from artistic consideration. It might be argued that perfect integration is similarly an ideal limit,

[3] It also reveals itself in contemporary political and economic theory, notably in Fascist Germany and Italy; in the scientific simplism of Behaviorism and the metaphysical naïveté of Logical Positivism; and in such religious phenomena as the New Oxford Movement.

[4] The term "atomistic" is here used to signify the *complete* absence of artistic integration. A composition whose integration is merely inadequate may be described as "fractional."

valid as a point of reference but never permitting of actualization. Whatever the strength of this argument,[5] relatively few compositions give us this sense of perfect integration, and those which do are usually limited in scope, for the more ambitious the artist's creative program, the harder does he find it to weave together a multiplicity of ingredients with perfect artistic skill. It is sometimes possible to insist that the change of a single word in a sonnet, a single note in a song, or a single brush-stroke on a smaller canvas, would mar the artistic unity of the whole. It is seldom, if ever, possible to claim as much for an epic, a symphony, or a large and complicated painting.

Since artistic integration depends upon many different factors, it can, in any composition, be achieved in some respects and missed in others. For example, a statue may lack representational integration but exhibit a notable integration of non-representational three-dimensional pattern. Thus, an archaic Greek statue (Fig. 178), when compared with *Agias*, ascribed to a follower of Lysippus (Fig. 179), is very fractional in representational treatment. The head is not organically related to the neck; the neck does not flow smoothly into the shoulders, chest, and back; the arms and legs are not functionally attached to the trunk; the knees and calves are treated as relatively separate units; etc. Yet both in non-representational form and in expressed mood such statues may possess notable artistic integration. The fact that the same work can be integrated more adequately in some respects than in others explains many disagreements among critics regarding the artistic value of certain compositions. The modern enthusiast for African sculpture, for example, may value it for the integration and direct expressiveness of its artistic surface, while other critics attach greater importance to its representational fractionality and to the cultural naïveté of its expressed content.

The primary locus of artistic integration is artistic form, since the only vehicle of artistic expression is the formal organization of the media. Mere homogeneity of the primary medium or mere objective unity of the subject-matter can never *of themselves* endow a composition with artistically significant integration. A poem which is metrically unified though chaotic in subject-matter is, at least metrically, a work of art, however grave may be its interpretative deficiencies; whereas a poem dedicated to a single subject, but

[5] Cf., below, pp. 397*f*.

wholly unsuccessful in achieving unity through formal organization, lacks all artistic quality and is therefore not a work of art at all.

The greatest art is integrated at every level. The sensuous characteristics of the primary medium employed are artistically consonant; the primary and secondary media are adapted to one another; the form imposed upon the media is congenial to them and they to it; and the form itself, consisting as it does of a pattern of elemental and ideational relationships, is hierarchically organized with subordinate elements brought together in simple unitary ideas, these into more complex ideas, and these combined finally into a fused and integrated whole. A richly integrated artistic form, in turn, is the only fitting artistic vehicle for profound artistic content.

Examples of notable integration and fractionality will readily suggest themselves to the reader. Raphael's *Transfiguration* (Fig. 184), for instance, is clearly more unified in compositional pattern than his *Coronation of the Virgin* (Fig. 183), the upper and lower portions of which are hardly brought together by the upward gaze of the spectators. Some of Marin's more recent water-colors (Fig. 157) illustrate the use of artificial structural lines to achieve a unity of representational effect which other painters have achieved more indirectly and perhaps more subtly. In sculpture, "*The Tyrannicides*," i.e., *Harmodius and Aristogiton* (Fig. 181), intended as a single composition, may be contrasted with *Orestes and Electra* (Fig. 182), which, though in the same compositional pattern, is obviously more integrated. In architecture, *Alexander Hall*, on the Princeton Campus may be contrasted with *Notre Dame la Grande*, at Poitiers, in the same general style. Diaghileff's production of *L'Après-Midi d'un Faune*, as rendered by Nijinsky, is a notable example of integration in the ballet; Shakespeare's *Romeo and Juliet* possesses greater inner coherence than *Much Ado about Nothing*; while the loosely knit symphonies of Philipp Emanuel Bach are certainly less unified than Beethoven's *Fifth* or than César Franck's *D Minor Symphony*.

Artistic integration must not, of course, be identified with insipid harmony or with mere symmetry devoid of inner dynamic tension. Such easy harmony is the mark of prettiness and deserves the contempt which critics usually accord it. Artistic integration is essentially the resolution, not the denial, of inner conflict—the achievement of unity *amid* complexity, not unity in an artistic vacuum. Indeed, one way of measuring artistic achievement is in terms of how much diversity, discord, or inner conflict has been successfully welded into a state of formal integration so as to produce a rich synthetic effect. This criterion is valid, if for no other reason, because life and reality as we know them are themselves so rich in contrasts and discords. If art is to be significant it must express this aspect of our world, and it can do so only by making visible or audible, and by thus "bringing home" to us through artistic form, the dynamic complexity of human experience and of the reality which it mediates.

It should be noted, finally, that fractionality in art is never, of itself, artistically expressive. The expression of chaos cannot itself be chaotic. Fractionality is often a symptom or manifestation of disorder, but it cannot artistically express disorder. When an angry man hacks at a block of marble in a blind rage, or babbles incoherencies, or flings paint onto canvas with reckless abandon, the results will be symptomatic of his mental state. But they will not be art. To express such mental states artistically the artist must discipline both himself and his medium. He must create a work whose formal order is artistically eloquent, and not merely symptomatic, of the thought and emotion he wishes to express. In this endeavor he may be only partially successful. Parts of his composition may be expressive while other parts, or the work as a whole, fall short of perfect integration. Critical judgments of artistic integration must therefore be discriminating. Blanket approval and condemnation are seldom judicious.

3. *Artistic rhythm*

To explore exhaustively the nature and function of rhythm in the several arts would involve a thorough reexamination of all the categories of artistic form, since all art *qua* art is rhythmic in formal organization. I must content myself with a brief indication (a) of the distinction between natural and artistic rhythm, and (b) of the manner in which artistic rhythm manifests itself in the temporal and non-temporal arts respectively.

(a) If natural rhythm be defined as regular recurrence or periodic movement, nature abounds in rhythmic manifestations—in the movements of the heavenly bodies and the recurrence of the seasons, in intra-atomic activity, in the cycle of organic germination, growth, and decay, in such phenomena as breathing and the beating of the heart, etc.

Strictly speaking, natural rhythm characterizes only temporal events. It is essentially a temporal phenomenon manifesting itself in spatial movement. But the time factor may be introduced by the observer in the process of passing a number of static objects successively in review and in noting recurrent similarities and differences. Thus, a mountain range which is itself immovable may appear rhythmic to an observer who surveys the succession of rises and depressions. The wave-like undulations on the surface of a sand dune may appear rhythmic as our eye passes rapidly from ridge to ridge. Nature may therefore be said to be rhythmic in two senses—in a literal sense, when the recurrent phenomena are themselves in repetitive or cyclical motion, and metaphorically, when they are themselves static but are so ordered as to produce a rhythmic effect in us when we observe them in temporal succession.

But neither type of natural rhythm is in itself artistic, nor can it acquire an artistic character by being incorporated without change into a work of art or into artistic response. Natural rhythm, like other non-artistic phenomena, is merely part of the artist's raw material, or, in proportion as he recognizes its artistic potentialities, part of his artistic medium. In both the temporal and the non-temporal arts, natural rhythm acquires an artistic character by being artistically transformed and controlled.

Thus, the "tempo" of a musical composition is the rate of speed at which it is performed, its "beat," the regular sequence of temporal intervals; and both, regarded as purely physical phenomena, can be measured with scientific precision. Both are essential ingredients of the primary raw material of music and both enter constitutively into musical rhythm. But to acquire musical significance both must be submitted to musical control. Musical rhythm, moreover, is never *merely* a function of tempo and beat but is determined also by the musical relation of larger and smaller musical units to one another and by innumerable melodic, polyphonic, and harmonic devices which, in combination, give the composition its dynamic forward-moving momentum and its musical vitality. Similarly in the visual arts, the rhythm of a building, a statue, or a picture is based, so far as artistry can be said to depend upon the pre-artistic, on volumes and areas, shapes, colors, and "values," and upon their physical relation to one another. But the *artistic* rhythm of a colonnade, a statue, or a picture is the product of artistic organization carefully designed to lead the eye of the sensitive observer from one unit to another and thus to create in him an artistic sense of continuity and climax. Thus, a colonnade compels the eye to move horizontally from column to column; a slender column supporting an arch or vault draws the eye upwards, first rapidly and then more slowly, until it comes to rest for a moment before resuming its exploration; while the complex rhythm of an entire architectural interior or façade is the synthetic product of many minor rhythms produced by the artistic relation of vertical to horizontal, solid to void, light to shade, in reiterative and developmental organization.

Artistic rhythm, then, is a product of artistic form. But the vitality of artistic form is the product of rhythmic organization. This interdependence of form and rhythm in art can best be described by saying that rhythm is the inner life of artistic form, the source of art's expressive vitality. A composition which lacks artistic rhythm fails to awaken and hold our interest; the more vital it is, the more powerfully are we impelled to explore it; and the more we sense its rhythmic sweep, the more unerringly do we follow the artist's lead until we finally achieve a single embracing intuition of it as a vital artistic whole.[6]

(b) The two types of natural rhythm already described, i.e., the "actual" or "literal" rhythm of natural motion and the "empathic" or "metaphorical" rhythm of static phenomena which appear rhythmic as a result of empathic response, have their artistic analogues in the "artistic" rhythm of the temporal and non-temporal arts respectively. A composition in one of the temporal arts is apprehended as being itself in movement, and its rhythm as being an integral aspect of this objective temporal succession, whereas a

[6] The term "rhythmic" is sometimes restricted to certain specific types of artistic rhythm or to its more pronounced artistic manifestations. Metrical verse is thus occasionally said to be rhythmic and literary prose to lack rhythm, or music with a pronounced beat to be intrinsically more rhythmic than music in which the measured beat is less overt. This restricted use of the term is to be deplored. Artistic rhythm should be defined generically to include every type and degree of rhythmic manifestation in art. For only if artistic rhythm is thus defined can its essential contribution to artistic vitality be appreciated. Its more specific manifestations in the several arts and genres can then be distinguished, and the various degrees of rhythmic intensity in various compositions differentiated. All art is rhythmic in some sense and to some degree, even though rhythmic vitality manifests itself very differently in different arts and genres, and far more powerfully in some compositions than in others. Cf. Frank Jewett Mather, Jr., *Concerning Beauty* (Princeton: Princeton University Press, 1935), chap. IV.

composition in the non-temporal arts is apprehended as being itself static and unchanging, and its rhythm as being a function of its immobile organization. In nature, a running brook is seen to be itself in motion, a quiet pool, at rest; in art, a musical composition or a poem, as heard, or a dance, as seen, are apprehended as running themselves off in time, whereas a building, a statue, or a picture appear to be unchanging and at rest. Hence, the artistic rhythm of the former possesses a type of objectivity which the latter does not possess; the rhythmic character of the non-temporal arts, though dictated by the artistic form of the composition, can be apprehended only with the aid of empathic response to an objectively static pattern.

This basic difference between the temporal and non-temporal arts is of great importance for artistic creation. For in the temporal arts the creative artist must forever keep in mind the fact that the several parts of his composition must be apprehended in objective temporal sequence *before* the composition can be intuited as a whole, whereas, in the spatial arts, the larger outlines of the whole present themselves to the observer *at the start*, and the subsequent exploration of the parts is oriented to a continued (and progressively enriched) apprehension of the whole. In the temporal arts the auditor must therefore be made to rely on his memory of what has gone before, if, at the conclusion, he is to be able to apprehend the whole *as* a whole. This necessitates a studied use of repetition and recapitulation based on a careful consideration of the auditor's psychological aptitudes, i.e., his ability to assimilate new material, to remember what has already been presented, and to pass from one experience to another. The artistic problem of the architect, sculptor, and painter, in contrast, is so to construct the whole as to make possible an initial unified apprehension which, as the several parts are examined with greater and greater care, is not progressively negated but rather articulated and intensified. In the non-temporal arts, in short, artistic apprehension (though itself as temporal a process as in the temporal arts) starts with the whole and keeps returning to the whole while the parts are successively explored, whereas, in the temporal arts, the parts are apprehended first in the order of *their* successive presentation, and the structure of the whole comes only gradually into view as the composition unfolds itself in time, so that the entire composition stands revealed only at the end of the performance and thus only in retrospect.

This difference between the temporal and non-temporal arts, itself a function of their respective primary media, dictates a different type of artistic rhythm in the two cases. In the former, the rhythmic factor is physically more actual and coercive. In music, for example, the auditor has no control over the order in which the successive tones are heard, nor can he, as auditor, control the tempo, i.e., the rate of speed at which the composition is played. Even the performer should obey the instructions of the composer and render the composition in the order and at the tempo directed in the score. And since these factors enter constitutively into the artistic rhythm of the composition, this rhythm is actualized in the composition itself and is rooted in a temporal sequence as objective and coercive as that of any natural phenomenon.

In the non-temporal arts, in contrast, the order and rate of exploration is not dictated with such coercive finality. We can, at least theoretically, approach a building from any angle, explore its several parts in any order, and determine for ourselves how rapidly or slowly to pass from one portion to another. Its rhythmic character, moreover, is metaphorical rather than physically actual. Columns and arches do not actually "soar"; a colonnade is physically as immobile as a blank wall; the sculptural or pictorial representation of movement is not itself in motion, nor is a "dynamic" pattern of colored areas physically less static than a single colored area. The rhythmic factor in these arts is partially a product of sensitive artistic response, which in turn, is the artistic variant of pre-artistic empathic and associative responses to visible phenomena themselves static and immobile.

The task of the creative artist differs correspondingly in the two cases. In the temporal arts he must so control the rhythmic character of the successive portions of the composition as to facilitate their reconstruction in the auditor's memory so that, at the end of the performance, he may possess a cumulative impression of the several parts in their relation to one another and so achieve a sense of the rhythmic character of the whole. In the non-temporal arts his task is rather to stimulate in the spectator the requisite artistically controlled empathic or associative response, by making the composition as a whole arouse in him at the outset a sense of its larger rhythmic unity which is then confirmed, intensified, and enriched by the subsequent more or less leisurely exploration of the several artistic units and relations.

But it would be a great mistake to overemphasize this important difference between the temporal and non-temporal arts, or to overlook what they have in common and what is common to all artistic response to a work of art as such.

In the first place, all artistic apprehension is itself a temporal process in the sense that it "takes time" for a work of art in any medium really to be explored and assimilated. It takes time really to "see" a building, statue, or painting, and it takes far more time really to assimilate a musical composition, a dance, or a poem than is required for a single reading or rendition. Adequate artistic comprehension involves a time-consuming exploration of the parts in their relation to one another and to the whole, and of the whole in its complex and synthetic structure. This fact is of greater artistic importance than the fact, just discussed, that in the temporal arts the parts present themselves to us *seriatim* and the whole only as a cumulative effect, whereas, in the spatial arts, apprehension of the whole tends to precede exploration of the parts. For in *both* cases *adequate* artistic intuition comes only at the *end* of a more or less *prolonged* period of analysis and synthesis. No poem, dance, or musical composition of genuine artistic merit can be grasped with adequacy, even by the most sensitive critic, in a single presentation. It must be read, seen, or heard again and again and its every detail studied in its relation to other details and to the whole, if a true sense of the complex whole is to be achieved. Similarly, no significant building, statue, or picture can possibly be understood in all its subtle complexity at a single glance. Here too the parts must be studied and digested in their relation both to each other and to the larger whole. In the light of what is thus ultimately required of the observer in both cases, the difference in order of investigation comes to assume a relatively minor artistic importance.[7]

In the second place, the skillful architect, sculptor, or painter controls the order and even the tempo of our artistic exploration in a manner somewhat analogous to the control exercised by the artist in the temporal arts, though less coercively and in a less uniform and

[7] The fact that it takes an appreciable time to approach a building, to walk around it, to enter it, and to examine its interior, and the additional fact that the exterior must be viewed before the interior is seen and that the exterior and the interior cannot be seen simultaneously, makes architecture more of a "temporal" art than either sculpture or painting. Some of the characteristics of the temporal arts are thus applicable to architecture in a unique way.

all-embracing fashion. He does so mainly by suggestion, although at times this suggestion resembles a command in its insistence and is unmistakable even to the relatively insensitive layman.

A well-planned building, for instance, has its approach carefully laid out in such a way that our first view of it as a whole shall be as effective as possible (Figs. 68-71). Our successive impressions of it as we draw nearer are similarly controlled by the approach and the surrounding landscaping. We are guided by walks and by larger traversable areas in our exploration of its exterior from various angles. These pointed suggestions may, of course, be ignored. We can sometimes, for example, get our first view of a building from an adjoining building, or from an aeroplane, i.e., from a perspective not contemplated by the architect. Photographs taken from such unusual angles are often arresting in their distortion of normal architectural perspective, but they are correspondingly misleading in their interpretation of the architectural structure and rhythm of the building itself. (Comparable infelicities are as possible in the temporal arts.) The architect also guides us in our exploration of the interior by indicating the main entrance and by such devices as aisles, halls, and staircases. This guidance is again not as coercive in most cases as is the inexorable temporal sequence in the temporal arts; yet frequent indication is given of where to start, where to go next, where to hurry on and where to pause, etc., and these indications will not be missed or ignored by the sensitive observer.

The same type of guidance is evident in many pictures and statues. Most pictures have one or more "points of entrance," "lines of movement," and "centers of interest," all of which help to determine their rhythmic structure. The competent observer is thus led into a picture, guided from unit to unit, here invited to linger and there to move more rapidly, frequently to retrace his steps at a faster or slower tempo, etc., until every detail has been thoroughly explored. Similarly, a skillfully composed statue draws the eye to certain points of interest and guides it from one artistic unit to another. It is only through obedience to these artistic instructions that the rhythmic character of a picture or a statue can assert itself.

In Poussin's *Et in Arcadia Ego* (Fig. 136), for instance, it is only because the eye is quickly caught by the white upright figure of the shepherdess, passes from her to the first and then to the second shepherd, pauses for a moment at the tomb upon which their gaze is fastened, and is then drawn upward to the trees and horizontally from right to left along their boughs, that the rhythm of this subordinate repetitive idea is perceived and felt to echo, in reverse, the stronger rhythm of the standing figures. Similarly, it is only when the eye, focused upon the seated figure in the right foreground, is quickly guided by the powerful curves around the corner and back into the center of the picture, where it is invited to make a second, more leisurely, and more deviating journey, that other rhythmic patterns become evident. Here too the guidance offered is more psychologically and artistically than physically compelling. But guidance is provided analogous to that of which we are so acutely aware in the temporal arts.[8]

The *expressive significance* of formal complexity, integration, and rhythm, meanwhile, is evident only when artistic form is regarded as the vehicle for artistic content, and when the question is raised as to what type of artistic content can achieve artistic expression in the several primary media.

[8] Cf. the analysis of Watteau's *Embarkation for Cythera* (Fig. 235), above, pp. 209-10.

PART III

ARTISTIC CONTENT

CHAPTER XII

ART AS AN EXPRESSIVE VEHICLE

1. Art possesses cognitive significance

NO attempt has been made thus far to formulate a comprehensive definition of artistic content or to analyze its distinguishing characteristics. I have merely described it as "that which finds expression *via* artistic form in an artistic medium." This general description indicates (i) that the content of art is not wholly to be identified with its form or with its medium, and (ii) that it is functionally related to both. But it fails to explain the crucial term "expression," and it tells us nothing about the positive character of artistic content or the distinctive types of content which art is able to express.

The central thesis which I shall try to defend is that, in a work of art, (a) *reality* is (b) *interpreted*, and (c) *expressed in a distinctive way.*

(a) The true artist, I shall argue, has never conceived of art as an escape from reality into an ivory tower. He has attempted to come to grips with reality in his own way, and the more serious the artist, the more resolute has been this attempt. Only the "aesthete" has subscribed to the thesis of "art for art's sake"; the motto of the conscientious artist has been "art for life's sake." In attempting to apprehend reality in his own way the artist resembles the scientist and the philosopher, the moralist and the theologian. Art is one among other significant human enterprises, and, like them, derives its significance[1] from the artist's preoccupation with what man accepts as real. To ignore this basic characteristic of art is to do violence to its historical character and to rob it of much of its human import.

(b) But the true artist has never striven merely to duplicate reality or to copy it with slavish fidelity. He has recognized the need for interpretation. From primitive times to the present creative artists have offered us in their art a series of interpretations of human life and of man's physical and spiritual environment, and the critics in

[1] The term "significance" has a dual meaning, i.e., (i) importance or value, and (ii) reference or signification. My thesis is that the significance (importance) of art is essentially conditioned by its signification of (or reference to) something other than itself, though such reference does not of itself suffice to endow the work of art with value.

the main critical traditions have emphasized the importance of this interpretative factor.

(c) Art differs from science, morality, and religion in its generic approach to, and interpretation of, reality. Its subject-matter, broadly considered, embraces every *kind* of reality known to man. But only certain *aspects* of reality interest the artist; his approach to it, like that of other specialists, is selective. Unlike the scientist, he apprehends reality in terms of individuality and value, not in terms of abstract generality, and his goal is not the mere conceptual apprehension of truth for its own sake but rather the comprehension of reality in its relation to man as a normative and purposive agent. On the other hand, art resembles science and differs from morality and religion in being essentially contemplative. It is not the primary function of art as such to initiate action or to induce spiritual commitment. Hence, though art does, like science, concern itself primarily with universals rather than mere particulars, it does so in its own peculiar way, and though it makes an essential contribution to moral and religious insight, it refrains, at its best, from every form of propaganda. Furthermore, the artist "expresses" his distinctive insights in a distinctive way which differs in essential respects from the way in which nature "manifests" her character to us and also from the way in which the scientist "formulates" his apprehensions of natural order.

A work of art may accordingly be re-defined as a distinctive expression, in a distinctive medium, and by means of a distinctive type of formal organization, of a distinctive type of interpretation of man's experience and of the real world to which this experience is oriented.

Since the artist's attitude and objective, his mode of expression, and the content of his art are all intimately related as functions of a single organic process, their analysis and exposition raises all the difficulties incidental to the analysis of any organic situation. Any order of exposition is in a sense arbitrary, since no one aspect of the total situation can be fully understood prior to an understanding of other functionally related aspects. I have chosen, on purely pragmatic grounds, to examine first the *differentiae* of the artist's generic approach to reality (Chapters XIII and XIV), next, the distinguishing characteristics of artistic expression (Chapter XV), and, finally, various generic types of artistic content as exemplified in the six major arts (Chapters XVI to XIX). Since this investigation will presuppose the expressiveness of art, a word of explanation should be offered in support of this presupposition.

2. *Art is essentially expressive*

If the true artist seeks to express in his art an interpretation of some aspect of the real world of human experience, every genuine work of art, however slight and in whatever medium, must have *some* subject-matter. It is not *merely* an aesthetically satisfying organization of sensuous particulars. The entire history of the fine arts and literature, from the earliest times on record down to the present, offers overwhelming evidence that art in the various media has arisen from the artist's desire to express and communicate to his fellows some pervasive human emotion, some insight felt by him to have a wider relevancy, some interpretation of a reality other than the work of art itself in all its specificity.

The history of ornament may be taken as a test case, since ornament is frequently non-representational and since it appears in every society and culture. To the untutored eye, an ornament is nothing but a more or less agreeable pattern which reveals nothing and signifies nothing beyond itself. Yet a study of the types of ornament characteristic of any specific culture and period tells a different story.[2] An ornament which is indigenous to a culture, or which, though borrowed, has been assimilated by a culture, is as highly stylized as any self-contained work of art in any of the major artistic media. Now style can, as we shall see,[3] be defined only by reference to the point of view adopted by the artist towards his subject-matter. Style is a function of artistic expression; a wholly inexpressive object is devoid of style. To admit the stylistic character of artistic ornament, accordingly, is to admit its expressive character, hence its artistic content, and so the fact that even an ornament is, in its own limited way, a revealing cultural document. The reader is referred, for empirical evidence of the way in which ornament can express the spirit and temper of a culture, to illustrations of ornamental designs characteristic of different cultures (Figs. 1-3, 8, 9).

But, granting that all art is in essence expressive, it might be argued that what it expresses is not an interpretation of objective reality but merely the unique personality and point of view of the individual artist, or even, as it has sometimes been urged, merely

[2] Cf. A. Riegl, *Stilfragen* (Berlin: Georg Siemens, 1893).
[3] Cf., below, Chap. XXI.

the artist's passing mood or fancy. Is this interpretation of art tenable?

To limit the subject-matter of art to the artist's fugitive mental states divorced from his more enduring personality and outlook is to revert to a type of atomistic psychology now happily outmoded. It is recognized today that human consciousness is not a mere aggregate of unrelated mental states, but that, save in extreme pathological cases, consciousness is at each instant a function of a more enduring self, however personal identity be defined. Selfhood transcends psychological atomicity and implies a vital continuity of experience, i.e., the influence of an experienced past and an anticipated future upon each present moment of awareness. Consciousness is a function of a "self" persisting in time as a relatively enduring pattern of memories, habits, impulsions, etc. Every mental state must therefore be regarded as pertaining to, and in its own way reflecting, the character of a self which maintains its identity amid the flux of inner and outer change. "Self-expression" in art is therefore, even in its most restricted forms, the expression of more than a passing mood, idea, or impulse. It must to some extent express the artist's enduring personality.

But every human being, and therefore every individual artist, resembles other human beings and reflects in his own way his physical and cultural environment. As Leibniz would express it, man mirrors the world of which he is a part. Like other finite creatures (but more completely, because of his complex nature) man transcends himself in being what he is, and the richer his personality, the more richly does he reflect his total environment. When, therefore, an artist expresses *himself* in his art, he simultaneously and necessarily expresses certain aspects of the *environment* that has formed him, and the more spiritually significant his personality and outlook, the more does his art reveal the forces which have made him what he is. Thus even the doctrine of art as self-expression implies that the subject-matter of art is, in any concrete instance, not merely the enduring self of the creative artist but as much of the objective world as the artist has assimilated in the development of his own personality.

Finally, to assert that artists throughout the ages have been concerned merely to express what uniquely characterized their individual personalities is grossly to misread the historical record and the empirical evidence at our disposal. The more petty the artist and the more egoistic, the more anxious has he been, no doubt, to exhibit himself to the world as a unique individual. Instances are on record of artists so absorbed in their own inner states that their chief desire was to indulge in autobiographical self-revelation. But the more significant the artist, the stronger has been his conscious or unconscious preoccupation with some aspect of universal human experience and the more compelling has been his desire to employ artistic form as a vehicle not for mere self-expression but for what he has felt to be a true and revealing interpretation of some aspect of his environment.

The critical tradition in western Europe, to say nothing of similar traditions in other cultures such as the Chinese, supports this interpretation of the artist's motives and achievements. From Greek and Roman times, through the Middle Ages and the Renaissance, and down to the modern period most of the critics who have achieved distinction and whose names have endured have been those who were not content to bask in the pleasing "aesthetic surface" of art, but who sought rather to delve beneath this surface to the interpretations of human life and objective reality which, they believed, specific works of art expressed. It is only in periods of cultural and spiritual decadence, periods characterized by a loss of inner assurance in spiritual values, that the "aesthete" (in the narrow and derogatory sense) has made his appearance and proclaimed that art is *reducible* to aesthetically agreeable patterns of sound and color and is therefore in essence an escape from reality, mere play, an object of aesthetic delight and nothing more.

It is of course essential that the aesthetic surface of a work of art should satisfy the strictly aesthetic criterion. It is also true that beauty, and beauty alone, is the proper object of "pure" aesthetic taste, and that "pure" taste, as Kant so cogently argued, is man's aesthetic response to this quality and to nothing else. What must be combated in an age of cultural instability such as ours is the attempt to *reduce* art to mere formal beauty and to consider the production and enjoyment of such beauty not only as an end in itself (which it certainly is) but as the only end, or even the chief end, of art. Just as the true scientist, however great his enthusiasm for logical consistency, is never content merely to play with concepts and propositions according to the rules of logic, but seeks to use his reason and his logic for the attainment of scientific truth, so the true artist, though enchanted with the beauty which he and others can occasion, is never willing to be a mere creator of beauty but always strives to express, in terms of beauty, his interpretation of a wider reality and a richer experience. And just as scientific truth involves not merely logical consistency but also correspondence to the real world of spatio-temporal events, so too does artistic truth demand not only the presence of formal beauty but the expression of a true understanding of certain aspects of human experience and reality. The doctrine of "art for art's sake" has at times, as at the end of the nineteenth century, been of great value as a reminder that art is not a mere reproduction of reality, that subject-matter and artistic content are not identical, and that aesthetic objects in general, and works of art in particular, are distinguished from other objects of awareness by their aesthetic surface. But this has never been regarded by the main critical traditions as an adequate formulation of the nature of art at its best.

Philosophers of art have, as a rule, agreed with the critics in this respect. Plato never succeeded in formulating a clear and adequate account of art as an expressive vehicle. But his moralistic strictures in the *Republic* demonstrate his belief that both music and literature affect man more profoundly than they could if they were mere exemplifications of beauty, in the *Phaedrus* and the *Symposium* he explicitly recognizes art's expressive power. Aristotle, standing on his master's shoulders, recorded his interpretation of the drama in the famous dictum that "poetry is something more philosophic and of graver import than history"[4]—a dictum which, applicable as it is to all art, raises art far above the category of the merely aesthetically agreeable. Kant isolated pure taste and pure beauty in order to determine their *differentiae*, and it is noteworthy that his best examples of "free" (as opposed to "adherent") beauty are flowers and sea-shells, which are not works of art at all, and wall-papers and arabesques, which, in comparison with other forms of art, are limited in expressed content. It is also noteworthy that Kant held no very high regard for mere formal beauty as such. He valued natural beauty chiefly as "the symbol of the morally good,"[5] and denied spiritual significance to art which merely satisfies formal

[4] *Aristotle on the Art of Poetry*, tr. with commentary I. Bywater (Oxford: The Clarendon Press, 1909), p. 27. The reference is to the *Poetics*, IX, 1451 b, 5-6.

[5] *Kant's Critique of Judgement*, tr. J. H. Bernard (London: Macmillan, 1914), p. 250.

aesthetic criteria.[6] Hegel, unlike Kant, was from the first primarily concerned with art rather than with beauty in and for itself, and was anxious that his analysis of art should do justice to the great masterpieces of Oriental and Western culture. He was accordingly led to define art in all the several media as being in essence expressive of the artist's interpretation of reality itself in one or other of its manifestations.

More recently, we are indebted to Croce for a renewed insistence on the expressiveness of art. His formula, "art = intuition = expression," is at once too simple and too comprehensive to be wholly acceptable. But it clearly indicates his recognition of the fact that art has a subject-matter which the artist seeks to interpret. The expressiveness of art has been recognized by other contemporary philosophers of art with varying degrees of emphasis—by Bergson and Alexander, Dewey and Parker, and even by Santayana, especially in his critical essays on literature. Despite several dissenting voices, the general verdict of philosophers through the centuries may thus be said to have sustained the judgment of the critics and the conviction and practice of the creative artists themselves, namely, that art has been and should be essentially expressive of the artist's interpretation of reality and human life.

As we have seen, the several arts differ in their characteristic subject-matter, and these differences are dictated by their respective primary media. But despite these differences, the arts are alike in their generic approach to their subject-matter. The generic subject-matter of art, in turn, is not distinctive at all; it is identical with that of ethics and theology, science and philosophy. The artist is preoccupied with the same world of objective existence and the same human experiences which concern the other cognitive disciplines. He merely approaches this world and these experiences in a distinctive manner and with a distinctive goal in view. This approach and goal must now be examined with some care.

[6] *Ibid.*, p. 214. "If the beautiful arts are not brought into more or less close combination with moral Ideas, . . . they then serve only as a distraction. . . ."

CHAPTER XIII

THE ARTIST'S APPROACH TO HIS SUBJECT-MATTER

THE artist approaches reality in an attitude of "artistic contemplation" which can best be described by contrasting it with the attitudes of "active participation and commitment" and of "dispassionate and impersonal inquiry." Both as a biological organism and as a human being, man must repeatedly commit himself to some specific course of action. As a pure scientist, man investigates nature in a spirit of dispassionate research. The artist's characteristic attitude resembles, yet differs from, each of these. It is a kind of Aristotelian mean between passionate participation and dispassionate inquiry.

1. The attitudes of active participation and of scientific detachment

Participation and commitment are necessitated by man's dependence upon his physical, social, and spiritual environment. As a normative agent immersed in a temporal process, he cannot avoid action and commitment. He is forever being confronted with alternatives between which he must choose, and each decision entails its own inescapable consequences.

As a physical being he must adapt himself to his physical environment if he is to continue to exist. He must conform to natural necessity and, so far as possible, adapt physical objects and events to his own needs. His behavior is determined partly by reflexes, instincts, and habits, partly by reflection and deliberate decision. But whatever the method of adaptation, biological survival involves specific behavior in specific situations, and the results of such behavior are irrevocable. Even at the level of biological existence a non-committal neutrality is impossible.

As a social being man is under a similar necessity to act and to abide by the consequences of his actions. If he is to flourish in society he must adapt himself to an economic and social order. He is daily confronted with concrete situations which make decisions unavoidable. He cannot merely be a spectator; in one way or another he must participate in the life of his community and accept the results of his social behavior.

But man is also a being sensitive to moral values and capable of a religious response to the supernatural. If he is to realize his humanity he must acknowledge the value of human personality and recognize moral rights and duties. This again involves a series of concrete decisions whose moral implications are far-reaching and inescapable. Every known religion, in turn, insists on the necessity for active spiritual commitment. And even the atheist and the agnostic must, in the very act of disbelief or of suspended judgment, adopt a credal attitude towards ultimate reality.

It is clear, then, that at every level of human experience adaptation to environment, participation in the temporal process, and positive commitment are unavoidable. Timeless disembodied spirits, if such there be, may be exempt from this necessity and may be able to contemplate eternal essence with perfectly non-committal impartiality. But the temporal process is for us an inescapable fact; we are at every instant confronted, whether we like it or not, with the either/or of finite existence. Commitment need not be conscious or deliberate; many of our responses are determined by forces of which we are quite unaware. We can also deliberately refuse to consider alternatives, and let events mould us as they will. But even this conscious decision not to make a choice is a commitment. Thus participation and commitment are unavoidable in all practical affairs, in the pursuit of happiness, and in the realization of moral and religious ends.

As a human being the scientist cannot, of course, ignore the social and moral implications of his own inquiries. And even as a pure scientist he is committed to the search for truth. He must assume the responsibility for choosing to investigate some particular set of natural phenomena, and during these investigations he must repeatedly exercise choice in the selection and interpretation of observable evidence. Even the scientific enterprise is a human enterprise subject to the conditions of finite existence.

Yet the pursuit of scientific truth for its own sake is characterized by a kind of objectivity and dispassionate aloofness which distinguishes it clearly from man's practical and spiritual pursuits. The scientific attitude is one of temporary detachment from utilitarian and spiritual concerns. The scientist transforms himself, so far as possible, into an impersonal observer, intent on the discovery of truth *irrespective of its human import.* He makes every effort to suppress all scientifically irrelevant emotions[1] and to ignore, at least for the time being, moral and religious considerations, and he is not satisfied until he has apprehended his data and formulated his conclusions in quantitative terms. He thus partially mirrors in his own attitude the regularity, impersonality, and disregard for human hopes and fears which natural processes, the object of his investigations, themselves exhibit.

2. The attitude of artistic contemplation

The attitude of the artist mediates between that of an "agent" entering into life as an active participant, and that of an "observer," or disinterested spectator, refraining from practical commitment.[2] His first reaction to his complex environment resembles that of the common man, save that his perceptions are more catholic and acute and his emotional responses more intense. But from the very outset he participates in the generic forms of human experience primarily through his imagination, and this participation is motivated primarily by a desire to contemplate rather than to achieve the ends which other men are intent on achieving. In these respects his attitude resembles that of the scientific inquirer rather than that of the man of affairs, the sensualist, the moralist, or the religious worshipper. Yet, despite this comparative aloofness, the artist is not interested in truth merely for its own sake, irrespective of its human import, but in the significance of things for human life. He views reality *sub specie humanitatis.*

However powerful the artist's imagination, it cannot function *in vacuo.* It must be provided with materials to work with. Furthermore, if the artist is to achieve in his art a significant interpretation of human experience and of the objective world, he must establish first-hand contact with his subject-matter. He does so in two ways—partly through immediate participation and partly through sympathetic observation. He participates in life by actually experiencing jealousy and fear, bereavement and good fortune, and the like. His observations, in turn, will be productive of real understanding only

[1] The emotions immediately associated with scientific inquiry itself (e.g., fear of failure, joy in success, anger at scientific dishonesty, etc.) are integral to the search for scientific truth.

[2] In Baumgarten's terms, aesthetic "approval" mediates between practical "desire" and scientifically objective "contemplation."

if his own experiences are sufficiently rich and varied to provide a clue to the qualitative character of what observation reveals. A man who has never experienced friendship cannot hope to understand this relationship merely on the basis of observation.

The youthful artist, however, is apt to exaggerate the importance of living through the experiences he wishes to interpret. The weaker the artist's re-constructive imagination, the greater is his dependence upon autobiographical material; the more powerful his imagination, the greater is his ability to extend and develop imaginatively his own necessarily partial and fragmentary experiences. Indeed, too whole-hearted participation in certain types of experience precludes participation in, and comprehension of, other types. No man can be both chaste and lascivious. Shakespeare could not possibly have been all the characters in his plays, or experienced at first hand all that he made these characters experience. His own experience must indeed have been extraordinarily varied. He must have been able to find in himself, as latent tendencies, the impulses and dispositions which his characters possess to a marked degree. But he must have observed far more than he was actually able to participate in during a single lifetime, and what he observed he was able to interpret with unusual imaginative power.

The artist's imagination not only supplements his first-hand experience; it gives him an insight into human experience *superior* to that afforded by first-hand participation, however vivid or intense the latter may be. This is Proust's central thesis—that life is truly comprehended only when re-lived in recollection.[3] The more poignant the concrete situation, the more powerfully is the experiencing agent driven to act and feel rather than to reflect. Action and passion, not comprehension of what the situation signifies, is the dominant motif of first-hand participation in human affairs. The agent is too absorbed in his own joy or sorrow, too fascinated by the passing sensation, too deeply concerned over the practical implications of his conduct, fully to appreciate the complex and subtle nature of his own emotions, sensations, and volitions. At the moment, he cannot introspect with lucidity and candor. And even after he has lived through the experience in question and is free to direct his attention to the nature of his own psychological processes and the objective situations which occasioned them he will be unable, unless he is an

[3] Cf. Wordsworth's "emotion recollected in tranquillity."

artist, to reconstruct them with sympathetic insight. His normal impulse is to forget the past and to attend only to the present and the future, and if he does indulge in recollection his memories will usually be a mere uninterpreted re-living of certain fragments of his past.

The artist, in contrast, knows how to view life with an objectivity akin to (though not identical with) the objectivity of scientific apprehension, and, simultaneously, with an immediacy, warmth, and intimacy akin to (though not identical with) that which distinguishes first-hand participation. Because his approach to life is primarily imaginative, he escapes the blinding effect of immediate participation and commitment. And because it is imaginative and human, and not merely ratiocinative and impersonal, he apprehends what the scientist as such can never apprehend; he escapes the frigidity of conceptual abstraction and impersonal calculation. The common man is too close to life to see it in perspective without subjective prejudice. The scientist is too far removed from life to comprehend its human quality and import. Only the artist is able to mediate between these extremes and to view life as a human being, yet not merely as an individual agent; with passionate intensity, yet with dispassionate lucidity; intimately and with due regard to the idiosyncratic, yet also from a more universal and catholic point of view. In this sense the artist is *par excellence* a humanist. Through his reliance upon an informed and disciplined imagination he is able, as no one else, to apprehend the man in men and to speak to us with a profoundly human impersonality.

Bullough's well-known doctrine of "psychical distance" is in essence an account of "artistic objectivity," and, as developed by him, is equally applicable to the artist's apprehension of reality and to our aesthetic enjoyment of art and nature. He points out that too great "nearness," that is, too natural and immediate a response, on the one hand, and, on the other, too great "distance" or aloofness, both destroy the possibility of genuine aesthetic apprehension. The psychical distance requisite to effective aesthetic insight is a mean between these extremes. Though it can be somewhat increased or diminished without being destroyed, there is an ideal "distance" for each individual in any concrete situation. This applies to the artist in his imaginative apprehension of reality. It applies also to our response to his art. Here the requisite "distance" is dictated by the work of art itself. And it applies, finally, to our aesthetic response to nature. In such response we must achieve the requisite objectivity without assistance. If we are to apprehend nature aesthetically we must adopt towards it, on our own initiative, the artist's attitude. The reader is referred to Bullough's masterly discussion[4] of "psychical distance" for an elaboration of what I have entitled "artistic objectivity" and "artistic contemplation."

[4] Edward Bullough, "'Psychical Distance' as a Factor in Art and an Aesthetic Principle," *British Journal of Psychology*, Vol. V (1912), pp. 87-118.

CHAPTER XIV

THE GOAL OF ARTISTIC COGNITION

NOT only does the artist's generic attitude differ from that of the scientist; he seeks to attain and express a different kind of insight from that which the scientist strives to attain and formulate. I will discuss the nature and criteria of artistic *versus* scientific truth in a later chapter. Here I am merely concerned with the cognitive goal of artistic endeavor.

Art and science focus upon different aspects of reality and human experience, and the farther they advance, the more pronounced the difference between them becomes. But they resemble one another in being, each in its own way, extensions of man's normal every-day cognitive experience. Both the scientist and the artist not only start with the apprehensions of the common man; they are at pains not to lose contact with the world of ordinary sense-perception. I must accordingly preface my analysis of artistic and scientific insight with a brief summary of certain familiar characteristics of ordinary sense-perception and its objects.

1. Perceptual and non-perceptual awareness

The "world" of sense-perception is characterized by both change and permanence, novelty and order, similarity and difference. It is a spatio-temporal world of objects and events[1] which possess a relatively enduring identity amid ceaseless external and internal change. Every object, regarded as a relatively self-contained entity, enjoys a certain degree of permanence and endures as "the same" object for a certain length of time. But even while it endures it is subject to continual alteration, so is its environment, and so, consequently, are its relations to its environment. Again, the visible world manifests both novelty and order, recurrence and the emergence of the new. Every object and event is unique in certain respects, and new types of objects and events occasionally make their appearance. Yet the new always appears in a more or less orderly

[1] No philosophically rigorous distinction between objects and events is here intended, but merely the "common-sense" distinction between relatively enduring perceptual objects and transitory happenings.

manner and resembles the old and the familiar in certain respects. These resemblances and differences vary in importance, some possessing (within any specific frame of reference) major significance and others appearing as trivial. Every classification of perceptual objects must be based on what are regarded as crucial generic similarities and differences, and under them are subsumed more specific and less important variations. I shall attempt to describe these characteristics of the perceptual world in terms of the concepts of "universality" and "individuality" because these concepts will be found to be particularly helpful in the analysis of artistic content.

A "universal" may be defined as a recurrent quality, character, state, or relation which manifests itself, or might manifest itself, in two or more individuals and on two or more occasions. So defined, the term "universal" is applicable to the common characteristics not only of perceptual objects and events but of all possible objects of apprehension, and I shall presently want to use it in this wider sense. A perceptual universal may be described as a recurrent quality, character, state, or relation by virtue of which two or more perceptual objects or events resemble or differ from one another, whether actually or potentially. Perceptual universals are of many different types. Some are sensuous qualities, such as redness, sweetness, and smoothness; some are relational, as signified by the words above, below, far, and near; some are quantitative and invite measurement, e.g., size, volume, weight, and intensity; some are natural or man-made types, such as animal and dog, tree and cypress, table and chair; some are types of processes or characteristics of processes, such as growth and vitality, energy and momentum; etc. There is no need to attempt an exhaustive classification of these universals, if indeed such a classification is possible. Nor need we explore the many ways in which universals are related to one another, though they are clearly not mutually exclusive, animality, for instance, being definable only in terms of other universals such as color, size, weight, and life. Nor, finally, need we raise the vexing philosophical problem of whether or not universals in general, and perceptual universals in particular, have any reality apart from their spatio-temporal manifestations. Plato, we know, tended to hypostatize them in his doctrine of Ideas and to endow them with a reality independent of and superior to the reality of objects and events in space and time, while nominalists have gone to the other extreme and have sought to identify them with the words which we use to describe our experiences and to articulate our ideas. We can avoid this controversy by conceiving of universals simply as recurrent aspects of the objects of human awareness. As such they are as "objective" as are the objects which they qualify.[2]

An "individual" may be defined as a unique temporal or spatio-temporal embodiment of a more or less complex pattern of universals.[3] So defined, every individual has the following characteristics.

(a) It has two basic ingredients, that of universality and that of particularity or specificity. It "participates" in, or manifests, certain universal traits, that is, it possesses certain characteristics which it shares, or might share, with other individuals. Thus a red rose participates in such universals as "flower," "rose," and "redness," and therefore resembles other individual flowers, roses, and red objects. But it is a unique spatio-temporal embodiment of these universals, that is, it is characterized by spatio-temporal particularity or specificity—it is *this* individual rose and no other. In the language of Whitehead, it is an "occurrent," unique in its here-and-now specificity or particularity.

(b) Every finite individual endures for a finite period of time and maintains its identity during this period despite both inner and outer change. Its identity is a function of those universals whose embodiment is taken to constitute its "essential" nature. What is judged to be "essential" to the continued identity of any specific individual will depend upon how the class of individuals to which it belongs is defined, and this, in turn, depends upon the observer's interest and frame of reference. But however a rose be defined, any given rose will be judged to be the "same" rose so long as it continues to satisfy the conditions laid down by this definition. It can maintain its identity despite all changes in its environment and all inner changes which do not affect what is accepted as its essential nature.

(c) Individuals vary in complexity in two ways, first, with respect to the universals which they embody, and, second, with respect to their temporal or spatio-temporal constituents. (i) The simplest

[2] The meaning here assigned to the term "universal" must not be confused with the different though related meaning of "omnipresent" or "widespread," as opposed to "non-existent" and "rare." All omnipresent or widespread qualities or characteristics are "universals" as I have used the term; but some "universals" (in my sense) are much more widely exemplified than others. Thus many more objects in nature are green than pink; but "pink" is as truly "universal" (as here defined) as is "green."

[3] This definition applies only to finite or phenomenal individuals. If individuality is to be ascribed to Deity it would have to be defined somewhat differently.

individual necessarily embodies a hierarchy of universals just because universals are themselves hierarchically related to one another. Thus a single undifferentiated rectangular patch of red embodies not only the universal "redness" but the universals "color" and "quality," and not only the universal "rectangularity" but the universals "shape" and "area." Since the hierarchical interrelationships of universals are inexhaustible, the simplest individual is, with respect to the universals which it embodies, itself inexhaustible. But some individuals are, none the less, more complex than other individuals because they embody more universals. Thus a human being embodies more universals than does the petal of a rose. (ii) Individuals differ also in the number and complexity of their parts or constituents. Thus a rose is more complex as an individual occurrent than a single petal, and a man, than a rose. Every individual entity (save hypothetical "irreducible" entities) is composed of parts which have an individuality of their own, and every individual, however complex, is part of one or more inclusive individual entities.

(d) Conceptual apprehension of an individual entity involves the recognition of the universals which manifest themselves in it and the manner in which these universals are, in it, related to one another. The temporal or spatio-temporal uniqueness, specificity, or particularity of an individual entity, in contrast, is ineffable, i.e., conceptually inapprehensible and inexpressible. It can be "known" only through immediate intuitive awareness. As Professor Loewenberg has expressed it: ". . . Particulars—things that are 'here' and 'now,' endowed with 'individual' qualities and relations—are essentially unutterable. We are obliged to introduce universals, 'general' qualities and relations applicable to heterogeneous existences, in any attempt to describe the particular objects we experience. We perceive, for instance, a particular rose, but the description of it in terms of fragrance, shape, and color is general, relevant to every kind of flower. We never succeed in specifying the particular save in terms that define the *type* or the *class* of things to which it belongs. Perceptual immediacy and discursive language are incompatible. The immediate is ineffable; descriptions are compendious and catholic, never disclosing what is individual and incommensurable in the objects directly apprehended. Speech inevitably signifies the dominance of the common denominator."[4]

[4] J. Loewenberg, in the "Introduction" to *Hegel, Selections* (New York: Scribner, 1929), pp. xxiv-xxv. I shall presently (cf., below, Chap. XVIII, §5) argue that it is one of

The world of sense-perception can therefore be described as a world of more or less enduring, yet ever-changing, individual objects and events each of which exhibits both universality *and* particularity.

If we turn from the objects of sense-perception to the cognitive process by which these objects are apprehended, sense-perception appears, prior to all analysis, to be a simple act of immediate awareness. It is this characteristic of our every-day perception of objects which the naïve realist emphasizes, and in his naïveté he declines to analyze the situation further. But if perception is analyzed it is found to be a complex process involving both moment to moment sensations and conceptual interpretations of these sensory data. These complementary processes are not noticed by the layman because they are so perfectly fused in ordinary sense-perception. But they may be distinguished as follows.

The object of "pure" sensation is a specific sensory quality, quale, or datum, e.g., a red patch; and only through sensation do we become aware of the specific sensory qualities and configurations of the perceptual world. The primary object of "pure" conception, in contrast, is an abstracted universal. Sensation and conception differ, then, in their characteristic "objects." They differ also in that "pure" sensation is an ideal limit which can be approximated but never reached, whereas "pure" conception is possible and actually takes place in the purest "abstract" thinking. It is psychologically impossible to have a sensation without consciously or unconsciously interpreting it in some way. We are bound to relate it to other sensations and to set it in a perceptual frame of reference.[5] But we can think abstractly, that is, isolate a universal or a pattern of universals and conceive of it as abstracted in thought from its perceptual context. Even the common man makes use of abstractions in his daily experience, as language testifies, for every word he employs, except demonstrative words (e.g., "this" and "that") and proper names,

the functions of art to do what cannot be done in the medium of discursive language, that is, to express particularity in all its ineffability. The foregoing characterization of individuality, meanwhile, is as applicable to a work of art as it is to any other individual entity. The limitations of the conceptual analysis of art, to which I have repeatedly referred, are thus seen to be merely a specialized instance of the universal limitations of all analysis and discursive description of individuality in any of its manifestations.

[5] Only in pathological cases and in moments of extreme mental lethargy, as, for example, immediately prior to falling asleep, is interpretation reduced to a minimum, and even then sensation is not entirely "pure."

signifies one or more universals—it is this conceptual meaning of words which the dictionary attempts to define.

Perception can therefore be defined as a fusion of sensation and conceptual interpretation. It is, at each instant, a complex of specific sensations which are interpreted by the percipient in terms of remembered past sensations and in terms of various types of universals. But the characteristic "object" of a perception is neither a specific sensory quality nor an abstracted universal, but an individual "thing," namely, *these universals as particularized in this concrete individual.*

Man's "inner" experiences and their "objects" exhibit, on analysis, a character analogous to that of his "outer" experiences and their objects. All experience is, of course, "inner" in the sense of being a psychological process which reveals itself directly only to the introspective agent. But we shall find it convenient to distinguish between man's sensory perception of an "outer" world of spatial objects and events and his non-sensory cognition of "inner" objects.[6]

These objects of inner experience, in turn, are of two different types. One type, which includes all images, all acts of conscious awareness, and all emotive, conative, and affective states, is essentially private to each individual. The other, which consists of universals apprehended in conceptual abstraction, is as public as is the perceptual world of nature. I alone can become immediately aware of the products of my own creative and re-creative imagination. I alone can, by an act of introspection, know at first hand my own cognitive processes, my own volitions, emotions, and feelings of pleasure and pain. But such mathematical relationships as $2+2=4$ are not private to me. Images and universals are alike in being apprehensible without self-conscious introspection, whereas man can become explicitly aware of his own processes of awareness and his own conative, emotive, and affective states only by observing himself introspectively while he is in the act of apprehending or of experiencing the volitions, emotions, or feelings in question.

The objects of man's private inner experiences (i.e., the images, the emotive, conative, and affective states, and the processes of awareness which he alone can directly intuit) can, like the objects

[6] Cf. Kant's distinction between "inner" experience as temporal, and "outer" experience as spatial and temporal.

of his outer experiences, be described in terms of particularized universality. Each of these objects is, in itself, a specific occurrent. My present emotion is a specific emotional state, the visual image which I now see in my mind's eye is a specific image, and my present act of perceptual, imagistic, or conceptual awareness is always a specific act of cognition. But each of these individual occurrents resembles other individual occurrents in my own experience. Each may therefore be regarded as a specific manifestation of one or more universals, i.e., as a specific instance, "here and now," of some recurrent trait of man's inner experience. Meanwhile, these states and processes never occur (save approximately in pathological cases) in complete isolation but always as interrelated aspects of that complex process which we entitle the "stream of consciousness," and since this stream is permeated with a sense of personality they can be described as particular moments or fragments of someone's individual consciousness.

This cursory description of man's inner and outer experiences and their respective objects will suffice as a basis for the comparison which I must now attempt to make between the characteristic objects of scientific and artistic cognition and between the kind of truth sought respectively by the scientist and the artist.

2. Scientific inquiry

I have said that science and art are both specialized extensions of man's everyday experience. What science does is to develop, and presently to transcend, man's perceptual knowledge of natural objects and events by sharpening sensory observation and refining conceptual interpretation. The chief objective of science is a precise conceptual apprehension of the uniformities of spatio-temporal events. The scientist is not interested in individual phenomena as such. He is interested only in their generic characteristics and in the underlying natural structures and processes which serve to explain their behavior. He focuses his attention upon universals—upon the skeletal structure of nature and upon the types of processes which, in combination, constitute natural order.

The scientist does not, of course, ignore the particular sensory manifestations of structural uniformity and dynamic regularity. He does not evolve his theories *in vacuo* without empirical evidence. The whole technique of scientific observation has been developed to render more precise his first-hand sensory contacts with nature and to provide empirical verification for his theoretical constructions. But he values specific observations of individual empirical phenomena only as clues to underlying structure and types of invisible dynamic process. Nor can he completely ignore the objective individuality of the phenomena which he is investigating. In astronomy, for example, the individuality of the heavenly bodies and of our universe is recognized and studied for its own sake; in geology, individual geological formations are investigated; and the psychologist and the social scientist are becoming increasingly aware that the individuality of men and women and of societies and cultures cannot be ignored. Yet even in these sciences final emphasis falls upon recurrent characteristics rather than upon individual phenomena as such, while in such sciences as physics and chemistry the individuality of specific physical entities is almost completely ignored.

Universals are thus abstracted by the scientist from their particular manifestations and apprehended conceptually. Every effort is made to pass from vague description and generalization to conceptual formulations of maximum clarity, precision, and rigor. Hence the importance which is attached to quantitative measurement and to mathematical formulae. Hence also the tendency to regard these quantitative formulations as more correct than mere perceptually descriptive judgments. For gradually there emerges a sharp distinction between Eddington's "two worlds," the qualitatively rich and varied world of normal sense perception, and the cold, bloodless, and abstract world of scientific theory; and it is not strange that some scientists and scientifically-minded philosophers should be led to regard the latter as the "real" world of nature and the former as no more than its psychologically conditioned "appearance."

The scientist's characteristic interpretation of man's normative experiences reflects his general interests, methods, and objectives. His approach is that of an external observer, not that of a participating agent. There is only one type of normative experience in which the pure scientist participates with genuine sympathetic insight, namely, his own eager search for scientific truth.[7] All other values he investigates "from without" rather than "from within." This is the case even in those "scientific" disciplines whose subject-matter is human nature and human conduct in their individual and social

[7] Aesthetic values which enter into strictly scientific inquiry are integral to the scientific enterprise.

manifestations. The psychologist, anthropologist, and sociologist, for example, must concern themselves with practical, aesthetic, moral, and religious values because the men whose behavior they are trying to investigate are emotive, affective, and volitional agents who devote themselves to the attainment of practical ends and spiritual values, create and delight in beauty, enter into moral relations with their fellow men, and worship a deity in whose objective reality they believe. But in proportion as they aspire to "scientific objectivity" and seek to emulate the natural scientist's dispassionateness and conceptual aloofness, they study man merely as the most complex of natural phenomena. They observe *that* men indulge in acts of evaluation, and they describe with conceptual precision *what* it is to which men have attached, or wish to attach, value under specific circumstances and in specific cultures; but they never, *as pure scientists*, are able really to comprehend any of these values with aesthetic sensitivity, moral insight, or religious reverence. They accept man's normative experiences as psychological and sociological facts, just as the natural scientist accepts as a fact man's perception of such secondary qualities as color, sound, and odor. But just as the physicist *qua* physicist translates these qualities into air waves, light waves, and the like, explains our perception of them as a psychological phenomenon occasioned by the impingement of these waves upon our physical organism, and is then tempted to deny that natural objects "really" possess the qualities revealed to sense-perception, so likewise does the scientifically-minded student of human nature seek to explain man's normative impulses as specific manifestations of physiological, psychological, climatic, economic, and other principles, to reduce all values to subjective pleasures, and then tend to deny objectivity to values by asserting the complete subjectivity and relativity of all human evaluations.

The scientist's external approach to values and his scepticism regarding the objective validity of man's aesthetic, moral, and religious beliefs is not unrelated to his usual indifference to individuality. For individuality and value seem in our experience to be functionally related. The act of evaluation is commonly focused upon something which, at least during the act itself, is apprehended in an individual context. Men normally value not abstractions but individual objects, events, and processes. What occasions our aesthetic delight is not abstract beauty but specific objects and scenes in nature and individual works of art. Morality divorced from individual men and women and from specific motives, dispositions, and actions is an abstraction without meaning or coercive power. The religious consciousness apprehends the object of worship as possessing the attribute of individuality, if not of personality. And even in his practical life and his hedonistic pursuits man values the attainment of specific ends and derives pleasure only from concrete actions and situations.

It is true that values, like the primary and secondary qualities, are universals, since they manifest themselves in different individual contexts. It is also true that, unlike mere natural uniformities, they have a transcendental character, for they are always apprehended by the normative agent as ideals never perfectly attainable by man and never adequately realized in space and time. And, finally, man does conceive of values abstractly and does manifest loyalty to them as transcendental ideals. But although values can be thus conceptually apprehended and even cherished as timeless essences independent of phenomenal existence, they can take on empirical reality for us only in an individual context. Individuality is the empirical locus of value. Individuals, in turn, acquire significance only through participation in values and through the manifestation of value, for "significance" in this sense[8] is definable as "possessing value or worth." The principles of individuality and value, in short, condition one another as complementary principles in man's normative experience. It is not strange, accordingly, that the scientist's disregard for the individuality of persons and events should prevent him, as a pure scientist, from first-hand comprehension of all values other than the one which is integral to the scientific enterprise.[9]

[8] As opposed to its other and more technical meaning of "signification." Cf., above, p. 229, n. 1.

[9] An attempt might be made to defend the possibility of genuine scientific knowledge of values in the following way. It might be pointed out that the scientist (for example, the physicist) must rely upon ordinary sense-perception, however sharpened by the use of instruments and however controlled by scientific hypotheses, for first-hand empirical contact with the world of nature—in short, that in his attempt to discover natural uniformities he must approach nature as a perceptual "agent" and must apprehend nature's sensuous qualities and configurations with immediate and "sympathetic" percipient "insight." It might then be argued that, similarly, in the study of man and of the objects of man's normative experiences, the scientist can and should enter sympathetically into man's normative experiences, apprehend their objects with first-hand "sympathetic insight," and *then* proceed to interpret them with a dispassionateness and

3. The artist's apprehension of reality

The scientist, I have said, is interested in individual phenomena only as clues to nature's underlying structure, while the common man, impelled as he is to maintain life in a difficult environment, regards individual objects chiefly with an eye to their practical import and only with sufficient care to adapt himself to them. The artist, in contrast, is unusually sensitive to the specificity of his physical environment. He delights in specific colors and sounds, textures and odors, and revels in their sensuous immediacy and particularity. So keen is his appreciation of these qualities that he is frequently able to shake them loose, as it were, from their perceptual context and to enjoy them for their own sake, temporarily neglectful of other characteristics of the objects in which they appear, and indifferent for the moment to their practical import. This interest in the specificity of perceptual objects extends itself to the objects of inner experience. The artist is unusually sensitive to specific moods and feelings, images, desires, and cogitations as unique events. Their uniqueness fascinates him in and for itself; he never wearies of observing them, both within himself and indirectly in others, and of considering to what use he can put them in his art.

But even greater is his interest in the more complex individuality of natural objects and of human beings. His professional interest in nature differs radically from that of the scientist. He does not analyze a natural object into its physical and chemical constituents, translate its sensory qualities into quantitative terms or numerical

a conceptual rigor analogous to that which characterizes interpretation in the natural sciences.

This is not only possible, it is the procedure which students of art, morals, and religion have always adopted. The disciplines of artistic and literary criticism, ethics and theology, and the more general investigations which are commonly entitled the philosophies of art, morals, and religion, are, at their best, disciplines of precisely this type. Whether they should be called "sciences," however, depends entirely upon how the term is defined. If we define it to include all cognitive disciplines, those concerned with man's normative experiences and their respective objects can, of course, be called sciences. But in the text I have, following English and American usage, defined science more narrowly to include only those disciplines which attempt to model themselves on physics, the most rigorous of the natural sciences. And it is surely not strange that methods expressly devised for the exploration of impersonal nature should fail to throw light upon those aspects of human experience which most sharply distinguish human beings from natural objects and processes as such. A recognition of the limitations of scientific methodology facilitates the recognition of the validity, *within* these limits, of the scientific approach and of scientific knowledge. Cf., above, Introduction.

ratios, isolate generic universals from their individual contexts, and apprehend them in conceptual abstraction. He does not abandon the perceptual world of individual objects for a world of scientific abstractions. His world of nature is from first to last our every-day world of complex individual objects and events. Human beings are similarly apprehended by him as unique persons whose uniqueness enhances their intrinsic value. The true artist strives to enter into the lives of those whom he encounters with sympathetic insight, and he studies their unique dispositions and personalities with the keenest interest.

This concern for individuality in all its forms is accompanied by a profound interest in values of every type and by a genuine understanding of man's normative experiences in all their variety. He studies men and women as beings who normally believe in objective values and strive to realize ideal ends. The true artist will therefore not attempt to "reduce" man's moral strivings or religious aspirations to an unconscious search for hedonistic satisfaction, or to translate pleasure into its physiological concomitants. He accepts man's normative experiences at their face value and seeks to interpret them with sympathetic insight. Every artist must, indeed, have his own "philosophy of life" and his own scale of values, and this philosophy of life will not only determine his choice and his interpretation of his subject-matter but contribute greatly to the significance of his art.[10] But the true artist realizes the need for a catholicity of outlook in all his observations and interpretations—a catholicity which can enable him to share imaginatively in man's most conflicting normative experiences and to achieve a sympathetic understanding of man's most varied beliefs and modes of conduct.

Yet despite this interest in individuality, the artist, like the scientist (though in his own distinctive way), is primarily concerned to apprehend and interpret the more universal characteristics of human nature, human experience, and man's complex environment. He selects from among his own experiences and those of his fellow men the experiences which seem to him to possess universal meaning and significance. He realizes that if his art is to endure and to be intelligible to a wide and varied audience he must transcend, without neglecting, the merely particular and idiosyncratic. For only thus can he hope to interpret his subject-matter (which in each

[10] Cf., below, Chap. xxiv.

specific work of art must necessarily be specific) in a manner intelligible to others. To make a legitimately universal appeal he must set in relief those aspects of his subject-matter which are or might be universally experienced. In his preoccupation with unique individuality he must not lose sight of significant universality.

This is true even in the case of portraiture.[11] The explicit subject of a portrait is the sitter as a unique and actually existing individual. To deny the artistic relevance of this fact (as is done by some theorists) is not only to contradict the testimony of the great portraitists and the well-nigh unanimous verdict of leading critics, but to ignore the distinctive characteristic of portraiture as such. The portrait painter *is* deeply concerned to catch the unique individuality of his sitter, and the artistic value of his portraits depends to a considerable extent upon his success in doing so. But in all portraiture worthy of the name the artist is *also* interested in the universals which his individual subject-matter manifests. These two interests need not conflict, though it requires artistic genius to satisfy both at once. The less competent portraitist tends to sacrifice objective individuality to generality, or, alternatively, generality to individual verisimilitude. But the great portraitist knows how to catch the characteristic likeness of his sitter and, simultaneously, to portray him in such a way as to reveal those universal human traits which most clearly manifest themselves in him. Indeed, he achieves each of these objectives in the very process of achieving the other. For his understanding of the universals in question is derived in part from his intensive study of their manifestation in this particular individual, while his insight into the individuality of his sitter is conditioned by his knowledge of the universals which, in unique combination, constitute his individuality. Thus Raphael's portrait of *Angelo Doni* (Fig. 249) is a revealing portrait of this particular man partly because it so clearly exhibits his humanity, and it is also a revealing study of a young man because youth and manhood so clearly manifest themselves in the person of Angelo Doni.

The artist's interest in universals differs profoundly, however, from the scientist's interest in universals, on the one hand, and from man's active allegiance to ideals, on the other. His primary objective is artistic revelation, not scientific exploration or passionate participation. The truth of which he is in search is not the abstract

[11] Cf., below, Chap. XVIII.

conceptual truth of science, and the goal to which he is committed is not practical or spiritual commitment. Some of his observations may have a scientific interest, but this is always accidental and irrelevant to his main objective. The more profound his spiritual insights, the more richly will they contribute to man's spiritual life, but even this contribution is incidental to artistic endeavor as such. For in proportion as the artist assumes the primary rôle of prophet, moralist, or evangelist he abandons his calling as an artist and renounces artistic insight for its own sake.

Thus the artist seems to say to us: "Behold mankind and nature. Consider human experience and man's environment in all its individuality and universality. This is the situation as I find it, good and bad, beautiful and ugly, orderly and chaotic, but, whatever its character, intrinsically interesting to me and to all men who can approach it with an artistic attitude. I, as artist, have not attempted to view this complex scene with scientific impartiality, and I have not hesitated to offer you my interpretation of it. But in interpreting it, I have attempted to exhibit what seems to me to be its true nature and its universal human import. My object has been to apprehend it concretely, not abstractly, and I regard this apprehension as an end in itself, not merely as a means to action. Hence, however you may ultimately interpret human life and the realities which confront you, I offer you an artistic record of my observations and interpretations. Enjoy it for itself, and learn to contemplate life, as I have, with artistic objectivity. Then, if you care to do so, put whatever fresh insight you have derived from me to any use you like."

CHAPTER XV

ARTISTIC EXPRESSION

THE distinguishing characteristics of artistic expression can most easily be set in relief by comparing the way in which the artist expresses himself with the ways in which the scientist, on the one hand, and the moral agent, on the other hand, express themselves. These human modes of expression, in turn, must be distinguished from mere natural manifestation.

1. Natural manifestation and human expression

By "nature" I mean the sum-total of spatio-temporal objects and processes constituting the physical world of sense-perception and, in addition, all the psychological processes which accompany the lower and higher forms of life. The concept of nature thus embraces the entire actual and potential subject-matter of scientific inquiry. It includes whatever can be observed, perceptually or introspectively, and interpreted in terms of scientific principles. This world of nature "manifests" both individuality and universality. What are the *differentiae* of this manifestation?

In manifesting itself to man nature is passive, unconscious, and non-purposive, whereas human "expression" is in essence active, conscious, and purposive. Nature merely *exists* as a possible object of awareness. It makes no effort to reveal its secrets to man and is indifferent to his inquiries. It exhibits itself to him but offers him no assistance in his attempt to understand its structure or interpret its behavior. It "answers questions" if questions are put to it in the form of observation and experiment, but it volunteers no information and takes no initiative in aiding man to satisfy his curiosity. It does, indeed, continually intrude itself upon his consciousness and coerce him, often to his discomfort, into conformity to its laws. But its impact upon him is mechanical, not purposive. It does not adapt itself to him; he must adapt himself to it. Philosophical naturalists like Bertrand Russell who interpret nature with scientific objectivity are quite right in describing it as "omnipotent but blind," "a trampling march of unconscious power."[1]

[1] "Blind to good and evil, reckless of destruction, omnipotent matter rolls on its re-

Organic nature, it is true, does manifest an unconscious purposiveness. The members of a living organism contribute to the life of the organism as a whole and, in turn, depend for their vitality upon the entire organism. The leaves and roots of a tree simultaneously condition and are conditioned by the entire tree. But the goal of biological adaptation is sheer biological survival and nothing more. It is also true that nature as a whole has been interpreted by philosophers, theologians, and poets as the expressive revelation of a larger cosmic purpose. Both Plotinus and Berkeley, each in his own way, conceived of nature as a "divine language." Christian theologians have repeatedly found in nature evidence of a Divine plan. But, as Kant convincingly argued, nature *in and of itself* neither suggests nor validates such a teleological interpretation. If we come to nature already persuaded that it is created and sustained by a Divine power we can, indeed, interpret it in terms of a cosmic teleology. But if we approach it without prior religious commitment and with scientific objectivity we will be unable to discover in natural order any justification for such a teleological interpretation. The "voice of nature" is, in and of itself, singularly inexpressive of any conscious purpose or ultimate normative objective. It merely manifests itself to man in all its individuality and universality.

To say that natural manifestation is passive is to recognize the fact that what is manifested in nature "becomes manifest" only to the discerning eye. What nature does is to present us with a mass of observable data which *we* must interpret through our own efforts. Strictly speaking, what is immediately "given" to us at each instant of sensory or introspective awareness is merely a specific pattern of sensuous or non-sensuous particulars, and it is only when we compare these particulars with other particulars that they become for us manifestations of universality. Thus a particular patch of yellow manifests the universal, "yellow," *to us* only when *we* become aware of its similarity to other patches of color. Similarly, a specific emotional state is directly apprehended by the emotive agent as a specific emotion. It becomes *for him* an exemplification of "fear" or of "emotion" only as the result of more extended introspection and interpretation. The individuality of more complex natural phenomena manifests itself to us in the same way. The complete individuality of a complex natural object or event is never revealed

lentless way." Bertrand Russell, *Mysticism and Logic* (London: Longmans Green, 1921), p. 56.

to us at any given instant. All that is thus revealed is a specific pattern of particular qualities. Complex individuality manifests itself therefore only in the temporal *succession* of immediately given patterns and therefore only to a mind endowed with memory, imagination, and reason, that is, only to an intelligent observer.

Strictly speaking, then, nature is at each instant of immediate sensuous or introspective awareness a congeries of particular appearances which manifest universality and more complex individuality only to beings endowed with the appropriate cognitive capacities. These capacities are requisite not only to scientific inquiry but to ordinary sense-perception, i.e., to the perception of similarities and differences and to the apprehension of perceptual objects and events as complex individual entities and processes. We perceive, moreover, only what we have learned to perceive; both the individuality of natural objects and their universal traits manifest themselves to us only in the form in which, and to the extent to which, we have learned to apprehend them. The same factors, *mutatis mutandis*, condition our awareness of ourselves and of other selves as highly complex individuals, as well as our apprehension of the universal characteristics of man's inner experiences. In both "worlds," the "inner" as well as the "outer," universals are actually present as the pervasive traits of real individuals, but in neither world can either universals or more complex individuals be apprehended as such save in and through selective observation and disciplined reconstruction.

Expression differs from mere manifestation in being a product of man's conscious, normative experience. It is only because man is capable of interpreting his environment that he has anything to express, and he resorts to expression partly to clarify his own thinking, partly to share with other human beings his interpretative apprehensions. Expression is in essence consciously and purposively motivated.

Man may express himself spontaneously without explicit awareness of what he is doing and without any explicit motive or intention. But his behavior is expressive only if it reflects, however indirectly, his conscious and normative processes. When human behavior fails to reflect these processes, as in the case of purely reflex action, we do not call it expressive; it is merely the agent's physical response to his physical environment. Human expressiveness is most clearly exemplified, on the other hand, in man's deliberate attempt to express his own ideas, emotions, feelings, and volitions in some appropriate medium.

Again, communication need not be the explicit motive of expression. We can and do express ourselves without reference to an actual or even a potential audience. But normally the motive of human expression is communication. It is imperative for us, as human beings, to communicate our experiences to others and to share in their experiences, and such inter-personal communication is, in its very essence, consciously and purposively expressive. Even when we express ourselves in solitude we assume, for the moment, the double rôle of expositor and recipient. We attempt to realize ourselves to ourselves by expressing our own thoughts, feelings, emotions, or desires for our own benefit. And only a reflective and purposive being can indulge in such solitary self-revelation. Expression, then, whether directed to social communication or not, is essentially a human activity.[2]

2. *Three types of expression*

The three main types of expression are most clearly exemplified in scientific inquiry, artistic creation, and moral conduct.

(a) *Scientific* expression is chiefly characterized by its abstractness, its precision, and its lack of emotive, affective, and conative overtones. It is essentially conceptual, for it is only by means of concepts that universals can be abstracted from their empirical context and so apprehended. And it aims at maximum precision, both in the description of what is scientifically observed and in the theoretical reconstruction of nature's basic structure and typical dynamic processes.

This desire for scientific precision motivates the scientist's continual resort to measurement and dictates his use of words and mathematical formulae. When he uses terms which are current in ordinary discourse he tries to employ them in a non-emotive and non-conative manner. But, wherever possible, technical terms are invented which are free from emotive and conative associations and which, as scientifically defined, connote exactly what the scientist wishes them to connote. For still greater conceptual precision the

[2] If the lower animals can be said on sufficient evidence to express themselves in an analogous way, this merely indicates the absence of any absolute boundary between man and other living creatures. We can leave it to the psychologist to determine the precise degree of similarity between human and non-human organisms in this respect.

scientist employs mathematical equations. He also makes use of illustrations to facilitate conceptual apprehension, but these are always made as schematic and diagrammatic as possible, and even so they are regarded as inferior in scientifically expressive power to precise verbal description, and greatly inferior to mathematical formulae. They are merely concrete visual aids to abstract conceptual apprehension. They are seldom scientifically expressive in their own right; they resemble allegories in requiring translation into abstract conceptual terms. The more advanced a science, the more inadequate are such images and diagrams, and the more does the scientist insist that his ideas can be expressed accurately only in the language of scientific prose and mathematical formulae.[3]

These characteristics of scientific expression deprive it almost entirely of biographical flavor. Individual scientists have no individual style comparable to the individual style of an artist. Some scientists do have an expressive style which distinguishes their writings. But the ideal of scientific exposition is impersonal and objective, transcending personal, racial, cultural, and epochal variations. Since scientists and mathematicians are not disembodied intelligences but finite human beings living in specific periods and cultures, their work does tend to mirror their own interests and tastes and those of their social environment. But this is a tendency which the pure scientist strives to rectify. If further proof is needed, compare the contributions to a scientific journal with the poems in a literary journal or the pictures in a contemporary exhibit. The former will, for the most part, be found to be so impersonal in manner of expression that no one can tell, merely from the mode of expression, whose contributions they are, whereas a good poem or a good picture exhibits in its artistic form unmistakable indications of its authorship.

These generalizations regarding the scientific mode of expression are, of course, inadequate. I have ignored, for example, the aesthetic factors of "elegance" in mathematical demonstration and of craftsmanship in the construction and manipulation of apparatus in scientific experimentation—factors to which mathematicians and scientists attach importance and which the philosopher of art might profitably investigate.[4] I have also ignored the fact that distinguished

[3] Cf., in this connection, A. S. Eddington, *The Nature of the Physical World* (New York: Macmillan, 1928), pp. 209-10.

[4] Cf., below, p. 430, on "medial felicity."

scientists have not hesitated to make *occasional* use of a more literary mode of exposition. Professor E. A. Milne, for instance, in his *Relativity, Gravitation, and World-Structure,*[5] introduces into his highly technical argument a passage rich in imagery and emotive overtones. Discussing the future of our universe, he says:

". . . Though each local system evolves, decays, and possibly in some sense grows cold and dies, yet the universe lives for ever, [and] knows no death in time. For however large is t, we can always find a nebula so swiftly moving that events on it, observed by us now, are arbitrarily early in time. However small is t' and however large is t, the answer is simply $V = c(1 - t'^2/t^2)^{1/2}$. However old we ourselves may be, our experiences always contain events as early as we please in local time. These events we place near the expanding frontier of the universe. For observers at them, experiencing them, the universe to them has hardly embarked on its career of evolution. For them, time is still young. They are experiencing the early history of the universe. The infinite number of nebulae contained in the universe include an unending sequence of arbitrarily young experiences. There, near the confines of the visible universe, is the coming generation. There, we find the sons of the morning. The confines of the universe constitute, as it were, a layer of cosmic protoplasm, expectant of evolution. As I have elsewhere quoted, there the world is

> For ever piping songs for ever new,
> For ever panting and for ever young.

In our vision, time there stands still, like Grantchester clock in Rupert Brooke's poem. . . . Once started, the system goes on for ever. Each constituent has a temporal experience—each observer lives in time but the universe as a whole knows no time history. It is the same yesterday, to-day, and for ever. 'Time like an ever-rolling stream bears all its sons away.' Death and decay in our midst, for us; but for the world, immortality. The totality of things created knows no terminus in time, no decay, no asymptotic strangulation of the surge of life. Always there is a future vista, and since we need suppose no exact parallelism of the evolutionary trends on any two nebulae, there are unending opportunities for variety of local experiences. . . . The world ever sows at its frontier the seeds for its own future. Each individual nebula reaps the harvest of its own

[5] Oxford: The Clarendon Press, 1935, pp. 137-8.

experiences, and passes to the winter of decay. But ever anew the seasons recur. There at the confines of the visible universe, at the world's inaccessible edge, the music of the spheres is the song of a new dawn, the dawn of the world's perpetual birthday."

Such literary expression would seem to have value even for the scientist. But Professor Milne would be the first to insist that the burden of his scientific analysis and proof must be expressed, as he himself has expressed it, not in a literary but in a strictly scientific and mathematical form.

(b) The passage just quoted exemplifies some of the generic *differentiae* of *artistic*, as opposed to scientific, expression. The sentence containing the mathematical equation illustrates what I have described as the characteristically scientific mode of expression, while, in the rest of the passage, the same thought is expressed in non-technical prose with generous reliance on poetic imagery and metaphor. The translation of a poem into scientific prose would provide an equally good illustration of this basic difference. The most conventional and "classical" of literary compositions, provided it has true literary quality, differs in kind from a strictly scientific treatise. The former must be felt to be really understood, while such feeling is irrelevant to strictly scientific comprehension. Where rigorous scientific exposition is cold and impersonal, artistic expression is warm and personal; where the former is abstract and conceptual, the latter is concrete and imagistic; where the former eschews emotive and conative overtones, the latter exploits these overtones to the full; where the one is innocent of an individual style, the other is essentially stylistic.[6]

Not only does the artist seldom conceive of universals abstractly; he never expresses his interpretation of them in a purely abstract way, but always concretely, i.e., in an individualistic setting. Every work of art exhibits individuality in three distinct ways. I have discussed[7] its "specific form," which I have defined as the unique organization of the work's specific primary and secondary artistic media. This formal uniqueness conditions the uniqueness of the expressed content of every work of art, since what is expressed by a work of art is expressed only in and through its specific form. A work of art is highly individual, then, both in artistic form and in artistic content. But it is individual in still another way. However concerned

[6] Cf., below, Chap. XXI, on style.

[7] Cf., above, Chap. VIII.

the artist may be with the generic or universal aspects of his subject-matter, the specific subject-matter with which he deals in any work of art is introduced as having an individuality of its own. This is true even in the abstract arts and in literature, but it is most immediately evident in the case of the representational arts of sculpture and painting.

All sculptures and paintings (except pure abstractions) not only have a representational subject-matter but treat this subject-matter in a highly individualized manner. The painter, for example, does not discourse abstractly about trees or mountains or about their generic perceptual qualities. He depicts an *individual* mountain or tree in such a way as to emphasize certain of its generic qualities (Figs. 138, 212, 185-193). He does not discuss human characteristics as types in symbolic abstraction. He creates individual men and women on canvas and portrays them in such a way as to emphasize not only their individuality but also those generic human traits which interest him (Figs. 223-229, 245, 249, 263). Whether the representational objects which he employs for this purpose are more or less faithful portraits of actually existing individuals, or whether they have been only indirectly suggested by nature and are in large measure products of the artist's creative imagination, is here irrelevant. What is relevant is their individuality in his art and the use he makes of them as vehicles for the interpretative expression of universals.

As regards the abstract arts, it is clear that the musical composer makes as little use of conceptual abstractions in the apprehension and expressive interpretation of his subject-matter as does the painter. The emotive-conative states which constitute his subject-matter in any specific composition are specific states whose individuality is quite lost sight of when they are prosaically and crudely classified as "joy," "hope," "resignation," "sorrow," and the like. What the music itself expressively interprets is a succession of highly particularized moods and conative states which, in turn, exemplify with unusual intensity and clarity certain emotive and conative universals. The composition arouses in us *specific* emotions, moods, and feelings, and it is only in experiencing them that we achieve a new understanding of this *kind* of inner mental state. In pure music this effect is achieved entirely through the use of highly individualized, non-representational tonal patterns, whereas in sculpture and painting the subject-matter is introduced representationally and the emotive-conative states are primarily suggested indirectly through the depiction of conscious individuals. The painter and the sculptor rely far less than does the composer upon the immediate expressiveness of formal patterns in the primary medium.

Architecture resembles music in not relying on representation. The architect depends rather on the power of architectural form to arouse an immediate empathic and emotional response. But the architect, unlike the composer, is, as we have seen, primarily concerned to give architectural expression to the building's social function. The social function of any specific building is, once again, a specific social function. A building is built to satisfy a specific social need in a specific community and in a specific culture. Hence the distinctive subject-matter of architecture, like that of the other arts, is an individual subject-matter, and the architectural form in which it is interpreted is a correspondingly individualized form.

Literature which does not make use of images can validate a claim to literary quality only if the concepts which it invokes are themselves played one against another in such a way as to emphasize their varying degrees of generality and if, in addition, language is used with regard not only to conceptual meaning but also to emotive and conative overtones. But most literature not only uses images of one type or another; it employs them in a manner integral to literary expressiveness. Here they require no translation (save in pure allegory) but function immediately through fruitful metaphorical interplay with associated concepts. But images, like pictorial representations, are effective only in proportion as they are individualized. The perfect literary image is the very opposite of a scientific illustration or diagram, for it is at once individualized and immediately expressive of the universals it was created to invoke. This use of literary images, meanwhile, does not begin to exhaust the rôle of individuality in literary expression. A narrative or plot, for instance, must be individualized if it is to serve its literary purpose. Literary characters must be endowed with individuality if they are to function as expressive revelations of recurrent human traits. If nature is treated descriptively it must be described not in abstract but in concrete terms. If an author wishes to create a mood or atmosphere he can do so not by marshalling conceptual abstractions but only by recording interpretatively the individual reactions, whether his own or those of his characters, to specific natural objects and occurrences. Whatever his specific subject-matter or manner of treatment, the literary author must invoke the principle of individuality at every turn in giving artistic expression to his interpretation of human experience and its objects.

The artist, then, is as consistent as the scientist in his treatment of individuality. Though he also apprehends the universal traits of objects and events, he does so not primarily by means of conceptual abstraction but rather by noting their natural manifestations in individual contexts. And he expresses his normative interpretations of these universals not in abstract unstylistic prose but, whatever his artistic medium, in stylized works of art whose individuality is directly a function of the specific artistic form and, indirectly, of the specific subject-matter, whether this subject-matter be a mood, a representational object, a social function, or a literary image, character, or plot.[8]

(c) Only those characteristics of *moral* expression which serve by contrast to set the *differentiae* of artistic expression in relief need to be described here. I have used the phrase "volitional actualization" to indicate the major concern of the moral consciousness. Volitional behavior is of course not restricted to moral conduct. The scientist wills to know and deliberately acts in such a way as to promote scientific knowledge;[9] the artist wills to know in his own normative way and deliberately expresses his insights in his art; the practical man acts voluntarily to achieve his utilitarian ends. On the other hand, the moral consciousness is not indifferent to cognition, for moral insight is an absolute prerequisite to genuinely moral action. Yet the moral attitude, like the practical, differs generically from the artistic and scientific in its preoccupation with the will, and it differs from the practical in its prime concern for ultimate values and objectives. Kierkegaard has recorded in his *Journal* why he was unable to write a story about his love for Regina while in the throes of that relationship: ". . . I cannot poetize it, the instant I essay to do so there comes over me an anxious dread and an impatience to act." And, again: "A real love-affair . . . always grips a person so profoundly that he is brought into the ethical sphere."[10] Here we have

[8] For a further consideration of the rôle of individuality in art, cf., below, Chap. XVIII, §5.

[9] Cf. A. N. Whitehead, *The Function of Reason* (Princeton: Princeton University Press, 1929), p. 30: "There is a strong moral intuition that speculative understanding for its own sake is one of the ultimate elements in the good life."

[10] Quoted by Walter Lowrie, *Kierkegaard* (London: Oxford University Press, 1938), p. 241.

the clue to the essential difference between art and morals. For the artistic consciousness, insight and the appropriate expression of such insight are ends in themselves. Moral conduct, in contrast, involves *being* the kind of person we should be and *acting* towards others as we should act. Art may thus be said to emphasize appearance, if (but only if) by "appearance" is meant artistic expression, while morality emphasizes reality, if (but only if) by "reality" is meant the actual possession of a moral character and the actual performance of moral acts. The artist portrays men as they are, with all their virtues and vices, *and* as they ought to be; the moralist is actively concerned to eradicate vice and to foster human virtue. The artist as artist is content to understand human nature with all its potentialities and limitations, and to reveal his insight through his art. Man as a moral being feels under obligation to translate his moral ideals into the phenomenal actuality of inner attitude and overt behavior.

If this basic distinction between art and morals is kept in mind we can profitably note their mutual dependence. Conduct which is not based upon a fine understanding of human nature in general and of the concrete human situations to which such conduct must be oriented lacks genuine moral value. Professor Fite is quite correct in insisting upon genuine sympathetic moral insight as essential to moral goodness.[11] And this insight, in turn, though not wholly artistic in character, is closely akin to artistic insight, for it is not abstract or purely conceptual, but simultaneously conceptual, imaginative, and emotive. The initial approach of the moral agent to human beings is similar to the artist's initial approach to them. The moral agent and the artist differ only in ultimate motivation and in the use to which such immediate apprehension is put. Furthermore, the artist's specific insights, as these are expressed in his art, are invaluable to the moral agent, while art in general aids morality in strengthening the imagination.[12] If morality is taken to include all that concerns man's true nature, his human relations to his fellows and his apprehension and realization, in whatever form, of goodness as a normative ideal, morality may be said to constitute art's ultimate subject-matter.

But man's moral consciousness differs from his artistic consciousness in expressing itself not only in an initial sensitivity to human situations but also in conceptual apprehension of moral laws and

[11] Warner Fite, *Moral Philosophy* (New York: Lincoln MacVeagh, 1925).

[12] Cf. Shelley's *Defence of Poetry*. See below, pp. 469-70.

principles, in the transformation of his inner attitude towards himself and his fellows, and in the resolute attempt to translate moral principles and ideals into phenomenal actuality. Ethical theory, like scientific theory, is abstract and formal, while moral conduct, though often expressive in the manner of art (as when a man exhibits his sympathetic understanding of another in an expressive gesture or other revelatory action) may take the form of prosaic, inexpressive behavior.

These comparisons of artistic expression with the modes of expression typical of science and morality must suffice to indicate the more important generic similarities and differences between them. I have in this chapter used the term "expression" in its more generic sense, partly in order to conform to common usage and partly to distinguish expression as such from natural manifestation. But since art attaches such peculiar importance to expression, and since I am here primarily interested in artistic expression, I shall, in the remaining chapters, restrict the term to the expressiveness of art and refer to the other two modes of expression as "description and formulation" and "volitional actualization" respectively.

CHAPTER XVI

TYPES OF ARTISTIC CONTENT

BEFORE attempting to classify the main types of universals and individuals to which an artist can give interpretative expression in an artistic medium it will be well briefly to recapitulate the chief characteristics of artistic content in general.

(a) The content of any specific work of art is unique, since it is a function of the work's specific or unique form. Yet artistic content, like artistic form, has a generic character which can be analyzed.

(b) The content of a work of art is *not* (i) its specific primary medium. Yet specificity plays an important rôle in all artistic expression.[1] Neither is this content (ii) the work's specific artistic form, though this form is the artist's only expressive vehicle. Nor is it (iii) the beauty or formal aesthetic quality of the composition's specific form. Formal beauty is the *conditio sine qua non* of artistic content, but it is neither identical with this content nor the sufficient condition of artistic expressiveness. Again, the chief content of a work of art is normally *not* (iv) the individuality of the artist. The artist is bound to express himself in the work of art as a whole, i.e., in the selection and organization of his primary medium and in the selection and interpretation of his subject-matter.[2] But although an artist can, if he chooses, also make his own unique individuality the main subject-matter of his work, most artists, and certainly the great artists, have been primarily concerned, though not always consciously or explicitly, to express in their art their interpretation of some aspect of man's generic experience and of that wider reality to which this experience is oriented.[3] Finally, the content of art is never (v) merely the artistic individuality of the specific subject-matter. The specific subject-matter of a work of art, whether in portraiture or non-portraiture, is indeed always artistically individualized. But in non-portraiture this individualized subject-

[1] Cf., below, Chap. XVIII, §5.

[2] This type of self-expression, which is integral to all art as such and the source of an artist's individual style, must be distinguished from that type of self-expression which originates in the artist's deliberate intent to make his own unique personality his chief subject-matter and its interpretation the chief content of his art.

[3] Cf., above, pp. 231*ff*.

matter functions solely as a vehicle, within the work of art, for the artistic expression of universals, and in portraiture it is a vehicle for the expression not only of universals but of the artist's interpretation of the objective individuals portrayed.

(c) The chief content of a work of art consists of the artist's interpretation of certain universals, plus, in the case of portraiture, certain objective individuals, as this interpretation has been expressed by him *via* artistic form in an artistic medium. These universals and individuals are normally not apprehended abstractly either by the creative artist or by the re-creative observer. The artist usually apprehends them in their individual objective contexts without explicitly abstracting them in thought, and he usually expresses his interpretation of them directly in his chosen medium without prior explicit conceptual formulation. The observer's artistic response, in turn, recapitulates the stages of the artist's creative process but in the reverse order. He starts with the work of art and, subjecting himself to its guidance, seeks to apprehend the interpretation which the artist has already expressed in it. He may then, as professional critic, attempt either to formulate this content in non-literary prose or else to re-express it, however inadequately, in literary prose. Meanwhile, both the critic and the layman find themselves referred by the re-created work of art back to those generic experiences and objects which first inspired the creative artist to undertake his artistically interpretative labors. But, as sensitive observers, they will not cease to contemplate the work of art itself. For it is *during the very process of re-creating and appraising it* that they are impelled to reflect upon that wider human experience (including their own) and that wider reality (including the objects of their own past experience) to which the work of art itself directly or indirectly refers them.

(d) Unless this unique manner in which both universals and complex objective individuals enter into art's expressed content is explicitly and continuously kept in mind, the following classification of the main types of artistic content will lead to a serious misapprehension as to the nature of this content and of the whole artistic enterprise—the misapprehension, namely, of supposing that artistic creation and re-creation are explicitly conceptual and that the content of a work of art is itself an explicitly conceptual content.

This classification does not purport to be either philosophically rigorous or empirically exhaustive. Its justification must be wholly pragmatic. It is offered here merely as a preliminary basis for the critical analysis of the content of works of art in the several artistic media.

Since the artist expresses in his art an interpretation of certain aspects of human experience and of the objects of human awareness, the natural basis for a classification of the main types of artistic content is the generic character of human experience itself and of the objects to which it is oriented.[4]

The two main types of human experience are "outer" and "inner" experience. I shall from now on designate "outer" experience as "perceptual" and "inner" experience as "spiritual,"[5] defining the former to include all those experiences whose objects are available to sense-perception, the latter, all those experiences whose objects are not directly evident to the senses. The objects of both perceptual and spiritual experience, in turn, manifest both universality and individuality. The generic content of art can accordingly be said to be the interpretative expression of various types of perceptual and spiritual universals and the interpretative portrayal of various types of complex human and non-human individuals. The artist also emphasizes the sheer specificity which characterizes the objects of man's perceptual and spiritual experiences; but how this specificity, so emphasized, can be said to constitute part of art's expressed content is a question which must be postponed.[6]

These preliminary distinctions[7] can be indicated diagrammatically as follows:

- artistic content
  - universal (non-portraiture)
    - perceptual
    - spiritual
  - individual (portraiture)
    - human
    - non-human

[4] Cf., above, Chap. xiv, §1.

[5] The term "spiritual" is here used in its broadest generic sense to signify all that concerns the human spirit, i.e., that in man which is not purely physical.

[6] Cf., below, Chap. xviii, §5.

[7] These categories, like other categories listed in this book, imply one another in

The expressed content of specific works of art could profitably be analyzed merely in terms of these categories. But analysis can be sharpened by a further discrimination between perceptual and spiritual universals and individuals.

1. Perceptual universals

A perceptual universal may be either a typical, relatively self-contained, perceptual object or a typical quality, relation, state, or occurrence manifested by such an object. I shall, for convenience, entitle the former type of perceptual universal "substantival" and the latter "adjectival."[8] Mountains and streams, plants and animals of different species, and the human body, all considered as types of phenomenal objects, are examples of substantival perceptual universals, while sensuous qualities such as color and odor, spatial and temporal relations, states of rest and motion, and all visible natural occurrences such as the overt behavior of men and animals and the sensuous appearances of the four seasons, are, again considered as types, examples of adjectival perceptual universals.

2. Spiritual universals

Spiritual universals may be "religious," "social," or "introspective." This three-fold distinction is based upon the fact that man's inner or spiritual experiences can be either religiously or socially oriented and that man can also focus his attention upon himself and his own inner processes; that is, he can worship a deity, enter into relation with his fellow men as a conscious human being and a moral agent, or reflect upon his own inner nature, life, and destiny.

Man's spiritual experience is, indeed, seldom if ever exclusively religious, social, or introspectively self-conscious. No religion is completely divorced from social intent and conduct; man's social relations frequently assume religious character and value; and a consciousness of self not only pervades all conscious awareness but is itself, in turn, conditioned by a consciousness of other-than-self. Yet

various ways. Thus perceptual universals may be either human or non-human; human individuals are both perceptual and spiritual, etc.

[8] This distinction between substantival and adjectival universals, i.e., between "things," regarded as types, and their typical attributes, states, and modes of behavior, is a common-sense distinction congenial to ordinary sense perception and useful in the criticism of art and literature. This justifies its use in the present context. Whether or not such a distinction is ultimately defensible from a strictly scientific or a rigorously philosophical point of view is here irrelevant.

our spiritual experiences are often *predominantly* religious, social, or introspective in character, and in each case, the generic traits may be described as religious, social, or introspective universals.

The universals of each of these three types are of course as numerous and diverse as the experiences and objects which manifest them. What I have called the religious experience, for instance, includes all such religious emotions and attitudes as awe and reverence, contrition and conversion, petition and a sense of forgiveness, all the activities associated with religious worship, and all of man's imagistic and conceptual interpretations of Deity. But all experiences classifiable as religious have the generic character of being theocentrically oriented, whether the deity to whom the finite agent seeks to relate himself be an idol, a human being endowed with divine attributes, the world of nature, the mystic One, or the God of theism. It is this theocentric orientation which distinguishes religious from social (or anthropocentric) and from reflective (or egocentric) experiences. Accordingly, the content of a work of art may be said to be religious in proportion as it expresses, *via* artistic form, this theocentric attitude in any one of its innumerable and diverse manifestations.

Man's social experiences are as various and complex as are his religious experiences, ranging all the way from the crudest to the most refined relations between persons. When a man is treated merely as a physical organism, or when, alternatively, a human being is endowed with attributes of divinity in a unique sense, he ceases, so far forth, to be an object of social concern. But within these limits man relates himself socially to his fellow men in innumerable ways—economically, politically, hedonistically, in friendship, in love between the sexes, in parental and family relationships, and the like. But whatever its specific form, man's social experience is an inner or spiritual experience, since its object is essentially man's inner or spiritual nature. Social experience, to be human and not merely sub-human, must be a relation between finite persons and must presuppose some sense of human personality. The content of a work of art is social, then, in proportion as it reflects this generic social attitude in any of its typical manifestations.

Our experience becomes predominantly self-conscious and egocentric when we withdraw from the world and reflect upon our own inner nature and our own life and destiny. Here again we must distinguish between two types of reflective self-awareness. We can reflect upon our relation to a deity, to our fellow men, or to the world of nature, with special reference to the significance of this relationship *for us*. Each of us tends, in his more introspective moments, to consider his own life and welfare primarily in terms of that aspect of his environment which has impressed itself upon him most vividly and which therefore seems to him to be of crucial importance to himself. Thus the practical man of affairs tends in moments of reflection to consider his business prospects; the reflections of the engrossed scientist tend to be scientifically oriented; the religiously devout tend to concern themselves primarily with their own spiritual welfare; and so forth. But these orientations are ancillary to the reflective agent's primary egocentric orientation, for here he is concerned not to worship God but to consider his own prospects in a world controlled by a divine power, not to investigate nature but to reflect on the bearing of such an investigation upon his own life and happiness, etc. His basic preoccupation is egocentric. The question which controls his thoughts is: How do these entities and relationships concern me?

But man can also, in moments of reflective introspection, concentrate his attention more narrowly upon his own inner emotional and conative states and, in the process, recognize their universal character. It is chiefly reflection of this type which provides the musical composer and the lyric poet with their distinctive subject-matter. These moods and feelings, hopes and fears, do not, indeed, present themselves to us entirely unmotivated. They are always associated with some aspect of our environment and related to other aspects of our stream of consciousness. Yet it is these inner states themselves, in all their immediacy, of which we are for the moment primarily aware. The artist, in turn, expresses them interpretatively in his art as universal human emotions and conations, moods and feelings.

In order to distinguish between these two types of introspective awareness and between the universals which characterize each type, I shall describe the first type as "objectively," the second as "subjectively," oriented.

3. *Human portraiture*

A work of art can be described as a portrait in proportion as the artist attempts to portray in it the individuality of an actually existing "historical" individual. Even the theorists who insist that such objective reference never possesses artistic value must admit the expressive importance, in what is commonly called portraiture, of the individuality of the subject-matter as depicted in the works of art themselves, and they must also recognize that these "artistic" individuals fall into certain classifiable types. My present concern is merely to differentiate between these types, whatever the final verdict concerning the importance for art of the objective individual reference.[9]

Individuality (in contrast to mere particularity) manifests itself most richly and significantly in human beings; human beings can be depicted in a predominantly religious, social, or reflective attitude; and each of these expressed attitudes can be interpreted in a variety of ways. It is also possible for the portraitist to depict the unique individuality of human events and the significantly unique products of human creation or construction. Historical paintings, novels, and poems exemplify the first of these types of portraiture, paintings and literary descriptions of buildings, the second. Since the distinctive individuality of these events and objects is conditioned by the human beings who participate in them or bring them into being, works of art of these two types can also appropriately be classified under the general heading of human portraiture.

4. Non-human portraiture

Non-human portraiture includes all artistic interpretations of animate and inanimate objects designed to emphasize their unique individuality. That such portraiture actually exists can easily be shown. But the more primitive the organism and the more simple and elemental the natural phenomenon, the more impoverished is its individuality and the less well adapted is it to serve as the subject-matter of portraiture.

These additional distinctions can be indicated diagrammatically[10] thus:

[9] Cf., below, Chap. XVIII.

[10] Whatever the importance or unimportance of the reference in portraiture to actually existing individual persons, objects, or events, we must remember that the category of portraiture is much less extensive in denotation than the category of non-portraiture. The abstract arts do not lend themselves to portraiture at all, while pictorial, sculptural, and literary portraits are greatly outnumbered by compositions which are not portraits. We must also remember that the expressed content even of a portrait is predominantly universal. Unless this is realized, the symmetry of this diagram will be seriously misleading.

TYPES OF CONTENT

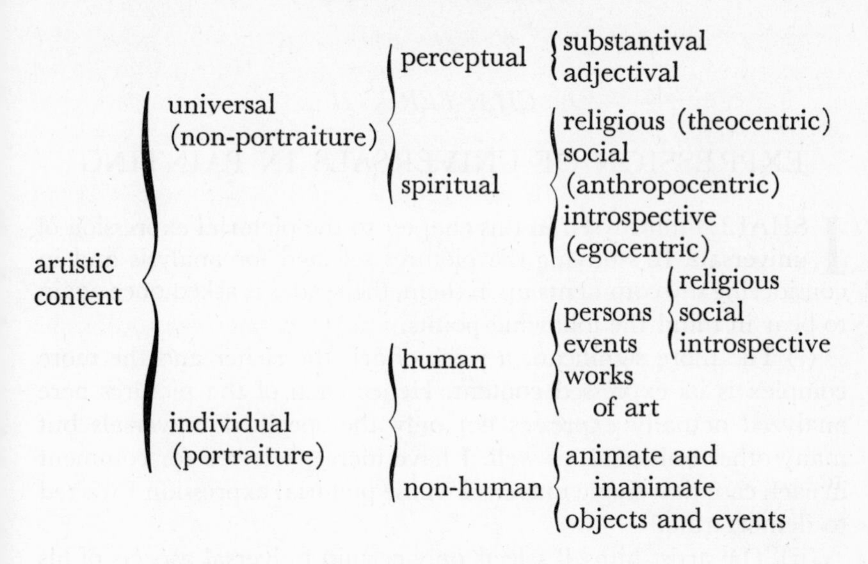

CHAPTER XVII

EXPRESSION OF UNIVERSALS IN PAINTING

I SHALL limit myself in this chapter to the pictorial expression of universals. In studying the pictures selected for analysis and in considering my comments upon them, the reader is asked once again to bear in mind the following points.

(i) The more significant a work of art, the richer and the more complex is its expressed content. Hence each of the pictures here analyzed actually expresses not only the specified universals but many other universals as well. I have merely selected for comment in each case that single universal whose pictorial expression I wished to demonstrate.[1]

(ii) The artist himself selects only certain universal aspects of his subject-matter for artistic interpretation, and when the chosen universal is itself complex, he emphasizes only certain aspects of it at the expense of other aspects. No work of art tells the *whole* story about anything. Nor can a work of art ever be said to express *the* essential property or quality of its subject-matter, since what is judged to be essential depends upon the point of view adopted. What art does is to reveal *certain* aspects of its subject-matter with unrivalled clarity and power.

(iii) The content of a work of art can be comprehended adequately only in and through *artistic* response, and what is so comprehended differs in essential ways from what is comprehended by means of conceptual analysis. The very act of picking out this or that type of universal as constituting part of the content of a work of art does violence to the work and partially distorts its nature. We shall succeed in "seeing" what the artist wishes us to see only if we really look at the picture with artistic intuition and use prosaic analyses merely as indications of what to look for.

(iv) We must not forget how very much is lost in a photographic reproduction. No photograph can do more than reproduce certain

[1] A critic or commentator may accurately be said to "demonstrate" the correctness of his interpretation of a picture by confronting us with the picture, appealing to our trained sensitivity, and inviting us to "see" in it what he "sees."

aspects of a painting. No final test can be made save in the actual presence of the work of art itself.

(v) The reader is again asked not to attach special importance either to my selection or to my critical interpretation of the illustrations cited. These pictures have been chosen and, wherever possible, reproduced, because they seemed to me to demonstrate the points at issue. But if the reader disagrees with my choice or interpretation he is invited to substitute examples which, in his opinion, demonstrate the point in question more clearly.

1. Perceptual universals

(a) *Substantival universals.* Trees are a favorite subject-matter of landscape painters because they lend themselves quite ideally to pictorial treatment. They vary endlessly in color, leaf pattern, structure, and size, and every tree is obviously a unique individual. Yet trees resemble one another both in genus and species. Here, then, is a rich field for artistic selection and interpretation. No two painters have painted trees in exactly the same way, but every competent painter who has attempted to express a revealing interpretation of trees has succeeded in expressing certain of their distinctive characteristics. Thus, Théodore Rousseau (Fig. 187) is preoccupied in his careful drawings and paintings with the multiplicity of leaves and the intricacy of leaf, bark, and branch patterns. The oak is one of his favorite subjects as best exemplifying these arboreal characteristics. Corot, in his later style (Fig. 188), emphasizes the softness of the foliage and the way in which it seems to melt into the surrounding atmosphere. Birches and willows are his favorite subjects. Henri Rousseau (Fig. 189), unlike Corot, takes pains to delineate each individual leaf and delights in constructing patterns of leaves in which each leaf exists as a stiff, relatively self-contained, object. Tropical vegetation lends itself to such treatment, and this is one reason, though doubtless not the chief reason, for Rousseau's love of tropical forests. Cézanne (Figs. 185, 212), in his treatment of trees as of other perceptual objects, is interested in their three-dimensional solidity and, particularly in his later years, in the manner in which they contrast visually with their background. I need not discuss the technical devices by which he attained his ends. What concerns us here is merely the extraordinary sense of reality which his pictures convey. Witness the strength of his tree trunks, the dynamic thrust of his branches, the manner in which his foliage relates itself to its supporting branches, and the way in which his trees exist as individual entities in three-dimensional space. He is also interested in the endless play of light and shadow, and of warm and cold color, which trees in the sunlight so clearly manifest. André Derain (Fig. 190) resembles Cézanne in many ways, but in the illustration here reproduced he emphasizes the sinewy, tensile, almost rubbery character of the twisting branches. Matisse (Fig. 191), to cite but one more example, is always primarily interested in the two-dimensional decorative character of perceptual objects. His trees clearly exhibit this interest. They are represented less for their own intrinsic character than as occasions for, and aids to, the creation of an interesting pictorial design. Yet even Matisse catches some of the flair and sweep of tree trunks and branches.

That painting, like the other arts, is essentially interpretative is evident from these illustrations. If further evidence is needed, a Cézanne landscape and an un-retouched photograph of the same scene (Figs. 185, 186) afford, by contrast, a clear illustration of the way in which the painter makes use of selection, simplification, and even distortion in order to emphasize just those aspects of his subject-matter which he wishes to set in high relief. Corot's early painting of Chartres, when compared with a photograph of that cathedral, demonstrates the same point (Figs. 38, 39. Compare Figs. 32-35).

Most painters show us *less* of the objects depicted than would be apparent to ordinary visual perception, though the traits which are exhibited are made more prominent and inescapable than they are in nature. This is typical of painting in general, as it is of the other arts. The artist's normal procedure is to select and omit and, by these devices, emphasize. But an artist, and notably a painter, can move away from "literal reproduction" in the opposite direction. That is, he can portray in a single picture *more* aspects of his subject-matter than would be apparent to momentary sense-perception; he shows us what would be visible in actuality only at successive instants and from different points of view. This procedure is best illustrated in the work of Jan Van Eyck. In his painting of St. Francis (Fig. 218), for example, the kneeling saint, the attendant monk, and the landscape in the nearer and more distant background appear at first sight as they would in actuality if we were ten feet away from the human figures, twelve or thirteen feet from the rocks on the right, one hundred feet or more from the rocks on the left, and several hundred yards from the cluster of buildings in the more distant background. Yet the grass and flowers around St. Francis and the monk, as well as the apparently more distant rocks, are painted as they could only appear to us if we were a foot or so from them, so minute are the depicted details. Van Eyck has thus compressed into a single picture more than could actually be seen *either* at close range *or* from a greater distance. The perceptual experience which is mediated to us is thus not so much heightened as enriched; the intention is to telescope several normal perceptions into one synoptic perception. Meanwhile, Jan Van Eyck is clearly interested in offering us an interpretative account of nature itself; he is by no means indifferent to the perceptual universals which actually manifest themselves in his subject-matter. The fact that, in the picture of St. Francis, his interest in nature is subordinated to a profounder interest in the contrast between nature and spirit, the temporal and the eternal, in no way diminishes his concern with nature. On the contrary, he must portray nature as he does in order visibly to demonstrate this contrast which constitutes the picture's major expressed content.

(b) *Adjectival universals.* Adjectival universals are related to substantival universals as the perceptual qualities, states, and relations of a perceptual object are related to the object itself as a relatively self-contained individual entity. The former distinction, accordingly, is no more absolute than the latter, but it is useful for critical analysis just as the distinction between a "thing" and its states, relations, and qualities is useful in normal sense-perception and even in science.

But no picture can express universals of one type without simultaneously expressing universals of the other type. In the landscapes which we have been considering, for example, each painter has had to exhibit many of the adjectival characteristics of trees in the process of interpreting the universal, "tree." He has also, in his interpretation, emphasized certain adjectival universals at the expense of others. And, conversely, the painter who is particularly interested in adjectival universals for their own sake cannot express them representationally without portraying to some extent the objects in and through which they manifest themselves. The distinction, then, between the expression of substantival *versus* adjectival universals reduces itself to a matter of emphasis. Some painters emphasize the substantival type, others, this or that adjectival quality. In our pictures of trees the chief interest seems to center upon trees *as trees*, though now this and now another aspect of trees receives special attention, and though the pictures vary in the degree to which they convey to us a sense of the reality of the entire tree as a living organism. (Compare, for example, Cézanne's trees with those of Matisse, or even with those of Henri Rousseau.) But there are paintings which, in contrast, emphasize some adjectival universal at the expense of the substantival universal and which depict perceptual objects primarily to exhibit some adjectival universal *for its own sake.*

Monet, for example, in his haystack studies, his studies of Reims Cathedral, and his pictures of the Houses of Parliament and the Doges' Palace (Fig. 35), was primiarly interested in the portrayal of light and luminous color. These qualities cannot be represented all by themselves. They can be depicted only in conjunction with colored objects which reflect light. Monet was therefore compelled to paint solid objects such as haystacks and buildings in sunlight, shadow, or fog. Yet it is clear that he was not interested in the stacks or the buildings as perceptual objects, but only in the luminous color which they exhibited at different times of day.[2] The architectural structure of his buildings quite disintegrates under this treatment. They are structurally amorphous; his stone lacks lithic quality, and his solids are almost porous, as though the thick, luminous, color-saturated atmosphere not only bathed them but flowed through them without resistance. Here, then, the perceptual universal, "a stone architectural façade," is in large measure *sacrificed* in the effort to portray light and color for their own sakes; only enough of the solidity and structure of the perceptual object is introduced to achieve the desired effect. As a result, Monet's pictures are magnificent expressions of these adjectival universals. Having learned to see them here, we can see them again, though with diminished intensity, whenever we look at an uneven surface in bright sunlight or luminous shadow.

This emphasis upon some sensuous quality at the expense of perceptual representation can be carried even further than it is by Monet. The representational forms can be simplified and distorted almost beyond recognition. Some of Corinth's landscapes illustrate a stage in this process (Fig. 192); his colors (the reader not familiar

[2] It is on record that, during this period, he would work on a picture for only a short time each day and return to it the following day at the same hour in order always to observe his subject in the same light.

with his paintings must take my word for it) are glorious, particularly his blues and reds, but they are as brilliant as they are partly because the objects which they purport to qualify are indicated in the most sketchy manner. In Gauguin's paintings (Fig. 194), in contrast, though flat colored areas predominate, though the colors are so selected and contrasted as to emphasize their character as color, and though the effect is usually more two-dimensional and decorative than three-dimensional and perceptually realistic, crucial outlines are emphasized sufficiently to involve less sacrifice of perceptual universals than in Corinth. For an exclusive emphasis on color contrasts and harmonies, with no perceptual content whatsoever, we must turn to such abstractions as those of Kandinsky (Fig. 98).

A variant of this adjectival tendency is to be found in the work of those painters who, in their use of the brush and the palette knife, emphasize the sensuous universals immediately manifested in pigment. This can be done more or less at the expense of perceptual representation, as sometimes happens in the paintings of Rouault (Fig. 196), or it can be done without this sacrifice, as in the later pictures of Franz Hals. In Hals' *Hille Bobbe* (Fig. 195), for example, a broad and visible brush stroke endows the painting with much of its freshness and charm and introduces into its expressed content some of the sensuous universals present in oil pigments. But these strokes are employed primarily for their representational effect. With an amazing economy of means Hals manages to express the old woman, her owl, and her tankard, not only as perceptual objects but as objects themselves expressive of spiritual universals.

The contrast between a manipulation of the primary medium productive of an immediate sensuous effect, on the one hand, and a handling of this medium which results in an emphasis upon the sensuous character of the representational subject-matter, on the other, is evident from a comparison of one of Renoir's nudes with Rubens' *Toilette of Venus* (Figs. 199, 200). In Renoir's picture, the colors as colors, and the way in which they have been applied to the canvas, are primarily responsible for the picture's sensuous content. In Rubens' picture, in contrast, the color is so smoothly applied, and the brush stroke so subdued, that we forget the painted surface and attend only to the female figure. She, in turn, is so portrayed as to emphasize every sensuous quality of female flesh to an almost painful degree. Both pictures are notably sensuous in content (though the sensuous universals in the two cases are by no means identical). But this content is expressed primarily through pure surface pattern and texture in the first case, and chiefly through expressive representation in the second.

Those adjectival universals which are primarily functions of space and time enter into the expressed content of all pictures in which emphasis falls upon the relation of solids to one another in space (that is, upon perspective in its infinite variations) or upon the movement of solids in space. Renaissance paintings which betray an intense interest in perspective (at the time an exciting new discovery) such as, for example, Mantegna's *Dead Christ* (Fig. 198), are as good illustrations as any and require no comment. But the pictorial expression of movement calls for special analysis.

A painter can express movement in two ways, either representationally or compositionally, that is, either by painting objects in such a way as to indicate that they are themselves in motion, or else by inducing in us, through the compositional organization of his primary and secondary media, a sense of movement which we then unconsciously read back into the picture. In both cases the movement is, of course, actually read into the picture which, as a physical object, is a perfectly static pattern of colors and shapes. But, in the first case, the representational figures are seen to be *themselves* following the path which the eye is compelled to travel through the picture, whereas, in the second case, the coerced movement of our eyes gives us a sense of directed movement which the represented objects are not themselves following.

Rubens' *Peasants' Dance* (Fig. 204) illustrates the first type. Not only are the peasants moving in the foreground from left to right, and in the background from right to left, i.e., in a counter-clockwise circular path; the tempo varies at different points in the circle. The girl in the immediate foreground is almost, though not quite, at rest; the figures to the right of her (from our point of view) hurry with ever-increasing acceleration; the distant figures in the background, to the left of the break in the circle, are running so fast that those behind them have broken loose and fallen behind; and the remaining figures on the left are gradually slowing down again. Here obviously the peasants are themselves dancing along the path which our eyes follow again and again in exploring the picture. The movement is, as it were, "objective," i.e., actually represented, and not merely suggested. (*Vide* also Fig. 206.)

Rubens' *Castor and Pollux* (Fig. 203) illustrates the expression of "subjective" movement through dynamic composition. Here too the horses and the human figures are in motion, but they are not themselves moving in the picture along the path which our eyes follow. The head of the gray horse at the right impels us to look to the right and down; this visual movement is strengthened by the woman's outstretched hand and by the forelegs of the horse; our vision is pulled around by the drapery flowing over the woman's leg, then upward by the movement of the legs of the horse and the woman, until our eye is caught by the putto; the latter promptly impels us to re-enter the composition along the head of the black horse and head of its rider, etc. This is not, of course, the only visual path through the picture, though it is certainly the dominant path. For the picture is compositionally a wheel supported by the lower female figure as a fulcrum. But the figures also exist in a three-dimensional space which we too, therefore, seek to explore. Yet the powerfully expressed movement, which is an essential part of the picture's sensuous content, is suggested by the compositional arrangement of the figures and not by the representation of them as themselves moving along any of the dominant paths of visual motion.

Rubens' *Battle on the Bridge* (Fig. 205) combines both devices for expressing motion. Here the eye travels across the bridge from left to right, then down, and then out under the bridge. Yet the figures themselves clearly follow no more than broken segments of this revolving circular path. The fallen horse and rider at the right, for example, have fallen from the bridge, but have no prospect of moving rapidly from right to left and back under the bridge. The same applies to the figures on the left. We are, as it were, hurried along by jerks as each group of figures carries us a short distance and then turns us over to the next group.

2. *Spiritual universals*

(a) *Religious universals.* The religious experience, though characterized by a generic attitude common to all forms of religion, always involves specific beliefs and practices. Every genuine religion is a specific religion with a creed, a symbolism, and a form of worship of its own. It is natural, then, that the best examples of religious art should express not religion in general (save in so far as the specific is always a manifestation of the generic) but some particular religion such as Christianity. But Christianity is itself much too complex a phenomenon to find complete expression in any single work of art. A painter, for example, must limit himself to the expressive interpretation of some aspect of the Christian experience and express this aspect in terms of one or more specific events, persons, or doctrines in the Christian tradition. But the more religiously significant the episode, person, or doctrine, the more profound will be the revelation, as mediated by the picture, of what is crucial to Christianity; while the higher Christianity itself stands among the religions of the spirit, the more eloquently will the painting manifest, to the discerning eye, the inner nature and significance of religion in its richest flowering. In a word, since all truly religious art is incarnational,[3] making visible the invisible and figuring forth the spiritual to sense, the more profound this incarnational revelation, the more significant the work of art becomes for all who are at once artistically sensitive and religiously minded.

Painting can express religious universals in two ways, either symbolically or representationally. In order to reduce symbolism to its simplest terms, and with an eye to its specific rôle in art, I defined a symbol[4] as anything to which a more or less arbitrary meaning has come to be attached by convention, and which, accordingly, becomes intelligible to us only in proportion as this conventional meaning is known and conjured up when the symbol is employed. Pure (i.e., "primary") symbolism was then distinguished from presentational and representational (i.e., "secondary") symbolism by defining a pure symbol as any visible or auditory sign whose only referential meaning is that meaning which has been attached to it by linguistic convention, and by defining a presentational or representational symbol as any image or representation which has acquired, in *addition* to its perceptual or presentational reference, a *further* symbolic meaning. Thus, non-onomatopoetic words are pure (or primary) symbols, whereas the images which they, singly or in combination, conjure up become presentational (or secondary) symbols when an additional symbolic meaning is attached to them. For example, the pack on Christian's back in *Pilgrim's Progress* symbolizes the burden of sin. Similarly, the pictorial representation of a sheep is normally the mere expressive likeness of a sheep; but in Christian

[3] Cf. the author's "Art as the Vehicle for Religious Worship," in *Religion in Life*, Vol. VII (1938), pp. 93-105.

[4] Cf., above, Chap. VI, §2.

iconography it becomes, in addition, the symbol of Christian discipleship.[5]

Most of the symbolism used in religious painting is not primary but secondary symbolism. But it is often difficult to decide exactly at what point, in a religious painting, mere non-symbolic representation passes over into secondary symbolism. Since this problem is crucial to the analysis of the pictorial expression of religious content, and since, moreover, the same problem reappears in the other arts whenever secondary symbolism is invoked, I must attempt to clarify the issue. This can be done best by analyzing a concrete example, such as the famous *Pietà* of the School of Avignon (Fig. 211). To what extent does the painter here make use both of primary and of secondary symbolism? And to what extent does an adequate comprehension of the picture's content depend upon an acquired knowledge of Christian iconography and the Christian tradition?

In the first place, the circular halos around the heads of the three central clothed figures are pure or primary symbols. To ordinary sense-perception they are mere geometrical circles which only distantly suggest halos of light emanating from the three heads. Hence they can have no meaning for us unless we know (i) that they are "halos" and (ii) that, in Christian iconography, halos signify that

[5] Strictly speaking, actual sheep are, in the Christian tradition, primary symbols of Christian discipleship, just as the crescent is the primary symbol of Mohammedanism, the rising sun, the primary symbol of Japanese imperialism, etc. Hence, primary symbols may be either arbitrary signs made by man (e.g., marks on paper), or natural objects (e.g., sheep, the moon, the sun, etc.). I am concerned here, however, merely with (i) non-representational signs devised by man for recording and communicating his ideas (e.g., letters of the alphabet, words, etc.), (ii) non-symbolic sculptural or pictorial representations (Fig. 2) and non-symbolic literary images, and (iii) such *additional* symbolic meanings as may become attached either to artificial signs or to literary images and visual representations. In what follows I shall refer to these arbitrary signs as "primary symbols," to representations as "representations," and to both primary symbols and representations which have acquired additional symbolic meaning as "secondary symbols." Thus, alpha and omega are mere primary symbols when regarded merely as the first and last letters of the Greek alphabet, but they become secondary symbols when, in Christian iconography, they are made to symbolize the Person of Christ (Fig. 3). Similarly, any pictorial or sculptural representation of a perceptual object is, in itself, a mere representation and not a symbol at all; but any such object, e.g., the grapevine or the peacock, as represented, becomes a secondary symbol when it is introduced into a symbolic context, e.g., made to symbolize Christ's relation to His disciples, and eternal life. *All* iconographic symbolism is "secondary" symbolism as here defined.

the persons whose heads they encircle are persons of special religious significance.

The halo around the head of the recumbent figure is only slightly more representational; an untutored observer would probably see merely a regular pattern of gilt lines. Only in proportion as we are able to "see" these lines as rays of light mysteriously emanating from the head does it become for us a secondary symbol, that is, a recognizable representation with an additional symbolic or iconographic reference.

It is clear that the figures themselves can have no *religious* meaning for us unless we are familiar, on the one hand, with the Christian story, and, on the other hand, with the representational conventions of Christian art. Without this knowledge the picture is merely the representation of a kneeling middle-aged man in a white robe, with a rapt expression on his face, apparently unaware of the other figures; of a seated woman with deep sorrow depicted on her face; of the obviously dead body of a man on her lap; of a male figure possibly absorbed in thinking about the dead man; and of a weeping female figure. An observer wholly ignorant of the Christian tradition and Christian iconography, but artistically and humanly sensitive, could respond to the picture's expressive representation of human sorrow in the presence of death. He would, however, be puzzled by the picture's apparent lack of representational and compositional coherence. He would not know what to make of the curious combination of a very realistic three-dimensional figure on the left foreground and a flat, unatmospheric, completely unrealistic, gold background. He would also be at a loss to explain how the figure at the extreme left was related to the group, i.e., why he was so indifferent to the other figures, living and dead, and what he was absorbed in. Interpreted merely as a human document and without any religious reference, the picture would have both artistic value and human meaning for him, but, at this level, it would seem to be deficient in psychological motivation and would exhibit certain deplorable compositional inconsistencies.

If, on the other hand, we come to the picture equipped with the requisite historical and iconographic knowledge these inconsistencies disappear, the requisite motivation is supplied, and the whole picture takes on profound religious meaning and significance. For now the dead body is seen to be that of the God-man, the Incarnation of God in the historical Jesus, whose humanity is here expressed in the realism with which the body is portrayed, and whose divinity is indicated by the unique halo. The seated woman becomes the Virgin Mary holding on her knees the body of her dead Son and grieving for Him like a human mother. The figure on her left is identified as Mary Magdalene with her pot of ointment, and instantly there comes to mind the Biblical story of her encounter with Jesus and His treatment of her. The figure at Christ's head is John who does not grieve for his Master as dead but adores Him as the living Christ. Finally, the figure in white, at the extreme left, is seen to be that of the donor of the picture (whose presence is in conformity with Medieval and Renaissance pictorial convention). But he is not merely the donor; he typifies the human Christian who is conversant with the doctrine of the Incarnation and accepts it as of supreme religious significance. He is not looking at the group, or at the figure of Christ, because they exist for him not as physical beings but as persons in the divine epic. He needs only to reflect upon them and to worship his dead and risen Lord. The group is for him, as it is intended to be for us, not a realistic representation of ordinary men and women, but an icon, that is, a pictorially expressive vehicle for worship.[6] Hence the flat gilt background, which in Christian iconography is always indicative of eternity as opposed to our world in space and time. Hence also the three-dimensional plasticity of the donor and the planear treatment of the two Marys.[7] The picture

[6] An icon, properly conceived, is an artistic incarnation of Deity, not to be worshipped as divine, but to be reverenced as a visible embodiment of a Deity who, in actuality, is spirit, and not flesh. Thus an icon differs essentially from an idol, which, by definition, is *itself* the Deity which is worshipped.

[7] Note the fine gradations from the plastic to the planear which, in this picture, are motivated by both compositional and iconographic considerations. The donor, as the most completely human figure, is most plastically and realistically portrayed. John is next most realistic, partly because he is closest to the donor in the composition, and partly because he is most fully aware of his own humanity *in contrast to* Christ's divinity, though his historical significance as one of Christ's disciples, and as a major figure in the Christian tradition, is symbolized by the halo. The Marys are least "realistically," i.e., plastically, portrayed, partly because they are farthest from the donor in the composition, and partly because of their religious significance for the donor, and therefore for us—hence the halos. What makes them religiously significant is not that they themselves fully realize Christ's divinity, but merely the fact of their close association with Christ in history and tradition. Finally, the body of Christ Himself in the center of the composition is handled with a brutal realism (since Christ was "very man") and yet, simultaneously, portrayed in a highly stylized posture and with a pronounced stylized halo (since Christ is "very God").

thus expresses with great eloquence the Christian doctrine of the Incarnation; and this expression is perfectly evident to anyone equipped with the requisite knowledge, but remains completely hidden from the wholly untutored observer.

Two other types of knowledge, meanwhile, are requisite to an adequate comprehension of this picture. In the first place, no one wholly unfamiliar with the phenomenon of death and human sorrow could understand the picture even as a human document. A being capable of sense-perception, but devoid of the feelings and emotions typical of human experience, could not interpret the faces and gestures of the two Marys as indicative of sorrow. And, in the second place, a being who was either incapable of sense-perception or unable to recognize a more or less stylized pictorial representation of perceptual objects could not even interpret the picture's two-dimensional pattern of lines and colored areas as a representation of one undraped and four draped human bodies. Thus, even the apprehension of the picture as a picture of a corpse and four sorrowing or contemplative persons involves interpretations which presuppose a knowledge acquired partly from first-hand participation in man's outer and inner experiences and partly from social convention.

The aesthetically minded abstractionist makes every effort, in the presence of such a picture as this, to ignore not only its historical and religious significance but even its representational character, and tries to confine himself entirely to the picture's non-representational aesthetic surface. So viewed, the picture, like all good pictures, will afford him genuine aesthetic satisfaction, for the colors do contrast and harmonize and the lines and areas do relate themselves to one another in a more or less aesthetically satisfying way. Yet, at this level, the picture must be judged to lack artistic perfection, since the robe of the donor, the loin cloth of Christ, and other light areas are too glaringly white and too violently opposed to the rest of the composition to make for purely aesthetic harmony. That this contrast is religiously motivated and religiously expressive could of course not enter into the pure aesthete's perceptions.

Let us now return to the problem of pictorial symbolism. What portions or aspects of this picture are symbolic, whether in a primary or a secondary sense, and what portions are representationally but not symbolically expressive? Where shall we draw the line between the acquired knowledge which is requisite to the interpretation of a symbol (whether primary or secondary), and that which is requisite to the apprehension of a non-symbolic representation? *Some* interpretative equipment is requisite at *each* of the stages of apprehension which I have described—aesthetic sensitivity, for the appreciation of abstract artistic pattern; a knowledge of the relevant perceptual and social experiences and a familiarity with the conventions of artistic representation, for a comprehension of the picture's perceptual and social subject-matter and content; and, finally, a familiarity with Christian tradition and iconography, for an understanding of the picture's religious meaning and significance. Which of these types of acquired knowledge is symbolic, and which is not?

This problem can only be solved by means of a more precise definition of terms. As I have said, a primary symbol is non-representational. A representation, in turn, becomes a secondary symbol if its "symbolic" meaning has been attached to it by explicit human convention—a convention which must therefore be learned before the representational object can function as a symbol for the observer. A halo, for example, whether representational or purely geometric, became a Christian symbol when it was first used deliberately as a visible indication of Divinity, or association with Divinity; and it continues to function as a symbol with this symbolic meaning so long as it is used and accepted in this manner. Its symbolic character manifests itself, moreover, in the fact that its symbolic meaning is hidden from any observer who is unaware of the convention and who is therefore unable to translate the symbol into the idea symbolized. But if symbols are defined in this way, then not only the halos but the figures and, indeed, the picture as a whole must be regarded as *religiously* symbolic. The various distinguishable areas of the picture, in turn, are representational in proportion as they actually portray (instead of merely indicating by means of primary symbolic reference) some aspect or aspects of the visible appearance of perceptual objects. Thus the circular halos are almost wholly non-representational and the gold background is entirely so, while everything else in the picture is more or less representational.

It follows, then, that symbolism and representation are not incompatible in painting. Indeed, a secondary symbol is by definition *both* symbolic and representational. It is also evident that religious painting uses both symbolism and representation as its expressive vehicles, and, in the case of secondary symbolism, simultaneously. That pictorial representation can be immediately and vividly expressive needs no argument. A symbol, in turn, is expressive to the extent to which its symbolic meaning is *instantly* available to the artistic observer without *conscious* translation. Here the equipment of the observer constitutes the crucial variant. An observer brought up in the tradition of medieval Christian iconography would find such symbols as the ram, the dove, the tongues of fire, the sheep, and the vine as familiar as his own mother tongue. These symbols would therefore be immediately intelligible to him without explicit translation. The average American undergraduate, in contrast, is unfamiliar with these symbolic conventions. Hence, prior to intensive education, they simply do not exist for him as meaningful symbols, and the picture must therefore present itself to him correspondingly impoverished in expressed content. Nor will it suffice merely to possess the requisite conceptual knowledge of the relevant conventions and traditions. These symbols can become expressive for us as they were for men in the Middle Ages only after we have truly assimilated their symbolic meanings and have made them so completely our own that the symbols can speak to us with an immediacy unimpaired by the paraphernalia of scholarly learning and conscious, laborious translation.

This analysis of the rôle of symbolism in religious painting is equally applicable to religiously expressive compositions in the other artistic media. In architecture, for example, forms like the Gothic arch have acquired, lost, and reacquired religiously symbolic meaning; each step and gesture in a religious dance can be endowed with ritualistic meaning and religious value; while religious poetry is peculiarly rich in religious symbolism of every type.

Both primary and secondary symbols are, of course, used more extensively in some paintings than in others. Schongauer's *Crucifixion* (Fig. 162), for example, is rich in secondary symbolism: note the angels catching the precious Blood of the Sacrament in the Chalice, the skull and bones of Golgotha, the inscription on the cross, and the crown of thorns. Dürer's *Crucifixion* (Fig. 163) relies more heavily upon a representational depiction of grief. Here, in addition, shadow and atmosphere become expressive vehicles, though not as powerfully as in Rembrandt's magnificent etchings (Figs. 215, 216). Giotto, in his *Entombment* (Fig. 221), relies less on explicit symbolism than either Dürer or Schongauer. He uses, rather, the more universal language of stylized pictorial representation, and he uses it with extraordinary simplicity and power.

Pictures differ also in richness of artistic content and in penetration and sincerity of religious insight. Tintoretto's *Crucifixion* (Figs. 213, 214), of truly epic proportions, elaborates the historical event with great dramatic intensity. Millet's *Angelus* (Fig. 223), in contrast, expresses the more general attitude of religious worship with great simplicity and without appeal to traditional religious figures. He merely represents two peasants pausing to pray at the sound of the angelus, and the only symbols used are the folded hands, the bowed heads, and the distant spire. A similar though more intense effect is achieved in Zurbarán's *Kneeling Monk* (Fig. 217), while Jan Van Eyck's *St. Francis* (Fig. 218) is less dramatically intense, more interpretative, and richer in historical associations. Raphael's *Madonna del Prato* (Fig. 177), in contrast, though Christian in subject-matter (note the cross and the halos), is at best only mildly expressive of a religious content. Finally, pictures like Dürer's *Adoration of the Trinity* and Raphael's *Dispute of the Sacrament* (Fig. 219) illustrate respectively the pictorial interpretation of theological doctrines and the discussions concerning them in the Christian Church. The religious expressiveness of such pictures is clearly less than that of most of the other pictures which we have been considering because the subject-matter, though rich in religiously emotive associations, is primarily abstract and conceptual and, to that extent, devoid of immediate emotional appeal.

(b) *Social universals.* The contrast between religious and social content can best be demonstrated by two sets of comparisons. The first is that between Millet's *Angelus* (Fig. 223) and his *Gleaners* (Fig. 224). In both cases we see peasants in the fields; but in the *Gleaners* they are at work, while in the *Angelus* they have not only stopped working for a moment but are in a posture of prayer. Millet's *Sower* (Fig. 225), meanwhile, is a much more eloquent expression of manual toil. The act of casting the seed upon the ground is a happy choice of subject-matter for the theme of labor, while the figure of the sower has been finely executed in a free and vigorous manner.

Or compare Giotto's *Meeting of Joachim and Anna* (Fig. 222) and his *Entombment* (Fig. 221). A superficial interpretation of the former might suggest that merely because these figures are Biblical characters and therefore, as the halos indicate, of religious interest, the expressed content of the picture must therefore be religious. But, despite the Biblical associations which contribute to the picture's content, the chief content of the picture is social rather than religious. What is here so sensitively and eloquently expressed is tender human affection. Note the inclination of the figures of Anna and Joachim towards one another, an inclination which is reinforced and interpreted by the strongly modelled folds of Joachim's robe and the gentle sweep and curve of Anna's dress. Note the heads and facial expressions of both figures, and, above all, the hands—Joachim's grasping Anna's shoulder with masculine energy, Anna's engaged in one of the gentlest caresses to be found in painting. If this picture is compared with the *Entombment* or with any of the *Crucifixions* which have been cited, the contrast in expressed content is indisputable.

We must also be careful not to assume that a picture with a predominantly social subject-matter is, merely on that account, expressive of social content. For example, Meissonier's *Napoleon III at Solferino* (Fig. 268), though military in subject-matter, is only feebly expressive of the martial spirit; his *Retreat from Moscow* (Fig. 269) catches the spirit of the great retreat more expressively; while Rubens' *Battle on the Bridge* (Fig. 205) is a magnificent expression not only of movement but of fierce combat to the death. Delacroix's *The 28th of July, 1830* (Fig. 270) illustrates in an interesting way the effective use of both realism and symbolism in the artistic expression of man's militant struggle for freedom from oppression. The figure of Liberty, holding the flag, fits perfectly, thanks to the faithful rendering of the semi-nude body, into the highly realistic scene of soldiers and civilians, yet remains the conventional symbol of the French Revolution. These pictures, taken in conjunction, clearly show (i) that the choice of subject-matter is of great importance for artistic expression, but (ii) that the expressed content of a picture is determined not by subject-matter as such but by the way in which it is handled.

The following pictures may be cited as exemplifying the effective pictorial expression of various types of social content. Jordaens' *The Concert* (Fig. 226) expresses lusty and somewhat vulgar conviviality; Adrian Brouwer's *The Gamesters* (Fig. 227), violent and earthy rowdyism; Greuze's *The Village Bride* (Fig. 228), sentiment or sentimentality, depending upon the observer's perspective and his scale of values; and Hogarth's *Marriage à la Mode* series (Fig. 229), shrewd and satiric comment on human frailty. Géricault's *The Raft of the Medusa* (Fig. 230) might be classified under the heading of illustration rather than expressive painting; but, despite its romantic celebration of a stirring contemporary event, it expresses with great dramatic power the anguish of human disaster and the hysterical hope for rescue. Delacroix's *Dante and Virgil* (Fig. 231) exemplifies the attempt to re-express in pictorial terms what has already been expressed by another artist in another medium. The elder Peter Breughel's *The Blind Leading the Blind* (Fig. 232), though frankly allegorical, is obviously much more than a mere pictorial allegory whose meaning can only be determined by faithful translation with the aid of a key. It tells its story without reliance on commentary and tells it in an unforgettable manner.

(c) *Introspective universals.* The painter can express the inner state or mood of introspective reflection most unequivocally by portraying human beings whose visual appearance reflects this state or mood. A natural scene may, indeed, arouse in us an attitude of contemplation and the landscape painter can express this attitude on canvas (Fig. 138). But nature itself is unreflective. Only man is able to reflect and only he can directly manifest, in his own person, the objective presence of introspective universals. His conscious processes are most clearly mirrored, moreover, in facial expression. Hence the clearest pictorial expressions of introspective universals are to be found in portraiture, though, even in portraiture, the pose of the body and the whole pictorial setting can reinforce and interpret the expression of the face.

Watteau's *Gilles* (Figs. 233, 234) perfectly illustrates the way in which a painter can give artistic expression to introspective universals. It is significant that the clown is an idealized self-portrait of the painter. It is also significant that the clown's facial expression is the most expressive portion of the picture. But this facial expression is pictorially motivated and interpreted by the entire scene. The clown is portrayed in a dual rôle—first, as a clown among clowns, whose profession it is to arouse laughter and careless gaiety, but second, as a human being who reflects upon the fate of human solitude. Thus the clown typifies, and the picture as a whole expresses, a spirit of introspective withdrawal from social intercourse. A moment ago Gilles was indulging in his clownish antics, but now, while the merrymakers are still laughing at him, he has become aware of his own human nature and human dignity.

In his *Embarkation for Cythera* (Fig. 235) Watteau expresses not an escape from life but rather the distinctively pastoral theme of delightful contrast between the contemporary here and now and the idyllic realm of the imagination. The handling of the trees and the foreground, and of the nearer courtiers and ladies in the costumes of the period, emphasizes one aspect of this dichotomy, namely, the realm of the actual and the concrete present, whereas the dimmer figures gradually disappearing behind the knoll, and the hovering putti who imperceptibly resolve themselves into the luminous atmosphere, carry us on the wings of the artistic imagination to the idyllic land of Cythera in the distance. The picture is thus an eloquent expression of man's perennial longing for the permanently good.

This exploration of the realm of the imagination is one aspect of what I have described as the reflective mood. Watteau's *Embarkation* comes as close as painting can to the articulation of human desire and aspiration. For a still more articulate expression of man's ideational preoccupation with his own life and destiny as it is affected by his physical, social, and spiritual environment we must turn to reflective poetry and prose. It will not be amiss, however, to cite one more example of reflective painting. One of Giorgione's pictures (Fig. 236) depicts, on the right, a woman nursing her child, on the extreme left, a man gazing abstractedly into space, and, in the background, a landscape containing two broken columns, a bridge over a stream, houses, trees, and a dark sky, with a streak of lightning breaking through the clouds. The picture's outstanding characteristic is, on the one hand, its color harmonies and, on the other hand, its lack of specific motivation. The failure of critics and historians to agree on a name for the picture testifies to this lack; some call it *The Tempest*, others, *The Soldier and the Woman*, etc. Their inability to find in the picture any one specific theme that might appropriately dictate a title is significant. In motivation the several portions of the picture are curiously unrelated to one another. The seated woman is not attending to the child at her breast; the man, who may be a shepherd, or a soldier, or something else, is not looking at the woman, or, indeed, at anything in particular; and the presence of the two columns is pictorially unexplained. Even the sky, though dark with clouds and broken at one point with a white streak of lightning, is not really an angry sky and certainly fails to disturb in the slightest the placid atmosphere of the near and middle foreground. Nothing is really happening; nothing stands in realistic or dynamic relation to anything else; everything is, as it were, detached and aloof from its surroundings. And yet the picture as a whole is not only amazingly unified in color and compositional form; the mood that it expresses is a perfectly consistent mood of revery and reflective contemplation. This mood expresses itself most vividly, perhaps, in the human faces and postures. But the rest of the scene expresses it too, for the trees and sky, the houses and broken columns, are all depicted as one would see them, without anxiety or curiosity, in a spirit of contemplative detachment. The real theme of the picture is revery—a revery "poetic" in its charm, yet oriented (in its own detached way) to a world of real objects and people as Watteau's *Embarkation* is oriented both to a world of the imagination and the world of actuality.

There are those, meanwhile, who would argue that the reflective mood in its purest and most detached form is best expressed not in figure compositions or landscapes but in pictorial abstractions, on the score that line and colored area, properly handled, can be as immediately and powerfully expressive as can a musical pattern of melodic lines and harmonies. I have already acknowledged that abstract form in painting is somewhat expressive, and some of Picasso's abstractions (Fig. 100) might be cited as examples of reflective content in this genre. But that any pictorial abstraction can rival music in this respect I cannot admit, nor can I grant that the expressive potentiality of representational subject-matter is ever ignored in painting with impunity. Let the reader compare, with respect to expressed content, his favorite musical nocturne, his favorite pictorial abstraction of this type, and any apposite representational painting such as Whistler's nocturnal *Battersea Bridge*, and ask himself which of these seems to him to express most effectively the reflective mood.

CHAPTER XVIII

THE PORTRAYAL OF INDIVIDUALS IN SCULPTURE AND PAINTING, AND THE RÔLE OF SPECIFICITY IN ART

PORTRAITURE, defined as the artistic interpretation of objectively existing individuals, raises two problems. (i) How does the portraitist express the unique individuality of persons, objects, and events, and how, in the portrait, is this expressed individuality related to artistically expressed perceptual or spiritual universals? (ii) What, if any, is the artistic importance (as opposed to the merely historical interest) of this objective reference in portraiture to an actually existing individual?

(i) The nature of portraiture can best be demonstrated empirically by comparing the portrait of a man with an ordinary photograph of the same individual, e.g., one of Cézanne's self-portraits with a contemporary photograph (Figs. 239, 240). A good photograph is an accurate record of the individual's visual appearance at one particular instant, but it can exhibit only as much of his enduring personality as happens to manifest itself during the snap of the shutter, and, if we ignore the factor of photographic artistry, it offers no interpretation whatever of his character. A good portrait, in contrast, sacrifices momentary verisimilitude to the more permanent and significant traits of the individual in question. Thus, by means of simplification and distortion, Cézanne has blocked in his own features with great power and directness, and, in the process, revealed himself to us as a man of homely virtues, forthright, irascible, an individualist, keenly observant but not much given to social intercourse, industrious and unwearied in his artistic quest, and his own severest critic. If this portrait is compared with Cézanne's other self-portraits and with portraits of him by other artists it will be clear that a portrait, like other works of art, never expresses *the* essence of its subject-matter but merely certain *aspects* of this essence. In no one of his self-portraits does Cézanne attempt an exhaustive pictorial autobiography, or even an exhaustive portrayal of his own character and appearance on any particular day.

Now this facet of his own physiognomy and character interests him, now that. But this does not contradict the assertion that every serious portrait by a competent artist does express some aspect of the sitter's unique individuality.

The more pronounced this individuality, the richer the portraitist's opportunity.[1] Hence the ideal subject for a portrait is a human being, and more particularly a man or woman with a well-defined personality and a revealing countenance. Portraits of very young children are never as interesting as those of more mature people, since there is less to reveal and interpret. This limitation is of course greatly intensified as we descend from children to animals and from animals to plants and inorganic objects.

Every portrait necessarily expresses, in the act of portraying an actual individual, certain substantival and adjectival universals, both perceptual and spiritual. There is no such thing as a portrait which is *nothing but* a portrait of a unique individual, for no individual is unique in the sense of manifesting no universals whatever. But representational works of art differ markedly in emphasizing now the individual, now this or that universal. A few illustrations will make this plain. Saint Gaudens' *Adams Memorial*, usually entitled *Grief* (Fig. 237), illustrates one extreme. This enigmatic figure, far from being a portrait of any actual man or woman, is so modelled as to leave its sex quite indeterminate. Yet it is indubitably human and certainly expresses human grief with great artistic power. Here the entire emphasis falls upon the expression of human bereavement in its most universal form. Compare this statue with David's portrait of *M. Seriziat* (Fig. 242), or Doré's statue of *D'Artagnan* (Fig. 241), the one, the portrait of a living man, the other, of a character in fiction. Both of these portraits emphasize the sitter's momentary appearance somewhat at the expense of his more abiding personality, and his individual uniqueness somewhat at the expense of more universal human traits. Most of the portraits referred to in the following pages fall between these extremes and illustrate an emphasis both upon the individuality and upon the universality of their respective subjects. Rodin's bust of *Victor Hugo* (Fig. 256)

[1] Whitehead is right in insisting that *every* individual occurrent, a rock as well as a human being, is "conceptually inexhaustible," for the enumeration of any finite number of universals manifesting themselves in it must fail to exhaust its entire nature. But this need not exclude the possibility of recognizing different orders or kinds of infinite complexity.

and Raphael's *Angelo Doni* (Fig. 249) are good examples. We know that these are genuine portraits, both in intention and achievement. Yet they are more than mere portraits of historical persons. They express, in the one case, the urbane man of the world and all that that implies, in the other, the reflective mood of a mature thinker.

(ii) Is the attempt of the portraitist to do justice to the objective individuality of his subject-matter of any artistic moment? The answer will depend upon how "art" and "artistic response" are defined—whether narrowly, with sole reference to their *differentiae*, or more inclusively, with an eye to *all* their major characteristics.

The narrowest definition of art would reduce it to mere aesthetic surface, and the analogous definition of artistic response would restrict such response to the functioning of pure aesthetic taste. This approach to art has its merits. Kant, for example, made a notable contribution to aesthetic theory by analyzing "pure" beauty and "pure" taste. But it leaves completely out of account art's expressed content, both universal and individual, ignores the artist's intent to create not merely beauty but expressive beauty, and reduces the rôle of the critic to that of the trained aesthete.

It is also possible to define art as the expression of universal content without admitting that the distinctive characteristic of portraiture as such, i.e., the portraitist's attempt to interpret and portray the individuality of specific men and women, events and objects, has any artistic relevance. This is a tenable interpretation of the art of portraiture, but it is, I believe, incorrect because it violates the basic principle of critical and philosophical appraisal, namely, that every factor which seems to the creative artist to be of artistic importance, and which actually registers itself in his art, should be regarded by the critic as artistically relevant, and that whatever is judged to be critically relevant should be accepted as relevant by the philosopher of art. Now a portraitist is, by definition, an artist who, *as an artist*, is intent on expressing in his medium his interpretation of the unique individuality of his subject. This is the only definition which does justice to what we know about the way in which portraitists have thought and worked. Most critics have taken this unique objective of portraiture into account and have not felt that, in doing so, they have exceeded their prerogative as critics. And no philosopher of art has ever advanced a coercive reason for rejecting as artistically irrelevant what portraitists as artists and critics as critics have accepted as relevant. It is true that the content of an expressive portrait is not *merely* the artist's interpretation of the individuality of his subject-matter, and that the greater the portrait, the more significant is its universal content. But this is no reason for excluding the additional factor which distinguishes portraiture as such. It is also true that the critic is often unable to check the correctness of the portraitist's interpretation of his individual subject-matter. But this difficulty does not differ *in kind* from that of checking an artist's interpretation of universals; and in any case, a practical difficulty of this type should not be permitted to coerce our definition of portraiture as a distinctive genre.

In the ensuing analysis of portraiture in sculpture and painting, I shall be primarily concerned with the way in which various universals are expressed in portraiture rather than with the measure of success which has attended the portraitist's attempt to interpret the unique individuality of his subject.[2] I shall examine, in turn, human portraiture which is predominantly religious, social, and reflective; the portrayal of human events and of man's artistic products; and, finally, the portrayal of animate and inanimate objects and events in nature.

1. *Human portraiture*

Mino da Fiesole's relief of the *Duke of Urbino* (Fig. 243) is a useful point of reference for our analysis of other portraits. The portraits which we shall be considering in a moment have been chosen because in each case the sitter is portrayed in a religious, social, or reflective attitude. The Duke of Urbino, in contrast, is portrayed with a wholly impassive countenance. The portrait does, of course, express Mino's interpretation of the Duke's character. He is portrayed as unimaginative and insensitive, assured, self-complacent, and smugly self-contained. The portrait is therefore by no means an inexpressive work of art. But we scrutinize the mask-like face in vain for any hint of the trend or orientation of the Duke's thoughts. Piero della Francesca's portrait of the Duke (Fig. 244) depicts him in precisely the same manner in the pictorial medium.

(a) *Religious reverence*. The Duke's impassivity enhances, by contrast, the marked religious expressiveness of Hugo van der Goes' *Portrait of a Young Man* (Fig. 245), Jan Gossaert's portrait of *Jean*

[2] The latter task must be left to the art-critic and the art-historian, since the critical and historical analysis of particular works of art falls definitely outside the province ot the philosopher of art.

Carondelet, and the figure of the donor in the *Avignon Pietà* (Fig. 211). In all three cases the praying hands give us a clue to the artist's expressive intent. But such clues, taken by themselves, provide no guarantee that the artist's intention has been artistically realized, or even that he intended to express genuine religious reverence. In his portrait of *Two Clerics*, for example, Antonio Moro (Fig. 248) has depicted the priest with the folded hands as quite as secular-minded as his brother cleric, who is frankly staring us in the face. He either intended to depict him in this way, or failed, through incompetence, to portray him in an attitude of sincere religious communion. The actual artistic content of a portrait, then, can be determined only through immediate artistic response to the portrait as a whole, regarded as an artistically expressive vehicle. So apprehended, Dürer's *Praying Hands* (Fig. 246) are in themselves religiously expressive artistic "ideas," and the portraits by van der Goes, Jan Gossaert, and the Avignon master are eloquent portrayals of genuinely pious individuals in the act of sincere religious worship.

(b) *Social interest.* Raphael's portrait of *Angelo Doni* (Fig. 249) exemplifies a pronounced social orientation. Here the sitter is neither reflectively preoccupied with his own inner thoughts nor religiously enthralled, but is directly aware of us as his human audience. Angelo Doni regards us with extraordinary human comprehension. A predominant social interest can also be expressed in group portraiture. In Largillière's study of himself and his wife and daughter (Fig. 250), for example, the painter is looking at us and thus enters into immediate relation with us; his wife is looking at her husband, though in a somewhat abstracted manner; and the daughter is shown in a romantic pose, intended, as the gesture and the sheet of music indicate, to celebrate her father's artistic genius. Thus all three figures are socially oriented, though each in a different way. A still greater variety of social orientation is evident in Rembrandt's *Anatomy Lesson* (Fig. 251). Dr. Tulp is portrayed in the act of pedagogical exposition and is aware of his hearers, but he is also posing for his portrait, i.e., he is aware of us.[3] The man at his immediate right is absorbed in the discourse; his right-hand neighbor is gazing at the cadaver, as is, with less absorption, the man behind him; while the two figures in the background, as well as the figure farthest but one to our left, exhibit different degrees of interest in us as their

[3] It is always possible to construe the painter as the object of interest; but even this interest is social in character.

pictorial audience—degrees varying all the way from casual awareness to intent fascination.

(c) *Reflective contemplation.* The contrast between a predominantly social and a predominantly reflective content must be illustrated with some care. It is strikingly exemplified in a comparison of Roger van der Weyden's *Man with the Arrow* (Fig. 258) with Raphael's *Angelo Doni* (Fig. 249). The sitter in both cases is a young aristocrat, but the expressed mood and inner attitude are utterly different in the two portraits. A more familiar contrast is afforded by Michelangelo's famous statues of Giuliano and Lorenzo in the *Medici Chapel* (Figs. 252, 253). There exists, as Professor Erwin Panofsky has shown,[4] abundant archaeological evidence to show that the former was intended by Michelangelo to express the Jovial, the latter, the Saturnian disposition.[5] "The contemplative Saturnian is '*closed to the world*'; he is morose, taciturn, *entirely concentrated upon his own self*, a friend of *solitude* and darkness, and avaricious or at least parsimonious. The active Jovial is '*open to the world*'; he is alert, eloquent, *companionable*, *interested in his fellow-beings*, and unlimitedly generous. In the Medici Chapel this antithesis is indicated, in a general way, by the contrast between the 'open' composition of the Giuliano statue and the 'closed' composition of the 'Penseroso,' as well as by the two pairs of personifications with which the two statues are grouped together. . . . But the Saturnian and Jovial connotations of the two portraits are emphasized by more specific features. Like the face of Dürer's *Melencolia*, the face of the 'Penseroso' is darkened by a heavy shadow suggesting the *facies nigra* of the Saturnian melancholic. The index finger of his left hand covers his mouth with the gesture of Saturnian silence. His elbow rests on a closed cash-box, a typical symbol of Saturnian parsimony; and, to make the symbolism still more explicit, the front of this cash-box is adorned

[4] Erwin Panofsky, *Studies in Iconology* (New York: The Oxford Press, 1939), pp. 210-11. The author's notes have been omitted and certain phrases of peculiar interest have been italicized.

[5] This contrast is clearly expressed in Pico della Mirandola's Commentary on Benivieni, from which Professor Panofsky quotes (pp. 209-10) the following passage. " 'Saturn signifies the intellectual nature which is only devoted to and intent on understanding and contemplating. Jupiter signifies the active life which consists of superintending, administering and keeping in motion by its rules the things subjected to it. These two properties are found in the two planets called by the same names, viz., Saturn and Jupiter. For, as they say, Saturn produces contemplative men, while Jupiter gives them principalities, government, and the administration of peoples.' "

with the head of a bat, the emblematic animal of Dürer's engraving *Melencolia I*. Giuliano, on the other hand, holds a princely sceptre and with his open left he offers two coins. Both these motifs symbolically [contrast] him who '*spends*' *himself in outward action with him who* '*shuts himself off*' *in self-centred contemplation*. . . ." This analysis, which I have quoted at some length partly for its relevance to the present argument and partly because of the light it throws on the use of symbolism in the representational arts, certainly enriches our understanding and appreciation of the subject-matter and so, though only indirectly, of the expressed content of the two statues. Yet this objective evidence merely confirms, as did the praying hands, the correctness of the impression which is directly conveyed, quite apart from the symbolism, by the faces and postures of the two figures. For even to an observer ignorant of this symbolism, Lorenzo is clearly lost in contemplation and unaware of his physical and social milieu; Giuliano, in contrast, though portrayed in an attitude of repose (as is appropriate for a tomb) is obviously the man of affairs, aware of his social environment and concerned to adapt himself to it in princely fashion.

The transition from a social to a reflective content is also exemplified by three portraits by Reynolds. In his portrait of John and Theresa Parker, the children are aware of their audience, but John more so than his sister. In *The Young Fortune Teller* the boy gives us a shy, smiling glance while the girl continues with her fortune telling, though she too betrays some realization that she is being observed. Finally, in *The Age of Innocence* (Fig. 261), the child's abstracted gaze and folded hands express the oblivion to the external world characteristic of a pleasing day-dream.

These comparisons indicate the preeminent rôle in portraiture of facial expression. Rodin's *La Pensée* (Fig. 254) offers further confirmation of this fact, for here quiet contemplation is expressed entirely by a single head. This expression is, indeed, intensified not only by the inclination of the head but by the sharp contrast between the smoothly modelled face and the rough-hewn block of stone. But this latter device is also used by Rodin to express a very different kind of content; in his *Danaïde* (Fig. 255), for example, it is used to reinforce the expression of a predominantly sensuous content. In *Le Penseur* (Fig. 257), on the other hand, where not the face but the convulsed pose and violent modelling of the body is the chief vehicle, the expressed content is not so much reflection as the ineffectual struggle of bone and sinew to engage in an uncongenial activity. If we compare the brutality of this statue with the spirituality of *La Pensée*, or with the rugged intelligence of *Victor Hugo* (Fig. 256), the great importance of the face for the sculptural expression of spiritual universals is evident.

I have said that, while reflection may be directed introspectively to the passing mood, it is more often religiously or socially oriented. Because of its primary medium, literature can indicate easily and precisely the type of reflection in which a literary character, whether biographical or fictitious, is indulging. Sculpture and painting, in contrast, must resort to indirection in order to motivate a reflective facial expression. The means at the disposal of the representational arts are either symbolic, as in the case of the Medici statues, or representational, i.e., reliance upon a revealing sculptural or pictorial setting. The relatively detached figure of Mary Magdalene in the *Entombment* at Solesmes (Fig. 210) is, taken by itself, expressive of deep sorrow, but, divorced from the sculptural group, it gives us no clue as to the occasion of this sorrow. We can be quite sure that the woman is not asleep and that the sorrow manifested in her face is an enduring grief that will never cease. But the instant the figure is apprehended in its sculptural setting (Fig. 209) we realize not only that she is at present absorbed in intense contemplation but that this contemplation is religiously motivated. The figure thus becomes expressive of an attitude of Christian worship. Thus the expressiveness of a single figure can be sharpened and interpreted through artistic association with a representational setting.

In Raphael's portrait of *Pope Julius II* (Fig. 259), in Rembrandt's *Man with the Helmet* (Fig. 260), and in Daniel Chester French's *Abraham Lincoln* (Fig. 262), on the other hand, the only clues we have to the orientation of the reflective mood are, respectively, the clerical robes, the soldier's helmet and armor, and the symbols of government on Lincoln's chair. These clues justify the assumption that each man's revery is appropriate to his calling. But this is as far as reasonable interpretation can be pushed. Sculptural and pictorial portraiture do not lend themselves to a more articulate expression of man's inner life and thoughts. Only in literature can these thoughts be specified and elaborated.

The ability to reflect is man's peculiar faculty; it is preeminently this capacity which distinguishes him from the brute. But this withdrawal into oneself may be the occasion or the symptom of mental collapse. If man alone is able to reflect, he alone is subject to the disease of madness. Madness may be defined as failure to maintain normal and healthy contact with reality. The madman may manifest his madness in an inability to adapt himself advantageously to nature, or to indulge in fruitful human intercourse, or, in some cases, to believe in and worship a divine being. His madness accordingly condemns him to the solitude of his own futile reflections and to the torment of his own frustrated desires and consuming emotions. This pathological phase of man's reflective life has also been expressed in portraiture, notably in the later paintings of Van Gogh. If Van Gogh's paintings are studied chronologically they will be found to record the successive stages of his mental illness. His madness is clearly expressed in his later *Cypresses* (Fig. 193), while a self-portrait (Fig. 263), painted in October, 1888, and annotated by Van Gogh "à mon ami, Paul G[auguin]," shows us a man still artist enough to express on canvas the inner madness which he was sane enough to observe and interpret correctly. The picture has thus a double interest, first, as the vivid expression of the reflective attitude become self-destructive to the point of madness, and second, as striking evidence of the dual personality which resides in every artist. In the sane artist this duality expresses itself in his ability to step, during his interpretative and creative labors, into the rôle of artistic observer and to view his subject-matter (and, in portraiture, even himself) with "artistic objectivity." In mad Van Gogh this dualism manifests itself in its most extreme form. For even when, as a human being, he was correctly judged by others to be insane, as an artist he was sane enough to recognize his own insanity, and sufficiently gifted as a painter to express this insanity with pictorial lucidity.

2. *The portrayal of historical events*

The transition from *bona fide* human portraiture to the portrayal of historical events is a gradual one. It would be easy to select a number of pictures exemplifying intermediate stages between these extremes and to arrange them in such a way that the difference in type of subject-matter and expressed content between any two adjacent pictures would be negligible. The position in the series to which any of these pictures should be assigned would depend upon the *degree* to which individual personalities, on the one hand, and individual historical events as events, on the other, were emphasized in the picture in question. Thus David's *Death of Marat* (Fig. 265) is partly a portrait of Marat, but it portrays him at the dramatic moment of his death. The emphasis falls, as the title of the picture indicates, upon the event of his murder rather than upon his personality.

Yet despite this frequent overlapping of the genres of human portraiture and historical painting, the latter has its own generic characteristics and its own distinctive problems. The special subject-matter of an historical painting is an event which, *as an event*, is seen in historical perspective to possess an individuality of its own and, as such, to be of interest and importance to man. The problems which the historical painter, like other artists who deal with historical subject-matter, e.g., the writer of an historical narrative, must solve are (i) the selection of an event which permits of being treated in an artistically and humanly significant manner, (ii) the circumscription of the event (since actual events flow into one another without clearly established boundaries) and the apprehension of its historical individuality, and (iii) the interpretation of this event in such a manner that both its unique individuality and its more universal character and import are expressed with insight and artistic clarity. These problems are, it is evident, specific variants of the more general problems of portraiture as such, i.e., the *significant* portrayal of objective *individuality*. Like the pure portraitist, the historically minded artist must avoid undue emphasis upon the merely idiosyncratic and momentary, on the one hand, the merely general or universal, on the other.

The problem is intensified in historical painting by the fact that the temporality of an historical event, i.e., its essentially transitory character, so largely determines for us its nature and significance. The distinction between an event and an individual object, such as a human being, is, no doubt, merely one of degree, since both, as individual entities, are spatio-temporal occurrents embodying timeless universals. Without exploring the philosophical intricacies of the problem, however, it is evident that our primary interest in a human being, as the subject of a portrait, is his *relatively enduring* character and its *recurrent* appearances, whereas our primary interest in an historical event as such is its *transitive* and *unique* character. In short, we normally entitle an occurrent an "event" when its transitiveness is our chief concern, an "object," when its relatively persistent identity is in question. Meanwhile, the primary medium of the painter is "non-temporal" or "static." The painter's difficult task, accordingly, is to decide how to portray interpretatively, in a static medium and in a single representation, a subject-matter whose objective character, viewed in historical perspective, is in very essence "temporal" and "dynamic."

Since these problems are all closely interrelated, we can, like the historical painter who must solve them simultaneously, consider them in conjunction with one another. Delaroche's *The Execution of Lady Jane Grey* (Fig. 264) illustrates a type of solution which stresses the particular moment rather than the more embracing event, and historical verisimilitude rather than universal significance. It falls quite definitely, therefore, into the category of historical illustration and expresses artistically little more than sentimental pathos. Such crucifixions as Dürer's or Rembrandt's (Figs. 163, 215, 216), in contrast, largely ignore historical verisimilitude and emphasize the lasting significance to man of an historical event of supreme religious importance. Delacroix's *Crucifixion* (Fig. 220), in turn, contrasts sharply with these three because it so completely loses sight of the distinctively religious character of the event portrayed. Delacroix emphasizes historical verisimilitude no more than do Dürer and Rembrandt, but he does emphasize the merely human rather than the humanly divine, and the particular rather than the universal. What we here see portrayed is not a Divine event of profound religious significance but merely a human event, and, furthermore, not universal "anguish" but the particular sufferings of a particular man and the particular sorrow of those who are attached to him by love and friendship. David's *Coronation of the Empress Josephine* (Fig. 267) resembles *The Execution of Lady Jane Grey* much more closely than it does the crucifixions of Dürer and Rembrandt in the historical fidelity with which the costumes, the architectural setting, and even the faces are portrayed. But the coronation, itself an event of greater historical significance than the death of Lady Jane, is depicted in such a way as not only to emphasize its wider historical import but also effectively to convey a sense of universal regal grandeur. In the same artist's *The Oath of the Horatii* (Fig. 266), or his *Sabine Women*, he achieves still greater generality. In both these pictures he makes every attempt to handle the costumes, military accoutrements, and architectural details with archaeological accuracy, but the compositional organization of the pictures is dictated entirely by interpretational considerations and expressive intent.

The latter tendency is even more pronounced in the historical paintings of Poussin; his *Rape of the Sabines*, for instance, emphasizes the expression of timeless universals to such an extent that the historical subject-matter is little more than an occasion for the portrayal of typical physical movement and human passion.

Notable for their success in catching the peculiar temper and spirit of an event of major historical importance are Delacroix's *The 28th of July, 1830* (Fig. 270) and Rude's *Le Départ des Volontaires* (Fig. 271). They also illustrate an important difference between the representational potentialities of sculpture and painting. Painting lends itself far more effectually than sculpture to the expressive representation of historical events as such; sculpture is limited by its primary medium to the expression of the more universal and suprahistorical. Thus, Delacroix is able, without descending to historical triviality, to give us an interpretation of the spirit of the French Revolution which is not only rich in universal meaning but is a vivid interpretation of a specific historical event. Rude, on the other hand, though he employs the same symbolic figure of Liberty associated with the French Revolution, is compelled by his medium (in order to avoid the merely picturesque) to generalize this figure and to portray the figures marching in front of it without reference to date or place. Thus Rude's composition really expresses the universal spirit of war rather than that of the French Revolution and is therefore, according to pictorial standards, not primarily an historical study, whereas Delacroix's picture is preeminently historical, though it also possesses a more universal meaning and significance.

Finally, it should be noted that each of the pictures here discussed attempts to solve the problem of representing a temporal event in a "timeless" medium by depicting this event, whether with historical verisimilitude or in a more generalized fashion, at the moment when it manifests both its individual nature and its universal significance most clearly. Here again, then, the choice of specific subject-matter is of great importance. But even more depends upon how this specific subject-matter is interpreted, that is, upon how successfully those characteristics which are manifest are set in relief and expressively treated. For undue fidelity to historical detail reduces art to mere illustration, while a complete lack of historical sense results in the abandonment of the historical genre. The historical painter, like the portraitist, must combine an historical sense of the characteristically individual with a philosophical sense of the universal and the abiding.

3. The portrayal of other works of art

Historical events derive their distinctive character from the human beings who participate in them and from the human societies which constitute their frame of reference. Works of art, in turn, derive most of their peculiar individuality and human significance from the hands of their creators, the artist having impressed on each of them an individuality largely foreign to the primary and secondary raw materials which he has employed. Accordingly, when a painter elects to paint a picture of a building which already possesses an artistic individuality and character of its own, his problem is strictly akin to that of the portrait painter. He can, of course, largely ignore the building's own artistic quality, as did Monet in his cathedral studies and his painting of the *Doges' Palace* (Fig. 35). But if, in the spirit of portraiture, he wishes to catch the distinctive individuality of a building which has a style and character of its own, he must solve the difficult problem of how to do justice to this individuality without disrupting the artistic unity of his own composition. Antonio Canale and Bernardo Belotto (both called Canaletto), the fashionable and highly competent painters of famous buildings in the eighteenth century, were notably successful in the solution of this problem (Figs. 33, 12). They were as literal in their representation of the visible details of a façade as the pictorial medium well permits, and relied almost entirely on the angle and range of vision, and on the handling of the foreground, the sky, and the lighting, which they were able to control, for the creation of a pictorial composition with artistic individuality and merit of its own.

The solution of this problem is, of course, facilitated by the necessary translation of a three-dimensional object onto a two-dimensional canvas—a necessity which, though in one sense a limitation of the pictorial medium, is actually its chief representational asset, since what is translated can also be interpreted and controlled. The exercise of this control is finely exemplified in Cézanne's *Puget's Cupid* (Fig. 275) and in Corot's paintings of buildings, e.g., of Chartres (Fig. 39), the Colosseum, the Roman Forum, or the Belfry of Douai. Bonington's paintings of buildings exhibit a greater latitude of interpretation and technique, his *Doges' Palace* (Fig. 34) and his *Parterre d'eau at Versailles* (Fig. 274) illustrating two possible extremes *within* the limits of pictorial unity. The former, despite its architectural fidelity, is itself a lovely and expressive landscape. The latter, despite its cavalier treatment of the palace, is not only a charming landscape but, in addition, an admirable expression of the sweep and atmosphere of the actual architectural setting and the spirit of the architectural milieu.

The problem of fusing one work of art in another, where the former is made the representational subject-matter of the latter, is still more acute when the work of art which is representationally introduced into a painting is itself a painting or a group of paintings. That such a procedure seriously threatens final pictorial unity is painfully apparent in the younger David Teniers' *Picture Gallery of Archduke Leopold William* in Brussels (Fig. 273). Whatever this painter's technical competence, his composition must surely be judged to lack both compositional and expressive unity. Watteau's solution of the same problem in his *Gersaint's Signboard* (Fig. 272) is interesting. Despite the fact that this picture was cut in two shortly after it was painted, and each half hung for years as a self-contained composition, the picture as a whole is completely unified. The unity is technically achieved by a number of coordinate devices—by perspective, by the street in the foreground which helps to establish the three-dimensional unity of the room, by the central doorway in the background, the arrangement of the two groups of human figures, the color harmonies, etc. But what especially concerns us here is the care which Watteau has exercised *not* to paint the pictures on the walls in such a way as clearly to reveal their subject-matter, i.e., his deliberate *suppression* of *their* artistic individuality. This solution, as well as the non-existence of pictures in which the individuality of other pictures is emphasized without disastrous results, suggests that there are limits beyond which portraiture cannot go with artistic success, and that the pictorial representation of other pictures tends to be a case in point.

4. The portrayal of animals and things

To pass from the human to the sub-human is at once to discover a marked diminution of objective individuality, or, more accurately, to discover that animals, plants, and inanimate objects (apart from those which man himself has fashioned) possess an individuality which is less rich and complex and, for that very reason, less interesting to man. This is clearly revealed in paintings of animals and trees and of the objects which are representationally introduced into still lifes.

Animal portraiture is by no means unknown. We have all seen pictures of Derby winners painted in the true spirit of portraiture, and we have doubtless found them very dull unless we happened to be particular fanciers of horse-flesh. Such pictures are, indeed, seldom painted by imaginative artists. But even an artist of great competence cannot reveal what does not exist to be revealed. However much we may love a dog or cat as a household pet, and though we may prefer its company on occasion to that of human beings, what we describe as its personality falls so far short of human personality as to preclude the possibility of using animals as a suitable subject-matter for serious portraiture.

A comparison of two roughly contemporary paintings in the Dutch School may serve to demonstrate this. Paul Potter, in a picture entitled *The Young Bull* (Fig. 276), has painted the animal with portrait-like affection and fidelity. The evidence for this is not only the pictorial treatment of the bull but the way in which the other animals, the tree, the flying bird, the distant landscape and immediate foreground, and in particular the cowherd, have also been painted. Everything in the picture betrays the artist's unusual interest in the unique individuality of every object in the visible world. The picture is actually a portrait study of a group of animals and their keeper in a highly realistic setting. Now Potter's technical competence is undeniable, as is his sense of composition. The picture is a perfectly good picture unless one wishes to condemn it on the score of too meticulous "realism." But then a host of excellent Dutch interiors, with or without figures, must be condemned as well. What really bores us in Potter's picture is the fact that it is a portrait study of a subject-matter which cannot sustain or justify such treatment. Consider, by way of contrast, Aelbert Cuyp's handling of a similar subject-matter in his *Young Herdsman with Cows* (Fig. 277). Here again animals and human beings are depicted in a landscape setting, but now not in the spirit of portraiture but rather in the spirit of true landscape painting. The significant subject-matter here is the scene as a whole, not the individual figures in it, whether human or animal. The two men are well in the background and play a very minor, though not a wholly negligible, rôle, and the cattle, despite their number, size, and prominence in the picture, are yet subordinated to the depiction of the countryside in the evening light. They make an important contribution to the total pictorial effect, but the true subject-matter of the picture is the landscape *with* cattle, *not* the cattle in a landscape. As a result, the picture is artistically expressive as Potter's is not.

Turning to pure landscape painting, we must acknowledge the possibility of emphasizing, as does Cézanne in his familiar paintings of Mont Ste.-Victoire, the distinctive silhouette of a mountain, or, like Théodore Rousseau in some of his paintings and sketches, the characteristic arboreal configurations of individual trees or groups of trees. This type of emphasis, if duly subordinated to the larger interest, i.e., to the expression in a landscape of various types of universals, does, no doubt, enrich the total expressed content of the picture. But it is essential to successful landscape painting that this element of portraiture be kept well subordinated, for actual mountains and trees possess in themselves a less rich and interesting individuality than do even animals (*vide* Fig. 104). The individuality we so value in a landscape is primarily that of the pictorial representations themselves, not that of actual trees and mountains. The strictures of those critics who refuse to acknowledge the value of objective individual reference in portraiture as such *do* apply to landscape painting in which the emphasis of portraiture is at all pronounced, though they do not, I believe, apply to human and historical portraiture.

Finally, the objects represented in a still life normally possess so impoverished an individuality of their own that they can hardly be said to provide a suitable subject-matter for portraiture at all. Our interest in a Chardin still life (Fig. 280), for example, is directed exclusively to the individuality of the pictorial objects on the canvas and the universals which these objects express. We entirely ignore the particular eggs, onions, pipes, or kitchen utensils which Chardin presumably arranged on a table as his model. This applies equally to still lifes painted in a free impressionistic manner and to the meticulous still lifes of a DeHeem (Fig. 281), in which every dewdrop and tendril is depicted with painstaking fidelity. Whatever the artistic significance of a still life in whatever style, this significance must be the product of factors other than the factor of objective individual reference.

There is, so far as I know, only one exception to this rule, namely, when an inanimate object is so painted as to suggest that it possessed for the painter, and therefore can possess for us, a personality of its own. Van Gogh's *Yellow Chair* (Fig. 286), which must be described *not* as a still life but as a portrait study, is a case in point. What makes it interesting as a portrait is the intimate individuality which the chair has acquired. We see it portrayed as a chair which has become beloved of its owner. Nor does it seem fanciful to suggest that Van Gogh painted a pipe and an open paper of tobacco on the seat of the chair to enforce this very interpretation. For there are few inanimate objects in common use which are richer in intimate human associations than a pipe. This, then, is not just a kitchen chair but some human individual's chair (presumably Van Gogh's), and it is this association which, from the representational point of view, justifies its being made the subject-matter of a portrait.

But even in Van Gogh's *Portrait of a Chair* the *chief* emphasis falls upon the expressed universals and on the compositional design of line and colored area. Still lifes are too various to permit of easy classification, but in general they tend to emphasize one or other of these factors. Chardin, for example, stresses perceptual and spiritual universals (for he too knows how to introduce the factor of intimate human association), while modern painters like Matisse and Braque (Figs. 282, 283) emphasize the more abstract design and the total decorative effect of the composition's non-representational "aesthetic surface." The special merit of Cézanne's still lifes (Fig. 284) is their extraordinary fusion of both these factors, the representational and the decorative. There is no fruit more real than his, if by "reality" we mean the eloquent expression of perceptual universals, but also no compositions more decorative or with a more immediately expressive "aesthetic surface."

5. The rôle of specificity in art

My analysis of artistic content would be incomplete without explicit recognition of the unique emphasis in art on particularity, or specificity, *as such*. Since this contribution is especially evident in pictorial still lifes, let us briefly reexamine this genre with this problem in mind.

When we stand in front of a good still life we are not only aware of the picture's universal content and of its decorative quality, but respond with interest and delight to its sensuous and compositional specificity. That is, we are vividly aware of its specific colored areas and the pictorial objects that constitute its specific representational subject-matter. "What a lovely bit of blue and ivory," we exclaim;

and again, "Notice the way in which the artist has handled this particular apple, this onion, this shadow, this perspective, this contrast or harmony." What here arouses our interest is the factor of sheer pictorial specificity—*this* particular area of red (not universal redness), *this* apple (not apples in general or any generic characteristic of apples), *this* shadow (not darkness or colored luminosity of shadows as such), *this* specific solution of *this* compositional problem (not abstract principles of perspective, harmony, or dynamic contrast).

The artistic importance of specificity is especially noticeable in still lifes because of the absence in them of all reference to specific objective individuals and because of the relative poverty of their universal content. In looking at a fine portrait we are invited by the artist to transcend the *picture's* artistic specificity and to see in it the *objective* individual which its colored areas and representational forms portray. The more sensitive we are to the portrait *as* a portrait, the more are we impelled to "look through" the picture and apprehend its objective subject-matter as the artist has interpreted it. Similarly, in looking at pictures with a universal content of major import we are so impressed with this content that we tend not to be explicitly aware of the picture's artistic specificity. But still lifes are, as we have seen, not portraits, and the most expressive of still lifes can hardly rival a great landscape or figure composition in profundity of expressed content. The artistic specificity of a still life, i.e., its "aesthetic surface," is therefore most likely to engage our attention.

Now it is precisely this type of response which the champions of art's "aesthetic surface" are most concerned to emphasize. Indeed, this is the only response which they are willing to entitle genuinely artistic. To "transcend" a picture's specificity, or to "look through it," is to them anathema. For them a picture or a work of art in any other medium is, *as a work of art*, a specific pattern of sensuous particulars *and nothing more*.

I have been concerned throughout to refute this popular modern dogma which is, as I believe, not only empirically unsound and theoretically unjustifiable, but, in the light of art history, heretical. Here, however, I should like to emphasize the important element of truth in it.[6] Like most heresies, it is erroneous more in what it denies than in what it affirms. The pure aesthete is quite right (i) in recognizing that the artistic specificity of any composition is an *essential*

[6] Cf., below, Chap. xxv.

condition of its artistic quality, and that aesthetic response to this factor is a *sine qua non* of all artistic response, and (ii) in condemning any tendency to ignore this factor by literally "looking through" the work of art, as one might look through a pane of glass, or by "transcending" its aesthetic surface in the sense of leaving this surface behind.

Indeed, the artistic specificity of a work of art in any medium is an essential ingredient in its expressed content. Part of what every work of art should convey to us is a vivid sense of "this-ness." The specificity of a work of art is thus not only the necessary *vehicle* for artistic expression but part of the artistic *content* which it expresses. This fact, as much as any other, distinguishes a work of art from a mere phenomenon of nature, for the latter merely *manifests* its unique specificity in just being the spatio-temporal occurrent that it is, whereas a work of art not merely manifests but *expresses* specificity.

This accounts for the fact that artists are able to teach us to observe and enjoy the individuality of natural phenomena. Having lived for a while with a Cézanne still life, we are impelled to look at specific apples and folds of cloth with new eyes and to observe not only their generic but their specific qualities and attributes. Such quickening of normal sense-perception is one of art's most precious by-products. The painter of a still life could never have painted an apple with such loving attention to its *pictorial* specificity had he not first known how to observe and delight in individual apples in all *their* objective uniqueness. We, in turn, are first led to delight in the *picture's* specificity, and it is this delight which later impels us unconsciously to observe natural objects themselves in all *their* endlessly varied uniqueness. Thus, paradoxically, even a still life may be said to lead us indirectly beyond itself to a sharper and more sensitive awareness of the unique appearances of individual natural phenomena.

This recognition of the rôle of specificity in art—a recognition sufficiently emphatic, I trust, to satisfy even the aesthete—does not, meanwhile, impair in the least the validity of the claim that universals and (in portraiture) objective individuals constitute the major content of all significant art. No contradiction is involved because artistic specificity plays the dual rôle of necessary vehicle for artistic expression *and* of expressed content.

The precise interrelation between universality, objective individuality, and artistic specificity in painting can now be summarized as follows. (i) *Universals* can only be expressed in painting through the mediation of specific pictorial patterns (non-representational and/or representational). (ii) *Objective individuality* can only be expressed under the same conditions and, in addition, through the expression of relevant universals. And (iii) *artistic specificity* can only be expressed in a composition which also expresses certain universals and, in portraiture, objective individuals.

This analysis of portraiture, finally, suggests a fruitful way of describing the universal content of non-portraiture. A portrait refers us specifically to *one* completely determinate objective individual, however complex. In the non-portrait, on the other hand, the artistically individualized representation of a man, a landscape, an historical event, an apple, or any other perceptual occurrent refers us to *any* relevant objective individual, that is, to *all* specific individual occurrents *of this general type*. The individual tree or mountain on the canvas is strictly analogous to a "propositional function" in logic or mathematics. When a mathematician considers the properties of an isosceles triangle ABC, he refers to no one specific triangle but to all triangles which satisfy the requisite geometrical requirements. Similarly, in the proposition, "*x* is red," *x* refers to no one specific red object, to the exclusion of other red objects, but to all actual or possible specific objects which possess the universal quality, "redness." This interpretation is applicable to every type of universal content in art, whether perceptual or spiritual. *Any* specific subject-matter of a work of art, once selected and organized so as to become expressive of *any* given kind of universal content, is transformed by this process into an artistic propositional function which refers us to *all* actual or possible occurrents (but to no one specific occurrent) embodying the universal quality or relation in question. *This* musical interpretation of grief, *this* architectural interpretation of finitude in the presence of infinity, *this* literary interpretation of cruelty, etc., express universal grief, exaltation, and cruelty of this type as embodied in all actual or possible specific instances.

It is clear, then, that in non-portraiture artistic specificity, as expressive of artistic content, always involves an *indeterminate* reference to one or more actual or possible objective individual embodiments of the universals in question. This is precisely what the aesthete, who restricts himself to the artistic specificity of the work of art, ignores. Portraiture differs from non-portraiture merely in possessing an *additional determinate* reference to some one specific actually existing individual.

CHAPTER XIX

THE EXPRESSIVE POTENTIALITIES AND LIMITATIONS OF THE MAJOR ARTS

I MUST restrict myself in this chapter to a brief indication of the distinctive expressive potentialities and limitations of the major arts other than painting. It must be left to the reader to apply to the other arts whatever principles of pictorial expressiveness may be more generally applicable, and whatever new principles of wider applicability emerge in the following sections.

1. Sculpture

The range of sculptural[1] expressiveness can best be indicated by defining four boundaries which the sculptor cannot transgress without loss of sculptural quality and artistic expressiveness. Two of these relate primarily to free-standing sculpture, the other two to sculptural relief.

Free-standing sculpture loses sculptural quality and artistic expressiveness if it is either too abstractly geometrical or too literally reproductive. Karl Hermann's *Bewegung* (Fig. 95) and Brancusi's *Bird in Space* (Fig. 99) go about as far as possible in the direction of sculptural abstraction without complete loss of expressiveness. Hermann's composition is a pure abstraction except for certain faintly suggested representational associations. Yet its title, "Movement," is justified by the powerful upward thrust of the wave-like shape and the sense of movement which it arouses in us. It is still on the expressive side of the boundary between art and purely formal (here, geometrical) beauty, though dangerously near this boundary. A perfectly plain sphere, in contrast, must be sculpturally quite inexpressive, though it may be aesthetically satisfying (Fig. 94. Compare Fig. 93). The other boundary, which complements the boundary of geometrical (or purely formal) inexpressiveness, is that of inexpressive literal reproduction. Painted wooden statues, such as Günther's *Mary on a Cloud* (Fig. 125), approach this boundary but still possess great sculptural eloquence. Pratt's *Country School Boy*

[1] I shall here confine my attention to completely or relatively self-contained sculpture and ignore pure sculptural decoration.

(Fig. 105), in contrast, is so literal a copy of the artist's model as to be sculpturally quite inexpressive. It merely manifests in a wholly naturalistic manner as many of the universals actually manifested by a living barefoot boy as are possible in an unpainted statue. If we compare this statue with Rodin's *John the Baptist* (Fig. 106), a sculpture very similar stylistically to the *Age of Bronze* which was loudly declared by contemporary critics to be merely a cast of a living model, the presence of the interpretative factor in Rodin's statue, and its absence in Pratt's, is at once evident. Or, to cite two more contrasting illustrations, compare Bernini's *David* (Fig. 108) with another *David* (Fig. 107), here portrayed as an older man. The sculptural expressiveness of Bernini's statue is indubitable. The other figure, in contrast, is actually not a statue at all but a photograph of a living man. As a *retouched* photograph of a carefully *posed* model it possesses some slight artistic quality; but it is completely devoid of genuinely *sculptural* expressiveness.

The first of these boundaries is paralleled in painting by inexpressive pictorial abstractions, i.e., sheer two-dimensional geometry, as exemplified by Mondrian's *Composition in Black, White and Red* (Fig. 97), and requires no further commentary. The second would be paralleled in a two-dimensional medium by an untouched colored photograph which would differ from a "realistic" Dutch interior (Fig. 168) as the photographed *David* referred to above differs from Rodin's *John the Baptist* or Bernini's *David*.

The expressive potentialities of free-standing sculpture are best realized through the fullest sculptural exploitation of physical solidity and three-dimensionality. This involves a wise selection of subject-matter with an eye to its plastic solidity, as well as judicious simplification, generalization, and compositional arrangement. The *Theseus* and the *Fates* from the east pediment of the Parthenon (Figs. 115, 116) are superb solutions of the problem of how the sculptor can effectively select and interpret his subject-matter.

Sculptural relief remains sculptural only so long as it too realizes the solid three-dimensionality of its medium and refrains from a sculpturally disastrous imitation of painting. Sculpture that is *purely* linear is not sculpture at all but a drawing in an uncongenial medium. The primitive *Charging Mammoth* (Fig. 145), found in La Madeleine, is a case in point. The Egyptian relief representing Akhenaten worshipping the sun (Fig. 146), in contrast, though still predominantly in the linear manner of treatment, has unquestionable sculptural quality. A sculptor whose chief objective it is to approximate as closely to literal reproduction as the medium permits is simply renouncing his sculptural birthright (Fig. 101). Ghiberti's expressive panelled reliefs on the east doors of the Baptistry in Florence (Fig. 102), Girardon's delightful *Bathing Nymphs* (Fig. 112), and even Rodin's overwhelming *Porte de l'Enfer* (Fig. 153) all illustrate, in very different styles, the possibility of approximating to a pictorial effect without loss of genuinely sculptural quality.

These boundaries of sculptural relief suggest the corresponding boundaries of the graphic and pictorial arts in their relation to sculpture and architecture. Only the genius of a Michelangelo could emphasize sculptural plasticity as he did without loss of pictorial, i.e., fresco, quality (Fig. 133). Tiepolo's wall in the Palazzo Labia (Fig. 131), in which it is difficult to distinguish real architectural and sculptural forms from their pictorial representation, is a work primarily indicative of the artist's illusionistic skill in the Baroque style. Tiepolo's ceiling over the main stairway in the Residenz in Würzburg has far greater pictorial quality.

The sculptural technique lends itself best to the expressive interpretation of those perceptual universals which most clearly manifest themselves in the human body and in the bodies of the larger mammals. The glorious *Venus from Cyrene* (Fig. 201) in the Terme Museum in Rome is a perfect example of the expression in sculpture of the smooth, firm plasticity of the female figure. The quality of sensuous softness is intensified in Rodin's *Danaïde* (Fig. 255), that of muscular strength and firmness in Maillol's *Female Torso* (Fig. 202). The three-dimensionality and physical mass of the female figure achieves notable expression in Maillol's *Seated Woman* (Fig. 126), while these qualities are emphasized in a massively cubistic manner in Ahron Ben-Shmuel's *Seated Woman* (Fig. 128). In Gaston Lachaise's *Torso* (Fig. 129) a comparable effect is achieved by the mountainous breasts, enormous torso, and bulging thighs.

Sculpture also lends itself superbly to the expression of the vitality of the human body, whether in movement or in poised repose—both figures in Kolbe's *Heinedenkmal* (Fig. 120) declare the vitality of youth—and whether in a posture of graceful ease (as in Donatello's *David*, Fig. 117) or of violent physical struggle (as in Pollaiuolo's *Hercules and Antaeus*, Fig. 121). Sculpture can express movement at least as effectively as it can be expressed in painting, though the sculptor cannot make use of as many representational devices as can the painter. In order to be expressive of movement, the sculptural, like the pictorial, figure must be represented in one of the many postures which, in real life, are known to initiate, accompany, or complete bodily movement, i.e., they must be transitional postures rather than postures which can easily be maintained for an indefinite period. When the posture marks the transition from rest into motion, as in the *Nike of Samothrace* (Fig. 110), or from motion to rest, as in Giovanni da Bologna's *Mercury* (Fig. 119), the figure is particularly expressive of dynamic power. On the contrary, a pose fleetingly assumed by the body in active motion is expressive of motion itself rather than of its dynamic potentiality. The latter effect of actual motion is achieved in Donatello's *Singing Gallery* (Fig. 208) by the rhythmic repetition (with variation) of the poses of the nearer figures and by the contrary motion of the figures in the background. Sculpture can also, like painting, express continued motion along a definite path; note the circular movement of the dancing girls in Carpeaux' *La Danse* (Fig. 207).

In the expression of perceptual universals such as these, sculpture is unexcelled. But its perceptual subject-matter is seriously restricted. It is limited, in the sub-human realm, to animals of sufficient size, plasticity, and physical compactness to permit of unified sculptural treatment. Barye's statues of animals (Fig. 279) and the famous *Horses from St. Mark's* (Fig. 278) well exemplify the types of animals adapted to execution in this medium. They also admirably illustrate the nature of sculptural generalization.

In attempting to express spiritual universals the greater sculptors have invariably avoided a trivial subject-matter[2] and a too literal portrayal of visible details. A sculptor working in a heavy and durable primary medium will almost inevitably trivialize his art if he chooses as his subject-matter objects or events whose associations are trivial; witness Prof. Ernst Herter's *Circe* (Fig. 288). The major primary sculptural media dictate the choice of a subject of enduring human significance. Not only in monuments designed to immortalize the dead but in all secular and religious sculpture, human dignity is at a premium. Compare, for instance, the reflective

[2] i.e., a subject-matter which they, at least, could only interpret as trivial. Theoretically, no subject-matter is intrinsically trivial (cf. Tennyson's "flower in the crannied wall"); but, practically, some subjects resist a significant artistic interpretation more than others and remain stubbornly trivial even in the hands of artistic genius.

dignity of the *Youth of Tralles* (Fig. 238) with the comparative triviality of Rude's *Neapolitan Fisher Boy* (Fig. 287). If sculptural "scale" be defined as the sculptural expression of human dignity or divine majesty, a statue must have "scale" if it is to express a significant spiritual content. Such scale, in turn, can be achieved only through the avoidance of literality and through the expressive use of generalization. Compare, on this score, the expressive power of Donatello's *Crucifix* in S. Antonio in Padua (Fig. 289), Meunier's *The Puddler* (Fig. 290), or Michelangelo's *Deposition* (Frontispiece) with the inexpressive tinsel "realism" of the religious figures so often seen in Roman Catholic churches.

This basic sculptural demand that a significant subject-matter be interpreted with dignity and power does not, of course, exclude the possibility or the intrinsic value of sculpture created to express playful humor, grace, charm, etc., not only in terracotta, porcelain, and wood, but even in stone (Figs. 122-124).

The possibilities of sculptural portraiture of human beings, animals, and historical events have already been discussed and require no further comment. But it is interesting to note that there are no self-contained sculptural equivalents of pictorial still lifes. The reason for this is evident. A sculptural portrayal of objects suitable for a still life would itself too closely resemble a still life in the raw to possess genuine sculptural quality; the inevitable similarity of the representation, however stylized, to the subject-matter represented seems to preclude the possibility of sculpture in this genre. The art of ceramics might be considered the art of sculptural still life. But a terracotta bowl is obviously not the sculptural representation *of* a bowl but the bowl *itself*, and therefore, according to my definition of representational sculpture, not sculpture at all, though obviously still an expressive work of art in its own medium, i.e., that of ceramics.

2. Architecture

A building may be defined as a shell constructed out of building materials according to engineering principles for the express purpose of housing some social activity. An edifice which cannot be entered, or whose interior space cannot be put to a specific practical use, is not a building at all. A building, in turn, can be said to possess architectural quality only in proportion as it *expresses* its social function. Our problem is to determine how such architectural expressiveness is achieved.[3]

Engineering skill and utilitarian satisfaction of social functions are the necessary but not sufficient conditions of architectural quality. To be architectural, a church must not merely be constructed according to sound engineering principles and be capable of housing a religious congregation; it must *express* its distinctive religious character with respect both to its exterior and to its interior. Thus, the best Gothic and Baroque churches (Figs. 40-41, 64-65), Mohammedan mosques, and Chinese temples are architecturally expressive, whereas churches which look like barns, factories, or railway stations are not. Similarly, a private dwelling, to have architectural quality, must not only satisfy a family's utilitarian needs with engineering efficiency but *express* the human spirit in its domestic manifestations. Many of the cottages and manor houses in

[3] There are, of course, various types of structures, such as bridges, which do not strictly "enclose" space but which are constructed by engineers to perform specific social functions and which *can* be so constructed as to express this function in an architectural manner. I shall not here discuss structures of this type, but my analysis of architectural expressiveness should be applicable to them.

Some structures, such as mortuary monuments, are border-line cases which are sometimes not easy to classify either as sculpture or as architecture, even when the joint criteria of engineering construction and usable enclosed space are faithfully applied. *Grant's Tomb* in New York indubitably falls under the category of architecture rather than sculpture, and so, presumably, do the great pyramids, since they enclose a space which, however constricted, was intended to house the spirits of the dead. But what of a modern sepulchral vault whose only function is to serve as a dignified and accessible tomb? The *Washington Monument* should, I suppose, be classified as sculpture rather than architecture, since its function, like that of the *Gloriette* in Schönbrunn (Fig. 76), is to be decorative in a landscape setting and commemorative in the manner of symbolic sculpture, rather than useful and expressive in an architectural manner. The fact that it is actually hollow and that sightseers can ascend it by means of an elevator is fortuitous, not integral to its basic function. But what of the *Lincoln Memorial* in Washington, which, in one sense, is merely an elaborate architectural setting for Daniel Chester French's statue of Lincoln, and, as such, functions essentially like a niche built into a wall to receive and set off a statue, but which, in another sense, is a complete building built, like the *Parthenon*, to house a statue in an enclosed space?

I mention such border-line cases merely to suggest that they should not be allowed to confuse the basic issues or to impugn the validity of a definition which isolates the distinctive characteristics of architecture as such and is clearly applicable to the vast majority of architectural edifices. No definition, of course, either creates or effaces an empirical fact. All that it can do is to exclude certain objects from the class which it defines. But this exclusion does not deny the existence of these discrepant objects; it merely refers them to some other category.

the Cotswolds, near Oxford (Figs. 13-14), eloquently express the domestic life of tenantry and gentry, whereas many modern domestic houses merely manifest their strictly utilitarian function.

This architectural expressiveness of social function, far from being a mere additional factor which may be added as a luxury to satisfy man's purely aesthetic taste, is, rightly viewed, integral to a building's *real* usefulness. A religious congregation requires not merely a durable shelter from the elements but a meeting place in which it can *effectively* realize its main objective, i.e., the worship of God in its own distinctive way. Since the members of such a congregation are human beings more or less sensitive to the character of their artistic environment, such worship is notably facilitated by an appropriate and artistically expressive architectural setting and is correspondingly impeded by one which is inappropriate or inexpressive. The more ritualistic a religious service, the more pressing is this need, but even a Quaker must find it easier to worship God in his own way in one of the lovely Quaker meeting houses than in an empty barn. Similarly, domestic life requires not merely shelter and physical comfort but an architectural setting appropriate to and expressive of the individual family in its private social activities. The more genuinely human and spiritual the individual or the social group, the more vital is this need for an architectural environment which fosters man's spiritual life by expressing the spirit and temper of his social activities and attitudes.

A building expresses its social function in a truly architectural manner only if the primary expressive vehicle is architectural form rather than mere surface decoration. Appropriate architectural decoration does, indeed, greatly clarify and enhance a building's architectural expressiveness. But such decoration is appropriate and architecturally effective only if it is artistically integrated with the basic expressiveness of architectural forms as such. Our first problem must therefore be to discover how such forms can become artistically expressive of the spiritual universals which distinguish various types of social activity from one another.

A building can be architecturally expressive of spiritual universals only in proportion as it expresses certain of the perceptual universals which manifest themselves in building materials and engineering structure. I have said that although the architect may invoke symbolism and pictorial and sculptural representation to intensify and interpret the expressiveness of architectural forms, his edifice will possess *architectural* integrity and expressiveness only if the basic structure itself is expressive of the building's social function. But this basic structure can express such spiritual content only *through* the expression of certain adjectival perceptual universals which manifest themselves in building materials and engineering structure as such. At the strictly physical and utilitarian level, a building cannot be built to provide an efficient and usable interior space save by the efficient application of engineering principles to specific physical materials. At the artistic level, a building cannot express its social function architecturally unless the architect exploits the expressive potentialities of his building materials and his engineering forms in such a manner as visibly to proclaim their physical properties. The expression of these properties *alone* will not, of course, suffice to make the building expressive of its *social* function, but unless these properties *are* architecturally expressed, the building's social function cannot be given *architectural* expression.

To understand this dependence of truly architectural expressiveness upon the expressive exploitation of building materials and engineering structure, i.e., the dependence of the expression of spiritual universals integral to social function upon the expression of perceptual universals integral to engineering principles, we must bear in mind the architect's "audience" and the way in which this "audience" regards an architectural edifice. The artistically sensitive layman's response to architecture may be described as follows.

(a) It is primarily directed to a building's *perceptual* appearance, not to its invisible engineering structure. It is true that the concealed structure must conform to sound engineering principles if the building is to endure, but this requirement is essentially sub-architectural. What is important architecturally is its structural appearance. A well-built edifice which *looks* insecure is *architecturally* inferior to a badly built edifice which, while it lasts, *looks* secure.

(b) But to be perceptually satisfactory a building must, in both its exterior and interior appearance, satisfy certain requirements dictated by the observer's knowledge of relevant natural phenomena, e.g., weight or gravity, compression, tensile strength, and the like. The observer has spent his life adjusting himself to physical objects and therefore knows from experience that stone is heavier than wood, that a steel girder is more tensile than a wooden beam, that a heavy beam is stronger than a light one, and similar observable facts. Accordingly, every visible architectural form will arouse in the average observer certain basic motor reactions which enter significantly into his artistic response to the building as a whole.

(c) The architecturally competent observer is, from the strictly engineering point of view, a layman, not an expert, in engineering. Competence in architectural response presupposes architectural sensivity and training; and this training, in turn, will involve the learning of certain basic engineering principles of which the architecturally naïve layman may not be aware—principles such as that of the outward thrust of a heavy sloping roof. Gothic flying buttresses, like those which surround *Amiens* on three sides, must remain structurally unmotivated for anyone ignorant of this outward pressure. A critic of architecture, to be competent, must therefore possess whatever basic engineering knowledge is requisite to an understanding of the main visible architectural forms. But the more esoteric principles of engineering, however essential to the efficient construction of a building, need not be mastered as a prerequisite to its competent architectural apprehension.

(d) Finally, these basic natural phenomena and engineering principles of which the architecturally competent observer is aware must not only be visibly manifest but *architecturally expressed* if the building as a whole is to satisfy the requirements of architecture. The difference in architecture between mere manifestation and architectural expression is strictly analogous to the difference between the manifestation of certain universals in nature and their pictorial expression. The architect, like the painter, must decide which of the perceptual universals manifesting themselves in his materials and in his engineering forms require visual emphasis, and then decide how best to achieve this emphasis. Only thus can he heighten man's normal perceptions of load and support, thrust and counter-thrust, size and volume, in a manner requisite to architectural expressiveness.

Bearing in mind these factors which condition man's artistic response to architecture—factors which the architect who is properly sensitive to the social function of his own creations will himself consciously or unconsciously take into account—let us see how certain perceptual universals can not only manifest themselves in a building but receive architectural expression.

Two fundamental properties of building materials are their weight, i.e., their obedience to gravity, and their tensile strength, i.e., their ability to support weight and meet the pull of gravity.

Every building necessarily manifests these properties, but not all buildings express them. The *Temple of the Sphinx* in Ghizeh (Fig. 47) perfectly manifests, in its vertical monoliths and lintels, the support of a heavy load by massive uprights. It is impressive as an engineering feat, but it remains architecturally inexpressive in its stark simplicity. The Hall of the Ramesseum (Fig. 48), in contrast, expresses the same principle in its rows of unnecessarily heavy columns with their great flaring capitals and their massive bases.[4] In the lower entrance hall of the *Upper Belvedere* in Vienna (Fig. 58) the motif of a supported load is representationally expressed by the powerful sculptural figures straining to hold up the imposts of the rounded arches on their shoulders. In the *Salle de l'Aquilon* in *Mont St. Michel* (Fig. 59) the same effect is achieved by strictly architectural means, i.e., by the exposure of the heavy voussoirs, the massive masonry of the spandrels, walls, and vaults, and the stone courses of the columns. Similarly, the square piers and the heavy cubistic arches of the church at *Germigny-des-Prés* (Fig. 56) intensify our sense of great weight powerfully supported from beneath. A portion of the balustrade of the exterior gallery between the towers of Notre Dame (Fig. 77), on the other hand, produces in us the very opposite effect. Here the visible load requiring support is felt to be considerable, despite the lightening effect of the open tracery, and the pipe-stem columns, which have actually proved through the centuries to be sufficiently strong, *look* far too fragile to perform their supporting function. The colonnade, taken by itself, thus gives us an uneasy sense of a downward thrust disproportionate to the available support, although, as part of the entire façade, it functions as a screen with perfect artistic success.

In all these illustrations the expressive emphasis has been placed upon the pull of gravity and the more or less adequate neutralization of this pull by the supporting members. But architecture can also emphasize an upward thrust rather than a downward pull; witness the "lightness" of the pointed Gothic arch and the soaring "lift" of the unbroken pier shafts as they rise from the base of the piers up past the arcade, triforium, and clerestory, into the gloom of the ribbed vaults (Fig. 41). By these and other devices congenial

[4] The often alleged absence of conscious expressive intent or explicit artistic response on the part of the ancient Egyptians is irrelevant to the present argument. Man can achieve expressiveness without intending to create a "work of art" and without "artistically" appreciating what he has created.

to the Gothic style our gaze is drawn upward through measured intervals with an irresistible compulsion productive of a pronounced sense of lightness and upward movement. A comparable effect is achieved in the Baroque (Fig. 67) by the dynamic twisted column with its powerful upward thrust and by the innumerable curves of its architectural forms—an effect further intensified by sculptured figures and painted ornaments designed to minimize the sense of weight and intensify the sense of airy lightness.

Another physical characteristic of all buildings is, by definition, their enclosure of a space of specific physical dimensions. It is one of the functions of architecture as an expressive art to intensify our apprehension of this space by making it appear more or less extensive than it actually (physically) is, i.e., by qualifying it architecturally. This architectural control of space can be achieved in a variety of ways, only three of which can here be mentioned.

The first is the use of a colonnade, arcade, or other repetitive architectural "idea." The *Piazza* of St. Peter's (Fig. 64), for example, looks a great deal larger than it is partly because the eye is compelled to travel horizontally along the curved colonnade with its four rows of columns. The visual length of the interior of *S. Paolo fuori le mura* (Fig. 62) is similarly magnified by the arches on either side (as well as by the row of windows in the clerestory) along which the eye must move before it reaches the apse.

The second way in which the architect can heighten our sense of space is by controlling the fundamental compositional arrangement which determines the shape of the enclosed area. Thus, the size and dignity of the Piazza of St. Peter's is intensified by its oval shape as seen from the entrance, while the grandeur of the church's façade is visually increased by the reversed wedge approach from the Piazza, an effect further intensified by the arrangement of the steps. The height and length of Amiens (Fig. 41) is similarly intensified by the narrowness of the nave, the vaulted ceiling, and the rounded and vaulted apse.

A third device is the control of interior light. This control takes two forms, first, the determination of where the light shall enter the building, and second, the use of colored glass. In *Hagia Sophia* (Fig. 63), for example, the sense of enormous spaciousness is achieved partly by the introduction of light through a circle of windows at the base of the dome. This leaves both the main body of the church and the apex of the dome in comparative gloom and makes the dome look as though it were as light as an eggshell. As a result, the interior looks a great deal larger than it actually is. A similar effect is observable in the interior of the *Pantheon* in Rome (Fig. 60), where the bright and even illumination from the oculus helps to affect the visual dimensions. The wise use of stained glass in Gothic architecture further intensifies the sense of immateriality in giving the space thus illumined a strange unreality, and in causing the vaults in the ceiling and in the aisles on either side of the nave to recede into a region of comparative darkness. Moreover, when the figures representationally portrayed in the colored windows are too indistinct to be seen clearly from the entrance or the nave, both the windows and the walls in which they are set seem to be farther off than they actually are, and this again affects the building's interior architectural dimensions.

I have referred to the fact that sculptural and pictorial decoration is used, particularly in the Baroque and Gothic styles, to strengthen the effect of lightness, movement, or distance which is initially achieved by structural forms and compositional arrangement. If we ignore the unhewn rocks on either side of the entrance, the façade of *St. John Nepomuk* (Fig. 66) illustrates the effective use of sculpture in the Baroque style, while the central portal of the west front of *Chartres* (Fig. 7) typifies an effective twelfth century use of stylized sculptured figures to accentuate and motivate the slightly pointed arch over a horizontal lintel. There are many buildings in each of these generic styles, however, which illustrate the danger incurred by a too lavish or otherwise injudicious use of architectural decoration. Decoration is injurious to the architectural effect if it obscures or otherwise renders visually ineffective the main structural forms upon which the building must depend primarily for its architectural expressiveness. The immediate expressive power of these forms is evident even in a photograph of a small section of the flying buttresses of *Mont St. Michel* (Fig. 29) and is unmistakable in the impressive wooden ceiling of *Procter Hall* in the Graduate College at Princeton (Fig. 28). In the *Chapel of Henry VII*, Westminster (Fig. 31), in contrast, the basic structural lines are largely obscured by the intricate carving, with corresponding loss of architectural integrity, and a similar result is effected by the use of both sculpture and painting in the vaulted ceilings of such church interiors as that of the *Church of the Propstei*, Birnau (Fig. 30). That the danger lies less in the amount of decoration than in its stylistic quality and its relation to the main architectural structure is evident in the west façade of *Rouen* (Fig. 8), or in the *Alhambra* in Granada (Fig. 9). In both cases the very elaborate sculptured decoration conforms to the respective styles of architecture and enriches, without weakening, the architectural effect.

The expressiveness of visible architectural forms can also be enhanced by a wise exploitation of the color and surface texture of the visible primary media. The color and design of the brick walls of the *Doges' Palace* in Venice (Fig. 32), contrasting as they do with the white marble arcades, the ornate central windows in each wall, and the cresting on the cornice, at once intensify and enrich the total architectural effect. The color, texture, and visible stone coursing in the manor houses in the *Cotswolds* (Fig. 14), or the richly weathered woodwork of fine half-timbered houses, exemplify the happy exploitation of adjectival perceptual universals manifest in the primary media of domestic architecture.

Let us now see how a building can express its social function *through* the expressive exploitation of its primary media and its engineering structure. Of the three main types of spiritual content, architecture lends itself primarily to the expression of religious and social rather than introspective universals. For architecture is essentially an art which adapts itself to the needs of a group rather than to the needs of an individual as such. Even a domestic dwelling, though on occasion built for, and adapted to, the use of a single individual, is normally the abode of a family, i.e., the elementary social group. It is therefore only in a subordinate unit of a building, e.g., in a private chapel or a study, that architecture expresses the mood of self-conscious reflection and withdrawal. That architecture can express with great eloquence many varieties of religious and secular corporate activities needs no prolonged demonstration. The grounds and buildings of *Versailles* provide examples of several different types of such expressed content. The magnificent eastern approach to the palace, as well as the façade of the palace as seen from the gardens (Figs. 68, 69), exemplify the architectural expression of regal grandeur. The *Chapel* expresses, both on the exterior and in the interior, corporate religious worship as practised by the Court. The *Grand Trianon* (Fig. 70), built as a retreat for Louis XIV by Mansart, expresses in its reduced scale the more informal life of royalty. The *Petit Trianon* (Fig. 71), a favorite residence of Marie Antoinette, expresses, both in architecture and landscaping, still greater informality and intimacy. The *Hamlet* (Fig. 72) expresses the simple life of the laborer on the farm. It was here, we recall, that the ladies and gentlemen of the court of Louis XVI led a mimic peasant life under the inspiration of Rousseau and as a romantic escape from the magnificence of formal royal functions. Finally, the *Temple de l'Amour* (Fig. 73) and the other pleasure pavilions on the grounds express in a manner verging on the sculptural the spirit of informal dalliance and amorous intrigue.

To show how architecture expresses such spiritual universals as these *through* the expressive exploitation of its primary medium, i.e., through primary reliance upon architectural form (though with the help of decoration), let us consider two contrasting examples.

The *Palace of Versailles* (Fig. 69) taken in its landscape setting, is undoubtedly Europe's most eloquent architectural expression of royal magnificence. How is this expressive effect achieved? Partly by the building's artistic unity amid extraordinary multiplicity and diversity of parts. This unity is a function of architectural proportions—of height to length, of the balconies and steps to the façade, of the columns and pilasters to the sustaining walls, of the three tiers of windows and arches, of the individual windows and arches to one another and to the whole exterior, and so forth. The effect is also achieved by the elegant architectural expression of weight (note the heavy arches of the garden façade) and vertical upward thrust (note the slender columns and the window arches); by a magnificent control of exterior and interior space (Fig. 4); by exploitation of color and surface texture; and, in no small measure, by a rich use of exterior and interior decoration which is never allowed to obscure, but is always made to intensify, the main architectural effect. If *Versailles* is compared in these and other respects with most Italian and German palaces of the same period, as for example the palace at Caserta or the *Nymphenburg* in Munich, which were inspired by it, the regal elegance, taste, and expressive scale of *Versailles* will immediately be evident, as will the architectural and decorative devices which combine to achieve these effects.

The stone dwellings in the Cotswold region (Figs. 13, 14) provide an equally notable example of the architectural expression of the domestic life of English tenant farmers, squires, and prosperous business men. The solidity of these houses, architecturally expressed by the square-cut blocks of stone of which they are built, and by their durable slate roofs, offers visible testimony to the solidity of the

British character. The way these houses hug the soil and adapt themselves to its contours is equally expressive. The manor houses, in turn, proclaim not only the squire's greater wealth but his love of comfort, his fondness for smooth lawns and ancient trees, his reserve and hatred of ostentation, and, above all, his sense of social continuity and tradition. It is not hard to read the character of the British gentry from their architecture, or that of the British tenantry from theirs.

A word must finally be added concerning the architectural expression of individuality. A building, I have said, cannot express individuality representationally; and it cannot, save in some portion of the interior space, express, as can pictorial or sculptural portraiture, the inner reflective experiences of the individual. Individuality can, however, enter into the expressed content of architecture in a distinctively architectural manner. The architect can express the individual tastes of specific persons, or of social groups with individualities of their own, in the building as a whole. In domestic architecture, for example, a house commissioned for my private use and that of my family can be made to express the disposition and tastes of my family and myself. Similarly, the Gothic cathedrals express not only the spirit of mediaeval Christianity but the more local characteristics of the several communities in which they were built, and Versailles expresses the individuality of the court of Louis XIV and his successors.

The mechanization of our modern culture threatens the dignity of the private individual and tends increasingly to impoverish the spirituality of the social group. This tendency manifests itself in the typical "modern" private house (Figs. 89, 90), which is often as impersonal and unindividualistic as a well-planned factory. It manifests itself also in modernistic church architecture. Compare, for example, the interior of the *Roman Catholic Church* in Bischofsheim (Fig. 83), as an architectural expression of Christian worship, with the interior of any of the great architecturally expressive churches such as *St. Peter's* in Rome (Fig. 65) or *Amiens Cathedral* (Fig. 41). If the church at Bischofsheim is compared with the *Hangar* at Orly (Fig. 82), it is at once evident that what are here manifest and partly expressed *via* pure architectural form are merely perceptual universals and engineering principles. There is hardly a suggestion of the spiritual universals so integral to Christian worship (*vide* also Fig. 88). The skyscraper (Figs. 85-87) and the modern suspension bridge (Fig. 80), in contrast, express in their own eloquent way the temper of our modern society, with its passion for size and mechanical efficiency and its aversion to that human dignity so valued by other periods and cultures.

3. Music

The dependence of artistically expressed content upon acquired associations and conventions, though demonstrable in all the arts, is most evident in music. For music is the most "artificial"[5] of the arts because its primary medium, i.e., the system of tones based on any given scale, as well as its generic forms, have meaning only in a musical context. That is, this meaning attaches to them only by association and convention. I have already remarked that the *ethos* (or emotive-conative associations) of one scale differs from the *ethos* of another scale within specific cultures and periods[6] and that these associations vary from one period and culture to another. Thus the Dorian mode, which to the Greek ear was strong and virile, is, to our ear, a minor scale with an entirely different set of emotive-conative associations, somewhat as white is the expressive symbol of death and mourning for the Chinese and Japanese, as black is for us. Similarly, every tone in a given scale has, for a given culture, an expressiveness of its own. The second, fifth, and seventh tones of our major scale, for example, lack for us the stability of the tonic and express a backward or forward pull towards the tonic or the octave of the tonic.

That some of our reactions to sound are more basic and universal than this is very likely. Men have probably at all times responded in essentially the same way to a quick as opposed to a slow beat; auditory rhythm is too deeply associated with man's basic physiological structure and responses to permit of pronounced cultural variations. But all the more refined and acquired associations which endow musical tones and scales with emotive-conative meaning are subject to conventional variations. And what applies to scales and tonal intervals applies of course in a progressively intensified manner to variations in timbre, to the more basic musical forms, and, finally, to the infinite variations of these forms; for the more elaborate and

[5] i.e., more of an artifact. Cf., above, pp. 54*ff*.

[6] Cf. the response of the ancient Greeks to their eight modes.

subtle music becomes, the more dependent upon conventional acceptance become its emotive-conative associations and expressed content.

This does *not* condemn us, however, to a pure subjectivism or relativism, nor does it preclude the possibility of genuine communication in this medium. For musical conventions and associations, like those of a verbal language, are sufficiently stable and enjoy a sufficiently wide acceptance in any period and culture to permit of communicatory exploitation. Not only the forms but the emotive-conative responses to these forms enjoy enough objectivity to make music an extraordinarily sensitive vehicle for the artistic communication of subtle and varied emotions and conations.

Bearing in mind that musical content is ultimately untranslatable into conceptual prose, let us consider what generic types of universals lend themselves to interpretative expression in this medium. Among the perceptual universals, substantival universals (i.e., perceptual types) cannot be expressed at all in pure music, even in program music. But this limitation is compensated for by the extraordinary power of music to express whatever adjectival universals manifest themselves in sound. Can any art express with greater directness, clarity, or subtlety of variation and individual emphasis such qualities as sweetness and gentleness, or harshness and strident contrast? Can even the dance express temporal direction and movement more eloquently or variously than music in its melodic lines and harmonic progressions, in its tempo, beat, and other rhythmic resources? The relational universals which music expresses are of course predominantly temporal. But music can also arouse in us artistically a genuine sense of spatiality. It can do so through the timbre of individual tones (compare, for example, the thinness and smallness of the sound of the piccolo or the highest registers of the violin with the space-filling fullness of the full organ), through "volume" (a loud passage sounds more space-filling than a quiet passage), and compositionally (note the "voluminousness" of a great chorus or a symphony). And what art, finally, can rival music in the expression of driving power or pulsing vitality?

Perceptual universals such as these achieve expression even in the most purely "decorative" of musical compositions. But in most music we also find expressed certain spiritual universals which naturally possess for us greater human significance. Association, convention, and training are again of crucial importance in determining what type of spiritual universals are expressed by musical forms, both generic and specific. Furthermore, spiritual universals are expressed in music (as in architecture) only *through* the expression of perceptual universals. Music can convey no sense of religious awe, despair, or exultation, of social conviviality, erotic passion, or martial fervor, of reflective withdrawal or contemplative brooding, save to an ear sensitive to timbre and rhythm, melodic line and harmonic relationship, i.e., to a person capable of immediate response to music's perceptual content. The spiritual content of music is invariably a function of its perceptual content; indeed, it *is* this perceptual content modified and enriched through the acquisition of additional emotive-conative associations.

Thus, to our ear, any slow and regular rhythm in a minor key expresses a general sense of restraint and melancholy, an unspecified retardation of man's normal tempo, a diminution of human vitality. In a funeral march this effect is so specified and so transformed as to arouse in us an emotive-conative response oriented to the thought of death and bereavement. Similarly, any soaring melodic line played at a rapid tempo with or without harmonic accompaniment in a major key quickens our heart-beat, induces muscular reactions in our hands and feet, and in general infuses in us a sense of movement, vitality, and animation. Dance music exploits these devices in such a way as to constitute the appropriate musical setting for an actual dance; it gives audible expression to the joy and spiritual exhilaration which the dancer directly expresses in bodily movement.

Religious music exemplifies a more subtle type of transformation. Man's religious experience is characterized from first to last by every conceivable type of emotive response. Each of these generic emotions can be expressed in music without awakening in us any specifically religious associations. But certain types of music have come to be so intimately associated by us with certain forms of religious worship that the emotions aroused in us by such music are felt to be "religious emotions," that is, identical with or similar to those emotional states which we experience, or feel we might experience, during actual credal participation in such worship. To the sensitive ear of one who is wholly ignorant of our Christian tradition, the music of the "Kyrie" in Bach's *B Minor Mass* could express no more than an unmotivated human anguish, and the "Gloria" and the "Sanctus" no more than a general sense of aspiration, hope, assurance, and triumph such as any human being might on occasion feel;

though in both cases these emotions are of course refined, varied, and intensified as is possible only in great music. But to Bach himself and to those of us who can bring to the hearing of this great *Mass* a requisite knowledge of the Christian tradition and an adequate capacity for religious comprehension, the "Kyrie" expresses the anguished cry of a *sinner*, the "Gloria" and the "Sanctus," praise of *Deity*, and the "Credo," the whole succession of emotive-conative responses through which the believing Christian passes in his affirmation of the successive articles of the *Creed*.

Again, it does not follow that because Bach's *B Minor Mass* means one thing to the secularly minded, another to the religiously minded, or one thing to the pagan and another to the Christian, the meaning of such a composition is therefore wholly subjective, or that we are at liberty to "read into the music" any type of emotive-conative response that we may happen or care to indulge in while the music is being played. Musically naïve auditors whose only response to music is sentimental, i.e., untutored and uninformed, may proclaim the complete relativity of all musical meaning, but the competent critic and the sincere music-lover recognize the sentimentality of such a pronouncement and simply repudiate it. For they realize that a genuine understanding of a musical composition depends not only upon a mastery of its "grammar and syntax" (i.e., its formal structure) but also upon the acquisition, through conscious or unconscious training, of a sensitivity to those emotive-conative associations which, prior to composition, constitute the composer's secondary raw material, and which reappear in the composition as the work's objective spiritual content. When Bach wrote the *B Minor Mass* he was not simply writing music in general. He was attempting to express in music the most characteristic emotions and volitions of the Christian's religious experience with specific reference to its articulation in the Christian Creed. And, since Bach's day, musically sensitive Christians as well as those who, though not themselves Christians, have understood the Christian experience with imaginative insight and have been able to recognize a musical interpretation of this experience, have been unanimous in acclaiming the extraordinary success of his attempt. Bach speaks to those who have the ears, mind, and heart to hear with unmistakable precision and power. His *Mass* is a vehicle of communication whose meaning is not only intelligible but eloquent in the highest degree. Our duty and privilege as listeners with a musical conscience is therefore clear, whatever our private religious beliefs or disbeliefs. We must attempt to respond to the *Mass* as Bach intended us to respond to it, of course with absorbed attention to its "aesthetic surface," of course responsive to its more general expressed content, but also and essentially responsive to its profound religious and Christian meaning.

In such music as Bach's *B Minor Mass* or his chorales and religious cantatas, the words for which the music was specifically composed not only provide indubitable evidence as to what Bach was himself seeking to express in this music, but, in addition, clarify this expression in verbal language. In many instances of music with words the words do, indeed, add little to the expressed content. But ideally, if words are used at all, they should make a positive contribution by giving the strictly musical content a verbally expressed motivation. Bach's *B Minor Mass*, Brahms' *Vier ernste Gesänge* and Schubert's *Songs* may be mentioned as examples of music whose musical meaning is verbally articulated and motivated in this manner. In opera at its best this meaning is further clarified and intensified by the acting and the stage setting. Pure music, on the other hand, must provide its own commentary.

The spiritual content of most of the serious instrumental music of the last century and a half has been increasingly personal and introspective. In its peculiar aptitude for this type of content pure music differs sharply from architecture which, as we discovered, is predominantly social in its orientation and lends itself only partially and indirectly to the expression of the introspective attitude. Architecture's limitation is music's chief potentiality; more than any of the other arts, music tends to arouse in us an attitude of solitary reflective contemplation.

In defining this attitude, I distinguished between that type of reflection which is more or less oriented to man's divine, human, or physical environment and that more introspective type of reflection which is more narrowly focused upon his immediate inner moods, feelings, emotions, and conations. Music excels in the expression of both types of reflection. On the one hand, the most explicitly religious or social music is simultaneously more reflective than are comparable works of art in other media. On the other hand, the attitude which finds expression in most of the great symphonies and sonatas, fugues, preludes, and fantasies is reflective in the narrower or more introspective sense. What the composers of these works have done is to explore with extraordinary subtlety man's feelings, emotions, and moods *for their own sake*, and with no more than an incidental suggestion as to a possible motivation for such inner states. Hence, to listen to this music is to discover emotive and affective potentialities within oneself previously undreamed of. Even though we are seated in a crowded concert hall, we listen in solitude and are absorbed in reflective contemplation of the moods and feelings aroused in us by the revelatory magic of the music.

But music of this type can take on expressive significance for us only in so far as we are able to regard our own moods and feelings as specific instances of universal human moods and feelings, for here, as elsewhere, man achieves a sense of dignity and worth only through participation in a wider experience and a common life. The joy or sorrow I reflectively apprehend while listening to music is indeed my own joy or sorrow, yet *not merely* mine but the joy and sorrow of other men and women. It is a universal joy and sorrow which I can share with others. Ignore the artistic *specificity* of the music itself, and all emotive response to it becomes, artistically considered, sentimental bathos. Refrain from *individual* emotive-conative response, and the music becomes a purely formal pattern, of interest only to the musical technician. Fail to recognize the *universal* character of the music's specific content and of the hearer's individual response, and the music loses its larger human significance. The music itself, as a complex pattern of meaningful sound, is objective to the hearer and, as such, demands his sensitive obedience to *its* behests; and what the music expresses is, in proportion to its profundity, a universal content even though, in apprehending it, we find ourselves withdrawing into ourselves more completely than in our response to any other type of art.

This must suffice to indicate the chief expressive potentialities of music. Its expressive limitations are too obvious to require more than a brief comment. The most successful "imitative" music can, at best, reproduce or suggest certain sounds in nature, such as the melodic line of a bird's song or the booming of distant guns. Undue reliance on such imitation betrays the musical poverty of the composer. The real objective of program music is the expression, in the language of music, of the *spirit* or *mood* associated with a non-musical theme, event, or natural scene. In expressing this mood, natural sounds need not be reproduced with fidelity. The music should rather express in a purely musical way those perceptual and spiritual universals which we associate with the theme, object, or event in question. Program music is the closest approximation in this medium to portraiture, that is, to the portrayal of some specific objective individual. But music, like architecture, cannot portray individuality as can the representational and literary arts. It can only express with musical abstractness certain universal characteristics of an individual person, object, or event, and it must, in the nature of the case, emphasize man's typical emotive-conative responses to this or that type of objective individuality. It can immortalize not Napoleon but only martial achievement and man's response to such achievement. Only in the case of persons and events of supreme religious significance in a given culture can greater specificity of reference be achieved, and even here the reference is much more general than in sculpture, painting, or literature. What applies to program music applies also to occasional music. The specific occasion which is celebrated is echoed in the music not in its specificity but only in its generic character and in terms of the generic moods and feelings which it tends to arouse in the observer.

Despite the almost insuperable difficulty of re-expressing in verbal prose the artistic content of a musical composition, the competent music critic can do something to indicate what a specific composition seems to him and has seemed to others to express, and he can also point out some of the technical devices by means of which this expression is achieved. The reader will find in a *Supplementary Essay* at the end of this volume an analysis, written at my request by Professor Roy Dickinson Welch, of the structure and musical content of Beethoven's *Eroica*. This analysis provides a more concrete illustration of some of the main types of musical content and of some of the ways in which music can express such content.

4. The Dance

We encounter more obstacles in studying the dance than in studying any of the other arts, not because the dance is in itself more subtle or elusive, but because a dance ceases to exist at the end of its performance and because we cannot appeal to available records of specific dances. A building, a piece of sculpture, or a picture endures and can be seen and studied by anyone, and though photographs of them do indeed distort them, certain of their essential characteristics can be caught by a photograph and preserved for more intensive study. A dance, in contrast, cannot really be photographed at all, since it "is not a succession of poses each of which has value in itself when frozen into inaction, but is actually composed of movement, which ceases to exist when confronted with any kind of static form. Merely to photograph the dancer, as is commonly done, is not necessarily to give any impression at all of his art."[7] The only photographic record of a dance comparable in adequacy to photographs of buildings, statues, or paintings would be a motion picture, preferably in color, but such records do not, for the most part, exist, and those that do exist are again not readily available. The musician can at least resort to the score in his analysis of a composition, however great the chasm may be between a musical score and music actually heard; but no useful system of dance notation is available. The student of the dance is thus limited to his own memory of whatever dances he may have been fortunate to see with his own eyes, and to the necessarily general and highly inadequate verbal descriptions of these and other dances in which critics have attempted to record and communicate their own analyses and impressions.

An additional obstacle in the way of any generalized discussion of the dance is the fact that it is so extraordinarily various in form and motivation. As one of the oldest and most universal of the arts[8] it has assumed, and still assumes, the greatest variety of forms,[9] and those who today devote themselves professionally to it as one of the

[7] John J. Martin, *America Dancing* (New York: Dodge, 1936), in a note preceding the sixteen admirable photographs by Thomas Bouchard reproduced in his book, to which the reader is referred. The photographs reproduced in the present volume (Figs. 293-299) have been selected to illustrate phases of the conventional Ballet and the Modern Dance. Bouchard's photographs, in contrast, were designed, as Mr. Martin has expressed it in his note, "to catch those transitional movements which contain in themselves both the fruits of the movement that has preceded them and the seeds of that which is to follow."

[8] "Dancing and building are the two primary and essential arts. The art of dancing stands at the source of all the arts that express themselves first in the human person. The art of building, or architecture, is the beginning of all the arts that lie outside the person; and in the end they unite. Music, acting, poetry proceed in the one mighty stream; sculpture, painting, all the arts of design, in the other. There is no primary art outside these two arts, for their origin is far earlier than man himself; and dancing came first." Havelock Ellis, *The Dance of Life* (New York: Modern Library, 1929), p. 34. The "dance" is here clearly taken in its broadest naturalistic sense (to include, e.g., the dance of the waves and of insects). But Mr. Ellis' chapter on the dance in this famous essay is an admirable account of the age, universality, importance, and variety of the dance in human culture. Cf., also, Curt Sachs, *World History of the Dance*, tr. by Bessie Schönberg (New York: Norton, 1937).

[9] Cf., above, Chap. III, Chap. IX, §2, and Chap. X, §2.

major arts, whether as actual dancers or as critics or dance enthusiasts, differ sharply in their interpretations of its true nature and objectives.

In the face of these difficulties, I shall confine myself to a brief account of the expressive potentialities of what, for lack of a better designation, is entitled the "Modern Dance," as the most significant contemporary development of the dance as a conscious art.[10]

The primary raw material of the dance is, as has been already pointed out, the human body in motion—"the dancer is essentially a nude figure upon which is placed the minimum of costume required to obtain a desired theatrical effect"[11]—and the dance itself is in essence the expressive movement of this figure or these figures. "All movement, however, is not suitable material for the creation of the dance. All dance is made of movement, but all movement is not dance; just as all music is sound, but all sound is not music; or all poetry is words, but all words are not poetry."[12] Hence, the dancer must select those movements which will best express what he wishes to express. Suppose it were "possible for all the movement of which a dancer's body is capable to be laid out before him. If he is an artist he must select from this what he is to work with. He must see at once that most of it is of no value to him. He must select the kind of movement that is not subordinate and subsidiary to physical necessity, but is the product of a mental, an emotional, a non-physical demand."[13] These selected movements must be organized for an expressive purpose. Form is as essential in the dance as it is in any of the other arts. As Havelock Ellis has put it, "The dance is the rule of number and of rhythm and of measure and of order, of the controlling influence of form, of the subordination of the parts to the

[10] In this analysis I shall lean heavily on the recent books of John Martin, one of the leading critical exponents of this movement. In his *America Dancing* Mr. Martin assumes, quite excusably, the rôle of protagonist as well as that of dispassionate critic, and it is primarily the assumption of this rôle which has led him to an attack upon tradition, some of the implications of which I shall have to reject. But his positive interpretation of the Modern Dance not only sets in admirable relief many generic characteristics of the dance as such; it also provides welcome confirmation of the major theses propounded in the present volume. Because of their dual interest to us, therefore, the numerous quotations, which he has kindly permitted me to use in this section, are included without apology.

[11] *America Dancing*, p. 135.

[12] *The Modern Dance* (Copyright 1933, by A. S. Barnes and Company, Inc., New York), p. 85.

[13] *Ibid.*, pp. 86*f*.

whole."[14] Both selection and formal organization, in turn, involve distortion in the interest of expressive emphasis. In the dance, as elsewhere, "distortion is the very basis of art; it is the quality which keeps art from being nature. . . . Not representation but interpretation is [the dancer's] business, his duty to nature itself; the abstracting into essences of those deep-rooted experiences of human living which appearances, surface truths, naturalism, cover and deny."[15]

Every dance also has some subject-matter which the dancer seeks to interpret, but though the dancer's choice of his theme or subject-matter is certainly of importance, what is of preeminent artistic importance is rather its interpretation. It is undoubtedly the layman's continual confusion of subject-matter with artistic content—a confusion which the dance, just because its primary medium is the actual living and moving body of the dancer, tends more than any other art to foster in the uninitiated—that leads Mr. Martin to insist with critical over-emphasis that "it is not subject that is important . . . , but content, and the two are many light years apart."[16] That subject-matter and expressed content differ in kind is indubitable; but Mr. Martin himself makes clear, in his account of leading contemporary dancers, how great an effort these dancers have made to select a subject-matter for each dance which would best lend itself to expressive exploitation for their particular purpose.

The final purpose of every serious dance, like that of every serious work of art in any medium, is to offer a new and vital interpretation of some aspect of man's inner emotional experience and of his generic emotive-conative responses to his complex environment. The true artist is "firm in the belief that he must set forth universal truths in terms of human experience. . . ."[17] "It is not the artist's purpose merely to stir up emotional states, but rather by means of this stirring up to lead the receptive mind to an enlarged experience, to a hitherto unrealized truth."[18] But truth can never be expressed in the dance, any more than in the other arts, wholly abstractly. It must be individualized by the dancer, both subjectively and objec-

[14] *Op. cit.*, p. xi.

[15] *America Dancing*, pp. 104*f.*

[16] *Ibid.*, p. 72. Cf. p. 33, where the subject is said to be "in itself of little consequence; it is content that is important, and content dictates outward form in any decent work of art."

[17] *Ibid.*, p. 84.

[18] *Ibid.*, p. 114.

tively. That is, he as an individual must *apprehend* specific truths in their individual manifestations from his own individual point of view, and he must then *express* them in his art with artistic individuation. We must remember that "every work of art is created out of one small individual's vision and experience of the universe, and that this vision and this experience are colored by . . . that tiny personal fragment of the universal from which he must deduce the great whole."[19] Moreover, "though human experience, returning always to the 'nature of man,' touches ever upon fundamentals that are perpetually operative, they cannot be dealt with in art generically but must be treated in specific manifestations. Love and hate, living and dying, good and evil, are not only platitudinous but actually inexpressible until they are individualized in concrete instances."[20] "It is impossible to paint a picture of love or hate, whatever the art medium; it must always be of some particular man loving or hating some particular object."[21]

The dance must achieve this expressive individualization in its own distinctive way. Though it has traditionally leaned heavily on music and will presumably continue to do so, "music is entirely secondary in any self-respecting form of dancing; it is an accompaniment, a background, not to be listened to for itself any more than a stage setting is to be concentrated upon after the actors come onto the scene."[22] When a dancer sets out to interpret music, as he so often does, his only safeguard is to *re*-interpret in his own medium the *spirit* of the music, that is the expressed content of the composition, without slavish subservience to individual musical phrases. But the dance can really be said to have come into its own only in proportion as the dancer first creates his dance in terms of his own medium and then proceeds to search for its most appropriate musical or auditory accompaniment. Musicians who are aware of the fact that our Western music came into its own only after it had been freed from its century-old bondage to a verbal text, i.e., with the exploitation of instrumental music for its own sake, should be the first to encourage the modern dancer to achieve an analogous autonomy, and to assist him in finding for his dances music that is really appropriate to them. Similarly, though dances have been

[19] *Ibid.*, p. 24.
[20] *Ibid.*, p. 67.
[21] *Ibid.*, p. 27.
[22] *Ibid.*, p. 98.

danced to a verbal accompaniment, exponents of the Modern Dance "do not dance literary texts. They lean in the direction of verbalism only when they are concerned with ballets of action and frankly programmatic works, which are not pure dance at all, but theatre dance."[23] It is essential that, whatever else he may do, the dancer should express himself in his distinctive medium, and that his audience should apprehend his meaning not in reliance upon, or through translation into, a literary medium, but through immediate response to the visible bodily movement on the stage.

The dance, like the other arts, can of course be indulged in as an act of sheer joyous self-expression. But as an *art* its primary function is to communicate an expressed content to others, and to do so it must be intelligible to an intelligent and responsive audience. Mr. Martin seems to me to understate gravely the requirements which the observer must satisfy if his response is to be intelligent.[24] It is of course essential that he should not bring with him false standards or distorting prejudices, and to be rid of these is indeed not easy. But surely he must also have acquired, whether by actual participation or by repeated observation and subsequent reflection, a familiarity with the expressive technique of the various schools and individuals —in short, with the language of the dance. Responsible critics in the other arts, all of whom can certainly not be dismissed as mere "academicians," are unanimous in their recognition of the need for such training. Is the dance really unique in being immediately intelligible to anyone who can bring to it no more than a sympathetic and open mind?

It is true that we acquire from the moment of birth an ever-increasing familiarity with the expressive significance both of the spontaneous and the more calculated movements of our own bodies and of those of our fellows, and that the dance at its best, far from denying these movements or falsifying their expressive significance, sets the most expressive of them in relief, and, by distortion and emphasis, underlines the emotive-conative experiences which find an outlet in them. It is also true that expressive movement is man's

[23] *Ibid.*, p. 90.

[24] Cf. *America Dancing*, p. 125: "There is nothing esoteric, nothing requiring learning, nothing demanding a struggle, about the perception of beauty or the remembering of it. We need only step out of the armor we have built of false attitudes, false education, false culture, and expose ourselves to it simply and honestly. That, perhaps, is a man-sized job."

most basic language, more basic even than the language of sound and certainly more primitive than verbal utterance or pictorial and sculptural representation. We need not minimize or deny man's universal capacity for empathic response to the observed movements of others, or the actualization of this response whenever it is not inhibited by habit and prejudice, or the kinaesthetic awareness of this response, or the spontaneous arousal in us of emotions, attitudes, and feelings which, in conjunction, constitute the immediate psychic counterpart to purely physical muscular reaction. These factors indubitably constitute, in aggregate, the *pre-artistic* communicatory vehicle which the dancer has at his disposal, waiting to be exploited. But this vehicle is in itself no more than what non-literary prose is to literary prose or poetry, or what emotionally charged sound is to expressive music. The dancer, like any other artist, must fashion his pre-artistic vehicle to his own artistic ends, and this involves the developing of an expressive technique with which, in turn, the observer must be familiar if he is to respond to the dance intelligently.

I shall consider in a moment the modern dancer's overwhelming preoccupation with this very problem of discovering and developing an expressive technique. And no one who has seen the Modern Dance at its best can fail to realize how far this technique has already been developed. The best of these dances are, as they should be, highly stylized, not naturalistic.[25] But in comparison with the other arts, and particularly with music, the dance has only taken a first short step in this direction. Its progress cannot be forced, and impatience is as childish as the attitude of supercilious contempt. But the need for indefinite progress in the direction of stylization, i.e., in the gradual development of an intelligible language of the dance, must be recognized—of a language not wholly private to each individual dancer (though each dancer must of course continue to create and dance in his own individual style), but sufficiently universal to permit of conventional acceptance and use, as are the accepted (yet ever changing) conventions and associations of music. In short, if it is true that "technique must remain a highly personal and plastic matter, in order to keep it at all times adequate to meet the ever changing demands made upon it,"[26] the best friends and admirers of the dance must also urge the pressing need for "that

[25] Martha Graham's *Frontier* is an especially fine example of evocative, stylized movement.

[26] *America Dancing*, p. 74.

fundamental technical practice for which the American dance is still waiting."[27]

Mr. Martin's summary of the basic principles of some of the leading exponents of the Modern Dance is of great interest because of the light it throws upon what these dancers themselves consider to be of crucial importance to significant creative dancing. "As Shawn has epitomized the four steps in the Denishawn method of composing, there was first, the idea; second, the bodily movement; third, the 'tonalizing' of the movement in terms of music; fourth, the costuming and scenery."[28] Hanya Holm's basic principles can likewise be grouped under four main headings which are, first, "an orderly and anatomically sound technical basis for the education of the body into an instrument of expressional movement"; second, "the evolution of a specific creative method by which the emotional experience of the individual is made to externalize itself in motor terms" (involving the technique of producing "first movements" from which subsequent movements flow with an inner, unintellectualized logic of their own); third, training in the conscious and intelligent use of space; and fourth, solution of the problem of musical accompaniment.[29] Doris Humphrey's compositions are based upon the conception of movement, as "the arc between two deaths." "On one hand is the death of negation, motionlessness; on the other hand is the death of destruction, the yielding to unbalance. All movement can be considered to be a series of falls and recoveries; that is, a deliberate unbalance in order to progress, and a restoration of equilibrium for self-protection. . . . Out of the alternation of unbalance and recovery, a rhythm develops which is kinetic rather than musical. Rhythm thus forms one of the three elements which can still be considered as structural. A second element is dynamism; that is, the variation in the intensity of movement as it progresses over its arc from motionlessness toward destruction. The third element is design. . . . In addition to these three structural elements, a fourth element appeared unsought; this was an element of meaning, a metakinetic element."[30] Finally Esther Junger is primarily concerned with three basic facts: gravity, space, and the human body. "These supply opposition as well as aid, and to ignore or attempt to

[27] *Ibid.*, p. 168.
[28] *Ibid.*, p. 158.
[29] *Ibid.*, pp. 182*f*.
[30] *Ibid.*, pp. 212*f*.

conceal them is to deprive movement of its vitality. Three general principles underlie the dancer's treatment of them. The first principle she calls resistance," involving the acknowledgment and dramatization of the opposition of space to movement, of gravitational pull, and of the counterpulls within the body itself. "The second principle, called sustained control, concerns itself more immediately with considerations of dynamism," i.e., with relaxation treated "as the letting out of the stream of life, the actual opposite of movement and not involved normally in the dance." Hence "movements which involve lyricism, far from being soft and relaxed, actually demand more control than those which are forceful and staccato. . . . The third principle is the use of the body as a unit. . . . A movement of one part shifts the center of gravity and requires compensatory movements elsewhere, so that ultimately every movement is seen to be a movement of the entire body."[31]

Even this bare indication of the overlapping theories of these dancers clearly indicates their ever-increasing preoccupation with choreographic technique and with what must certainly prove to be a salutary emphasis upon the basic principles of the dance as a distinctive language of expressive communication. However much they may agree or disagree[32] on technical methodology or immediate objective, these dancers are in notable agreement about the dangers which the Modern Dance must avoid if it is to realize its own potentialities.

I have already commented on the first of these, i.e., unselective and uninterpretative realism. This is perhaps the dancer's greatest danger, because he must use his own body as his chief expressive vehicle, and he is not safeguarded as are other artists by the necessity of translating his ideas into stone, or onto canvas, or into sound or words.

The opposite danger is that of meaningless abstraction, and it is this danger of which the aesthete is most likely to be unaware. "Any theory of dance that attempts to make use of the body as an instrument of pure design is doomed to failure, for the body is of all possible instruments the least removable from the associations of

[31] *Ibid.*, pp. 253*f.*

[32] "There has never been any fundamental struggle over technical methods; the interest centers rather in the purposes toward which the technical methods are directed." *Ibid.*, p. 61.

experience."[33] Hence the movements of the body "cannot be made into an abstraction of line and form under any circumstances."[34] "Abstraction as a basis for creation is devoid of all power to stir the mind of the spectator to a warmer, fuller realization of the life and times about him. Like literalism, its apparent opposite, it plays no part whatever in the modern dance."[35] This is a warning which "abstractionists" in other fields, both as creative artists and as theorists, would do well to heed.

The third danger to be avoided is self-expressionism, which is really a variant of uninformed realism. Fully recognizing that "the forms of creative art grow out of the reactions of the individual artists to [their] background and environment," and that "submergence of all differences in some sort of nebulous oneness means the negation of all the vital qualities and activities,"[36] Mr. Martin is clear and emphatic in condemning the notion that the dancer's chief function is merely to express himself. "The selfhood of the artist does not constitute the content of his art, but is merely the instrumentality through which perforce he manifests his ideas. . . . We do not want an artist to tell us what he is; even if it made any difference to us, he has not enough perspective for his opinion to be of any value. It is his business to tell us what he knows and what he sees that we have not known and seen. There is a common type of public nuisance who goes about psychoanalyzing himself perpetually and audibly, telling any available listener how he feels and why, using every circumstance available to reveal his peculiar sensitiveness. The method of the artist is the exact reverse of this; he uses his sensitiveness to reveal the circumstances of life about him."[37]

The fourth danger is, in a sense, akin to the second. It is the danger of mechanization. Such mechanization may arise from blind "academic" allegiance to traditional forms for their own sake, as has too often happened in the formal ballet, or from a mechanical pantomimic reproduction of mere external appearances. On the sterility of the "academic" worship of tradition Mr. Martin is eloquent, and many of his strictures are indubitably valid. We must

[33] *Ibid.*, p. 92. These associations should, of course, be artistically controlled and interpreted by the dance itself.

[34] *Ibid.*, p. 66.

[35] *Ibid.*, p. 94.

[36] *Ibid.*, p. 26.

[37] *Ibid.*, pp. 100*f.*

not forget, however, that no human achievement can be more than ephemeral unless it grows out of a tradition to which it, in turn, makes an original contribution. What the modern dancers and their sympathetic critics are actually doing is to attempt cooperatively to create an American choreographic tradition, studying with one another and learning from one another to this end. To this Mr. Martin would certainly agree, for he roundly castigates the "modernistic" search for novelty for its own sake, the devising of "deliberate incongruities and fantastic abnormalities for the sheer delight of causing a sensation."[38] We, in turn, can recognize the sterility of the "academic" attitude at its worst and sympathize with the determination of the modern dancer to infuse the dance with new life and new human significance through the creation of new forms better suited to the achievement of new objectives.

The same argument applies to pantomime. Despite its pitfalls it has, as a useful ingredient in certain types of dance, a rightful place, as Charles Weidman has recently demonstrated.[39] The difference between pantomime and the non-pantomimic dance, and the potential expressiveness of each, is admirably indicated in a passage from Havelock Ellis' *Dance of Life*. The passage relates to ancient religious dances and is poetic rather than analytical in character, but the distinction which it describes and the wider application of this distinction are evident. "These religious dances, it may be observed, are sometimes ecstatic, sometimes pantomimic. It is natural that this should be so. By each road it is possible to penetrate towards the divine mystery of the world. The auto-intoxication of rapturous movement brings the devotees, for a while at least, into that self-forgetful union with the not-self which the mystic ever seeks. The ecstatic Hindu dance in honor of the pre-Aryan hill god, afterwards Siva, became in time a great symbol, 'the clearest image of the *activity* of God,' it has been called, 'which any art or religion can boast of.' Pantomimic dances, on the other hand, with their effort to heighten natural expression and to imitate natural process, bring the dancers into the divine sphere of creation and enable them to assist vicariously in the energy of the gods. The dance thus becomes the presentation of a divine drama, the vital reenactment of a

[38] *Ibid.*, p. 116.
[39] *Ibid.*, p. 230. Cf. Charles Weidman's *Opus 51*, or his *Candide*.

sacred history, in which the worshipper is enabled to play a real part. In this way ritual arises."[40]

What, then, can the dance which avoids the dangers of literalism and self-expression, abstractionism and mechanism, express with special immediacy and power? Among the perceptual universals, bodily movement, of course, in all its varieties. The "pure" dance can also express the greatest variety of sensuous universals, both qualitative and relational. With the aid of pantomime the dance can portray not only many perceptual types but man's kinetic reactions to a still greater number of such types. But its chief spiritual significance derives from its amazing capacity to express man's most intense religious and social feelings as well as his more reflective moods. Finally, the dancer can express not only the distinctive spirit or essence of individual persons, animals, and things; he can also express, with the aid of pantomime, their more significant external manifestations. In short, the expressive potentialities of the dance are extensive in range and in dynamic power. Its limitations are akin to those of music and are most readily evident if the dance is compared with literature. Without pausing to catalogue the differences between these arts, let us consider, in conclusion, the distinctive expressive power of literature as an art.

5. Literature

The task of analyzing the expressed content of literature is in some respects the easiest, in others the hardest, of all. It is facilitated by the fact that every literary work which still exists in written or printed form is, at least theoretically, equally available to everyone and easily reproducible in a volume. Buildings, sculptures, and paintings have to be visited to be adequately apprehended at first hand. Music must be performed to be heard, and this involves dependence upon the performer who, in turn, must give the composition his own interpretation, since even the most complete musical score necessitates a type of interpretation which the written word does not. And the dance, as we have just seen, is the most ephemeral of all the arts and the hardest to record or possess permanently as one's own. But since the advent of the printing press anyone with the price of a book can own and buy a literary work more easily than a rich collector can buy and own a pictorial or sculptural masterpiece, and what he purchases is the work itself, so

[40] *Op. cit.*, pp. 38*f.*

far as a literary composition is identifiable with the written or the printed word.

Moreover, literature can boast a longer and richer critical tradition than any of the other arts. Critical interpretations of literature are more numerous and constitute a more venerable and more continuous tradition than do analogous interpretations in other media. Such interpretations greatly aid literary comprehension. Furthermore, though the re-creative literary critic is continually made aware of how extraordinarily difficult it is to interpret the expressed content of literature in critical prose, his task is, none the less, easier than that of other critics just because his critical medium resembles that of creative literature itself in being verbal. The translation involved in the critical re-creation of literature need not span quite so great a chasm as must be spanned by a verbal interpretation of music, the dance, or the visual arts.

But these advantages are offset by a corresponding hazard. For the printed poem, essay, or novel which we purchase in a bookshop is, after all, not the work of art itself in the sense in which a dance performed before our eyes, a musical composition actually heard, or a picture actually seen, are authentic works of art in all their sensuous objectivity. The poem, essay, or novel which awaits our artistic response does not exist on the printed page but only as *re-constructed by the imagination* from the verbal symbols. This constitutes a subtle distinction between literature and the other arts which merits more precise formulation.

A work of art in any medium must of course be artistically *re-created* in order to be apprehended for what it is. Artistic response is never a passive acceptance of what is merely "given." All that is ever "given" is a sensuous pattern whose artistic character and significance can be apprehended only through an act of the artistically re-creative imagination. But literature is unique among the arts in possessing, as we have seen, a dual primary medium which is essentially symbolic in character. That is, the visible symbols must first be translated into their appropriate sounds, and the sounds which are uttered must then be associated with their appropriate symbolized meanings, for the literary work to come into existence as an object awaiting artistic apprehension and appraisal. *Before* he attempts to "re-create" the poem as a work of art the reader must himself actually "reconstruct" it both vocally (or sub-vocally) *and* ideationally.

The term "ideationally" indicates the inescapable *added* factor in all literary response. Once the musician has translated a musical score into actual (or imaginary) sound, the composition exists for him as a sensuous object (with due allowance for the interpretative factor); whereas the reader of a poem who has translated the printed symbol into vocal (or sub-vocal) sound is confronted with merely a part, and that, much the lesser part, of the poem. The poem comes into existence for him as an object for artistic response only *after* he has associated these sounds with their appropriate ideational meanings.

Moreover, each individual *must* take this second all-important step in literary reconstruction *for himself*. A musical composition which is publicly performed from a printed score exists objectively as a pattern of sound available to everyone in the audience who is equipped with the requisite auditory capacity; whereas a poem read aloud to an audience from the printed page, though existing objectively, like music, as an audible pattern of sounds, and though, as such, immediately available to all who have ears to hear, does not exist *ideationally*, i.e., as a *meaningful* pattern of sound, save as *each individual* himself translates the audible sounds into the meanings which convention has associated with them. Whereas, during a concert, the members of the audience are in the presence of *one and the same public* pattern of sound (however various may be the capacity of different members of the audience really to "hear" the music with *musical* comprehension), during the public reading of a poem each member of the audience is in effect apprehending the *private* poem which he himself is forced to reconstruct from the successive public sounds of the reader's voice.

A literary composition must therefore always be subjected to a type of reconstruction peculiar to literature and not required in any of the other arts. For the writer, the poem is, in the first instance, a *new* construction which he symbolically records on paper. But having once recorded it, even he can continue to possess it only by *re*constructing it anew in his own mind from the written or the printed word. For the reader, the poem exists from the first only as a reconstruction from the printed page. Thus a literary composition differs in kind from works of art in other media in never being immediately "given"[41] to sense-perception.

[41] What from one point of view is immediately "given" may, from another point of view, be itself a reconstruction. Thus, the statue we are now looking at is immediately

This fundamentally "reconstructive" character of a literary work of art must not be confused with the "re-creative" process which conditions all *artistic* response. Artistic re-creation is requisite to the apprehension of the artistic character of any work of art in any medium. But in the other arts, what is thus re-created is a "given" perceptual object whose perceptual characteristics are themselves essential ingredients of the work of art itself. What we see in a picture with our physical eyes is an integral part of the picture regarded as a work of art. Hence, when we apprehend a picture as a work of art we become aware, by an act of the artistic re-creative imagination, of the artistic character of the picture as an actually visible, i.e., a "given," object of sense-perception. In literary apprehension, in contrast, the object upon which the artistic re-creative imagination operates is *itself* the product of the reconstructive imagination. Thus the imagination of the reader must perform a double task. It must first reconstruct the work from the printed symbols and endow it with an objective reality analogous to the "given" reality of the perceived picture prior to all artistic response. This reconstructive activity is accordingly strictly pre-artistic. The imagination must then artistically re-create this reconstruction if the work's *literary* character is to be apprehended, just as the painting must be re-created artistically if its *pictorial* quality is to be apprehended.

These two distinct acts of the imagination, which often take place simultaneously and are always ultimately fused, can be distinguished for purposes of analysis by entitling the first the "reconstructive," the second, the "re-creative," act of the imagination, and by designating the result of the first act as the "reconstructed" poem, that of the second, the "re-created" poem. It is the historical critic's primary task to facilitate accurate reconstruction in the light of historical evidence, whereas the re-creative critic's task is to help us to re-create with artistic comprehension what has been correctly reconstructed.[42]

"given" as a sensuous physical object in a way in which a poetic image is not; but the statue, regarded as a perceptual object, is itself the product of a perceptual reconstruction—a process which, as we have seen, involves the interpretation of successive and qualitatively various sense-data with the aid of memory and in terms of various concepts. But this does not affect the present argument.

[42] This distinction is valid and useful even though historical and re-creative criticism are not actually distinct but are always cooperative and mutually conditioning aspects in a single process. Cf., below, Chap. xx.

The term "reconstructive" signifies, I have said, the "translation" of printed or written symbols into their auditory equivalents, and then a more important "translation" of these auditory symbols into their ideational meanings. This second act is indeed a translation, but in genuinely literary response it is not merely a translation. It is rather a vital and sustained association in which the sound is not left behind or forgotten but is apprehended along with its meaning. A literary phrase is a pattern of sound *and* a pattern of meaning fused into a single organic whole. The creation and fusion of this whole in response to the stimulus of the printed page is, to repeat, the act of the reconstructive imagination here operative at a pre-artistic level.

A poem, considered for the moment merely as a reconstruction, is in one way inferior to a musical, choreographic, architectural, sculptural, or pictorial composition regarded as a "given" perceptual object. As an ideational reconstruction (though not as a mere auditory or visual pattern), it lacks the sensuous immediacy and vividness of a sculptural or pictorial representation of a perceptual object, for no object of inner awareness can possess the *kind* of vividness or immediacy which visual representations possess. This is evident if we compare, for example, a literary description of dancing figures with an actual dance, or a literary description of a landscape with a pictorial landscape. But this loss is offset by a corresponding gain both to the creative writer and to the reader.

The gain to the writer is strictly analogous to the advantage, already referred to, which the painter enjoys over the sculptor. Here, as there, what the imagination creates it can control. The painter must create three-dimensionality and light because he is working on a two-dimensional surface. But, as a result, he has a unique control over the light and space which he representationally creates. Similarly, the writer must construct, through the instrumentality of verbal symbols, whatever subject-matter he wishes to treat. But what is thus constructed can be selected, combined, and used for expressive purposes with a degree of freedom from external circumstance and a measure of artistic control far greater than is possible in any of the other arts.

The reader's reward is that greater intimacy and vividness which may distinguish the products of man's reconstructive imagination from the "objects" of his sensory awareness. It is true that men differ in capacity for imaginative reconstruction far more than they differ in capacity for sense-perception (which is itself a reconstructive process of a more elementary type). We can all observe, and most of us can be impressed by, the brilliance of a sunset. We can all see buildings and statues as real objective entities and even apprehend pictures as pictorial representations of perceptual scenes. But most of us find much greater difficulty in reconstructing an abstract argument, an image, or an emotive-conative state from the printed page or from the spoken word. Yet, in proportion as we are able to indulge in such reconstructive activity, what we have thus reconstructed is nearer to us, more really our own, more of a vital possession, than any perceptual object can ever be to us. Hence the more than life-like reality of a literary image, character, or event for one whose reconstructive imagination is unusually sharp and active, provided of course that the writer whose work is being read has himself created this image, character, or event with literary clarity.

But this reconstructive factor in literature raises a unique difficulty for the literary critic. Quite apart from variations in *subsequent artistic* interpretation and appraisal which arise in the field of literature as in other fields of art, what assurance can he have that he and his audience, i.e., those who have read the poem which he is discussing, are talking about and seeking to understand the same thing? This is a serious problem which the literary critic must face, but it is one which permits of solution. Precise and reliable communication is possible in literature (a) because of the "symbolic clarity" of the primary medium, and (b) because of the contribution of literary criticism.

(a) The "symbolic clarity" of literature is a function of the conceptual symbolism of its primary medium. I have pointed out[43] that every word (except proper nouns and demonstratives) has a core of conceptual meaning, i.e., a symbolic reference to some distinguishable recurrent quality, relation, or pattern, and that, furthermore, this conceptual meaning functions even when words are used for the construction (by the writer) and the reconstruction (by the reader) of images or for the evocation and reconstructive apprehension of emotive-conative states. In this fundamental sense the primary literary medium is uniquely conceptual among the primary artistic media. The effect of this primary conceptual symbolism upon the generic character of literary composition is a distinctive type of referential specificity which I have called "sym-

[43] Cf., above, Chap. VI.

bolic clarity." The nature of this quality can perhaps best be indicated by comparing the effect upon us of music and poetry respectively and the manner in which this effect is achieved in the two cases.

A musical composition presents itself to us first as an intrinsically satisfying pattern of sound, and these related sounds arouse in us instantaneously, as they are played, a continuous pattern of specific emotions, feelings, and impulses. This happens without our attaching any conceptual meaning to individual tones or musical phrases. Our first and basic response to music is definitely non-conceptual. Conceptual interpretation takes place, if at all, only *later*, when we try to express in words what the music has meant to us. It is only then that we think and speak of universals like "joy" or "sorrow" as entering into the expressed content of the music.

In our response to a poem, in contrast, this order is reversed. In reading a poem we do, indeed, first perceive the marks on paper (as, in music, we may first read the score) and then translate these marks into their appropriate sounds (as we do in music when we play or sing from a musical score). But our apprehension of the poem really begins only when we translate these sounds into their ideational meanings. The apprehension of these meanings is, as we have seen, an essentially conceptual undertaking because the central meaning of each word is its conceptual reference to a universal. And this apprehension of each word's specific conceptual meaning conditions, in turn, all apprehension of the more complex ideas which words in combination connote, whether these ideas are themselves new concepts, or images, or expressions of emotive-conative states. Thus the conceptual query,

> Tell me where is Fancy bred,
> Or in the heart or in the head?

or the description of an emotion and its manifestations, such as

> My love is strengthen'd, though more weak in seeming;
> I love not less, though less the show appear . . . ,

can be apprehended reconstructively only if we understand the conceptual meaning of each word.

The *final* effect of an individual passage or of a complete composition, on the other hand, may be either primarily conceptual or primarily imagistic, emotive, conative, hortatory, etc. That is, complex concepts may be developed without appeal to imagery, or complex images, without conceptual interpretation, while an emotion may be described directly or evoked in a more indirect way. These varying expressive emphases are achieved in a variety of ways. The Metaphysical poets make relatively little use of imagery and rely primarily on the "metaphorical" interplay of more general and more specific concepts with their associated overtones, whereas poetry which lies closer to the main poetic tradition employs both concepts and images, plays these off against each other in metaphorical relation, and controls the emotive-conative associations of both alike. Whenever words are used in literature not to elicit images or to evoke emotive-conative states but primarily for their conceptual reference, whatever ideational clarity results may be entitled "conceptual clarity." But this clarity, which has its counterpart in "imagistic clarity" and "emotive-conative clarity," is only one possible effect of "symbolic clarity," and must not be confused with it.

But whatever the dominant character of the final expressed content of a literary composition, this content will continue to reflect the symbolic nature of its verbal origin. The cumulative effect will be achieved, as in a mosaic, from the collection, interrelation, and fusion of innumerable specific references which constitute the very essence of verbal language; and this effect, so achieved, will never cease to have that specificity of conceptual reference, that mosaic-like primary symbolic clarity, which can be achieved only in a conceptually symbolic medium.

One of the distinguishing hall-marks of the competent writer is his ability to exploit this characteristic of words and to endow his writing with this "symbolic clarity." This is obvious in science and philosophy. The specialist in these fields is able to use words more precisely for his purposes than is the common man. But it is equally true in creative literature. The competent creative writer is able to use words with a nice regard for their conceptual meanings and, as a result, not only to refer to universals but to create images and evoke emotive-conative overtones with far greater precision or "symbolic clarity" than can the average individual. For, in his own way, the creative writer too is a specialist in the use of words; like other specialists he too is able to give verbal expression to his ideas with unusual symbolic clarity. This makes it possible for any number of readers to reconstruct precisely and uniformly what he has expressed with literary precision.

(b) Were linguistic and literary conventions identical in all nations, periods, and cultures, reliable literary reconstruction would depend merely upon the writer's and the reader's mastery of the primary verbal medium. But these conventions are, as we know, in a continual state of flux. This applies to ordinary discourse, and it applies also to the languages of the specialists. Even the common man cannot be understood by others unless both he and they employ the same linguistic conventions. But at the level of non-specialized verbal discourse the practical exigencies of survival in a social group effect in man a partly unconscious, partly conscious, adaptation to such conventions and verbal habits as are requisite to inter-subjective communication. In the art of literature this adaptation is not so easy. Like the common man, the poet is subject to the ordinary linguistic traditions and conventions of his age. But, like other specialists, he is also subject to the conventions of his special calling. The writer is therefore dependent for his specialized literary equipment upon his predecessors and upon the whole literary tradition of which he is a part. Even when he revolts against this tradition, the quality and temper of his revolt are in large measure determined by the tradition which he is renouncing. In this sense, literary creation (despite the contribution of original genius, whose importance is of course undeniable) is, like artistic creation in other fields and ultimately like all human endeavor, a cooperative venture, however unconscious may be the writer's indebtedness to tradition and however unpremeditated his use of literary conventions.

But if the language of all creative literature is as specialized as this would indicate, and if the poet must come into his literary inheritance in order to express himself with literary adequacy, we, his audience, will not be able to understand him and reconstruct his ideas from the verbal symbols he uses unless we too can bring to the reading of his works the requisite linguistic equipment and traditional orientation. It is just at this point that the literary critic comes to our aid. His first contribution is to set a literary movement in its proper historical and traditional context, i.e., to explain how the language, the literary conventions, and the whole intellectual and spiritual atmosphere of one age differ from those of another age and, more specifically, from our own. His second contribution is to relate the specific writer to his specific literary tradition with all its distinctive national, epochal, and ideological characteristics. And he must then try to interpret the ideational meaning of particular literary compositions in the light of this historical orientation.

I shall have more to say in the next chapter on the nature and function of criticism as such. Here I need merely note the contribution which the literary critic is able to make to our accurate reconstruction of a literary composition. Historical criticism cannot of itself, of course, insure adequate artistic re-creation in this or in any other artistic medium. It is merely a propaedeutic to such re-creation. But, as such, it is invaluable. For with the aid of the competent historical critic it is possible to learn the distinctive language and the cultural background of older literary works and to reconstruct, with great accuracy, the literary composition whose artistic expressiveness we wish re-creatively to apprehend.

The solution to the critic's problem is now apparent. Different individuals *will* be able to reconstruct the "same" literary composition in proportion (i) to the adequacy of their historical orientation in the relevant literary tradition, and (ii) to their innate capacity for the reconstruction of ideas from verbal symbols—the two conditions operating strictly in conjunction. At least ideally, the critic is unusually well equipped in both respects, and the more competent he is, the easier will it be for the layman, with the critic's aid, to approximate to an accurate reconstruction of literary compositions for himself.

Because of the unrivalled scope and diversity of the secondary medium of literature, most literary compositions have a much richer and more complex artistic content than compositions in other primary media. This makes it unusually difficult to cite individual literary compositions to illustrate the literary expression of this or that type of artistic content, for each composition is likely to exemplify a great number of types with almost equal clarity. The following passages and complete compositions are cited merely as instances of various expressive *emphases* on some of the main generic types of artistic content, as these types have been classified in Chapter XVI (*vide* particularly the chart on p. 275).

(a) *Perceptual universals, substantival and adjectival.* Carl Sandburg's *Fog* is a poetic interpretation of fog as a "perceptual object."

The fog comes
on little cat feet.
It sits looking
over harbor and city
on silent haunches
and then moves on.

Compare Shelley's *To a Skylark*, *Ode to the West Wind*, *The Cloud*, and *To the Moon*. H. D.'s (Hilda Doolittle's) *Heat*, in contrast, is concerned with heat as an "adjectival quality."

O wind, rend open the heat,
cut apart the heat,
rend it to tatters.

Fruit cannot drop
through this thick air—
fruit cannot fall into heat
that presses up and blunts
the points of pears
and rounds the grapes.

Cut through the heat—
plow through it,
turning it on either side
of your path.

But this distinction is often hard to draw, since perceptual objects can be described only in terms of their attributes, as in Keats' *Ode to Psyche*:

'Mid hush'd, cool-rooted flowers fragrant-eyed,
Blue, silver-white, and budded Tyrian . . .

For other poetic expressions of perceptual universals, see Andrew Marvell's lines, in *Thoughts in a Garden*:

Annihilating all that's made
To a green thought in a green shade,

Samson's lament on his blindness in *Samson Agonistes* (lines 67-109), James Thomson's *Seasons*, the "topographical poetry" of the eighteenth century, and, in general, all expressively descriptive passages in prose or verse, as, for example, in Wordsworth's *Prelude*.

(b) *Spiritual universals, social, religious, and introspective.* The transition from "perceptual" to "spiritual" universals is evident if we compare the works just cited with Wordsworth's sonnet, *Westminster Bridge*, William Blake's *London*, and Carl Sandburg's *Chicago*, in the order named. Wordsworth sees London still asleep in the early morning, when the city possesses a personality of its own almost apart from its inhabitants.

> Earth has not anything to show more fair:
> Dull would he be of soul who could pass by
> A sight so touching in its majesty:
> This City now doth like a garment wear
> The beauty of the morning; silent, bare,
> Ships, towers, domes, theatres, and temples lie
> Open unto the fields, and to the sky;
> All bright and glittering in the smokeless air.
> Never did sun more beautifully steep
> In his first splendor valley, rock, or hill;
> Ne'er saw I, never felt, a calm so deep!
> The river glideth at his own sweet will:
> Dear God! the very houses seem asleep;
> And all that mighty heart is lying still!

Blake, walking through the streets of London, sees on every hand the weakness and woe of its individual inhabitants.

> I wander thro' each charter'd street,
> Near where the charter'd Thames does flow,
> And mark in every face I meet
> Marks of weakness, marks of woe.
>
> In every cry of every Man,
> In every Infant's cry of fear,
> In every voice, in every ban,
> The mind-forg'd manacles I hear.
>
> How the Chimney-sweeper's cry
> Every black'ning Church appalls;
> And the hapless Soldier's sigh
> Runs in blood down Palace walls.

But most thro' midnight streets I hear
How the youthful Harlot's curse
Blasts the new-born Infant's tear,
And blights with plagues the Marriage hearse.

Sandburg, like Wordsworth, personifies an entire city, but in a different way. His Chicago is essentially a city of human activity and lusty, laughing vigor.

Hog Butcher for the World,
Tool Maker, Stacker of Wheat,
Player with Railroads and the Nation's Freight Handler;
Stormy, husky, brawling,
City of the Big Shoulders:
. . . Laughing!
Laughing the stormy, husky, brawling laughter of Youth, half-naked, sweating, proud to be Hog Butcher, Tool Maker, Stacker of Wheat, Player with Railroads and Freight Handler to the Nation.

Variant social emphases, some relatively simple and some very complex, are evident in the following poems. Chaucer, in the *Canterbury Tales*, depicts different types of persons and their relation to each other with literary objectivity and insight. Pope, in the *Essay on Man*, dissects human nature in the light of relatively abstract principles of social behavior, though not without the use of image and metaphor. William Langland's *Vision of Piers Plowman* early strikes the note of social reform, as does Shelley in the nineteenth century in his *Mask of Anarchy* and, in contemporary literature, Archibald MacLeish and Stephen Spender in their proletarian poetry. Andrew Marvell's *To his Coy Mistress* treats of a more subtle and less easily recognizable type of social relationship. A highly civilized seventeenth century gentleman addresses himself to his mistress with a wealth of sophisticated social overtones. A somewhat similar artistic content, reflecting a modern approach, is found in T. S. Eliot's *Love Song of J. Alfred Prufrock* and *Portrait of a Lady*, in both of which the individual portrayed has a strong sense of his social *milieu*. The primary expressive emphasis in most novels is predominantly social; compare, for instance, Dostoievski's *Brothers Karamazov*.

Such Psalms of praise as *Psalm 100*, "Make a joyful noise unto the Lord, all ye lands"; *Psalm 103*, "Bless the Lord, O my soul: and all that is within me, bless his holy name," or *Psalms 146* to *150*, which begin with, "Praise ye the Lord," clearly exemplify a religious emphasis genuinely "theocentric" in orientation. Though equally religious in expressed content, *Psalm 54*, "Save me, O God, by thy name," *Psalm 59*, "Deliver me from mine enemies, O my God," and *Psalm 61*, "Hear my cry, O God," are more "egocentrically" oriented. This egocentric orientation is characteristic of most "reflective" religious poetry, for example, of Robert Herrick's *Litany to the Holy Spirit*, John Donne's *Hymn to God, my God, in my Sickness*, and portions of T. S. Eliot's *Ash Wednesday*. Yet when Henry Vaughan, in *The World*, sings,

> I saw Eternity the other night,
> Like a great *Ring* of pure and endless light,
> All calm, as it was bright . . . ,

he points

> The way, which from this dead and dark abode
> Leads up to God. . . .

George Herbert's *The Altar* (note the visual pattern of the printed text) is even more theocentrically oriented.

> A BROKEN ALTAR, Lord, Thy servant rears,
> Made of a heart, and cèmented with tears;
> Whose parts are as Thy hand did frame;
> No workman's tool hath touched the same.
> A heart alone
> Is such a stone,
> As nothing but
> Thy power doth cut.
> Wherefore each part
> Of my hard heart
> Meets in this frame,
> To praise Thy name:
> That, if I chance to hold my peace,
> These stones to praise Thee may not cease.
> O let Thy blessed SACRIFICE be mine,
> And sanctify this ALTAR to be Thine.

Compare also the closing canto of Dante's *Paradiso*.

Wordsworth's familiar lines in *Tintern Abbey*,

> And I have felt
> A presence that disturbs me with the joy
> Of elevated thoughts; a sense sublime
> Of something far more deeply interfused,
> Whose dwelling is the light of setting suns,
> And the round ocean and the living air,
> And the blue sky, and in the mind of man;
> A motion and a spirit, that impels
> All thinking things, all objects of all thought,
> And rolls through all things.

express a deeply religious response to nature, whereas Section XI of Tennyson's *In Memoriam*, taken by itself, gives poetic expression to a reflective mood oriented to nature without any religious overtones:

> Calm is the morn without a sound
> Calm as to suit a calmer grief,
> And only thro' the faded leaf
> The chestnut pattering to the ground. . . .

Hamlet's soliloquy (III, i, 56-88) is reflective in a more "philosophical" sense. In his sonnets, Shakespeare treats the theme of love now with relative detachment, as in *Sonnet CXLI*,

> In faith, I do not love thee with mine eyes,
> For they in thee a thousand errors note. . . .

or in *Sonnet CXLVII*,

> My love is as a fever, longing still
> For that which longer nurseth the disease. . . .

and now with more impassioned fervor, as in *Sonnet XVIII*,

> Shall I compare thee to a summer's day?
> Thou art more lovely and more temperate. . . .

This passion receives still more intense utterance in the brief speech of Troilus in *Troilus and Cressida* (III, ii):

> I am giddy, expectation whirls me round.
> The imaginary relish is so sweet
> That it enchants my sense. What will it be
> When that the watery palate tastes indeed

Love's thrice-repured nectar? death, I fear me,
Swounding destruction, or some joy too fine,
Too subtle-potent, tun'd too sharp in sweetness
For the capacity of my ruder powers. . . .

or Shelley's *Indian Serenade*,

I arise from dreams of thee
In the first sweet sleep of night. . . .

or Browning's lines, from the Dedication to *The Ring and the Book*,

O lyric Love, half angel and half bird,
And all a wonder and a wild desire. . . .

In none of these poems is the emotion left wholly unmotivated, but it is treated in most of them primarily in terms of its own immediate nature and without elaboration of what has occasioned it. Similarly Tennyson's lines from *The Princess*,

Tears, idle tears, I know not what they mean,
Tears from the depth of some divine despair. . . .

express a nameless melancholy whose occasion is indicated only in the most general way.

(c) *Literary portraiture*. In literature, as in the other arts, the expression of "individual," as opposed to "universal," content is artistically less significant but not on that account devoid of artistic interest. Biographies and autobiographies are *bona fide* literary genres, the equivalent, in this medium, of sculptural and pictorial portraits and self-portraits. They rise to literary heights in Isaak Walton's *Life of John Donne* and *Life of George Herbert*, Boswell's *Life of Johnson*, Newman's *Apologia pro vita sua*, the autobiographies of Rousseau and Ruskin, and Lytton Strachey's *Eminent Victorians*. For a shorter literary portrait of an historical figure, see Roger Ascham's famous portrait of Lady Jane Grey in his *Schoolmaster*. In verse, the biographical note may be deeply personal, as in Edgar Lee Masters' *Anne Rutledge*:

Out of me unworthy and unknown
The vibrations of deathless music:
"With malice toward none, with charity for all."
Out of me the forgiveness of millions toward millions,
And the beneficent face of a nation
Shining with justice and truth.

I am Anne Rutledge who sleep beneath these weeds,
Beloved in life of Abraham Lincoln,
Wedded to him, not through union,
But through separation.
Bloom forever, O Republic,
From the dust of my bosom!

But it may also be satirical, as in Pope's portraits of Addison and Lord Hervey in the *Epistle to Dr. Arbuthnot*, or in Dryden's portraits of Shaftesbury and Buckingham in *Absalom and Achitophel*. Browning paints Saul in a Rembrandtesque manner in *Saul*, and in *Fra Lippo Lippi* he expresses his interpretation of the spirit of the Renaissance in his portrayal of the painter. The soliloquies of Dr. Faustus and Hamlet may be read as poetic self-delineations of quasi-historical persons, while Wordsworth's *Prelude* is the poet's own spiritual autobiography.

Literature can also celebrate historical events. Witness Walt Whitman's description of the passage of Lincoln's funeral cortege through the countryside in his noble elegy, *When Lilacs last in the Dooryard Bloom'd*, part of a group of stanzas which Whitman entitled *Memories of President Lincoln*. Other examples that come to mind are the epics of Homer and Virgil, where the historical orientation is not lacking in literary significance, the old English poems, *The Battle of Brunanburh* and *The Battle of Maldon*, Shakespeare's historical plays, Milton's *On the Late Massacre in Piedmont*, Tennyson's *Ballad of the Revenge*, and, in our day, Spender's *Vienna*. Gibbon's *Decline and Fall of the Roman Empire* and Carlyle's *French Revolution* are notable examples of literary prose in the field of history.

Literature also abounds in the celebration of other works of art, in the same and in other media, as in Chaucer's account of the temples of Mars, Venus, and Diana in *The Knight's Tale*, Spenser's description of tapestries in The House of Busyrane in *The Faery Queen*, Keats' *On First Looking into Chapman's Homer* and *Ode to a Grecian Urn*, and Tennyson's *Palace of Art*. Pater's classic description of the *Mona Lisa* in *The Renaissance*, and many of Ruskin's descriptions of Turner's paintings and his description of *St. Mark's* in the *Stones of Venice* possess a degree of literary expressiveness which justifies their inclusion in this list.

As we would expect, attempts at literary portraiture of animate and inanimate objects, whose individuality is hardly rich enough to sustain such treatment, are usually satirical, as in John Skelton's *Philip Sparrow*, Thomas Gray's *Ode on the Death of a Favorite Cat* (Horace Walpole's), and William Cowper's famous description of the sofa in *The Task*. In Kipling's *Jungle Books* and *Just So Stories*, the animals are personified in a spirit of playful humor. When the writer becomes preoccupied with the world of organic and inorganic objects, emphasis on the objective individual tends to give place to perceptual universals with an invocation of spiritual overtones. We are thus brought back to our starting point.

These examples of various types of expressed content in literature will, I hope, suffice to suggest to the reader ways in which he can document the foregoing analysis more fully for himself. They should at least serve to demonstrate the inexhaustible diversity and richness of literary content. Any composition of literary merit will exemplify a number of the generic categories of artistic content, and some, all or nearly all of these categories. Milton's *Lycidas*, for example, only 193 lines long, and so distinguished for its intensity and unity that it is often called the greatest lyric poem in the English language, can, without unreasonable stretching, be said to express each of the generic types of literary content here enumerated. Lines 37-49, 134-151 (the flower passage), and 154-164 abound in expressed perceptual universals, both substantival and adjectival. Lines 165-175, on the resurrection, are religiously oriented. Lines 113-131 deal with social corruption in places of duty and trust. Lines 64-84 are a reflection on fame, with an autobiographical suggestion. The biographical reference to King, the subject of the poem, is implicit throughout (*vide* particularly the reference to King and Milton and their tutor Chappell in lines 23-36). In lines 186-193 Milton is voicing his determination for his own future. In lines 130-131 he prophesies the destruction of the corrupt clergy (*vide* his own statement, in a published foreword, that he "foretells the ruin of our corrupted Clergy, then in their height"). And, finally, in lines 103-107, he treats specifically of the river *Cam*. This bald indication of the wealth of subject-matter and expressed content in a single poem may suggest the comprehensiveness and complexity of literary content. It should also remind us that the categories here distinguished are of value to literary analysis and re-creation merely as signposts to what each individual must discover for himself in the presence of actual compositions as literary works of art.

PART IV

PRINCIPLES OF CRITICISM

CHAPTER XX

THE NATURE AND CRITERIA OF CRITICISM

1. *The three aspects of criticism*[1]

A WORK of art is a unique, individual whole—a self-contained artistic "organism" with a "life" and reality of its own. But it is also an historical phenomenon—the product of a specific artist in a specific school, period, and culture, and an exemplification of stylistic characteristics which it shares with other works by the same artist and of the same school, period, and culture. Finally, works of art vary in artistic excellence, truth, and significance: every work of art possesses its own degree of perfection and its own measure of truth or falsity, triviality or greatness.

The competent critic takes all three aspects of the work of art into account, and so, though with less systematic and historical rigor, does the artistically sensitive layman.[2] He apprehends the individual work of art in all its self-contained uniqueness through sensitive artistic re-creation. But to re-create it adequately he must understand the artist's "language," and this implies familiarity with the generic style of the composition and its cultural setting. Historically oriented re-creation, in turn, does not exhaust critical response, for such response also implies appraisal of the work of art with respect both to its artistic quality and to its truth and spiritual significance. Criticism has therefore three aspects, the historical, the re-creative, and the judicial. Each aspect relates itself to a corresponding aspect of the work of art itself—historical criticism, to the work's historical character and orientation; re-creative criticism, to its unique artistic

[1] I am especially indebted to Professor A. E. Hinds for the following analysis of artistic and literary criticism. Professor Hinds is at present engaged in writing a book on literary criticism in which these distinctions will be examined both systematically and historically.

[2] The difference between lay and critical response to art is one of degree rather than of kind. Ideally, at least, the critic differs from the layman merely in possessing greater artistic sensitivity, a more accurate and a richer historical orientation, and a capacity for more objective judicial appraisal. That some laymen surpass some professional critics in one or other of these respects is irrelevant to my argument. My only concern is to formulate the basic principles of artistic response as these are exemplified in artistic and literary criticism at its best.

individuality; and judicial criticism, to its artistic value. These aspects of criticism are mutually conditioning factors of a single organic process: their relation to one another is strictly analogous to the interrelation of style, individuality, and value in the work of art itself.

The special task of historical criticism is that of determining the nature and expressive intent of works of art in their historical context. It involves, on the one hand, the authentication of texts and monuments, and, on the other, their interpretation in the light of available biographical, social, cultural, and other types of evidence. It is only thus that we can hope to understand, so far as lies in our power, what it was that the authors or makers of works of art intended to express, and to interpret this intention in the light of *their* interests and cultural background.

The special task of re-creative criticism is that of apprehending imaginatively, through sensitive artistic response, what the artist has actually succeeded in expressing in a specific work of art. The re-creative critic will inevitably, and quite properly, *also* relate what he thus apprehends to his own interests and needs. But this act is not in itself integral to re-creative criticism, save in so far as it contributes positively to the critic's understanding of the work of art itself and *its* expressed content. The prefix "re," in the term "re-creation," is of crucial importance.

The special task of judicial criticism is that of estimating the value of a work of art in relation to other works of art and to other human values. This determination of value involves, as we shall see, an appeal to at least three distinguishable normative criteria—a strictly aesthetic criterion of formal artistic excellence, an epistemic criterion of truth, and a normative criterion of larger significance, greatness, or profundity.

It must be emphasized that these three aspects of criticism are in reality three complementary approaches to the work of art, and that each approach can be explored effectively only in conjunction with the other two. Historical inquiry divorced from sensitive re-creation and judicial appraisal can merely produce an uninspired chronicle of "objective" historical "facts" which, by themselves, must fail to determine the artistic nature and value of the works of art under consideration. The effort to re-create a work of art without any understanding of its historical context must fail to be truly *re*-creative and must remain a purely subjective reaction. And man's aesthetic response to art must lack all artistic significance if it is not accompanied by an appraisal of it in terms of appropriate artistic standards. But this evaluation of a work of art must remain purely academic, scientific, or moralistic, if it is undertaken without historical perspective and without artistic sensitivity.

Thus, re-creative apprehension and judicial appraisal are both conditioned by historical orientation. Really to *re*-create a work of art is to apprehend the content which its author actually expressed in it, i.e., to interpret it correctly as a vehicle of communication. Such apprehension implies not only a general understanding of the medium employed but a familiarity with the artist's language and idiom, and these, in turn, are determined by his school, period, and culture as well as by his own personality. It also implies a knowledge of the artist's times and of his intellectual and spiritual environment. Without such historical orientation no critic, however artistically sensitive, can escape critical "sentimentality," that is, an illegitimate intrusion into the work of art of what does not exist in it and a failure to apprehend certain of its essential ingredients. Judicial appraisal, in turn, must be arbitrary and unfair unless it is based upon an historically objective understanding of what is appraised. The question, What is it worth? presupposes the question, What is it? and this question can be answered only within an historical frame of reference.

Similarly, the re-creation of a work of art in all its individuality is essential to both historical and judicial criticism. It conditions the work of the historian of art and literature because the subject-matter of such historical study can be determined only in terms of immediate artistic response. Only man's artistic sensitivity can reveal what is and what is not a "work of art," and so, what does and what does not constitute the appropriate subject-matter of artistic and literary history. On the other hand, only that can be subjected to valid artistic appraisal[3] which has been faithfully re-created. Appraisal cannot be based on rules or principles permitting of a purely mechanical application. We must "feel" what we would judge; our appraisal must be based upon an immediate artistic experience in the presence of the work of art itself.

[3] i.e., appraisal which purports to be an objectively valid estimate of the work of art itself. Without such re-creation, appraisal is irrelevant to the work of art in question and records either a merely subjective preference or a merely mechanical application of academic rules.

Finally, though judicial appraisal is in a sense the culmination of criticism, it actually pervades the entire critical enterprise. Try as we may to postpone appraisal until the historical and re-creative tasks have been completed, we shall discover that we have been appraising the objects of artistic contemplation from the very outset. We are inescapably normative in all our thought and conduct. No sooner are we confronted with what purports to be a work of art than we evaluate it, however incipient may be this evaluation and however often this preliminary judgment may be revised in the light of new historical evidence and fresh re-creative discovery. This normative compulsion is not only inescapable; it is essential to profitable historical inquiry and to fruitful artistic re-creation. For historical investigations which are not guided throughout by a sense of values and standards, both artistic and non-artistic, i.e., which lack normative perspective, tend to be trivial and inconsequential.[4] Significant historical research, in art as in other fields, must be guided by normative principles if it is to produce significant results. Artistic re-creation, in turn, can be no more than idle, self-indulgent play if the artistic quality and the truth and significance of art are ignored. Even the aesthete, who deprecates the categories of artistic truth and greatness, is, at his best, aware of "pure" artistic quality and prides himself on the refinement of his aesthetic taste.

The ideally all-round critic, then, is equally proficient in orienting himself historically to the work of art, in re-creating it, and in appraising it; and no critic can afford to be entirely deficient in any one of these three respects. But critics tend, as the result of temperament and training, to be predominantly historical, re-creative, or judicial in their basic approach to works of art in the several media. This predominant critical aptitude and interest, in turn, tends to identify them more or less closely with one or other of the great critical movements of a given culture. These movements, distinguished from one another by a major emphasis upon some aspect of the critical enterprise, may persist for centuries, but they acquire special importance during certain periods in history. Thus, in our modern European culture, "neo-classic" criticism, which was preponderantly judicial and which was distinguished for its allegiance to Aristotelian principles derived from the *Poetics*, flourished in the

[4] When the minute researches of a factually-minded scholar unearth facts which more synoptic minds can use and interpret profitably, these discoveries must be regarded as happy accidents. It is clear that the best historical research is not conducted in this way.

seventeenth and eighteenth centuries. "Romantic" criticism, which was preponderantly re-creative and which was distinguished for its interest in original genius, its emphasis upon the conceptually unanalyzable character of artistic quality, and its belief in the intuitive character of artistic apprehension, was the dominant critical movement of the first half of the nineteenth century. Finally, modern historical scholarship in literature and the fine arts achieved increasing importance during the second half of the nineteenth century and is still the dominant critical approach to art. These movements, I must repeat, differ from one another only in major emphasis, and the greatest figures in each movement owe their distinction to their unusual aptitude for all three types of criticism. But even the greatest critics tend to reflect the intellectual climate of their period and culture and to exhibit an affinity with one or other of the great critical movements.

If the ultimate interdependence of these three aspects of criticism is steadfastly borne in mind, it is profitable to note that their logical order of priority differs from their psychological order of priority. Historical inquiry logically precedes artistic re-creation as its necessary (though insufficient) condition, because a work of art, especially when it belongs to another age or culture, simply cannot be understood without the requisite historical orientation. Re-creation, in turn, is the necessary (though insufficient) condition of judicial appraisal, since only that can be significantly appraised whose nature has been re-creatively apprehended. Psychological interest tends to reverse this order. We normally take pains to re-create what, at first glance, arouses our artistic interest (i.e., elicits a preliminary, more or less favorable, judicial estimate), and historical research in the realm of art is usually motivated by the desire to understand more adequately what we have already partially re-created and enjoyed.[5]

[5] It might perhaps be argued that the professional critic's special prerogative is to offer and defend judicial estimates, and that the layman's chief interest in art is properly confined to artistic re-creation and enjoyment. But such a distinction between the layman and the critic would, if pressed, radically distort the unitary nature of man's response to art. In actuality, the layman is continually appraising what he apprehends and enjoys, and most professional critics have chosen to be critics, partly at least, because of their unusual capacity for artistic re-creation and enjoyment. The more we consider the matter, the more inescapable is the conclusion that everyone who approaches art seriously, i.e., both re-creatively and judicially, is really a "critic," even though his critical equipment be more or less deficient.

2. Artistic style, perfection, truth, and greatness

Our analysis of artistic style and of artistic perfection, truth, and greatness will be facilitated by a preliminary definition of each of these concepts and a brief indication of their relation to one another.

The style of a work of art is a function of the composition as a whole, regarded as an historical phenomenon. Every artist has his own individual style (or styles), and so has every school, nation, period, and culture. Style is thus essentially a generic manifestation of the individual temper and outlook of the artist and of his social and cultural milieu. The works of any given artist manifest stylistic similarities and differ stylistically from the works of other artists; the style of one school differs from that of another; and when the art of one nation, period, or culture is compared with that of another, distinctive stylistic similarities and differences become apparent. Of course, these several stylistic characteristics overlap, for a work of art simultaneously manifests the style of the artist, of the school to which he belongs, and of his nation, culture, and period. Thus a painting by Rubens illustrates his individual style as well as the Flemish variant of the seventeenth century Baroque. Hence, when we say that a work of art is "in" this or that style, the term "style" signifies a complex, historically determinate, generic character which must be interpreted in both a narrower and a wider frame of reference.

When, on the other hand, we say that a work of art "has" style, we declare it to be more or less *successfully* expressive in the manner of art. Style in this sense is synonymous with artistic quality or expressiveness. The artistic quality or perfection of a work of art is definable as pure artistic merit, i.e., as proportional to the success with which an artist has succeeded in expressing, *via* artistic form in an artistic medium, what he wished to express, irrespective of the truth and the significance of the expressed artistic content. The work of an artist who has nothing to express must, by definition, be wholly inexpressive and therefore wholly lacking in artistic quality or merit. It will therefore "have" no style whatever because it is not a work of art at all. As a result, it will not be "in" any historical style in any really significant sense; it can be no more than a "manneristic" imitation of certain superficial generic characteristics of genuine works of art by other artists.

Style as an *historical* phenomenon and artistic quality as artistic *merit* are thus intimately related. The former not only presupposes the latter; it *is* the latter regarded from the historical point of view. When we consider a work of art stylistically we ask: To what extent does it express the individual outlook of its author and thus resemble his other creative compositions? In what ways does it manifest the generic traits and express the pervasive attitudes of his school, nation, period, and culture? On the other hand, when we consider its artistic merit, we concentrate our attention upon the composition as an artistic achievement, and ask: How successfully, according to artistic criteria, has its author expressed in this composition what he set out to express, i.e., how appropriate is the work's specific form to the artist's expressive intent? These two questions, though clearly different in focus and objective, both relate to the work's distinctive mode of expression. The former is designed to establish generic similarities and differences between the work in question and other compositions, and these similarities and differences are viewed in historical perspective. The latter is designed to determine the degree of the composition's individual artistic excellence without *specific* reference to its larger historical orientation or to the artist's larger productivity. But the second question cannot be answered adequately save within a wider stylistic framework, since re-creation and evaluation are, as we have seen, dependent upon historical orientation; and, conversely, the generic style of a work of art cannot be determined without both artistic re-creation and judicial appraisal of the composition itself and of other compositions with which it is compared.

The truth and the greatness of a work of art, in turn, depend upon, yet transcend, both its stylistic character and its strictly artistic quality. Two compositions can be in the same style and yet vary greatly in truth and significance, and one may express a profound insight into human experience, the other, a distorted or superficial interpretation of human life. Thus the painting of Watteau and Boucher, though both artists were Frenchmen living in the eighteenth century and though both painted in the Rococo style, differ greatly in expressed significance. Again, two compositions may be similar in artistic quality or degree of perfection, expressing with equal competence the content which each artist wished to express, but the content of the one may be slight, that of the other, rich in human import. A Callot line drawing (Fig. 154) is as perfect of its kind as one of Rembrandt's etched crucifixions (Figs. 215, 216), but the expressed content of the latter is certainly richer in human significance than that of the former. The truth and significance of a work of art are thus primarily functions of the work's expressed content; its artistic quality or perfection is primarily a function of its specific expressive form; its style is primarily a function of its historical and generic character.

Style, perfection, truth, and greatness are thus distinct but complementary concepts. Style is *primarily* an historical concept, while artistic perfection, truth, and greatness are *primarily* normative concepts. The standard of artistic perfection is *primarily* aesthetic or infra-philosophic, while the standards of truth and greatness are *primarily* supra-aesthetic or philosophic in character. All four concepts are applicable, positively or negatively, to all art. They are explicitly invoked by most critics, and implicitly invoked even by the layman in his response to art. The fact that they are seldom defined with precision or distinguished clearly in concrete application imposes upon the philosopher of art a peculiar obligation to clarify their meaning and determine as precisely as possible how they are related.

None of the critical concepts can be understood adequately save in its relation to the other three. But the general relation in which they stand to one another suggests the order in which they can most profitably be investigated. Style conditions but does not guarantee artistic merit; a work can be artistically expressive without being truthful in the manner of art; and the artist's expressed insight can be truthful without being profound. That is, artistic greatness presupposes artistic truth, artistic truth presupposes artistic quality, and artistic quality is necessarily a function of generic style. I shall, accordingly, start with a general analysis of style and then proceed to investigate in order the concepts of artistic perfection, truth, and greatness.

CHAPTER XXI

ARTISTIC STYLE

A TRUE artist is bound to reveal himself in his works, and, in revealing himself, he inevitably reflects his social and cultural milieu. This individual and cultural revelation constitutes the essence of artistic style. Style manifests itself in the work of art apprehended as an organic and individual entity but interpreted as a more or less typical member of a class of artistic objects which resemble one another in various ways. Its *primary* locus is artistic form. But since artistic form is a function of the work of art *as a whole*, every distinguishable aspect of the work of art contributes to the composition's distinctive style. The artist's choice of his primary and secondary media, his formal organization of these media, and the resultant content of his art—all these factors, *taken in conjunction*, are of genuine importance in determining the style of a work of art.

1. Style and artistic form, the artist's intent, and his choice of media

Style manifests itself directly in artistic form. But this form is dictated by the artist's intent. And this intent, in turn, not only determines the artist's organization of his media, but conditions his choice of specific media for formal organization. Bearing in mind the organic unity of the completed work of art, let us consider first some concrete examples of the way in which a style manifests itself in architectural form. Wölfflin, to whose *Principles of Art History*[1] the reader is referred for a masterly analysis of the Baroque and High Renaissance styles, has defined five principles of formal organization and has distinguished these two styles in terms of these principles. We are not here concerned with the correctness of Wölfflin's analysis. That is a problem for the art historian. What concerns us is merely the fact that different styles do manifest themselves in different types of formal organization.

Wölfflin points out (a) that the Renaissance style is primarily linear and tactile, the Baroque, primarily painterly (*malerisch*) and visual. In the former the emphasis falls upon clearly defined out-

[1] Heinrich Wölfflin, *Principles of Art History*, tr. M. D. Hottinger (New York: Holt, 1932; George Bell and Sons, London).

lines and edges, in the latter, upon relationships of color and luminosity. "In the former case the stress is laid on the limits of things; in the other the work tends to look limitless. Seeing by volumes and outlines isolates objects: for the painterly eye, they merge. In the one case interest lies more in the perception of individual material objects as solid, tangible bodies; in the other, in the apprehension of the world as a shifting semblance."[2] (b) In the Renaissance style the plane is emphasized; in the Baroque, the visual third dimension. "Classic [i.e., High Renaissance] art reduces the parts of a total form to a sequence of planes, the baroque emphasizes depth."[3] (c) The Renaissance emphasizes the closed, the Baroque, the open form. "Every work of art must be a finite whole, and it is a defect if we do not feel that it is self-contained, but the interpretation of this demand in the sixteenth and seventeenth centuries is so different that, in comparison with the loose form of the baroque, classic design may be taken as *the* form of closed composition."[4] (d) The Renaissance emphasizes the multiplicity of parts, whereas the Baroque stresses the felt unity of the whole. "In the system of a classic composition, the single parts, however firmly they may be rooted in the whole, maintain a certain independence. It is not the anarchy of primitive art: the part is conditioned by the whole, and yet does not cease to have its own life. For the spectator, that presupposes an articulation, a progress from part to part, which is a very different operation from perception as a whole, such as the seventeenth century applies and demands. In both styles unity is the chief aim . . . , but in the one case unity is achieved by a harmony of free parts, in the other, by a union of parts in a single theme, or by the subordination, to one unconditioned dominant, of all other elements."[5] (e) The Renaissance strives for "absolute," the Baroque, for "relative" clarity. Here the contrast is between the "representation of things as they are, taken singly and accessible to plastic feeling, and the representation of things as they look, seen as a whole, and rather by their non-plastic qualities. But it is a special feature of the classic age that it developed an ideal of perfect clarity which the fifteenth century only vaguely suspected, and which the seven-

[2] *Ibid.*, p. 14.

[3] *Ibid.*, p. 15. The word "classic" (*Klassisch*) is used by Wölfflin to signify the art of the High Renaissance.

[4] *Ibid.*, p. 15.

[5] *Ibid.*, p. 15.

teenth voluntarily sacrificed. Not that artistic form had become confused, for that always produces an unpleasing effect, but the explicitness of the subject is [no] longer the sole purpose of the [presentation]. Composition, light, and colour no longer merely serve to define form, but have their own life."[6]

These contrasting types of formal organization, in turn, are motivated by a distinctive outlook and interest. It is *because* the Baroque artist saw the world and interpreted life as he did that he gradually evolved those stylistic forms which would most effectively enable him to express what he wished to express: the forms were dictated by the artist's intent. What he wished to express was an emotionally vivid sense of human finitude in the face of cosmic infinity, and this relation was apprehended in a characteristically seventeenth century manner. The Baroque style, as is well known, became, among other things, the eloquent vehicle of the Counter-Reformation, whose spirit achieved literary expression in Loyola's *Spiritual Exercises.*[7] What Loyola was so passionately concerned to acquire and transmit was a vivid sense of man's spiritual relation to Deity and his dependence upon God. He was not content with mere theological abstractions, and would willingly have endorsed Thomas à Kempis' statement: "I had rather feel contrition, than know the definition thereof."[8] Nor had he any use for a vague and inchoate mysticism; the relationship of God to man and of man's duties to God were, he believed, clearly established by Christian doctrine and therefore apprehensible without confusion. God was to him not indefinite, not Hegel's "bad infinite," but the God who had revealed Himself to man in Christ, and who, in this revelation, had made perfectly explicit the relation of the Infinite to the finite and of sinful mortals to their holy Redeemer. What the most typical religious painters, sculptors, and architects of the Baroque period set themselves to accomplish, accordingly, was the vivid architectural, sculptural, and pictorial expression of this spirit and belief, which differed so markedly from the typical spirit and outlook of the Renaissance. Employing such formal devices as those which Wölfflin

[6] *Ibid.*, pp. 15-16. I have substituted "no" for "not," and "presentation" for "presentment," as closer to the German text.

[7] *The Spiritual Exercises of Saint Ignatius Loyola*, tr. W. H. Longridge (London: Robert Scott, 1919).

[8] Thomas à Kempis, *Of the Imitation of Christ* (London: Oxford University Press, 1916), Book I, Chap. 1, p. 2.

has described, they painted pictures, carved statues, built buildings, whose effect upon the observer is powerfully dramatic, and what was expressed with such dramatic fervor was the evangel of the Counter-Reformation as formulated in Jesuit doctrine.

Andrea Pozzo's ceiling in *S. Ignazio* in Rome (Fig. 132) is a perfect example of religious motivation and artistic accomplishment in the Baroque style. We can interpret this extraordinary work with additional assurance because we know that Pozzo was a Jesuit priest familiar with, and committed to, the doctrines of Loyola, and also because we have in our possession Pozzo's own famous *Perspectiva Pictorum et Architectorum*,[9] written while he was painting this ceiling. This work is a technical treatise devoted entirely to the analysis of architectural principles requisite to the achievement of desired architectural effects. His whole emphasis, like Loyola's, falls upon the need for the study of principles, for discipline, and for practice. But Pozzo's motivating interest is, again like Loyola's, quite unmistakable. Loyola's goal is religious conversion and salvation: Pozzo's is the eloquent visual expression of man's relation to God. The elaborate perspective of his ceiling is so painted that it can be seen without distortion from only one spot—a spot marked by a circle in the marble floor. Pozzo did this deliberately in order to emphasize the relation of each individual finite mortal to infinite Deity as the Creator of the cosmos and the Savior of mankind. If we gaze upward from this one spot, we discover that all the lines of perspective focus not upon an infinite point in space but upon the Cross, the Christian symbol of God's redemption of man. Pozzo has obeyed his own injunction to "the Lovers of Perspective": "Therefore, Reader, my Advice is, that you chearfully begin your Work, with a Resolution to draw all the Lines thereof to that true Point, the Glory of GOD."[10] It is to this end, the celebration in architecture and painting of man's worshipful recognition of the glory of God, that this religiously motivated Baroque architect and painter exercised such dynamic control over exterior and interior space by means of architectural form, by the manipulation of light, and by pictorial and sculptural ornament. Everything he did had its function in producing the right dramatic effect upon the spectator. "Baroque architecture ultimately derives the grandeur of its expressive scale from the largeness of its basic belief, namely, that the

[9] Published in Rome, 1693, and translated into English by John James, 1707.
[10] *Op. cit.*, "To the Lovers of Perspective."

cosmos is infinite and yet is submitted to divine and human measure."[11]

Much Baroque art is of course secular rather than religious in motivation, and not all religious Baroque art is as expressively successful as is Pozzo's ceiling. Few Baroque artists were as explicitly aware as was Pozzo of what they were trying to express. But all Baroque art, in whatever medium, is expressive in its own way of that diversified, yet curiously distinctive, spirit which permeated the seventeenth century. This spirit expresses itself differently in different portions of the century, in different countries, and in the work of different individual artists; but its generic character persists amid infinite major and minor variations, and leaves its mark upon the most diverse products of the period.

Stylistic form, then, is motivated by the artist's conscious or unconscious intent. But this intent also determines in large measure the artist's choice of his primary and secondary media. Some primary media lend themselves better than others to a Baroque treatment, or, to state the case more accurately, a style as pronounced as the Baroque invites the special exploitation of certain aspects of each primary medium. It also invites the use of several media in combination: note the extensive use in Baroque architecture of sculpture and painting. Baroque style exercises a similar selective control over the secondary medium. The more dramatic religious events, for example, are peculiarly susceptible to Baroque interpretation. Witness, for instance, Bernini's *Ecstasy of S. Theresa* (Fig. 113); Bernini's choice of this subject is as characteristic as is his sculptural treatment of it. In a word, the Baroque style manifests itself not only in artistic form and in the artist's intent but also in his selection of subject-matter and in his exploitation of available primary media.

2. *Sympathetic and antipathetic styles*

The relation of one style to another may be primarily one of sympathy or of antipathy, or it may be partially sympathetic, partially antipathetic.

Some styles, as I have already pointed out, are predominantly sympathetic. Though differing both in denotative scope and in con-

[11] Quoted by permission from an unpublished work on architectural scale by Professor George Forsyth, to whom I am also indebted for the preceding interpretation of Pozzo's ceiling.

notative character, they exhibit an integral affinity which makes it possible for them to fuse and to manifest themselves simultaneously in a single stylistically unified work of art. The style characteristic of a particular artist is usually sympathetic to the styles of his school and nation, period and culture. This relationship is not, of course, accidental. It is the natural result of social influence and cultural development. Since Rubens was not merely a unique individual but also a Fleming endowed with something of the Flemish temperament and outlook, and, in addition, a seventeenth century European, sensitive to the dominant temper of his century and continent, it was inevitable that his style should exhibit not only his own individuality but that of his social environment and cultural tradition.

But styles also stand in antipathetic relation to one another. This antipathy obtains in proportion as the basic motivating *Weltanschauung* differs. Thus Rembrandt differs stylistically from Rubens in essential ways, as does the Dutch school from the Flemish School, the Baroque from the High Renaissance, and the European from the Egyptian, Indian, or Chinese. These differences vary, of course, in degree and importance. For example, Rubens and Rembrandt have more in common than have Rubens and Raphael: the Dutch and Flemish schools of the seventeenth century exhibit a greater affinity than exists between either school and, say, the school of Duccio. But stylistic similarities and differences, affinities and antipathies, must not be interpreted superficially, since the animating spirit and underlying motivation is, as we have seen, of great importance in the determination of a style. Thus, despite important and easily recognizable differences, the paintings of the late sixteenth century artist, El Greco (Fig. 291), exhibit a deep stylistic affinity to those of his contemporary, Rubens (Fig. 292).[12]

Human nature being what it is, no two styles are wholly antipathetic. The most typical Chinese outlook has *something* in common with the philosophy and temper of western Europe, and the most diverse of individual temperaments exhibit at least *some* common traits. Hence there is a certain affinity between all styles in every artistic medium. But since cultures, periods, and individual artists also differ from one another in significant ways, no two styles are

[12] Some of these basic affinities are explored in Karl Scheffler's fascinating *Der Geis der Gotik* (Leipzig: Insel-Verlag, 1929).

wholly sympathetic to one another, and some are much more antipathetic than others. It is one of the chief tasks of the critic of art and literature to study these affinities and antipathies and to do the fullest justice to both.

No culture or society, meanwhile, is static, and no individual artist, however pronounced his individuality, is immune to cultural and social influences. Societies and individuals alike are continually undergoing internal change, partly as a result of external contacts, partly in obedience to the logic of their own inner development. These changes of outlook are reflected in the emergence of new styles, in their progressive evolution, and in their eventual destruction or radical transformation. Thus artistic style is as subject to the flux of historical emergence, change, and decay as any other historical phenomenon. The categories of relative permanence and change, of inner evolution and response to environmental influence, are, like the categories of universality and individuality, as applicable to style as they are to other spatio-temporal phenomena. A second equally important task of the critic of art and literature, accordingly, is to explore the complex patterns of stylistic change, to determine the external and internal causes of such change, and to correlate the appearance, development, and decay of specific styles with the emergence, evolution, and disappearance of those more basic human attitudes which constitute the underlying basis of style. The history of art is in essence a history of artistic style, and this, in turn, is but one aspect of the more synoptic discipline of human history as such.

The critic who engages in such historical investigation will discover, finally, that a style is the joint product of genuine originality and healthy assimilation of sympathetic elements in other styles. In the absence of all assimilation (were this possible) nothing could emerge stylistically but freakish novelty, whereas the complete absence of originality or innovation marks the crystallization and ultimately the death of style. Eclecticism in the bad sense may be defined as the arbitrary juxtaposition of antipathetic stylistic factors or, alternatively, as the use in a single work of art of unassimilated aspects of sharply divergent styles. The impact of his cultural and artistic environment upon an individual artist will be artistically fruitful only in proportion as the artist is able to fructify his own original thought and creative activity through vital contact with the thought and productivity of other men.[13] A third task of the critic, accordingly, is to analyze various styles with an eye to their inner integrity and vitality and to discriminate between the spurious art of superficial eclecticism and the genuine art of healthy stylistic development.[14]

3. *Stylistic vitality*

All generic styles are, by definition, complex universals which characterize, and achieve embodiment in, specific works of art. From the re-creative point of view, the individual work of art is the basic fact, and in proportion as we emphasize this fact, we must regard a generic style merely as a common characteristic of two or more works of art and, as such, judge it to be wholly dependent upon them for its reality and significance. Historically considered, however, styles seem to possess a certain vitality and dynamic power of their own. Since the creative artist is himself a relatively enduring personality with a relatively stable outlook and a technique which, despite variations, exhibits a degree of constancy, his individual style is actually operative throughout the period of his productivity. Each of his successive productions reveals the influence of his dominant stylistic bent: his work is what it is in large measure because of the dynamic influence of his own unique style. Similarly, schools, nations, periods, and cultures are all characterized by pervasive attitudes, traditions, and conventions which, despite continual modification, exhibit an enduring core of identity over a longer or shorter period of time. These relatively enduring attitudes and conventions influence the thought and actions of individual men and women, and so of individual artists, in a profound way. Hence,

[13] What happens when a building in a well-defined style is imitated without architectural comprehension is well illustrated in the *Kaiserpalast* in Strasbourg (Fig. 25), patently in imitation of Le Vau's exquisite *Château de Vaux-le-Vicomte* (Fig. 24). Note the loss of architectural proportion, the inappropriate use of sculptural figures, etc.

[14] The relation in which any particular style stands to other styles can be indicated schematically with the aid of a spatial metaphor. If any given style is symbolized by a horizontal line, all styles primarily sympathetic to it can be symbolized by parallel lines, and all primarily antipathetic styles, by vertical lines. The factor of developmental influence can then be symbolized by diagonal lines flowing into the original horizontal (to indicate the influence of other styles upon the style in question) and out of this horizontal (to indicate the impact of this style upon subsequent styles). The angle of incidence in each case can be made to symbolize the degree of sympathy and antipathy between the style under investigation and the related styles, whether antecedent, contemporaneous, or subsequent to it in time.

styles must be interpreted by the historian, however cautiously, as dynamic forces whose tangible effects are evident in the works of art of the school or nation, period or culture, in question.

A style seldom manifests itself exhaustively in any single work of art.[15] Thus, certain aspects of the styles of Rubens and Rembrandt fail to achieve adequate embodiment in any one of their paintings. The richer a style, the more various and partial are its specific manifestations, and the more necessary is it, if we are to know it for what it is, to apprehend it in terms of its inner essence. Such apprehension is not primarily conceptual, though critics are bound to attempt conceptual formulation as an aid to stylistic analysis. What the critic actually does is to develop an "eye" or an "ear" for stylistic similarities and differences. He learns to recognize, for example, that distinctive stylistic quality which we associate with the Baroque or the High Renaissance, or with an individual musician or poet. He may be at a loss to know how to formulate these distinguishing stylistic traits with conceptual precision, but like Wölfflin he must, as critic, attempt to isolate and define the significant hall-marks of a distinctive style, and this attempt may, as we know, issue in illuminating conceptual definitions and descriptions. What he is analyzing, meanwhile, is not the lowest common denominator of all works of art "in" the style in question, or even the mere aggregate of all recognizable stylistic hall-marks: it is a universal with a life and integrity of its own, which is best described in terms of a pervasive attitude and which expresses itself in subtle artistic relationships not reducible to conceptual formulae. Wölfflin's analysis of the Baroque and Renaissance styles, for all its clarity and penetration, is but a halting formulation of what the author, as a sensitive and informed critic, has felt and seen, and he himself would be the first to admit the inadequacy of his own or any other verbal accounts of these or any other styles.

The artistic vitality of a style is conditioned by the spiritual vitality of the artist and of his cultural background. The more integrated an artist's personality, and the more coherent his outlook, the more artistically eloquent (other things being equal) is his style. An artist whose style changes often and radically during his lifetime

[15] This is because a style is, philosophically considered, a complex universal with many constituent and interrelated aspects. A work of art may, accordingly, manifest some of these aspects without manifesting others, i.e., it manifests a given style more or less adequately.

will be found to have failed, as an individual, to develop steadily; the violent revolutions in his style reflect correspondingly mercurial changes in his basic outlook and betray an incapacity for genuine spiritual development. The consistent stylistic development of such artists as Titian or Beethoven, in contrast, mirrors the ever-increasing profundity of their insight into the nature and meaning of human life. The clever but shallow artist may develop a facile style early in life, but he is likely to devote the rest of his days either to the imitation (with minor variations) of his own work or else to a restless search for novelty—a search frequently issuing in superficial eclecticism. Thus an artist's style mirrors his personality as an enduring and changing individual. The unpredictable activity of artistic creation can objectify in successive works of art what would otherwise never achieve objectification, but it cannot produce stylistic significance out of nothing. Only that can be expressed in the language of art which in a sense already exists in the realm of the spirit, and the stylistic character of the final product is necessarily determined by the artist's inner spiritual capacity and history.

This applies, *mutatis mutandis*, to the more generic styles of a school or nation, period or culture. In each case, the vitality of the style is ultimately proportional to the spiritual cohesion and wisdom of the social group. The historic styles in art are, accordingly, accurate indices to the temper and spiritual atmosphere of the social group. Internal confusion, doubt, and despair promptly manifest themselves in the art of the period: witness the almost complete absence today of a generic style comparable in inner vitality to the Gothic or the Roman Baroque. The chief trends of modern painting, from Dadaism at one extreme, through the various types of abstractionism, to proletarian and fascist art, at the other, exhibit the modern temper in its violent revolt against tradition, its search for novelty, its cynicism, its desperate attempt to save itself by this or that totalitarian or individualistic device. Though we admit, as notable exceptions, the work of certain rare and solitary individuals wiser than their times and able to tower above their fellows in spiritual and artistic stature, the art of any social group and tradition is a true measure of what the group or the tradition has itself been able to achieve. Thus, the art of ancient Egypt is as static as Egyptian culture itself through forty centuries. The art of Greece clearly reflects, in its archaic, classical, and hellenistic periods, the cultural and spiritual evolution of the inhabitants of the city states. The typical art of Rome objectifies Rome's imperial majesty. A major task of the art-historian, accordingly, is to interpret diverse styles, and the individual works of art which manifest these styles, in the light of a more synoptic historical apprehension. Works of art, in turn, suitably dated and interpreted, provide the historian of human cultures with an invaluable source of historical information.

4. Stylistic variations

Despite the close affinity of sympathetic styles to one another, these styles can and do vary independently of one another. There have been periods, such, for example, as the archaic period in Greece, when the entire emphasis was on conformity to a traditional generic style and the submergence of the artist's own individuality. And there have been other periods, like our own, in which the dominant desire for self-expression has led to a contempt for tradition and an indifference to the development and preservation of older styles. In every age, moreover, the chief artistic contribution of some artists has been their sensitivity to tradition, of others, their capacity for originality and revolt. As a result, the dominant style in some works of art is the artist's own individual style, in others, the characteristic style of a school, and in still others the more pervasive style of a nation or cultural epoch. Even the works of a single artist can vary in this respect; some may chiefly exemplify the artist's individual style, others, a more generic outlook.

Styles vary in richness and complexity. This type of variation is conditioned by two factors—underlying spiritual attitude and expressive technique. If, on the one hand, the philosophy of life which underlies a style is superficial and lacking in inner coherence, or if, on the other hand, the available artistic conventions are undeveloped and crude, the resultant style will be correspondingly impoverished. A rich and humanly significant style is the artistic product of profound insight powerfully canalized by tradition and effectively implemented by a versatile and expressive technique. Compare, on this score, the primitive art of central Africa, whose congeniality to modern artists and critics testifies to the sophisticated infantilism of our post-war culture, with the stylistic profundity, subtlety, and richness of ancient Greece, the Middle Ages, the Renaissance, or the Baroque period. Or compare the individual styles of the great masters in any medium with the styles of their uninspired followers or of minor rebels and innovators.

Any such estimate of contrasting styles depends, of course, upon how style is defined. If it is defined as a lowest common denominator, its connotative richness will vary inversely with its denotative scope, for the more numerous and diverse the representatives of a style, the less will they have in common. If, on the other hand, it is defined, as I have suggested that it should be defined, as the distinctive manifestation in art of a coherent spiritual outlook, a generic style like that of the thirteenth, fifteenth, or seventeenth centuries in Europe will necessarily be richer than the style of any human individual, whatever his spiritual and artistic stature.

CHAPTER XXII

ARTISTIC QUALITY AND PERFECTION

1. The general nature of artistic quality

THE concept of style is, as we have seen, primarily an historical concept. That of artistic quality or perfection,[1] in contrast, is primarily a normative concept. Every genuine work of art must, by definition, "be" in one or more styles. But individual works of art in the same style or styles differ in artistic merit. The same artist will express himself with greater artistic skill in some of his creations than in others, and the works of one artist in a given generic style will be superior to those of another artist in the same style. It is even possible to compare works of art in radically different styles, and when this is done, one work will often be found to surpass another in sheer artistic quality. We must now examine the nature of artistic quality by analyzing some of its determining conditions.

I shall not try to do here what I have insisted repeatedly cannot be done, i.e., to *reduce* artistic quality to other more primitive qualities.[2] The unique character of the artistic quality of a work of art can only be immediately intuited, and though it can be exhibited and denoted, it cannot be defined or even described. As a simple and ultimate quality it eludes analysis as inevitably as do sound and color. The artistically sensitive and trained observer will be able to recognize and appraise it with great assurance when he is in its presence; and the more artistically sensitive he is, the more will he appreciate the inescapable limitations of all formal analysis. But though analysis cannot define artistic quality itself, it can exhibit some of its determining conditions. It is these which I shall attempt to indicate.

[1] The concept of "artistic quality," like other normative concepts, signifies both a generic quality and an ideal limit. All works of art have, by definition, some degree of artistic quality, but some approximate to the ideal of artistic perfection more closely than others. In the text I have sometimes employed the terms "artistic quality" and "artistic perrection" synonomously, but, as a rule, I have used the former term to signify the generic quality, the latter, to signify the artistic ideal or norm.

[2] Cf. G. E. Moore, *Principia Ethica* (Cambridge: Cambridge University Press, 1929), p. 7, on the irreducibility of "simple notions."

I have said that the artistic merit of a work of art is proportional to the success with which an artist succeeds in expressing in it whatever he desires to express, irrespective of the truth or significance of this expressed content. What are the implications of this statement?

The first is that artistic quality is always a function of the success with which artistic form is adapted to artistic intent. It is a characteristic of the work of art as a whole, not merely of its formal pattern as such. To manifest artistic quality, the form of a work of art must be expressive, and this expressiveness is partly conditioned by the artist's expressive intent, even though this intent is often unconscious and is seldom explicitly formulated by the artist himself prior or subsequent to the act of artistic creation. In appraising artistic quality, accordingly, the critic must take the artist's intent into account, divining it, for the most part, from the expressed content of the work of art itself.

Hence artistic quality must, secondly, be distinguished from formal beauty as such, just as beauty must be distinguished from mere aesthetic quality. I have throughout this volume[3] used the term "aesthetic" to signify that generic quality which is the object of generic aesthetic response. *Any* object of awareness which arouses in the aesthetically sensitive observer a feeling of aesthetic delight and invites continued contemplation should, I believe, be said to possess aesthetic quality. Thus even a single sound or color, prior to all artistic selection or manipulation, may be aesthetically pleasing. Beauty, on the contrary, has been described as a function of formal organization. It belongs to the genus "aesthetic quality," because it too makes an immediate appeal to the sensitive observer; but it is a distinctive species of this genus because of its dependence upon formal organization and structural relationships. Artistic quality, in turn, is a distinctive kind of beauty, and therefore, *a fortiori*, a very distinctive kind of aesthetic quality. Like other types of beauty, it too is a function of form; but, unlike other types of beauty, it is a function of artistically expressive form. The problem of expressive intent does not arise in the apprehension and appraisal of beauty as such: all that is required is sensitive aesthetic response to mere formal organization. But artistic beauty cannot be divorced from expressive intent, since a work of art must be apprehended as an expressive

[3] Cf. pp. 5*ff*.

vehicle. The aesthetic, the beautiful, and the artistic are thus related to one another as genus to species to sub-species.

The third implication is that artistic quality is primarily a function of artistic form. The special locus of artistic quality is not the primary medium prior to its formal organization, nor the expressed content as such, but the pattern into which the medium is organized for expressive purposes. Certain sounds and colors possess aesthetic quality, i.e., make an immediate aesthetic appeal, whereas others do not; but artistic (as opposed to mere aesthetic) quality makes its appearance only *after* the primary medium has been formally organized for expressive purposes. The content of a work of art, in turn, is, as we shall see, the primary locus of the work's artistic truth and its larger human significance;[4] but in itself it cannot be considered the locus of artistic quality. What determines the purely artistic merit of a work of art is not what it says but how it says it, not its expressed content but its expressive form.

In the fourth place, artistic quality is a function of the specific form of a work of art, not of the generic forms which the work of art more or less faithfully exemplifies. The appraisal of a composition's specific form must, it is true, involve a recognition of the use here made of various types of generic form; and it is quite legitimate to criticize an artist for violating principles relevant to a given manner of treatment or compositional pattern, if it is clear that he has chosen to invoke these principles. But what is of crucial importance is not the artist's obedience to the canons of this or that generic form, but rather the artistic vitality and perfection of the specific form of the work of art as a unique composition. Since every work of art is a unique solution of a unique problem, the critic must ask: How successfully has the artist solved his particular problem in this particular work of art? How appropriate is this specific form to the artist's specific intent? In this sense every critical judgment recording an appraisal of artistic quality is necessarily a singular judgment.

Finally, artistic quality is dependent upon certain universal conditions, and its appraisal necessitates an implicit appeal to a universal standard of artistic perfection. That this is the case can be shown both theoretically and empirically. Considered theoretically, the concept of artistic perfection is by definition a normative concept. This means that every appraisal of a work of art, though

[4] Cf., below, Chaps. XXIII and XXIV.

necessarily a singular judgment relating to the specific work of art in all its uniqueness, involves an appeal to a standard universally applicable to all works of art as such. On the other hand, empirical analysis of the most diverse works of art reveals the fact that whenever artistic intuition discovers artistic merit in a work of art, the work in question is actually found to satisfy, in proportion to its artistic merit, certain determining conditions of artistic quality as such.

This chapter will be devoted to a consideration of some of these conditions of artistic quality. We shall discover that something can be done to indicate what factors the critic must take into account in all his critical appraisals, and what conditions have been violated by an artist when a work of art is deficient in artistic merit.

2. *The analysis of artistic perfection in terms of Aristotle's doctrine of the mean*

A work of art which arouses interest is often said to be "alive"; its "vitality" is frequently made the measure of its artistic merit. To describe a work of art as "alive" is, of course, to resort to metaphor, but the application of the concept of vitality to art is appropriate and illuminating. No other concept serves as effectively to indicate the most essential characteristic of genuinely expressive artistic form. For such form clearly reflects the creative vitality of its author. Just as man differs from a machine in being alive, so a work of art, which is his handiwork, differs from the product of a machine in being the eloquent sensuous expression of the artist's creative imagination. Whenever a competent artist warms to his work and prosecutes it with spirit and disciplined enthusiasm, the work of art itself bears the unmistakable marks of such effort. Whenever, in contrast, an artist lapses into mechanical passivity and works without imaginative concentration, his work will show a corresponding lack of vitality. A work of art which possesses artistic vitality moves us, if we are sensitive, to a correspondingly vital artistic response, whereas, in proportion as it lacks artistic vitality, it "leaves us cold" and fails to arouse us to artistically re-creative activity.

Artistic vitality is always a product of a synthetic resolution of conflicting tendencies any one of which would, if uncontrolled, destroy all artistic merit.[5] The analysis of this reconciliation of polar

[5] For an illuminating analysis of vitality as a function of dynamic tension and as a condition of artistic quality, cf. Kurt Riezler, *Traktat vom Schönen* (Frankfurt am Main,

extremes will be greatly facilitated by the application to art, with suitable modification, of the Aristotelian doctrine of the mean.[6] To demonstrate the relevance to art of this doctrine, I shall first summarize the four aspects of the ethical mean which Aristotle emphasizes, and then indicate how his formulae must be modified to make them applicable to artistic perfection.

Aristotle describes the mean of virtue, first, as an "intermediate between excess and defect." As such, it is *one* state or condition, whereas excess and defect allow of *many* variants. "It is possible to fail in many ways . . . , while to succeed is possible only in one way. . . ."

He points out, in the second place, that the mean in ethics is not "the intermediate in the object," i.e., a mean which is "equidistant from each of the extremes" and "one and the same for all men," but rather the "intermediate relative to us," which is "not one, nor the same for all." The "intermediate in the object" is, he says, the intermediate "according to arithmetical proportion": this type of mean may be symbolized by a point *X* mid-way between the two ends of the line *AB*, thus:

$$A \overset{X}{\text{———·———}} B.$$

The "intermediate relative to us," in contrast, cannot be defined in any such mechanical fashion. ". . . If ten pounds are too much for a particular person to eat and two too little, it does not follow that the trainer will order six pounds; for this also is perhaps too much for the person who is to take it, or too little—too little for Milo [a famous wrestler], too much for the beginner in athletic exercises. . . . Thus a master of any art avoids excess and defect, but seeks the intermediate and chooses this—the intermediate not in the object but relatively to us."

In the third place, the mean of virtue is itself an extreme, not permitting of excess or deficiency, while the extremes, i.e., the moral

Klostermann, 1935). Cf., also, Ananda Coomaraswamy, *The Transformation of Nature in Art* (Cambridge, Mass.: Harvard University Press, 1935).

[6] Cf. *Ethica Nicomachea*, 1106a-1109b. The quotations in the text are taken from W. D. Ross' translation (Oxford: Clarendon Press, 1925). For a clear exposition of this doctrine and a discussion of its wider orientation in Aristotle's thought, cf. Whitney Oates, "The Doctrine of the Mean," *Philosophical Review*, Vol. XLV (1936), pp. 382-98. I am not primarily concerned in the following analysis to defend Aristotle's account of moral virtue. I merely wish to indicate the applicability of his doctrine of the mean, duly modified, to the concept of artistic perfection.

vices, possess no virtuous mean. It is not possible ever to be right with regard to badness: spite, shamelessness, envy, adultery, theft, and murder are "themselves bad, and not the excesses or deficiencies of them"; they are always wrong. Contrariwise, and this is the important point, ". . . there is no excess and deficiency of temperance and courage because what is intermediate is in a sense an extreme": a mean can have neither excess nor deficiency. The mean of virtue may therefore by symbolized by a perpendicular line *XY* to distinguish it from the point *X*, which merely symbolizes a neutral mid-way point.

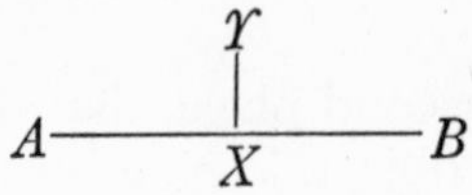

$$
\begin{array}{c}
Y \\
| \\
A \text{———————}\, X \,\text{———————} B
\end{array}
$$

Finally, Aristotle points out the difficulty of arriving at the mean in any particular case. (All moral decisions, since they are "relative to us," *are* particular decisions.) "It is no easy task to be good. For in everything it is no easy task to find the middle . . . ; so, too, anyone can get angry—that is easy—or give or spend money; but to do this to the right person, to the right extent, at the right time, with the right motive, and in the right way, *that* is not for everyone, nor is it easy; wherefore goodness is both rare and laudable and noble." The decision, moreover, "is not easy to determine by reasoning . . . ; such things depend on particular facts, and the decision rests with perception." By "perception" Aristotle here means moral perception, which is the product of suitable capacity subjected to suitable discipline and training.

Let us now see how this doctrine of the mean may, duly interpreted, be applied to the analysis and appraisal of artistic perfection. Aristotle himself explicitly recognizes the legitimacy of such application. "It is thus," he says, "that every art does its work well—by looking to the intermediate and judging its works by this standard (so that we often say of good works of art that it is not possible either to take away or to add anything, implying that excess and defect destroy the goodness of works of art, while the mean preserves it; and good artists, as we say, look to this in their work). . . ." What Aristotle here calls the "goodness" of works of art I have called their "perfection," i.e., that which makes it impossible "either to take away or to add anything" without injury; and the artistic analogue to "virtue" is "artistic quality."

(a) Artistic perfection, like moral goodness, is a mean between extremes. And it is always a single state, whereas the possibilities of artistic defect are multiple. There is in art, as in morals, only one correct solution to any specific problem, but many incorrect solutions. The dictum, "It is possible to fail in many ways . . . , while to succeed is possible only in one way . . . ," is as applicable to art as to moral conduct. This solitary solution in art is also, as in morality, an "intermediate" between excess and defect. The multiple possibilities of artistic imperfection are always analyzable as degrees of excess or defect with respect to a mean which mediates between them. I shall examine in some detail in the next section three notable types of artistic excess and defect, and the manner in which artistic perfection mediates in each case between these types of artistic imperfection.

(b) Artistic perfection, like moral goodness, is not a function of mere arithmetical proportion; it is not determinable, either by the creative artist or the critic, in a mechanical fashion by the mere application of universal rules. It is always the unique solution of a unique problem.

Aristotle describes this aspect of the moral mean by contrasting the "intermediate in the object," which is "one and the same for all men," with the "intermediate relative to us," which is "not one, not the same for all." The former is determinable by the mere application of a rule and without reference to the concrete situations, whereas the latter is essentially a function of these concrete situations. The "right" amount of food for a specific athlete can be determined only in terms of *his* specific needs: "rightness" is relative to each individual moral agent and cannot be deduced *a priori* from abstract rules or principles.

This analysis is analogically applicable to artistic perfection. The locus of moral value is human thought, character, and conduct, whereas the locus of artistic quality is the work of art. But just as, in morals, it is the uniqueness of the moral agent and of his situation which, in each case, determines the mean of virtue, so, in art, it is the specific work of art in all its uniqueness which determines the mean of artistic perfection. In both realms the unique situation is the crucial frame of reference. And just as a virtuous action is never precisely the same on two occasions (since the agents and the circumstances in which they find themselves are never identical, however great their similarity), so artistic perfection, despite similarities between its several manifestations, is always a function of the specific work of art, that is, of the artist's specific intent and of his specific primary and secondary media. What is artistically "right" in one work of art is never identical with artistic "rightness" in any other work of art.

This account of the mean does *not* commit us to a complete relativism of either moral or artistic value. Aristotle is careful to point out that there is actually *one and only one* completely virtuous course of action for any specific individual in any concrete situation, and this course of action *is* objectively valid and morally compelling. The same is true of art. The artistic perfection of any specific work of art is objectively valid in its specific frame of reference, and, as such, artistically compelling. Its "rightness" is not indeterminate. It is a function of an objective situation; each work of art has its own objective norm or τέλος. This conception of objective rightness in a unique situation is perfectly intelligible and defensible. What is relative to a unique frame of reference need not, on that account, be "merely" relative. It can be *absolutely* valid *in that specific context*. If *Q* is valid for S^1 and *R* for S^2, *Q* and *R* are *not* absolutely valid *without qualification*; but *Q is* none the less absolutely valid *for* S^1, and *R for* S^2. This is precisely what Aristotle asserts regarding the mean of virtue. A given act (*Q*), he says, is *absolutely* right for a specific individual (S^1) in specific circumstances, while another act (*R*) is equally right for another individual (S^2) under similar circumstances (or for the same individual under other circumstances), though neither act is unqualifiedly right for all moral agents under all possible circumstances. Similarly, a specific artistic form is absolutely right for a specific work of art and wrong for all other works of art.[7]

(c) Aristotle describes the mean of virtue as itself an "extreme." Here he is calling attention to the fact (i) that since the mean is an absolute norm, i.e., the one and only virtuous course of action in any concrete situation, it is impossible to be too virtuous—there is no excess of the mean; and (ii) that it is impossible to deviate from the mean and still be truly virtuous—there is no defect of the mean. The

[7] Unless we assume the possibility of two identical works of art with an identical artistic intent. In this case, however, we should actually have not two works of art but only one: whatever may be claimed for the metaphysical possibility of exact duplication, each work of art must, for artistic response, be regarded as possessing a *de facto* uniqueness.

vices differ radically from virtue in this respect. For (i) the vices have no absolute norm of their own—there is no ideal of vice. Vice is definable and determinable solely by reference to the norm of virtue. And (ii) there are an indefinite number of possible deviations from virtue, all of which, *qua* deviations (whether by excess or defect of some component element) are vicious. Virtue is thus autonomous as vice is not, and it is single in any specific situation whereas the vices are, in essence, multiple in character.

This does not mean that virtue cannot be more or less indefinitely approximated. On the contrary, few actions, if any, are perfectly virtuous; it is very difficult to get angry "at the right person, to the right extent, at the right time, with the right motive, and in the right way." Men can be, and are in actual practice, more or less virtuous in the sense of approximating more or less closely to the norm of perfect or genuine virtue. All that Aristotle is insisting is that true virtue, *as an ideal or norm*, is single and autonomous, and that this perfect virtue itself permits of no equally virtuous alternatives.

The mean of artistic perfection is describable in strictly analogous terms. Since, in any specific work of art, the formal organization of the medium which constitutes its perfection is, for that work of art, an absolute norm, i.e., the one and only absolutely right solution of the artist's unique problem, it is (i) impossible to come too close to this norm—there is no excess of the artistic mean; and it is (ii) impossible for the work of art in question to deviate from this norm and still be truly perfect—there is no defect of the artistic mean. Artistic imperfection, in contrast, (i) has no norm of its own—there is no such thing as ideal imperfection: imperfection in art is definable and determinable solely by reference to the norm of ideal perfection. And (ii) there are an indefinite number of possible deviations from artistic perfection, all of which, *qua* deviations (whether by excess or defect of some component element) are all equally imperfections. Artistic perfection is thus autonomous as imperfection is not, and it is single in every specific work of art whereas the possibilities of imperfection in any work of art are indefinitely numerous.

Yet a work of art can more or less closely approximate to its own ideal norm. Few works, if any, are absolutely perfect. It is theoretically possible for a work of art to express with complete success what the artist intended to express. But when we say that a work of art is "perfect" (as we sometimes do) this may well indicate merely *our* inability to imagine any alteration which would increase its artistic value. The artist himself may, in such a case, be able to improve his own work in a way which the most competent critic could not possibly anticipate. Compare, for example, Rembrandt's earlier and later versions of his *Crucifixion* (Figs. 215, 216). And even if the artist himself cannot improve on his own work, and actually judges it to be perfect, this still would not make it absolutely certain that the work of art in question was in fact perfect. When we say that a work of art is "perfect," then, we usually mean (i) that it is deeply satisfying, and (ii) that no *defect* is discernible by the critic (or even by the artist himself); we do not mean, or should not mean, that no improvement is possible. Perfection, if possible at all, may indeed be more possible in art than in morality, and man as an artist may be able to give himself and others complete satisfaction more often than man as a moral agent. None the less, the norm of artistic perfection must be defined as an ideal norm to which actual works of art can merely approximate more or less closely, just as the mean of moral virtue is defined by Aristotle as an ideal seldom, if ever, perfectly attained. What must be emphasized is that, *as an ideal*, it is unitary for each work of art and permits of no equally perfect alternatives.

(d) When Aristotle remarks upon the difficulty of hitting the mean he has in mind the fact that virtue is not only an intermediate between extremes of excess and defect (which are defined with reference to it as the ideal norm) but that—and this is the point to notice here—these extremes are conflicting tendencies, or, more accurately, modes of conduct which lure the moral agent from the path of moral rectitude. Courage, for example, is not only a mean between cowardice and foolhardiness; these extremes, which may be defined as excess and deficiency of caution, or as deficiency and excess of recklessness, are tendencies to which the moral agent is tempted to yield and to which he must refuse to yield if he is to achieve the mean of genuine courage. The mean of virtue is therefore always describable as the resolution of a dynamic tension. This is, I believe, a correct account of the psychology of moral conduct. The moral agent does find himself continually drawn towards one or other extreme, each of which, if embraced, would constitute vicious rather than virtuous conduct. The difficulty with which he is here confronted is, as Aristotle points out, partly cognitive and partly volitional. It is hard to *know* what course of action to pursue, and even when moral insight points the way, it is hard to make one's actions *conform* to one's best insight. The doctrine of the mean is thus a recognition of the function of tension and conflict in the moral life. Aristotle does elsewhere insist that the *perfectly* virtuous man will not be tempted by vice but will be able without effort to envisage and pursue the path of virtue, manifesting no doubts or hesitations. But this is a humanly unattainable ideal. Finite creatures that we are, we cannot expect to escape from the necessity of moral conflict; we can never hope to approximate to the mean without making a cognitive and volitional *effort* to avoid the non-virtuous extremes.

This situation is perfectly paralleled in the realm of art. The extremes of artistic imperfection are not in themselves forces with a dynamic power of their own; they are merely states of imperfection. But they possess for the creative artist a perverse fascination, tempting him to favor now one and now the other to the detriment of his art. If he is to be successful in his creative labors, he must exert every effort to *recognize* them as states of imperfection, and to *resist* their psychological appeal: he must use all the artistic acumen and will-power at his disposal to achieve a clear apprehension of his artistic goal and to translate his insight into the sensuous pattern which it dictates. The more competent he is as an artist, the less will he be tempted by the non-artistic extremes to which lesser artists so frequently succumb. But even the greatest artist, since he is still a finite and fallible mortal, cannot hope to transcend the necessity for such conscious effort.

This conflict of extremes, meanwhile, largely determines the vitality of the actualized mean, for the latter is now seen to be a *dynamic* resolution of a *dynamic* situation. As Aristotle puts it, it is because the mean is hard to hit that "goodness is both rare and laudable and noble." Conduct which does not represent a victory over vice lacks human vitality, even though effortless achievement be the ultimate objective even for mortals. Similarly, a work of art which does not represent a victory in the face of genuine artistic obstacles and temptations fails to manifest that artistic vitality which we prize.

And this, in turn, exhibits still another aspect of the mean. Objectively considered, its essential nature and value is a function of those very factors, states, or tendencies which, in and of themselves, constitute moral vice or artistic imperfection. Thus, the virtue of courage and the vice of foolhardiness have in common a fearlessness in the presence of danger, and courage and cowardice are alike in the recognition of danger and the sense of caution. Courage combines fearlessness and caution, transforming each into an organic ingredient of the *new quality* which is characterized, as Plato would put it, by a knowledge of what is and what is not to be feared. Virtue is not merely a negative repudiation of the opposing vices. It is rather the assimilation of what in each vice is vicious simply because it appears in isolation or excess. Without those very qualities which distinguish the opposing vices from one another and endow them with their positive character and reality, the mean of virtue could not be what it is. Its value is in large measure a function of the factors which it combines and, in combining, transforms into aspects of a new organic whole: the vitality of virtue is conditioned by *those very factors* whose reconciliation it is so hard to achieve and preserve.

Similarly, in art, the actualized mean of artistic perfection will manifest artistic vitality only in proportion as it embodies those factors, states, or tendencies which, if yielded to without restraint, issue in artistic imperfection, but which, in happy fusion, make a positive and essential contribution to artistic perfection. I shall explore certain aspects of this dynamic fusion in the next section.

Aristotle's final contribution is his recognition that the mean of virtue can be discovered not by mere deductive reasoning but only by practical wisdom and moral perception. This doctrine is the analogue in ethics to the view I have already urged, that artistic quality is discoverable only by artistic wisdom and insight. Only the good man, says Aristotle, can perceive the moral mean, and only that man is good whose innate capacity for virtue has been suitably cultivated and disciplined. The conditions of sound artistic judgment are perfectly analogous. Artistic quality will reveal itself only to the man who has cultivated whatever native artistic capacity he may have, by subjecting it to the requisite historical and systematic discipline. Both types of insight are specialized (it is the trainer, i.e., the athletic expert, who prescribes the athlete's diet), and each is adapted to its respective object—moral virtue in the one case, artistic perfection in the other. These qualities must never be identified; nor, whatever their similarities, must moral wisdom ever be confused with artistic insight or with other types of specialized awareness. But just as the mean of virtue is discoverable not by *a priori* reasoning but only by moral wisdom, so too can the ideal of artistic perfection be apprehended only by artistic wisdom and intuition. Rational analysis can do no more in either realm than explore structural relationships and formulate basic principles of moral and artistic achievement. It can neither discover virtue and artistic quality in specific contexts, nor reveal the moral or artistic perfection manifested in concrete instances.

One final remark must be added. The fact that the mean, whether in morals or in art, is always determined by the unique moral or artistic situation, and that it is itself, accordingly, always unique in this sense, does not preclude the possibility of comparing the conduct of different individuals with reference to their respective degrees of approximation to their respective moral objectives, or the possibility of comparing different works of art in terms of their respective degrees of artistic perfection. Since works of art fail of perfection in varying degrees, it is quite possible for a discriminating critic to compare two works of art with reference to their measure of perfection, i.e., to the closeness with which *each* approximates to *its* ideal of artistic expressiveness, even though the specific norm of perfection must of necessity be determined in each case with specific reference to the specific medium, expressive intent, and other essential aspects of each work of art under review. In other words, the relative degree of perfection which any given work of art manifests in comparison with other works of art is an objective fact for artistic perception. It is therefore one which the discerning critic can establish with considerable precision, and regarding which he can achieve notable agreement with his fellow critics.

3. Artistic perfection as the resolution of three polar tensions

The concept of artistic perfection as an Aristotelian mean can now be elaborated in terms of three specific polarities or tensions which must be resolved if a work of art is to possess artistic merit. These are (a) the polarity of simplicity *versus* complexity, whose resolution is the mean of organic unity; (b) the polarity of order *versus* novelty, whose mean is expressive originality; and (c) the polarity of the denial *versus* the idolatry of the medium, whose resolution is the expressive exploitation of the medium. These polarities and means are all equally applicable to works of art in any medium, but the third is explicable, by its very nature, only with reference to the several artistic media. These three means, in turn, are obviously aspects, or factors, of the single organic mean of artistic perfection as such.

(a) *Simplicity, complexity, and organic unity.* I have already discussed artistic unity as an aspect of artistic form.[8] But its essential nature can be described with greater precision if it is regarded as an aspect of the dynamic mean of artistic perfection.

The vital unity of a work of art is an intermediate between the extremes of tiresome simplicity and bewildering and confusing complexity. A work of art may be too complex to be apprehensible as a unified whole, or it may be too simple to engage and hold our interest. It approaches perfection only in proportion as it manifests both the simplicity (or unity) and the complexity (or richness) of genuine organic unity.

This ideal unity is not a mere "arithmetical" mean or mechanical compromise between the too complex and the too simple. It cannot be achieved by the creative artist through mere obedience to formulae or rules, for it is the product of the creative imagination. A certain kind of unity can, no doubt, be attained by mere technical proficiency and obedience to canons. But such unity is sure to lack artistic vitality and to differ qualitatively from that type of artistic unity which the sensitive artist seeks to create and which the sensitive critic prizes. Unity of this type is the product of "original genius." Perfect artistic unity is always a unique function of the specific work of art in all its uniqueness. Each work of art has its own ideal unity to which the unity which it actually possesses more or less closely approximates. Hence the question as to how successful, with respect to artistic unity, any particular work of art is, is a question which can be answered only in terms of the work of art itself, that is, in terms of what *this* work of art seems to permit and demand. Only the creative artist can decide (if anyone can) what *more* might have been done in the interest of greater unity: the critic can merely approve or censure what the artist has already accomplished.[9] Such appraisal, though it inevitably reflects the critic's familiarity with other works of art, and is to this extent necessarily a comparative judgment, is always primarily and essentially an appraisal of specific

[8] Cf., above, Chap. XI.

[9] When the critic judges a work of art to be deficient in this or that respect, this judgment in no way obligates him to determine how this deficiency might be remedied. It is his primary task to appraise what others have created, not to improve on their creation. This is the task of the creative artist, and if he is unable or unwilling to undertake it, no one else can hope to make good his failure.

accomplishment with reference to the problems set by the specific work of art.

Artistic unity, like other aspects of the mean of artistic perfection, is itself an extreme. No work of art can possess too great artistic unity, and every deficiency in artistic unity, however great or small, is an artistic imperfection. Each work of art has only one ideal unity, but the possible deviations from this mean, i.e., the possible degrees and varieties of lack of unity, are indefinitely numerous.

Artistic unity is vital in proportion as the work of art is an artistic fusion or synthesis of simplicity and complexity. It must possess a *kind* of simplicity and a *kind* of complexity of its own. The "simplicity" at which the artist aims and which the critic prizes is not, as Plato supposed,[10] mere homogeneity of the primary medium or mere paucity of formal relationships, but rather an organization of parts, however numerous and diverse or few and homogeneous, such that every part stands in evident relation to the whole and clearly contributes to the total effect. Artistic "complexity," in turn, is not mere multiplicity or diversity of parts and relations, but rather artistic inexhaustibleness. We judge that art to be artistically "rich" in which we can forever discover new aspects and new relationships. What we demand of art is the "simplicity" of artistic *unity of effect* and the "complexity" of artistic *subtlety* and *richness.*

The vitality of genuine artistic or organic unity is thus in large measure the product of a happy resolution of the dynamic tension between the extremes of empty simplicity and unorganized complexity. A distinguished work of art combines the simplicity of artistically eloquent organization with the complexity of artistic richness. It might be described as the successful solution, in the realm of artistic form, of the problem of the one and the many; it is a resolution of the conflicts between mere empty unity and meaningless variety, between insipid balance and painful irregularity, between dull homogeneity and disorganized heterogeneity. The artist is continually tempted, in his creative labors, to sacrifice the one for the other—to achieve unity *at the expense* of variety, contrast *at the expense* of unity. Such solutions are inevitably lacking in artistic vitality; what is achieved is not vital unity but dead and meaningless simplicity, not vital richness but mere variety and opposition devoid of artistic significance. What we admire in the masters is their ability

[10] Cf. *Republic*, 399.

to create works in which so many artistic units and relations are fused into so organic an artistic whole, in which so many variations are introduced not for their own sake but as contributory factors to the final unity of artistic effect. The greater the tension, the greater the vitality of the work; the greater the pull in the opposing directions of sheer simplicity and sheer complexity, the greater the unity *and* richness, i.e., the artistic vitality, of the final result.

The difficulty of achieving such artistic unity is obvious. Complete attainment of perfect artistic unity is theoretically possible. But since man is finite, the likelihood of such an achievement is negligible; and in any case, neither the artist himself nor his critics can ever be sure that perfect unity has actually been achieved. In appraising the unity of a work of art the critic must rely on artistic "perception," not abstract reasoning; he cannot invoke scientific principles or appeal to the authority of rules or formulae. Relying on this perception, he must first appraise the unity of each specific work of art in terms of its own specific frame of reference. But he can also compare different works of art, in the same or in different media, in terms of the *degree* of unity which each possesses in relation to the others.

It would be possible to describe and illustrate in great detail the manifestations of artistic unity in the several major and minor arts, in the several manners of treatment, and in the many different types of compositional pattern. The reader may be referred to almost any critical discussion of artistic form for a more particularized application of the basic principle of artistic unity which I have tried to formulate.[11]

(b) *Order, novelty, and expressive originality.* Vital artistic quality is also a mean between the extremes of mere order or regularity, on the one hand, sheer novelty for its own sake, on the other.

By "order" is meant obedience to rule, convention, and tradition. Such order is a necessary factor in all art. For every art has its own technique by which alone its medium can be effectively exploited. The artist must be a craftsman before he can be an artist; mastery of his medium is a *sine qua non* of effective artistic creation. Every art, moreover, has its own conventions which have been developed by successive generations of artists and which have been recognized and sometimes codified by theorists. These conventions are in part a

[11] Cf., for example, D. H. Parker, *The Analysis of Art* (New Haven: Yale University Press, 1926), Chap. II, "The Problem of Aesthetic Form."

pervasive cultural heritage, in part the hall-marks of a more limited artistic school or movement, and in part the more or less established professional habits of the individual artist. No art is innocent of such conventions. They play as essential a rôle in art as they do in science and morals, politics and religion. The youthful artist is inevitably subject to their moulding influence; his artistic education consists in large measure in acquiring a familiarity with them and an ability to use them with skill. Even the most pronounced innovation or violent revolt is negatively conditioned by them. Originality in art can have no meaning save by reference to an artistic tradition which must be defined in terms of past conventions and various types of order.

But mere obedience to convention can never produce artistic quality. The product of such obedience is merely a manifestation of uninspired orthodoxy and the mark of mere proficiency in artistic technique. A composition in any medium which (*per impossibile*) was wholly unconventional would be quite unintelligible; but a composition wholly devoid of novelty is utterly dead, i.e., devoid of artistic vitality. Significant artistic originality, however, must not be identified with sheer novelty. Novelty is a genus of which only certain specific instances possess artistic significance.

Novelty *per se* is nothing but the appearance in time of radical difference. It is mere uniqueness. In one sense every object and event is unique. No leaf, no pebble on the beach, is in *all* respects identical with any other leaf or pebble. To be a particular is to be in some sense different and distinguishable from all other particulars. We normally use the term "novelty," however, to signify (i) a more *pronounced* difference, and (ii) an *unpredictable* difference. We describe those objects or events as novel which differ in some fundamental way from prior objects or events, and whose appearance we feel we could not have predicted. *Significant* originality, in turn, whether in art or in other realms, differs in kind from sheer novelty, however pronounced, unexpected, or unpredictable;[12] significance or value

[12] "When novelty is altogether separated from the conception of worth and utility, it makes but a slight impression upon a truly correct taste. Every discovery in nature, in the arts, and in the sciences, has a real value, and gives a rational pleasure to a good taste. But things that have nothing to recommend them but novelty, are fit only to entertain children, or those who are distressed from a vacuity of thought. This quality of objects may therefore be compared to the cypher in arithmetic, which adds greatly to the value of significant figures; but, when put by itself, signifies nothing at all." *The*

can never be defined merely in terms of newness or difference. But this is not the place to undertake an analysis of the concept of significance.[13] It must suffice to describe it here as always pertaining to a pattern of relationships by virtue of which the object or process in question points beyond itself and leads the mind to new insights and deeper apprehensions. All genuine originality in art is significant in this sense, but not all innovation is significant. The new may be a blind alley leading us nowhere, blocking the imagination and frustrating every attempt at revealing interpretation.

In art, then, significant originality is an Aristotelian mean between sheer order or convention and sheer novelty or emergent difference. Once again, it is not merely an "arithmetical" mean between these extremes. Yet it is indubitably a function of both factors. The vitality of art depends, at least in part, upon how much order is combined with how much novelty. The greater the originality of the artist *within* the framework of convention, and the more highly articulated and precise the order through which his originality has expressed itself, the more vital and dynamic (other conditions being satisfied) is the resultant composition. The great artists in each of the major media are great partly because they have been able so successfully to combine tradition and inventiveness, orthodoxy and heterodoxy, order and novelty. They have drawn richly on the past without being subjugated by it. They have used what their predecessors have discovered and perfected without themselves becoming mere imitators. The fruitfulness of their original contributions to art, in turn, is attested by the profound influence which they have had upon subsequent generations of artists. The work of each of the great masters has been, to a greater or less extent (depending upon various historical circumstances), both a culmination and a new beginning—a consummation of one tradition and the initiation of another. Every great artist is in some ways heterodox with respect to the past, orthodox with respect to the future. Men of lesser talent, in contrast, have always tended towards one extreme or the other—towards uninspired academic correctness or clever superficial novelty, towards mere traditional observance of established principles or mere ingenious novelty devoid of artistic significance. True artistic originality is extraordinarily

Works of Thomas Reid, ed. Sir William Hamilton (Edinburgh: Maclachlan and Stewart, 1863), Vol. I, p. 494.

[13] Cf., below, Chap. XXIV.

difficult and rare; or perhaps it would be more accurate to say that it is relatively easy for the rare man of genius, and impossible for all devoid of true creative ability. Anyone with normal intelligence and industry can achieve some measure of correctness, and the greater our ignorance or ineptitude, the more novel will be our attempts at composition in any artistic medium. Significant artistic originality is the unique product of disciplined genius.

Such originality is likely to manifest itself in strange and unpredictable ways. Not only are the works of some artists infinitely more original than those of other artists, but the works of the same artist may differ notably in this respect. It is only the greater artists who are able to avoid a stereotyped imitation of their own earlier work; innumerable instances come to mind of artists who have eventually become imitators of themselves, that is, whose spring of originality has ultimately run dry.[14] One of the surest tests of great artistic genius is the evidence of not only continued but ever intensified originality. Witness the last compositions of Beethoven and Bach, Titian and Cézanne, Michelangelo and Shakespeare. Genuine originality, finally, can no more be discovered by abstract reasoning or subjective whim than it can be produced by mere orthodox conformity or undisciplined ebullience. It too reveals itself only to cultivated artistic perception.

(c) *Denial of the medium, over-insistence on the medium, and expressive exploitation of the medium.* A third inter-medial polarity conditioning artistic quality relates to the use of the medium, both primary and secondary. I have already discussed the nature of the primary and secondary media in the six major arts; it remains to consider how, in general, artistic quality is a function of these media and of their use. Let us examine first the rôle of the primary medium.

Artistic quality is, in part, the product of the effective exploitation of the primary medium. By its "effective exploitation" is meant the full recognition of both its artistic potentialities and limitations. Artistic quality is always a manifestation of the artist's sensitivity to

[14] Collectors and other patrons of the pictorial arts often exert an unfortunate influence upon contemporary artists in this respect. An artist comes to be known as the author of works in a given style, and the collector frequently insists on having works typical of this style in his collection. Similarly, the art-conscious public tends to demand of the artist more compositions in the style to which it has become accustomed. The artist must often, as a result, pay a high price for continued originality, and the lesser artist often succumbs to the demand for repetition with only minor variations.

and love for his medium, and the potentialities of the medium are revealed in all compositions of genuine artistic merit. What I have referred to as the aesthetic character of the primary medium as such is intensified by skillful formal organization. The artist makes clear to us his appreciation of this immediate aesthetic quality and helps us to realize it as we never did before. Thus, the successful composer exploits the aesthetic character of timbre, tonality, and dynamic variation, and the musical significance of rests. In good architecture, the aesthetic character of evident tensile strength, weight, color, and surface-texture of the materials employed, and of the geometrical proportions of space and light, are all artistically realized. The competent dancer is acutely aware of his body as a potentially expressive vehicle, and uses it in such a way as to reveal its structure, form, strength, and pliability in motion and at rest. The skillful painter uses his paint in a manner appropriate to paint and his pencil, pen, or etching tool in a manner appropriate to the instrument and the surface to which it is applied. Good sculpture exhibits the lithic character of stone, the distinctive qualities of wood, and the like. And the writer whose compositions possess artistic quality betrays in every line his "sense of language," that is, his sensitivity to the sound of the spoken word and the musical rhythm of a phrase, the conceptual meaning of words, both single and in combination, and their emotional and imagistic associations. This "sense of the medium," this ability artistically to exploit to the full its artistic potentialities, is one of the hall-marks of creative artistic ability in every art.

Here too the mean lies between extremes—the extremes of under-exploitation (or "denial") of the medium and of over-emphasis upon (or "idolatry" of) the medium. The first of these extremes expresses itself in the failure to exhaust the relevant potentialities of the medium in question. The medium is, as it were, unjustifiably allowed to lie partly fallow; it remains less artistically productive than would be possible with adequate cultivation. Music which emphasizes formal pattern but ignores timbre and dynamic variation, or which emphasizes tonal "color" at the expense of more formal tonal relationships; architecture whose surface conceals or denies underlying engineering structure of potential expressive significance, or which emphasizes this structure at the expense of other pertinent architectural values; a dance whose sole merit is the proficient execution of a single type of step with minor variations; stone sculpture which visually denies its medium and is made to look as though it were composed of some other physical material; painting which fails to recognize the immediate aesthetic appeal of line, color, and shape, and does not exploit their potential artistic expressiveness; literature which ignores either the expressiveness of sound or the importance of conceptual and imagistic meanings:—these are all instances of failure to exploit the expressive potentialities of the primary medium. In a word, the primary medium remains unexploited in proportion as the end in view in any specific composition could be more effectively achieved through a richer and more effective use of this or that aspect of the medium in question.

Such under-exploitation of the medium is normally the result of sheer incompetence. The feeble artist is unable adequately to appreciate the immediate aesthetic appeal of his primary medium, and he is therefore unable to turn this aesthetic quality to account in his composition or to realize its expressive potentialities. But such failure must be sharply distinguished from the deliberate neglect of certain aspects of a given medium in favor of other aspects. In the one case, the artist fails through ignorance to accomplish what he himself would like to accomplish. In the other, he decides, wisely or unwisely but none the less intentionally, to make use of only this or that aspect of the medium in this or that specific way. Such selection is *in itself* clearly not subject to criticism, for *some* selection is *always* necessary in any specific composition. No artist can possibly exploit all the potentialities of his medium in any one work, and even the richest work of art is bound to exploit certain aspects of the medium at the expense of others. Here again, final appraisal of the measure of success or failure must rest with artistic perception. If we, as competent critics, feel that the medium has been wisely chosen and used to achieve the desired effect, we are judging the work to possess artistic perfection in this respect; if not, we judge it to be more or less deficient in artistic quality.

In proportion, meanwhile, as an artist restricts himself to the exploitation of only certain aspects of his medium, he is likely to "force" those aspects, i.e., to try to compel the medium to do more than it is capable of doing. For example, a writer who ignores the meanings of words tends to emphasize their auditory "values," and in extreme cases he may go so far as to rely on the "music" of the spoken word almost as exclusively as the composer of "pure" music relies on abstract musical patterns. Not content to recognize and exploit the sound of words and the immediate aesthetic appeal of vocal timbre, accent, and auditory rhythm as *contributory* factors, he takes the part for the whole and writes poetry as though he were writing "pure" music. Abstractions in sculpture and painting are generally characterized by a similar forcing of the primary media. The representational potentialities of these media are ignored and the attempt is made to create abstract two-dimensional or three-dimensional patterns which are intended to be as immediately expressive as are the equally abstract tonal patterns of music. Critics may differ as to whether this does constitute a forcing of the medium beyond its proper limits; but in any case a part is asked to do the work of the whole. Similarly, program music is in continual danger of straining the medium of pure sound in the effort to imitate natural sounds. Architecture which aims at representation is invariably grotesque[15] (Figs. 16-19). The free dance may defeat its own ends either by too exclusive reliance on non-pantomimic, silent motion, or, alternatively, by too great reliance either on musical accompaniment or on pantomime. Whether or not the medium *has* been forced in any specific composition in these media cannot be determined by an appeal to rules but only by immediate artistic perception. For everything depends upon the artistic effect of the specific composition upon the sensitive critic. If the effect is convincing, no "forcing" can be said to have taken place, but if the work appears to be a *tour de force* (Fig. 109), expressiveness must be said to have been sacrificed to virtuosity.

This "forcing" of the medium is, of course, a type of over-exploitation of the medium, or rather of one aspect of it at the expense of other aspects. It is a failure to recognize the expressive *limitations* of the medium in question. But the more usual form which such over-exploitation takes is simply an emphasis on the medium and its technical manipulation *for its own sake*. This extreme can accurately be described as a type of idolatry. I have said that the difference between a religious icon and an idol is that an icon, correctly defined, is an image which is revered as a symbol, representation, or expression of deity, whereas an idol is an image identified with deity. An icon leads us beyond itself and is essentially a *means* to a higher end, whereas an idol is thought of as *itself* possessing intrinsic religious value and power. Idolatry, however, is obviously not limited to

[15] Cf., also, architecture which, as frequently happens in the Gothic, denies the physical character of its medium (Fig. 77). Flamboyant Gothic corrects this defect.

religion. The veneration for logic or scientific method, for political organization, or for social conventions and institutions, *for their own sake* (as contrasted with a proper esteem for them as invaluable *means* to ends other than themselves) is equally idolatrous. Art too permits of idolatry of various types, and one of the most common today is the artistically unjustifiable emphasis on the primary media for their own sake. The lithic character of stone may be so stressed that the chief, and almost the only, impression we get of the work is this lithic quality. Music may be so exclusively colorful or structurally ingenious that it becomes mere sound without significance. It is the virtuoso in every art who is most likely to succumb to the allurements of this extreme. Technical proficiency simultaneously conditions and threatens genuine artistry. Meaningless musical brilliance, too facile execution of intricate steps or acrobatic leaps in the dance, sheer engineering skill and inexpressive architectural ingenuity, undue preoccupation with the polished surface of stone or metal, or with brush-stroke or etching line, artistically nugatory skill in illusionistic painting or sculpture, and love for verbal harshness or sweetness, conceptual clarity or imagistic vividness, *for their own sake*—all are manifestations of this extreme, i.e., of idolatry of the primary medium as such.

Here, as in the polarities already discussed, the mean is a happy fusion of tendencies which become extremes, deficient in artistic quality, only from over-emphasis. Ideally, the medium should be exploited to the full, yet not for its own sake or in the spirit of mere virtuosity but always as a means to the end of significant artistic expression. This mean can also be determined only by reference to the specific work of art. Our first question in the presence of any work of art must be: Might the artist have achieved what he appears to have intended to achieve more effectively through a richer exploitation of his medium, or, alternatively, through a less short-sighted preoccupation with his medium for its own sake? If our answer is affirmative, we must judge the work to be correspondingly deficient in artistic quality. If, on the other hand, there is reason to believe that a work of art which seems to us to incline towards either extreme does actually express exactly what the artist *meant* it to express, i.e., does emphasize, on the one hand, or neglect, on the other, just what he meant to emphasize or neglect for his expressive purpose—if we feel that, *given his objective*, the artist has exploited his medium in exactly the right way, we must then judge it to be (at least in this respect) "perfect" or ideally rich in artistic quality. Should it seem to us, on the contrary, to lack *all* expressed content and to be merely an exhibition of technique or craftsmanship, it must be judged to fall outside the category of art altogether. This is not to say that objects of this type necessarily lack all aesthetic quality or formal beauty (as opposed to artistic quality). I would suggest that most (if not all) so-called "machine art" (Fig. 93) falls into this category. A utilitarian, machine-made product may delight us with its technical perfection, surface, and shape. Such delight is not idolatry (as I have used the term) if no attempt is made to regard it as *art*. Here the honest and competent craftsman who takes pride in his work and who indulges in no artistic pretensions gives us our cue. It is only when cooking utensils and typewriters, bathroom fixtures and billiard balls, are put on exhibition and heralded as "art" that the charge of idolatry in art is justified. The mere craftsman merits our praise as a technician but our neglect as an artist.

So far I have been considering artistically effective and ineffective exploitations of the primary medium. The secondary medium, it will be remembered, is to be distinguished from the primary medium by the fact that it can never be used by the artist directly, but can only be introduced indirectly through suitable organization of a primary medium.

This means that effective exploitation of the secondary medium involves a wise decision as to what aspects and ingredients of the available secondary medium permit of effective use in the chosen primary medium. The latter, accordingly, tends to exercise a kind of negative censorship; certain kinds of secondary media do, and other kinds do not, lend themselves to effective use in this or that primary medium.[16] Certain kinds of subject-matter, for example, can be more effectively represented in painting than in sculpture; music lends itself to representation but poorly, architecture not at all.

Effective exploitation of the secondary medium can be described more positively in terms of the relation of the secondary medium itself to the artist's expressive intent. The creative artist approximates to the mean in proportion as he is wise in selecting and using his secondary medium as a vehicle for artistic expression. The subject-matter of a sculptural composition or painting, for example, is

[16] Cf., above, pp. 40*ff*.

wisely chosen if it provides the artist with the best possible opportunity for expressing the artistic content which he desires to express. *Within* the limits set by the primary medium the artist has a wide choice of subject-matter. He may choose carelessly and then attempt to express, in terms of what he has chosen, a content not effectively expressible in this way. Or, alternatively, he may become fascinated by his secondary medium in all its unillumined particularity, and content himself with as literal and uninterpretative a rendition of it as is technically possible (Figs. 101, 103, 104, 105, 107). In the latter case, as in the former, the potential significance of the secondary medium fails to achieve artistic expression. The mean of artistic excellence, in contrast, involves choosing the *right* subject-matter and employing it in the *right* way according to criteria dictated by the expressive intentions of the artist.

4. Application of these polarities to the six major arts

Each of these three polarities, whose respective means are aspects of the generic mean of artistic perfection, naturally manifest themselves in different ways in the several major arts, since each art has its own distinctive primary medium, its characteristic secondary medium, and its own intra-medial generic forms. That is, each set of extremes and each resultant mean must be interpreted, in the presence of any specific work of art, with reference to the art to which it belongs.

(a) *Music* without words and the pure *dance* are, I have said, the simplest of the arts. Unlike architecture, they need not adapt themselves to specific utilitarian needs; unlike sculpture and painting, they are not representational; unlike literature, their primary media are not in essence symbolic. Both achieve expressiveness directly through the non-representational and non-symbolic ordering of their primary media, and both have as their distinctive subject-matter man's emotive-conative states. This comparative simplicity is in a sense a limitation. The musician and the dancer cannot interpret many aspects of reality and human experience which other artists are able to interpret. But within the limits prescribed by their primary media, both music and the dance can express certain universals with unrivalled eloquence. They can do so, however, only if they exploit their respective primary media and their common subject-matter with imaginative power. This exploitation involves unusual sensitivity to all the sensuous attributes of sound and bodily movement, unusual discernment of familiar associations, and genuine understanding of man's emotional and impulsive nature.

Both music without words and the pure dance can err in the direction of tiresome and empty simplicity, on the one hand, confusing and unintegrated complexity, on the other. The desirable mean in both arts is obviously an organic richness which even the most sensitive observer cannot exhaust. Both arts, again, must be on their guard against mere conventionality, tradition, and mechanical order, on the one hand, mere unintelligible novelty, on the other. The great artist in these media is original *within* the framework of established convention. Not that this framework is not itself continually subjected to modification: witness the evolution of musical systems and forms and the healthy revolts in the dance against choreographic traditions. But some intelligible and familiar order is requisite to communication, as imaginative originality is requisite to artistic interest and vitality. Each of these arts, finally, must exploit its distinctive primary medium to the full if the latter is to be used with maximum artistic effect—music, the infinite variety of sounds in tonal, temporal, and dynamic relation; the dance, all the movements and postures of the human body. For example, a specific charge brought against the formal ballet by the exponents of the modern dance is its failure to exploit innumerable expressive bodily movements, while the protagonists of both the ballet and the modern dance condemn pure acrobatics as mere emphasis on bodily agility for its own sake. More generally, the incompetent dancer is unable to use his body as an effective vehicle for artistic expression; the agile dancer, in whatever school, is in danger of lapsing into mere virtuosity.

In the dance with musical accompaniment, and in music with a verbal text, a new factor is introduced which in each case complicates the respective media and creates new dangers to be avoided and new objectives to be achieved. The dancer must avoid undue subordination to the music, on the one hand, indifference to or defiance of the music, on the other. The composer, similarly, must avoid slavish and mechanical subservience to the text as well as blindness to its expressive potentialities.

Finally, pantomime introduces still another factor into the dance, and this new factor is parelleled in music by the element of representation in program music. The twin dangers and the new potentiality which result from these factors are perhaps more pronounced in the dance than in music, for the dance lends itself to pantomime better than does music to the representation of natural scenes or sounds. Undue emphasis upon these factors is peculiarly painful in both arts, and there are those who would argue that both factors should be avoided at all cost. But the most successful pantomimic dances, and program music at its best, both exhibit the expressive potentialities of these factors, provided they are introduced with imagination and artistic restraint.

(b) Artistic quality in *architecture* differs from that of the other arts chiefly through the introduction of a new factor which *may* appear in specific compositions in the other arts but *must* appear as an essential condition of architectural excellence. This factor is what architects entitle the "program," and what I have referred to as its "social function." I have pointed out that all art possessed of larger significance for man must, by definition, have a social function in a wider cultural sense. The truth of this is emphasized in the doctrine of "art for life's sake" (as opposed to the doctrine of "art for art's sake"). The social function which distinctively characterizes architectural quality is narrower; the term "general social function" has reference to the more limited type of social use (e.g., religious, civic, domestic, etc.) to which a building may be put, and the term "specific social function" to the still more limited, historically conditioned, social activities which it is meant to house (e.g., a seventeenth century Roman Catholic service, the official life of the court of Louis XIV, or the family life of John Smith). I have argued that whereas an artist in any of the other arts *may* have a "general" or "specific" social function in mind (as in the writing of "dance" music or "occasional" music) but *need* not do so, the architect, on the contrary, *must* know in advance at least what general social function the building which he is designing is intended architecturally to satisfy, and he *should* often know, if he is to achieve the highest architectural quality, the more particular use to which the building is to be put.

As regards the latter requirement, we must distinguish those social functions which change relatively little from age to age from those whose temporal or historical rhythm is shorter and more varied. Catholic Christianity, for example, possesses a relatively unchanging creed and form of worship. Hence, a cathedral which is architecturally expressive of this religion in one age is likely to express it in other ages, although even here stylistic changes which reflect changes in cultural and religious outlook must be taken seriously into account. Domestic architecture, in contrast, is (or should be) expressive not only of domestic life in general but also, e.g., of John Smith and his family, with their unique personal tastes, needs, and social outlook. But though this distinction is valid so far as it goes, it would certainly be foolish to insist on drawing a sharp line between the more general and the more specific social functions of architecture. It is far more important to recognize the essential importance of the "program" as such, that is, as defined to include both of these types of social function, and to see precisely how this factor enters into architectural quality.

Here the extremes are, on the one hand, architecturally inexpressive, purely utilitarian (i.e., non-artistic) satisfaction of a social requirement and, on the other hand, architectural form wholly unrelated to actual or possible social use. An architectural edifice designed without reference to any specific or possible use to which it might be put and which (to complete the description of this extreme limit) could be put to no use whatever, whether religious or secular, would be necessarily devoid of architectural quality. A building, on the other hand, which satisfied certain of man's needs in a purely physical way, but which completely failed to express these needs architecturally, would illustrate the opposite extreme. It is impossible to cite specific instances of pure architectural formalism, though the reason for this is fortuitous; no one would ever have the incentive to build or pay for a perfectly useless building. The *Gloriette* in the grounds of Schönbrunn in Vienna (Fig. 76) is perhaps as close an approximation to this extreme as we are likely to find; it is of no possible use save as a piece of architectural decoration in a formal palace garden. Even it, however, serves the very specific function of completing an important vista from the *Belvedere*, and is thus in a real sense part of the landscape setting of the palace. On the other hand, the world is full of buildings which lack all architectural expressiveness, though they are well adapted to man's strictly utilitarian activities: witness the average apartment house or factory, garage or private dwelling, as well as innumerable churches and public buildings.

The mean between these extremes may be entitled "expressive social functionalism." It is "socially functional" in that a building satisfying the requirements of the mean is well adapted to the use for which it has been designed; it is "expressive" in that this use is reflected in the architectural form. For example, a church which possesses artistic quality is not only equipped to house the ceremonial activities of the congregation, but, in addition, "looks like a church": an architecturally successful private dwelling is not only livable but proclaims its domestic function to the sensitive eye.

This aspect of architectural quality raises three problems. The first relates to stylistic convention. A building may look like a church in one period, when certain stylistic conventions have become established, and not look like a church according to other stylistic criteria. The language of architecture changes from age to age and differs according to locality, just as verbal languages change and differ. To deny the possibility of architectural expressiveness on this score would be as foolish as it would be to deny the possibility of verbal communication because no language is universal or eternal. This characteristic of the language of architecture, as of every language which artists use, is one of the factors which make historical criticism essential to all critical endeavor.

The second problem may be formulated thus: Is it possible architecturally to express *all* of man's manifold activities which require some kind of housing? That the best religious architecture does in its own way express the spirit of religious worship, and the best domestic architecture, the nature and dignity of family life, will hardly be denied. But what of industrial, business, and analogous social functions? The function of a factory building is to house and facilitate manufacture, of a garage, to protect a car against the elements. *Can* these functions be given *architectural* expression?

Finally, there is the problem, already mentioned, of how much importance should be assigned by the architect to the expression of more general social function and how much to more specific and temporary social requirements. Granted that a private dwelling should architecturally express both domesticity in general and the more specialized needs of John Smith, where should the emphasis fall?

The polarity of social functionalism in architecture is paralleled by the polarity of engineering functionalism.[17] Here the extremes and the mean are not far to seek. The extremes to be avoided are, on the one hand, the failure to exploit the expressive potentialities of visible engineering structure and building materials and, on the

[17] The two distinctive architectural polarities thus relate, respectively, to the exploitation of the distinctive secondary and primary media of architecture.

other, a non-expressive idolatry of these factors. The Rococo style in southern Germany in the eighteenth century was prone to the first of these extremes; modernistic architecture is prone to the second. The mean, which will manifest itself differently in different styles and different buildings, is of course the expressive exploitation of engineering structure as well as of the color and surface texture of building materials.

(c) The most distinctive characteristic of artistic quality in *sculpture* and *painting* relates to their capacity for representation. If these arts are conceived to be essentially representational, the relevant polarity and mean are easy to define. The mean of expressive representation lies between the extremes of (i) wholly non-representational abstraction and (ii) the most literal reproduction possible in the primary medium in question. The best illustrations of these extremes in painting are wholly abstract designs and entirely unstudied photographs; in sculpture, three-dimensional abstractions and faithful wax models, painted and clothed to achieve verisimilitude.

I have observed that strictly literal reproduction is impossible, since the very process of translation into a medium, whether in sculpture or in painting, necessitates some modification, and since, moreover, some selection of subject-matter, angle of vision, and the like, is unavoidable. This does not mean, however, that either the selection or the act of translation need involve the introduction of artistic quality. The news photographer selects his subject and records its visual appearance at a particular instant without, as a rule, achieving any of the artistic expressiveness possible in the art of photography. His purpose is not to create a work of art but to capture a particular scene in all its unrelieved specificity. As regards the opposite extreme, I have already admitted the possibility of achieving some measure of artistic expressiveness in pure abstractions. Criticism of such abstractions must therefore be based upon the claim (i) that these primary media (unlike music) do not effectively lend themselves to such treatment, and (ii) that a rich medium is left relatively unexploited if no use is made of its representational possibilities.

The distinctive mean of artistic perfection in these representational arts must be defined, then, as a unified, original, and vital exploitation of both primary medium and representational subject-matter for the sake of artistic expressiveness. The subject to be represented must be selected with an eye to its usefulness as a potentially expressive vehicle, and it must be so treated as to transform this potentiality into an artistically vital actuality. This transformation, in turn, can be effected only through skillful use of the primary medium. The most expressive sculpture and painting (quite apart from the larger significance of what is expressed) approximates closely to this ideal. Appraisal of artistic quality in these arts, as elsewhere, involves reference to the presumed intention of the artist and to the particular problem which he has set himself in the particular composition.[18]

(d) If music and the pure dance are the simplest of the major arts, *literature* is certainly the most complex. The secondary medium, as has already been noted, includes most, if not all, of the secondary media of the other arts, and a great deal besides. It includes all possible subjects which permit of effective literary treatment, namely, the whole world of man's inner and outer experience. Our problem is to determine how this subject-matter may be taken into account in a description of the conditions of literary quality. Again, the primary medium of literature is, as we discovered, itself complex, consisting, on the one hand, of sensory symbols, i.e., spoken (and written) words, and, on the other hand, of the meanings which these words possess individually and in syntactical relation. Both of these aspects of the primary medium of literature—the sound of the spoken word and the meanings of the words as symbols—must be kept in mind in any analysis of the conditions of literary quality. The media of literature are accordingly too complex to make possible the formulation of a single literary polarity and mean: as in the case of architecture, at least two polarities and means, relevant to the primary medium, must be invoked.

The first of these concerns the relation of the sound of the spoken word to the meaning symbolically conveyed. Language may be used (as it is in science) with sole reference to the meanings which the words, spoken or written, evoke. This marks one extreme or pole. At the other extreme, the "music" of the spoken word, or (to take account of all possibilities) the visual pattern of the written or printed word, is emphasized without any reference whatever to its symbolic meaning. Both of these extremes lack all true *literary* quality. The goal of science differs from that of literature, and the

[18] Cf., above, pp. 317-21, 407-13.

linguistic means to be approved in each case differ correspondingly. The literary author must take into account a factor which the scientist quite properly ignores, to wit, the immediate expressiveness of sound. The opposite extreme would be most closely approximated in verse which was pleasing to the ear but which meant nothing ideationally because the words used were not real words but mere nonsense syllables. Such verse would have a certain aesthetic quality, and might even possess some slight artistic value *as music*, but it would *not* be literature. It too would lack literary quality in any accepted sense of the term. A finely written or printed page which is grateful to the eye but whose text is wholly incomprehensible would merit an analogous appraisal.

The mean between these extremes must include both factors, duly transformed through organic fusion. Literature is excellent (other conditions being satisfied) in proportion as the expressive potentialities of the spoken word (and of the written or printed word, though this is a minor factor) are exploited in such a way as to reinforce and clarify the meaning which these words express. How these factors of sound and meaning are to be weighted, and how each factor is to be used in relation to the other in any specific composition, must depend upon the artistic intention of the individual writer—an intention which, so far as it can be ascertained, must be taken into account by the literary critic. Stylistic characteristics of periods, movements, and individual authors, meanwhile, are often describable in terms of greater emphasis, now on one factor, and now on another. All that can be demanded more generally is the presence of *both* factors in happy combination. Finally, the mean, though deriving its artistic vitality from the dynamic interplay of both factors, differs qualitatively from each extreme. A melodious line of poetry is not merely melody *plus* meaning, but meaning intensified and clarified by sound, sound rendered meaningful in a literary manner.[19]

The second polarity which contributes to literary quality relates specifically to the meaning of the words employed. Three types of meaning have been distinguished: (i) conceptual meaning, as recorded (so far as possible) in the dictionary definition of individual words, but including also, and more particularly, emergent con-

[19] Cf. S. Alexander's comparison of Wordsworth and Spinoza: "In the second case the words only catch fire from the subject matter; in the other the words are themselves on fire." *Beauty and Other Forms of Value* (London: Macmillan, 1933), p. 60.

ceptual meanings brought into being by a judicious combination of words; (ii) imagistic meaning, present in all cases in which a word, or a group of words, conjures up an image of any type in the mind of anyone familiar with the language and psychologically capable of entertaining such images; and (iii) emotive-conative overtones, which tend to attach themselves to all words under favorable circumstances, but which vary greatly from word to word and from one individual or one social group to another. In making this distinction, I pointed out that the scientist does his best to introduce into his discourse only conceptual meanings, and that, when he does appeal to imagery, he limits himself to images, e.g., diagrams, carefully chosen and scientifically (or mathematically) defined. He also tries hard to exclude scientifically irrelevant emotive-conative overtones. The literary author, in contrast, makes rich use of overtones and, indeed, conceives it as part of his task to create new overtones through skillful selection and use of words with emotive and conative associations. He can introduce and control these associations, meanwhile, by suitable manipulation of both concepts and images, or, more specifically, by using both together in "metaphorical" relation. It is this relation which is found, on analysis, to constitute the specific locus of the second polarity of literary quality.

This polarity can be described most simply as the dynamic contrast and interplay of concept and image. The extremes or poles are (i) pure abstract concepts, best exemplified in logical analysis or mathematical reasoning, and (ii) concrete images in all their unrelieved particularity. Both extremes, conceived of as ideal limits, are devoid of literary value and, *in themselves*, arouse no emotive-conative overtones of explicit artistic significance. It is only when they are effectively combined, that is, so related that the image takes on wider significance through conceptual interpretation, while the concept is simultaneously given concrete application in an image, that vital literary quality comes into being. To describe the result as "vital" is to recognize the emergence of new meanings and new emotive-conative overtones. For these are an all-important *product* of the metaphorical dimension which constitutes the second mean of literary excellence.

This description of the mean in terms of the effective interplay of concept and image is accurate up to a point, and is directly applicable to most literature which possesses literary quality. Compositions differ greatly, however, in both literary type and historical style, and, consequently, in their use of this metaphorical dimension. Most of the world's great literature achieves literary merit through the employment of both concepts and images. But there are notable examples (for instance, in the writings of the Metaphysical poets) of genuine literary quality achieved through the effective interplay of more general and more limited concepts; while, near the other pole, individual passages and even entire literary compositions owe their undeniable literary power primarily to an interplay of more general and more specific imagery. Not to leave out of account these relatively rare, yet not unimportant, ways of achieving artistic quality in literature, the metaphorical literary polarity should be re-defined as a fruitful interplay of the more general and the more particular, as expressed in the medium of words.

This more inclusive characterization of literary quality has the additional merit of indicating the similarity of literature to the other arts. For, clearly, artistic quality in each of the arts might well be described in terms of the effective interplay of the more general and the more particular. This formula, in turn, suggests what may be made a fitting summary of my entire analysis of the conditions of artistic quality. Artistic quality is generically identical in all the artistic media; and it is the conditions of this common character which I have been at pains to analyze in the foregoing account of the three inter-medial polarities. These conditions differ from one art to another only in so far as the primary media differ, these differences, in turn, dictating corresponding differences in the respective secondary media. Empirical investigation of intra-medial conditions of artistic quality in the several arts reduces, therefore, to a more specific and *seriatim* application of the third inter-medial polarity, which concerns the effective exploitation of the primary medium. Thus, the two distinctively literary polarities which I have just described are merely particularized applications of the principle of exploiting the primary literary media effectively for purposes of literary expression.

What has been achieved in this analysis is neither the formulation of rules mechanically applicable to specific works of art for the determination of their artistic quality, nor an immediate first-hand perception of artistic quality as such. All that I have been able to do has been to explore some of the *conditions* of artistic quality whose neglect seems inevitably to result in artistic insufficiency. That elusive something which we entitle artistic "vitality" or "perfection" remains, like other ultimates, as inaccessible to conceptual analysis as its appearance is unpredictable. All that reason can do in its presence is to exercise its peculiar prerogative of self-limitation, i.e., to confess its own impotence and to acclaim the power of disciplined and oriented artistic intuition to discover, enjoy, and appraise artistic beauty in its innumerable specific manifestations.

CHAPTER XXIII

ARTISTIC TRUTH

IF we conceive of art as being in essence expressive, and if we believe that what a work of art expresses, through the organization of a primary artistic medium, is an interpretation of some subject-matter, it follows by definition that what is thus expressed may be either true or false. Furthermore, the applicability of these categories to art is actually assumed by every artistically sensitive person, whether critic or layman, who regards a work of art not only as an object of intrinsic delight but as a vehicle of communication. Thus, when we say that a poem "rings true," we credit its author not only with sincerity but with insight. In some sense or other we are endorsing his interpretation of his subject-matter. And, conversely, when we describe a picture or a musical composition as "shallow," "superficial," or "sentimental" (in the derogatory sense), we are not primarily impugning the artist's sincerity but are accusing him of lack of understanding. We are in some sense repudiating his interpretation of his subject-matter. Thus the categories of truth and falsity are actually invoked in all artistic response to art; and this invocation is completely in harmony with the definition of artistic content as an artistically expressed interpretation of reality in its relation to human life. Our task in this chapter is to examine the concept of artistic truth and to attempt to formulate its criteria.

Since the claim that artistic content may be true or false can be taken seriously only if the terms "truth" and "falsity" are used not in a radically misleading sense but in a manner conformable to common usage, I must attempt to show that the "truth" which is here claimed for art is genuine truth and not something entirely different, masquerading under the name. It will therefore be necessary to indicate, however briefly, the *generic* nature and criteria of truth as such. But whatever truths achieve expression in art reflect a distinctive approach to reality and are expressed in one or another of the distinctive artistic media; and this approach and these media differ, as we have seen, from other approaches, such as the scientific, and from other media, such as conceptual prose and mathematical symbolism. Hence, however we define the generic nature of truth and its criteria, the truths which science and art respectively express will differ from one another in significant ways, and the generic criteria of truth will be applicable to works of art and to scientific propositions respectively only as restated in a more specialized form. That is, the *specific* criteria of truth which are applicable in the one case are not applicable in the other. A validation of the concept of artistic truth must accordingly take into account the *difference* between artistic and scientific truth, as well as their *similarity* as species of a common genus.

1. The generic nature and criteria of truth

The age-old dispute among philosophers as to the generic nature and criteria of truth testifies to the extreme complexity of the problem. It is a problem whose solution must depend ultimately upon metaphysical as well as epistemological considerations, and no simple statement can be formulated which is at all adequate to the situation. The following brief analysis is offered merely as a basis sufficient for the subsequent analysis of artistic *versus* scientific truth. The entire chapter is no more than a preliminary indication of how the concept of artistic truth might profitably be explored.

The position here adopted concerning the nature, locus, and criteria of truth in general may be summarized as follows.

Truth and falsity are here conceived of as *properties*[1] of one and only one type of entity, namely, of *propositions*. They are properties of a proposition according as it does or does not accurately describe what it purports to describe, i.e., the "object" to which it "refers."

Hence the *locus* of truth and falsity is always a proposition. To make this clear, and to guard against certain common errors, it is necessary to note the following.

(a) A proposition is *not* a judgment. The latter is a conscious act of averment which has a proposition as its object. It is the *affirmation*

[1] I need not here discuss the question as to whether truth should be defined as a quality or as a relation, i.e., as an adjectival or a relational property, or in what sense it should be conceived of as a value. This problem is of importance for a more synoptic metaphysical and epistemological inquiry, and its solution would of course be relevant to the problem of artistic truth. But here I am merely concerned to show that a work of art, defined as a proposition or set of propositions expressed in a distinctive communicatory medium, may be *as* true or false as a scientifically expressed proposition, that is, that the categories of truth and falsity are, *mutatis mutandis*, *as* applicable to art as they are to science. If this can be established, any more adequate analysis of truth would be *as* relevant to the artistic as to the scientific (or other) cognitive enterprises.

or *denial* of a proposition. Hence, despite common usage, a judgment as such is never true or false; it is merely (to follow C. D. Broad) *correct* or *incorrect*. It is correct when a true proposition is asserted to be true, or a false proposition, false: incorrect, when a false proposition is asserted to be true, or a true proposition, false.

This distinction between a judgment and a proposition is important because in appraising the truth or falsity of a work of art we are concerned only with the truth or falsity of the *meaning* it expresses, and not with the problem as to whether the creative artist himself has wished to affirm or deny what he has expressed in his art. It also rules out *a fortiori* all questions concerning the artist's sincerity.

(b) As the object of a judgment, a proposition is always expressed in *some* (though not, as we shall see, in *any*) medium. All cognition, of whatever type, and therefore every possible judgment, requires an expressive vehicle or language. Croce is right in insisting that apprehension ("intuition") involves expression in some appropriate medium. Thought and its expression are aspects of a single organic process. We do not *first* apprehend a situation and *then* express our apprehension of it in some medium; we apprehend it from the very outset only in and through some cognitive and expressive medium, e.g., in conceptual prose, in mathematical symbols, in one of the artistic media, or in some other medium or combination of media. The statement: "I know what I mean but I can't express it in any medium whatever," simply indicates faulty introspection.[2]

(c) The medium in question may or may not be a medium of inter-subjective communication. It may be a medium already in use as a communicatory vehicle. Or it may be a newly invented language (e.g., a new type of symbolism) which, though for the moment known only to its inventor and therefore not yet available for purposes of communication, is of such a character as to permit of general acceptance and use. Or, finally, it may be a medium which, in the nature of the case, is and must remain wholly private. Subjective images as such constitute such a medium. It follows that a proposition which could only be expressed in a medium of the third type must necessarily remain irrelevant both to art and to science. For to have either artistic or scientific relevance, a proposition must be available to public scrutiny and criticism, if art and science are con-

[2] This does not, of course, entail that propositions cannot be subsistent entities whose reality is independent of their relation to mind. The autonomous subsistence of propositions is irrelevant to my argument.

ceived to be (as they usually are) *public* universes of discourse. Hence, the only propositions with which we are here concerned are those which are, or might be, expressed in a medium which is already, or which might become, a medium of inter-subjective communication. In what follows, the term "proposition" will accordingly be used to mean a "proposition which can be expressed in a medium which is actually or potentially a medium of inter-subjective communication."

(d) This restriction of truth and falsity to propositions may suggest an implication which I must specifically repudiate—the implication, namely, that propositions are identifiable with their formulation in a conceptual medium. If we ask a philosopher what he means by a proposition he will usually cite as typical propositions what are asserted in scientific, mathematical, or logical judgments, and then define a proposition in terms of abstract conceptual relationships. But if propositions are conceived of in this manner, and if truth is then described as a property of propositions, it follows necessarily that man can apprehend and express the truth with precision and adequacy only in and through a conceptual medium. The thesis here defended, in contrast, is that certain aspects of reality can be apprehended and expressed most adequately and precisely in and through the artistic media, and that what is thus apprehended and expressed *cannot* be translated into a conceptual medium without vital loss. The possibility of expressing many true propositions in a conceptual medium is not for a moment denied. What is challenged is the denial that truth and falsity are applicable to art, and the assertion that a work of art can at best merely express inaccurately and vaguely what can be expressed precisely only in a conceptual medium. In making propositions the locus of truth, accordingly, I am conceiving of propositions much more broadly than they are commonly conceived of; I would include *every* proposition about reality which can be expressed with precision in *any* medium of communication, including the several artistic media.

I must also attempt to indicate, however briefly, the theory of knowledge and reality which underlies my entire account of truth and its criteria. I am assuming (i) the existence of a complex and diversified objective reality with a character of its own; (ii) the possibility of establishing direct empirical contact with various aspects of this reality, i.e., of acquiring empirical data which, in and of themselves, give us an immediate (if restricted) insight into some aspects of reality itself, and which, in addition, provide clues to other aspects of the real; and (iii) that reality is of such a character that rational interpretation of available data can give us a genuine understanding of its complex and diverse nature. The *ultimate* "facts" to which a proposition or set of propositions must correspond in order to be true are the relevant aspects of objective reality itself. But our empirical contacts with this reality are partial and fragmentary, and the only "facts" *immediately* available to us are more or less atomistic empirical "data" of one type or another, which we assume to be not only immediately revelatory of very restricted regions of reality but also indicative, as clues, of the complex and universal character of the real.

If we were able to know reality in all its complexity and sweep in a single comprehensive intuitive experience, such knowledge would be entirely by "direct acquaintance," and the only criterion of truth which we would have to invoke would be that of correspondence between the propositions entertained and reality itself as exhaustively intuited. We should merely have to compare these propositions and the aspects of reality to which they referred in order to test their truth. If, on the other hand, we had no direct empirical contact with reality whatsoever, we would have no way of testing the extent to which any given proposition corresponded with its ultimate referendum, and would therefore have no way of knowing whether our beliefs were correct or incorrect. Availability of reliable empirical evidence as to the existence and nature of the real is thus a necessary condition of all human knowledge. In actuality, our knowledge mediates between these hypothetical states of complete and immediate intuitive apprehension of reality as a whole and of complete and incorrigible ignorance.

All human knowledge of reality is "re-constructive" (save when it concerns an immediate datum and nothing more) because we are compelled to re-construct the complex nature of the real from our successive and fragmentary empirical contacts with it. This re-construction takes the form of rational interpretation of available empirical data. This is why mere correspondence is not a sufficient criterion of truth, and why the criterion of consistency must also be invoked. But these two criteria, taken in conjunction, suffice to determine the truth of propositions entertained by man, if we assume, as all but the most sceptical positivists would be willing to do, that immediate empirical data, wisely interpreted, do indicate, in however fragmentary a way, the existence and nature of the complex real. We *can* come to know something about reality itself with some degree of assurance, provided we pay scrupulous attention to all relevant empirical data and provided we interpret these data in a rational, i.e., consistent, manner.[3]

We are now in a position to discuss the generic criteria of truth. An expressed proposition can be accepted as true if it satisfies the joint criteria of "consistency" and "correspondence." By consistency is meant, in general, the satisfaction of the several conditions requisite to the clear expression of ideas in any medium. By correspondence is meant the satisfaction of, or conformity to, all relevant empirical evidence. *Both* criteria are essential to the validation of propositions expressed in any medium, and both are found, on examination, to be complex.

The criterion of consistency is complex in two respects: first, because it applies, *mutatis mutandis*, both to the use of the expressive medium and to the ideas which are expressed in the medium, and second, because it has, in both cases, a positive as well as a negative aspect.

Here I must pause for a moment to justify the analytical distinction between ideas and their expression in some medium. I have subscribed to the Crocean thesis that apprehension and expression are two aspects of a single organic process. But this close interdependence of reflection and expression in a medium does not preclude the possibility of distinguishing analytically between the media of expression and the ideas expressed and expressible in these media, or between a correct and effective use of a medium, on the one hand, and ideational non-contradiction and coherence, on the other. Moreover, it is essential that this distinction be drawn, for only thus can the fact be recognized that consistency is conditioned by *two* factors, the one relating to the use of the medium, the other, to the ideas which are expressed in and through it. Let us consider first the applicability of the generic criterion of consistency to the use of the medium.

[3] Cf. the author's "A Critical Examination of Mr. Stace's Solipsism," *Journal of Philosophy*, Vol. XXXII (1935), pp. 197-216. The view here adopted is in essence an extension of the position defended by Bertrand Russell in *The Problems of Philosophy* (New York: Holt, 1919).

(i) A proposition satisfies the *negative* criterion of medial consistency if the rules, conventions, or laws of the medium are not violated. This type of consistency may be entitled *medial correctness.* Thus, I use the English language correctly if I do not violate any of the rules of grammar, i.e., if I conform to all syntactical requirements.

(ii) A proposition satisfies the *positive* criterion of medial consistency in proportion as the relevant expressive potentialities of the medium are exploited. This type of consistency may be entitled *medial felicity.* I exploit the medium of English prose adequately in proportion as I choose my words wisely and combine them in a manner appropriate to the ideas which I wish to express.

Medial correctness is the necessary but not the sufficient condition of medial felicity. The relevant expressive potentialities of a medium cannot be effectively exploited in thoughtless defiance or ignorance of grammar and syntax.[4] But a use of language, though correct, may be inept, impoverished, and even nonsensical. Medial correctness and felicity, in turn, are both necessary but not sufficient conditions of ideational consistency, whether positive or negative.

(iii) As regards ideational consistency, two propositions are *negatively* consistent if they do not contradict each other, however close or distant their relevance to one another. Thus, the proposition, "the moon is not made of green cheese," and the proposition, "Caesar crossed the Rubicon," do not contradict one another because they belong to such different universes of discourse; they stand in no discernible relation to one another. But the proposition, "the moon is not made of green cheese," is also consistent with innumerable scientific propositions concerning the constitution of the heavenly bodies, as is the proposition, "Caesar crossed the Rubicon," with innumerable historical propositions. What is common to these propositions is the *absence* of contradiction. It is consistency in this negative sense which is formulated in the classic Laws of Thought.[5] Let us, for convenience, entitle it *ideational non-contradiction.* No proposition or set of propositions can be accepted as true which violates this basic requirement of rational reflection.

[4] When liberties are taken with linguistic conventions they must be taken consciously, and for expressive effect, not irresponsibly.

[5] i.e., the law of identity (*A* is *A*); the law of non-contradiction (*A* is not both *B* and non-*B*); and the law of excluded middle (*A* is either *B* or non-*B*).

(iv) But the several propositions which, in combination, constitute an illuminating interpretation of any given subject-matter are, in addition, *positively* related to one another as members of an integrated ideational pattern. The interrelation of these propositions need not be one of strict implication, for it may not be possible to deduce one from the other *a priori*. They are, none the less, organically related in that each constitutes a description of one of several aspects of the given subject-matter, and so makes an essential contribution to the synoptic description of this subject-matter in its several aspects. This organic interrelation of propositions is a unique type of relationship. Let us entitle it *ideational coherence*.

These negative and positive forms of ideational consistency are related to one another as medial correctness is to medial felicity. Ideational non-contradiction is the necessary but not the sufficient condition of ideational coherence.

These four distinguishable types of consistency can be described in a less technical manner as follows. Every language has its own grammar and syntax. If we are to express ourselves clearly in a given language, we must either use the language correctly or else depart from this usage only for good and sufficient reasons. But the more complex and subtle the ideas we wish to express, the more imperative is it that we not only avoid grammatical errors but exploit the relevant expressive potentialities of the language as richly as possible. Meanwhile, the ideas which we express must not contradict one another. But this again is not enough. For the goal of all discourse is the expression of ideas which complement one another in the sense of combining, as organic members of an ideational pattern, to constitute a complex synoptic idea. In short, we can express ourselves correctly or incorrectly; if correctly, then felicitously or infelicitously; if felicitously, then in an unilluminating or illuminating and coherent manner. The ideal of complete consistency must accordingly be defined in terms both of the use of the medium and of the ideas expressed in the medium, and, in each case, both negatively and positively. Ideal consistency in the meaningful expression of ideas is approximated in proportion as all four aspects of consistency, two formal and two ideational, are satisfied.

So defined, consistency is a necessary criterion of truth[6] and the sufficient criterion of rational discourse, if the latter is defined with-

[6] On the assumption, here accepted without argument, that the reality which we are

out reference to truth. As a generic quality, consistency is identical in all its manifestations, and sensitivity to it is a necessary condition of all intelligent reflection and all intelligible communication. Its essential nature can be apprehended only by immediate intuition, though we can become indirectly assured of its presence or absence in certain contexts, e.g., in logic and mathematics, by a mechanical application of rules. But since its specific manifestations differ in different media, it can be achieved and apprehended in any medium only by those who have mastered the medium in question. We may therefore be equipped to express ourselves consistently, and to recognize consistency, in one medium while lacking the requisite equipment in other media.

But mere consistency, though a necessary criterion of truth, is not its sufficient criterion. To be true, a proposition or set of propositions, whatever the expressive medium, must in addition "correspond" to the "facts." It must "describe" its referendum. What is expressed must in some sense "conform" to "what is actually the case." It must set forth in its own way whatever characteristics of its referendum it purports to exhibit. Thus, a perfectly consistent geometry may be inapplicable to our spatio-temporal world; an historical reconstruction of past events may be internally consistent but historically untrue; a consistent theology may give a false account of the objective reality to which it refers.

The generic criterion of correspondence has, like the criterion of consistency, both a negative and positive aspect.

(i) It requires, on the one hand, that nothing be affirmed (i.e., that no proposition be accepted as true) which is *discrepant* with *any* reliable available evidence. I shall, for convenience, label this *negative* criterion of correspondence *the avoidance of empirical discrepancy*. A proposition must be regarded as false if it is discrepant with (i.e., contradicts, in whatever manner a proposition can contradict an empirical datum) any available empirical evidence that is reliable. Thus, the proposition, "the moon is made of green cheese," is disproved by positive scientific evidence and must therefore be rejected as false. The negative character of this criterion is analogous to the negative character of the ideational criterion of non-contradiction. Its satisfaction does not of itself guarantee the truth of

striving to apprehend is itself rational and orderly. If this assumption is invalid, rational reconstruction and apprehension of reality are impossible.

any proposition, but its non-satisfaction suffices to establish the proposition's falsity.

(ii) The positive counterpart of this negative criterion of correspondence is the demand that *all* available empirical evidence which is both relevant and reliable be taken fully into account. I shall entitle this *positive* criterion of correspondence the *adequate satisfaction of all empirical evidence*. This criterion differs from the negative criterion as follows. The latter demands that a proposition, to be true, must not *contradict any* single item of empirical evidence: the former, that *all* available relevant and reliable evidence shall be *satisfactorily* accounted for. Here the terms, "reliable," "relevant," and "available," which must be invoked to explain the meaning of "adequate satisfaction of all empirical evidence," require some elaboration.

(α) If correspondence can be tested only by an appeal to immediate observation or first-hand cognitive experience, it is essential that such observation be accurate, i.e., *reliable*. How, then, can the accuracy of an observation be tested? Only, in the last analysis, by a direct critical scrutiny of its clarity and vividness. In actual practice, we test the correctness of an observation by repeating it under favorable conditions, just as we test the consistency of a proposition by immediate scrutiny, and of an argument, by reviewing its successive stages until we are satisfied that no error has escaped us. We do, indeed, derive great additional assurance from collaboration with other competent observers—I say "competent," because, in every universe of discourse, we inevitably and properly value only the confirmation of experts, that is, of those in whose competence we have assurance. No mathematical theory is actually judged to be indubitably consistent until it has been subjected to the scrutiny of several experts, and no scientific observation is accepted as reliable until several trained observers have confirmed the initial observation. But such social confirmation, though of the utmost practical value, is merely ancillary to both rational and empirical verification. In the last analysis, every responsible investigator must rely on his own immediate observations for final assurance; and each investigator can test the accuracy of an observation only by applying to it the Cartesian test of clarity and distinctness.

(β) Meanwhile, the only clear and distinct observations to which we are justified in appealing, in the application of both the positive and the negative criterion of correspondence, are *relevant* observations. Our basic presupposition is that reality, in its endless diversity and complexity, reveals different aspects of itself to us as we approach it in different ways. The characteristic approaches of the scientist and the artist, respectively, have been described in an earlier chapter.[7] Each approach, moreover, if successfully explored, issues in specific types of experiences and observations which may differ in kind from the experiences and observations resulting from an alternative approach. Thus, vision differs in kind from touch, hearing, and smell; mere sensory perception (though it conditions moral insight, scientific discovery, and aesthetic apprehension) is not identifiable with any of these specialized modes of cognition; and each of these types of cognition, in turn, has its own distinctive empirical data. The more refined an observation, the more specialized does it become, and the more sharply is its immediate relevancy restricted to those propositions which are formulated to describe just that aspect of reality which is revealed by just this particular type of observation. Scientific observations, accordingly, need not be (though they may be) immediately relevant to artistic insight, and cannot properly be invoked in direct confirmation of the truth of propositions which achieve artistic expression and constitute the expressed content of specific works of art; and, conversely, the observations of the artist need not be (though they may be) directly relevant to the verification of a scientific theory. In short, a proposition can be directly tested for correspondence only by the immediate application to it of empirical data which are strictly relevant to it, and not by data relevant to a radically different universe of discourse.

But this must not be construed to mean that propositions (and their supporting data) in different universes of discourse are of necessity wholly unrelated to one another. On the contrary, the more inclusive or philosophical our perspective, the more imperative is it that *all* discoverable relationships between diverse propositions and sharply contrasting data be explored. For our apprehension of reality as a whole is strictly proportionate to the degree with which we are able to relate propositions which satisfy widely different experiences of different aspects of reality. Every specific proposition acquires new and important meanings in being related to other propositions and new data, first, in its own universe of discourse, and then, more generally, to propositions and data directly related to other aspects of reality. Within the confines of any specific cognitive

[7] Cf., above, Chap. XIII.

enterprise, our procedure is to modify any interpretation of a given set of data whenever new data necessitate such a modification; and when a proposition contradicts other propositions whose truth we accept, we make every effort to modify it in such a way as to make it consistent with these other propositions while still doing justice to the data which it and they purport to interpret. This interrelation of propositions and data within a restricted universe of discourse can be extended to define a more catholic notion of empirical relevancy. Though a given datum x is not *immediately* relevant to proposition P but only to proposition R, a relation, however distant, between P and R implies the *indirect* relevancy of x to P. Hence, a new indubitable observation in *any* universe of discourse may precipitate a modification not only of the propositions most immediately relevant to it, but also of more distantly related propositions which have been accepted as valid interpretations of entirely different data. From an ultimate philosophical perspective, i.e, in a philosophically coherent interpretation of reality as a whole, *every* verified datum and accepted proposition must therefore be regarded as in some sense, however remotely, relevant to every other verified datum and accepted proposition.

(γ) Finally, the term "*available*" is important in the formulation of the criterion of correspondence, because it directs our attention to the inconclusiveness of all human knowledge. Knowledge is conditioned by two basic factors, the nature of reality as possessing an objective character of its own, and the potentialities and limitations of man's cognitive response to it. When the reality in question is itself a temporal process productive of genuine novelty, man's empirical knowledge of it cannot, by definition, ever be complete, since in the nature of the case new empirical data, indicative of novel objective states, continue to present themselves indefinitely. But even when the reality to be known is not itself in process of transformation and productive of novelty, our apprehension of it is itself a temporal process consisting of successive acts of empirical awareness and successive interpretations of the resultant empirical data. Accordingly, the more complex an object of apprehension, however stable, the less likely are we to be able to experience all of its several empirical aspects in any finite time. We cannot doubt that many relatively stable objects of empirical awareness, including works of art, are cognitively inexhaustible.

Hence, no human apprehension of objects in the existential world can boast absolute completeness or finality. For, in the first place, I, as an individual cognitive agent, can hardly be aware of all the evidence referable to any aspect of reality which is now actually available to mankind; I must almost inevitably remain unaware of directly relevant data in the possession of other minds. And, in the second place, man's corporate experience of existential reality is incomplete, and must remain so to the end of time, partly because of the finite nature of all human apprehension, and partly because of the pervasive factor of objective novelty. This means that the truths which human beings are privileged to know are in essence finite truths, forever susceptible of further correction, further enrichment, and further clarification. Absolute Truth is an empty ideal, invaluable as a point of reference (for only by reference to it is the finite and imperfect nature of human truth intelligible) but, none the less, forever unattainable by human beings.

But this does not commit us to a vicious relativism. For there is no reason to impugn the correctness, *within limits*, of any specific interpretation of specific available empirical data. This is a point on which we must be clear. Given a set of data, any proposition which is internally consistent and which does full justice to these data is a correct (though restricted) interpretation *of these data*, and any subsequent interpretation of these data, taken in conjunction with other data which throw new light upon the situation, must take not only the original data but the original consistent and correspondent interpretation of them into account. This is precisely what is meant by the statement that individual intuitions are, in a sense, absolutely true. For if we define an intuition as an act of cognitive apprehension in which the mind is focussed with unusual clarity upon certain empirical data, and in which these data are interpreted with complete and self-evident internal consistency, every genuine intuition is absolutely true (according to the criteria of consistency and correspondence) *within the limited framework of this particular act of intuitive apprehension.* In a more inclusive framework the earlier interpretation must, indeed, yield to a more synoptic interpretation, and the original narrower intuition to a more inclusive intuition of a larger whole. But what was originally observed with observational clarity remains an empirical "fact," and the original intuition remains valid with respect to its original referendum, however much we subsequently extend the range of our empirical experience and the scope of our interpretation of it. Thus Einstein has not destroyed the validity of Newtonian mechanics *within* the Newtonian frame of reference, and every verified observation which the Newtonian interpretation had to satisfy must still be satisfied by the Theory of Relativity. Subject to the limitations of human cognition at any given moment, accordingly, human judgments may be accepted as correct or incorrect depending upon the extent to which the asserted propositions satisfy the joint criteria of consistency and correspondence.

This must suffice to explain the generic nature and criteria of truth. The several distinguishable criteria may be diagrammatically indicated as follows:

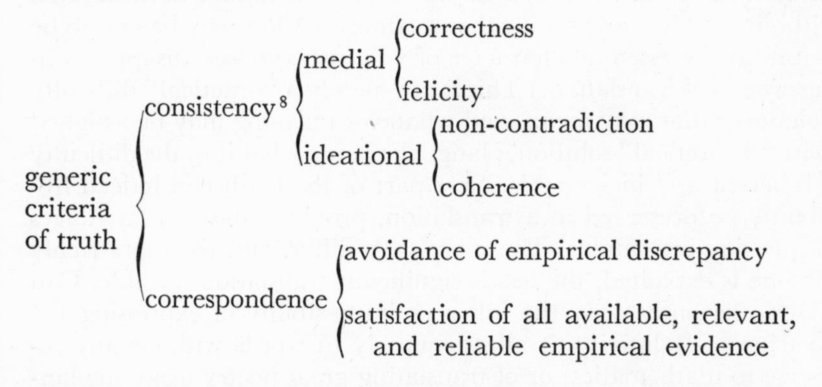

Before considering the applicability of these generic criteria to scientific judgments and to works of art, let us briefly explain the distinction here envisaged between scientific and artistic truth as species of a common genus.

The justification for this distinction lies in the fact that the various media of inter-subjective communication differ radically in expressive power. We can express in some media what we cannot express in other media—in mathematical symbols, what we cannot express in words; in scientific prose, what we cannot express in music; in music, what we cannot utter in words; etc. Each of these languages has its own expressive potentialities *and* limitations. And since reality itself is infinitely various and complex in character, certain aspects of it lend themselves far better to apprehension and interpretation

[8] Attention is called to the fact that "consistency" is here used more broadly than in ordinary philosophical usage. The term is usually made to designate what I have entitled "ideational non-contradiction."

in and through a given medium than any other. Thus the artist, apprehending human experience and its objects in and through an artistic medium, can grasp their individuality and human significance as the scientist cannot, whereas the scientist can apprehend and express the skeletal structure of the phenomenal world with a precision which art cannot rival. Each gets what the other misses, and what one apprehends and expresses in his medium cannot be apprehended or expressed with even comparable adequacy in any other medium.

Hence, when a master of any language has expressed himself adequately in that language by richly exploiting its expressive potentialities, the truth which he has expressed cannot be translated without vital loss into some other medium. (A loss may be said to be "vital" if the essential character of what is expressed disappears in the process of translation.) This is not merely a "practical" difficulty (whatever that may mean, and whatever meaning may be assigned to its "theoretical" solution); language being what it is, the difficulty is inherent and inescapable. *Some* part of the truth can indeed frequently be preserved in a translation, provided the two languages in question are similar. The more they differ, and the more richly the one is exploited, the less is significant translation possible. Can anyone seriously deny the inherent impossibility of expressing the doctrine of Relativity at all adequately in words without any recourse to mathematics; or of translating great poetry from one language to another without vital loss; or of re-expressing the expressed content of music or of the plastic arts in anything like an adequate manner in cold conceptual prose?[9]

It follows that although truth, generically defined, is indeed one, the artist and the scientist (to consider only these two) apprehend such different aspects of reality and express these apprehensions in such different media, that the distinction is amply justified between "scientific truth" and "artistic truth" as distinguishable species of a common genus.[10] Let us, then, consider these two types of truth and their respective criteria in turn.

[9] A mathematician once said to me, in discussing my claim that a particular poem expressed genuine insight: "I'll consider your claim if you will re-express in the language of mathematical physics what the poem seems to you to say,"—a remark which invited the answer: "I, in turn, will consider the truth of a mathematical theorem if you will translate it into music." The absurdity of both requests illustrates the point at issue.

[10] Professor W. T. Stace has challenged this distinction (cf. "Comments and Criti-

2. The nature and criteria of scientific truth

Scientific truth is a property of propositions (i) which are expressed in the communicatory media of mathematics and scientific prose, (ii) which describe the skeletal structure of the existential spatio-temporal world, and (iii) which satisfy the specific criteria of scientific consistency and scientific correspondence.

To be consistent, scientific propositions must be correctly expressed; the linguistic conventions of the media employed must not be violated. But the more subtle and precise the ideas which the scientist wishes to express, the more important is it that he exploit to the full the expressive potentialities of his linguistic media. The expert scientist expresses himself not only in a correct but in a scientifically felicitous manner. Here, as elsewhere, medial correctness is a necessary but not a sufficient condition of medial felicity.

If scientific propositions are to satisfy the criterion of consistency, it is necessary that the ideas expressed be consistent with one another. Since scientific interpretation is explicitly conceptual in character, the requisite ideational consistency, both "negative" and "positive," must be explicitly conceptual. Two contradictory concepts (e.g., round and not-round) must not be equated in a single proposition, and two propositions which describe the same referendum in contradictory ways cannot both be accepted as true. But the mere avoidance of contradiction will not suffice. The goal of

cisms," *Journal of Philosophy*, Vol. XXXV, 1938, pp. 656-61; portions of my answer to his criticism are here incorporated, with alterations, with the *Journal's* kind permission) on the ground that there is "only one kind of truth, which consists in the correct ascription of a predicate or relation to a subject," and that since whatever a work of art expresses can, at least theoretically, be re-expressed in a verbal judgment, there is no radical distinction between artistic and scientific truth. Professor Stace admits that translation is often difficult. But he minimizes the importance of this difficulty by regarding it as merely "practical," and as being occasioned by the fact that "language is a very crude instrument of expression." I should answer that verbal language is an excellent medium for the expression of certain kinds of truth, that is, for the expression of the truth regarding certain aspects of reality, and a very inadequate medium for the expression of other types of knowledge concerned with other aspects of reality. Professor Stace argues that "if you were a perfect master of a perfect language you could infallibly express in words every conceivable truth." Since no one can know how such a "perfect" language might be constituted, it is impossible to defend or attack this proposition. But it seems clear that the more perfectly any existing expressive medium is mastered and exploited, the less possible is it to translate what has been thus expressed into any other existing medium, however flexible this second medium, and however perfectly it has been mastered.

scientific inquiry is the formulation of a number of propositions, each descriptive of some aspect of the same complex referendum, which complement one another and so, in organic ideational relationship, offer a synoptic interpretation of the referendum in all its complexity. Whether or not a series of scientifically expressed propositions does or does not satisfy this fourfold criterion of consistency can be determined only by immediate and expert scrutiny.

The interdependence of medial and ideational consistency is as evident in science as in other universes of discourse. Like other men, the scientist can clarify his own ideas only by expressing them clearly in his scientific media.[11] Ideational confusion invariably reflects itself in medial confusion, and a deficient mastery of the expressive medium prohibits ideational clarity and precision.

It goes without saying that a scientific theory which is not based on scientific evidence is not worthy of consideration. A scientific proposition or set of propositions can be accepted as true only in proportion as they do not repudiate relevant scientific evidence and in proportion as they satisfy all available evidence which is both relevant and reliable.

The technique of obtaining scientifically reliable evidence has been so perfected by the natural scientists that, for precision and reliability, it is unrivalled in other cognitive disciplines. Not only have the scientists' direct observations of natural processes been greatly extended in scope and sharpened in precision by the invention of scientific instruments; a complicated experimental method has been evolved for the securing of observations under the most favorable conditions. The scientist has learned how to isolate phenomena and how to exclude or compensate for disturbing factors. He has also devised a technique of measurement whose flexibility makes it adaptable to a great variety of empirical observations. Nor has he been content with mere direct observation; he has learned how to detect phenomenal occurrences not immediately manifest, even with the aid of instruments, by noting and interpreting their observable effects. Scientific observation and empirical verification have thus become, particularly during the last few decades, highly refined and specialized activities.

The immediate relevance of observational data to any given scientific inquiry is determinable with great assurance because of

[11] These media are *always*, at least potentially, public and communicatory.

the equally specialized character of scientific theory. Every observation is made and every experiment is conducted with the explicit purpose of confirming, modifying, or disproving some specific hypothesis. The scientist goes to nature with definite questions and, as a result, is able to obtain from nature definite answers supported by immediately relevant empirical data. Meanwhile, more specialized scientific theories are continually being related to one another within a wider scientific frame of reference, with the result that data immediately relevant to a specific theory become relevant to a more synoptic theory and thus, indirectly, to other restricted theories. The inevitable tendency of all scientific inquiry is towards a more and more synoptic and organic interpretation of the whole world of natural phenomena. For, since nature is one, subject to universal laws and composed of interrelated aspects and processes, no single aspect or process is ultimately intelligible in isolation. A single phenomenon can, indeed, be described with relative self-sufficiency (though even here the general technique of scientific observation and description is invoked), and any given group of phenomena can be interpreted with great precision within a restricted frame of reference. But ultimately no specialized branch of a science can be divorced from the other branches of that science, and no more embracing science can survive the neglect of other major scientific disciplines. In this sense, scientific truth is a function of the whole set of propositions dealing with the phenomenal world as a whole, and standing in ideationally organic relation to one another. Scientific truth is not a mere aggregate of unrelated truths, but a function of a coherent pattern of propositions which, as a coherent pattern, describes the complex order of nature in all its length and breadth.

A scientist is under peculiar obligation, in any specific scientific enterprise, to acquaint himself with all the relevant data now available and, in addition, to devise experiments and make observations productive of new relevant evidence. But since his subject-matter is infinitely complex, he can never be assured that all the evidence is in; he must anticipate the discovery of new evidence which may necessitate a modification of his theories. Hence scientific knowledge is necessarily finite and incomplete. None the less, it is possible for specific scientific "intuitions" to be perfectly correct *within* a restricted frame of reference. No future observations can invalidate any precise observation, and no more synoptic interpretation can destroy the validity of a more restricted interpretation, *within its own limited perspective.*

It is clear, then, that the truths achieved in science are highly specialized manifestations of generic truth, and that the scientific criteria of consistency and correspondence are specialized applications of the generic criteria. This brief analysis of scientific method is relevant to our investigation because it indicates the specialized nature not only of the scientist's approach to reality but of his observations and interpretations of those aspects of reality which he elects to investigate and describe.

Let us now see whether generic truth, as here defined, is as relevant to works of art as it is to scientifically expressed propositions, and whether the generic criteria of truth, duly re-interpreted, can be applied to propositions expressed *via* artistic form in the several artistic media.

3. The nature and criteria of artistic truth

The chief differences already considered between artistic and scientific cognition may be summarized as follows. The artist apprehends and exhibits the universal characteristics of his subject-matter in a highly individualized context, whereas the scientist concerns himself with the skeletal structure of phenomenal processes and exhibits these, so far as possible, in abstraction from their individual manifestations. The artist's basic orientation is anthropocentric and normative, whereas the scientist is interested in phenomenal structure for its own sake. The artist expresses his insights and interpretations in the warm and vital language of art, which is as perfectly adapted to the mediation of his normative apprehensions as are scientific prose and mathematics to the formulation of the scientist's impersonalized apprehension of the quantitative aspects of nature's skeletal structure. Finally, the type of objectivity requisite to artistic insight differs from the objectivity requisite to scientific discovery. These differences suggest that the *specific* criteria of artistic truth will differ from the *specific* criteria of scientific truth.

But we must also keep in mind those characteristics which we have found the artistic and scientific enterprises to have in common. In the first place, the artist, like the scientist, has a subject-matter which he interprets in his own way. If his interpretation is to be illuminating, he must, like the scientist, really comprehend this subject-matter and, like him, express his interpretation of it in some appropriate medium. The fact that the artist indulges in a type of evaluation foreign to scientific interpretation does not relieve him of the responsibility for comprehending the objective character of his subject-matter honestly and intelligently, since no evaluation in any universe of discourse, including art, can be significant unless it is based upon a true understanding of the material which is evaluated. No artist can exhibit the human import of anything which he radically misapprehends. And if his evaluations are to be relevant to the lives and experiences of other men, the artist must, in addition, achieve a genuine understanding of man's normative experiences, and be able to apprehend and interpret the values to which men do attach, or should attach, importance. In short, the artist must be wise with respect both to certain aspects of the objective nature of his subject-matter and to its actual or potential human import.

Secondly, the artist, like the scientist, can clarify his own apprehensions of his subject-matter only in the act of expressing them as clearly and eloquently as possible in his own artistic medium. In art, as in science, clarity of thought and clarity of expression are complementary aspects of a single process. Formal inexpertness simultaneously reflects and occasions ideational confusion, and *vice versa*. Moreover, if a work of art is defined (as I have defined it) as a vehicle of actual or potential communication, the artist must express himself in a language which is at least potentially intelligible to others.

These similarities, which might be indefinitely elaborated, between the artistic and the scientific enterprises justify the presumption that artistic truth, like scientific truth, should be regarded as a specific variant of generic truth, and that the generic criteria of truth, when re-interpreted, should be as applicable to art as they are to science. The correctness of this presumption can be established only by a more detailed consideration of artistic truth and of the application to art of its specific artistic criteria.

If a work of art has "anything to say" it must be regarded as the expression, in an artistic medium, *via* artistic form, of a proposition (simple or complex) which is both factual and normative, that is, which not only describes an objective situation but formulates an evaluation of it. Since the only objects which I have been concerned to analyze in this book are genuine works of art, i.e., works which are artistically expressive and are not *merely* decorative or aesthetically agreeable, I can therefore re-define a work of art as the artistic expression of one or more descriptive and evaluative propositions with a discoverable referendum. These artistically expressed propositions are what I have previously entitled artistic content. Accordingly, if truth can be correctly assigned only to propositions, and if propositions, artistically expressed, constitute artistic content, it follows that artistic truth is necessarily a function not of the artistic medium as such, or of the artistic form as such, but of the content of a work of art. The *locus* of artistic truth is artistic content.

It is also possible to regard a work of art as a judgment, that is, as an assertion by the artist that what he has expressed is true and not false. We normally interpret specific works of art in precisely this manner; we assume the artist's sincere commitment to the normative interpretation of reality and life to which he has given expression. But artists, like other men, can give expression to propositions whose truth they neither deny nor assert, and artists can also express propositions which they believe to be false. A work of art *need* not, therefore, record the artist's own private convictions regarding either the nature or the human import of his subject-matter. A recognition of this fact does not involve a repudiation of my earlier description of "serious" art as the expression of the artist's sincere convictions. Most works of art are correctly interpreted as the considered judgments of their authors. But the interpretation of "serious" art, though very important in other contexts, is not strictly relevant to the present inquiry into the nature and criteria of artistic truth. Our sole concern here is the kind of truth which can correctly be attributed to artistic content as such, and the manner in which this truth can be tested, irrespective of whether or not the creator of this or that specific work of art can reasonably be believed, in the light of available evidence, actually to have committed himself to the truth of his own artistic utterances.

The *differentiae* of artistic truth are determined not only by the distinctive character of the artistic media but by the artist's cognitive approach and goal. In analyzing these two aspects of the artistic enterprise we discovered,[12] first, that the artist's approach is highly individual, yet never wholly idiosyncratic. An artist's outlook and mode of interpretation manifests *significant* originality in proportion as it is simultaneously new *and* shareable, individual *and*

[12] Cf., above, Chaps. XIII and XIV.

universal. If his apprehension of reality is so unique that no one else can learn to see his subject-matter through his eyes or comprehend his interpretation of it, his vision must, by definition, remain incommunicable. This would not of itself necessitate the conclusion that his apprehension was illusory, or his interpretation of it, false; it would be theoretically possible that his insight was so subtle, refined, and exalted that no other human being could share it with him, and that the artist himself could test the validity of his own insight by applying to it the specific artistic criteria of truth. But however articulate he found his expression of his artistic insight, it would, by definition, be unintelligible to others, and the content of his art could therefore not be accepted by anyone else as meaningful or, *a fortiori*, true. The only art whose truth we need therefore consider is that art whose expressed content is intelligible to the competent observer. But to be intelligible this content must, again by definition, express an approach to reality and an interpretation of it which other men can share. In short, the artist's approach, if the category of truth is to be applicable to his art, must be not only individual but also, and simultaneously, universal. That is, it must express an insight which, though original in the sense that the artist was the first to achieve it, must be such that others, following in his footsteps, can more or less closely approximate to it.

This is precisely the presupposition of all artistic re-creation. The critic goes to the work of art expecting to find in it new insights, new observations, new interpretations, new appraisals of a more or less familiar subject-matter. This means that he expects to be able to share in these new insights and to comprehend them with some measure of adequacy. And this expectation is justified in the case of all art which comes, in time, to be accepted as true and significant art. Indeed, it comes to be accepted as such just because it expresses a fresh yet intelligible outlook, an insight which is new and individual, yet shareable by others. Artistic truth is thus a characteristic of artistically expressed propositions which the individual artist has been the first so to apprehend and express, but which, once apprehended and expressed by him, can be re-apprehended by the sensitive and trained observer.

The nature of artistic truth is also determined by the artist's distinctive modes of expression, and, specifically, by his reliance upon the principle of artistic individuality. The propositions to which the artist gives utterance are never formulated by him in abstract conceptual terms[13] but are always expressed in a highly individual context. Artistic truth must therefore be defined as a function of artistically expressed insights, and the criteria of truth in art must be so defined as to be applicable only to propositions expressed in an artistic medium.

This general description of the nature of artistic truth can be sharpened and amplified by a consideration of the specific criteria of artistic truth and their applicability to art in the several artistic media.

The criterion of *artistic consistency* must be defined with reference both to the organization of the specific artistic media and to the way in which the ideas expressed in and through these media are related to one another. Here, as in science, we must distinguish analytically between the ideas expressed and their expression, though, in the actual work of art, form and content are fused aspects of one and the same organic whole. I have already described artistic quality as the dynamic mean (i) of organic unity (as opposed to the extremes of mere simplicity and mere complexity); (ii) of expressive originality (as opposed to mere order and mere novelty); and (iii) of the expressive exploitation of the medium (as opposed to its denial and its overemphasis). I have also pointed out that, so conceived, artistic quality has its *primary* locus in artistic form, though formal excellence can be appraised only with reference to the artist's expressive intent. Artistic "integrity," in contrast, has its primary locus in artistic content, though the integrity of art, so conceived, is necessarily conditioned by formal artistic excellence. Artistic quality may thus be equated with medial and formal consistency; artistic integrity, with ideational consistency; and both are requisite to complete artistic consistency. Artistic consistency, in turn, is the condition of artistic style. But a work of art may perfectly exemplify a coherent style and still fail to satisfy the criterion of artistic truth defined in terms of consistency *and* correspondence. In short, both consistency (or stylistic excellence) and correspondence (the product of artistic insight) are requisite to artistic truth. Let us examine these conditions and criteria of artistic truth in turn.[14]

[13] Though propositions may, as we have seen, be formulated in this manner in literature. Even here, however, such formulation constitutes only a part of the artist's total expression of his ideas.

[14] These distinctions are summarized diagrammatically on p. 458.

The artistic criterion of *linguistic*[15] *consistency* must be defined with reference both to the pre-artistic character of the primary medium and to the formal organization of this medium.

(i) The negative criterion of *linguistic correctness* is the artistic requirement of conformity to relevant pre-artistic and artistic rules and conventions. A work of art satisfies this criterion in proportion, first, as the basic principles of the chosen medium are not violated, and, secondly, in proportion as the formal implications of the manner or manners of treatment, and of the compositional pattern, adopted in it, are not disregarded. Thus, a musical composition is artistically correct if, first, the principles of the musical system, expressible in a scale, which the artist has selected as his primary medium of expression are obeyed, and secondly, if the musical manner or manners of treatment (e.g., the harmonic, or the melodic and harmonic in combination) and the generic compositional pattern or patterns (e.g., the sonata form) are correctly employed. Similarly, an English poem is artistically correct if the English language is used correctly, and if one or more of the literary manners of treatment (e.g., the lyrical) and the poetic form adopted (e.g., the sonnet) are employed in an artistically consistent manner. In short, every primary artistic medium has a characteristic structure and distinctive conventions of its own, and each of the arts has its own manners of treatment and its own compositional patterns. A work of art satisfies the negative criterion of correctness in proportion as it does not violate the medial conventions, the manners of treatment, and the compositional pattern to which the artist has, in this specific composition, committed himself.

[15] From here on I shall use the more general term "linguistic" instead of "medial" in this context. In the foregoing discussion of medial consistency, the term "medial" was used generically as a synonym for "linguistic," and "medium" as a synonym for "language"; and no attempt was made to distinguish between the basic structure and syntax of a language and the more general conventions of formal linguistic organization. But in Parts I and II this distinction, as it applies to art, was developed in considerable detail, by contrasting the pre-artistic organization of a primary artistic medium with the generic artistic forms in the several arts, e.g., between a musical system expressible in a scale, on the one hand, and the musical manners of treatment and compositional patterns, on the other. In what follows we are concerned with *all* the linguistic facilities at the disposal of the artist, both medial (in the narrower sense) and formal. The term "linguistic" will therefore be used to signify both "medial" *and* "formal," as these latter terms have been defined in Parts I and II. The several non-artistic languages, e.g., the language of mathematics, will be found, on analysis, to possess analogous "medial" *and* "formal" characteristics.

The academician tends to misconceive this negative criterion of linguistic correctness by making certain linguistic conventions absolute and demanding universal obedience to them. This error can be avoided by conceiving of artistic excellence in Aristotelian terms, i.e., by appraising the artistic correctness of any given work of art in terms of those conventions to which the artist has actually committed himself in any particular composition. The academicians forget that significant artistic originality has always involved linguistic innovations. But those who have revolted against academic tyranny have tended to forget that an artist, to be intelligible (even to himself), must conform to *some* linguistic conventions, that his intelligibility to others is conditioned by his obedience to conventions which his audience already accepts or might be induced to accept, and that every departure from more or less established pre-artistic and artistic conventions must be artistically justified. Sheer incompetence can produce nothing but artistically meaningless novelty and unintelligible chaos.

(ii) This negative criterion must be supplemented by the positive criterion of *linguistic felicity*. We expect an artist to be not merely consistent in following out the implications of his own artistic premises, and not merely competent in the use of those conventions to which he has committed himself—we expect him to be felicitous in his selection and exploitation of his primary medium, and fertile in the creation of new specific artistic forms. We expect his composition, in short, to manifest organic unity, expressive originality, and effective medial exploitation. An artist can avoid linguistic incorrectness without achieving linguistic felicity. Thus, a composer can obey the rules of harmony and counterpoint and construct a correct sonata or fugue without manifesting a spark of musical originality. Even though his work exemplifies various principles of formal unity, its aesthetic surface may lack organic unity. He may have expressed himself correctly in his chosen idiom and still have failed to exploit adequately the expressive potentialities of his medium. His work may be correct in a negative sense without being positively felicitous or inspired. Artistic correctness is a necessary but not a sufficient condition of artistic felicity.

In applying both of these criteria to art, the critic must therefore take into account the uniqueness of each individual work of art; each work must be appraised in terms of its own individual frame of reference. The first question to be answered is the question as to whether the artist has correctly and felicitously realized the linguistic implications and possibilities of *his own* starting point. But the appraisal of linguistic excellence is also a comparative appraisal, since we must also ask: Is this composition more or less successful in this or that respect than other compositions? The first question involves appeal to a standard which must be defined anew for each individual work of art; the second, to a standard of excellence which is applicable to many works of art in the same and in different media. In actual practice these two questions are frequently not distinguished, and when this happens the critical issues are usually confused. The critic is therefore well-advised to distinguish these two questions, for the neglect of either constitutes a failure in critical analysis and appraisal.

The most extreme formalist in art must acknowledge the applicability to art of these two criteria of linguistic correctness and felicity. But the more preoccupied he is with the aesthetic surface of art and its immediate aesthetic appeal, the more will he tend to define these criteria without reference to expressive intent and with sole reference to the formal beauty of the sensuous design. So defined, they are for him criteria of nothing but self-sufficient medial and formal aesthetic excellence. If, on the other hand, linguistic excellence be conceived of not merely as an intrinsic value but *also* as a necessary condition of artistic expressiveness, linguistic correctness and felicity must both be defined with reference to what the artist, in any given work of art, is trying, consciously or unconsciously, to express. Any organization of a primary medium must then be said to be artistically correct and felicitous in proportion as it effectively expresses, *in an artistically satisfying manner*, the ideas which the artist wishes to express.

(iii) An expressive work of art satisfies the negative criterion of *ideational non-contradiction* if the expressed propositions, or interpretations of the subject-matter, do not contradict one another. Every creative artist and every critic knows how hard it is to avoid contradiction of this type. The amateur painter, for example, finds it almost impossible to be consistent in his handling of representational objects in any specific composition. He finds himself unwittingly emphasizing one aspect of trees (for instance, their three-dimensionality and color) in one part of a landscape, and other aspects (for instance, the delicacy of their foliage or the distinctive thrust of their branches) in another part of the same composition. In short, he fails to maintain a consistent approach to his subject-matter.

This failure is essentially an ideational confusion (though it is of course partly conditioned by technical incompetence). To illustrate this type of contradiction in an extreme, indeed, a fantastic manner—suppose we were to find in a single composition different representational objects treated in the manner of Corot, Cézanne, Matisse, and Henri Rousseau. The result would be utter ideational chaos. We would exclaim: "The painter has contradicted himself in almost every stroke." And what applies to representational painting applies equally to the other arts. Imagine a characteristic passage of Debussy inserted into the middle of Bach's *B Minor Mass*, or a *Barrack Room Ballad* into *Paradise Lost*, or a modernistic architectural motif into the *Sainte Chapelle*. But it should not be necessary to appeal to such grotesque examples of ideational contradiction in art; the world is full of art which the competent critic must condemn in terms of this criterion.

It goes without saying that such contradiction must not be confused with deliberate and artistically eloquent contrast. The donor in the *Avignon Pietà* (Fig. 211) is deliberately painted in a markedly plastic manner to emphasize his humanity and to distinguish him from the religious group which is treated in a markedly planear manner. Here the artist is not guilty of ideational contradiction, for he is emphasizing contrasting characteristics of his subject-matter in order to depict its complex nature. Nor is ideational contradiction in art reducible to mere logical contradiction, for the ideas which in art contradict one another are not given explicit conceptual expression. The contradiction, when it occurs, is an artistically expressed contradiction and is discoverable, accordingly, only by the artistically sensitive observer.

(iv) But in art, as in science, the absence of ideational contradiction does not, of itself, guarantee positive *ideational coherence*. For such coherence is achieved only in proportion as all the interpretations of the several portions of the specific subject-matter *complement* one another so that the work of art as a whole expresses a complex and coherent commentary on the nature and import of the entire subject-matter in question. Every great work of art which is stylistically consistent through and through exemplifies such artistic coherence, as is evidenced by the sense of organic unity of outlook which we derive from it.

A work of art manifests artistic "integrity," accordingly, in proportion as it expresses in an artistically felicitous manner a genuinely coherent interpretation of a given subject-matter. Because of the close mutual dependence of expressive form and expressed content, i.e., of ideas (or propositions) expressed and the manner of their expression, linguistic felicity and ideational coherence can only be distinguished for purposes of analysis. Whatever degree of consistency characterizes the work characterizes it as a whole. Ideational incoherence and contradiction manifest themselves only in and through linguistic inconsistencies, and these, in turn, are invariably indicative of ideational confusion. If the work is to possess formal consistency, every element in the composition must have its ideational *raison d'être*. But the artist can achieve the requisite ideational clarity and consistency only in the act of expressing his ideas in his chosen artistic language. If we restrict ourselves, with the pure formalists, to a non-expressive aesthetic surface, artistic integrity must be identified with medial and formal felicity. But if we regard artistic form as a vehicle of artistic expression, artistic integrity becomes essentially a function of felicitously expressed artistic content.

In an earlier chapter, style was examined primarily as an historical phenomenon. We are now in a position to define its essential structural character. The vitality and integrity of a style, regarded as a dynamic universal, reveals itself in the ideational coherence (or artistic integrity) and the linguistic felicity (or artistic quality) of its most adequate exemplifications. The hall-marks of a generic style are a typical mode of formal organization expressive of a typical ideational pattern. The more coherent this pattern and the more felicitous its formal expression, the greater the integrity and perfection of the style in question. Meanwhile, a specific work of art is "in" a generic style in proportion as it conforms to the medial and formal conventions, and expresses the characteristic outlook, of that style. And, finally, any work of art "has" style in proportion as it expresses a coherent interpretation of its subject-matter with linguistic felicity. It follows that individual works of art may "have" more or less style, and may also exemplify a given generic style more or less adequately, while a generic style, regarded as an historical phenomenon, may itself have more or less expressive integrity and linguistic felicity.

This definition of style in terms of felicitously expressed ideational coherence makes it possible to translate my account of artistic consistency into stylistic terms. Linguistic correctness now becomes stylistic correctness or absence of formal stylistic contradiction;

linguistic felicity becomes stylistic felicity, that is, a rich exploitation of medial and formal stylistic relationships; ideational non-contradiction becomes the absence of contradiction in stylistic expression; and ideational coherence becomes coherence of stylistic outlook, i.e., of the *Weltanschauung* of the style in question. Artistic consistency, in short, can be completely equated with stylistic consistency. I envisaged the possibility of this translation when, earlier in this chapter, I anticipated the necessity of re-defining the generic criteria of truth in more specifically artistic terms if they were to be made applicable to art. It is now evident that the generic criteria of consistency, translated into stylistic terms, *are* the specific artistic criteria of artistic consistency, i.e., of artistic integrity mediated by artistic perfection.

But stylistic integrity cannot, of itself, guarantee artistic truth. It is as possible for a stylistic interpretation of reality to be consistent, and yet false, as it is for a geometry to be consistent, yet inapplicable to the physical world, or for a theology to be consistent, yet fundamentally untrue. Artistic truth, like truth in other universes of discourse, must satisfy the criterion of correspondence as well as the criterion of stylistic consistency. How, then, should the generic criterion of correspondence be re-defined to make it applicable to the artistic enterprise?

The crucial factor which must determine the nature of this re-definition is, as has already been indicated, the artist's distinctive approach to his subject-matter. This approach in no way relieves the artist of the necessity of first-hand scrutiny of empirical data, both factual and normative. His interpretations, like those of other men, must be based on empirical observation and supported by empirical evidence. But this observation must take the form of *artistic* intuitions; and this empirical evidence, to be *artistically* relevant, must condition genuinely *artistic* insight. The generic concept of the availability of relevant empirical evidence may therefore be restated in artistic terms as follows. To possess artistic truth, the expressed content of a work of art must be based on positive artistic insight and on empirical data relevant to artistic interpretation. Availability of artistically relevant evidence is the first and most general condition of correspondence in art.

If we assume the availability of such evidence, (i) the *negative* aspect of the artistic criterion of correspondence is the *avoidance of discrepancy with artistically relevant evidence*, and (ii) its *positive* aspect is the *satisfaction of all artistically available empirical evidence which is artistically relevant and artistically reliable.* To understand the nature of these negative and positive aspects of artistic correspondence we must attempt to establish the precise meaning, within an artistic frame of reference, of the terms "artistically reliable," "artistically relevant," and "artistically available."

(*a*) In defining the *reliability* of artistic observation we must remember that the artist's observations of his subject-matter are determined by his artistic approach to it, that is, by his own cognitive and evaluative interests as an artist. He is not, for the most part, concerned with those aspects of his subject-matter with which the scientist is concerned; but he is concerned with other aspects of it, and these are as "objective" as are its scientific aspects, if by "objective" is meant "coercive, orderly, and, at least potentially, public." He exhibits this concern in his continual efforts honestly to discover and appraise these characteristics of his subject-matter; and the more sensitive his artistic conscience, the more anxious he is to do justice to them. But just as the scientist can test the accuracy of his own observations only by their immediate clarity and distinctness, so the artist can test the reliability of his own observations and decide whether he has done justice to his subject-matter only by an appeal to the test of observational clarity and distinctness. A single observation may suffice to give him assurance; if it does not suffice, he must repeat his observation. In either case, the appeal must be to the self-evident clarity of immediate intuition, and when this test is satisfied, the artist is as sure as a man can be who relies only on his own experience that he has accurately observed those characteristics of his subject-matter which he, as an artist, was concerned to discover.

We, in turn, can verify the reliability of his observations only by observing the same or a generically similar subject-matter from the artist's approach, as this approach is indicated by the work of art in question and by other works of art of the same artist. If an artist's approach to reality is so idiosyncratic that no one else can learn to approach it in the same way, his work must, by definition, remain unintelligible, and his observations wholly unverifiable. But the works of art whose truth we are here considering do not belong to this class. These works are intelligible because their authors' several approaches to reality, though highly individual and original, *are* shareable by all who have the requisite re-creative capacity.

That this is the case will be substantiated by every sensitive critic. He knows from his own experience that it is possible to be at first completely baffled by a novel artistic approach; then, with patience and effort, to become accustomed to its novelty and to learn to apprehend the artist's subject-matter through the artist's own eyes; and, finally, to find this approach so congenial and so revealing that he is able to apprehend in the artist's own way the same generic subject-matter in other contexts. We can, accordingly, test the accuracy of the artist's empirical observations, as these have been recorded in his art, by learning from his art to see his subject-matter through his eyes and then checking the artist's observations with observations of our own which are relevant to the artist's immediate cognitive interests. Thus, by studying a number of Cézanne landscapes, or even a single landscape of his (Fig. 212), we can become aware of his particular interest in color, in "edges," and in the three-dimensional solidity of physical objects. We can then go directly to nature, either in retrospect or by means of new perceptual observations, and test the accuracy of his recorded observations in terms of Cézanne's own cognitive preoccupation. This is what every sensitive critic does, consciously or unconsciously, if he takes seriously Cézanne's interpretation of natural objects and is not content merely to enjoy the surface pattern of his pictures. And if he tests Cézanne's observations in this manner, the critic cannot but be impressed by the objectivity of Cézanne's vision, or fail to realize that what Cézanne saw we too can see, and that what had significance for him can have significance for us. Accordingly, the ultimate test of the reliability of the artist's recorded observations is a twofold scrutiny, first, of his work as the artistic record of his observations, and second, of the generic or individual subject-matter which he has here interpreted. The critic must ultimately accept as empirically reliable those observations, whether of the work of art or of its generic or individual subject-matter, which are intuitively clear and distinct.

(β) The artistic *relevance* of an empirical datum must, in the first instance, be determined by the artist's generic and individual approach to his subject-matter. Since his generic approach differs from that of the scientist, no strictly scientific criterion of relevance is applicable to art, even when an artist handles some aspects of his subject-matter in a somewhat scientific manner (as, for example, when a painter is intent on achieving accurate perspective). But every artist whose vision is fresh and original will adopt, in addition to the generic artistic approach, one or more individual approaches to his subject-matter; indeed, the truly original artist will never interpret the same subject-matter in exactly the same way in any two compositions. The relevance of an empirical observation must, accordingly, be determined first and foremost by the unique artistic orientation recorded in the individual work of art, secondly, by the artist's characteristic interests during the period in which the work was produced, thirdly, by the more pervasive outlook expressing itself in all his work, and, finally, by the dominant interests of his school, period, and culture.

In this respect the artistic enterprise differs sharply from the scientific. In science, individuality of outlook is a fault which every competent scientist does his best to avoid or eradicate, whereas, in art, the individuality of the artist's approach to his subject-matter is integral to the very nature and value of artistic vision. A work of art is, accordingly, far more self-sufficient than any scientific theory; it is, to a notable degree, a self-contained universe with an autonomy of outlook not to be paralleled in science, since the scientific attitude is in essence impersonal and scientifically objective. Whatever objectivity can be attributed to artistic cognition and expression must certainly not be *identified* with scientific objectivity.

If a specific work of art, or all the products of a single artist, were wholly and immitigably unique, observational relevance would be correspondingly restricted. But, as we have seen, the more significant a work of art, the more universal is its expressed content, i.e., its interpretation of a given subject-matter. An artist is no true artist unless his work reflects his own original outlook; but sheer novelty must never be confused with significant originality. The artist's recorded observations and interpretations are significant for mankind only in proportion as they also reflect the "man in men" and express what other men can verify in their own experience. This means, on the one hand, that the more catholic and universal the artist's basic interests, the greater the field of relevant observations. But it also means that we, as critics, are entitled to regard as relevant to any specific work of art any observations and experiences which would have become applicable to the work in question had the artist explored his subject-matter more profoundly from the point of view which he himself has chosen to adopt in this particular work. For nature is so complex, and its parts are so interrelated, that it is literally inexhaustible from any individual point of view. Accordingly, even though we accept as the immediate frame of reference the individual point of view recorded in the specific work of art, it is always possible, at least theoretically, to bring to bear upon it experiences and observations which, though strictly relevant to it, have been ignored by the artist. And the more universal this frame of reference, the richer the field of potentially relevant empirical observation.

These two conditions of artistically relevant observation, i.e., the factor of individuality and the factor of universality, do not conflict. On the contrary, they are complementary, since the artist's approach is, at least in some degree, both individual and universal, and since his subject-matter, however restricted his individual approach to it may be, is inexhaustible. The only observations which are relevant to a particular work of art are sanctioned by the work's individual frame of reference; but the number and variety of observations relevant to this limited frame of reference are potentially infinite.

(γ) The insights of the artist, like those of the scientist, are conditioned by the *availability* of empirical evidence. It has been pointed out that no human truths are absolute in the sense of being complete and final apprehensions of their subject-matter, but that individual intuitions, in any universe of discourse, may be final and complete *within a limited frame of reference*. This applies to art as well as to science, but to each in a characteristic way.

Scientific theories interlock and condition one another's truth very extensively. Scientific investigation is essentially a cooperative enterprise. Scientists advance like an army along a wide-flung front, each scientist depending on his fellow scientists and promptly adapting to his own use their discoveries and interpretations. Even the greatest scientific genius is, in this sense, a collaborator; however revolutionary his empirical discoveries and theoretical interpretations, the former are essentially conditioned by earlier observations, while the latter are in large measure the crystallization of previous scientific reflection.

The value of art, in contrast, is to a notable degree a function of the individuality of the artist's outlook. Despite his technical and cultural dependence upon his artistic predecessors and contemporaries, his contribution to the sum of artistic insight is, in the nature of the case, far more individual than the contribution of any scientist to the sum of scientific knowledge. It follows (and this is the point to be noticed) that individual artistic intuitions, because of the relatively greater self-containedness of each individual work of art, enjoy a greater finality than do corresponding scientific insights. The best of scientific theories are subject to revision as the best artistic insights are not. A great work of art can be true for all time in a way in which no scientific theory can be eternally true, because, in the work of art, an individual approach to a given subject-matter is not as subject to correction by other individual approaches as is the case in science. Artistic intuitions enjoy a degree of autonomy unrivalled in the scientific enterprise.

But in proportion as the artist gives expression to insights which other men can share, and sets in relief universal aspects of his subject-matter, the more synoptic criterion of coherence must be admitted to be as applicable to art as it is to science. It is of course this type of coherence with which the philosopher is primarily concerned in all his inquiries into the nature of reality as a whole and in his interpretation of the relation of art, science, morality, and religion to one another. The philosophical doctrine of a pluralistic universe originated primarily in protest against a too facile and dogmatic assumption that the universe possesses a particular kind of unity, and that man's apprehensions of it must themselves be related in some particular way. As a safeguard against the slurring of vital distinctions, both with respect to reality itself and to our several generic ways of apprehending it, the pluralistic thesis has great philosophical value. But most philosophers, past and present, have rejected the suggestion that truths apprehended from one point of view can lack *all* relevance to truths apprehended from some other point of view—that scientific truth, for example, stands in no positive relation whatever to the truth of religious insight. As Kant pointed out, man is so constituted that he is satisfied with nothing less than the organization of *all* knowledge into a coherent and organic pattern.

If coherence is defined in this synoptic manner, the truths which achieve expression in art must indeed cohere not only with one another but also with the truths of science and of all other cognitive approaches to the real. In this wider frame of reference, these several insights, if valid, are seen not to contradict but rather to complement one another, each exhibiting aspects of reality which are ignored in other approaches. And from this more inclusive point of view, even the truths of art are seen to be finite truths which necessarily fall short of Truth as the prerogative of absolute omniscience. A work of art may well express an individual intuition which, within its own individual frame of reference, is unaffected by other intuitions of the same or other subjects. But if it is appraised with reference to the synoptic intuition of the philosopher, or judged in historical perspective, its characteristic limitations, both systematic and historical, are at once apparent. Thus artistic truth is, in terms of any ultimate criterion, no more final or absolute than the truths vouchsafed to man in other universes of discourse.

The specific criteria of artistic truth, and their relation to the concepts of style, artistic perfection, and artistic integrity, may be diagrammatically indicated as follows:

- specific criteria of artistic truth
  - artistic (or stylistic) consistency — style
    - linguistic (or stylistic) — artistic perfection
      - correctness
      - felicity
    - ideational (or stylistic) — artistic integrity
      - non-contradiction
      - coherence
  - artistic correspondence
    - avoidance of discrepancy with artistically relevant evidence
    - satisfaction of all artistically available, relevant, and reliable empirical evidence

Space forbids a detailed application of these specific artistic criteria to the several major arts. In discussing artistic correspondence I have referred, by way of illustration, to the art of painting because the differentiae of artistic observation are most easily indicated in this art. But the foregoing analysis is equally applicable to all the arts, since each art has a secondary medium or subject-matter which it interprets in its own characteristic way. Thus, the music critic tests the composer's interpretation of his subject-matter (i.e., man's emotive-conative states) for truth and falsity by comparing it with his own emotive and conative experiences and observations. Similarly, the literary critic must draw on his own experience if he would verify the observations and interpretations of reality and human experience which are recorded in specific literary compositions.

In each of the arts, the artist's empirical observations can be more or less accurate and penetrating, and his interpretations of his subject-matter more or less synoptic and universal, *within* his own individual frame of reference. What distinguishes artistic truth from scientific truth is preeminently this individual frame of reference; but despite this notable difference the artist, like the scientist, can give expression to accurate observations of certain objective characteristics of his subject-matter and can truly interpret these observations in his art. The artist's approach to reality, like the scientist's, is a highly specialized approach. Hence artistic truth, like scientific truth, can be tested only by an application of specific variants of the generic criteria of truth. In both cases, consistency and correspondence must be defined in terms of the distinctive characteristics of the specific cognitive enterprise. No intelligent person would dream of testing a refined scientific hypothesis by means of ordinary untutored sense-perception. To verify a scientific observation we must conform to the requisite technique and bear in mind the specific objective of the experiment or observation in question. And this requires natural aptitude, training, and the adoption of a distinctive observational approach. Why, then, should it be surprising that an analogous aptitude, training, and observational orientation are requisite to the enlightened verification of artistic insight? A layman, untrained in mathematics, is not able to detect an inconsistency in a complicated mathematical argument, and a person unfamiliar with modern scientific theory cannot distinguish clarity from confusion in advanced scientific thinking. Is it surprising, then, that a layman who is unfamiliar with the intra-medial forms and conventions of music, architecture, or any of the other arts, or even a critic who is unfamiliar with the more or less distinctive language of a particular artist, should be unable to judge whether the artist in question is contradicting himself in his work, or whether a specific composition is artistically confused or clear? Witness the proverbially incompetent judgments of the general public, and the bewilderment of even the critics, in the presence of a significant artistic innovation. What is imperatively required is a trained sensitivity to artistic expression in general and, more specifically, an understanding of the specific language used by the artist in the work in question.

The more profound the artist, meanwhile, the more profoundly moral will be his interpretations of human experience. Great art is not moralistic. Its primary function is not to preach or to inculcate specific moral doctrines. But the vision of an artist may confirm and deepen man's moral and spiritual insights. The problem of artistic greatness or spiritual profundity must now be examined.

CHAPTER XXIV

ARTISTIC GREATNESS

WE designate as "great" that art which moves us most profoundly and seems to us to mediate the richest and deepest human insights. Pater's distinction between artistic "goodness" (by which he seems to mean both "perfection" and "truth") and artistic "greatness" (his own term) exemplifies the critic's eventual appeal to a higher norm than that of artistic perfection or even artistic truth. "Good art, but not necessarily great art; the distinction between great art and good art depending immediately, as regards literature at all events, not on its form, but on the matter. . . . It is on the quality of the matter it informs or controls, its compass, its variety, its alliance to great ends, or the depth of the note of revolt, or the largeness of hope in it, that the greatness of literary art depends, as *The Divine Comedy*, *Paradise Lost*, *Les Misérables*, *The English Bible*, are great art. Given the conditions I have tried to explain as constituting good art;—then, if it be devoted further to the increase of men's happiness, to the redemption of the oppressed, or the enlargement of our sympathies with each other, or to such presentment of new or old truth about ourselves and our relation to the world as may ennoble and fortify us in our sojourn here, or immediately, as with Dante, to the glory of God, it will be also great art; if, over and above those qualities I summed up as mind and soul—that colour and mystic perfume, and that reasonable structure, it has something of the soul of humanity in it, and finds its logical, its architectural place, in the great structure of human life."[1]

It is of course possible to identify artistic greatness with mere formal consistency, i.e., artistic perfection considered without reference to expressive intent, or with artistic integrity, i.e., felicitously expressed ideational coherence, or with artistic truth, however

[1] Walter Pater, *Appreciations* (London: Macmillan, 1895), pp. 35-6. The difference between a rtistic perfection and greatness was recognized by Longinus when he distinguished between "flawlessness" (or "faultlessness") and "sublimity," though his concept of "flawlessness" emphasizes the negative aspects (i.e., formal correctness and ideational non-contradiction) of what I have called artistic perfection and integrity, while his concept of "sublimity" is weighted with more theological overtones than is the concept of greatness here defended.

trivial. If the greatness of art is defined in any of these ways, it is not a new artistic dimension but a synonym for one of the critical categories already considered. But there is ample evidence that sensitive laymen as well as critics of art and literature mean by artistic greatness something other than mere formal beauty, artistic integrity, or artistic truth. And their interpretation of art is, I believe, defensible. Just as a work of art may manifest perfection and integrity without giving a truthful interpretation of its subject-matter, so the insight expressed in a work of art may be truthful but trivial, correct so far as it goes but devoid of genuine greatness. What, then, are the *differentiae* of artistic greatness?

This problem, like the problem of artistic truth, could be dealt with adequately only in a comprehensive philosophical inquiry. As ordinary mortals, we are continually evaluating our experiences and their objects by reference to some ultimate standard, however vague this reference may be, however inarticulate our sense of this ultimate norm. The artist reinterprets man's experiences in terms of his own scale of values and ultimate objectives. The critic, in turn, interprets and appraises specific works of art on the basis of *his* normative reflections and beliefs. The task of the philosopher of art, accordingly, is to analyze these three levels of evaluation in their relation to one another and within the framework of a still more inclusive philosophy of value. But since philosophers of different persuasions still interpret values and the act of appraisal in diverse ways, each philosopher of art must formulate and defend his own philosophy of value and deal with the specific problem of artistic greatness in the light of the basic normative principles which he accepts. All that I can attempt to do in this chapter, however, is to consider briefly two generic factors which determine all human evaluation, and to examine the concept of artistic greatness in the light of these factors.

1. Factors determining artistic greatness

Our evaluations are conditioned partly by the emotional intensity and vividness of particular experiences, and partly by a sense of their larger implications. The less reflective the agent, the more will his evaluations be determined by the poignancy of each immediate experience; the more thoughtful he is, the more will he tend to evaluate his experiences and their objects in a wider frame of reference, i.e., in terms of their more ultimate import for himself and his fellow men. *Both* emotion and reflection are requisite to *adequate* evaluation. One of H. G. Wells' fantastic creatures from Mars, endowed with reason but devoid of all capacity for emotive response, could attach no greater significance to one experience than to another, and would regard all objects and events as equally devoid of import. A pure sentimentalist, in contrast, indulges in unrestrained emotional response to the most inconsequential occurrence and fails to sense the import of occurrences to which more thoughtful individuals rightly attach great significance.

Emotion and reflection are thus the two chief subjective[2] factors in human evaluation. Each individual's synoptic sense of value, in turn, may be entitled his "philosophy of life." This philosophy of life is normally not the product of professional philosophical inquiry. "The philosophy which is so important in each of us," says William James, "is not a technical matter; it is our more or less dumb sense of what life honestly and deeply means. It is only partly got from books; it is our individual way of just seeing and feeling the total push and pressure of the cosmos."[3] So conceived, a man's philosophy of life expresses itself in each of his particular evaluations; and it is the art lover's and art critic's philosophy of life which, in *some* sense, determines his appraisal of the greatness of a work of art. A work of art will be judged to possess profundity or greatness in proportion as it seems to the observer (his philosophy of life being what it is) to mediate a profound experience by expressing, *via* artistic form, some profound interpretation of its subject-matter.

The profundity of any artistic interpretation and evaluation must, in turn, be regarded as a function of the "depth" and the "breadth" we predicate of the artist's normative insight.[4] The depth

[2] I am prepared to defend the thesis that values are objective, since they present themselves to us coercively, in an orderly manner, and publicly, i.e., to all who possess the requisite normative sensitivity. According to this view, evaluation is an act not of invention or creation but of genuine discovery. Values are not mere hypostatizations, mere projections of our own emotions and feelings; they actually characterize objects of awareness, and our evaluations are correct or incorrect according as we ascribe or fail to ascribe to such objects the values which they actually possess. But since this objectivistic interpretation of value would be repudiated by many philosophers today, whereas no one would deny the fact that men do evaluate their own experiences and the objects to which they are directed, I have chosen to discuss the critical judgment of artistic greatness merely in terms of human evaluation.

[3] *Pragmatism* (New York: Longmans Green, 1922), p. 4.

[4] The terms "profound" and "profundity" are used throughout as synonyms for "great" and "greatness," where "greatness" is conceived of as a function of both

of his insight is proportionate to the adequacy with which he comprehends the nature and human import of any subject-matter, however limited, from any specific point of view, however restricted. Its breadth is proportionate to the scope of the subject-matter surveyed and to the catholicity of the agent's normative outlook. The greatness of a work of art can be determined only by reference to *both* of these complementary criteria.

A work of art is judged to be great, according to the criterion of depth, if it expresses a searching examination of, and an intense normative response to, the nature and immediate human import of those aspects of his subject-matter which the artist has chosen to explore from some particular point of view, irrespective of the scope of this subject-matter or the breadth of the artist's approach to it. The subject-matter of a still-life, as compared with that of a landscape or of a composition whose interest centers in human beings, is certainly restricted in scope. Yet some of the still-lifes of painters as different as Chardin, Cézanne, and Matisse (Figs. 280, 284, 282) may all be said to satisfy the criterion of depth because each painter has, from his own point of view, interpreted certain aspects of this restricted subject-matter with penetrating insight and imaginative intensity. The subject-matter of the work of Félicien Rops, in contrast, is more extensive in scope, but his approach to it is highly restricted by his predominant erotic interest; even according to very low standards of human decency his philosophy of life is morally perverse and spiritually diabolic. Yet there is nothing trivial or superficial in his art, for it expresses an intense imaginative understanding of human depravity in some of its most extreme forms. It differs in kind from cheap and tawdry pornography. Rops plumbs the very depths of human bestiality, and his specific evaluations are as authentic of their kind as are those of Milton's Satan crying, "Evil, be thou my good!" The imaginative power with which this aspect of human nature is apprehended and depicted makes these works genuinely great, if greatness be defined solely in terms of depth or penetrating insight.

But when the work of Rops is appraised in terms of a more comprehensive philosophy of life, the perversity of his moral outlook and of his transvaluation of man's spiritual values becomes at once apparent. And when the most inspired still-life or landscape without hu-

"depth" *and* "breadth." That is, "profundity" is *not* restricted to mere "depth" of insight.

man figures is compared with an equally inspired figure composition or landscape with figures, the intrinsic limitations of certain types of subject-matter cannot be denied. Ultimate greatness, in short, must be measured not only in terms of depth but also of breadth; and the breadth requisite to greatness in art, as in other fields, is a function both of the subject-matter dealt with and of the manner in which it is interpreted. If a work of art is to be truly great, its subject-matter must give the artist an opportunity to express his more comprehensive philosophy of life; and his interpretation of it must be commensurate to its scope and universal human import. The greatest artists in every medium have been those who have interpreted a significant subject-matter in a significant way. They have chosen a subject-matter which lends itself to the richest normative exploitation, and they have exhibited in their interpretation of it an unusual catholicity of outlook and degree of normative sensitivity. Witness the great symphonies and operas, the great basilicas and cathedrals, the sculptural and pictorial masterpieces, and the great epics, tragedies, and novels of our Western culture.

We must be careful not to misinterpret the contribution of the subject-matter to artistic greatness. It is obvious that subject-matter cannot *of itself* make a work of art either trivial or profound: the factor of artistic interpretation is of crucial importance. It takes a Chardin to paint a jug, a pipe, and a loaf of bread in such a way as to suggest the rich contributions which such homely objects make to our daily life and happiness. And mere complexity of subject-matter cannot make art great. A Maillol can express greater profundity of insight in a marble torso than a lesser artist could in an ambitious sculptural group. A love sonnet may be more profound than an epic, a song than a symphony, not only in depth but in breadth of expressed content. We might even go so far as to say that, *theoretically*, an artist with the requisite insight and imagination should be able to select *any* subject-matter, however restricted, and so interpret its relations to a larger whole as to endow it with profound human significance.[5] But in *actual practice* those subjects which normally possess deep significance for us lend themselves more easily to a profound artistic interpretation than do those subjects

[5] "One impulse from a vernal wood
May teach you more of man,
Of moral evil and of good,
Than all the sages can."—Wordsworth, *The Tables Turned.*

which we normally judge to be petty and trivial. It is not accidental that the works of art whose greatness is universally acknowledged are invariably interpretations of man's most poignant social and religious experiences and of the objects and events to which men generally tend to ascribe ultimate value.

We must also be careful not to confuse the breadth or catholicity of interpretative outlook requisite to the production of great art either with superficiality or with an incoherent and undigested eclecticism. Depth of insight and intensity of emotional response are necessary conditions of significant breadth, since a whole can never be adequately apprehended or evaluated save in and through an adequate normative apprehension of its parts. Nor will it suffice vividly to apprehend the parts in isolation from one another. Greatness of vision involves a coherent and synthetic intuition of the whole. Intuitions of a limited subject-matter from a restricted point of view do possess a genuine validity not only within this narrower frame of reference but even in a wider perspective, since a more synoptic intuition must take such narrower intuitions into account. Yet a persistent attempt to understand the nature and to determine the significance of anything, however trivial, is bound to lead to the investigation of its relations to other things. For since the objects of our several experiences are themselves interrelated in numerous ways, and since the values we assign to them (or discover in them) interpenetrate and condition one another, nothing can be apprehended or evaluated with real adequacy save in its relation to other things and in terms of a more comprehensive philosophy of life. Thus, depth of analytical and normative insight tends inevitably towards breadth of insight and evaluation; the more deeply we study anything, the more we are impelled to widen the scope of our inquiry. Narrower intuitions always tend to generate more inclusive intuitions.[6]

Artistic greatness, accordingly, is essentially a function of normative interpretation, but also, in actuality, of subject-matter. How-

[6] It might be argued *a priori* that breadth of outlook without depth of individual insight should be appraised as highly as depth without breadth. But though sheer breadth of interest may be impressive as a manifestation of human vitality, of itself it certainly approximates less closely to true greatness than does its opposite counterpart. For genuine depth of insight, even though restricted, possesses positive value and dignity, whereas mere scope or catholicity of interest can never compensate for shallowness and superficiality. These complementary deficiencies are by no means on a par.

ever rich and suggestive may be a painter's interpretation of a still-life, or a musician's interpretation of a light and carefree mood, or an architect's handling of some spiritually unimportant activity and attitude, the resultant work of art will hardly merit classification among man's greatest masterpieces. And however penetrating may be an artist's comprehension of one restricted aspect of a complex subject-matter, his interpretation of it must fall short of genuine profundity because of the limitation of his approach and the inadequacy of his spiritual outlook. We can do full justice to the positive intuitions of a Rops and still feel compelled to admit that Rops, unlike Bosch among the painters or Dante and Milton among the poets, has failed to express in his art a realization that man's erotic impulse is only one aspect of his nature, and that this impulse, given free rein, leads to a diabolical perversion of the human will. What Rops asserts is, within limits, true and significant. But he himself fails adequately to interpret this truth in terms of other truths, or to appraise erotic pleasures in terms of a more catholic and inclusive scale of values.

The chief factors which, functioning as variables, determine artistic greatness may accordingly be indicated schematically as follows:

artistic greatness—*a function of* (profundity)	"depth"—*a function of*	imaginative penetration intensity of normative response
	and	
	"breadth"—*a function of*	scope of subject-matter integrated catholicity of outlook

2. *The critical appraisal of artistic greatness*

Just as the greatness of a work of art ultimately depends upon the profundity of the artist's normative insight, and just as this insight is profound or superficial depending upon the artist's own philosophy of life, so the critic's response to artistic greatness must likewise be conditioned by his ability imaginatively to apprehend artistic greatness when he sees it, and this capacity must be regarded as a function of his own philosophy of life and scale of values. To be competent at this critical level, the critic must have two distinguishable but complementary capacities: first, the ability to share imaginatively in many different types of experience and to comprehend diverse interpretations and evaluations of these experiences; and second, the ability to evaluate the profundity or triviality of these experiences and their normative interpretations. That is, he must be able to apprehend with sympathetic insight both the trivial and the profound, and he must also be able to distinguish triviality from profundity. Such discrimination, in turn, necessarily involves an appeal to some standard or scale of values other than those of mere formal excellence, artistic perfection, or artistic integrity. As T. S. Eliot has expressed it, with specific reference to literature, "The 'greatness' of literature cannot be determined solely by literary standards; though we must remember that whether it is literature or not can be determined only by literary standards."[7] But where can the critic find such a standard save in his own sense of profundity, his sense of "what life honestly and deeply means," his feeling of the "total push and pressure of the cosmos"?

This general account of the critic's final estimate of artistic greatness is, I believe, correct. But it leaves unanswered three perplexing questions. (i) If the critic's appraisal of artistic greatness necessarily involves an appeal to some non-artistic standard, is such an evaluation part of the critical enterprise, or does the critic who attempts to evaluate art in these terms exceed his prerogative as a critic of fine art or literature? (ii) If, in judging artistic greatness, the critic must ultimately fall back upon his own philosophy of life, can any degree of objectivity be claimed for such a judgment? Is not such an appraisal necessarily as subjective as is the individual critic's private philosophy of life? (iii) Finally, does not the appraisal of works of art in terms of greatness necessitate invidious comparisons between masterpieces which express, in the manner of art, different philosophical attitudes? Until these questions are answered, the claim that artistic greatness is a legitimate and necessary norm of criticism cannot be said to have been satisfactorily validated. Let us deal with them in turn, and in the reverse order.

The difficulty which the third question raises can be expressed more concretely by imagining a critic under the necessity of deciding whether the *Avignon Pietà* or a Cézanne landscape (Figs. 211, 212) is the greater picture. Let us assume that the two pictures are equal in formal beauty, artistic perfection, and artistic integrity. Let us also assume that each picture expresses a truthful interpre-

[7] *Essays Ancient and Modern* (London: Faber and Faber), p. 93.

tation of its particular subject-matter—the *Pietà*, of the Christian Incarnation; the landscape, of a hilly countryside. And let us finally assume, for the sake of the argument, that the two paintings express, with equal artistic eloquence, two radically different philosophies of life—the *Pietà*, the Christian interpretation of man's relation to Deity; the landscape, a naturalistic interpretation of man's place in the cosmos.[8] How, then, is the critic to choose between these pictures? As I have described them, they differ only in ultimate philosophical outlook. But, according to the foregoing criterion of greatness, this difference would appear to necessitate an absolute choice. For from a consistently naturalistic point of view, the Christian interpretation of reality is false, since God is judged to be merely a projection and hypostatization of human desire; whereas, from the Christian point of view, the naturalistic interpretation of human life and its cosmic setting is either false or utterly inadequate. And the critic himself cannot be both a naturalist and a Christian, though he may be neither. Is it accordingly his duty *as a critic* to award the palm to the *Pietà*, if he be a Christian; to the landscape, if he be a naturalist; and, if he be neither, to neither of these pictures but to some third picture which satisfies all the other criteria of artistic merit and, in addition, expresses the particular philosophy of life which he himself happens to prefer? Would not any one of these three judgments commit the critic to a kind of comparison which he must find peculiarly odious? Can masterpieces like this be ranked and ordered according to any scale of values, objective or subjective, critical or non-critical?

A passage in Shelley's *Defence of Poetry* suggests by implication the way in which this question should be answered. Shelley is here discussing the function of poetry and the truly poetic attitude. "A man, to be greatly good, must imagine intensely and comprehensively; he must put himself in the place of another and of many others; the pains and pleasures of his species must become his own. The great instrument of moral good is the imagination; and poetry administers to the effect by acting upon the cause. Poetry enlarges the circumference of the imagination by replenishing it with thoughts of ever new delight, which have the power of attracting and assimilating to their own nature all other thoughts, and which

[8] If the reader finds it difficult to accept this interpretation of these pictures, he is invited to substitute examples which seem to him to conform better to the requirements of the argument, e.g., the epics of Dante and Lucretius.

form new intervals and interstices whose void for ever craves fresh food. Poetry strengthens the faculty which is the organ of the moral nature of man, in the same manner as exercise strengthens a limb. A poet therefore would do ill to embody his own conceptions of right and wrong, which are usually those of his place and time, in his poetical creations, which participate in neither. By this assumption of the inferior office of interpreting the effect, in which perhaps after all he might acquit himself but imperfectly, he would resign a glory in a participation in the cause. There was little danger that Homer, or any of the eternal poets, should have so far misunderstood themselves as to have abdicated this throne of their widest dominion. Those in whom the poetical faculty, though great, is less intense, as Euripides, Lucan, Tasso, Spenser, have frequently affected a moral aim, and the effect of their poetry is diminished in exact proportion to the degree in which they compel us to advert to this purpose."[9]

This passage, taken out of its context, might be interpreted to mean that the poet should refrain from giving artistic expression to his own deepest convictions. But such an interpretation would be a radical misconception of Shelley's actual belief as evidenced in other portions of this essay and in his own poetry. What he is urging is not silence on questions of supreme human import, else he could never have proclaimed the greatness of Milton. Nor is he advocating a poetic restriction to mere spiritual generalities. He was perfectly well aware that the poet must express his philosophy of life, if he is to speak with poetic eloquence, in specific attitudes to concrete situations, however imaginatively conceived these situations may be. What Shelley is here primarily eulogizing is the imagination, "the organ of the moral nature of man." And those whom he is attacking are the poets who "have frequently affected a moral aim," because "the effect of their poetry is diminished in exact proportion to the degree in which they compel us to advert to this purpose." In short, he is censuring the adoption by the artist of a *moralistic* attitude, and he is extolling that type of poetry which strengthens the faculty of the imagination by "replenishing it with thoughts of ever new delight, which have the power of attracting and assimilating their own nature to all other thoughts, and which form new intervals and new interstices whose void ever craves fresh food." He is thus conceiving

[9] *A Defence of Poetry*, World's Classics (London: Oxford University Press, 1932), pp. 132-3.

of artistic greatness not as the expression of any *specific* philosophy of life or scale of values but merely in terms of the depth and breadth of the artist's imaginative power and spiritual insight.

If this account of the true function of the poet (and so, by implication, of the artist in any medium) is correct, the true function of the critic must be described in analogous terms. Just as the artist is ill-advised to insist upon "his own conceptions of right and wrong, which are usually those of his place and time," at the expense of more universal truths, so the critic is ill-advised to insist on the correctness of his own individual philosophy of life, or to appraise the greatness of art solely by reference to any specific moralistic criterion. The moralistic attitude, like its religious and philosophical variants, is as illegitimate in criticism as it is in artistic creation. All that a critic has a right to demand of an artist is that he deal with *some* significant subject in *some* significant way, that is, that he exhibit in his art a genuine breadth of outlook and, simultaneously, a genuine depth of understanding which will reveal specific characteristics and values which had previously passed unnoticed. He can require of an artist merely that he explore *some* major phase of reality and human experience from *some* relatively inclusive point of view, and that this exploration be pursued with real imaginative power. And since there is no reason why many artists might not achieve this goal, and why many works of art might not possess artistic greatness so defined, the critic who restricts himself to this criterion need not make invidious comparisons between the world's great masterpieces.

Yet the critic cannot apply this criterion of imaginative depth and breadth without an appeal to what I have entitled a philosophy of life. For no critic can *recognize* genuine depth of artistic insight unless he has had profound experiences of his own, nor can he *appreciate* significant breadth of outlook unless his own outlook is catholic and integrated. If great art is the product of a great soul, only a critic of spiritual stature can hope to recognize and appreciate artistic greatness when he sees it. To the trivial all things are trivial. A critic with limited powers of observation, a weak imagination, and a restricted scale of values, must remain blind to artistic greatness and incapable of distinguishing artistic profundity from artistic triviality.

This does *not* mean that he should appraise the greatness of a work of art by reference to his own *specific* scale of values or pattern of beliefs. Such a procedure would involve the adoption of that moralistic attitude which Shelley rightly condemns. Yet unless he has *some* specific scale of values and *some* specific philosophy of life, he cannot hope really to comprehend *any* scale of values different from his own. And unless he himself has an integrated philosophy of life, based on deep insights and real breadth of vision, he cannot enter imaginatively into the expressed philosophy of life of the great artist. The specific doctrines to which he individually subscribes are not directly relevant to his appraisal of artistic greatness. All that is immediately relevant is their authenticity, their depth and scope. But his own spiritual outlook can have neither depth nor scope nor authenticity unless it takes some specific form and crystallizes itself in some specific scale of values. In this respect, but only in this respect, the critic's specific philosophy of life *is* relevant to his appraisal of greatness in art. Unless he believes in some scale of values he must remain blind to the nature and significance of scales of value to which he himself cannot subscribe; if his own philosophy of life is shoddy and unintegrated, he cannot hope to recognize the expression in art of any type of spiritual integrity in others. Yet, to repeat, it is only the depth and catholicity of his individual insights and outlook that are *immediately* relevant to his critical appraisal.[10]

But is it possible to reconcile this solution of our problem with the apparent dependence of artistic greatness upon artistic truth? It would seem obvious that an interpretation of reality which is believed to be false, either factually or normatively, can never be accepted as profound. Surely no interpretation and evaluation can be regarded as great if it is based upon what is judged by the critic to be a radical misconception of the object evaluated, or if the artist's specific scale of values is believed to be fundamentally unsound. Artistic truth would thus seem to be a necessary though not a sufficient condition of artistic greatness. Furthermore, my definition of artistic greatness as a function of depth and breadth of *insight* would itself seem to preclude the possibility of a critic's accepting as great any work of art expressing an interpretation of reality which he believes to be either factually or normatively deficient. But if truth is integral to artistic greatness, how can the critic refrain from appeal-

[10] It goes without saying that an artist may achieve greatness in his art without expressing it in his daily life. Witness Oscar Wilde's inability to make his conduct conform to the insight so eloquently expressed in the *Ballad of Reading Gaol*. Similarly, a critic's daily life need not adequately exhibit his deepest spiritual insights. We are here discussing not moral conduct but normative apprehension.

ing, in any appraisal of artistic greatness, to his own individual interpretation of reality and his own scale of values? More specifically, how can a Christian critic assert the greatness of a pagan masterpiece, or a naturalistically-minded critic, the greatness of a work of art which expresses a Christian philosophy of life? In short, are we not compelled, after all, either (i) to redefine artistic greatness so as to divorce it from truth, or (ii) to require the critic to indulge in that type of appraisal, already described, which he would certainly regard as invidious and odious, or (iii) to abandon the category of artistic greatness altogether?

Each of these three alternatives does violence to the critical enterprise. Most critics could not accept a radical divorce of truth and greatness in art with a good conscience. All sensitive critics would find the second alternative so distasteful that they would presumably decline to put it into effect. The third alternative is undoubtedly the most congenial to the modern temper, for the typical modern man has in large measure lost his sense of objective values, and is either reconciled to the subjectivity of norms or else prepared to champion its cause with enthusiasm. Yet even the modern critic, however explicitly he disavows the desire and the right to indulge in the appraisal of artistic greatness, continues to evaluate specific works of art, ancient and modern, in these terms, and there can be no doubt that in the great critical tradition critics have persistently sought to discover and interpret artistic greatness in the several artistic media. Before abandoning the category of greatness, therefore, let us attempt to redefine its relation to truth in such a way as to preserve its critical integrity.

The clue to this definition is to be found in the finitude of human knowledge. Were man capable of omniscience, were it possible for a critic to discover or invent a philosophy of life which was absolutely true and final, that is, perfectly correct in every detail and ideally compendious in scope, all works of art created by finite artists would have to be declared radically deficient in expressed insight and normative perspective. If an absolute standard of truth and value were available, and if the critic could appraise the truth and greatness of art according to this standard, it might be that no human work of art could ever be judged great.

But the philosopher should be the first to insist that no such standard is available. The wisest philosophers have failed, and will continue to fail, to apprehend absolute Truth or ultimate Value save as ideal limits of experience and inquiry. The critic can therefore certainly not be expected to possess perfect wisdom. What he is actually faced with is, on the one hand, a host of individual philosophies of life, as numerous and various as the sum and diversity of thoughtful individuals past and present, and, on the other hand, certain generic patterns of insight and belief which have been achieved cooperatively by the greatest minds through the ages, and to which multitudes of people have subscribed with varying degrees of comprehension. The mere fact that these more generic philosophies of life have stood the test of time suggests that each expresses some genuine insight and satisfies some basic interest and need of human nature. Each must be believed to reflect some relatively comprehensive, though partial and finite, normative intuitions. What the great artists have invariably done is to draw richly on one or other of these traditional philosophies of life, adding to them new insights which other men could share, and giving them new interpretations which others could find enlightening and ennobling. It is just this capacity to achieve *significant* originality, that is, freshness of outlook in essential harmony with some great tradition regarded as a heritage of universal[11] insights, which has made the world's greatest artists great according to finite standards of greatness. Their art is great not because it expresses omniscience, or because it is merely idiosyncratic, but, in the language of Pater, because of "its compass, its variety, its alliance to great ends, or the depth of the note of revolt, or the largeness of hope in it." Great art "finds its logical, its architectural place, in the great structure of human life" because "it has something of the soul of humanity in it."

Now *both* the *Avignon Pietà* and a Cézanne landscape (Figs. 211, 212), to revert to our earlier illustration, satisfy this criterion of greatness. Each in its own way manifests significant originality. Each gives expression to one of the persistent philosophies of life, yet not slavishly, but with genuine freshness of artistic interpretation. Neither proclaims the whole truth regarding reality or human experience; but each gives eloquent expression to certain universal insights which many thoughtful men have shared and which no one

[11] That is, expressive of what is *basic* in human nature and in man's environment, and, consequently, *apprehensible* by all who have the requisite sensitivity and acumen; but *not* "universal" in the sense of being *actually* apprehended as basic by all men. The deepest insights of Plato and Spinoza, Homer and Dante, Bach and Michelangelo, exemplify the type of universality here intended. Cf., above, p. 244, n. 2.

with imaginative sensitivity can afford to ignore. The *Pietà* expresses a belief which sincere Christians have cherished and continue to cherish with varying degrees of comprehension. The landscape expresses man's abiding sense of the impersonality of nature—a sense which has profoundly influenced human thought and behavior. Both paintings therefore express what many thoughtful men and women have regarded, and will continue to regard, as true insights into some major aspect of reality, and as valid evaluations from some relatively inclusive point of view. If either interpretation is accepted as all-inclusive, absolute, and final, the other must be condemned as false: if either painting is judged to be absolutely great, all other paintings must be judged to be relatively trivial or perverse. But if we exorcise this "Demon of the Absolute"[12] and approach both paintings with human understanding and catholicity of outlook, we shall be able to admit that each expresses certain deep-seated human beliefs and that each in its own way is genuinely great according to finite human standards.

We can profitably push this analysis one step further. The judgment of greatness is ultimately a function of evaluation, and evaluation is the explicit expression of a normative attitude—of man's "more or less dumb sense of what life honestly and deeply means," i.e., of his basic philosophy of life. No two individuals maintain identical attitudes; but there are certain generic attitudes which reappear again and again in human history. Man's normative attitudes, in turn, are partly conditioned by his endlessly varied experiences and by his varied interpretations of these experiences. But though no two individuals have identical experiences or interpret the objects of these experiences in identical ways, men do share certain basic types of experience and do accept certain generic patterns of interpretation. Now every specific work of art offers some specific interpretation, *via* artistic form, of a specific subject-matter, and expresses an individual normative attitude in a specific way. This factor of individuality is absolutely essential, as we have seen, to all artistic achievement. None the less, the greatness of art is primarily a function of the *generic* type of interpretation which underlies any specific interpretation, and of the *generic* attitude of which the specific attitude recorded in any particular work of art is merely a specific variant. It is always the universal shining through the particular

[12] Cf. Paul Elmer More, *The Demon of the Absolute*, New Shelburne Essays, Vol. I (Princeton: Princeton University Press, 1928).

which constitutes the greatness of art. But since human experience takes various generic forms, and since men adopt various generic attitudes, different works of art which express very different generic attitudes and interpretations of the same or different subjects may be judged by the critic to be equally great.

If artistic truth is conceived to condition artistic greatness in this manner, it is possible for the critic to appraise art according to the criterion of greatness without divorcing greatness from truth. He can declare any work of art to be great which, in its own unique and original way, gives expression to some basic human attitude, some synoptic scale of values, some larger interpretation of a significant subject-matter. He can insist that art, to be great, must indeed record a genuine understanding of human experience and its objects, and an evaluation whose limited truth and authenticity he and others can verify by reference to their own experience and to the history of human thought. But he must refrain from transforming *any one* specific pattern of beliefs, factual or normative, into an absolute criterion of objective greatness. His sense of human finitude must save him from such dogmatic presumption. Indeed, his realization that objective reality presents itself differently to different individuals and to different types of men, and that no one individual or group can claim omniscience, will make him welcome the artistic expression of diverse experiences and evaluations, if only they be penetrating and authentic from some relatively inclusive point of view, because such diversity enriches life and promotes our understanding of man and his inexhaustibly complex environment.

This conception of the critical attitude has the merit not only of relieving the critic of the painful necessity of making invidious comparisons between masterpieces which express different philosophies of life, but also of enabling him to achieve some degree of objectivity in his critical appraisals of artistic greatness. For if the critic refrains from making his own specific beliefs on ultimate questions the criterion of greatness in art, and if, instead, his own philosophy of life enters into his critical appraisals only as an adumbration of the generic nature of spiritual depth and breadth, his appraisals of artistic greatness will not merely reflect his personal idiosyncrasies or those of his "time and place." On the contrary, the greater his capacity for imaginative sympathy, the more catholic his outlook, the clearer his historical perspective—in short, the greater his awareness of *pervasive* human attitudes and *recurrent* patterns of belief, the more objective will be his appraisals of artistic greatness. It would be idle to pretend that the critic can achieve complete objectivity at this or at any other level of critical appraisal. Once and for all, he is debarred from omniscience by his human finitude. The only objectivity to which man can attain in *any* universe of discourse is a relative objectivity. But if the critical attitude is conceived of in the manner indicated, it should be possible to attain *as much* objectivity at the critical level of greatness as at the other critical levels.

This brings us, finally, to the question as to whether the critic does or does not exceed his prerogative *as critic* in attempting to estimate the greatness of art. Is it, or is it not, his duty to attempt to assess a work of art in terms of its artistic greatness?

My own answer to this question is implicit in what has gone before. The fact of crucial importance for the critic is the unity of the work of art itself. To do violence to this unity by ignoring as artistically irrelevant any element or dimension which is intrinsic to its nature as a unified whole is, I believe, to commit the unforgivable sin in criticism. And is not the ultimate significance or greatness of a work of art an essential aspect of its intrinsic nature? The artist himself believes that it is. He normally attaches great importance to the significance of his own expressed evaluations of his subject-matter. He is not content with mere formal beauty, artistic perfection, or even artistic truth. He is concerned to express interpretations of his subject-matter which he believes to be both true *and* significant. What right, then, has the critic *as critic* to refuse to take seriously, i.e., critically to appraise, the work's larger significance for mankind? Similarly, the sensitive layman, who constitutes the artist's chief audience, does not hestitate to respond to art as the artist would have him respond to it, that is, to judge it as trivial or profound. What right, then, has the critic, one of whose chief functions it is to help the layman to evaluate the work of art *as a whole*, to refuse his assistance where so frequently his assistance is most needed?

But even if the critic chooses to ignore, at his own risk, the insistent demand of the artist and of the layman that a work of art be judged also in terms of its measure of greatness, by what right can he ignore its intrinsic value as an interpretation of life and reality? For just as every work of art is, as we have seen, true or false irrespective of the artist's sincerity or the observer's insight, so too must a work of art be said to possess greater or less profundity, whatever the artist's ultimate appraisal of his own work and whatever society's reception of it. Its greatness or triviality, as these terms have here been defined, is as objective as is its truth or falsity, and as essential an ingredient of its objective nature. Hence, the critic cannot, I believe, be said to have completed his critical task of analysis and appraisal until, to the best of his ability, he has evaluated the work of art in terms of the norm of artistic greatness.

CONCLUSION

CHAPTER XXV

CONCLUSION

A REASONED defense of the category of artistic greatness, or of any other categories which a philosopher of art may believe to be norms essential to adequate critical appraisal, does not exceed his philosophical prerogative. But his primary task is that of analysis, not of persuasion. My chief concern in the preceding chapters has not been to persuade the critic to acknowledge the validity of these critical categories, or even to subscribe to my formulation of them. It has been rather to demonstrate the complex character of the critical enterprise and to formulate as precisely as possible the presuppositions and criteria of various possible critical approaches to the work of art. Such a formulation, provided it is thorough and consistent, should assist the critic to gauge the scope of his own critical activities and to realize more clearly the nature and implications of that type of critical evaluation to which he himself feels committed. It should also help critics of different persuasions to discover the basic critical principles on which they disagree, and either to arbitrate these differences or else to agree to disagree with greater mutual understanding. I shall conclude the present study with a brief consideration of the way in which the hierarchy of critical norms here described should serve to clarify certain critical perplexities.

I have distinguished five levels of critical appraisal, namely, (i) formal excellence or pure formal beauty, (ii) artistic quality or perfection, (iii) artistic integrity, (iv) artistic truth, and (v) artistic greatness. At each level the work of art is appraised according to a distinctive norm, i.e., with reference to the degree to which it possesses, or lacks, a distinctive property or attribute. The hierarchical relationship of these properties to one another can be interpreted in two complementary ways: first, logically, in terms of condition and conditioned; and second, teleologically, by reference to the essential nature and function of art.

(a) On the one hand, the first property is the necessary but not the sufficient condition of the second, the second of the third, and so on up the scale. Pure formal inexpressive beauty is a necessary, though not a sufficient, condition of artistic perfection (which involves a reference to artistic intent); artistic perfection is a necessary, though not a sufficient, condition of artistic integrity (which is a function not only of formal felicity but of ideational coherence); artistic integrity is similarly related to artistic truth; and truth, in turn, is a necessary, though not a sufficient, condition of artistic greatness.

This does not mean, of course, that a work of art must *completely* satisfy one norm before it can begin to satisfy the norm of the next higher level. It may not possess perfect formal excellence or beauty, and still be artistically expressive; it may be somewhat deficient in artistic integrity, and still express truthful insights, though the deficiency of ideational coherence must lessen the clarity of these expressed insights; and it may be truly great despite certain deficiencies at any or all of the subordinate levels. The precise manner in which these levels condition one another must rather be defined as follows.

(i) *Complete* deficiency at one level precludes all possibility of merit at the next higher level. Thus a work of art wholly devoid of formal excellence or formal beauty could not be at all expressive in an artistic manner, and, *a fortiori*, it would then have to lack all artistic integrity, artistic truth, and artistic greatness. Similarly, a work wholly devoid of truth could not be great; a composition which lacked all artistic integrity or ideational coherence could be neither true nor false; and a work completely devoid of artistic quality would, by definition, lack all expressed content and so all expressed ideational coherence.

(ii) The *greater* the artist's capacity at any of the first four levels, the greater the possibility of notable achievement at the next higher level. Thus, the more adequate the artist's apprehension of the truth, the greater the possibility of his achieving artistic greatness, provided he is also a man of spiritual stature; the greater his capacity for felicitous expression, the more likely is he, if he has a clear head, to achieve artistic integrity; the more sensitive he is to the aesthetic surface, the easier will he find it to express himself with artistic eloquence. In short, however notable the merit of the work of art as a whole, still greater success at any one of the levels would have made *possible* a still greater achievement at the next higher level.

Any property may be said to be more "fundamental" than another property (i) if it is *independent* of the property in question, and (ii) if it also *conditions* this property. (The property x is more "fundamental" than y if x can exist without y and if y cannot exist without x.) If "fundamental" be defined in this way, formal beauty is the most fundamental of the properties here considered, because it can make its appearance independently of all the other properties (as, for example, in a beautiful but inexpressive natural object or manufactured object), and also because it conditions their appearance in the manner already indicated. Artistic perfection is the next most fundamental property, because it is not dependent upon the properties higher in the series but conditions these properties; artistic integrity is more fundamental than artistic truth and greatness; and so on up the scale. The five norms are similarly related to one another, the norm of formal beauty being the most fundamental in the sense of being applicable to an object without reference to the applicability of the other norms, whereas their applicability is conditioned by its relevance to, and satisfaction by, the object in question; and so on up the scale of successive norms.

(b) But this hierarchical relationship can be interpreted not only logically, in terms of the more and less "fundamental," but also teleologically, that is, in terms of relative "importance," where "importance" is defined with reference to the τέλος, end, or function of art as such. So interpreted, the *higher* of any two adjacent properties both of which are accepted as essential to art, the greater is its importance because the greater its contribution to the value of the work of art as a whole. From this point of view, the most "fundamental" property is teleologically the least "important," "importance" here signifying "intrinsic value." Thus, assuming the validity of the five levels here distinguished, and of the order in which they have been arranged, the chief end of art would be artistic greatness, and all the other properties would have to be conceived primarily as means to the attainment of this end. If, on the other hand, the end of art is asserted to be the expression of artistic truth, irrespective of its profundity or significance, the attainment of this end would become the artist's ideal objective, the category of greatness would be discarded as invalid, and formal beauty, artistic perfection, and artistic integrity would all be interpreted primarily as means to this cognitive end. One and the same property could be simultaneously the most "fundamental" and the most "important," as these terms have been defined, only on condition that formal beauty (or some equivalent unconditioned property) was judged to be the only property requisite to synoptic artistic merit.

This teleological interpretation of the relative importance of the artistic properties at the several levels does not, of course, deny the intrinsic value of an artist's achievements at each of the lower levels of any accepted scale, since an artistic property can simultaneously possess both intrinsic and extrinsic value. The teleological subordination of aesthetic surface to the end of artistic expression, for instance, does not in the least preclude the recognition that this surface is in itself an object of intrinsic aesthetic satisfaction. Indeed, each subordinate property can make its appropriate contribution to the work of art as a whole *only* in proportion as it actually possesses an intrinsic artistic value of its own. Only an intrinsically satisfying aesthetic surface can mediate genuine artistic expression; only a genuinely expressive form can mediate an artist's ideational integrity, and so on. Whereas the teleological relationship in other realms frequently involves the subordination of certain constituent factors to the status of *mere* means without any intrinsic value, the teleological relationship in which the properties here in question stand to one another is one in which each property save the highest is *both* means *and* end—a means contributing to a richer and more inclusive achievement, but also itself a source of intrinsic satisfaction No integral artistic property is merely a means to an end, though the highest property in any accepted scale is pure end, since the ideal nature of art is defined in terms of the achievement of this end.

The logical and teleological relation in which the five properties and their respective norms stand in one another can be summarized as follows:

Relation of Logical Dependence	*Levels of Artistic Merit*	*Relation of Teleological Importance*
Going *up* the scale, each level is dependent upon the lower, or more "fundamental," level (or levels); independent of the higher level (or levels) ↑	artistic greatness artistic truth artistic integrity artistic perfection formal beauty	Going *down* the scale, the higher of any two levels is teleologically the more "important," since it constitutes the end to which the lower level is a means ↓

This interpretation of the hierarchical interrelation of the several critical levels and their respective objects and norms provides a basis not only for individual critical appraisals but for the settlement of various types of dispute among critics.

It makes clear that the individual critic must accept as his highest norm of artistic merit the norm appropriate to that level in terms of which he chooses to define the nature of art as such. If he conceives the ideal function of art to be the artistic expression of spiritual profundity, his highest and most "important" norm must be that of artistic greatness. If he defines the function of art in terms of artistic truth, integrity, or perfection, his highest norm must correspond to this definition. If he chooses to reduce all art to inexpressive surface decoration, his only norm of artistic merit will be that of pure formal beauty. The critic must thus decide upon art's ideal nature and function before he can attempt to appraise a specific work of art in terms of any clearly apprehended norm.

But, having once established this highest norm, he must also consider whether a work of art, to satisfy this norm, must also satisfy other subordinate norms, that is, whether it must, in order to possess the supreme *desideratum*, also possess other properties which artistically condition it and one another. If this question be answered in the affirmative, he is then under obligation as a critic to conceive of these properties in their relation to one another as clearly as possible and to formulate the relevant norms with maximum precision. For only thus can he hope to do critical justice to the artistic complexity of a work of art and to recognize its merits at each of the critical levels which seem to him to possess artistic validity.

The normal procedure of the individual critic who wishes to clarify his own principles of artistic evaluation is thus to start at the top of his hierarchical scale and work *down*, though he may reverse this order in his actual critical analysis of a specific work of art. If two or more critics, meanwhile, wish to discuss the merits of a work of art on some intelligible basis, they must first agree on some common scale of values. Their normal procedure will be to attempt first to agree on the most "fundamental" norm, and then work *up* the scale until they have discovered the highest or most "important" norm whose validity both can accept. For example, they might agree that a work of art should possess formal beauty, artistic perfection, and artistic integrity; but one might go further and define the ideal function of art in terms of artistic truth or even artistic greatness, while the other rejected these categories as inapplicable to art. They would then realize that a dispute between them as to the merits of any particular work of art at the two highest levels was idle—here they would simply agree to disagree. But they would still have a common basis for analysis and argument at the three lower levels.

Such a procedure would not, of course, put an end to all critical disputes. For critics will not find it easy to agree on how the several approaches to a work of art should be discriminated, or to formulate in an intelligible manner acceptable to all parties the norm relevant to each of these several approaches or levels. Nor are all critics likely to agree in their determination of the highest norm, that is, in their definition of the ultimate nature and function of art. And even if agreement could be reached on all these basic questions, the diverse aptitudes and backgrounds of different critics must continue to occasion differences of opinion as to the merit of specific works of art at any of the accepted critical levels. It would be foolish, therefore, to exaggerate the beneficial results which such a procedure might be expected to produce.

None the less, a common recognition that art can be appraised at different levels and in terms of different norms should do much to promote a more resolute endeavor to discriminate between these levels and to formulate these norms with maximum precision. And this endeavor should eventually discourage critical disputes in which the disputants unwittingly appeal to different norms or to norms which are inadequately apprehended by either or both of the parties concerned. Finally, a successful application of this procedure should enable critics of different persuasions to clarify the basis of their disagreement and to determine the levels at which argument is possible and agreement conceivable.

The foregoing analysis is offered primarily as a modest contribution to critical methodology. No finality is claimed for the scale of artistic values here defended, or for the formulation of the several norms of artistic appraisal. All I would urge is that some such method of analysis is requisite to an understanding of the basic principles of artistic and literary criticism, and that a wider recognition of these principles is essential to the vitality and integrity of the critical enterprise.

SUPPLEMENTARY ESSAY

BY

ROY DICKINSON WELCH

A DISCUSSION OF THE EXPRESSED CONTENT OF BEETHOVEN'S THIRD SYMPHONY

ROY DICKINSON WELCH

THE selection of one composition in which to observe the musical basis of Professor Greene's analysis and theory is difficult only because there is so great a number of works from among which the choice may be made. One might pick at random in the musical literature of the world with certainty that whatever example came to hand would serve as a satisfactory illustration of many of the points discussed in the foregoing pages of this volume. This fact confirms the validity and universality of Professor Greene's analysis.

In letting our choice of illustration fall upon the Eroica symphony of Beethoven there is no implication that many other works would not have served as well. This symphony illustrates as fully as any that comes to mind the points under discussion in this book, and it is easily available on phonograph records.[1] The present discussion of the work is not primarily addressed to technically trained musicians; it does, however, presume sufficient musical attentiveness and memory to perceive and retain musical ideas (motives, melodies, etc.). Readers with "ear enough to distinguish one tune from another and with wit enough to prefer order to incoherence" should, on turning from these pages to the music, be able to perceive those facts of musical experience which give this essay its excuse for being.

This symphony, like all significant musical compositions, has both a primary and a secondary artistic medium. The distinctive primary medium consists of the tones produced by a symphonic orchestra comprising flute, clarinet, bassoon, horn, trumpet, drums, violins, violas, violoncelli and bass viols. The distinctive secondary medium consists not only of all the subtle emotive-conative states directly evocable by the musical pattern as such, but, in addition, a complex, poetic, non-musical idea that brings the symphony close to the border, if not actually into the territory, of program music. We are

[1] Columbia recording by Felix Weingartner and the Vienna Philharmonic. Victor recording by Koussevitsky and the London Symphony.

dealing then here, first, with sound, its organization into expressive patterns, its manifold phenomena of loud, soft, high, low, simple, complex, and with patterns and forms established through relationships among tones and tonal groups; we are dealing, second, with suggestions of fairly definite emotional states partly dictated by an extra-musical idea in the composer's mind. We may, then, in this work, perceive purely musical materials and processes and also the expression through them of emotions and concepts derived from other than musical experience. We shall attempt to see the interaction of these two media.

Any attempt to define the emotions suggested by music is hazardous. From one point of view, music of any artistic significance is entirely self-contained and of interest apart from all emotional connotations other than those explicitly aroused by the technical skill of the composer or performer.[2] This is but one, and a limited point of view. It ignores, for the sake of distinguishing the purely aesthetic in music, other palpable components of musical experience, especially those emotions aroused by pure music in any musically sensitive person. For to avoid being so affected (if that be wholly possible) requires a consciously directed effort to discriminate one aspect of experience among several which coexist.[3] In certain kinds of study this effort must be made, and by such study a knowledge of the objective facts in any music, the instrumentation, the thematic materials, the forms, etc., may be acquired with little or no reference to coexisting emotional qualities. In the experience of music, however, these facts are but parts of a whole which includes some kind of emotional reaction.

But though the emotions suggested by a given composition may be apparent to most men, it is well-nigh impossible to describe them in words acceptable to all men. The emotion is so perfectly expressed by the music that words seem dilute or irrelevant—"Music begins where speech leaves off."[4] The difficulty of translating musically suggested feeling into words arises, as Mendelssohn pointed out, from the too great definiteness, and *not* from the indefiniteness, with which music expresses the greatest variety of emotions and impulses,

[2] Cf. E. Hanslick, *Vom Musikalish Schönen* (Leipzig: Breitkopf & Härtel, 1918).

[3] Cf. J. Combarieu, *Musique, ses lois et son évolution* (Paris: Flammarion, 1917), Chap. II, for a résumé of Kant, Hegel, Hanslick, Helmholz, etc., on this question.

[4] R. Wagner "Ein glücklicher Abend," *Gesammelte Schriften*, Vol. I, pp. 147-8.

moods and feelings. It is just because music expresses these states with such unexampled subtlety and precision that a verbal restatement of what a musical composition has already expressed is necessarily so inadequate. As Professor Greene has repeatedly urged, no adequate translation of artistic content from one medium to another is ever possible, and when the media are as different as are musical tones and verbal prose, this difficulty is well-nigh insuperable. Hazardous as the attempt is, however, to make a translation of musical impressions into words, it must be risked if a report of the whole experience of music is to be complete in important details. The emotional may not be ignored in such a complete report, even though it can at best be merely suggested and suggested as one man perceives it.

The Eroica had its inception, according to trustworthy records, in Beethoven's esteem for the person and career of Napoleon in the year 1803. The original, extant title-page bears an inscription to Bonaparte. One of the results of Beethoven's bitter disappointment in his hero, when Napoleon became emperor, was the partial erasure of this inscription. The printed editions of 1806 (parts) and of 1820 (score) bear a more general title: "SINFONIA EROICA Composta per festeggiare il Sovvenire di un grand' Uomo." Napoleon has now become simply "un grand' Uomo"; but the fact remains that the composer had in mind, and wished to convey, the emotions aroused by contemplation of an heroic figure.[5]

Yet the Eroica is not as programmatic as are many other compositions. There are no imitations of natural or other sounds (as in Beethoven's Sixth, *Pastorale Symphony*), no evocation of landscape (as in Mendelssohn's *Fingal's Cave*), no delineation of events (as in Berlioz' *Fantastique Symphony*). The Eroica is to be considered program music solely because we know that the emotions it evokes spring from Beethoven's intent to celebrate a specific hero. The work, however, does not depend for its effect upon this particular association. Whether it is essential to a complete understanding of the symphony that one know of its connection with Bonaparte is a debatable question. With or without this knowledge one would hear

[5] Cf. Albert Thayer, *Beethoven*, tr. H. E. Krehbiel (New York: The Beethoven Association, 1921), Vol. II, pp. 26*ff*., or J. Prod'homme, *Les Symphonies de Beethoven* (Paris: Delagrave, 1921), pp. 82*ff*.

the same music, and in any valid estimate of artistic worth it is the music itself and the emotive-conative states immediately evoked by the music that matter. Yet, knowing the title, and knowing that the figure of Napoleon was in Beethoven's mind when he was actually engaged in composition "one hears the work in an essentially different mental attitude from that in which one listens to the Fourth or Fifth or Seventh or any of the nine which has not a title. It is perhaps a confession of weakness, but there can be no doubt that with the majority of hearers anything that assists the imagination to raise some image during the performance of an elaborate piece of music aids them to understand it; and, when that initiative is given by the composer himself, it is a legitimate and very material help to the hearer."[6]

Some critics have been deceived into attempts to make descriptive story-telling music of this symphony, ascribing to its several movements ideas of battles, triumphal processions, a funeral cortège, popular rejoicings. More artistic men have perceived that the work does not lend itself properly to such anecdotal interpretations. Berlioz, for instance, saw "qu'il ne s'agit point ici de batailles ni de marches triomphales, ainsi que beaucoup de gens, trompés par le mutilation du titre, doivent s'y attendre, mais bien de pensées graves et profonds, de mélancoliques souvenirs, de cérémonies imposantes par leur grandeur et leur tristesse en un mot, de l'*oraison funèbre* d'un héros."[7] When we turn to the music itself we become aware that the musical facts, the materials, their treatment, their form suffice to express a pure musical content, however much or little the awareness of a program may induce an "essentially different mental attitude"; the work unaided by such suggestion is seen as one of the great artistic masterpieces in its medium. This, by any criteria of form, expression, details, or conception that may be invoked.

The symphony is in four major movements, the first moderately fast, *allegro con brio*, of large proportions and diverse musical material, the second, a *marcia funèbre*, also a long movement, the chief materials of which are two sombre melodies. The third movement is one of the most arresting of those many scherzi that appear in Beethoven's compositions of this period, energetic, swift-moving, incisive, mys-

[6] Sir George Grove, *Beethoven's Nine Symphonies* (Boston: Ellis, 1884), p. 33.

[7] H. Berlioz, *A travers Chants* (Paris: Calmann-Lèvy, 1862), p. 22.

terious. The last movement, *allegro molto*, is a set of elegiac variations which seem to expand in turn one or another of the moods which the theme suggests. Literalists, among those who attempt to see Napoleon's character and career mirrored in this music, have been perplexed by the appearance of a funeral march as the second movement. It is not easy to go on with the story convincingly after the hero is interred. The clearly perceptible content of these movements are spiritual universals which may be defined as heroic striving, grief, joy, exaltation, or in Wagner's words Action, Tragedy, Serenity, Love. Expressed in these terms the content is apparent to the perceptive ear and mature mind from a hearing of the music unaided by any association with Napoleon's career.

Let us now examine various portions of the work in some detail with special reference to its musical structure and the manner in which this structure expresses this musical content. The first movement suggests grandeur of conception, earnestness of thought and a wide range of ideas. Impulsive and sometimes inconsistent action are also evident and a relentless driving force—not Olympian detachment, nor a serene disregard of struggle, but rather involvement in conflict and a will to overcome. What are the palpable musical facts which express this sense of heroic virtue? The movement is one of the longest of its kind in all symphonic literature. Its 691 measures are divided into four major sections which reveal a monumental plan. The proportions are comparable with the design, large, balanced, embracing great diversity in a unifying framework and through organic relationships. Beethoven has been at pains to mark the major divisions clearly for the experienced and attentive ear. These divisions become as apparent as are the principal outlines of any fine architectural monument. In music large divisions in formal arrangement as well as the smallest unit of pattern must, owing to the nature of the art, be presented in time. What we are aware of at one moment must be set in memory against impressions of the next. We perceive conclusions, new beginnings, contrasts, reprise, only as we remember vaguely or vividly the details and effects of moments as they pass. Analogous qualities are present in the plastic arts but in these arts which are addressed to the eye—commonly a far more completely trained organ than is the ear—formal proportions, treatment of details and even expressive purpose are more readily and accurately perceived by most persons than they are in music.

The effect of this movement, however, depends less upon its length than upon its materials and their treatment. At the outset two sharply arresting chords seize the attention.[8] The auditor is aware that something serious is under way. There follows one of the most famous melodies in all music, a melody made of simple elements (largely the notes of the tonic chord in E flat major). It is stated gravely by the violoncelli accompanied softly by other stringed instruments. This melody is not permitted to run its course conventionally. At its fifth measure it comes out unexpectedly upon a tone (7) which seems to deflect its course and presently "the violins enter upon a high note. The harmony becomes clouded." Without a break a new melodic fragment enters, moving to its conclusion in flowing figures, to be overlapped at its end by a resumption of the original thought (Ex. 1).

Presently it reaches a passage abruptly interrupted by sharp accents and disturbed rhythms (25 to 35). Finally our original tune appears with full effect, eloquently stated by a large part of the orchestra. At this point we have proceeded but 45 measures.

Those who know the Eroica will agree that an understanding of what has happened in these 45 measures is of crucial importance to a perception of the work as a whole. Those who do not know the work should, if they wish to perceive its essential quality, begin by hearing repeatedly these 45 measures. What must be pointed out is, first, the naturalness and grave simplicity of the principal melody here, second, the fact that this melody is not allowed to complete itself before it has been mingled with apparently contradictory elements, third, the fact that the tune is not heard in its most com-

[8] The most profitable way to study this or any other involved music is either to hear it so frequently that all of its details and proportions become intimately familiar or—what amounts to quickening this process of familiar acquaintance—to follow the score while hearing the work. Measure numbers will be given throughout the following analysis of the several movements. Inexpensive editions of the score, published by Eulenberg and Kalmus, may be obtained from any music dealer.

plete form until after conflicting ideas have crossed its path. It is for such reasons as these that one feels a striving and action and energetic thrust in this movement.

In like manner we should take every self-contained passage of the whole symphony. Were we to do so we should see some of the qualities already suggested here, prevalent throughout.

The 45 measures we have examined are immediately followed by several small subjects each dwelt upon at some length. Quoted here in their simplest form, these themes reveal the essentially motival character of Beethoven's thought. Each, it will be seen, is restated many times (Ex. 2, 3, 4).

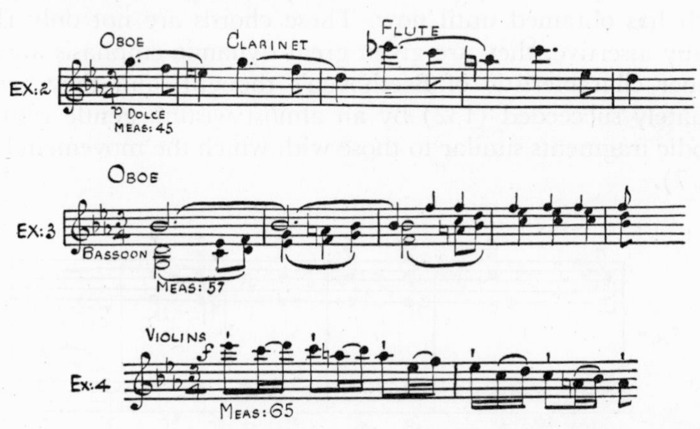

At about half way through the first major division in the movement (83), we come upon the first pause in the course of the work. All to this point has been a continuous and interrelated flow of ideas. Here there is a momentary point of rest, to be followed at once by a new subject (83) which though moving largely in chord structures is nonetheless propulsive in character. It does not pause (Ex. 5).

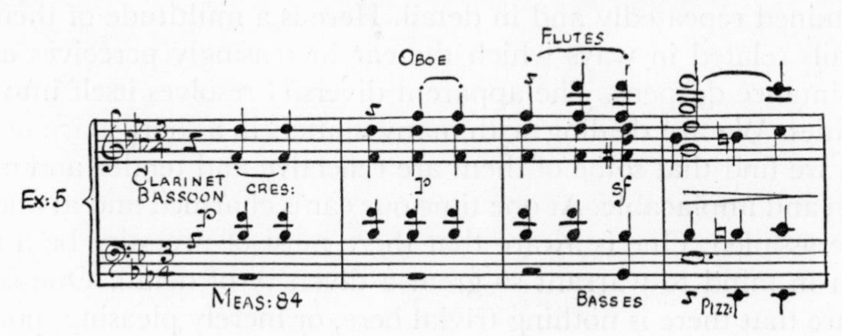

Once this is completed, we find we have gone on (109) to brilliant, assertive, dynamic material not unlike that with which we began, though more emphatic and more energetic (Ex. 6).

And then occurs one of the most singular and disturbing experiences in symphonic literature: reiterated chords (128) thrown off the beat in such a way that they seem to destroy the regularity of movement which has obtained until now. These chords are not only rhythmically assertive, they are given great dynamic emphasis and in a manner characteristic of Beethoven's thought, and they are immediately succeeded (132) by an almost wistful, gentle return to melodic fragments similar to those with which the movement began (Ex. 7).

With this the first major section of the movement (the Exposition) concludes, though that conclusion joins what follows by a resumption of rhythmic movement and melodic thought already familiar.

We should pause here. Like the brief passage of 45 measures over which we stopped above, this major division of the work should be examined repeatedly and in detail. Here is a multitude of thematic details related in ways which the ear increasingly perceives as acquaintance deepens. The apparent diversity resolves itself into similarities. We are dealing with many matters in a short space of time and we find that some of them are reflective and tender and others grim and implacable. At one time our ear is charmed and at another time assailed. One is aware that there must of necessity be a large plan in mind to warrant so great a diversity of detail. One is also aware that there is nothing trivial here, or merely pleasing, nothing histrionic or superficial. It is music of high seriousness and of immense intellectual power. It suggests, as was said earlier, grandeur of conception, earnestness, and complexity of experience.

Following this exposition is a lengthy section of 245 measures in which melodic and rhythmic thought now in mind is "developed." The course of events in this Development is traced below in outline.

(1) A passage, transitional in character, and based upon an inversion of the first melody (Ex. 1. Meas. 152-165).

(2) Now appears a treatment of a previously used motive (Ex. 2) to which is added an upward scale passage (Ex. 8. Meas. 167-178).

(3) Whereupon in the lower stringed instruments the first melody is resumed. In fragments it moves upward along the chromatic scale and is presently combined with another of the motives quoted above (Ex. 4). It is this last motive which supplies some material intervening between the statements of theme 1 and its repetitions (178-220).

(4) Then it gives way to a resumption of the material and treatment described at 2 above (220). A glance backward will show that thus far this development has a plan. A transition is followed by treatment of a certain idea. This idea and treatment return after intervening material. We have consequently here, following the transition, our familiar *A-B-A* arrangement.

(5) The development now embarks upon a new phase, a fugato (236) whose chief subject is derived from a striking passage heard earlier in the work (Ex. 9), to be interrupted by an extended treatment of those wide skips and rhythmic distortions of the basic movement that have earlier been seen (250).

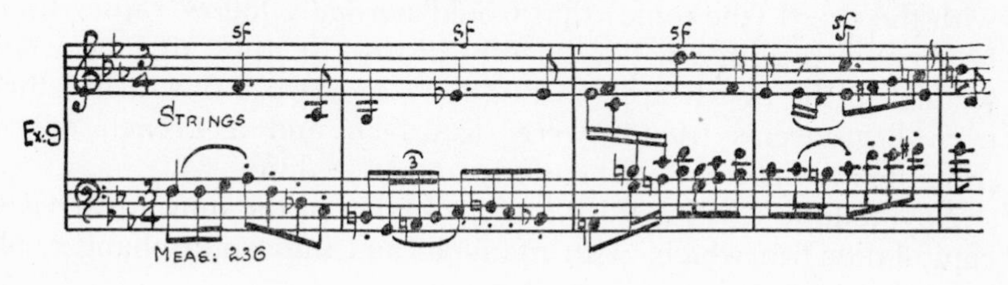

(6) We have reached another marked break in the flow of the movement (280). We draw up on an introductory chord which leads to an entirely new melody, an episode (Ex. 10. Meas. 285), which is repeated after an interruption by a passage returning to the first theme of the movement (300).

(7) At the conclusion of the second statement of this episode we return to the motives of ever widening intervals which characterize the climax of this whole development section, and this in turn dissolves into what is patently at once an end and a new beginning (366).

As we saw in the early part of this Development, so in the latter part, the material and treatment of the episode and its relation to contrasting material constitutes another *A-B-A* arrangement, this one introduced by the fugato with its succeeding climax.

This outline we have traced distinguishes certain major phases in the Development and it indicates also that for all the multiplicity of details and diversity in treatments—the moments of seeming preparation, of discussion, of increasing excitement, and of intense climax—there is a plan firmly ordered in the composer's mind and a plan which is very largely responsible for the effectiveness of what is presented.

Immediately prefacing a new division in the movement there is one of the most singular passages in the entire literature and one without precedent in Beethoven's time. At measures 392 to 398 the violins, tremolo, are announcing a chord prefatory to the resumption of the first theme, but this prefacing chord (the dominant seventh) is not completed before (measure 394) the horn intrudes with the chord (the tonic) that would normally follow rather than be combined with what is steadily heard (Ex. 11), making what seemed to the first hearers of this work so sharp a dissonance that even Beethoven's friends were disturbed, and a French editor prompted to "correct" the score in an early edition.

Now follows (397) a third larger division of the movement (Recapitulation) in which, with manifold and important changes, all

that was stated in the first 152 measures is restated. And at this point (555) when one would expect the movement to close, Beethoven sets forth upon another long passage (133 measures) which, like a second Development, treats in new ways, though with a sense of impending finality, many of the ideas that have already been so voluminously discussed.

Only with the entire movement in mind may one properly agree or quarrel with those words that have been adduced to describe the emotional suggestion of this piece. But whether or not these particular words seem the right ones, those that would seem fitting to any mature and competent judge must certainly suggest the same general range of thought as do the words that have here been used. The sustained and carefully planned proportions of the whole long movement should now be apparent. If not at first hearing, then certainly with familiar acquaintance, the plan of this work will become as apparent to the ear as is the plan, say, of Santa Sofia or Saint Peter's or Versailles, apparent to the visual sense. Comprehended in this large plan there is a great multitude of details and treatments. Moments of solemnity, of exuberant energy, of fierce assertiveness, moments of simple statements, of complex association of ideas, of mysterious implication, succeed one another, intrude one upon another. All this gives rise to a feeling that the movement embraces a complex, diverse, sometimes contradictory life experience. A hearing of the movement as a whole, with an awareness of the character of each detail and the relation of the details to one another, will evoke a sense of an heroic plan and action. There are few conventional startings and stoppings, no rhetorical flourishes. All is thematically vital, all is presented with vigor and conviction, and the whole moves with uninterrupted, propulsive force. These are reasons why the movement is spoken of as suggesting heroic conflict, or in Wagner's word, "Action."

The second movement, *Marcia Funèbre*, is marked *adagio assai*. The tempo here, the rhythm, the several melodies suggest, in Berlioz' words, an elegy. The solemn pace of the opening and concluding passages in C minor, the broken phrases of the melodic line and the appearance of triplet figures which emphasize the accents, give a sense of slow, sometimes halting, sometimes firm footfalls. The melody is heavy with grief.

The middle section (69 to 104) turns to the major mode. The melody here has been described as consolatory. It is certainly more gentle, more lyric, than that of the earlier part of the movement. It is discoursed successively by oboe, flute and bassoon, accompanied by steadily moving figures in the strings. Violent, fortissimo passages (76 to 79) suggest either protest or, perhaps, a reminiscence of military pageantry.

This gives way to a resumption of the original thought in minor (105) as at first and leading shortly to a new melody of upward inflection treated fugally (114 to 154). Here, after a hesitant fragment of the original funeral march, we enter upon a passage bold, grim and suggestive of inner struggle (159 to 181). Shortly afterward we are once more reminded of the mood of the early passages (209*ff.*), and at the end of the movement the original tune, now in broken, detached fragments, renews the sense of grief or tragedy which the opening measures suggested.

This is another of Beethoven's complex movements. But through all its complexity there is a prevailing mood. At moments there may seem to be a feeling of protest and at other times a feeling of military pomp. There can be no mistaking the majestic solemnity of the whole, nor the personal feeling with which it is imbued. Here is no mere spectacle. We are asked less to observe than to feel. This elegy, this funeral oration, is pronounced for a hero we love.[9]

[9] Cf. C. Bellaigue, "L'Héroïsme dans la Musique," *Revue des Deux-Mondes* (Nov. 15, 1892), p. 443: "Ce qui donne à la marche de *l'Héroïque* son incomparable grandeur, c'est d'abord la beauté de l'idée mélodique elle-même; c'est aussi une particularité de rythme: à la première moitié de chaque mesure, c'est l'arrêt, la défaillance qui coupe, de stations et comme de chutes douloureuses, la route menant à l'illustre tombeau. En dépit de quelques traits descriptifs: roulemens de tambours ou décharges de mousqueterie, ici encore l'inspiration de Beethoven est avant tout morale. A cet appareil de deuil, à 'ces tristes représentations,' comme dit Bossuet, il mêle ce qu'y mêlait aussi le grand orateur: la pensée de notre néant et celle du notre éternité. La délicieuse phrase en majeur, cette phrase de consolation, avec son accompagnement perlé, ses pures sonorités de flûte, ouvre le ciel à l'âme du héros. Plus loin, que sort-il de la fugue

A schematic outline of the movement is here given, an outline which like others of its kind comes to life only as it is traced during a hearing of the music. Its chief value will become apparent to those who hear and rehear repeatedly sections of the movement as they are described below until each major division and each detail within those divisions is clear to the ear.

The movement opens in C minor with the sombre melody of the march given to the low registers of the violins accompanied by the other strings (Ex. 12. Meas. 1-8). A short upward scale-wise group of tones in the basses on the strong accents gives the effect of heavy, reluctant tread, and is frequently repeated in the course of the movement.

The oboe repeats the melody, accompanied by clarinet, bassoon, horn, the strings repeating a triplet figure that emphasizes the accents. A second melody (17) now enters (Ex. 13),

followed (27-29) by a brief transition given to the violas without accompaniment and leading to a restatement of the first subject (31). These materials are used throughout the remainder of the first section (68).

The second section begins (69) after a brief transition, with a new theme in C major "a sudden ray of sunlight in a dark sky," given in

éclatante, de la mêlée où retentit un dernier echo des combats? Une voix plaintive, quelques notes désolées seulement, pour nous rappeler que 'rien ne manque dans tous ces honneurs, que celui à qui on les rend.' Puis une immense acclamation s'élève, qui semble 'vouloir porter jusqu'au ciel le magnifique témoignage de notre néant'; mais elle retombe aussitôt. Alors toute cette superbe douleur s'humilie, et le thème revient brisé, trébuchant à chaque note et comme à chaque pierre du lugubre chemin. Quelle fin qu'une pareille fin!"

turn to the oboe, flute, and bassoon. The strings meanwhile have a steady, animated movement (Ex. 14. Meas. 69-76).

Four measures (76-79) of vigorous rhythm, a loud roll on the drums and heavily pulsating chords introduce a second part of the melody (Ex. 15. Meas. 80).

A solemn transition (101-104) leads to a return of the opening melody (105).

The third section (C minor) begins as did the movement, but presently (114) a fugue on a new subject (Ex. 16)

replaces treatment given the original subject in the first section. This is built up to a great climax. Subsiding, the movement turns momentarily (154) to a whispered fragment of theme 1.

The fourth section begins fortissimo (158), the basses sternly reiterating a triplet figure, the horns and trumpet giving a kind of fanfare. Presently (171) the basses begin to "walk in darkness; the violins and flutes echo their vague tones so as to aggravate them tenfold."[10] Portions of the first theme are heard amidst this implacable movement and after a cessation of this driving impulse, there appears a new consolatory subject (213). The end is presaged by statements of fragmentary motives that seem to cry out in pain (231-237) and then the detached motives of the first melody (239-245) are concluded by a sudden loud outburst which dies away to a final lingering C minor chord.

[10] Sir George Grove, *op. cit.*, p. 51.

The third movement, Scherzo, has given story tellers more trouble than all the rest of the symphony. It fits into no logical plan save a musical one. It is manifestly analogous to hundreds of movements that occupy similar places in other symphonies. Wagner contended that "not a single feature of the development of the [Eroica] symphony can be said to have immediate outer connection with the fate of the hero." In no part of the work is this contention more clearly supported than in the Scherzo. The serenity which Wagner found in the movement has at best but dubious connection with any event or personal characteristic in the Napoleonic saga. The musical necessity for a gay movement at some point or points in a symphony had been realized by all who had written symphonies before Beethoven, and with few exceptions has continued to be admitted in the practice of Beethoven's successors. For two generations this lighter movement had been cast in the form of a minuet and trio, a movement that retained more or less the feeling of the stately dance. The Eroica is one of many cyclic works in which Beethoven supplanted the formal, conventional dance movement with a Scherzo. These Scherzi, whether gay or grim, boisterous or ironic, are more original, more personal, more poetic than the more formal, conventional dances they replace. The minuets are as elegant or as patterned as are the dances they spring from. The Beethoven Scherzi are as exuberant or mysterious or boisterous as were certain traits in Beethoven's character.

The Scherzo of the Eroica, by its almost uninterrupted, steady, lively flow, suggests a driving force in action. There is no hesitation here, no stopping to set off one aspect of thought from another. It begins softly, even mysteriously, moves with persistent energy to a brilliant climax, throwing off in its course, fragmentary melodies. It is not light-hearted nor careless. The mood is one of grave gaiety such as might be felt in the presence of matters at once exciting and earnest. Following the first major portion of the movement which is clearly terminated, there is a middle section or trio of which the most prominent features are passages for three horns where, as Sir George Grove remarks, "horns talk like flesh and blood in their own natural accents." Unmistakably solemn in import, these horn passages are followed by hushed dialogue between wood winds and strings that gives the impression of serious reflection on what has been said. The original Scherzo is resumed with many and important changes, and the whole brought to a brilliant conclusion.

A few of the important technical details may assist the hearer to a clear sense of the materials and their uses. The movement begins pianissimo, staccato, and allegro vivace in the strings. Presently the oboe is added and with the first violins completes the initial statement of the melody (Ex. 17. Meas. 1-14).

With this material the movement proceeds, reaching a fortissimo statement employing the whole orchestra (93-115). At this point an unpredictable shift of the accents disturbs for a moment the rhythmic flow (Ex. 18. Meas. 115-117, repeated at 123-126).

Driving upward through the entire scale the original movement and rhythm come out upon a fortissimo climax which is shortly followed by the concluding chords of this first major section. Then follows the Trio (167) of which the passages for the three horns are the most conspicuous features (Ex. 19).

Its hushed, portentous conclusion in held chords is one of the most impressive facts in the score (248-258). The Scherzo is resumed and is repeated substantially as it first stood, save that the distorted rhythms mentioned above now have great prominence; Beethoven changes the meter of the movement for four measures (381-385). The conclusion of the movement, beginning pianissimo on the drums (423) is brought from the barest whisper to a great fortissimo.

The fourth movement is a great set of variations with a brief, arresting introduction. Variations by their very nature are analytical. They deal with aspects of the subject in turn, or they isolate details of that subject for special treatment. A set of variations may do little more than exhibit what a composer has learned from predecessors or text-books of the possible skills traditional in the musician's craft. On the other hand variations may reveal the highest degree of originality and resourcefulness, resulting in a creation only superficially like anything else. While perfectly logical and constrained to be patterned on implications of the subject, they may be filled with unexpected turns of thought and with revelations of latencies in the theme that none but their composer could have imagined. A set of variations may also be a mere string of evolutions upon a theme, the succeeding treatments having little or no organic relation to one another, the whole having no essential aesthetic plan or climax. Another kind of variation, rare to be sure, but found in the works of great masters, is organic. One variation prompts another, or is related in treatment to it. The whole collection reveals a large plan in which repose, climax, balance in proportion are as clear and as logical as are the several ways in which the subject is discussed. Such is the movement in question.

The assertive, brilliant beginning which commands attention by its impetuous movement and its insistent chords forms a brief prologue to a hushed, ominous statement given by all of the strings, pizzicato, a statement which is not a tune but rather the basis of a tune. It is in fact the bass part of melodies which will subsequently follow. An eruptive, assertive fortissimo interrupts this mysterious shadow of a theme. There follow seven variations and a great conclusion. In all but the conclusion the original subject is somewhere present.

There are nearly as many moods suggested in this movement as there are variations or other divisions in it. The first two variations are quietly meditative. The third, with its new, exuberant melody (the main tune of the movement) quickens the pulse with a sense of exultation. A hard-driven fugue follows, which leads to a jubilant restatement of the melody. Then a passage of brilliant military splendor creates the climax toward which all has thus far moved. A new fugue disputes the original bass theme (inverted) through a long variation. And this, after a pause, gives way to a tenderly reflective restatement of the song-like theme, now poco andante.

There then begins a sober, noble epilogue which rarely loses sight of the main subject, turning what was so carefree and exuberant into an earnest, mature experience. A brief suggestion of the brilliant passage with which the movement opened announces the end in which there is triumph and assertive strength. If there be any one mood prevailing in all these changes, it is exultation, a quickening of senses and mind that well may seem to many men, as it did to Wagner, the inner experience of love.

A brief analysis of the score will suffice to indicate the main materials of the movement and its major divisions. The introduction (1-11) is directly followed by a statement in the strings, pizzicato, piano, of the subject which is to appear so frequently later as the bass (Ex. 20. Meas. 12). The vigorous interruptions are found at measures 29 and 37.

Variation I (44-59) adds to the bass theme graceful contrapuntal figures. Variation II (60-75) treats the bass in a similar way save that the figures now are in triplet groups. Variation III (76-107) adds the broad song-like melody which may be taken as the main theme of the work (Ex. 21). An argumentative transition (107-116)

draws up before Variation IV, a double fugue, which, after extensions, gives way to a new statement of the main theme (175-210), now in a new key and with an energetic conclusion. Immediately Variation V introduces the brilliant military tune and forms a climax to the movement (Ex. 22. Meas. 211-257).

A brief transition, using the main subject (258-265) is followed by Variation VI, a second double fugue, using the original bass theme inverted (266-348). This fugue is given a long concluding passage. Then Variation VII (349), poco andante, treats the main theme in a new tempo and a new rhythm. Presently (365) the melodic contour is greatly altered and there follows a long discussion of seemingly new ideas. At measure 431 the introductory passage with which the movement opened is suggested and leads to a brilliant conclusion in which the main theme is rarely lost sight of.

This brief analysis of the Eroica will perhaps serve to show what may (or may not!) be done in the way of finding words to express the more evident and arresting moods suggested by the music. Together with the effort to find words, reasonably adequate to the effect produced by a hearing of the score an effort has also been made to show precisely where in the music and by what means these effects are produced. Manifestly this is one of the major problems of musical criticism, a problem many critics will not or cannot face. Hanslick and his disciples to the contrary notwithstanding, musical experience is something more than the perception of arabesques in sound or the contemplation of pure beauty.[11] An enormous range of emotional reaction is prompted by music, and not always the same reaction at different times. Yet, it is certain that the Eroica "says" something in emotional terms that the Seventh Symphony does not, that a Bach fugue and a Chopin nocturne—any that may come to mind—are intentionally different in content and by perceptive minds regarded as different. Obviously, the opinions and emotional reactions of incompetent, insensitive, provincial minds are not here in question. The more intimately and technically the music is known, the more authentic will be the verbal exposition of its emotional

[11] Cf. J. N. W. Sullivan, *Beethoven, His Spiritual Development* (New York: Alfred A. Knopf, 1936), pp. 38 *ff*.

content. Words are not adding something to the music nor elucidating "what the music is trying to say." With regard to this symphony as in the case of other music, words can do no more than suggest what the music itself and it alone communicates with sure precision to the receptive and responsive hearer.

For further technical, historical, and critical discussion of this symphony see:

Grove, *Beethoven's Nine Symphonies*. Several editions available.
Prod'homme, J., *Les Symphonies de Beethoven*, Paris, Delagrave, 1921.
Berlioz, *A travers chants*, Paris, Calmann-Lèvy, 1862.
Wagner, *Gesammelte Schriften*, Vol. I, pp. 147, 148. "Ein glücklicher Abend."
Romain Rolland, *Beethoven the Creator*, New York, Harpers, 1929.
Tovey, D. F., *Essays in Musical Analysis*, Vol. I, London, Oxford University Press, 1935.

ILLUSTRATIONS

1. Project for a Warehouse — Frank Lloyd Wright

2. Architectural Frieze from the Forum of Trajan

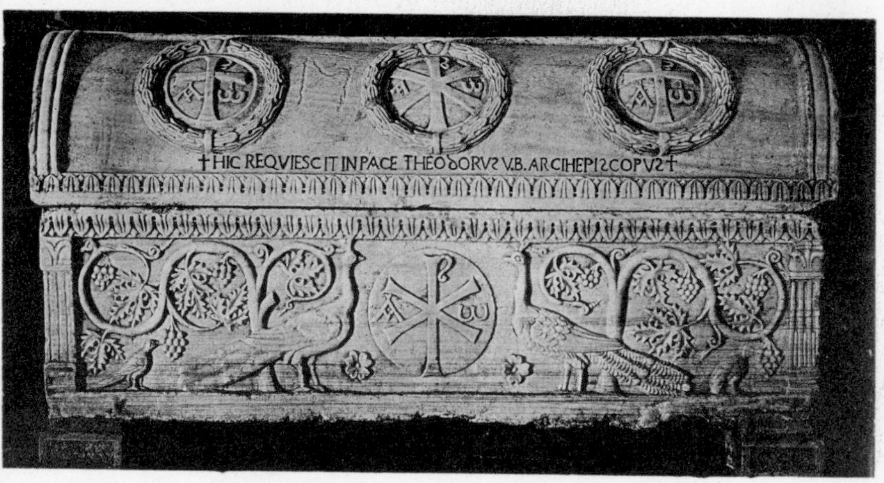

3. Sarcophagus, S. Apollinare in Classe, Ravenna

L. P. PHOTO

4. Galerie des Glaces, Versailles

L. P. PHOTO

5. Grand Foyer, l'Opéra, Paris

6. Interior, Louis XV Style

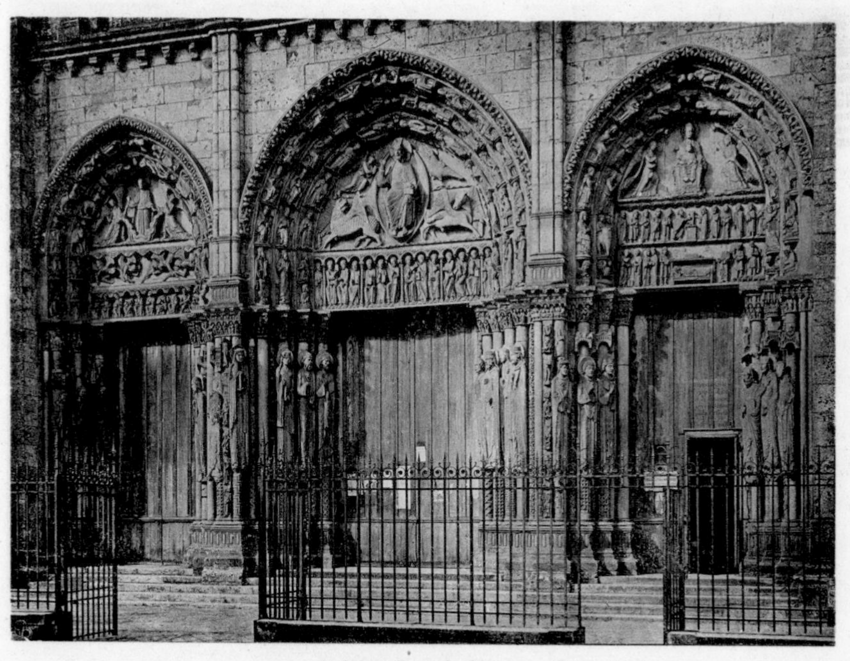

7. West Portal, Chartres Cathedral

BÄRENREITER-VERLAG

8. West Façade, Rouen Cathedral

BÄRENREITER-VERLAG

9. Archway, The Alhambra, Granada

BRAUN & CO.

10. Mont St. Michel

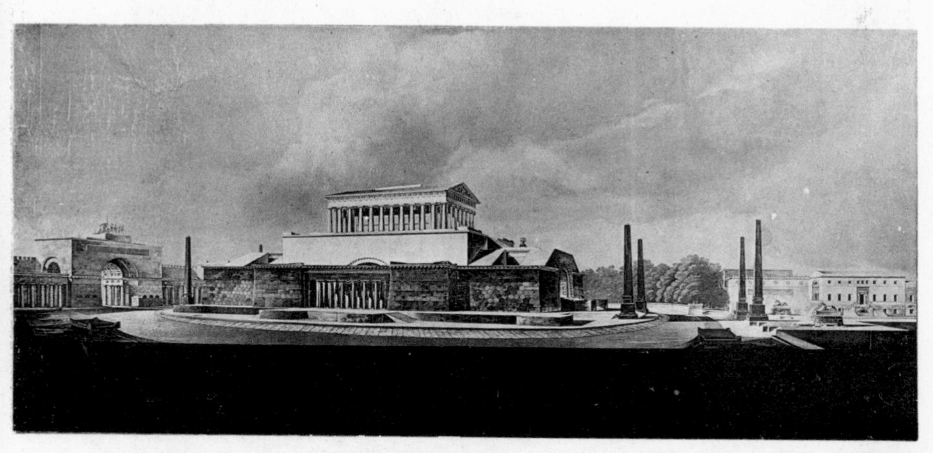

F. NITZSCHE

11. Project for a Monument to Frederick the Great F. Gilly

WOLFRUM

12. Gardens of Schönbrunn — Bernardo Belotto

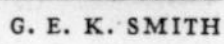

G. E. K. SMITH

13. Snowshill, Gloucestershire

G. E. K. SMITH

14. Daneway House, Sapperton, Gloucestershire

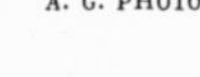
A. G. PHOTO

15. Grotte d'Apollon, Versailles

16. Laiterie, Rambouillet

17. Adolf Loos

18. Frank Fort

19. H. Mossdorf, H. Hahn, B. Busch

Projects for the Chicago Tribune Building, Chicago

20. Fonthill Abbey, West and North Fronts

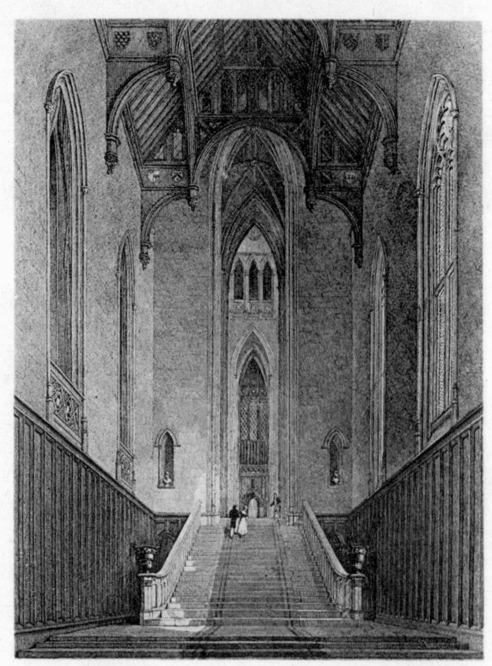

21. Fonthill Abbey, Great Western Hall

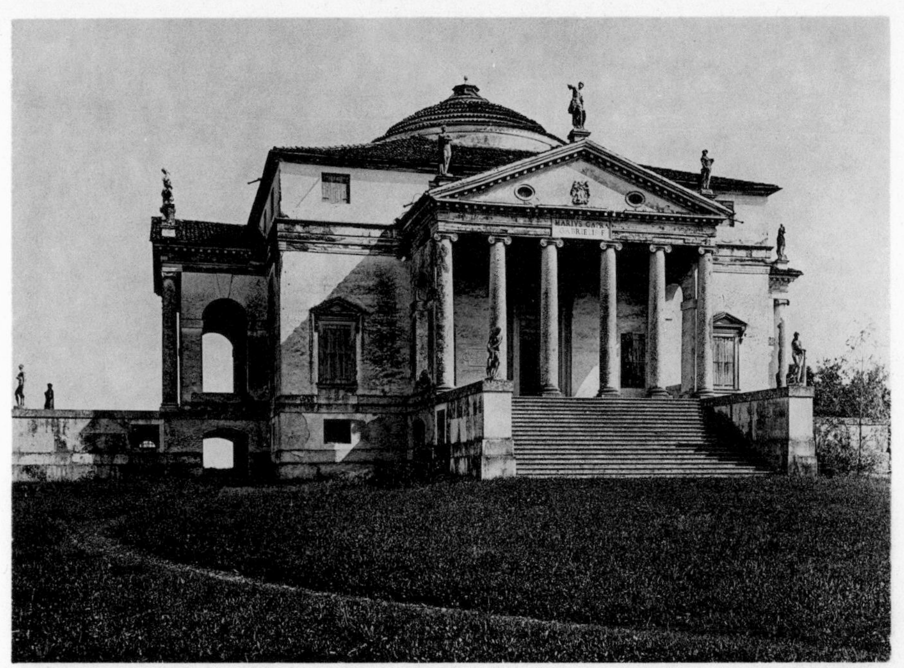

ALINARI

22. Villa Rotonda, Vicenza — Palladio

23. Mereworth Castle, Kent — Colin Campbell

24. Château de Vaux-le-Vicomte L. Le Vau

25. Kaiserpalast, Strasbourg Eggert

26. Pennsylvania Station, New York, Interior

27. Baths of Caracalla, Rome, Restoration

28. Procter Hall, Graduate College, Princeton

29. Flying Buttresses, Mont St. Michel

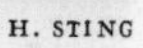

30. Church of the Propstei, Birnau

31. Chapel of Henry VII, Westminster

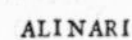

ALINARI

32. Doges' Palace, Venice

ANDERSON

33. Doges' Palace, Venice

Antonio Canale

34. Doges' Palace, Venice — R. P. Bonington

35. Doges' Palace, Venice — Claude Monet

ANDERSON

36. Palazzo Giraud-Torlonia, Rome

ALINARI

37. Palazzo del Grillo, Rome

BRAUN & CO.

38. Chartres Cathedral

BRAUN & CO.

39. Chartres Cathedral

Corot

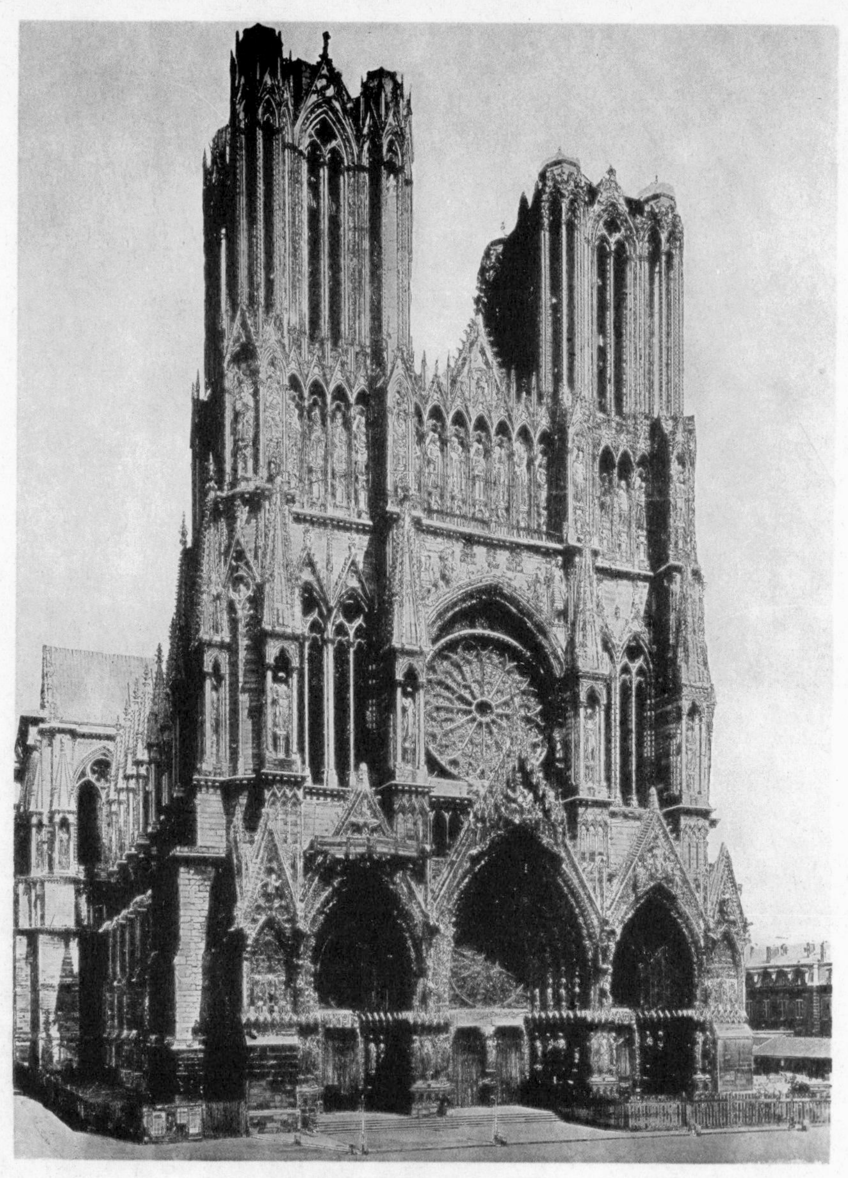

40. Reims Cathedral, Façade

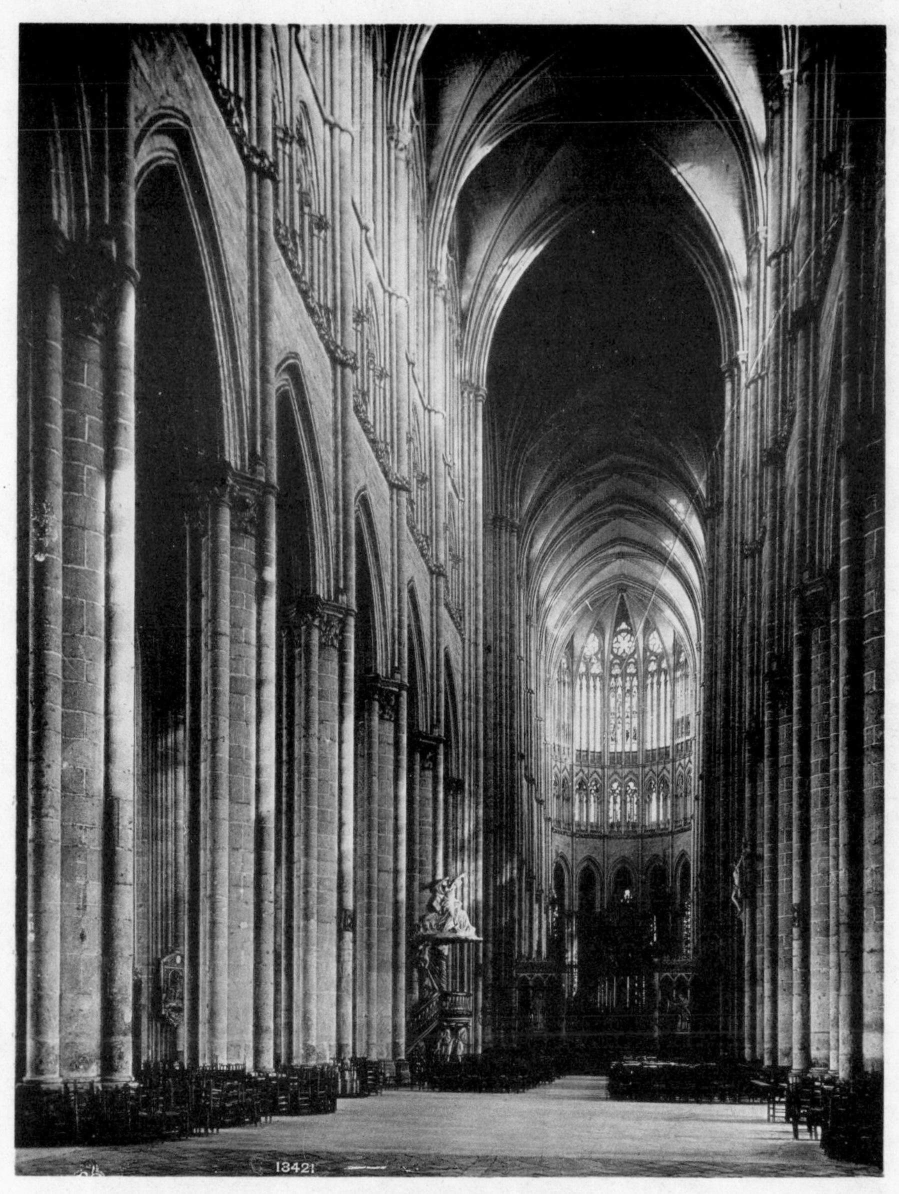

41. Amiens Cathedral, Interior

42. Bishop, Figure from a Trumeau

43. West Portal, Chartres Cathedral

44. West Portal, Amiens Cathedral

45. West Portal, Reims Cathedral

46. Chartreuse, Champmol, Dijon — Claus Sluter

47. Temple of the Sphinx, Ghizeh

G. E. K. SMITH

48. Hypostyle Hall, Ramesseum

49. Tomb, Beni Hasan

50. Palace of Minos, Knossos

51. The Parthenon, Athens

ALINARI

52. Temple of Nike Apteros, Athens

53. Temple of Zeus, Athens

54. Ishtar Gate, Babylon

55. Larkin Building, Buffalo — Frank Lloyd Wright

56. Church, Germigny-des-Prés

GERH. MERTENE

57 Chapel, Aix-la-Chapelle

A. SCHROLL & CO.

58. Hall, Upper Belvedere, Vienna

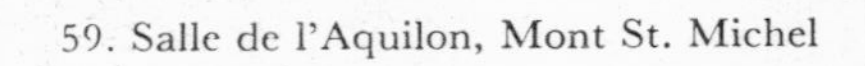

C. N. & CO.

59. Salle de l'Aquilon, Mont St. Michel

60. Pantheon, Rome, Exterior

61. Pantheon, Rome, Interior

BÄRENREITER-VERLAG

62. San Paolo fuori le mura, Rome

63. Hagia Sophia, Istanbul

64. St. Peter's Basilica, Rome, Façade and Piazza

ALINARI

65. St. Peter's Basilica, Rome, Nave

66. St. John Nepomuk, Munich

67. Chapel of the Residenz, Würzburg

"TEL"

68. Palace, Versailles, from the East

"TEL"

69. Palace, Versailles, Garden Façade

70. Grand Trianon, Versailles, Garden Façade

"TEL"

"TEL"

71. Petit Trianon, Versailles, Garden Façade

"TEL"

72. Hamlet, Petit Trianon, Versailles

73. Temple de l'Amour, Petit Trianon, Versailles

74. Dome of Chapel, S. Maria in Trastevere, Rome

75. Portico, S. Maria in Via Lata, Rome

76. Gloriette, Schönbrunn, Vienna

ALINARI

77. Tower Gallery, Notre Dame, Paris

78. Peristyle of the House of the Vettii, Pompeii

79. Railway Station, Stuttgart — Bonatz

80. The George Washington Bridge, New York

81. Stadium in Florence Pier Luigi Nervi

A. G. PHOTO

82. Hangar, Orly Freyssinet

83. Nave of Church, Bischofsheim Bohm

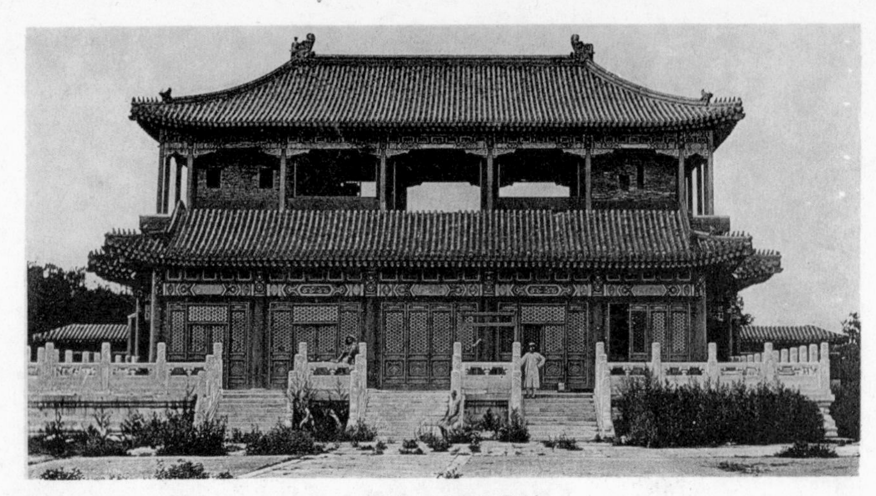

84. Chinese Hall, Pekin

85. Rockefeller Center, New York

86. Project, St. Mark's Tower
Frank Lloyd Wright

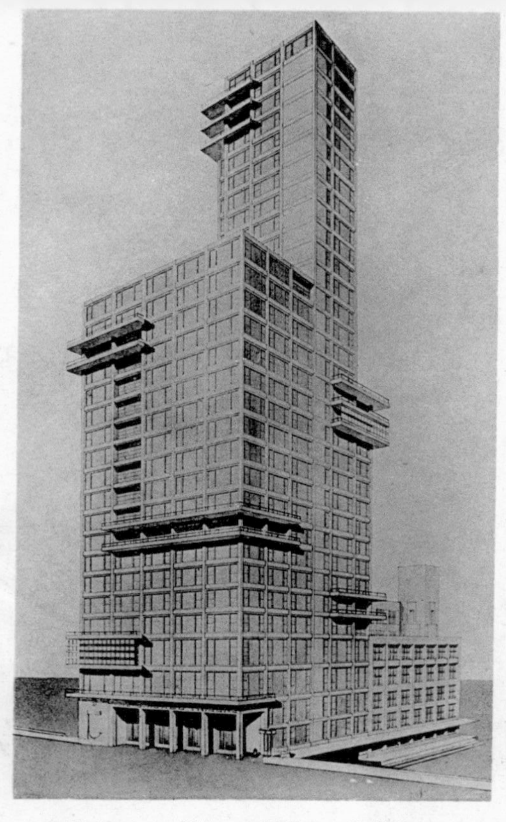

87. Project, Chicago Tribune Building
Walter Gropius

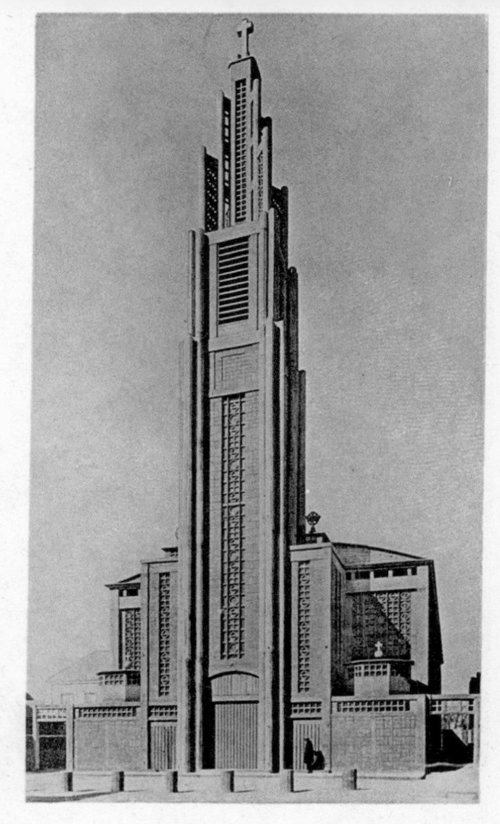

88. Notre Dame, Le Raincy
A. & G. Perret

89. E. Kaufmann House — Frank Lloyd Wright

90. Tugendhat, Brno — Mies van der Rohe

91. Schocken Store, Chemnitz — Mendelssohn

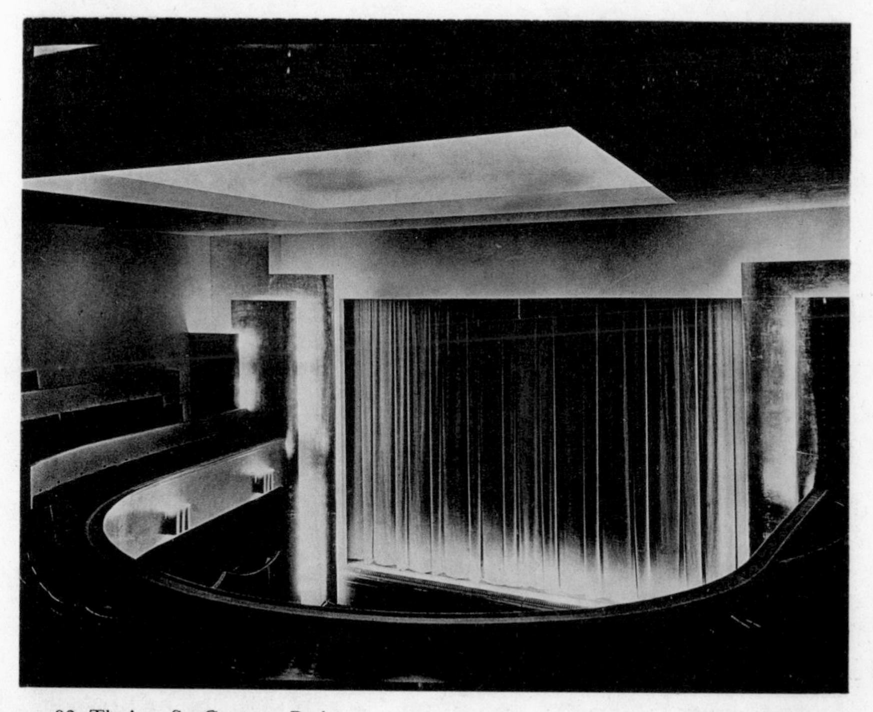

92. Theâtre St. Georges, Paris — Sicilis

93. Billiard Balls

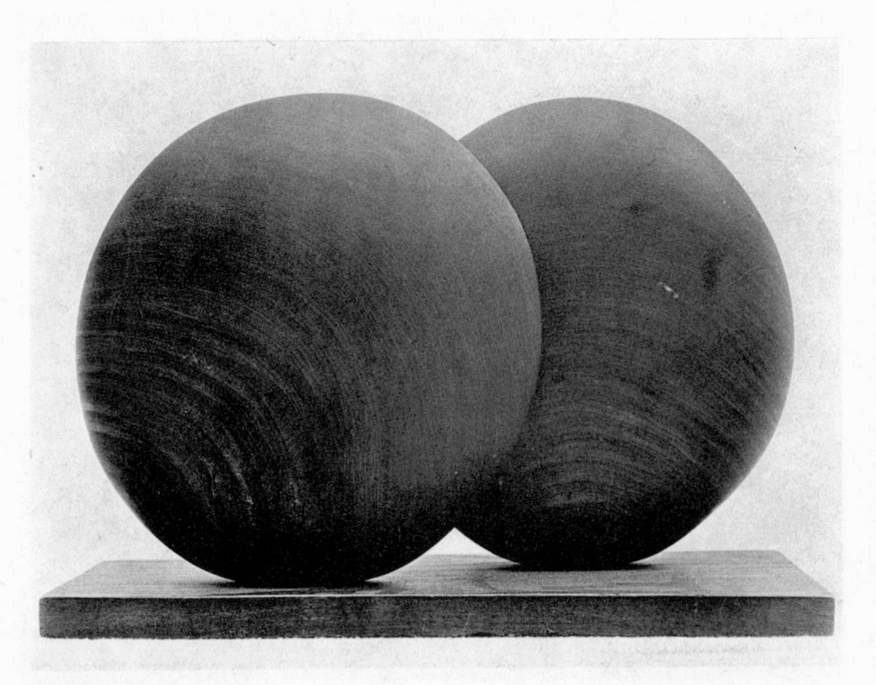

94. Sculpture — Barbara Hepworth

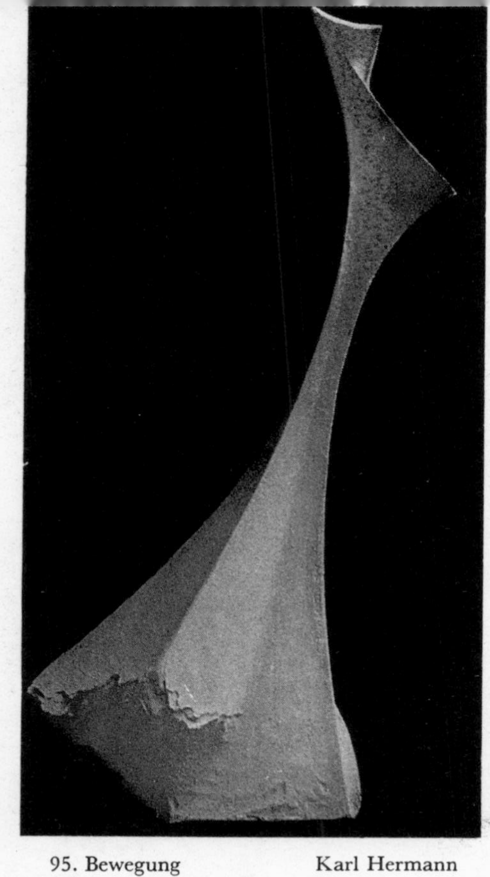

95. Bewegung Karl Hermann

96. Mobile Alexander Calder

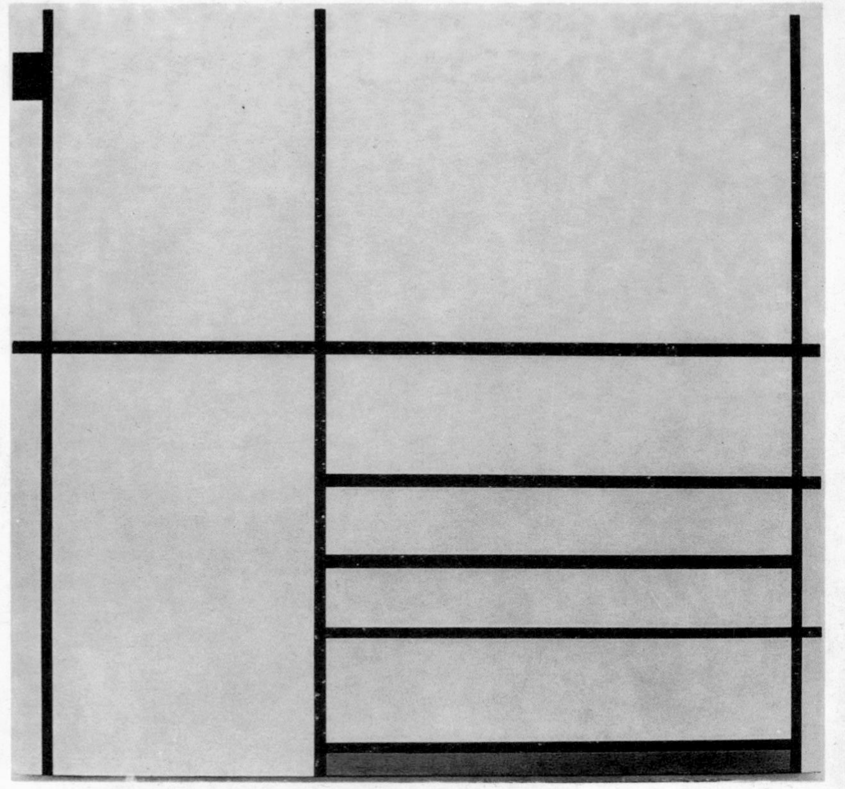

97. Composition in Black, White, and Red — P. Mondrian

98. Abstraction — Kandinsky

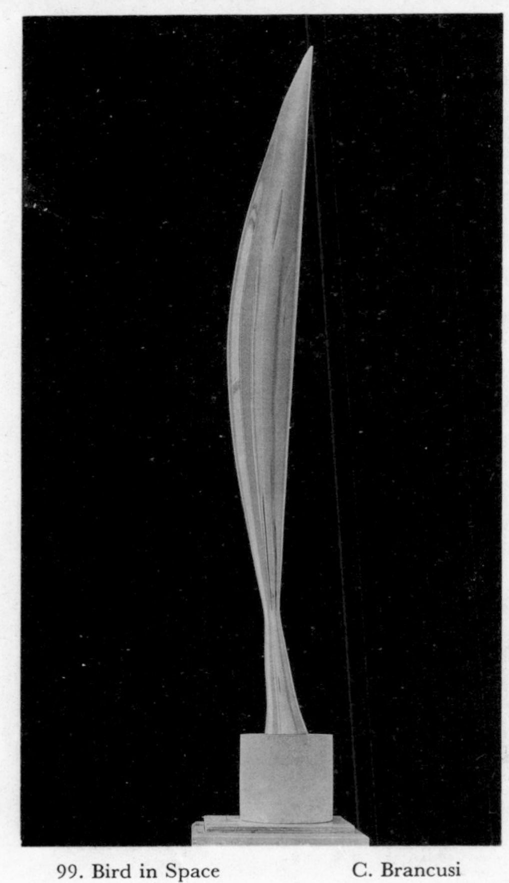

99. Bird in Space C. Brancusi

100. Abstraction Pablo Picasso

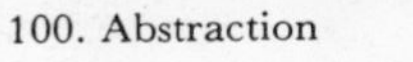

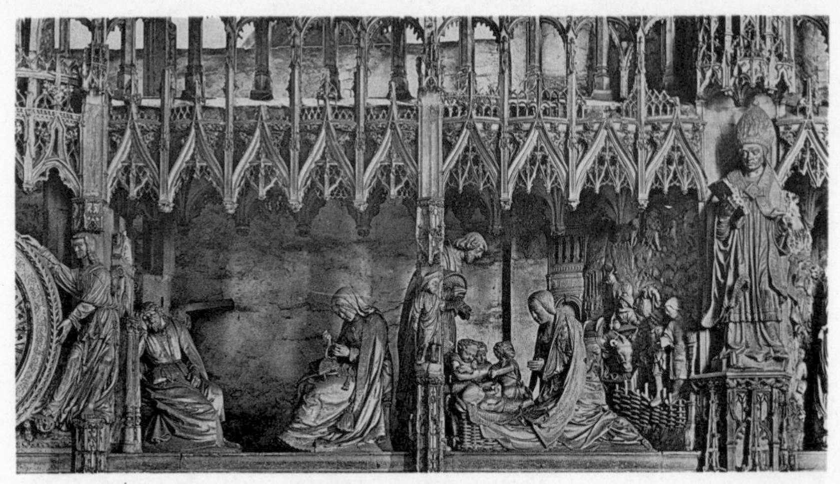

N. D. PHOTO

101. Choir Screen, Chartres Cathedral

ALINARI

102. Bronze Door, Baptistery, Florence — Ghiberti

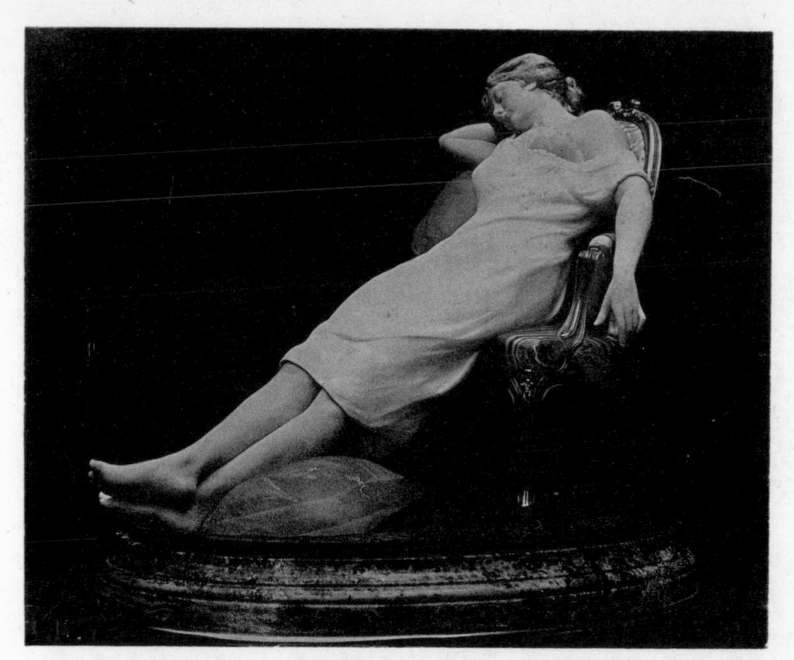

103. La Sieste L. Allouard

104. Tree John Constable

105. Country School Boy — Pratt

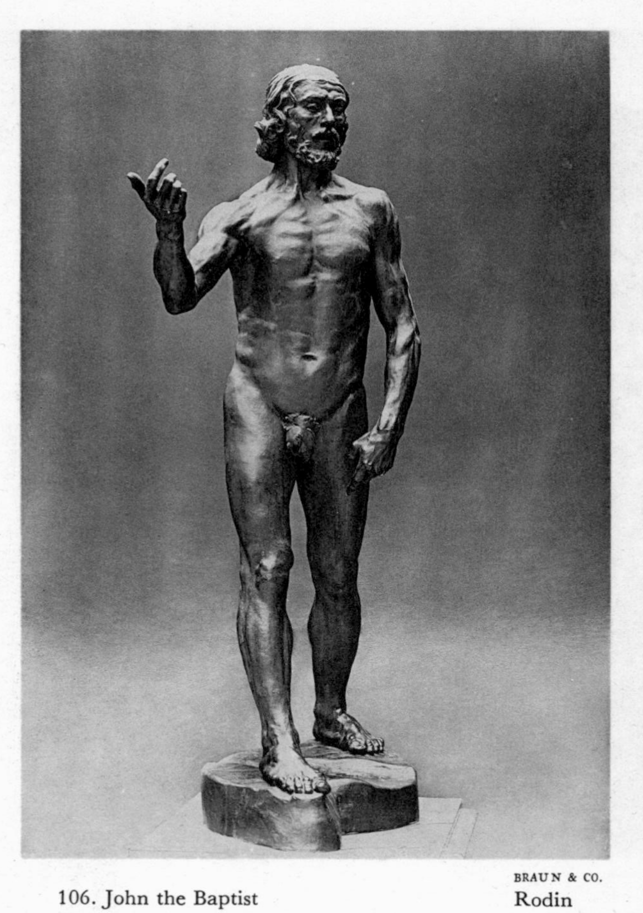

BRAUN & CO.

106. John the Baptist — Rodin

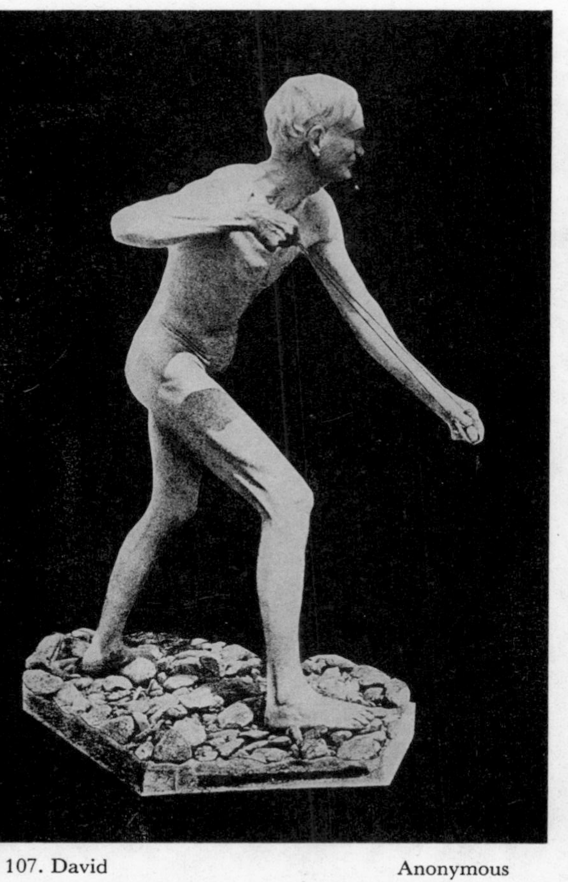

107. David Anonymous

108. David Bernini

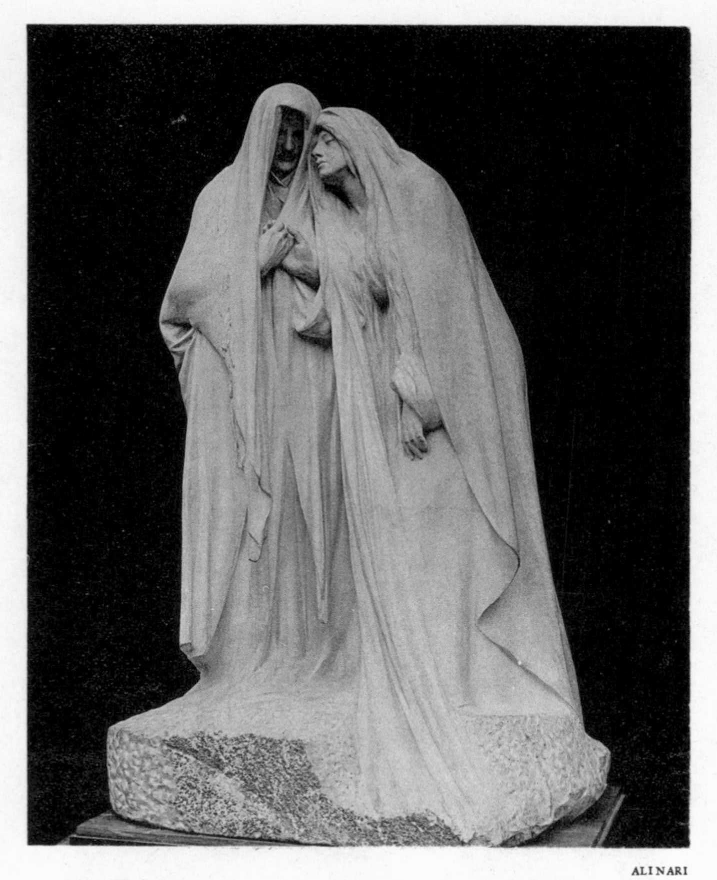

ALINARI

109. Two Mourners — Théodore Rivière

110. Nike of Samothrace

111. Horses of the Sun, Imprimerie Nationale, Paris — Le Lorrain

A. G. PHOTO

112. Nymphs Bathing, Versailles — Girardon

113. Ecstasy of S. Teresa Bernini

HANFSTAENGL

114. Seascape Jacob van Ruysdael

115. The Fates, East Pediment, Parthenon

116. Theseus, East Pediment, Parthenon

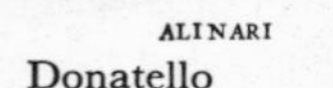

ALINARI

117. David Donatello

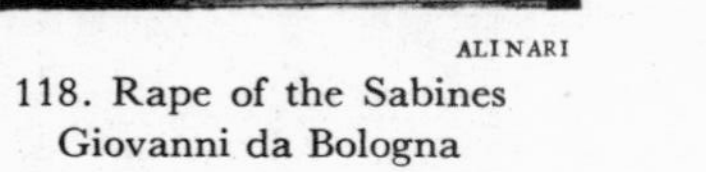

ALINARI

118. Rape of the Sabines
Giovanni da Bologna

ALINARI

119. Mercury Giovanni da Bologna

BÄRENREITER-VERLAG

120. Heine Denkmal — Georg Kolbe

ALINARI

121. Hercules and Antaeus — Pollaiuolo

122. Female Satyr, terracotta Clodion

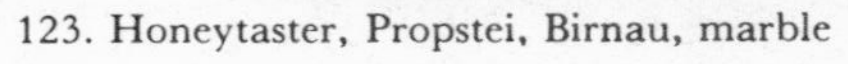

123. Honeytaster, Propstei, Birnau, marble

124. Minerva, porcelain — Melchior

125. Mary on a Cloud, painted wood — Günther

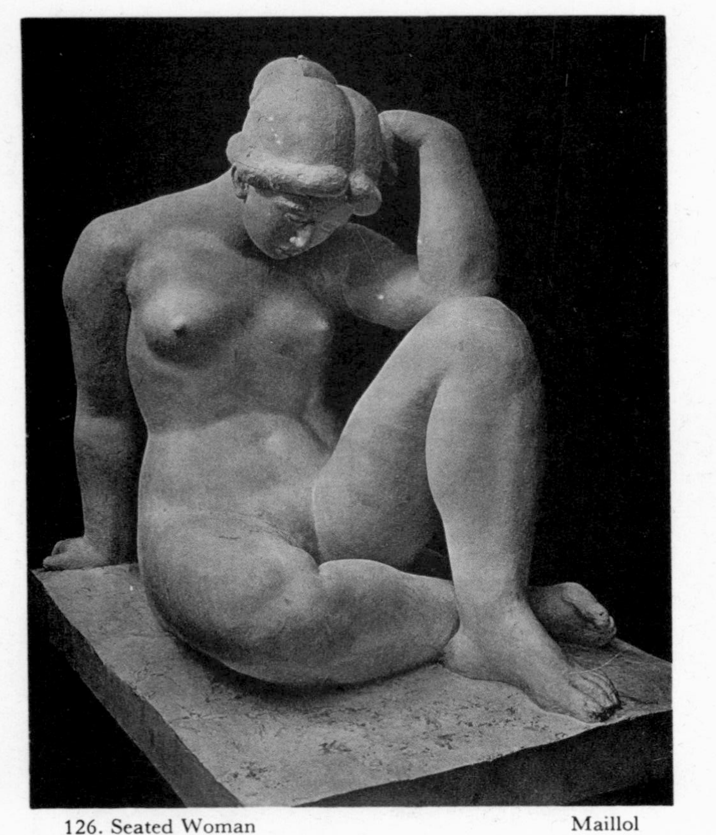

126. Seated Woman — Maillol

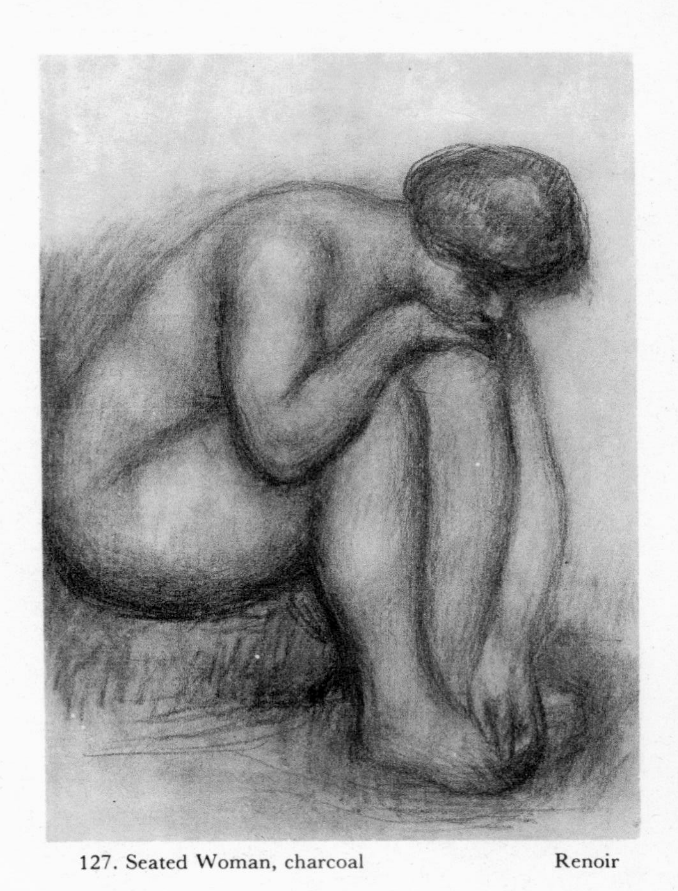

127. Seated Woman, charcoal — Renoir

128. Seated Woman — Ahron Ben-Shmuel

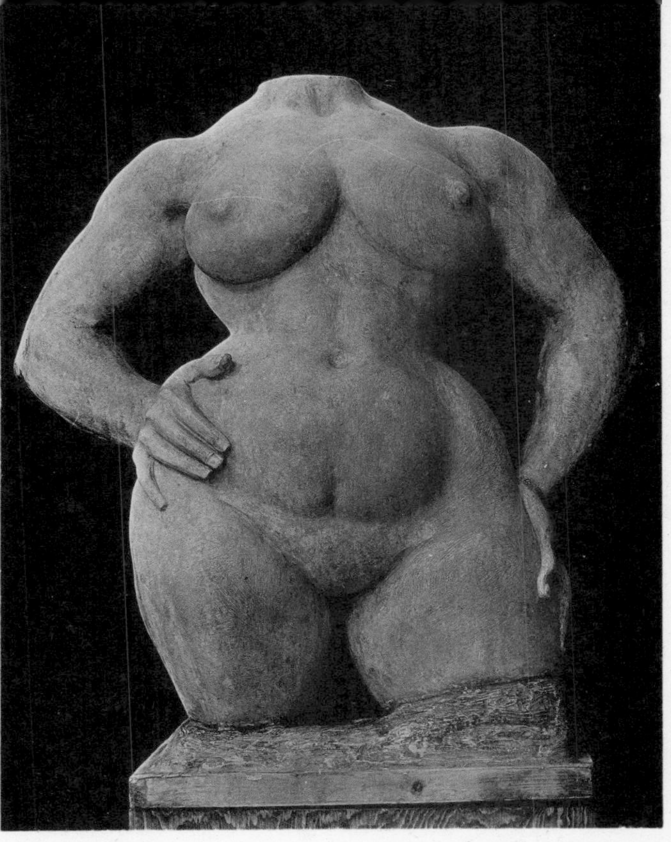

129. Torso — Gaston Lachaise

130. "Inter Artes et Natura" Puvis de Chavannes

ANDERSON

131. Decoration, Palazzo Labia, Venice Tiepolo

ANDERSON

132. Ceiling, S. Ignazio, Rome — Pozzo

ALINARI

133. Decorative Figure, Sistine Chapel — Michelangelo

SAUGEZ

134. Bound Slave — Michelangelo

ANDERSON

135. Longinus Bernini

BRAUN & CO.

136. Et in Arcadia Ego, Collection of the Duke of Devonshire — Nicolas Poussin

BRAUN & CO.

137. Shepherds in Arcady Nicolas Poussin

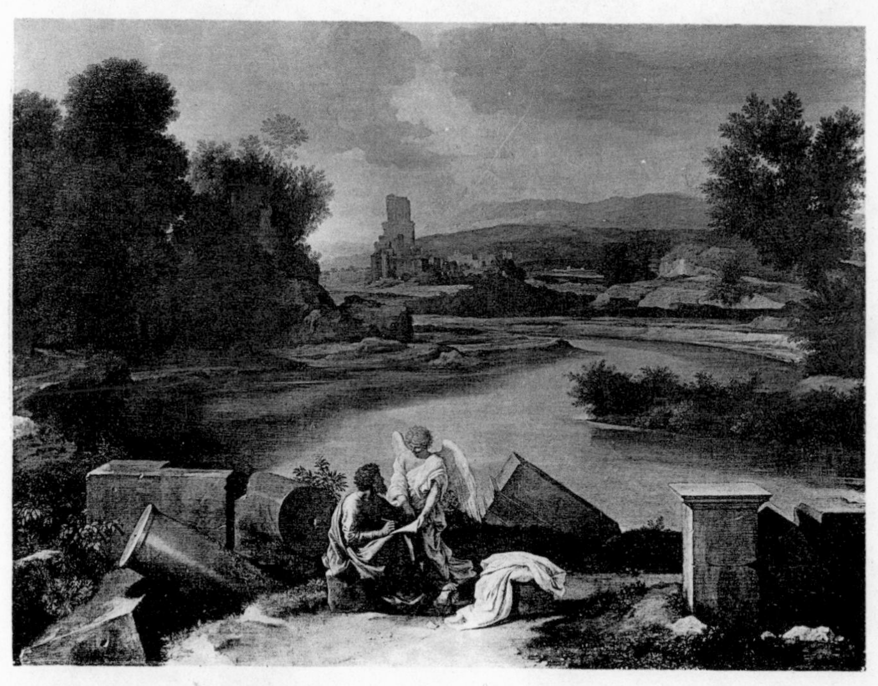

138. St. Matthew and the Angel Nicolas Poussin

139. Flora — Maillol

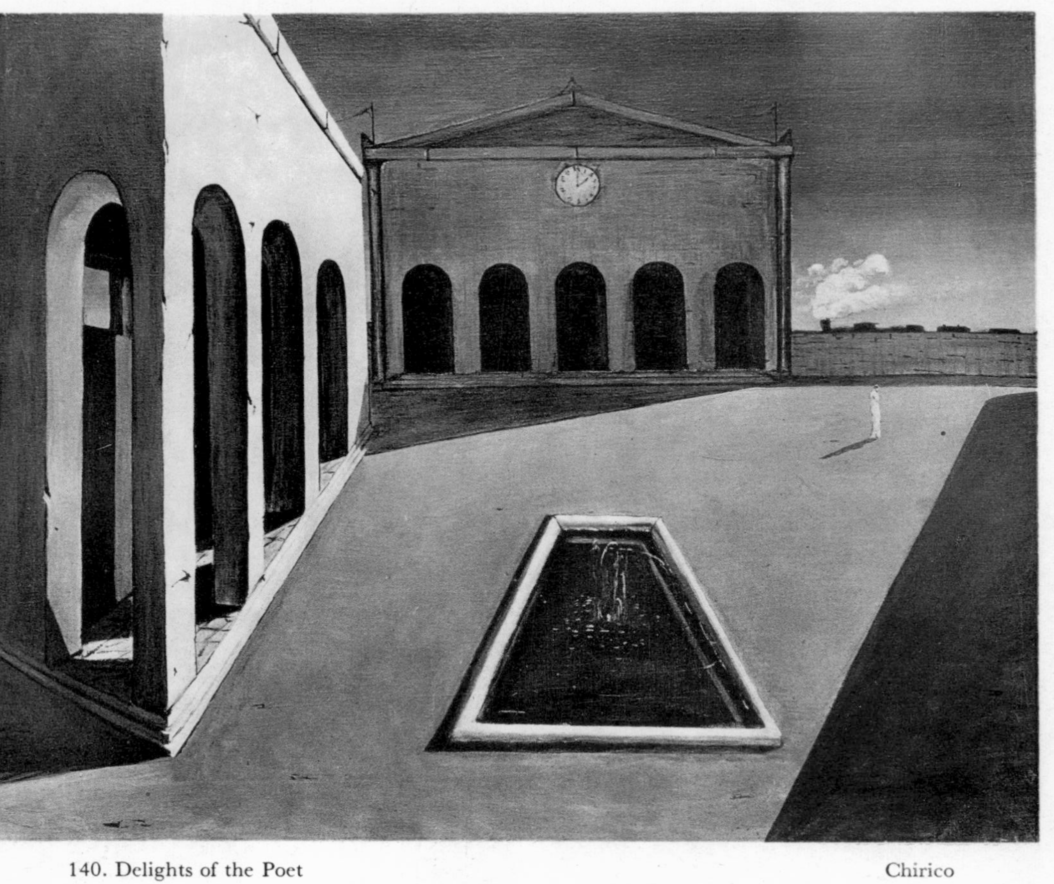

140. Delights of the Poet — Chirico

141. Wash Drawing for Bronze Angel Bernini

ALINARI

142. Bronze Angel, Chapel of the Sacrament, St. Peter's, Rome
Bernini

143. Longfellow Memorial Daniel Chester French

144. Death and the Young Sculptor Daniel Chester French

145. Charging Mammoth, La Madeleine

146. Akhenaten Worshipping the Sun, Cairo

147. Relief Bust of Scipio

148. Burning of the World, Perugia — Agostino da Duccio

149. Spartan Relief, Berlin

150. Dance of Salome, S. Giovanni, Siena Donatello

151. Statue of Chares, Miletus

152. War Memorial, Würzburg

R. KELLNER
Heuler

153. Porte de l'Enfer Rodin

154. Cavalier Callot

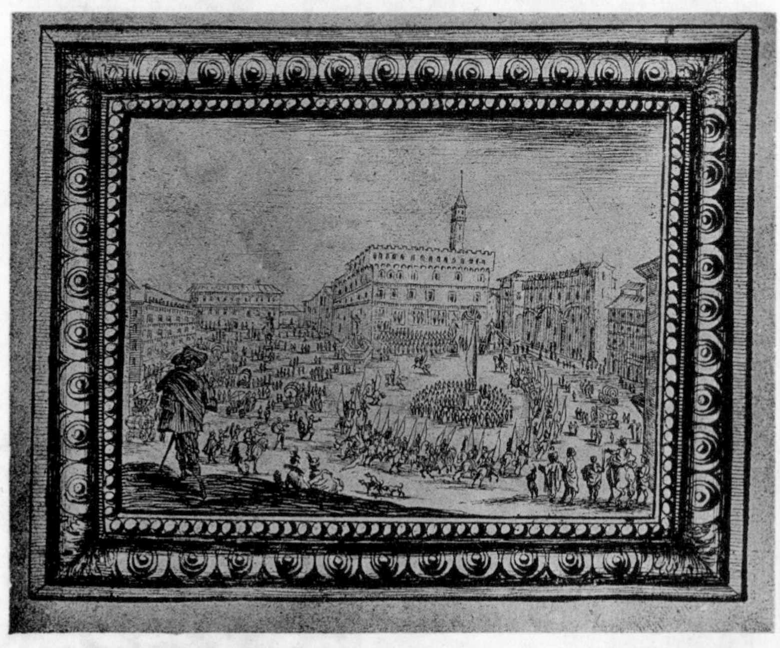

155. Piazza della Signoria, Florence Callot

156. Nude Figures — Pablo Picasso

157. Maine Islands — John Marin

BRAUN & CO.

158. The Fifer — Edouard Manet

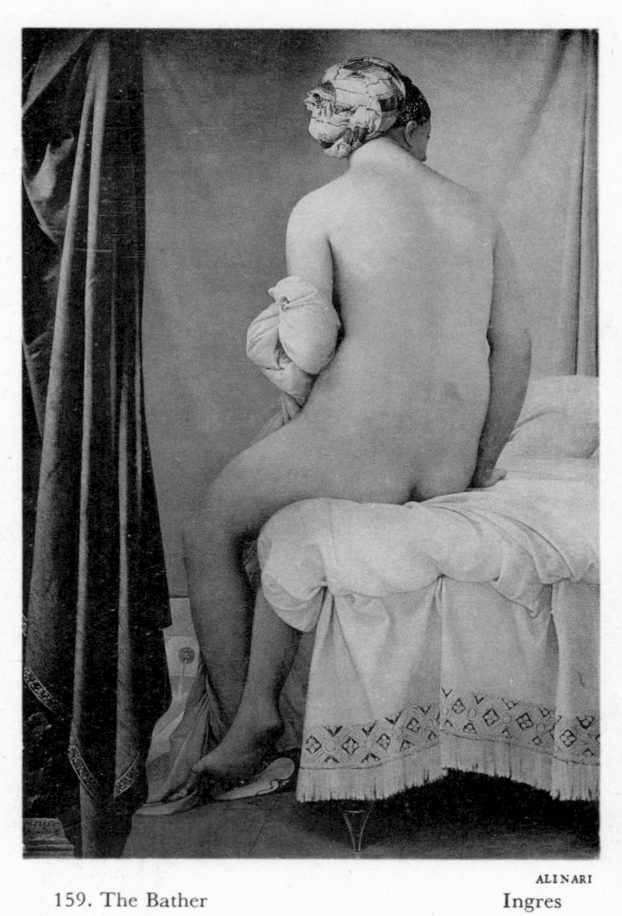

ALINARI

159. The Bather — Ingres

160. Coronation of the Virgin, Uffizi

BRAUN & CO.

Fra Angelico

161. St. John and Prochorus, Greek Gospels

162. Crucifixion — Martin Schongauer

163. Crucifixion — Albrecht Dürer

164. Erasmus — Albrecht Dürer

165. Ordination, Christ and Peter — Nicolas Poussin

166. Descent from the Cross Rembrandt

167. Supper at Emmaus Rembrandt

168. Woman at the Casement Vermeer

169. Norham Castle at Sunrise Turner

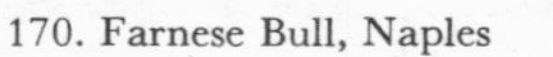

ALINARI

170. Farnese Bull, Naples

171. Laocoön, Vatican

172. Madonna and Child with St. John, London — Michelangelo (ALINARI)

173. Madonna of the Magnificat, Florence — Botticelli (ANDERSON)

174. Crucifixion　　　Perugino

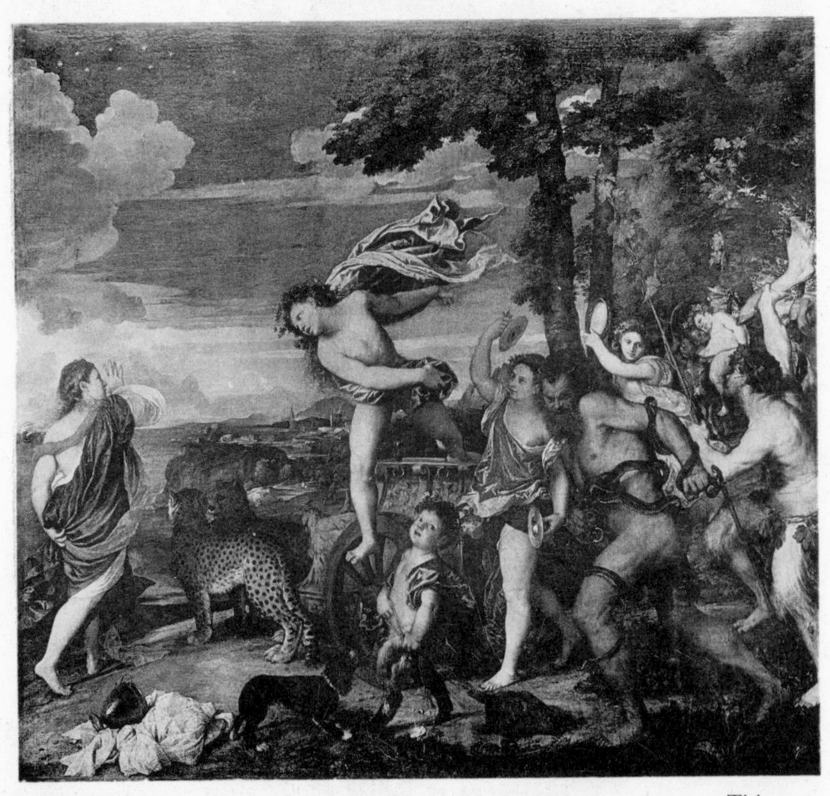

175. Bacchus and Ariadne　　　Titian

176. Madonna and St. Anne — Leonardo da Vinci

177. Madonna del Prato — Raphael

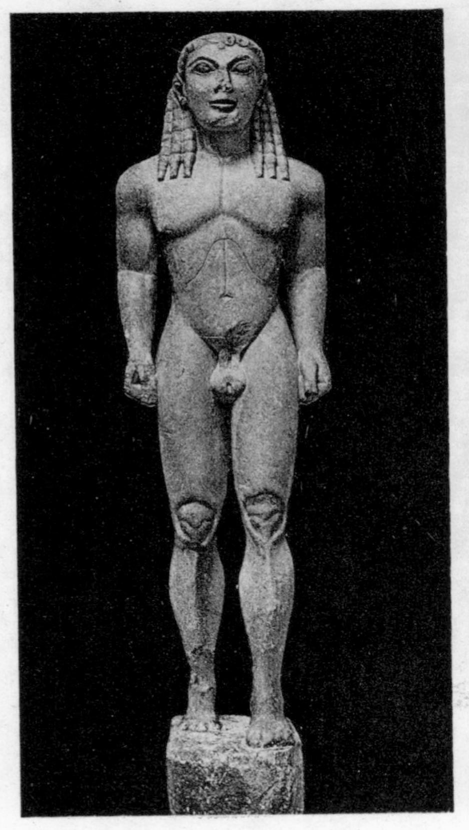

178. Young Man, Delphi

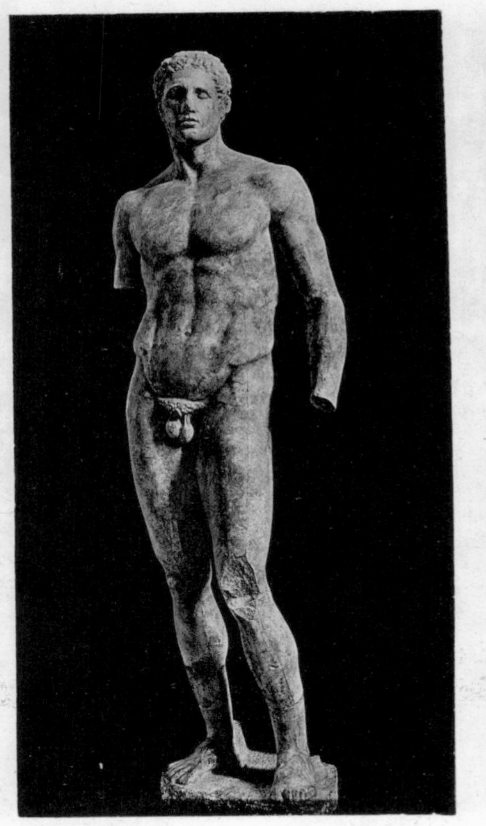

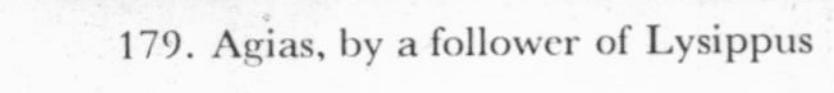

179. Agias, by a follower of Lysippus

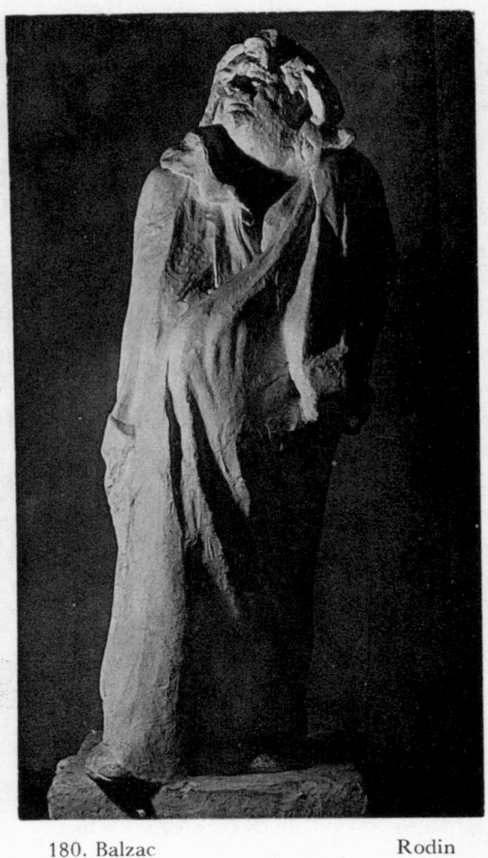

180. Balzac — Rodin

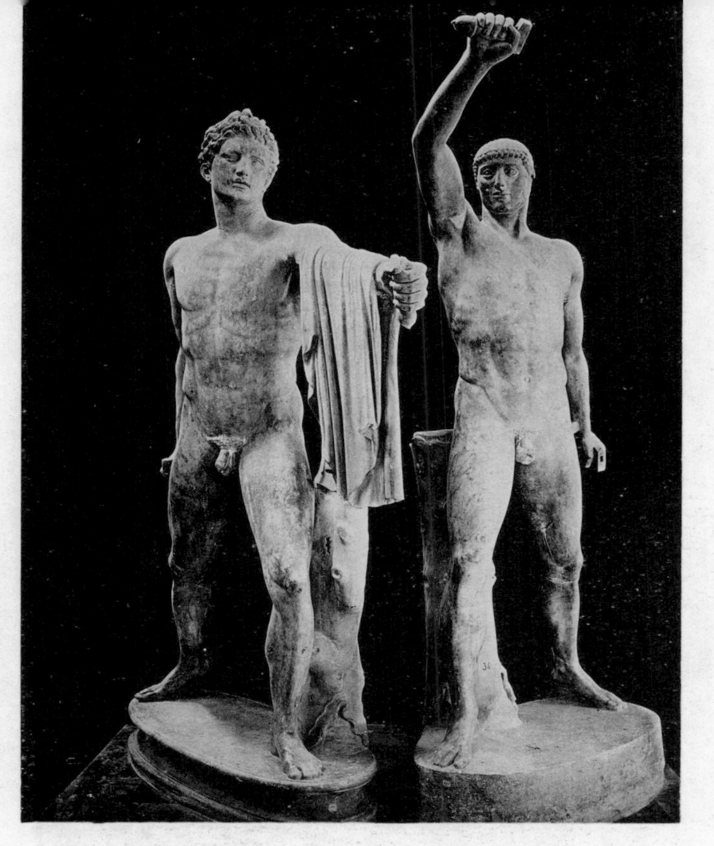

181. Harmodius and Aristogiton, Naples

ALINARI

182. Orestes and Electra, Naples

183. Coronation of the Virgin — Raphael

ALINARI

184. Transfiguration — Raphael

ALINARI

185. Avenue of Trees Cézanne

186. Photograph of the Subject

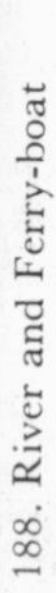

188. River and Ferry-boat — Corot

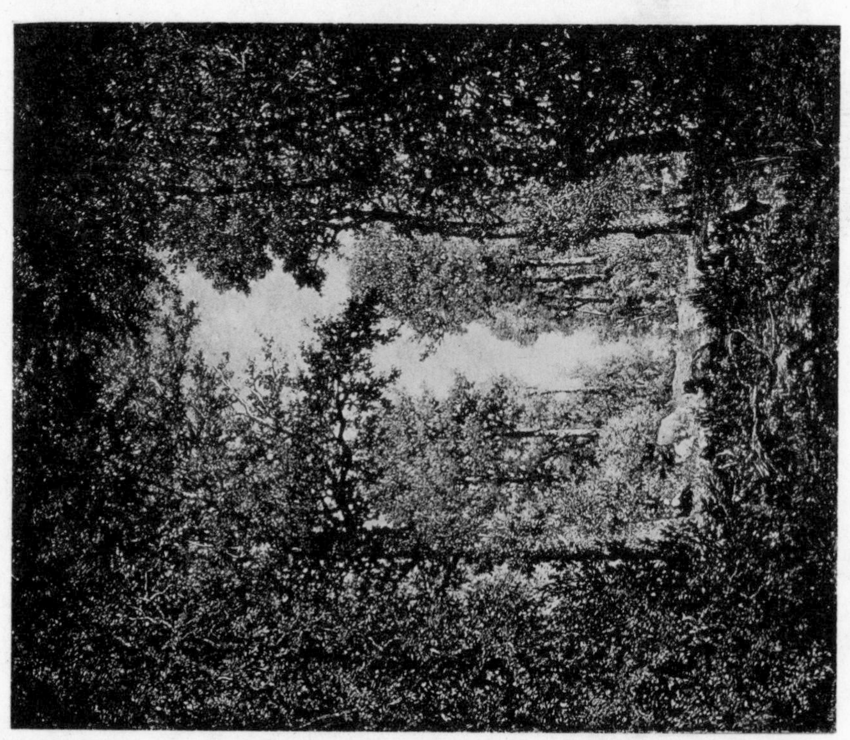

187. Woods and Cattle — Théodore Rousseau

189. Jungle Scene — Henri Rousseau

190. Pine Tree — André Derain

191. Landscape — Henri Matisse

HANFSTAENGL

192. Ostern am Walchensee — Lovis Corinth

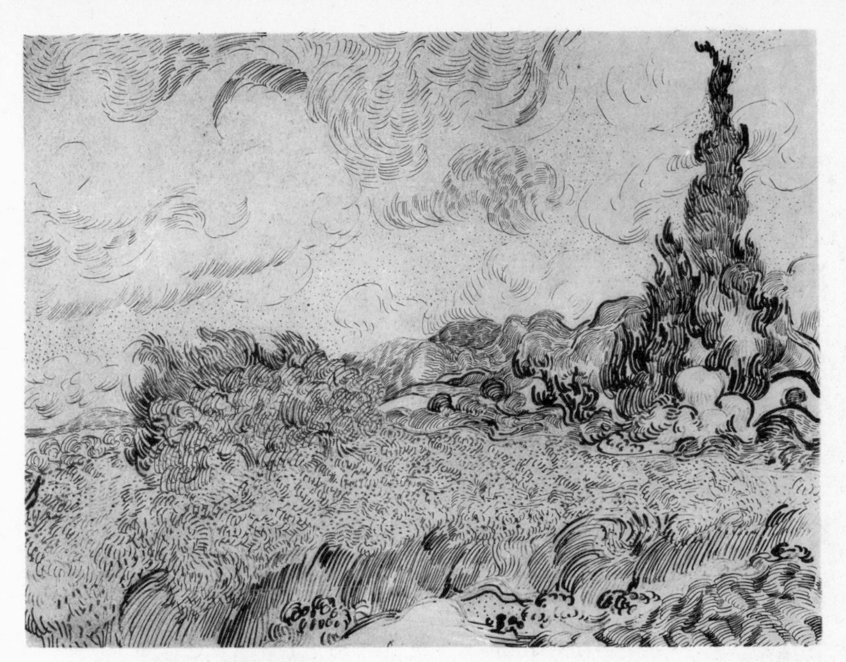

193. Cypresses, ink drawing — Van Gogh

194. Nude — Paul Gauguin

195. Hille Bobbe — Franz Hals

196. Le Clown à la Rose — Georges Rouault

197. Camera degli Sposi, Mantua

ANDERSON

Mantegna

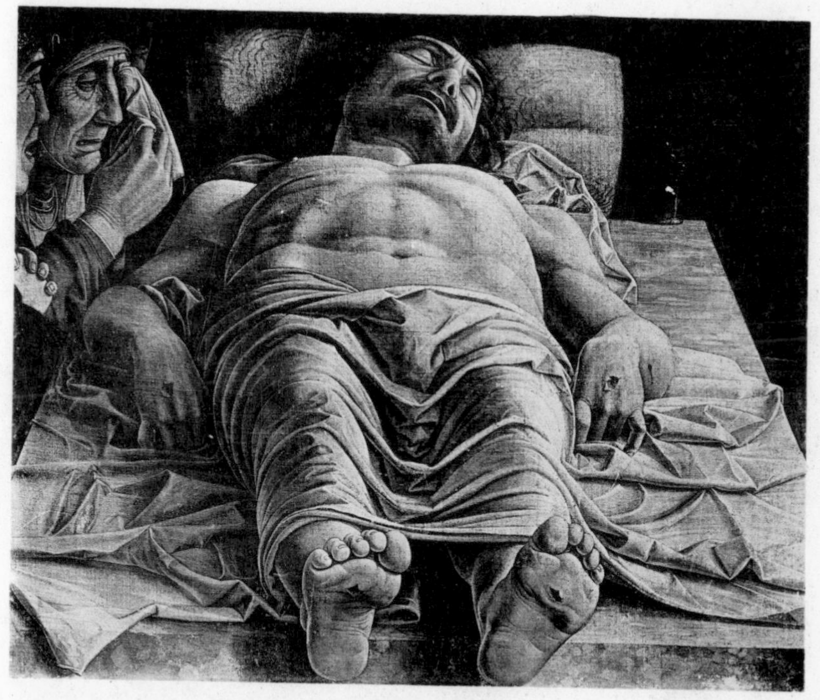

198. The Dead Christ

ALINARI

Mantegna

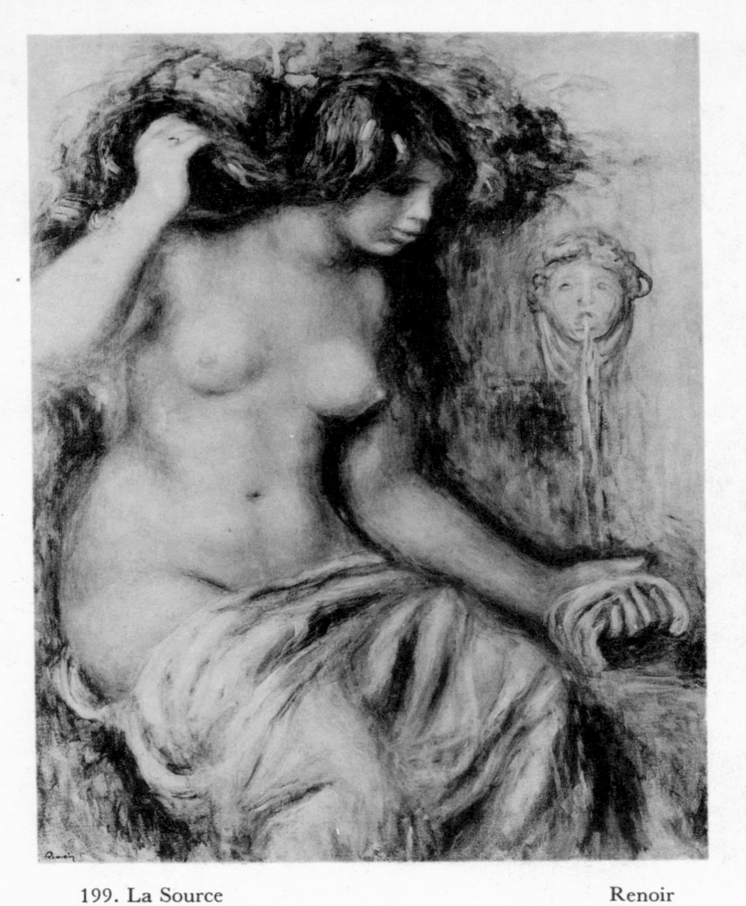

199. La Source — Renoir

200. Toilette of Venus — Rubens

ANDERSON

201. Venus from Cyrene, Terme Museum, Rome

202. Torso — Maillol

203. Castor and Pollux Rubens

204. Sketch for the Peasants' Dance Rubens

205. Battle on the Bridge — Rubens

206. Sketch for The Death of Adonis — Rubens

ALINARI

207. La Danse Carpeaux

208. Singing Gallery, Florence Donatello

A. G. PHOTO

209. Entombment, Solesmes

A. G. PHOTO

210. Mary Magdalene, Detail from the Entombment

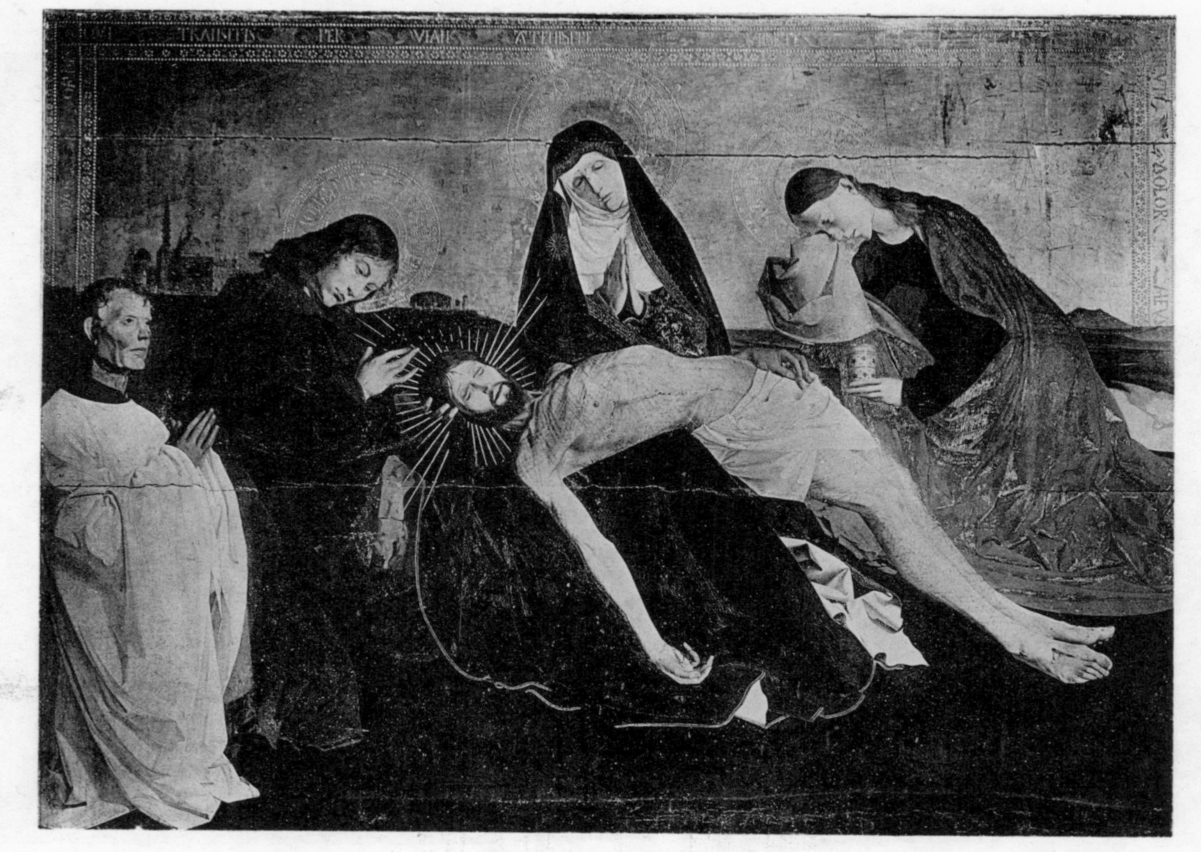

CH. EGGIMANN

211. Avignon Pietà, Louvre

212. House in Provence — Cézanne

ANDERSON

213. Crucifixion (detail) Tintoretto

ANDERSON

214. Crucifixion, Scuola di S. Rocco Tintoretto

215. The Three Crosses (first state) Rembrandt

216. The Three Crosses (fourth state) Rembrandt

217. Franciscan Monk — Zurbarán

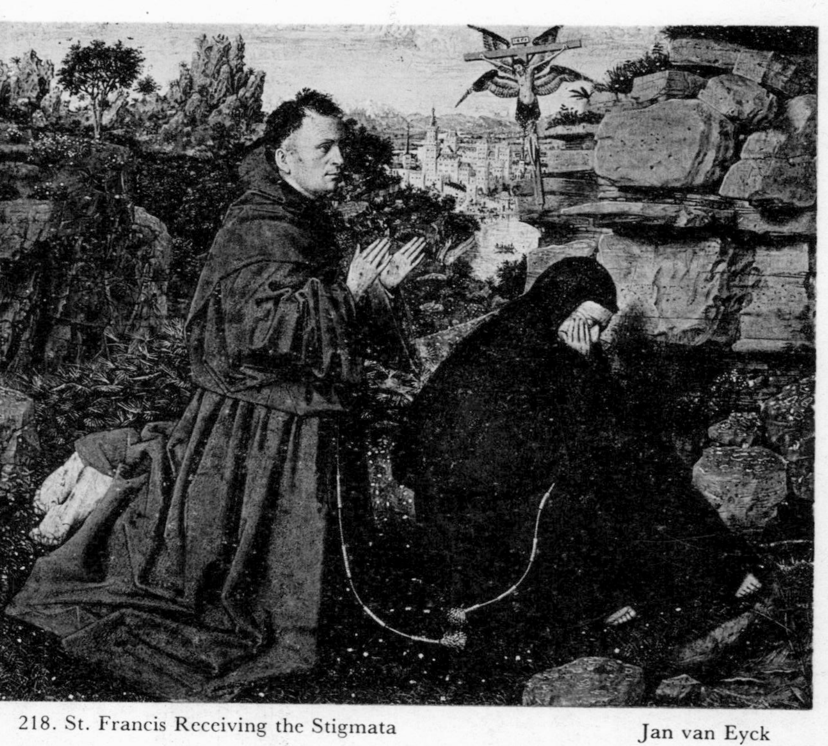

218. St. Francis Receiving the Stigmata — Jan van Eyck

219. Disputa

ALINARI
Raphael

220. Crucifixion

Delacroix

ALINARI

221. Entombment, Arena Chapel, Padua — Giotto

ALINARI

222. Meeting of Joachim and Anna,
Arena Chapel, Padua (detail)
Giotto

BRAUN & CO.

223. The Angelus J. F. Millet

BRAUN & CO.

224. The Gleaners J. F. Millet

225. The Sower J. F. Millet

226. The Concert ALINARI Jordaens

227. The Gamesters — Adrian Brouwer

228. The Village Bride — J. B. Greuze

ANDERSON

229. Marriage à la Mode (2) Hogarth

ALINARI

230. The Raft of the Medusa Géricault

ALINARI

231. Dante and Virgil — Delacroix

ALINARI

232. The Blind Leading the Blind — Peter Breughel, the Elder

233. Gilles

ALINARI

Watteau

234. Gilles (detail)

Watteau

235. Embarkation for Cythera

BRAUN & CO.
Watteau

ALINARI

236. The Tempest — Giorgione

237. Grief — Saint-Gaudens

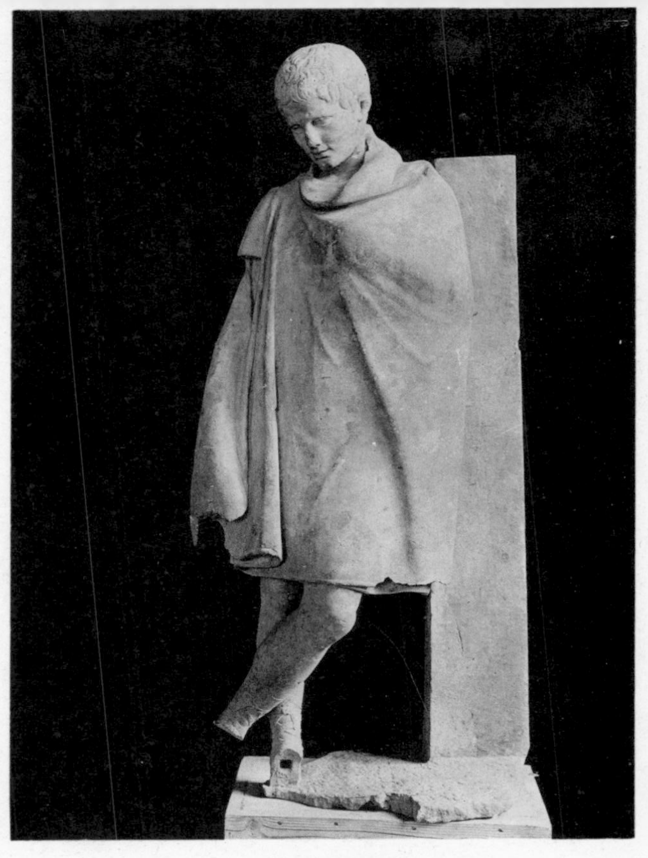

238. Youth of Tralles

239. Self-Portrait (1890-1894)

240. Photograph of Paul Cézanne (c. 1890)

241. D'Artagnan — Doré

242. M. Sériziat — BRAUN & CO. David

ALINARI

243. Federigo, Duke of Urbino — Mino da Fiesole

ALINARI

244. Federigo, Duke of Urbino — Piero della Francesca

245. Portrait of a Young Man — Hugo van der Goes

246. Praying Hands 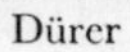 Dürer

247. Drapery Leonardo da Vinci

248. Two Clerics Antonio Moro

ALINARI

249. Angelo Doni Raphael

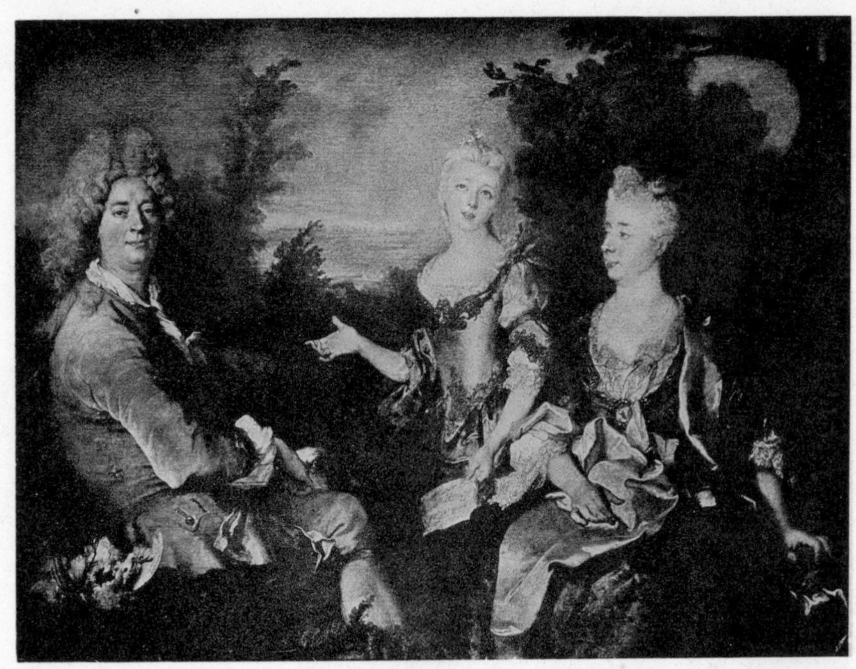

BRAUN & CO.

250. The Painter and his Family — Largillière

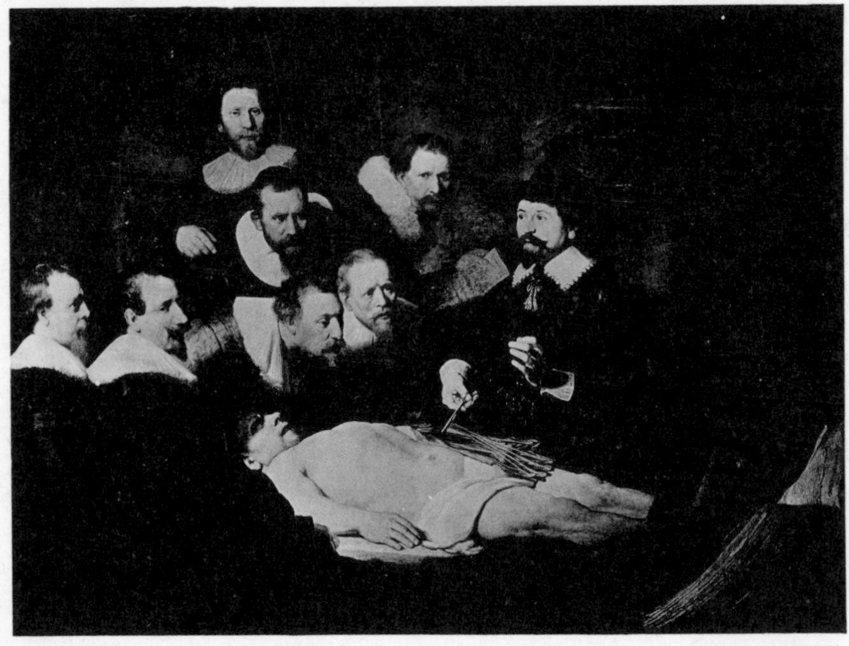

BRAUN & CO.

251. The Anatomy Lesson — Rembrandt

252. Giuliano de' Medici   Michelangelo

253. Lorenzo de' Medici   Michelangelo

254. La Pensée

ALINARI
Rodin

255. Danaïde

ALINARI
Rodin

256. Victor Hugo — Rodin

257. Le Penseur — Rodin

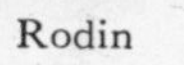

258. Man with the Arrow — Roger van der Weyden

ALINARI

259. Pope Julius II (detail) Raphael

HANFSTAENGL

260. Man with the Helmet Rembrandt

ANDERSON

261. The Age of Innocence — Reynolds

LEET BROS. CO.

262. Abraham Lincoln — Daniel Chester French

263. Self-Portrait Vincent Van Gogh

264. The Execution of Lady Jane Grey Paul Delaroche

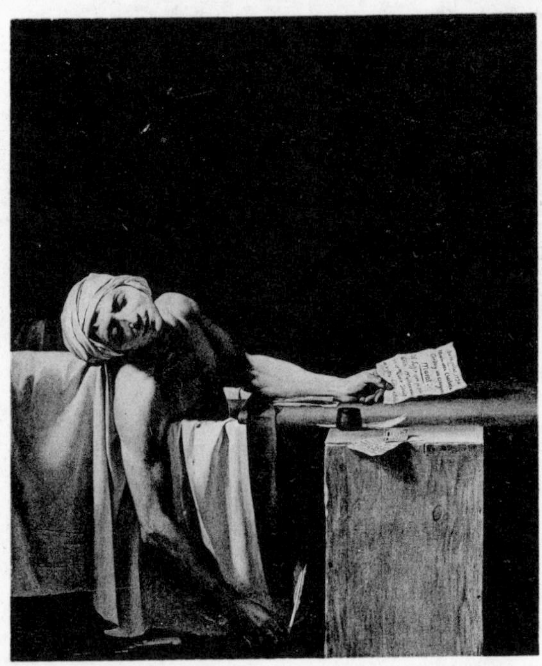

ALINARI

265. The Death of Marat David

266. The Oath of the Horatii

BRAUN & CO.

David

267. The Coronation of the Empress Josephine

ALINARI

David

ALINARI

268. Napoleon III at Solferino — Meissonier

269. Retreat from Moscow — Meissonier

ALINARI

270. The 28th of July, 1830 Delacroix

271. Le Départ des Volontaires Rude

272. Gersaint's Signboard — Watteau

273. Archduke Leopold William's Gallery — Teniers the Younger

274. Parterre d'Eaux, Versailles — R. P. Bonington

275. Puget's Cupid — Cézanne

276. Young Bull — Paul Potter

277. Young Herdsman with Cows — Cuyp

ANDERSON

278. Horses from St. Mark's, Venice

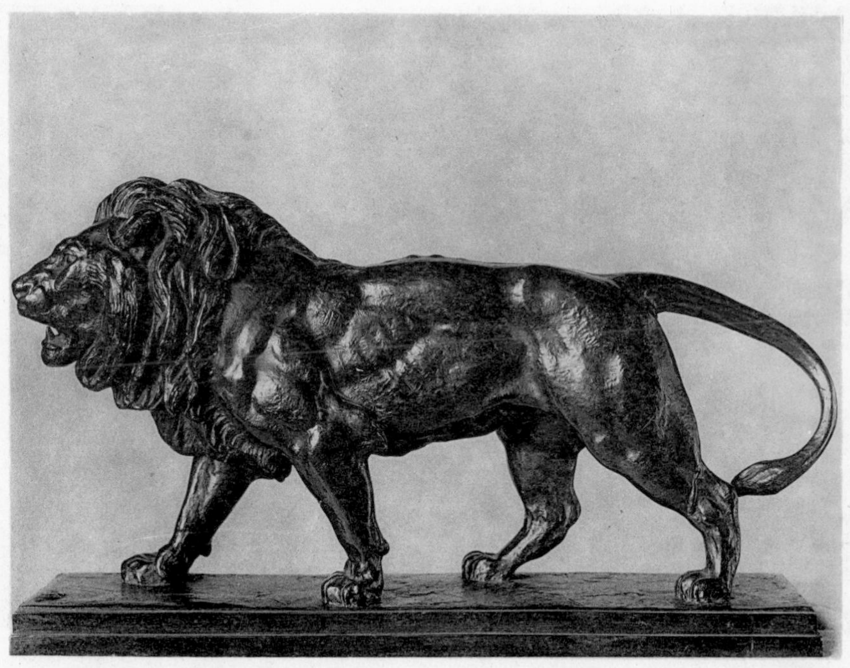

A. G. PHOTO

279. Lion

Barye

280. Still Life Chardin

281. Still Life De Heem

282. Still Life — Henri Matisse

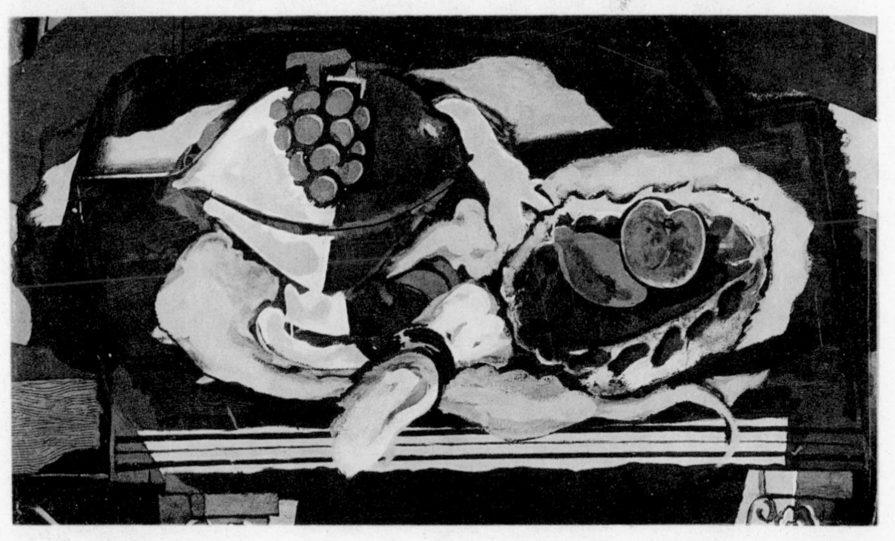

283. Still Life — Georges Braque

284. Still Life, oil Cézanne

285. Still Life, water color Cézanne

286. Portrait of a Chair — Vincent Van Gogh

287. Neapolitan Fisher Boy — Rude

ALINARI

288. Circe — Prof. Ernst Herter

289. Crucifix — Donatello

290. The Puddler — Meunier

ANDERSON

291. Crucifixion — El Greco

292. Coup de Lance Rubens

MAURICE SEYMOUR

293. Swan Lake after Petipa

Youskevitch and Danilova

MAURICE SEYMOUR

294. Le Coq d'Or Michel Fokine

Lazovsky and Algeranoff

MAURICE SEYMOUR

295. St. Francis — Leonide Massine

Panaieff, Guerard, Fenchel, and Massine

BENEDICT FRENKEL

296. Hanya Holm

WILLIAM STONE

297. Charles Weidman

298. Celebration — Martha Graham
Martha Graham Dance Group

299. With My Red Fires — Doris Humphrey
Doris Humphrey-Charles Weidman Company

INDEX OF PROPER NAMES AND TITLES

INDEX OF PROPER NAMES AND TITLES

References to reproductions in this volume are in italics.

INDEX OF PROPER NAMES AND TITLES

INDEX OF PROPER NAMES AND TITLES

INDEX OF PROPER NAMES AND TITLES

INDEX OF PROPER NAMES AND TITLES

INDEX OF PROPER NAMES AND TITLES

INDEX OF PROPER NAMES AND TITLES

INDEX